Forging a Nation

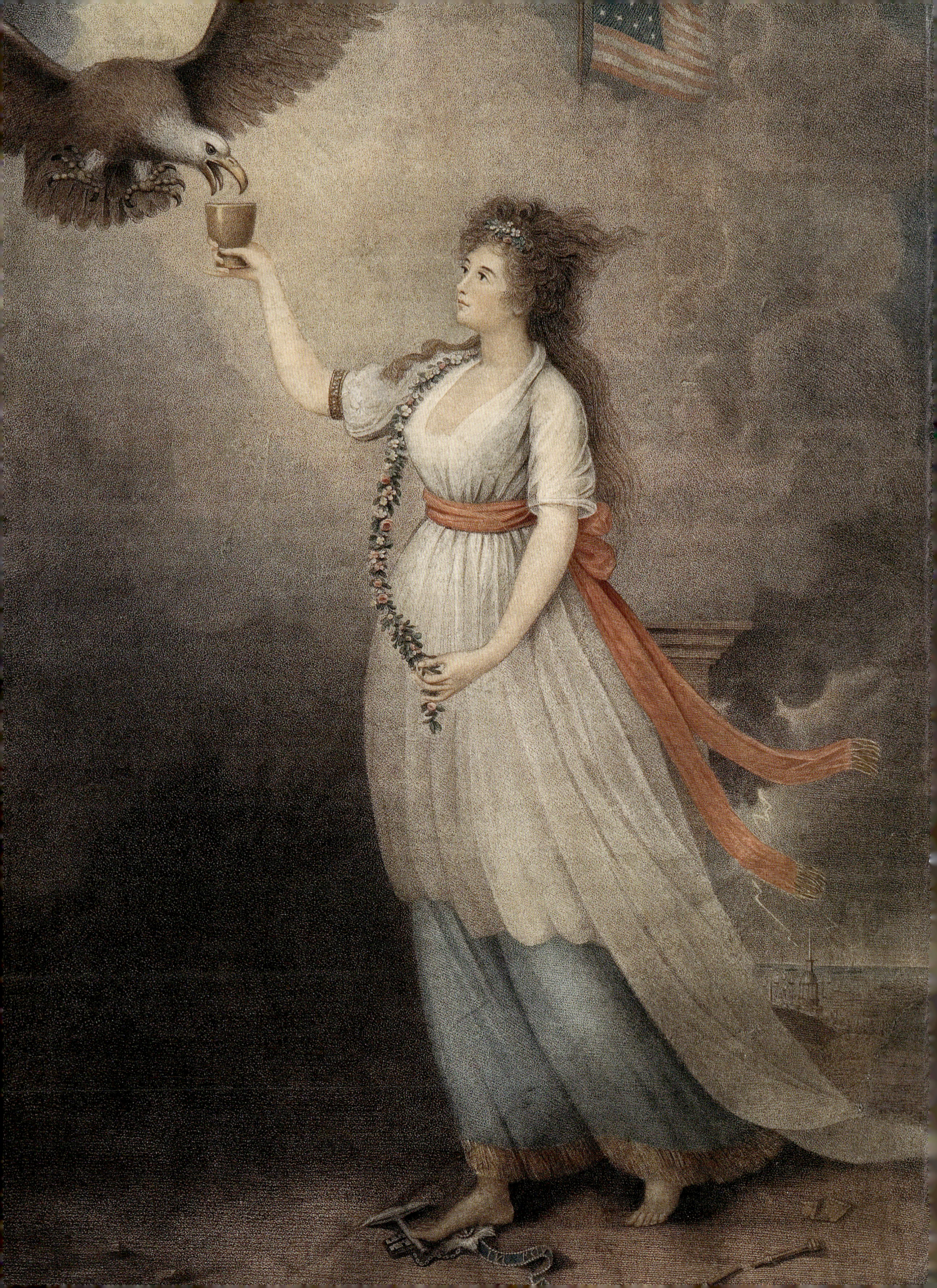

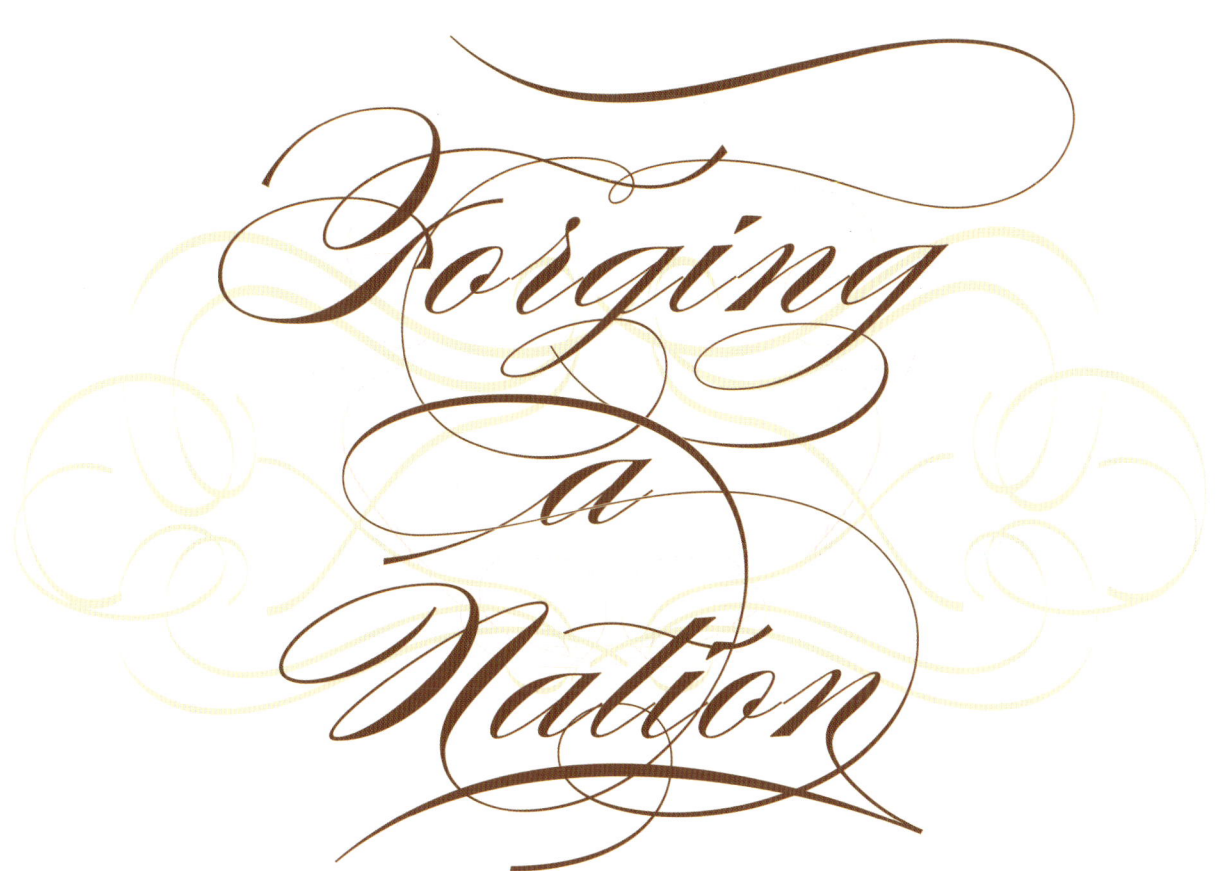

Forging a Nation

The American History Collection at Gilcrease Museum

FOREWORD BY DUANE H. KING

RANDY RAMER, KIMBERLY ROBLIN

AMANDA LETT, ERIC SINGLETON

GILCREASE MUSEUM | TULSA, OKLAHOMA

C.W. Titus Foundation

presents

America: Life, Liberty, and the Pursuit of a Nation

Additional support made possible by the

Grace and Franklin Bernsen Foundation,

H.A. and Mary K. Chapman Charitable Trust,

James D. and Cathryn Mayo Moore Foundation,

William S. Smith Charitable Trust, and

The Williams Foundation

Design, editing, and production: CAROL HARALSON DESIGN

Photography: ROBERT S. CROSS

ENDSHEET: DETAIL, ANGLORUMIN VIRGINIAM ADUENTUS. *Historia Americae Sive Novi Orbis, II*, 1634. GM 2975.1585

PAGE 2: LIBERTY, Edward Savage. Color engraving, 1796. GM 1526.272

Liberty is portrayed here in the form of the goddess of youth. Emblems of British constraint have been broken and are being disregarded by Liberty. She is surrounded by symbols of American independence, including the flag, liberty cap, and bald eagle. The flag of the United States was adopted by the Continental Congress on June 14, 1777. The Liberty cap was a soft conical item that in ancient Rome was given to a slave upon his release from servitude. It came to represent liberty in the 18th century. The bald eagle was adopted by Congress as a national symbol in 1784.

PAGE 6: ELECTRIC LIGHT BULB. Ca. 1890. GM 84.3408

PAGES 8-9: A NEW GENERAL MAP OF AMERICA. Ca. 1747. GM 3916.172

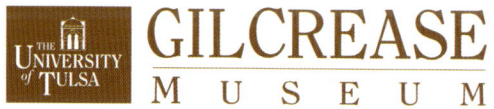

1400 NORTH GILCREASE MUSEUM ROAD

TULSA, OKLAHOMA 74127-2100

Gilcrease Museum is a University of Tulsa/City of Tulsa partnership.

The University of Tulsa is an EEO/AA institution.

"... And so we shall go on, puzzled and prospering beyond example in the history of man. And I do believe we shall continue to grow, to multiply and prosper until we exhibit an association, powerful, wise, and happy beyond what has yet been seen ..."

Thomas Jefferson to John Adams in a letter of January 21, 1812

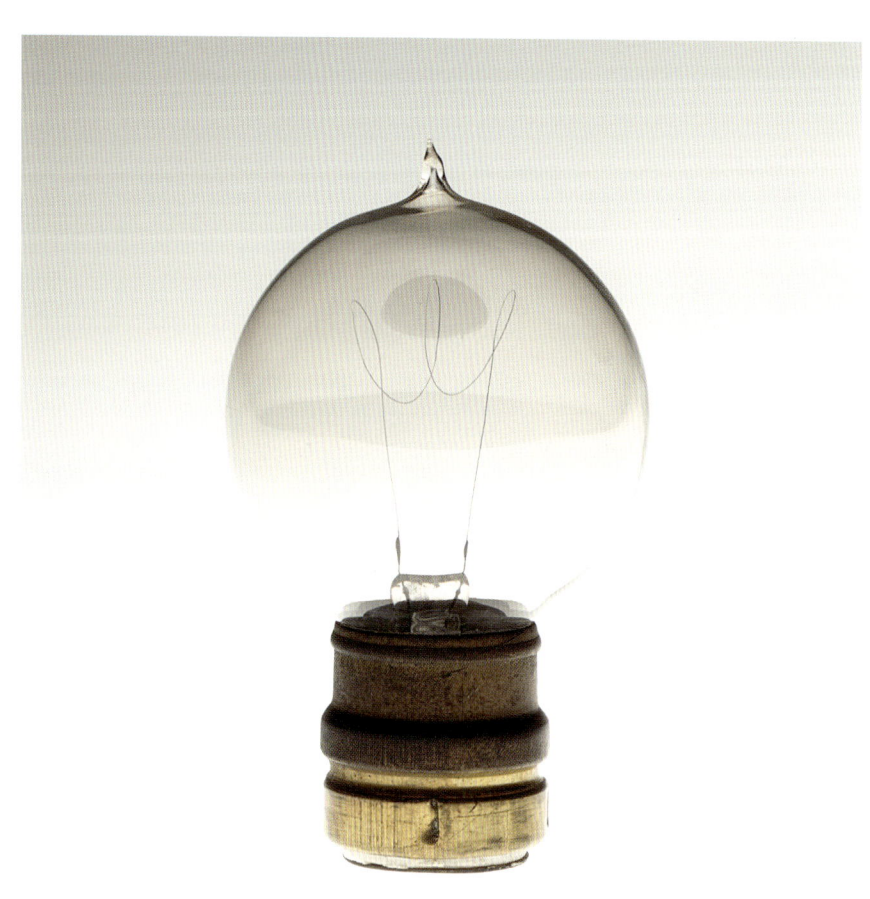

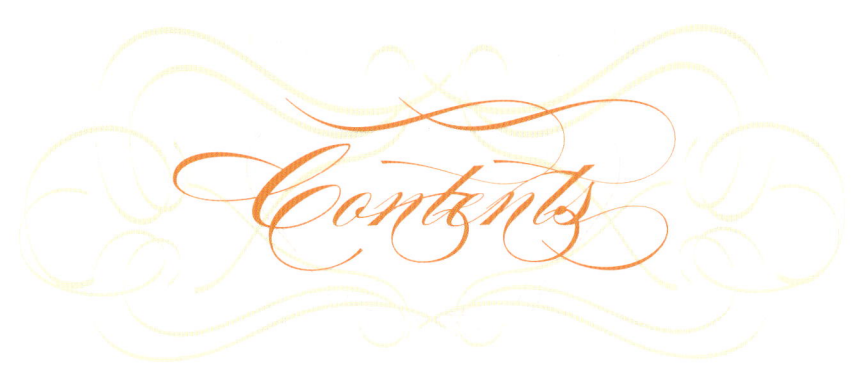

Contents

FOREWORD BY DUANE H. KING, PH.D.   10

A COLONIAL CONFLUENCE 18
KIMBERLY ROBLIN

EVOLUTION OF A REVOLUTION 48
KIMBERLY ROBLIN

TOWARD AN AMERICAN SELF:
SYMBOLS AND EARLY 19TH-CENTURY NATIONAL IDENTITY 88
RANDY RAMER

"THE COUNTRY OF THE FUTURE":
AMERICA IN THE MID-19TH CENTURY 126
AMANDA LETT

"NATIONAL SALVATION OR NATIONAL DESTRUCTION":
THE CIVIL WAR AND ITS AFTERMATH 158
AMANDA LETT

THE AMERICAN WEST AND THE WAR THAT SHAPED A NATION 198
ERIC SINGLETON

EPILOGUE BY RANDY RAMER 225

INDEX 235

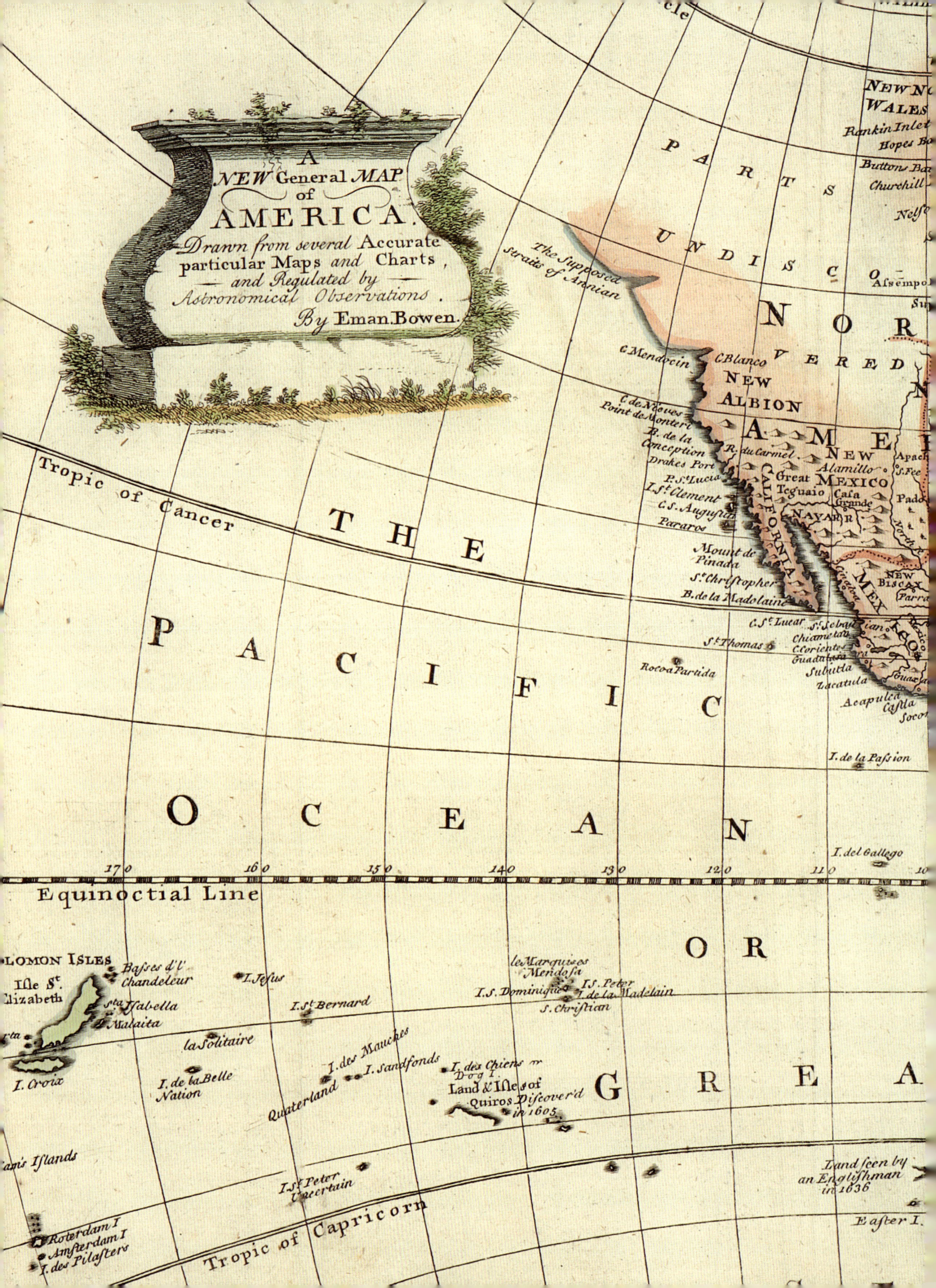

A NEW General MAP of AMERICA. Drawn from several Accurate particular Maps and Charts, and Regulated by Astronomical Observations. By Eman. Bowen.

NEW NO WALES
Rankin Inlet
Hopes Bo
Buttons Ba
Churchill
Nels

PARTS UNDISCO

The Supposed Straits of Anian

C. Mendocin
C Blanco
NEW ALBION
VERED
NOR

C. de N eves
Point de Monteri
B. de la Conception
Drakes Port
P. S. Lucia
I. S. Clement
C. S. Augusta
Pararos

R. du Carmel
Great Teguaio
NAYAR

AME
Alamillo
Casa Grande
NEW MEXICO
Apach
S. Fee
Pado

Mount de Pinada
S. Christopher
B. de la Madolaine

NEW BISCAY
Parra

C. S. Lucar
S. Thomas

S. Selba
Chiamet tat
C. Coriente
Guadicsa
Subutla
Lacatula
Acapulca
Castla
Socos

Rocoa Partida

Tropic of Cancer

THE PACIFIC OCEAN

I. de la Pass ion

I. del Gallego

170   160   150   140   130   120   110   10

Equinoctial Line

OR

LOMON ISLES
Isle S. Elizabeth
Basses d'l Chandeleur
I. Jesus
le Marquises Mendosa
I. S. Dominique
I. S. Peter
I. de la Madelain

sta Isabella
d. Malaita
I. S. Bernard
S. Christian

la Solitaire
I. des Mauches
I. de la Belle Nation
Quaterland
I. Sandfonds
I. des Chiens or Dog I
Land & Isle of Quiros Discover'd in 1605.

GREA

I. Croix

an's Islands

Land seen by an Englishman in 1636.

I. S. Peter Uncertain

Roterdam I
Amsterdam I
I. des Pilasters

Tropic of Capricorn

Easter I.

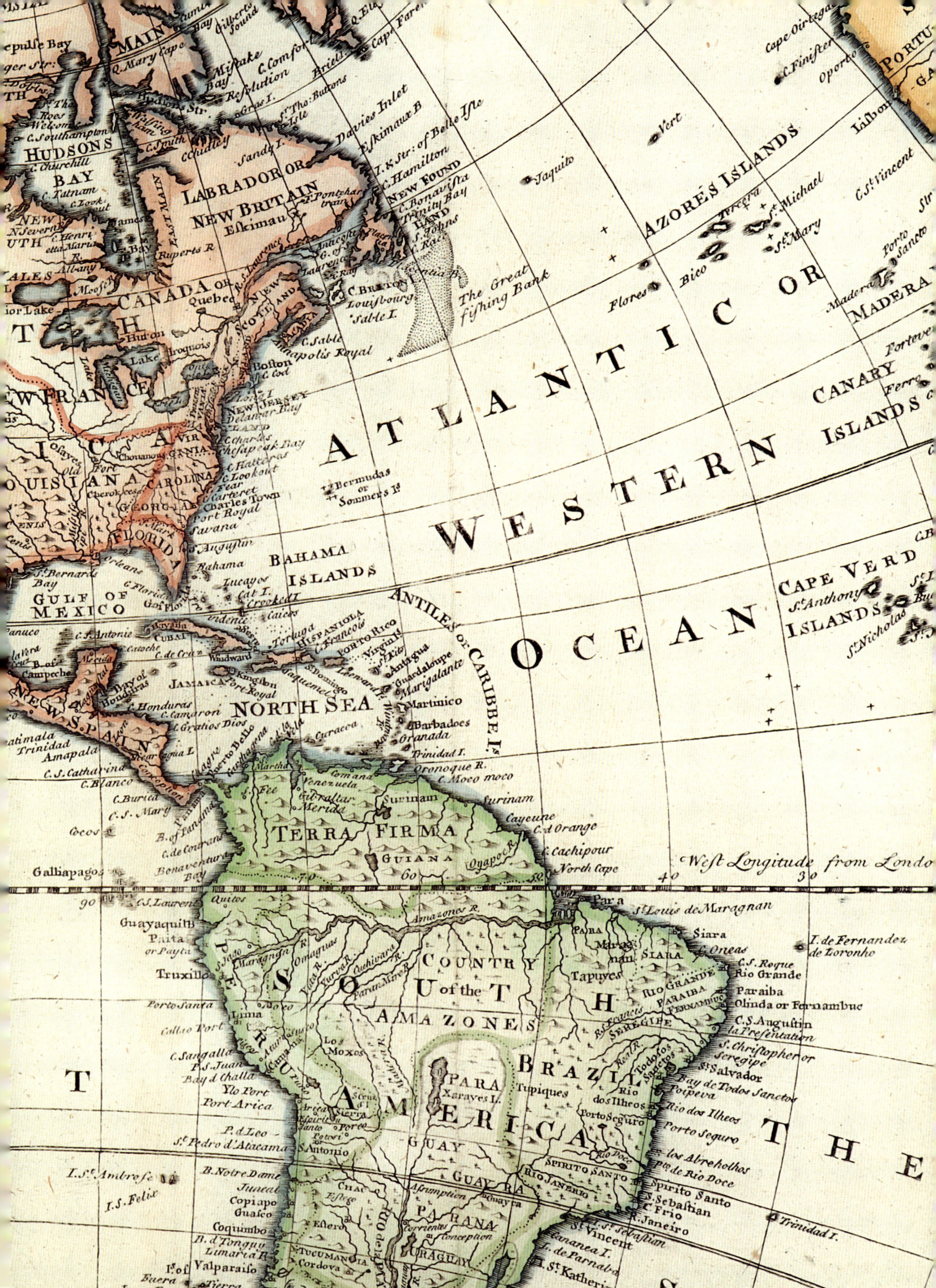

conclude Peace, contract Alliances, establish Commerce, and to all other acts & things which Independant States may of right do. And for the support of this declaration, with a firm reliance on the
Protection of Divine Providence, we mutually pledge to
each other our lives, our Fortunes, and our sacred honor.

Signed by Order and in Behalf of the
Congress,

John Hancock President.

Attest

Charles Thomson Secretary

A True Copy of the Original Declaration

Int

B. Franklin,

Deane

FOREWORD: IDEALISM V. REALITY

*From the certification of Paul Revere as a messenger
for the Massachusetts Committee of Safety in 1775
to a copy of the Emancipation Proclamation of 1863
that bears Abraham Lincoln's original signature,
it is amazing how much of this nation's history
can be written using only the archives of the
Gilcrease Museum.*

O ur United States of America is perhaps the only country in the world founded on moral principles. Throughout much of its history, these principles have served as the guiding light in attracting the "huddled masses" to our shores and have justified a claim to moral high ground in international diplomacy. The lofty ideals espoused by the framers of the Constitution give Americans and citizens of the world goals to aspire to, but the same ideals have often been difficult to reconcile with the reality of the American experience. This experience, replete with military and social conflict, ethnic cleansing, and racial and religious intolerance, has occasionally tested American idealism to the breaking point. Yet the resilience of the principles on which this country was founded continues to bring American political thought back to its center when challenged by fringe elements advocating social intolerance and political extremism. It might be argued that today America is closer to achieving the idealism on which it was founded than at any time in its history.

FACING: CERTIFIED
COPY OF THE
DECLARATION OF
INDEPENDENCE, 1777.
Attested and signed by Silas
Deane and Benjamin Franklin.
GM 4026.901

In this address, Washington promised the friendship of the
United States to members of the Delaware Indian Nation
and encouraged them to take any grievances to Congress.
Washington was only partly successful in gaining support for
the American cause as the Delawares were divided during
the war. He also reported that until recently the United States
fought the British alone, but recently the "Great King of
France is become our Good Brother and Ally…"
The document is signed "Commander in chief of all the
Armies in the United States of America."

During the Revolutionary War most American Indians
supported the British. The Royal Proclamation of 1763
established a boundary between Indians and settlers and
offered the best hope for Native people to maintain their
homelands. In the Treaty of Paris of 1783, the British made
no provisions for the many tribes who had supported their
war effort.

Nowhere are the ideals of America expressed more
clearly and succinctly than in the first document
produced by the founding fathers of this country, the
Declaration of Independence. The U. S. Constitution,
Bill of Rights, and Declaration of Independence
remain after more than two centuries the cornerstones
of our democracy and the foundation for American
identity and virtue. "We hold these truths to be self-
evident, that all men are created equal, that they are
endowed by their Creator with certain unalienable
rights, that among these are life, liberty and the pursuit
of happiness," states the Declaration of Independence.
It also proclaims "that to secure these rights,
governments are instituted among men, deriving their
just powers from the consent of the governed." At the
time, many of the signers of this important document
were slaveholders who defined "all men" as males who
looked, acted, believed, and spoke as they did. It would
be almost a century and a half before there was even
a pretense that full rights as Americans extended to
women, American Indians, and the descendants of
former slaves. How could the only country founded on
the basis of moral principles have so much difficulty
coming to terms with its own ideals?

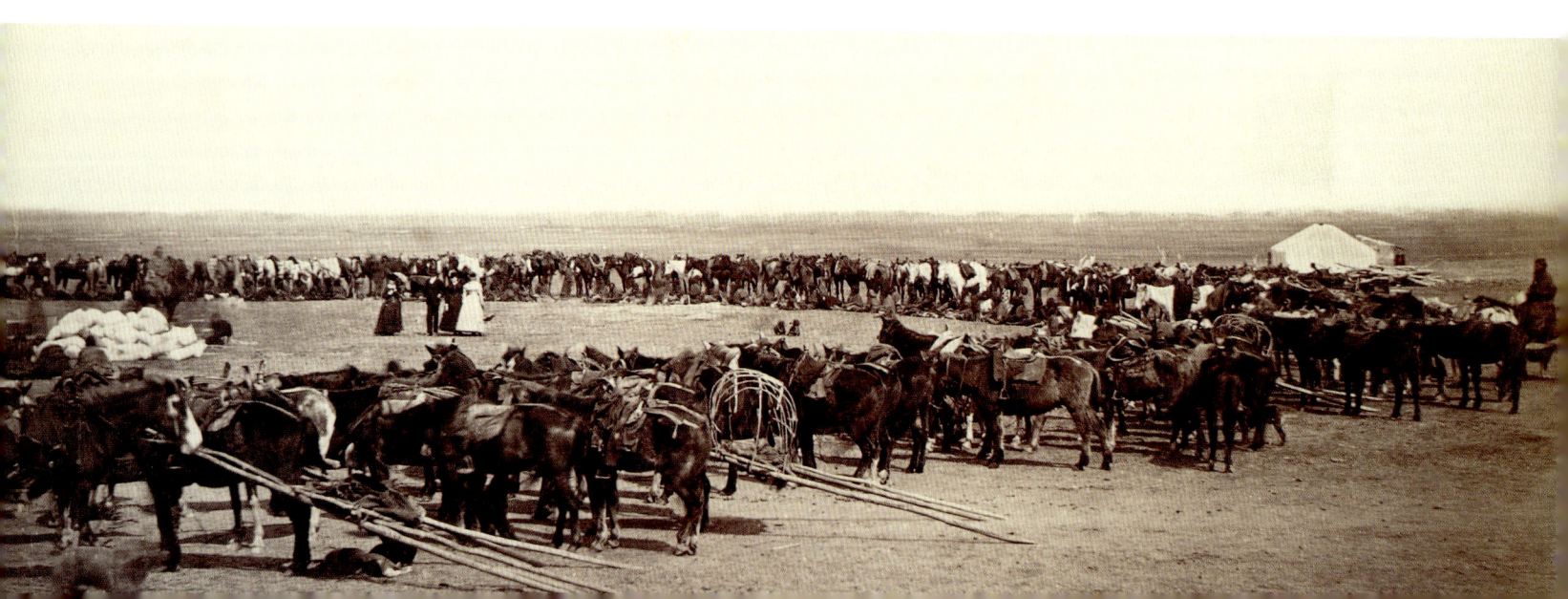

To the Chief Men, Deputies from the
Delaware Nation.

Brothers

    I am happy to see you here. I am
glad the long Journey you have made,
has done you no harm; and that you
are in good Health. I am glad also you
left all our friends of the Delaware Nation
well.

Brothers.

    I have read your paper. The things
you have said are weighty things, and I have
considered them well. The Delaware Nation
have shewn their good will to the United
States. They have done wisely and I hope
they will never repent. I rejoice in the
new assurances you give of their friendship.
The things you now offer to do to brighten the
chain, prove your sincerity. — I am sure
Congress will run to meet you — and will
do every thing in their power to make the
friendship between the people of those
States — and their Brethren of the Delaware
nation, last for ever.

Brothers.

    I am a Warrior. — My words are few
and plain; but I will make good what I say.
— 'Tis my business to destroy all the Enemies
of these States and to protect their friends. —
You have seen how we have withstood the
English for four years; and how their great

It might be suggested that the ideals on which this country was founded have ebbed and flowed with the personalities in power. George Washington and his secretary of war Henry Knox were very concerned about how the founders of this country would be remembered by history. They did not want to be viewed as similar to the Spanish conquistadors who trampled the rights and lives of indigenous people in Latin and South America. Instead they wanted to acquire Indian land through legitimate treaties and purchases and in the process turn Native Americans into "civilized-Christianized citizens" of the United States. Washington and Knox did not count on the possibility that some Indians might not want to sell their land nor did they foresee the total disregard that frontiersmen would have for Indian rights. Less than three decades after Washington's death, Andrew Jackson was elected president largely by a frontier population clamoring for Indian Removal.

KING JAMES II.

From *The Present State of His Majesties Isles and Territories in America*, 1687.

GM 2576.2050

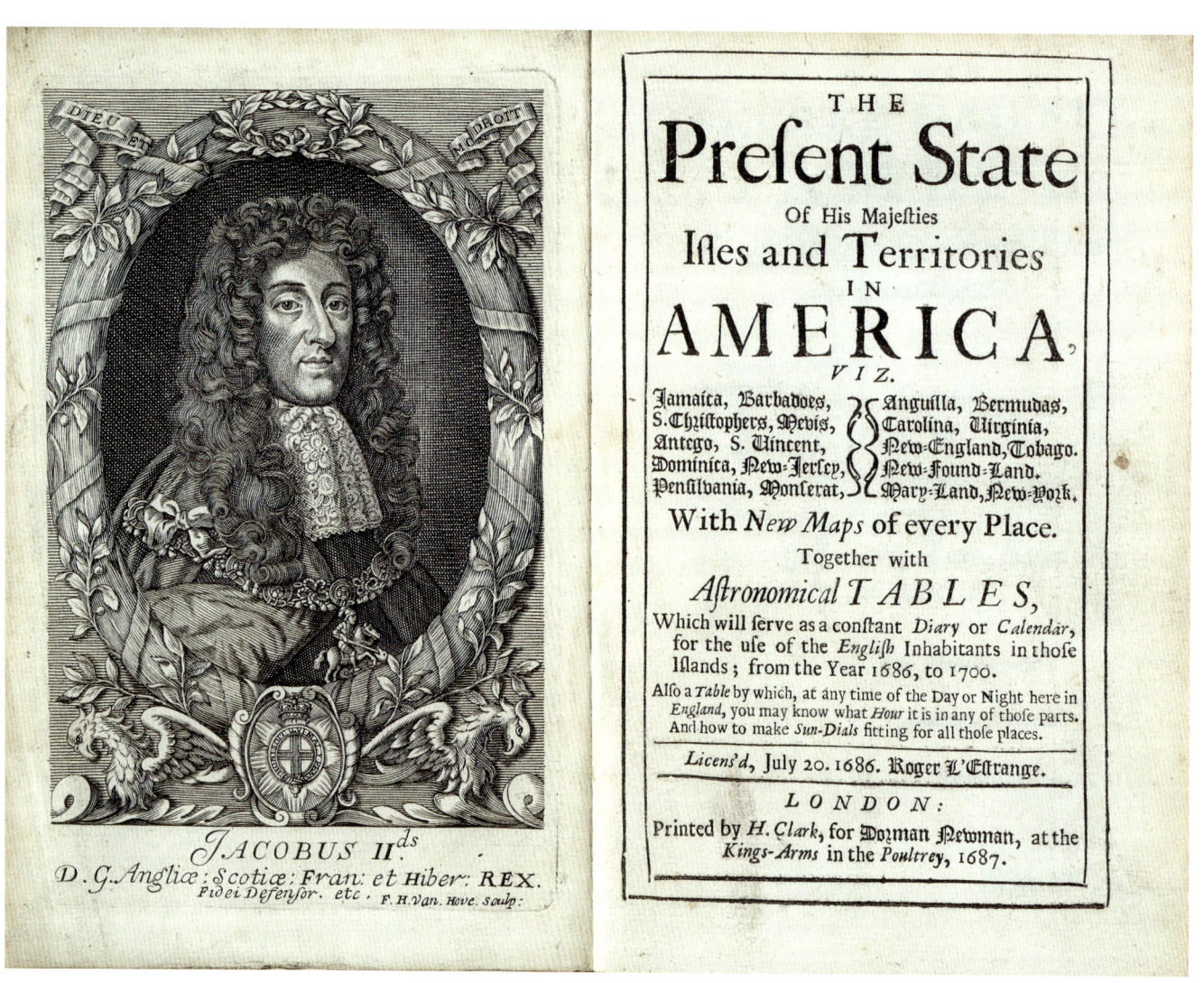

It is often said that when the mistakes of history are not remembered, they are repeated. For that reason and others, it is unfortunate that public education does not place a greater emphasis on history today. It is especially regrettable when some politicians with little sense of history embark on popular but short-sighted efforts that only repeat past mistakes.

American history is safeguarded by the libraries, archives, and museums of this country. Perhaps one surprising repository of American history is the Gilcrease Museum in Tulsa, Oklahoma. The depth of art, artifacts, and archival records in the museum's collection has been clearly illustrated in exhibits related to American history created by Gilcrease Museum. The exhibition *America: Life, Liberty, and the Pursuit of a Nation,* for example, covered a 300-year period from the founding of Jamestown to the closing of the western frontier at the end of the 19th century. More than 250 significant treasures from the Gilcrease Museum's permanent collection told the story of America's past through a deeply profound and moving narrative.

Only in a few places outside of Washington, D. C., could one expect to find so many art and archival riches related to the founding and early development of the United States. Among the national treasures in the collection are oil portraits of George Washington, James Madison, and John Marshall painted from life. Marble busts of George Washington, Benjamin Franklin, Marquis de Lafayette, Andrew Jackson, and others created by the most skilled sculptors of their time give us the most realistic likenesses of these historical figures extent from an age before photography.

The emergence of democracy in America is chronicled in the archives of the Gilcrease Museum through certified copies of the Declaration of Independence, the Articles of Confederation, and original correspondence between the founding fathers and powers of Europe. A letter written by Thomas Jefferson on July 1, 1776, comments on his political philosophy and "a Declaration" he was directed to draft. A letter written a century later by George Armstrong Custer discusses his plans to attack Sitting Bull. From the certification of Paul Revere as a messenger for the Massachusetts Committee of Safety in 1775 to a copy of the Emancipation Proclamation of 1863 that bears Abraham Lincoln's original signature, it is amazing how much of this nation's history can be written using only the archives of the Gilcrease Museum.

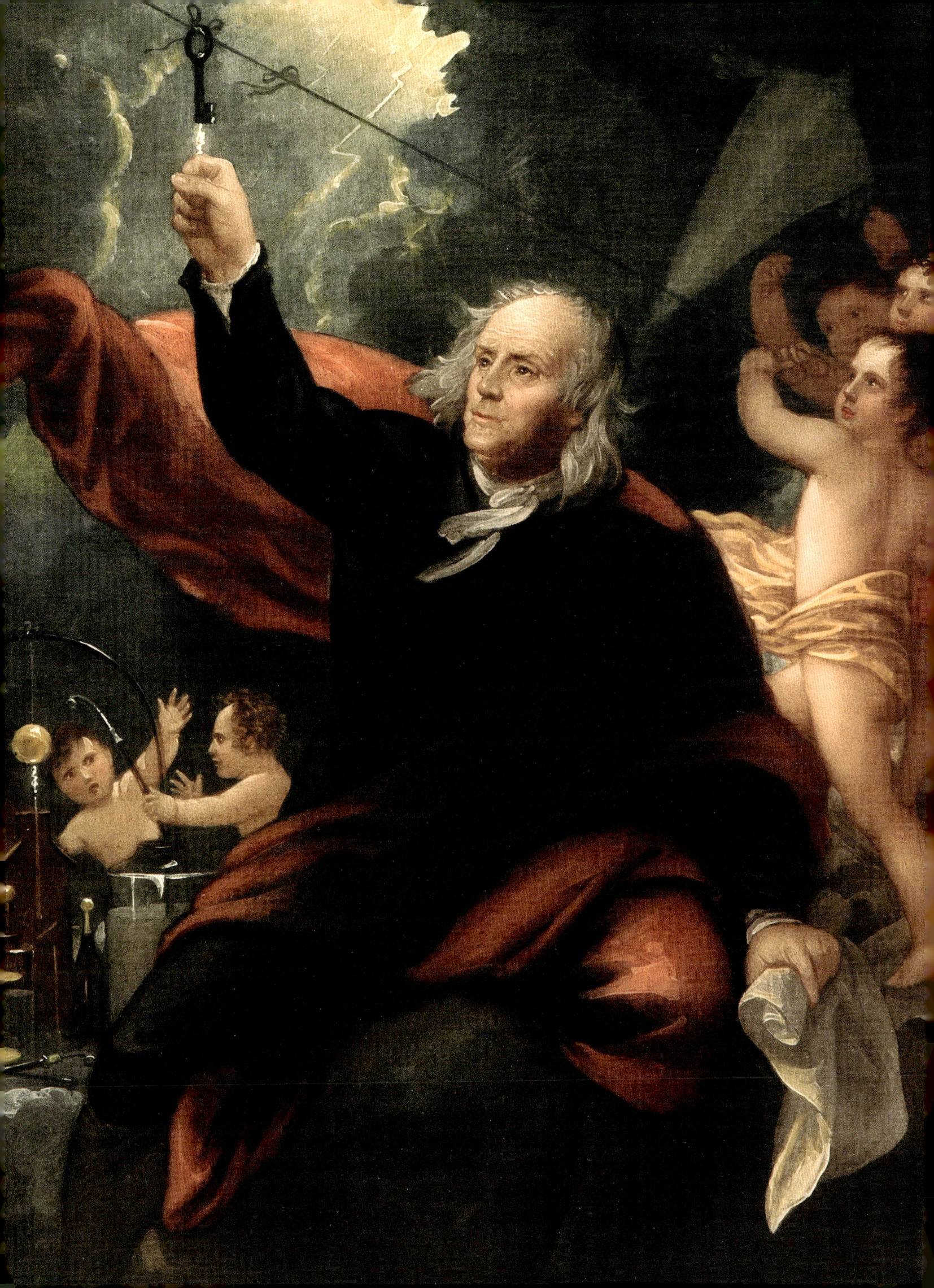

Many of the museum's treasures are so unique that it is difficult to put their significance in proper perspective since there are no comparables. For example, the Gilcrease archive has the only certified copy of the Declaration of Independence. The Declaration was drafted by Thomas Jefferson between June 11 and June 28, 1776. At the time, Jefferson was a political novice but a master with a pen, and his belief in "self-evident truths" and grievances against King George III were shared by most delegates of the thirteen original colonies. With minor editing by elder statesmen Benjamin Franklin and John Adams, the Declaration was essentially the work of the thirty-three-year-old Virginian. It is today perhaps the single most important document in American history.

The copy of the Declaration in the Gilcrease collection was handwritten with corrections by an unidentified scribe. It was sent to Baron von Schulenburg, minister to Frederick the Great of Prussia, by Benjamin Franklin and Silas Deane, American commissioners plenipotentiary, from their headquarters in Paris. Its authenticity is verified by an array of accompanying documents and the signatures of Franklin and Deane, who were desperately seeking support from France and other European powers for the American cause. As the only surviving certified copy of the Declaration of Independence, it has no comparable companions. Perhaps the closest document would be a Dunlap Broadside, one of the earliest published copies of the Declaration, of which there may be twenty-five extant copies today.

As much as we are inspired by these historical documents, we cannot help but admire the vision and persistence of Gilcrease Museum's founder, Thomas Gilcrease, who spent his life and his fortune collecting those items that best tell the story of America. As we study Mr. Gilcrease's passionately gathered treasures, we remember that to clearly see where we are going it is necessary to understand where we have been.

DUANE H. KING, PH.D.

EXECUTIVE DIRECTOR, GILCREASE MUSEUM

FACING: BENJAMIN FRANKLIN, Godfrey Mayer, after Benjamin West. Engraving, 1900. GM 1577.136

Both the image and the ideals of the American Enlightenment are included in this depiction of Benjamin Franklin. Surrounded by cherubs and scientific instruments, Franklin has electricity flowing into his extended hand from a key attached to a kite string. As Franklin unlocks the mysteries of science, a lightning bolt shines through an opening in the sky, illuminating a gray visage whose eyes remain riveted on this new discovery. In Franklin's other hand is a crumpled paper, signifying the myths of the past, ready to be discarded.

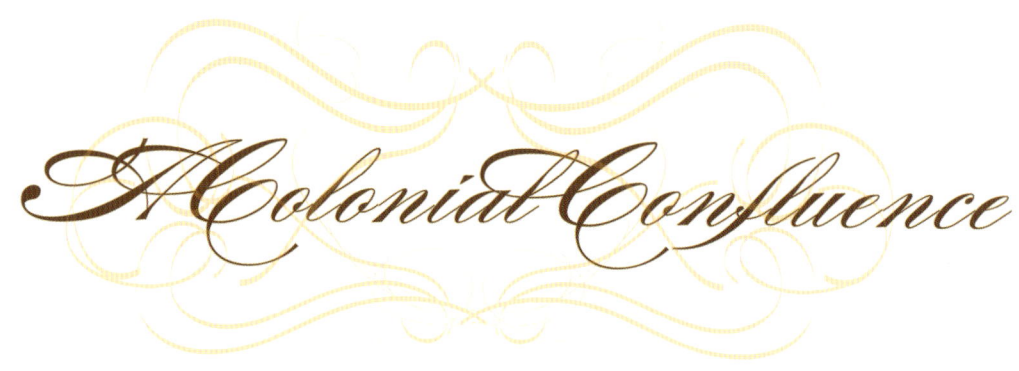

A Colonial Confluence

KIMBERLY ROBLIN

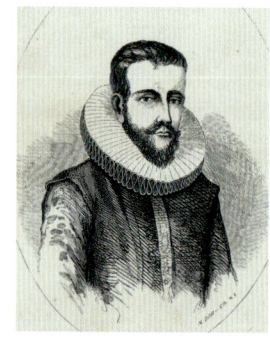

HENRY HUDSON,
unknown artist. Engraving.
GM 1526.381

Hudson, an Englishman
employed by the Dutch
East India Company,
was the first European to
successfully sail what is
today known as the
Hudson River.

**THE LANDING OF
CHRISTOPHER
COLUMBUS,**
Edward Savage. Engraving.
GM 1526.273

Within the pages of history we occasionally come across coincidences too extraordinary to be believable if they were written as fiction. In the summer of 1587, on the small island of Roanoke, a woman and her husband welcomed a baby girl, Virginia. The proud parents were among the over 100 English men, women, and children who had traveled across the Atlantic only months before to establish a British settlement. Virginia was the first Anglo-American child born in America, and the spirit of risk and adventure that would ultimately be synonymous with the country was uncannily captured in her surname—Dare.

It was a word that characterized the early interactions between Europeans and indigenous peoples after Christopher Columbus stumbled upon the "New World" in 1492 and ignited an age of exploration that ultimately would see the settlement and colonization of the Americas by newcomers. It was not the discovery of a new world but the meeting of two old worlds, and upon the later importation of African slaves, a third. The differing perceptions each held of the land was evident in their descriptions: our country to the Native Americans,[1] a distant country to the Africans,[2] and an unpeopled country to the colonists.[3]

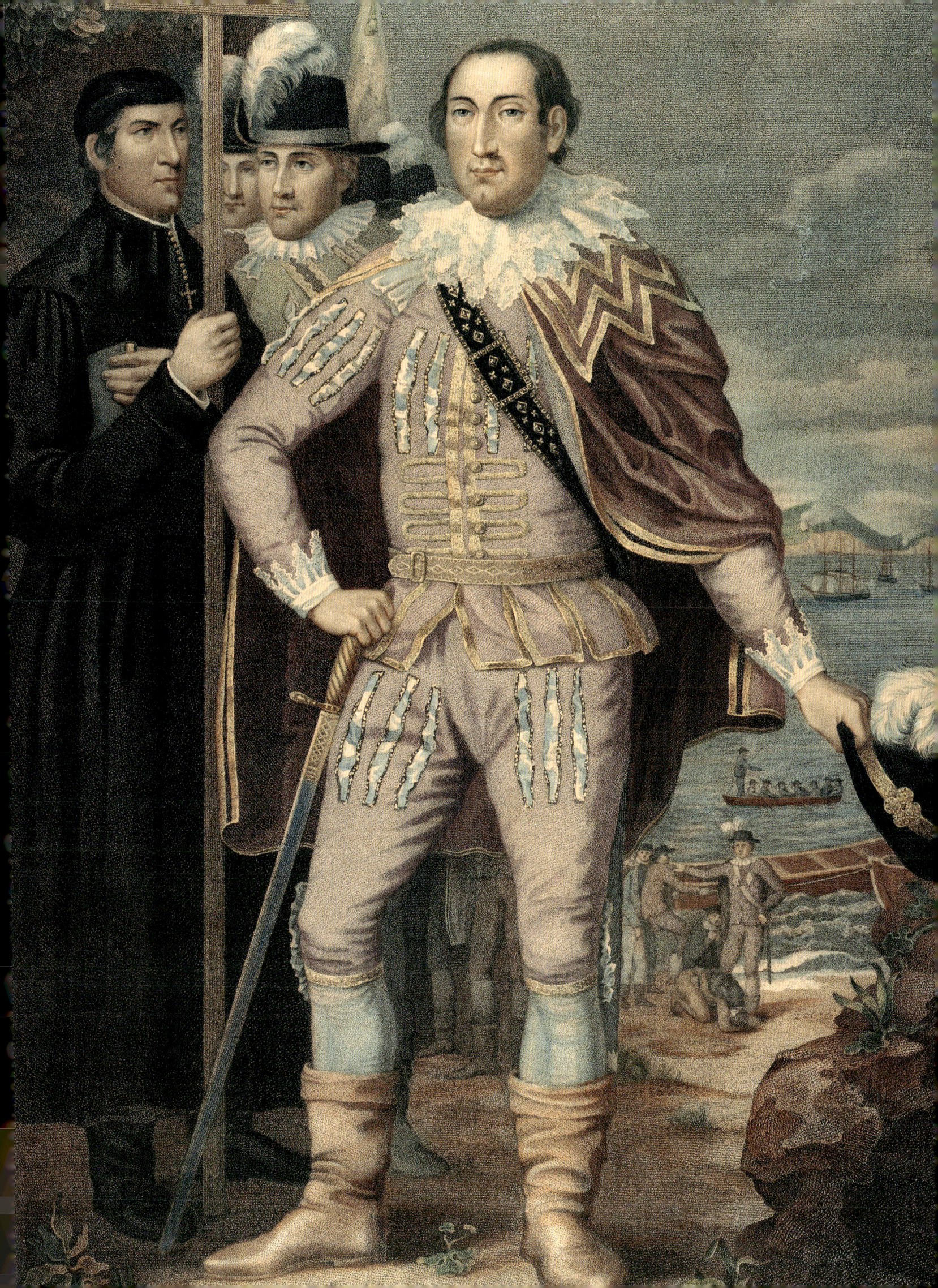

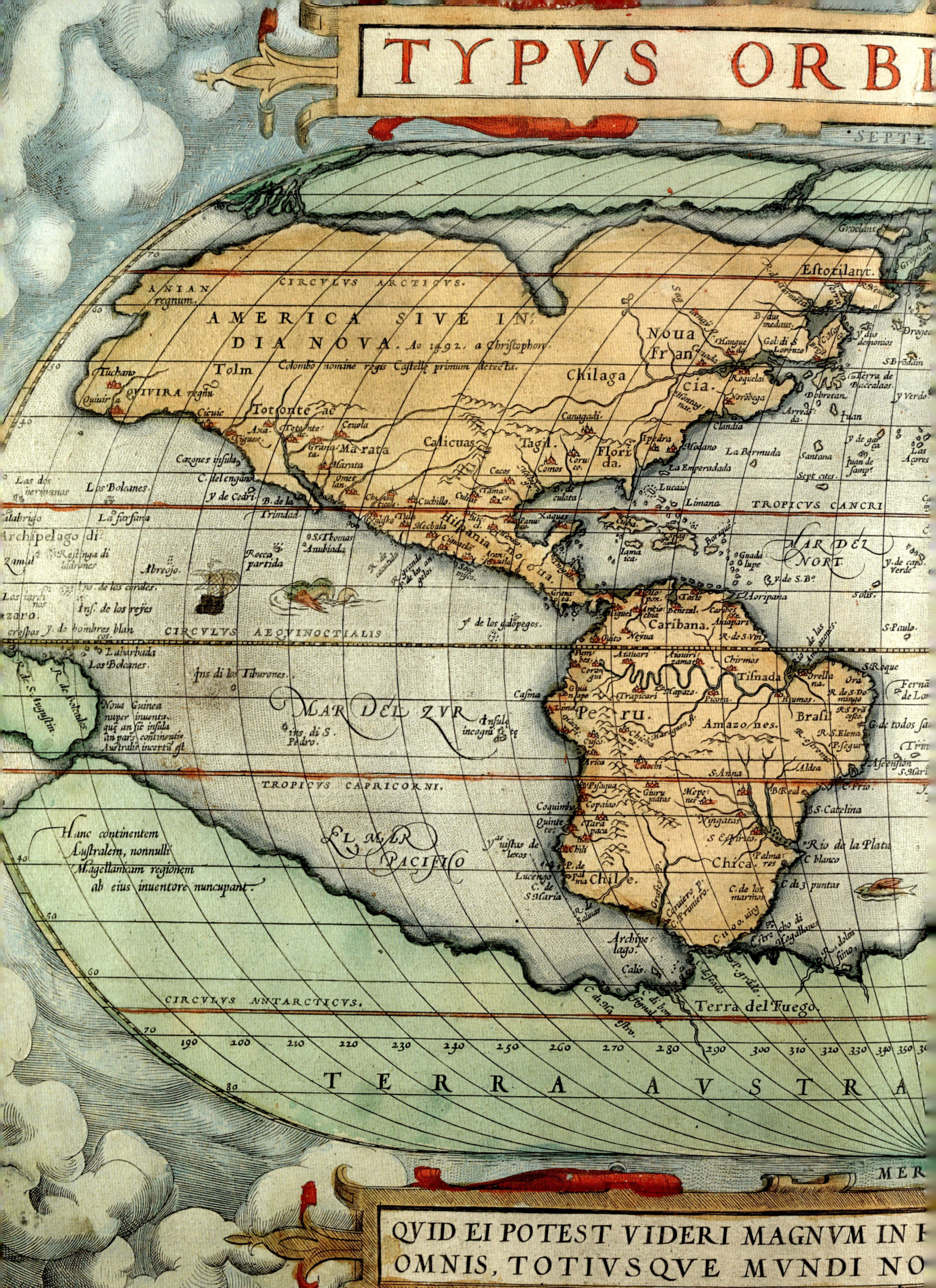

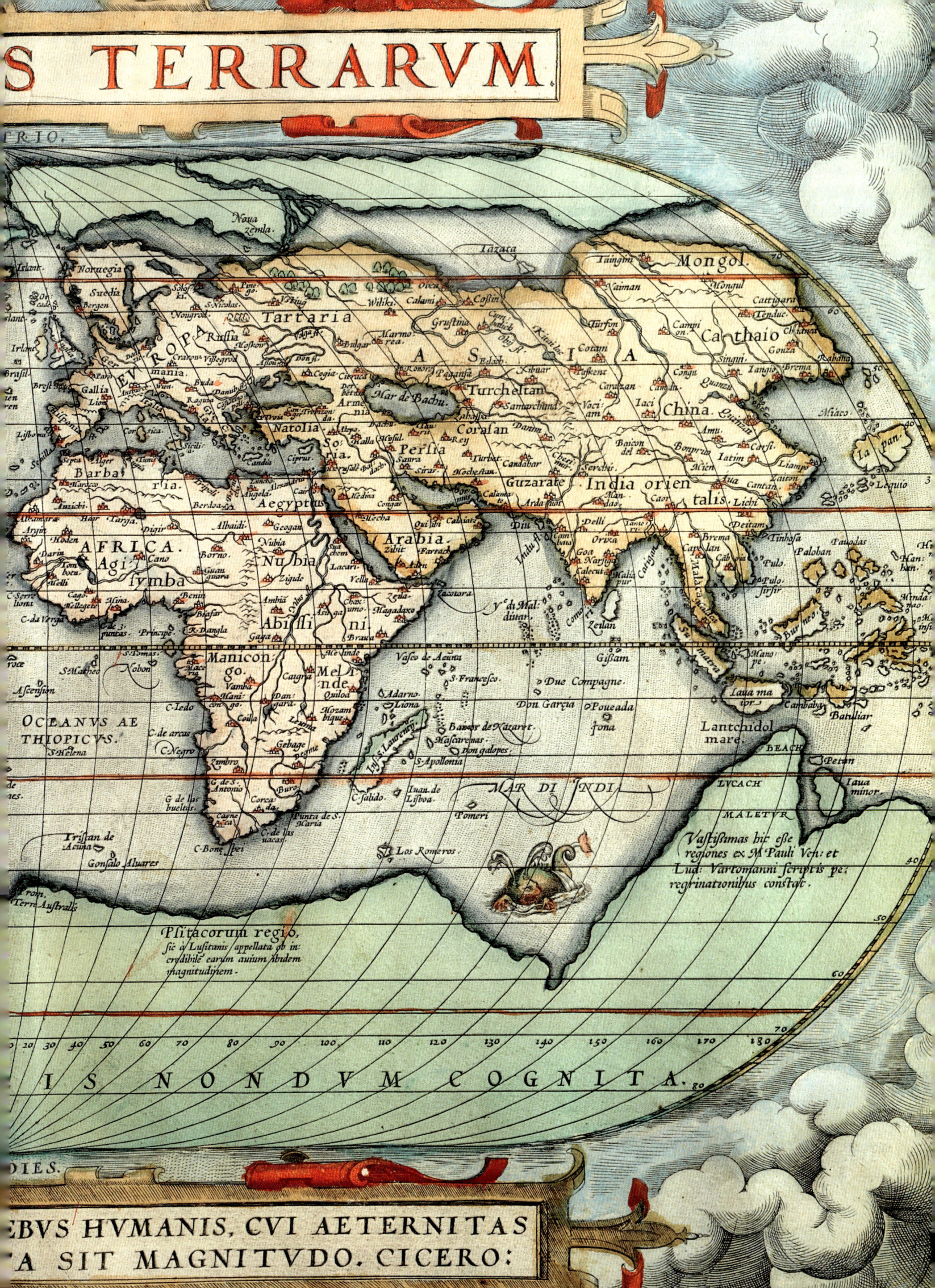

Land seene in the Bearing Dist.	Depth & sounding	Current & tide
	21 fad. four white sand.	
	200 fad.	
The Iland, noroest ——— SEbS — 9 or 10 lea.		ye Tide's setting uncertain
The Westermost part of ye Main in sight. N. — 5 or 6.		whirling round dark ½ hour
The said, westermost pt of ye Maine now. NNE. — 4 lea		
This part is noroest 15 le. from Resolution, b. NW, NWbW and		
and from this part of ye Maine ye Land — SEbE.		
falleth more Northward, being a smooth		
land, neither high nor low.		
		The flood setts to ye NW and
		setts strong in, then ye Ebb
		out here on ye North side
The Land hereabout is reasonable high.	32 fad. small sands &	The tide setts still to ye west
Many Ilands along this shore	shells.	ward.
The Land is only a mere blackrock all the hills	12 or 13 fad. by ye shore	At 1 in ye morn flowing wa
only some mossy banks in the valleys.	sandy	it highest about 3 foot in ½ ti
This 1 part of ye land (allowing war.) lieth NWbW & SEbE.	Many Ilands off in along ye	& 6 fad. more before high wa
Two great Ilands and a small one between them, be	shore, agreements at 50 fad.	ter. the whole flow 7 fo
tween us and ye Maine wch was distant some — 8 lea.		ye judgmt
Land off us S¼E, WbN½N. ye noroest 6 lea off		
Ilands between us & ye shore. { ye Westermost. 4e		
ye shore on ye Starboard ye America. { ye Southermost. 7 or 8.		
A good distance off very high land & craggy mountains		
Standing out to ye NE we saw the North shore		
being distant over from tother, some 14 or 15 Leags.		
it shewed like Ilands, being all broken Land.		
At VIII. at night		
ye Eastermost part bore — ESE½S		
ye Northermost — NE½E — 9 lea off	145 fad. small red stones	ye Current holpt us muc
ye Westermost land on ye E side — SW½W — 10.		
No land seen at noon but our Homark SWbW — 11 or 12 le.		
Salisbury I. seen. high land b. WbN. — 10 le. noroest		Great show off Strong tide
at VIII { ye Northermost part — nwbW.		setting out and in.
at night { ye Southermost — W¼S. — 9 or 10 off		
{ ye Body — WbN — 7 le		
The Maine bore — N — 12 or 13.		
At IX in the morning		
the SE pt of Salisb. I. bore NW¼N. — 4½ noroest		
the Northermost pt — NW¼N — 8 or 7½		
the Southermost pt — W¼N — 8.		
The Maine within — 4 or 5 le.		
Many small Ilands close aboard it.		
Another Iland beard off Salisbury NNW (a good dist. off		
it made in 3 parts as we came from ye Eastward, being		
ye Northern side very high land, dist from ye main 12 or 13.		
ye Northern pt of it lieth in Lat. 63.35. lon. 33.6 fro Orkny.		
The Eastermost pt of ye Main. NE½E — 14 or 15		
ye Westermost — nNW½W. 12 lea		
ye Eastermost pt of Salisbury I. SSW½ 6		
ye Westermost — WbS½S 7 or 8		
Mill Iland — nNW½W. 7		

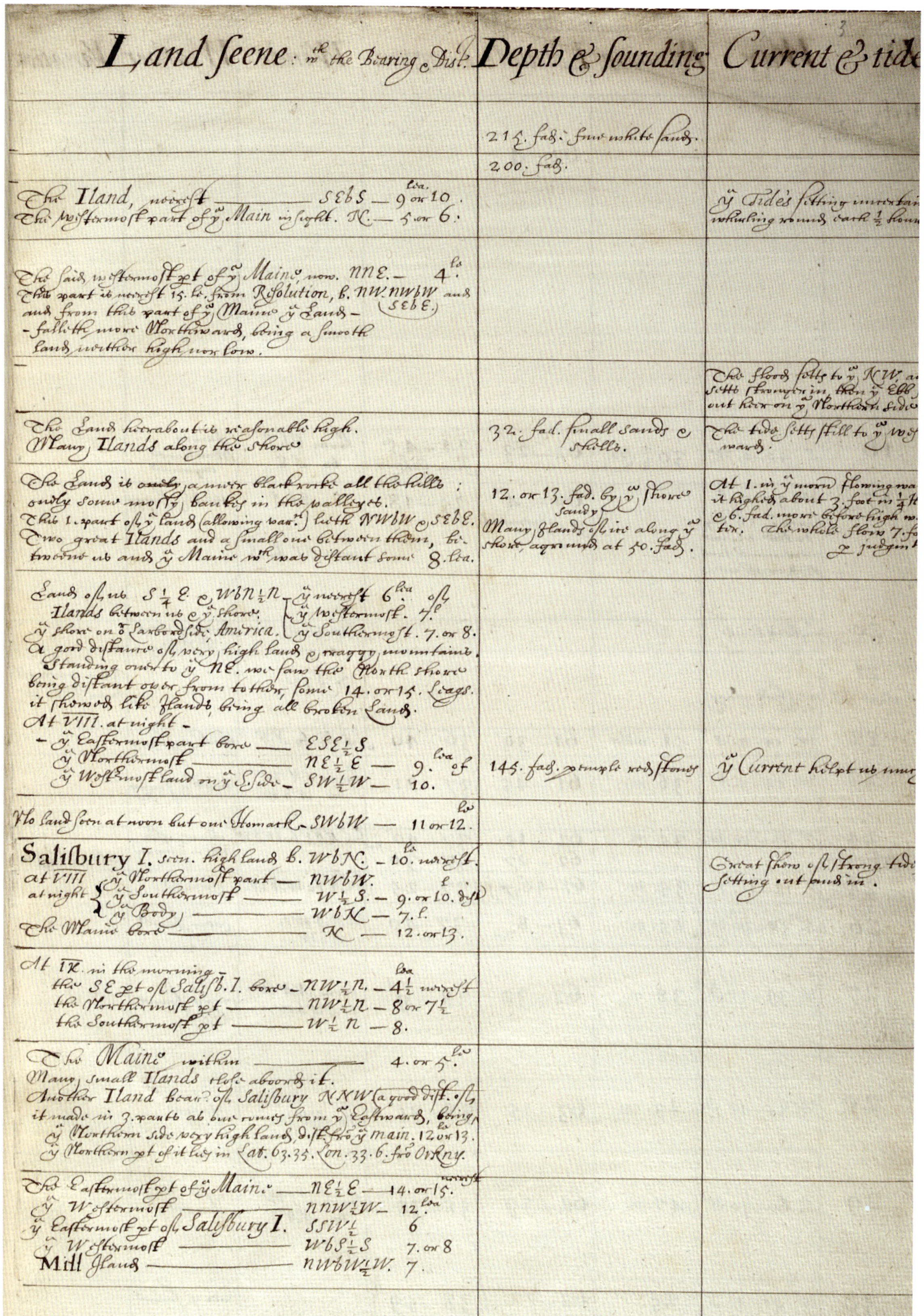

ABOVE AND FACING: LOG OF LUKE FOX, 1631. GM 3696.146

Luke Fox was an English explorer who set sail from England in May of 1631 with a crew of twenty men in search of the Northwest Passage. While he did not find the elusive route, he did become the first to circumnavigate Hudson Bay.

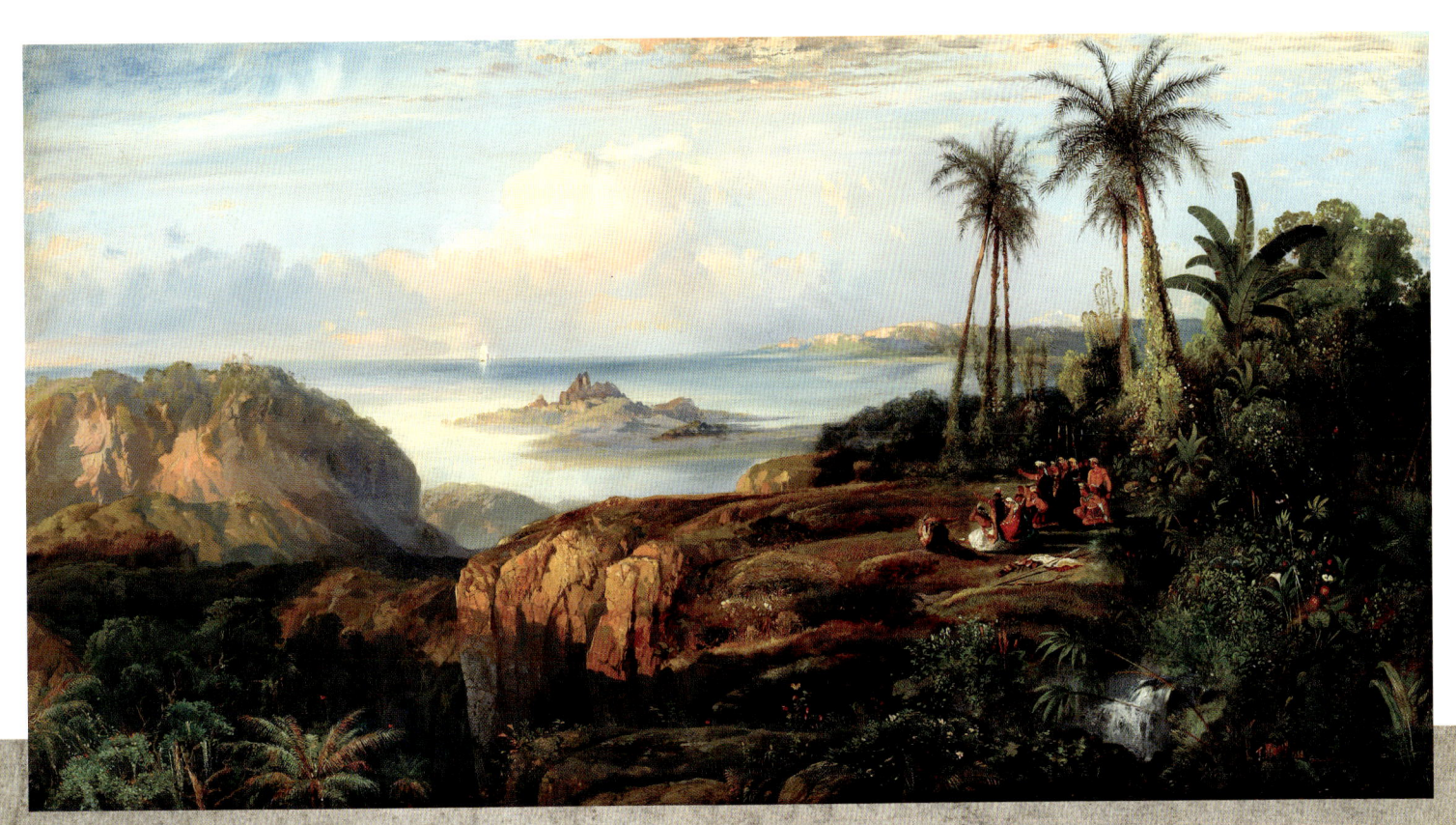

Y OURIN's
Journall.

NB This is the Traverse Book of some of the Officers
on board the Charles, Cap.t Luke Fox, who
was sent in quest of a NW Passage in y.e
Year 1631.
W.m Herbert.

j

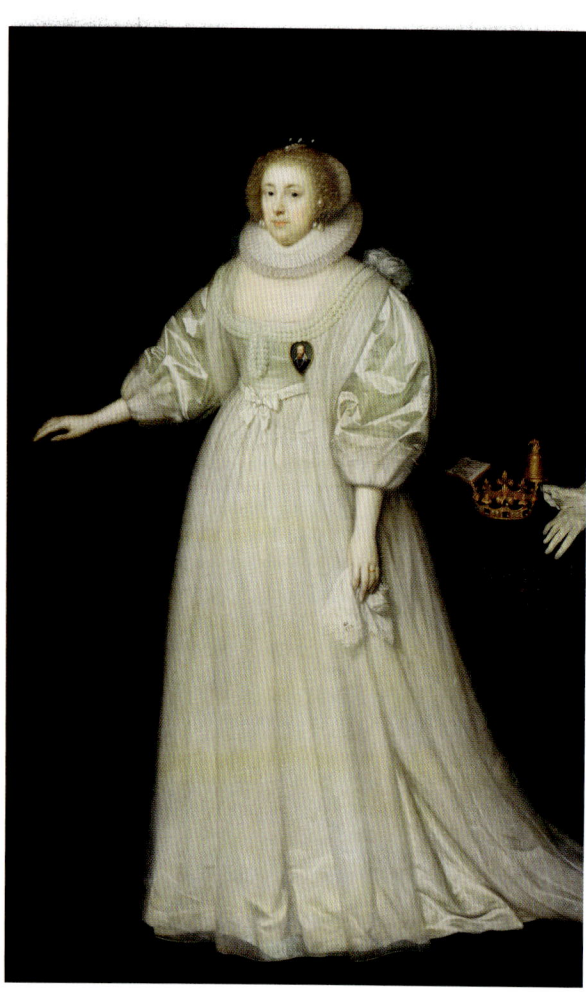

FRANCES HOWARD, DUCHESS OF RICHMOND AND LENNOX, Cornelius Johnson. Oil on canvas, 1635. GM 0176.1020

Frances Howard encouraged English interest in the exploration of the Western Hemisphere. As a patron of Captain John Smith, she financed his *Generall Historie of Virginia, New-England, and the Summer Isles,* printed in London in 1624. The "Epistle Dedicatory" in the volume, "Gratious hand, which hath given birth to the publication of this narration," is addressed to her.

The duchess was the daughter of Thomas Viscount Howard of Bindon. Twice widowed, she married her third and best-loved husband, Ludovic Stuart, Duke of Lennox, in 1621. Two years later her husband was created Duke of Richmond, and Frances became known as the "Double Duchess." Through wealth acquired from her husbands, she was one of the richest women in England. Happiness was to elude her, however, as the duke died in 1624. She mourned him the rest of her life. Cornelius Johnson painted her more than ten years later, still in mourning clothes and wearing a memorial broach.

For Europeans, this collision of worlds was an exercise in opportunity and ambition, not just for monarchies eager to secure valuable land and resources, but also for average citizens, particularly in Great Britain. Centuries of monarchical rule and absolute power had forged a rigid and repressive social structure. Similar to a caste system, it dictated that every person in the realm, from king to pauper, had a place within the hierarchy that determined social advantage or disadvantage. From birth, British subjects were taught to accept their stations and submit to any authority higher than their own,[4] and by the early 17th century, effects of this stringent system had become visible. The "wandering poor," members of the lower class who could no longer support themselves, moved from the countryside to the already crowded streets of London.[5] The dirty, disease-ridden city extinguished any quality of life they might have hoped for. While most were unwilling to stay, they were also unable to go, lacking the means to move again. The result was a population primed for the chance at a new life.

Colonization, however, was not easy, and England did not successfully establish a settlement until 1607, when John Smith and his men of the Virginia Company founded Jamestown. It was the first of several permanent British settlements that would spring up along the eastern seaboard in the following years. Different settlements drew different people, and as they established their towns, they also established the foundation for strong regional identities that would figure prominently in the country's future.

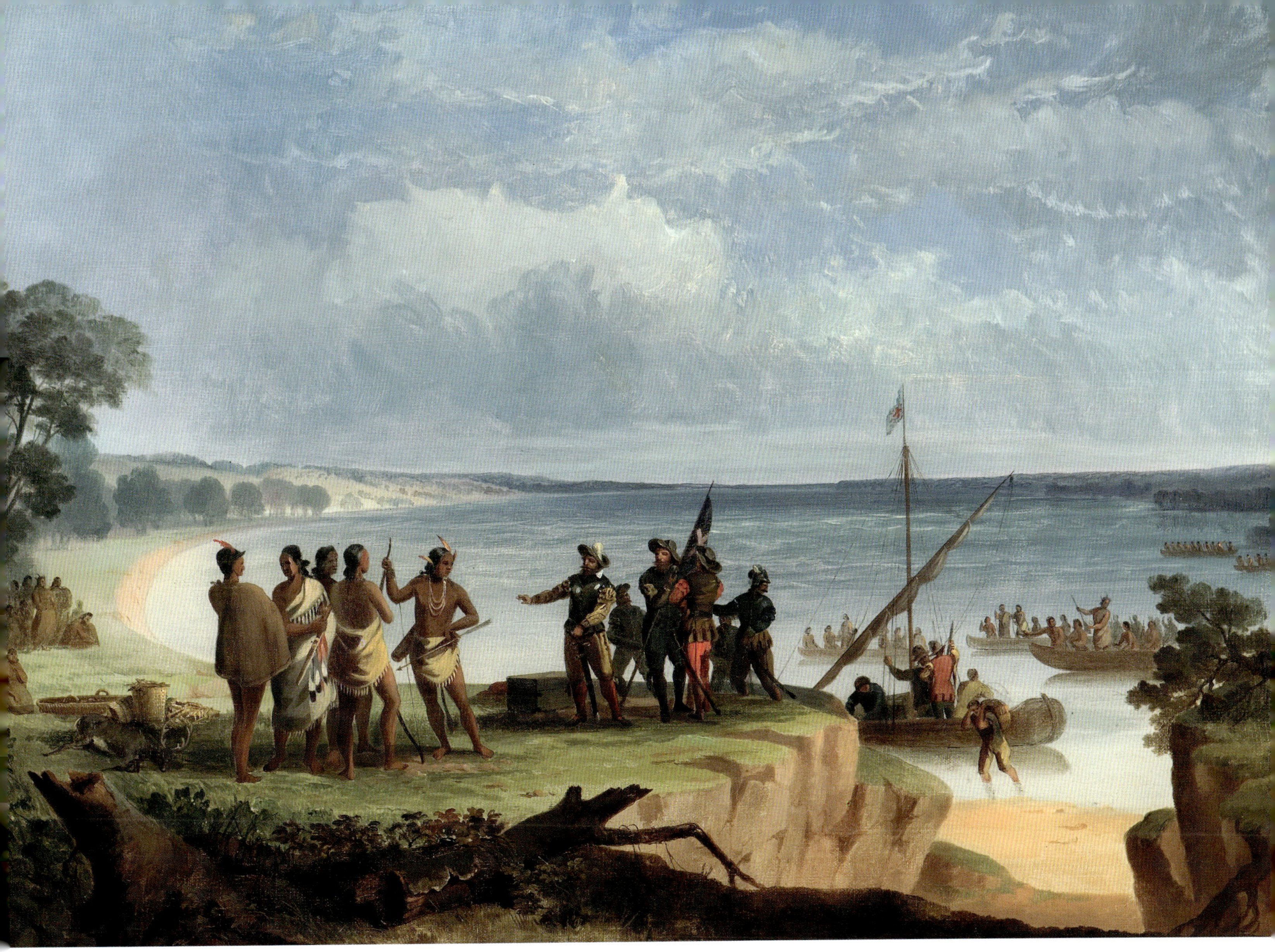

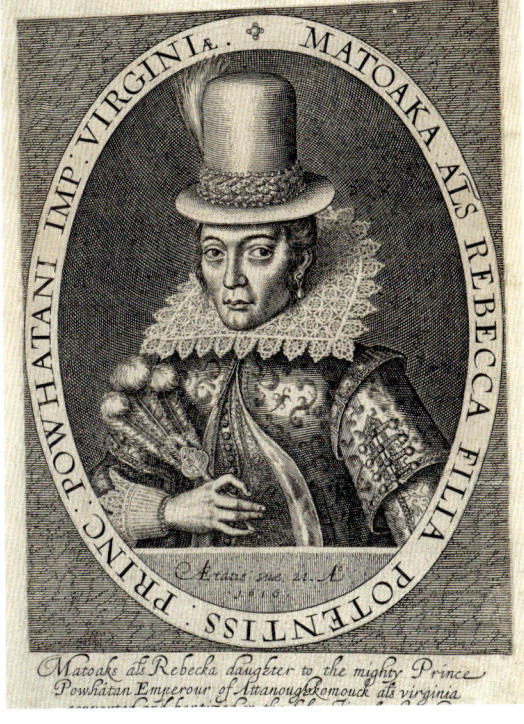

CAPTAIN JOHN SMITH AND PARTY LANDING AT JAMESTOWN MAY 14, 1607, John Mix Stanley. Oil on canvas. GM 0126.1145

In 1607, John Smith and his men of the Virginia Company established the first permanent English settlement in the Americas at Jamestown, Virginia.

POCAHONTAS. From *The Generall Historie of Virginia, New England, and the Summer Isles* by John Smith, 1624. GM 2576.2014

Daughter of Powhatan, Matoaka was a young girl of around ten when she first met John Smith and his fellow Englishmen. She was a frequent visitor to their camp, bringing food and other items to trade. In 1615, she met and married John Rolfe, a Jamestown colonist. The couple had a son together, Thomas, before Matoaka's death in 1617.

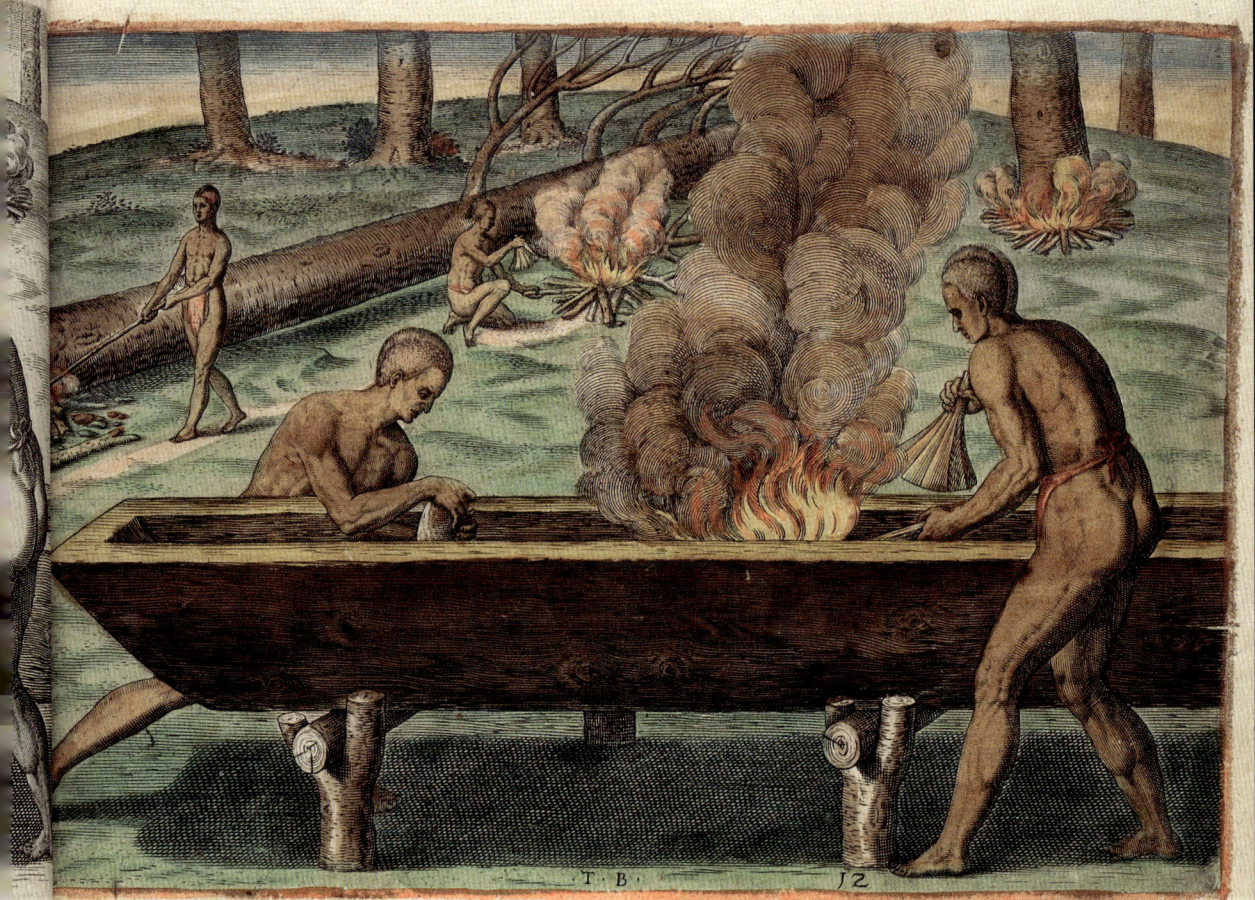

T.B.   J2

*RA est in VIRGINIA cymbas fabricandi ratio: nam cum ferreis
inſtrumentis aut aliis noſtris ſimilibus careant, eas tamen parare no-
runt noſtris non minus commodas ad nauigandum quo lubet per flumi-
na & adpiſcandum. Primum arbore aliqua craſſa & alta delecta, pro
cymbæ quam parare volunt magnitudine, ignem circa eius radices
ſumma tellure in ambitu ſtruunt ex arborum muſco bene reſiccato, &
ligni aſſulis paulatim ignem excitantes, ne flamma altius aſcendat, &
arboris longitudinem minuat. Pæne aduſta & ruinam minante arbo-
re, nouum ſuſcitant ignem, quem flagrare ſinunt donec arbor ſponte cadat. Aduſtis deinde arboris faſtigio & ramis, vt truncus iuſtam longitudinem retineat, tignis tranſuerſis ſupra furcas po-
ſitis imponunt, ea altitudine vt commode laborare poſſint, tunc cortice conchis quibuſdam adem-
pto, integriorem trunci partem pro cymbæ inferiore parte ſeruant, in altera parte ignem ſecundum
trunci longitudinem ſtruunt, præterquam extremis, quod ſatis aduſtum illis videtur, reſtincto igne
conchis ſcabunt, & nouo ſuſcitato igne denuo adurunt, atque ita deinceps pergunt, ſubinde vren-
tes & ſcabentes, donec cymba neceſſarium alueum nacta ſit. Sic Domini ſpiritus rudibus homini-
bus ſuggerit rationem, qua res in ſuum vſum neceſſarias conficere queant.

B 4

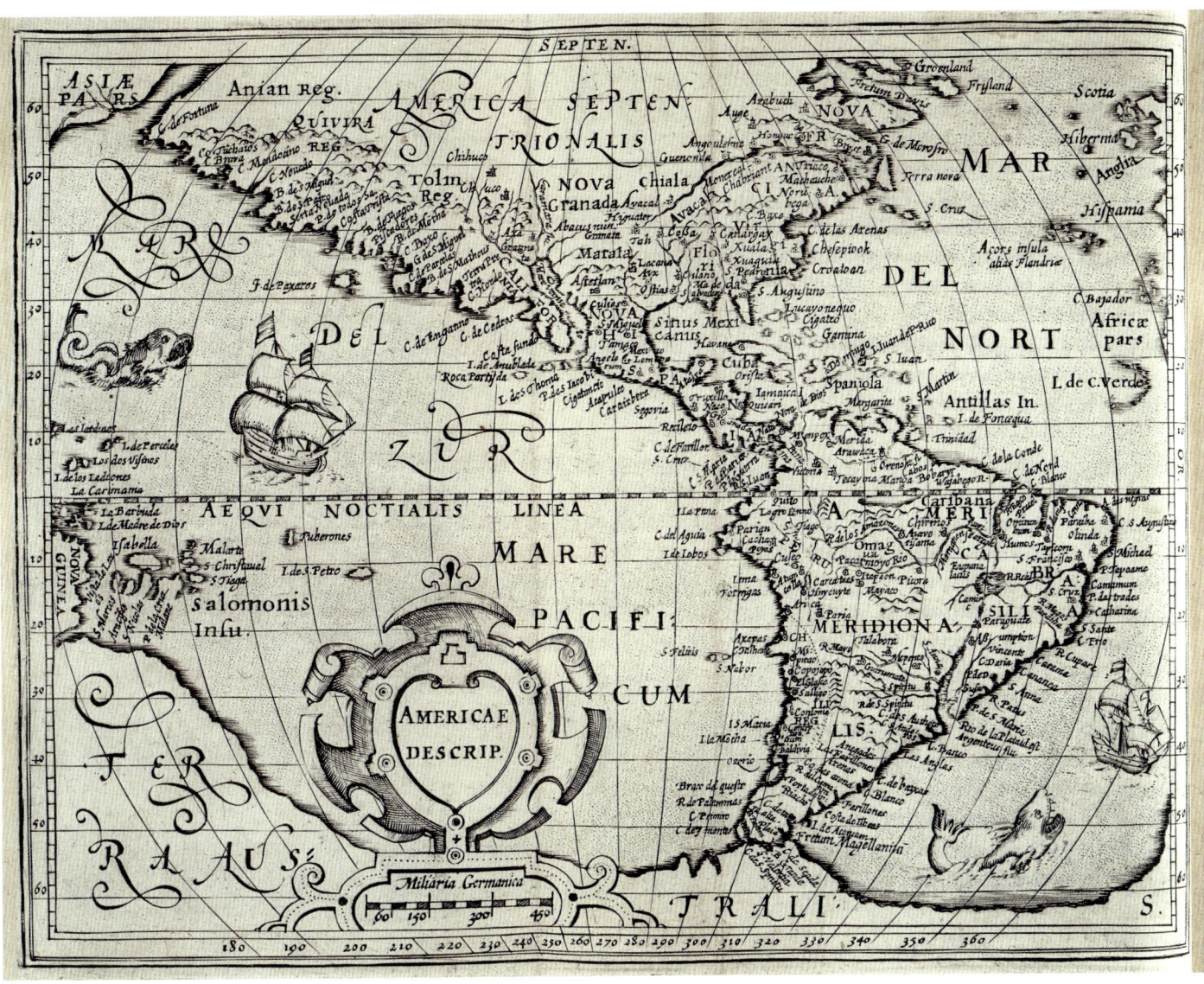

Regions with distinct demographic and economic signatures emerged. The initial waves of immigrants that populated these regions demonstrated a duality engrained in the later American identity—simultaneous diversity and commonality. The southern regions drew predominantly young, single men. While some came from relative wealth, many came from meager to modest origins, and saw in America a chance to make something of themselves.[6] In Britain a man was bound by birth, but in Virginia a man was bound only by ambition. Religion was present, but never pervasive in daily life, and livelihoods were largely made from farming individually owned acreage, with indentured servants or slaves providing labor for larger farms.

AMERICA. From *America Painted to the Life* by Ferdinando Gorges, 1659. GM 2576.2029

FACING: LINTRIUM CONFICIENDORUM RATIO. *Historia Americae Sive Novi Orbis, XII,* 1634. GM 2975.1585

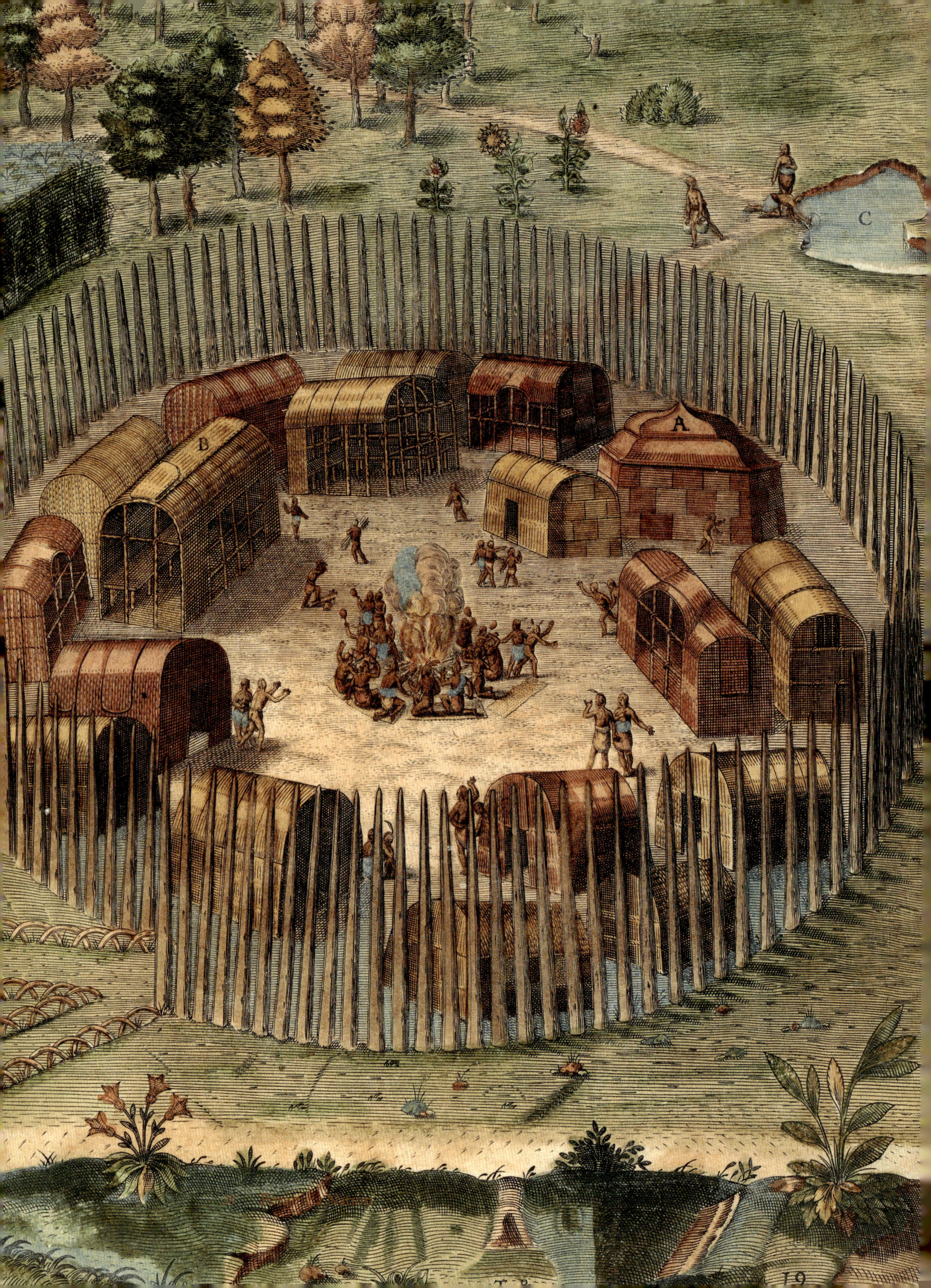

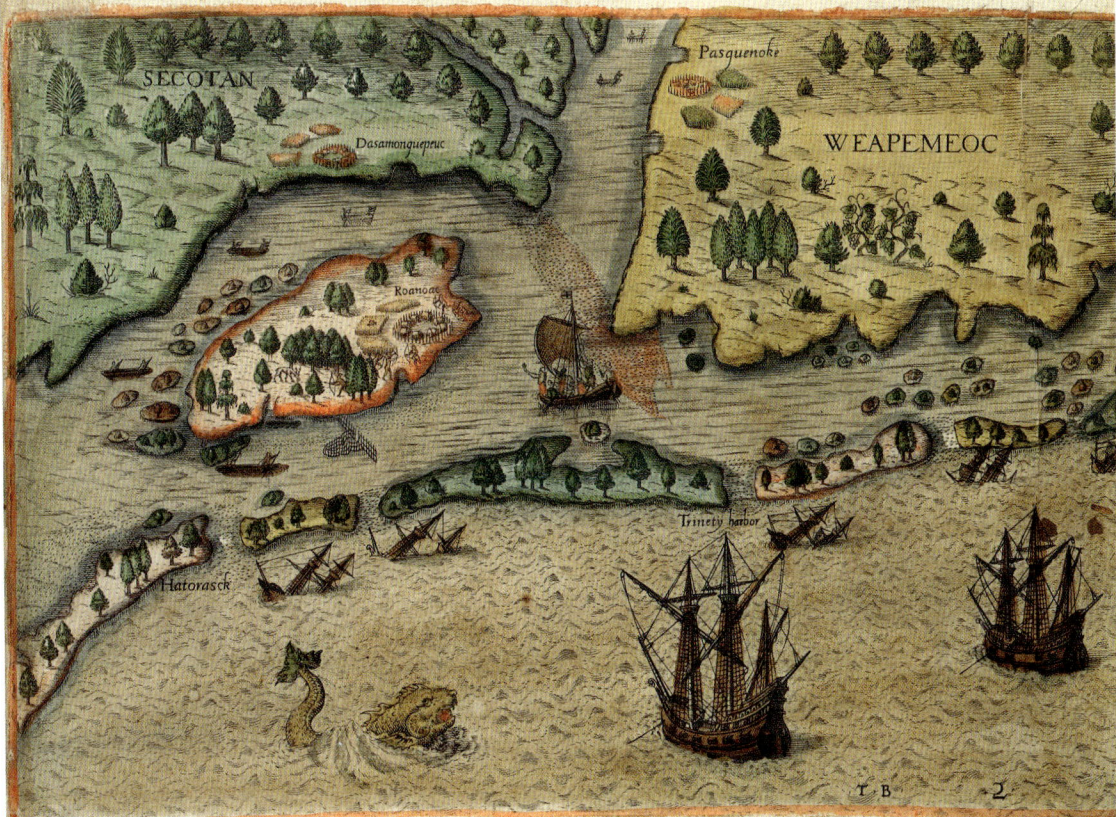

VIRGINIAE maritima Infulis abundant, quæ difficilem admodum præbent in eam regionem aditum: nam licet frequentibus & laxis interuallis fint inter fe difcreta, quæ commodum ingreffum polliceri videtur, magno tamen noftro damno expertifumus vadofa effe & vndarum breuibus infefta, nec vnquam interiora penetrare potuimus, donec multis & variis locis minore naui periculum faceremus: aditum tandem inuenimus loco quodam noftris Anglis bene cognito. Ingreffi igitur, & nauigatione aliquamdiu continuata, magnum flumen obferuauimus, è regione prædictarum infularum fe exonerans, quod tamen fubire non licuit, ob anguftias, arenarum æftu replente eius oftium. Longius igitur nauigationem profequuti, ad magnam infulam peruenimus, cuius incolæ, nobis confpectis immenfum & horridum clamorem tollere cœperunt, vtpote qui homines nobis fimiles numquam antea confpexiffent, & in fugam fe coniicientes, vlulatibus ferarum vel furioforum ritu omnia complerunt: fed amice reuocati, propofitifque noftris mercibus, veluti fpeculis, cultellis, pupis, & aliis quifquiliis, quas ipfis gratas futuras exiftimabamus, fubftiterunt, & obferuata noftra beniuolentia atque amicitia, blanditi nobis, & de aduentu gratulati funt: deinde in fuam vrbem ROANOAC nomine, atque adeo ad fuum WEROANS fiue Regulum deduxerunt, qui fatis humaniter nos excepit, noftro tamen confpectu attonitus.

Talis fuit nofter in eam Novi orbis partem, quam VIRGINIAM appellamus, aduentus: cuius incolarum ftaturam corporis & ornatum, victufque rationem, fefta, & conuiuia, figillatim vobis proponam.

FACING: VILLAGE.
Historia Americae Sive Novi Orbis, I, 1634. GM 2975.1585

ANGLORUMIN VIRGINIAM ADUENTUS. *Historia Americae Sive Novi Orbis, II*, 1634. GM 2975.1585

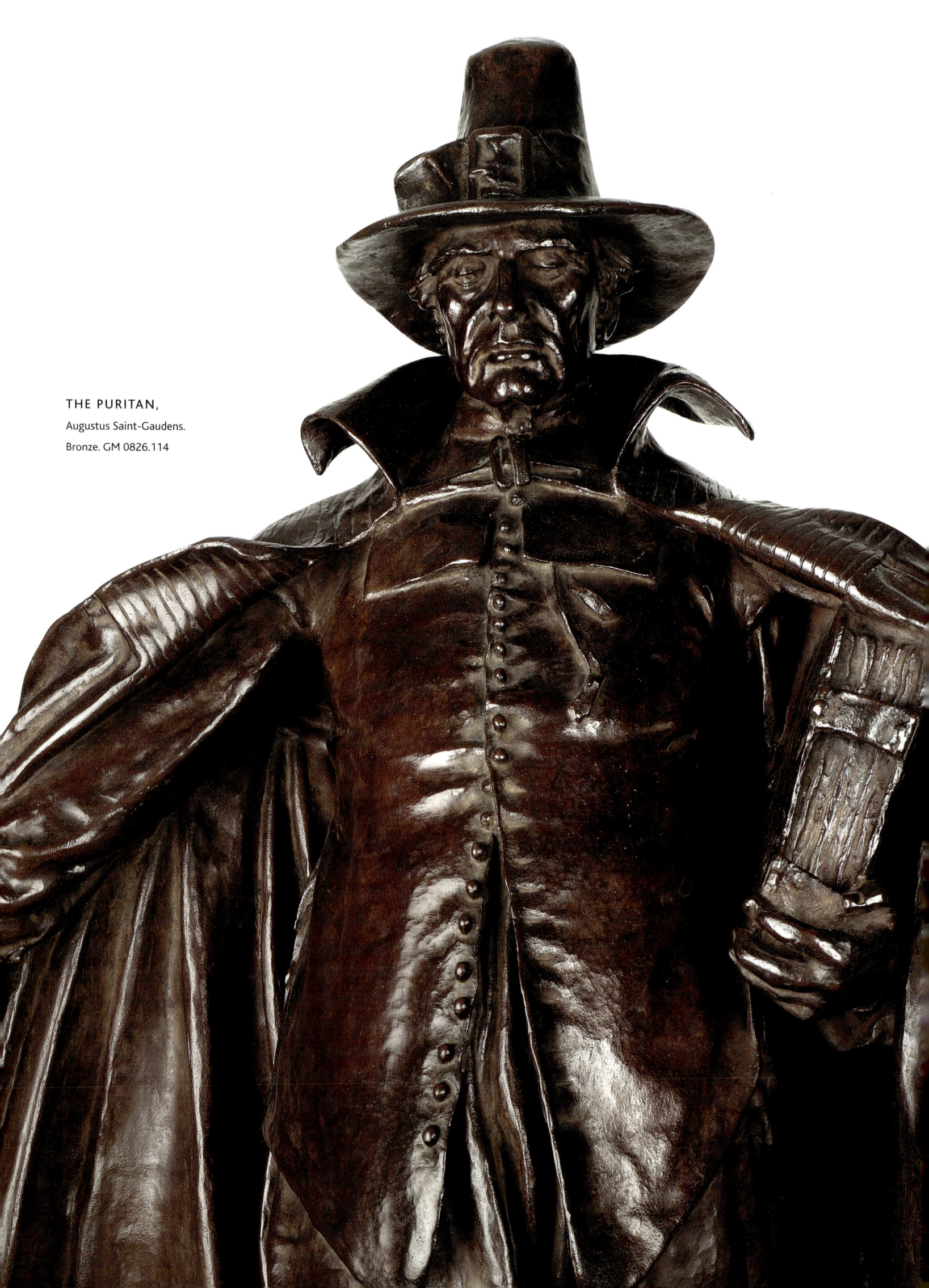

THE PURITAN,
Augustus Saint-Gaudens.
Bronze. GM 0826.114

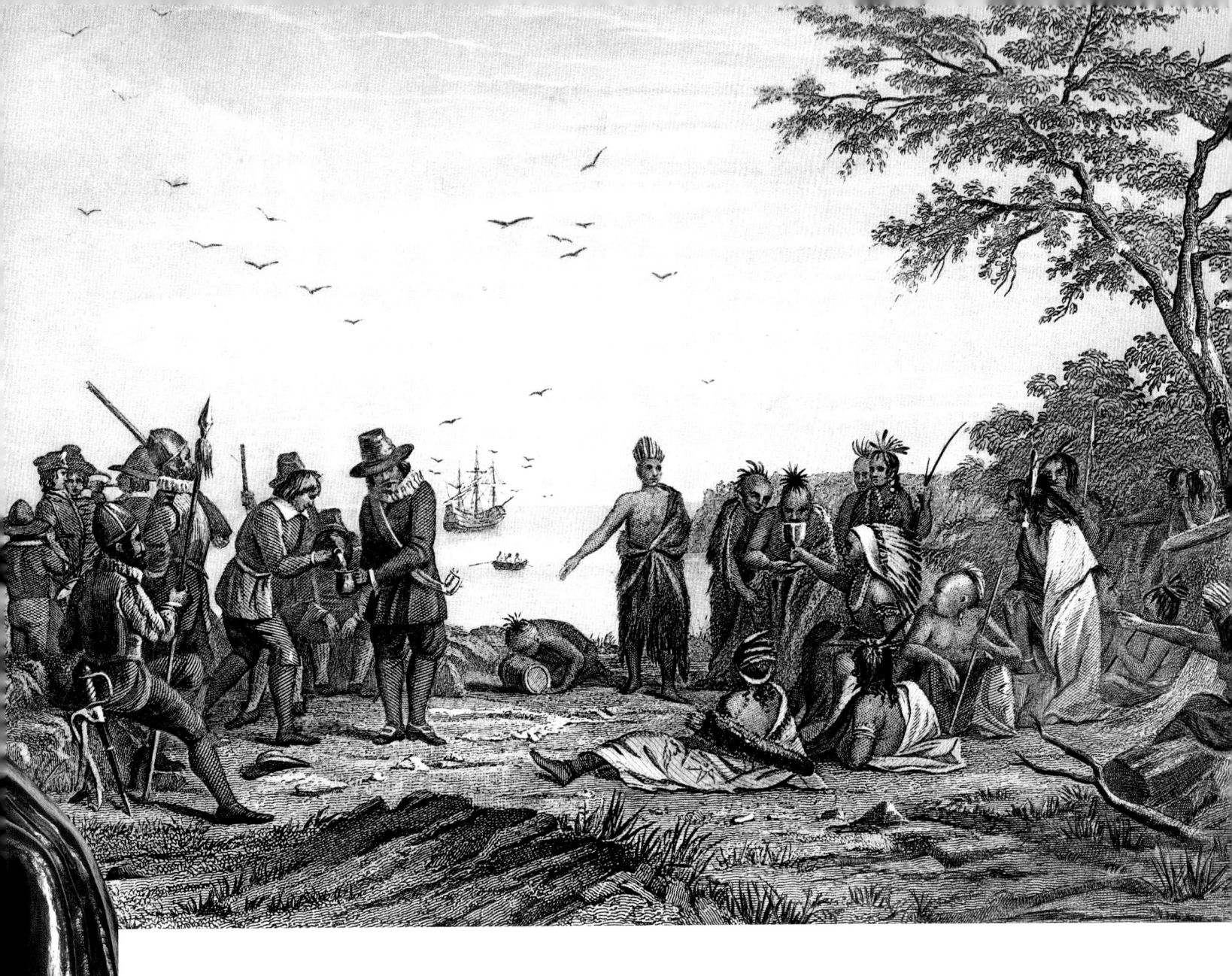

Deplorable conditions in London had left many desperate. Unable to afford the six pounds passage to the colonies, thousands signed contracts of indenture, stipulating they would work four to seven years as a servant.[7] Upon completion of the term, they would be free to pursue their new lives. The abundance of indentured servants and the low cost of maintaining them made them a favored work force over imported slaves, and by 1680, over 90 percent of the laborers in the southern regions were indentured servants.[8]

In contrast, economic and demographic diversity marked the middle and New England regions. Fleeing religious persecution, Pilgrims had settled Massachusetts Bay in 1620, followed by other Puritans in the following decade. Unlike the single men to the south, most came to the northern settlements with their families. Religion dominated every aspect of life, and emphasis was placed not on the individual but the community. Land was communally owned, and churches and

THE PILGRIMS MEET WITH MASSASOIT AND THE ALGONQUINS ON THE SHORES OF MASSACHUSETTS BAY, 1621, Gebbie & Husson Co., Ltd. Engraving. GM 15.1128

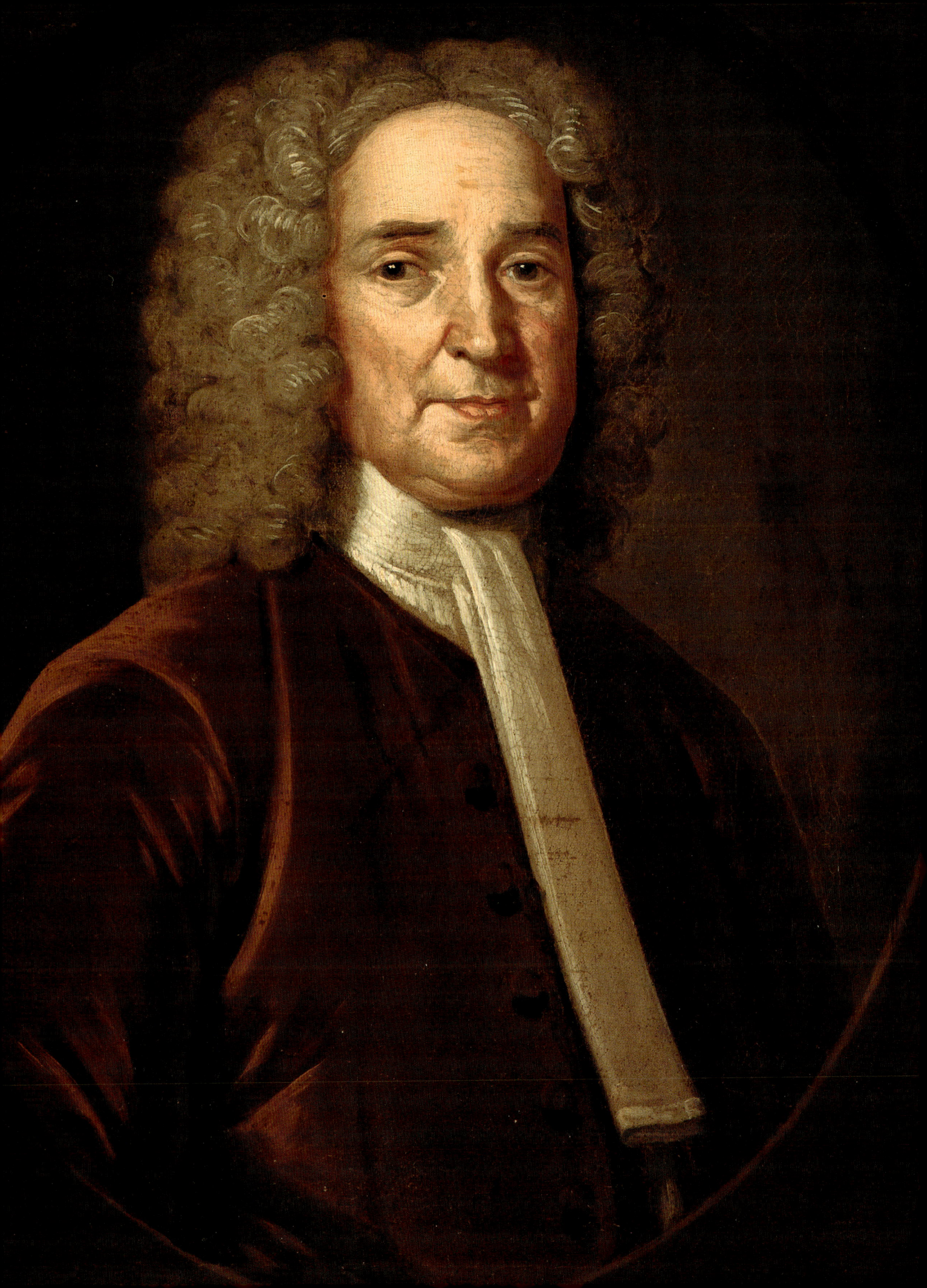

schools built for the betterment of the town.[9] They farmed, hunted, and raised livestock. Although they espoused more egalitarian principles than their southern neighbors, they still used servants and slaves for needed labor, Massachusetts becoming the first colony to legalize slavery in 1641.[10] Progress in the colonies very often came at the expense of others, particularly Native Americans and imported African slaves.

Although different in many respects, early colonists also shared fundamental similarities. Mainly, they were all immigrants who had been willing to abandon old lives in pursuit of the new and unknown. They were risk-takers and optimists who believed in the possibility of a better life that would never be theirs if they stayed in Europe. And so they left and endured six to twelve weeks in small, unsteady ships as they

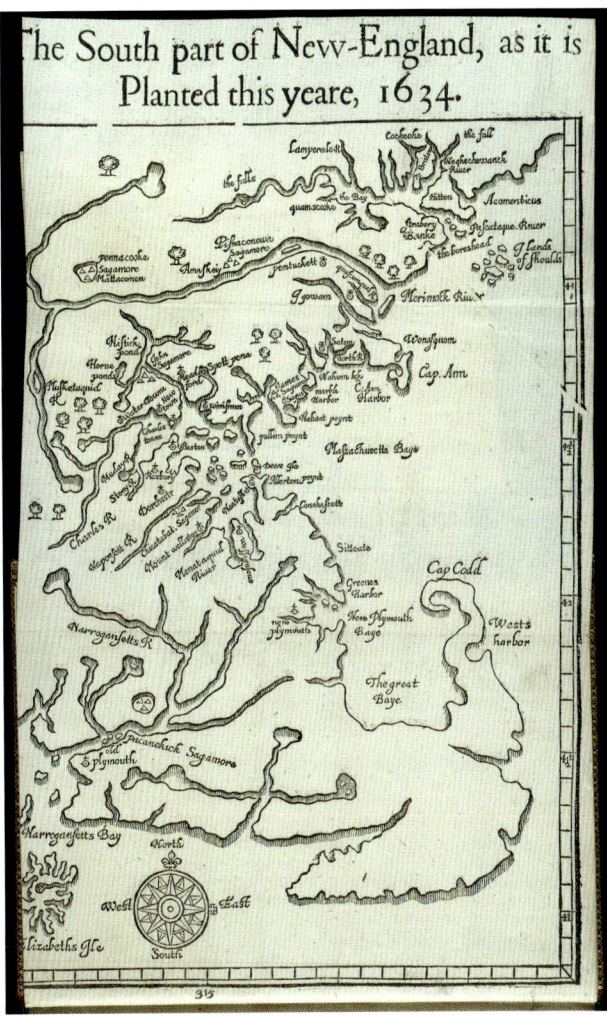

THE SOUTH PART OF NEW-ENGLAND, AS IT IS PLANTED THIS YEARE, 1634. From *New England's Prospect* by William Wood. GM 2476.2018.

FACING: PORTRAIT OF JOHN COTTON, John Smibert. Oil on canvas, ca. 1735. GM 0126.1004

John Cotton (1693–1757) was the minister of the Newton, Massachusetts, church when this portrait was painted. He graduated from Harvard in 1710 and was ordained as minister of the church at Newton in 1714. Cotton came from a long line of religious leaders, the first being a Puritan minister who arrived in New England as part of the Great Migration. The Cotton family flourished and during the colonial period there were at least six men named John Cotton. The family also included Cotton Mather, the Puritan clergyman, scholar, and author.

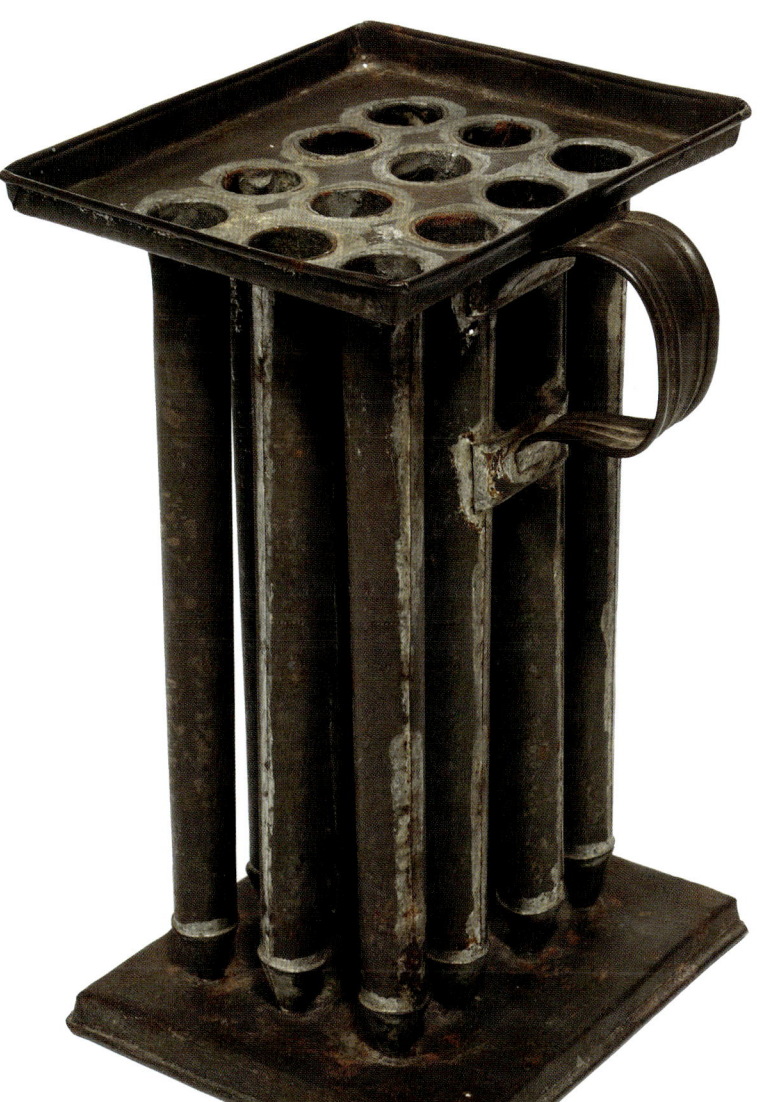

CANDLE MOLD. GM 69.222

crossed 1,600 miles of the Atlantic Ocean.[11] Once they disembarked, the struggle for survival began. For New Englanders, confronting this struggle was doing God's will and work.[12] All settlers, however, had to literally carve out their place, their home, in an unforgiving and unfamiliar world. Many did not survive. Some died from disease.[13] Others from violence. It was a hard existence that required people to be equally hard.

To bring some sense of normalcy to their new and difficult lives, the colonists relied heavily on familiar customs and practices. This was the second, major commonality among early settlers. Although the Netherlands and France had settlements, the majority of towns were British, and British settlers were quick to recreate British customs and culture. Towns and counties bore English place names such as Boston and Plymouth; local governments followed British models. Perhaps most interestingly, settlers wasted little time in reinstituting the rigid hierarchy they had fled. Class continued to be an agent of division, but with one significant difference. Social mobility, stifled and controlled in England, was now more open and offered the chance at higher stations. Authority was still an absolute and unquestionable element of colonial life, and the commonwealth continued as a model for every level of society, even in domestic settings. The king ruled the realm. The governor ruled the colony. The husband ruled the household. In Virginia, if a court convicted a woman of killing her husband, she was found guilty not only of murder, but also of petit treason.[14] This autocratic system also influenced the settlers' treatment of servants and slaves, and their relationships with Native Americans. Servants and slaves occupied the lowest social positions and were treated accordingly. Indians were regarded similarly.

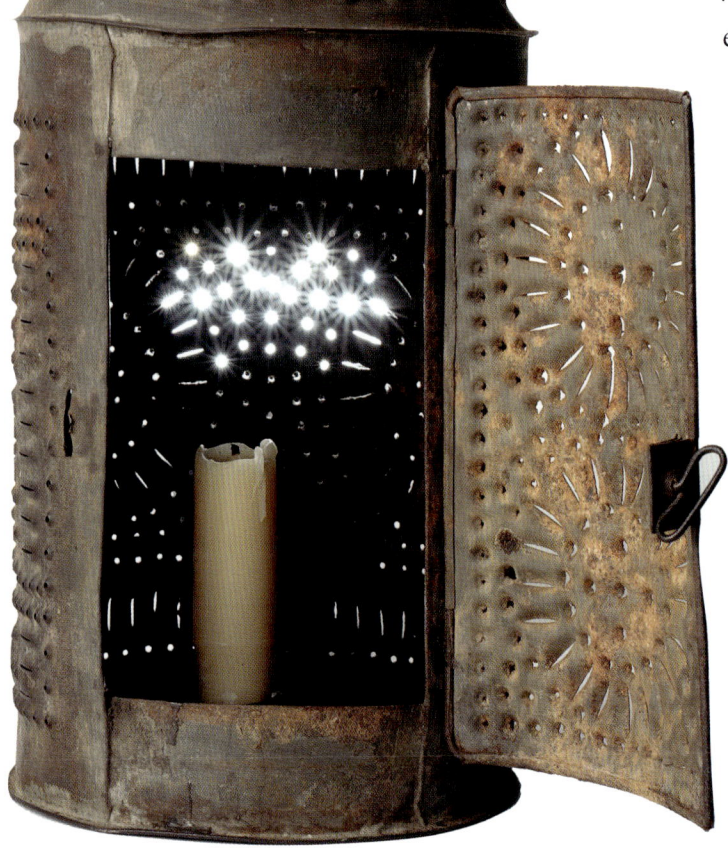

❧ By the King.

¶ A Proclamation prohibiting interloping and
disorderly trading to *New England* in *America*.

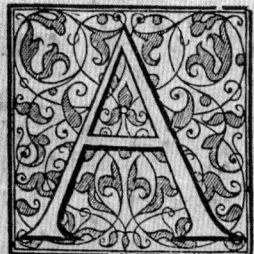

AS it hath euer beene held a principall Office of Chriſtian Kings, to ſeeke by all pious meanes the aduancement of Chriſtian Religion ; ſo the conſideration thereof, hath beene a ſpeciall motiue vnto Vs, from time to time, as often as cauſe hath required, to further, by Our Royall authoꝛity, the good diſpoſition of any of Our well affected Subiects, that haue a will to attempt the diſcouering and planting in any parts of the woꝛld, as yet ſauage and vnpoſſeſſed by the Subiects of any Chꝛiſtian Pꝛince oꝛ State. And now foꝛ that, by Gods ſacred fauour, there is likely to enſue great aduancement of his gloꝛy, Our Crown, and State, by reaſon of Our grant heeretofoꝛe made to the Counſell foꝛ the managing of the affaires of New England in America, being in bꝛeadth from foꝛty degrees of Noꝛtherly latitude from the Equinoctiall line, to foꝛty eight degrees of the ſayd Noꝛtherly latitude, and in length by all the bꝛeadth atoꝛeſayd, thoꝛowout the maine land from Sea to Sea ; We cannot but continue Our ſpeciall reſpect and fauour vnto them in their endeuours, and exerciſe Our Royall authoꝛity againſt the hinderers thereof. Wherefoꝛe, hauing receiued certaine infoꝛmation of many and intolerable abuſes offered by ſundꝛy interlopers, irregular and diſobedient perſons, that ſeeking principally their pꝛeſent and pꝛiuate pꝛofits, haue not only impeached ſome of the Planters there, of their lawfull poſſeſſions, but alſo taken from them their Timber without giuing any ſatiſfaction, as in iuſtice they ought to haue done : and not therewith contented, haue rined whole woods to the vtter ruine of the ſame foꝛ euer after ; as alſo, by caſting of their ballaſt in the harboꝛs of ſome of their Ilands, haue almoſt made them vnſeruiceable : And yet not ſo contented, by their pꝛomiſcuous trading, aſwell Marriners as Maſters with the Sauages, haue ouerthꝛowne the trade and commerce that befoꝛe was had, to the great pꝛofit of the Planters, and which were indeed their principall hopes foꝛ the aduancement of that plantation, next vnto the commodities that coaſt affoꝛds of Fiſhing : Neither heerwith ſatiſfied, but as if they reſolued to omit nothing that might be impious and intolerable, they did not foꝛbeare to barter away to the Sauages, Swoꝛds, Pikes, Muſkets, Fowling peeces, Match, Powder, Shot, and other warlike weapons, and teach them the vſe thereof, not only to their owne pꝛeſent puniſhment (diuers of them being ſhoꝛtly after ſlain by the ſame Sauages, whom they had ſo taught, and with the ſame weapons which they had furniſhed them withall) but alſo to the hazard of the liues of Our good ſubiects already planted there, and (aſmuch as in them lay) to the making of the whole attempt it ſelfe (how pious and hopefull ſoeuer) fruſtrate, oꝛ ſo much the moꝛe difficult. We, foꝛ refoꝛmation and pꝛeuention of theſe oꝛ the like euils heereafter, and foꝛ the moꝛe cleare declaration of Our Kingly reſolution and iuſt intents, both to maintayne Our Royall grant already made, and to vphold and encourage by all wayes and meanes the woꝛthy diſpoſitions of the vndertakers of thoſe deſignes, haue thought fit, and doe heerby ſtraitly charge and command, That none of Our Subiects whatſoeuer, (not Aduenturers, Inhabitoꝛs oꝛ Planters in New England) pꝛeſume from hencefooꝛth to frequent thoſe Coaſts, to trade oꝛ traffique with thoſe people, oꝛ to intermedle in the woodes oꝛ freehold of any the Planters oꝛ Inhabitants (otherwiſe then by the licence of the ſayd Counſell, oꝛ accoꝛding to the oꝛders eſtabliſhed by Our Pꝛiuy Counſell foꝛ the releeſe oꝛ eaſe of the tranſpoꝛtation of the Colony in Virginia) vpon paine of Our high indignation, and the confiſcation, penalties and foꝛfeitures in Our ſayd Royall grant expꝛeſſed : Leauing it neuertheleſſe, in the meane time, to the diſcretion of the ſayd Counſel foꝛ New England, to pꝛoceed againſt the foꝛeſayd offenders accoꝛding to the ſame, eſpecially, ſeeing we finde the armes of the ſayd Counſell to bee open to receiue into that plantation any of Our louing Subiects, who are willing to ioyne with them in the charge, and participate in the pꝛofits thereof.

Giuen at Our Court at Theobalds, the ſixt day of Nouember, in the yeere of Our Reigne of England, France, and Ireland, the twentieth, and of Scotland the ſixe and fiftieth.

God ſaue the King.

Imprinted at London by Bonham Norton and Iohn Bill, Printers to the
Kings moſt Excellent Maieſtie. M. D C. XXII.

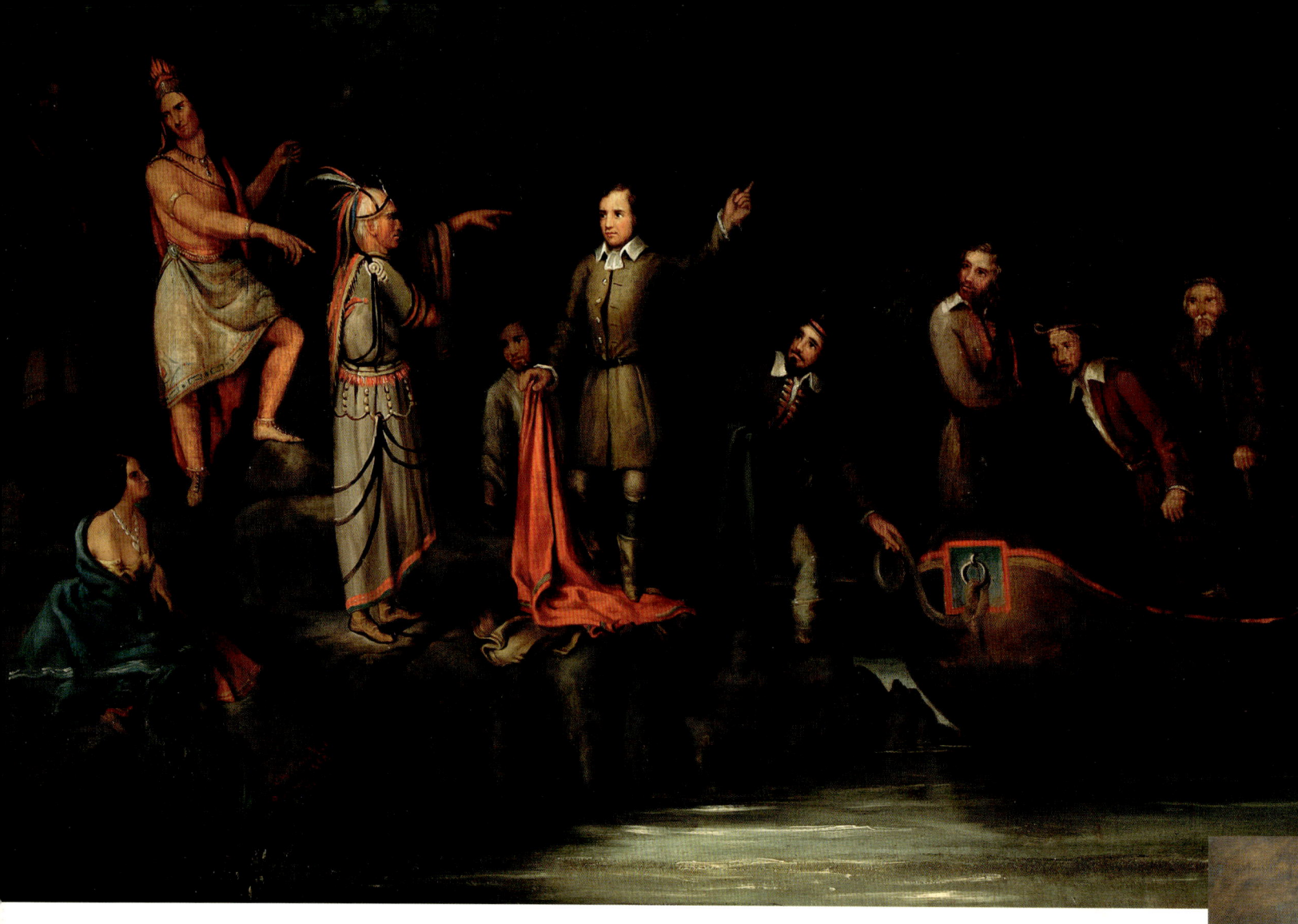

The sense of shared superiority resulting from this system encouraged unity among early colonists, enhancing their common identity. This typically authoritative approach was not without consequence. Too diverse for generalities, the relationships between settlers and non-Anglos ranged from civil at best to violent at worst. Curiosity between settlers and Native Americans drove early interactions that sometimes concluded without incident. As time progressed, however, distrust and retaliation replaced curiosity and a pattern of violence and conflict emerged. Such suspicions also characterized the relationship between colonists and slaves. If Africans survived the Middle Passage, they were sold as property upon arrival and forced to labor for a people they did not understand in a world they did not know. The fear that must have filled them plagued slave owners as well, as they worried about slave rebellions and violence. Such incidents did occur, and in the following century, it was not uncommon to read of such acts in the newspapers.[15]

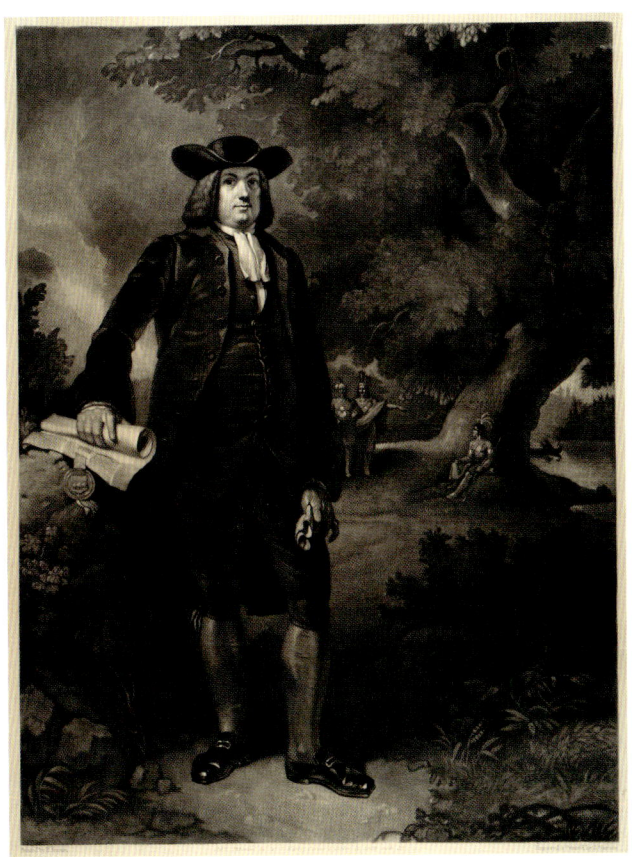

WILLIAM PENN, Henry Inman. Engraving. GM 1526.72

BELOW: PENN'S TREATY WITH THE INDIANS,
Benjamin West. Oil on canvas, 1809. GM 0126.1021

According to folklore, Quaker leader William Penn formalized the Great Treaty with the Delawares in 1682. The meeting was to have taken place under an enormous elm tree at Shackamaxon, now part of Philadelphia. The tradition of this meeting apparently grew from a letter written in 1733 by Voltaire in which the French philosopher praised Penn for an alliance that was "the only treaty between those people and the Christians that was not ratified by an oath, and was never broken." There is no evidence the event depicted here ever occurred, but the painting is an allegory of colonial America.

In reality, to promote peaceful coexistence, Penn often met with tribal leaders. The meetings were held outdoors at various council grounds and two such meetings were held at Shackamaxon. The depicted exchange of gifts was a customary practice at the conclusion of agreements.

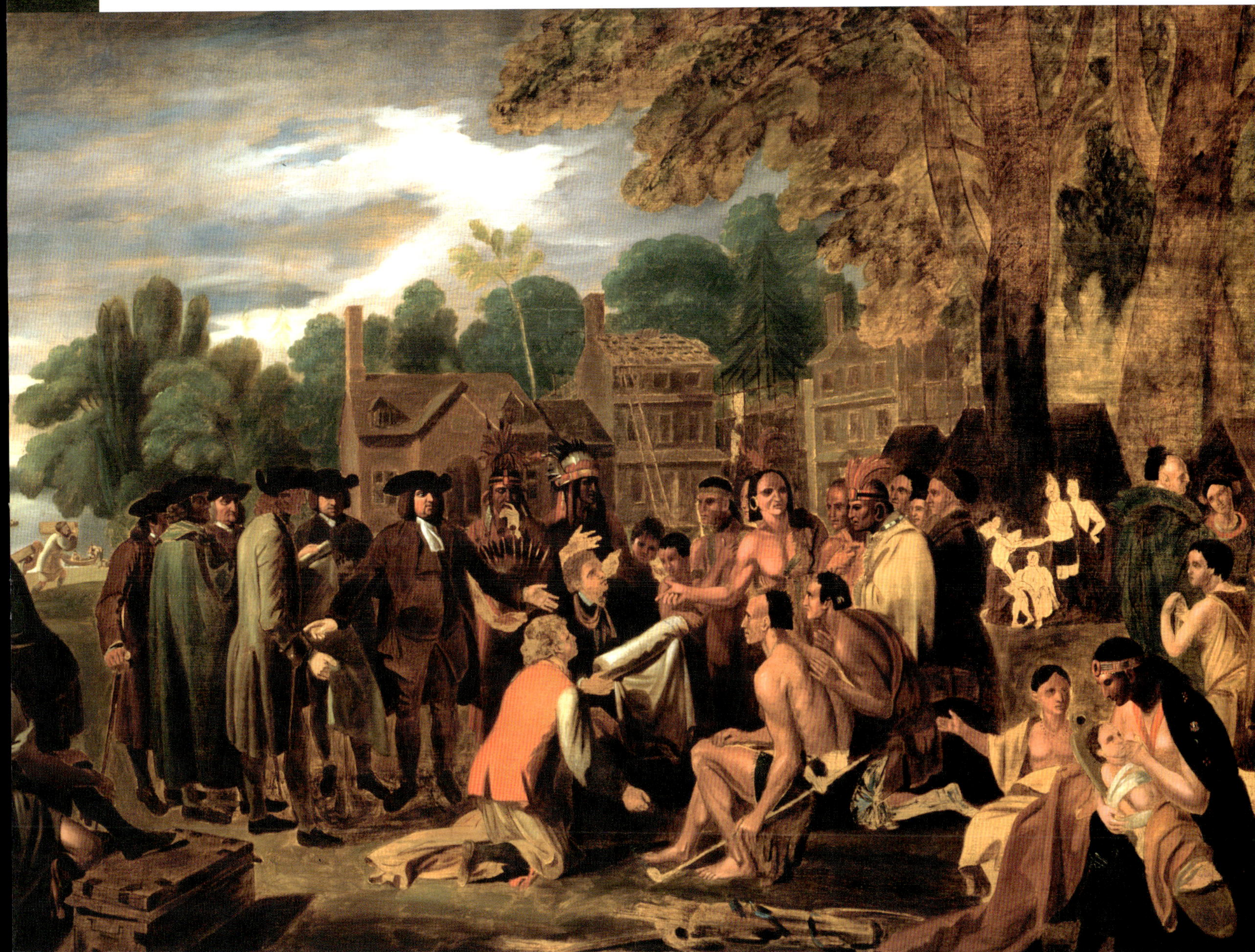

Propositions made by the Right Hon:ble
Francis Lord Howard Baron of Effingham his
Ma:tys Lieut: and Governour Generall of Virginia
To the Mayuase Oneydes, Onnondages and Cayouge
Sachims in the Court Hoys of Albany the 30th
Day of July 1684.

It is now seaven yeares since you (unprovoaked) came into
Virginia a Country Belonging to the great King of England, and
committed severall murthers and robberies, carrying our Christian
Women and children Prisoners into your Castles, all which injurys
wee had designed to have revenged upon you; But by the desire
of S.r Edm:d Androse then Governour Gen.l of this Country, wee
desisted from destroying you, And sent our Agents Coll: W.m
Kendall, and Coll: Southey Littleton, to confirme and make sure
the peace that Coll: Coursey of Maryland included us in, when
first he treated with you; Butt wee find that as you quickly forgot
what you promised Coll: Coursey, soe you have likewise wilfully
broake the Covenant Chaine, which you promist our Agent Coll:
Kendall should be both strong and bright, if wee of Virginia
would bury in the pitt of Oblivion the Injurys who had then done
Us, the which upon Govern.r Andros Intercession and your sub-
mission wee were willing to forgett, but you not at all minding
the Covenants then made, have ever since come into our Country
in a warlike manner, under pretensions of fighting with our
friends and neighbour Indians, which you ought not to have done,
our

As the decades passed, Indian populations significantly decreased from disease while settlements stabilized and their populations increased.[16] Colonies enjoyed relative independence, but the ascension of King James to the throne in 1685 adversely affected the relationship between the crown and the colonies. James ruled with a heavy hand and saw the colonies as little more than a revenue source. In an effort to exert more control over northeastern colonies, he consolidated Massachusetts, Plymouth, New Hampshire, Maine, Narraganset, Rhode Island, Connecticut, East Jersey, West Jersey, and New York into the Dominion of New England.[17] He also raised taxes and levied quit-rents, or land taxes, on personally owned land. Discontent rose among the population, and a Massachusetts reverend, John Wise, gave voice to the masses when he formally protested the taxes. In an argument famously associated with a later movement, Wise maintained that although they did not live in England, they were still Englishmen and as such retained the rights bequeathed to them by the Magna Carta, particularly the right to refuse any tax levied against them without their representative present.[18] No taxation without representation. The response from the Governor General Edmund Andros was swift and clear. The Magna Carta did not grant rights. The monarch did. Colonists could not misunderstand the message—that separate

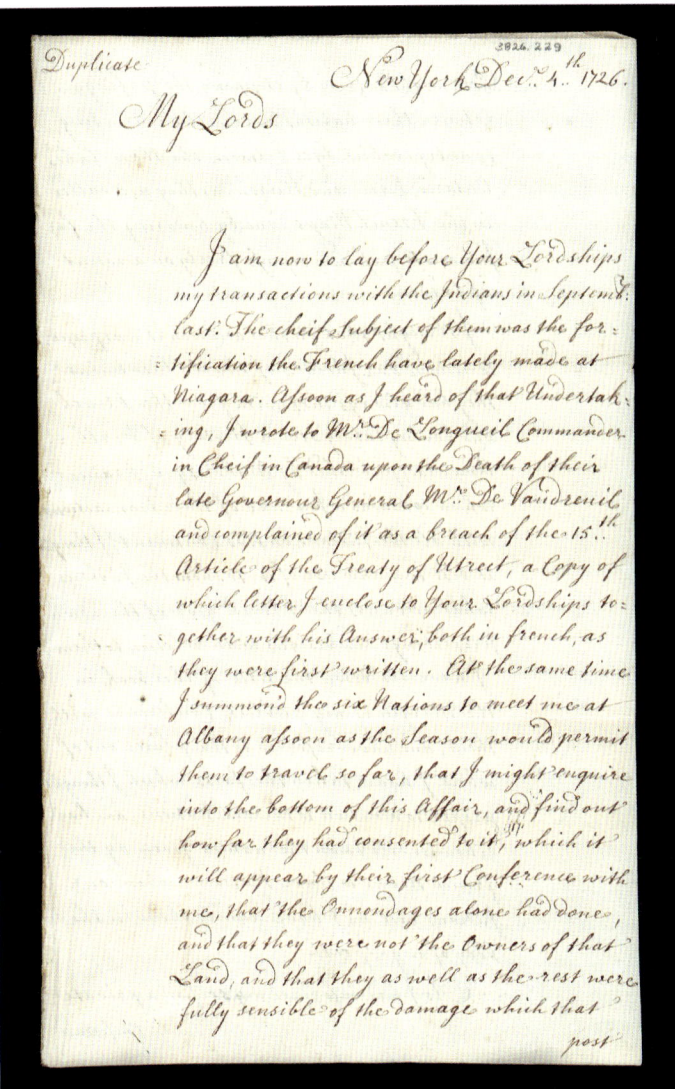

LETTER FROM GOVERNOR WILLIAM BURNET TO THE BOARD OF TRADE, DECEMBER 4, 1726. GM 3826.229

The son of an archbishop and the godson of William, Prince of Orange, and his wife Mary, William Burnet was born at the Hague in the Netherlands. He was appointed governor of New York and New Jersey in 1720. In this letter he discussed recent Native cessions of lands around Fort Niagara. He worried over the French maintaining the treaty, saying that "nothing has had a worse effect with our Indians than promising and not performing."

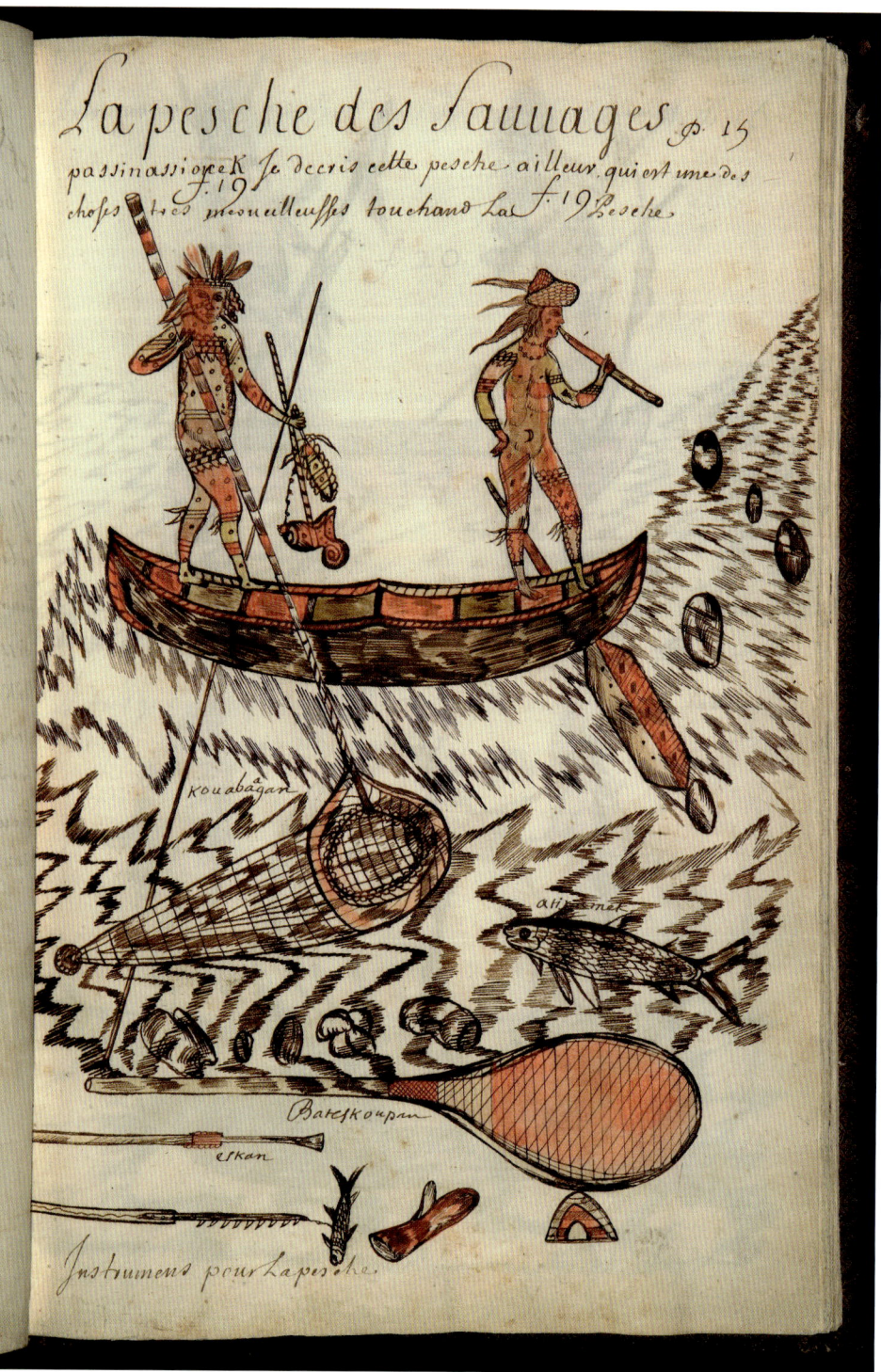

La pesche des Sauuages p. 15
passinassiopek Je decris cette pesche ailleur qui est une des
choses très merueilleuses touchand La F. 19 pesche

Kouabâgan

Ba...

Batchkoupan

eskan

Instrumens pour La pesche.

was not equal, and that they were seen as less than English. One dominion official even remarked that you have "no more privledges Left you than not to be Sould for Slaves."[19]

Relations between crown and colonists continued to decline as James became increasingly unpopular in England, culminating in the loss of his throne to William of Orange during the Glorious Revolution in 1688. News was slow to reach the colonies, but as reports trickled in, some saw a chance to rebel against the royal governors appointed by James. Massachusetts, a leading colony in the later American Revolution, raised a militia 2,000 strong and imprisoned twenty-six officials, including the governor general who had so sternly rebuked the populace for protesting taxes. The rebels dismantled the Dominion of New England, reaffirming their distinctive regional identities.[20]

Although crown-colonial relations were superficially renewed, a decisive shift had occurred. The settlers had demonstrated a defining aspect of the American identity—willingness to defend their freedoms when threatened. With the precedent of raising arms against the crown now set and the Dominion official's words still echoing, the colonists began to see themselves as something other than English.

The following year marked the beginning of another event that dramatically influenced the American identity—the Nine Years War between France and England. It was one in a long history of conflict between the two, and the cost was high.[21] Isolation from the fighting produced a contradictory result among the settlers; colonists felt united as English citizens against the French, yet they also felt simultaneously disconnected from England. Effects of the war, however, eventually reached the colonies when Britain began heavily taxing them to ease her financial burden. Britain also realized the economic advantages of commerce with the colonies. Cross-Atlantic trade dramatically increased, with the side effect of bringing more frequent news from the mother country in the form of newspapers and pamphlets. This access to current news helped reinforce the colonists' British identity at a critical time.[22] Trade also helped satisfy the colonial drive for material culture by providing British goods to the settlements.[23] In a society dominated by the display and validation of social status, material items were essential.

In the century since Jamestown, colonial identities had become complex and pulled in two directions. The news from Britain kept colonists physically and figuratively connected to the mother country, but individual, colonial, and class identities were intensifying as more people were now second- and even third-generation Americans, many never having stepped ashore in Britain.

FACING: CODEX CANADIENSIS, Louis Nicolas, ca. 1693. GM 4726.7015

Compiled by a Jesuit missionary, the *Codex* contains 180 illustrations of the peoples, flora, and fauna of 17th-century New France.

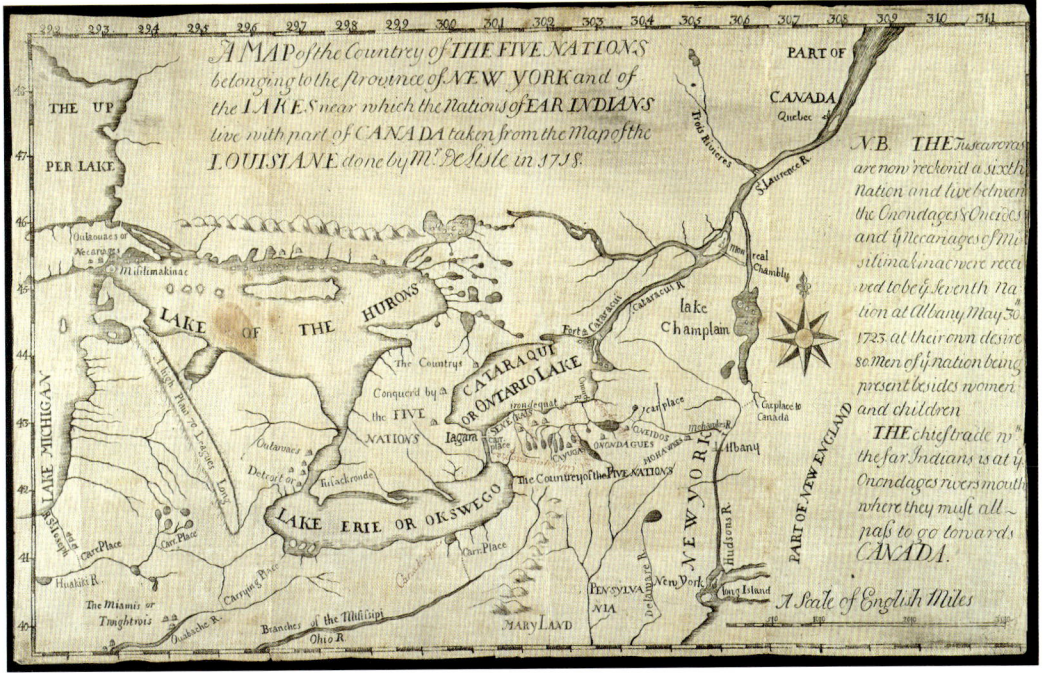

A MAP OF THE COUNTRY OF THE FIVE NATIONS, William Bradford, 1724. GM 3926.41

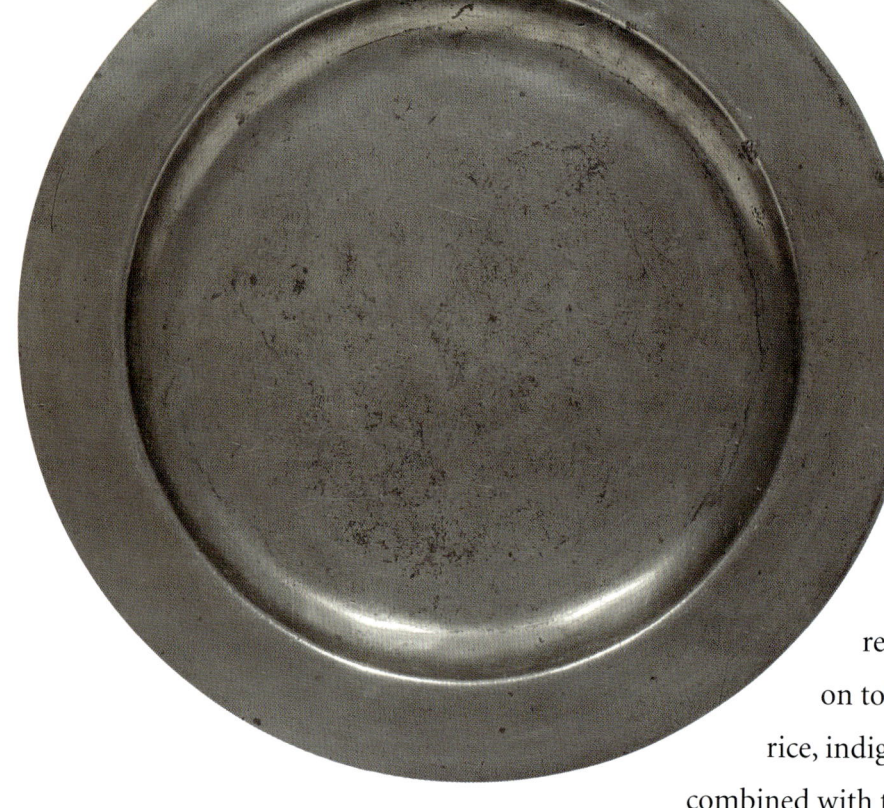

PEWTER CHARGER.
GM 67.30

Household items such as pewter chargers and plates were status symbols during early colonial times.

DOCUMENT OUTLINING THE SALE OF NEWISOCK, AN INDIAN SLAVE. 1750.
GM 4026.5897

Newisock was nine years old at the time of this contract.

The colonies were also becoming less English as European emigrants now constituted the largest percentage of arrivals.[24] Economically, the colonies were stronger than ever before. Fishing, whaling, logging, and shipping supported New England's growth, while southern economies relied on agriculture. No longer dependent on tobacco, they now profited from raising rice, indigo, and cotton. This farming tradition, combined with the use of indentured servants and an economic downturn during the 1680s, gave rise to a society marked by unequal distribution of wealth and the institution of slavery.

After completing their terms, indentured servants were usually granted or purchased small acreages, typically fifty acres. For a time they prospered, but during the economically troubled 1680s, they reaped less profit and with their farms further inland could not afford the high costs of moving their crops downriver to port. Large landholders capitalized on the situation and bought the small farms, creating extensive landholdings called plantations. To work these ever-expanding farms, plantation owners began relying on African slaves. The number of indentured servants had decreased, and as farmers had become wealthier, they could afford to purchase slaves. In 1700, enslaved people accounted for 13 percent of the population in the south; fifty years later they constituted 40 percent. Between 1700 and 1775, more slaves arrived in America than all European emigrants combined.[25] Plantation owners shaped the South and became America's landed gentry, using their positions to manipulate race relations to their advantage. They offered guns to Indians who brought in runaway slaves, yet they also instigated wars against Indians. The conflicts not only freed land for consolidation into even larger estates, but also defused the complaints of small-scale white farmers against plantation owners by uniting all against a common enemy.[26] Slavery became the foundation of the southern economy. While New Englanders determined social status and wealth through homes, clothing, and furniture, southerners determined social status by the number of slaves a person owned.[27]

To All Christian People to whom
these Presents Shall Come Know Yee that I
Nessamee of Sackhewack for and in Con=
sideration of the Sum of Thirty Pounds to me
in hand Paid before the Ensealing and Delivery
hereof by Jacobus Van Ess Abraham Fonda and
abraham P. van antwerpe Shonechtady Traders the
Receipt whereof I do hereby Acknowledge and
therewith my Self fully Sattisfied Contented
and thereof Acquit and Discharge the Said
Jacobus Van Ess Abraham Fonca & Abraham P. Van
Antwerpe their heirs Executors Adm.rs and Assigns
for Ever by these Presents Have Given granted
bargained Sold Alliened and Confirmed and by
these Presents do freely absolutely give, grant,
bargain, Sell, alien Convey & Confirm unto the
Said Jac.s Ess Abra. Fonda & abraham Piet.r Van
Antwerpe their heirs and Assigns for Ever one Certain
Indian Boy Called Newe'sock aged about Nine
years of Age To have and to hold the S.d Indian
Boy with all Priveleges to the Same belonging
to them the S.d Jac.s Ess Abraham Fonda Abraham
Piet.r Van antwerpe their heirs and Assigns for Ever
and to their only proper Use benefitt and behoof
In witness whereof I the Said Nessamee
have hereunto Sett my hand Seal this Ninth
day of July one thousand Seaven Hundred and
Fifty

Signed Sealed and Delivered
in the presences
of Us

Harmen J. Vissgher
Pet.r V. Driessen

        his
Nesa ✠ mee
        Mark

This Indenture made the Ten___ day of October ___
Yeare of the reigne of our Sovereigne Lord George by the grace of
God of Great Britaine ffrance & Ireland King Defender of the ffaith
&c Annoqz Dm 1715 Between Jonathan Chin an Indian man
of the one part and William Wanton of Newport in the Colony of
Rhoad Island & Providence Plantations Merchant of the other
part Witnesseth That the said Jonathan Chin ffor & in Consideration
of the Sume of ffifty Shilings already received of the said William
Wanton and alsoe of diverse Sumes of money, Which the said Jonathan
Chin owes, (and the said William Wanton has engaged to pay unto)
Jeremiah Wilcox, John Briggs, John Akins Benjamin Howland
& Daniel Wood, Testifyed by his Signing & Sealing hereof)
Doth Put & bind himself the sd Jonathan Chin a Servant unto
the said William Wanton his Exect Adm & Assignes & With him
to Serve as a Servant from the day of the date hereof unto the
full End & Terme of Two yeares and fully to be Compleate and
Ended During all Which said Terme The said Servant his
said Master shall faithfully Serve And in all things as a
good faithfull diligent & Obedient Servant shall ___ &
behave himself towards his said Master and all his during
the sd Terme In Witnesse whereof the sd Jonathan Chin hath
hereunto Sett his hand & Seale the day & yeare above written
And it is further Covenanted & agreed by the sd Jonathan Chin
That in Case the said Jonathan Chin should run away, he shall
Serve three Months longer then the Terme agreed upon

Sealed & Delivered   the marke of
in the presence of

Jeremiah Clarke   Jonathan ᴠ Chin

Ja: Martin

4026.1484

The concept of equality that is today synonymous with the United States was not present in 18th-century colonial America. Although anti-slavery sentiments arose in some colonies, such as Pennsylvania, most still saw no contradiction in espousing egalitarian principles while practicing slavery.

For the settlers, equality applied only to them—a perception demonstrated during Georgia's formative years. The funding company had wanted an economy founded on small farms, not on the disparate distribution of wealth that characterized Virginia and Carolina. To discourage such class divisions, and following recent parliamentary legislation, they banned slavery in the new colony. Georgia farmers, however, vehemently protested. Slavery was permitted in other colonies, they argued, so an inability to own slaves constituted inequality. The hypocrisy of the argument was lost on the contemporary audience. The Georgia Company relented, allowed slavery, and plantations and privilege soon marked the colony.[28]

Superficially, America was a land of promise, a city upon a hill. And it was a land of opportunity, but only for some. Poverty plagued most settlers who were predominantly "tillers of the earth," but America still attracted the downtrodden of Europe.[29] As news circulated overseas of the possibilities in America, more and more people began to make the trip, leaving their old lives behind. To regulate this surge of immigration, the Plantation Act of 1740 laid the guidelines for obtaining English citizenship. While it encouraged diverse immigration, it was not wholly inclusive and prohibited Catholic and Jewish immigrants from citizenship.[30] This act marked a significant transition in identity. To regulate citizenship meant to regulate membership in a specific group with a specific identity. America was no longer just a group of settlements on the edge of the known world but a real place, and the Plantation Act formally made the colonies an asylum of freedom.[31] The resultant society was pluralistic, no longer defined by an English majority, as many colonists claimed Dutch, German, Scots-Irish, and French roots, that strange mixture of blood, which you will find in no other country.[32] The religious climate was also transitioning through the Great Awakening, an evangelical movement marked by revivals and emotional sermons.[33] Led by Jonathan Edwards in New England, it espoused both a "scriptural and rational doctrine."[34] People were encouraged to contemplate their eternal souls and the very real risk of losing them to damnation. In England, a young Anglican minister named George Whitefield

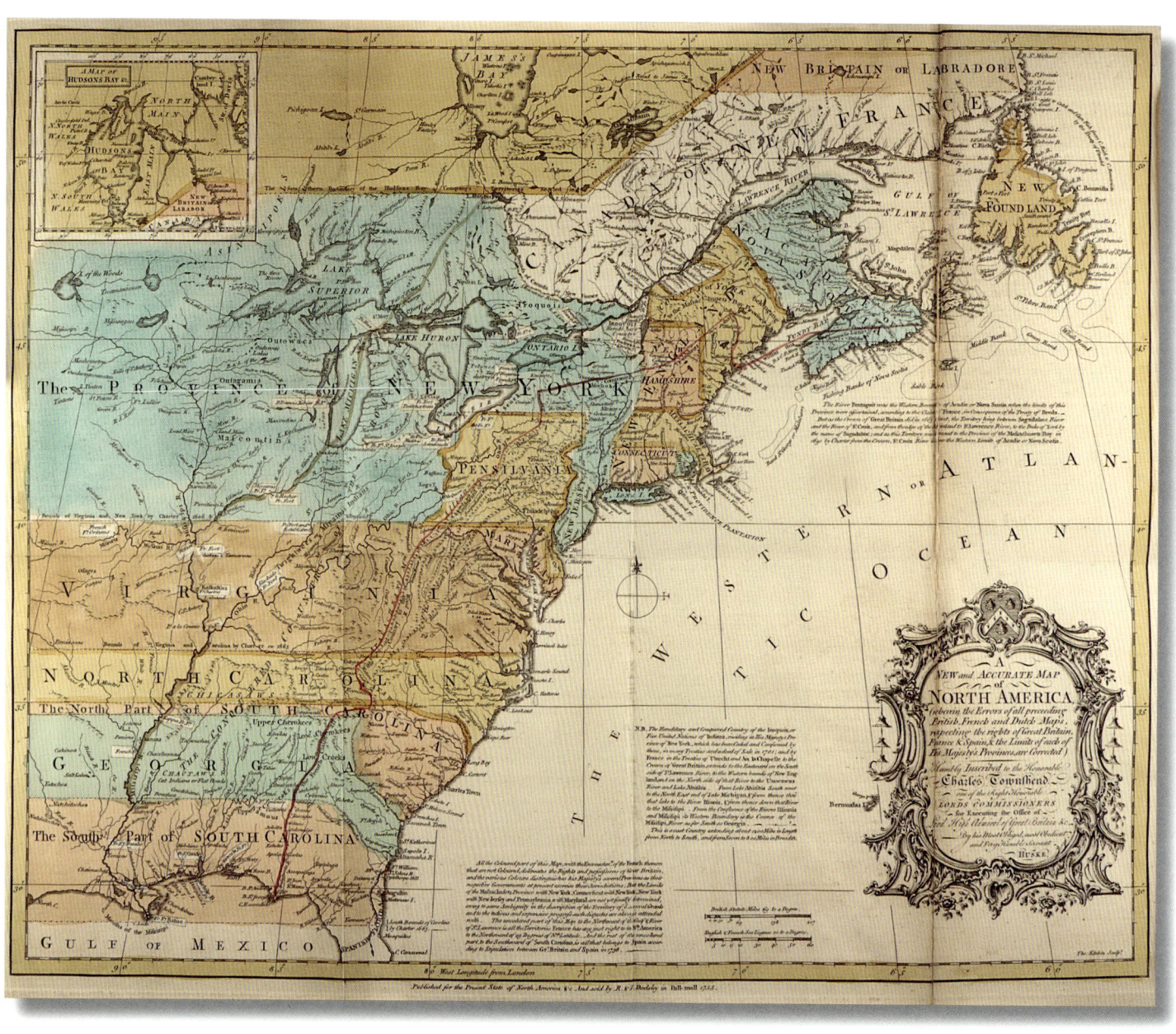

A NEW AND ACCURATE MAP OF NORTH AMERICA.

From *The Present State of North America*, 1755.

GM 2576.2144

led the movement, becoming so popular that when he came to the colonies in late 1739, he drew large crowds wherever he preached.[35] It was a progressive era in colonial history, marked by a new confidence and a renewed sense of possibility and optimism.

The cultural and chronological distance between Britain and her colonies continued to widen, however, and whether either recognized it, a crossroads was approaching. One last opportunity to resurrect the colonial English identity was close at hand, but for the time it remained endangered, as thin as the newspapers from abroad that provided the only reaffirmation of Englishness for the colonists. Once inherent, the identity was now imported.

NOTES

1. From *The Four Indian Kings' Speech to Her Majesty*, London, April 20, 1710. GM 5376.477.

2. *The Interesting Narrative of the Life of Olaudah Equiano, or Gustavus Vassa, the African*, Volume I (London, 1789), p. 76.

3. William Bradford, *History of Plymouth Plantation* (Boston, 1856), p. 24.

4. Alan Taylor, *American Colonies* (New York: Penguin Press, 2001), p. 119. Taylor provides a comprehensive history of colonial North America, discussing the sociocultural and geographic evolution of early settlements.

5. Karen Ordahl Kupperman, *Indians & English: Facing Off in Early America* (Ithaca, New York: Cornell University Press, 2000), p. 17. Using primary sources, Kupperman examines the relations between American Indians and English settlers during the 17th century, revealing the complexity and diversity of early interactions.

6. Taylor, *American Colonies*, p. 144.

7. Ibid., p. 142.

8. Jon Butler, *Becoming America: The Revolution before 1776* (Cambridge: Harvard University Press, 2000), p. 37. Butler examines the sociocultural revolution that shaped American identity and experience prior to the Revolution.

9. Taylor, *American Colonies*, p. 159.

10. *Slavery and the Making of America*, directed by Dante J. James, Thirteen Productions, New York, 2004, episode 1.

11. Butler, *Becoming America: The Revolution before 1776*, p. 19.

12. John C. Shields, *The American Aeneas: Classical Origins of the American Self* (Knoxville, Tennessee: The University of Tennessee Press), p. 33. Shields explores the influence of the classical world on shaping the American identity.

13. "Epidemical Fevers," *Publick Occurrences*, Boston, Massachusetts, September 25, 1690, issue 1, p. 1. In this report of a mortal fever occurring in and around Boston, and also of the prevalence of smallpox, it is estimated that around 350 died.

14. Taylor, *American Colonies*, p. 141.

15. "New York, January 26," *Boston News-Letter*, February 9, 1707, p. 2. The notice reports that a Mr. William Hallet, his pregnant wife, and their five children were murdered by their slaves, an Indian man and an African woman.

16. Butler, *Becoming America: The Revolution before 1776*, p. 11.

17. Taylor, *American Colonies*, p. 277.

18. Ibid., p. 277.

19. Ibid., p. 277.

20. Ibid., p. 280.

21. "France is to England what Carthage was to ancient Rome," *Boston Post-Boy*, Boston, Massachusetts, March 25, 1754, p. 1.

22. Taylor, *American Colonies*, p. 299.

23. "To be sold by Mr. William Price," *New-England Courant*, Boston, Massachusetts, August 14, 1725, issue 211, p. 1. The advertisement lists many items available for sale in Price's shop, including maps, prints, looking-glasses, tea-tables, and sconces.

24. "The Speech of Sir William Keith," *American Weekly Mercury*, Philadelphia, Pennsylvania, August 12, 1725, issue 295, p. 1. Sir Keith addressed Pennsylvania representatives on behalf of Germans wanting to settle permanently in Pennsylvania.

25. Butler, *Becoming America: The Revolution before 1776*, p. 40.

26. Taylor, *American Colonies*, p. 151.

27. Butler, *Becoming America: The Revolution before 1776*, p. 55.

28. Taylor, *American Colonies*, p. 243.

29. J. Hector St. John Crèvecoeur, *Letters from an American Farmer* (New York: Dolphin Press), p. 46. Crèvecoeur emigrated to America around 1750 and wrote a book in 1782 expounding on the state of America and what it meant to be an American. His letters reveal a society of contradictions, one that espouses equality and opportunity while still embracing slavery.

30. Taylor, *American Colonies*, p. 303.

31. Crèvecoeur, *Letters from an American Farmer*, p. 7.

32. Ibid., p. 49.

33. Taylor, *American Colonies*, p. 339.

34. "Lately Published," *New-England Weekly Journal*, Boston, Massachussetts, June 2, 1735, issue 426, p. 2. Advertisement for a new work written by Jonathan Edwards, pastor at Northampton. The work is deemed a "Scriptural and Rational Doctrine."

35. "Philadelphia," *Boston Gazette*, November 26, 1739, issue 1035, p. 3. "Rev. Mr. Whitefield preached at the Philadelphia Court-House" drawing a crowd of 6,000.

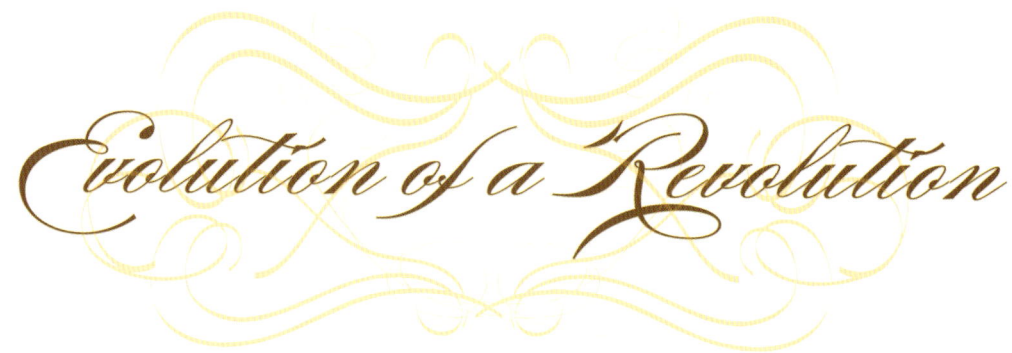

Evolution of a Revolution

KIMBERLY ROBLIN

July 4 — His nation at war, the young Virginian shifts uncomfortably in the heat and readies himself, contemplating the document he signed only hours before. He will become one of the key figures in American history, but for now the twenty-two-year-old can only lead his defeated British soldiers from Fort Necessity to the lilt of fifes and drums. George Washington will never surrender again.

BROWN BESS.
GM 62.173

For colonists, the mid-18th century was a time of pervasive uncertainty. With evolving identities based less on British ties and more on socioeconomic and regional similarities, colonists felt increasingly disconnected from the empire. In the summer of 1753, however, a renewed loyalty to Britain emerged with the onset of the French and Indian War. The western lands of the Ohio River had long been a source of local and international conflict as Natives and colonists clashed while Britain and France debated boundaries established by the Treaty of Utrecht.[1] For Britain, the Ohio River Valley represented an economic opportunity, but for France it was a link between its southern holding of Louisiana and New France. Governor Dinwiddie of Virginia appointed George Washington an emissary and sent him to offer a final warning to the French after they began building forts and harassing British settlers and traders.[2] It did not have the effect he planned. Washington reported their refusal and within months returned to the wilderness with a regiment of Virginia militia. By late May, he and his men had reached an area called the Great Meadows in southern Pennsylvania. There, early on the morning of May

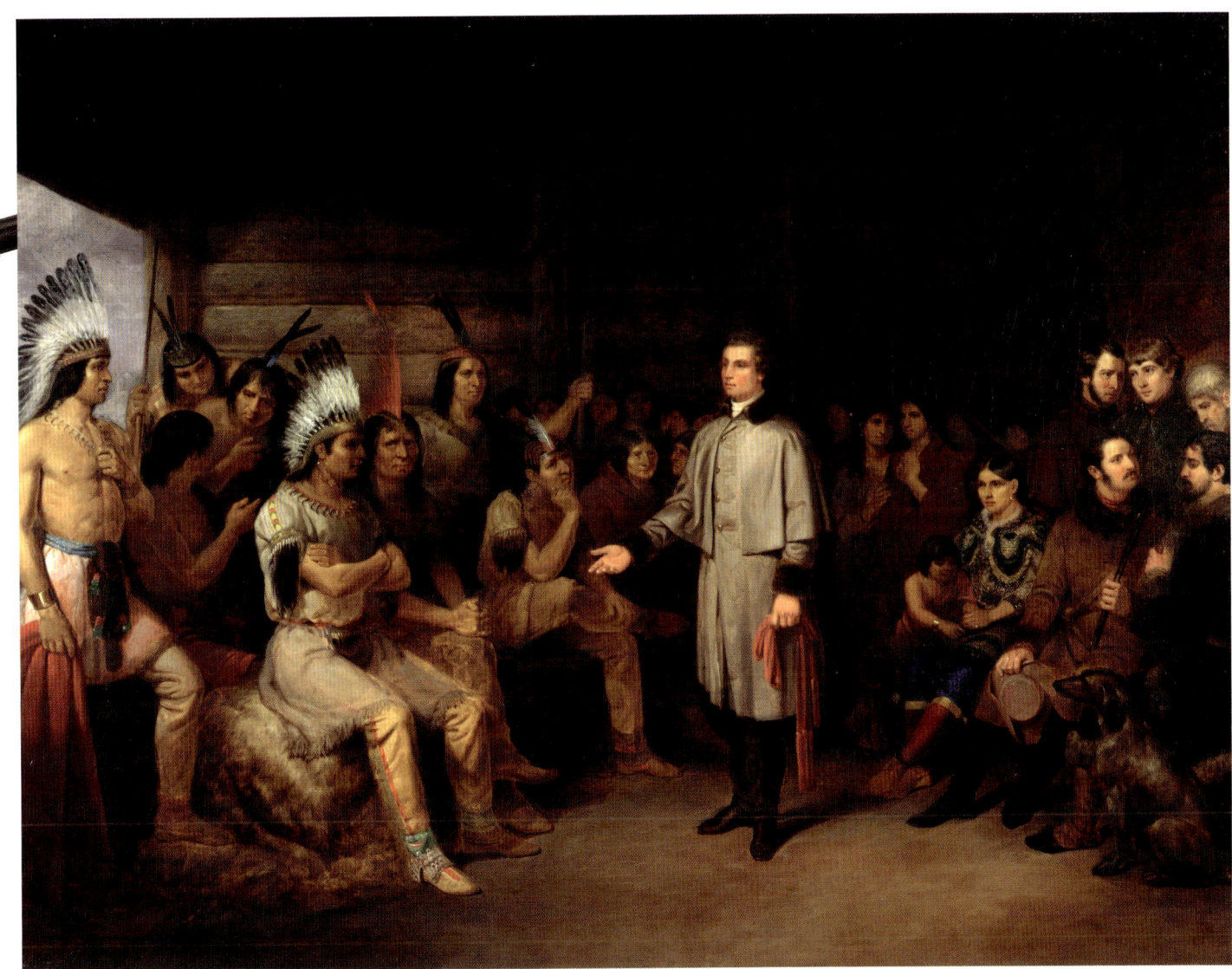

WASHINGTON IN CONFERENCE WITH REPRESENTATIVES OF SIX NATIONS,
Julius Stearns. Oil on canvas. GM 01xx.1514

28, Washington and his men fell upon a small French detachment. While details of the skirmish varied between sides, the outcome was inarguable. French soldiers had died, including Joseph Coulon de Jumonville, leader of the French detachment and brother to Captain Louis Coulon de Villiers.[3] Anticipating a retaliatory attack, Washington and his men constructed a garrison and named it Fort Necessity. The reprisal came one month later in early July when Captain Villiers and a force of 700 marched on the fort and captured it in less than a day, forcing Washington's surrender.[4]

The French and Indian War soon became part of an even larger struggle when the Seven Years War erupted

The League of the Iroquois, also known as the Six Nations, was one of the most important political forces in colonial America. Founded in the 15th century by Hiawatha and Deganawida, the original league included five nations from northern New York, the Mohawks, Oneidas, Onondagas, Cayugas, and Senecas. The sixth nation was the Tuscaroras, who migrated from North Carolina in the early 18th century. From the time of the league's founding, members did not raise arms against each other until the American Revolution. While the Mohawks, Senecas, Cayugas, and Onondagas allied with the British, the Oneidas and Tuscaroras allied with American forces. The American alliance, however, did not prevent theses Native groups from ultimately losing their land to the newly-formed United States government.

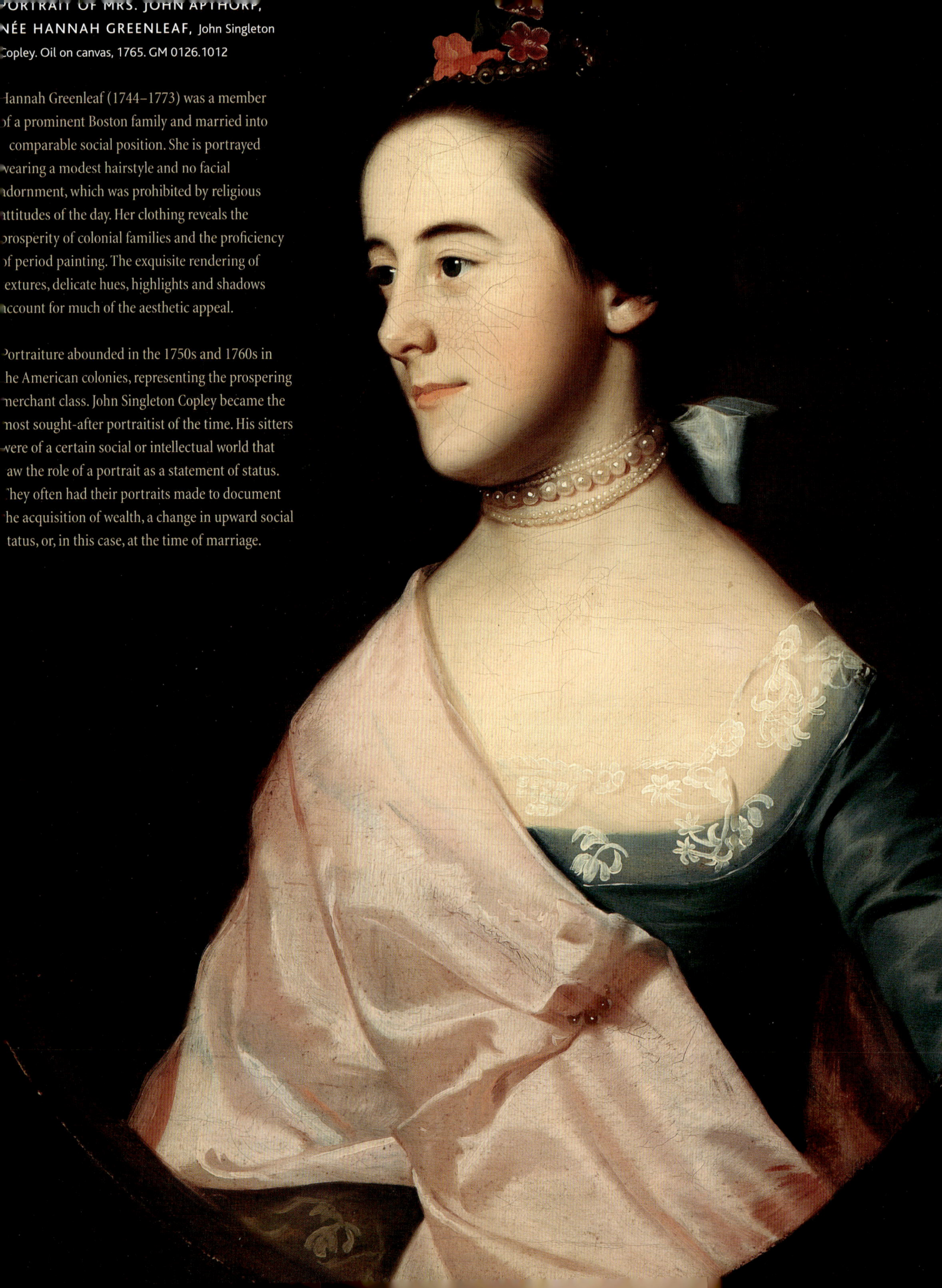

PORTRAIT OF MRS. JOHN APTHORP,
NÉE HANNAH GREENLEAF, John Singleton
Copley. Oil on canvas, 1765. GM 0126.1012

Hannah Greenleaf (1744–1773) was a member
of a prominent Boston family and married into
a comparable social position. She is portrayed
wearing a modest hairstyle and no facial
adornment, which was prohibited by religious
attitudes of the day. Her clothing reveals the
prosperity of colonial families and the proficiency
of period painting. The exquisite rendering of
textures, delicate hues, highlights and shadows
account for much of the aesthetic appeal.

Portraiture abounded in the 1750s and 1760s in
the American colonies, representing the prospering
merchant class. John Singleton Copley became the
most sought-after portraitist of the time. His sitters
were of a certain social or intellectual world that
saw the role of a portrait as a statement of status.
They often had their portraits made to document
the acquisition of wealth, a change in upward social
status, or, in this case, at the time of marriage.

between Austria and Prussia. While France allied with Austria, Britain aligned with Prussia, adding a new degree of urgency and importance to the conflict in America. The fighting continued until 1763, when both wars came to an end with the Treaties of Paris and Hubertusburg. France lost all North American holdings east of the Mississippi to Great Britain. The colonies gained a military hero in George Washington through his redemption in battle. And Britain, although victorious, faced the tremendous financial burden of waging two wars on two continents. Parliament looked across the Atlantic for revenue and passed two pieces of legislation that would exact a price far greater than the French and Indian War, and ultimately cost Great Britain her colonies.

The first was the Stamp Act in 1765 that taxed all pieces of printed paper. Intended to raise money for the protection of the Appalachian frontier and offset the cost of the war, it prompted swift and severe colonial reaction, neutralizing any renewal of British identity. Colonists argued that the legislation violated their rights on two counts—first, that the tax was not an economic regulator but a fundraiser, and, second, that they should not be made the sole contributors to a colonial defense fund, particularly since they had recently fought alongside British troops to protect British interests. Colonists had felt different from their British counterparts for some time and had even been called foreigners.[5] Parliament, however, had now explicitly validated the sentiment. Not only did the colonists feel different. They were seen as different from and less than British citizens.

Following boycotts in Boston, a cycle of action and reaction began between Britain and her colonies. Parliament reluctantly repealed the Stamp Act, only to pass the Declaratory Act the same day. Meant to reaffirm that body's authority, the act restated parliamentary power to make laws binding the American colonies *in all cases whatsoever.*[6]

MAN'S WAISTCOAT.
18th century. GM 84.3401

Clothing was an important indicator of social standing and status during the colonial era. High quality and expensive fabrics combined with intricate embroidery indicated wealth and privilege. American fashion was directly influenced and often, directly imported, from Europe.

Removal of the Stamp Act produced little effect since Parliament passed the Townshend Act the following year. Similar to its predecessor, the Townshend Act taxed imported glass, paper, lead, paints, and, infamously, tea. Boston again became the epicenter of protest with groups such as the Sons of Liberty, spurring boycotts and action. Dismissing the demonstrations as petulant disobedience, King George responded harshly.[7] He dissolved the Massachusetts Assembly for distributing incendiary pamphlets and sent British troops to Boston as a physical reminder of his absolute authority.

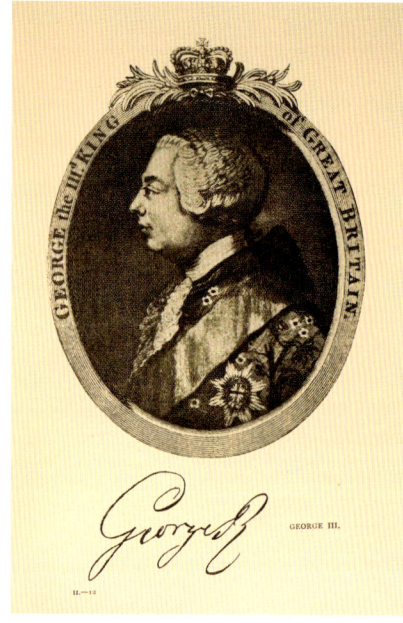

KING GEORGE III. From *A History of the American People.* GM 2527.4879

THE BOSTON MASSACRE.
From *A History of the American People.*
GM 2527.4879

On March 7, 1770, British soldiers outside the Customs House in Boston fired into a large crowd, killing five colonists. It was the culmination of increasing hostilities between Britain and her colonies. The redcoats stood trial and were defended by John Adams. Most were acquitted, but patriot propaganda succeeded in portraying the event as The Boston Massacre.

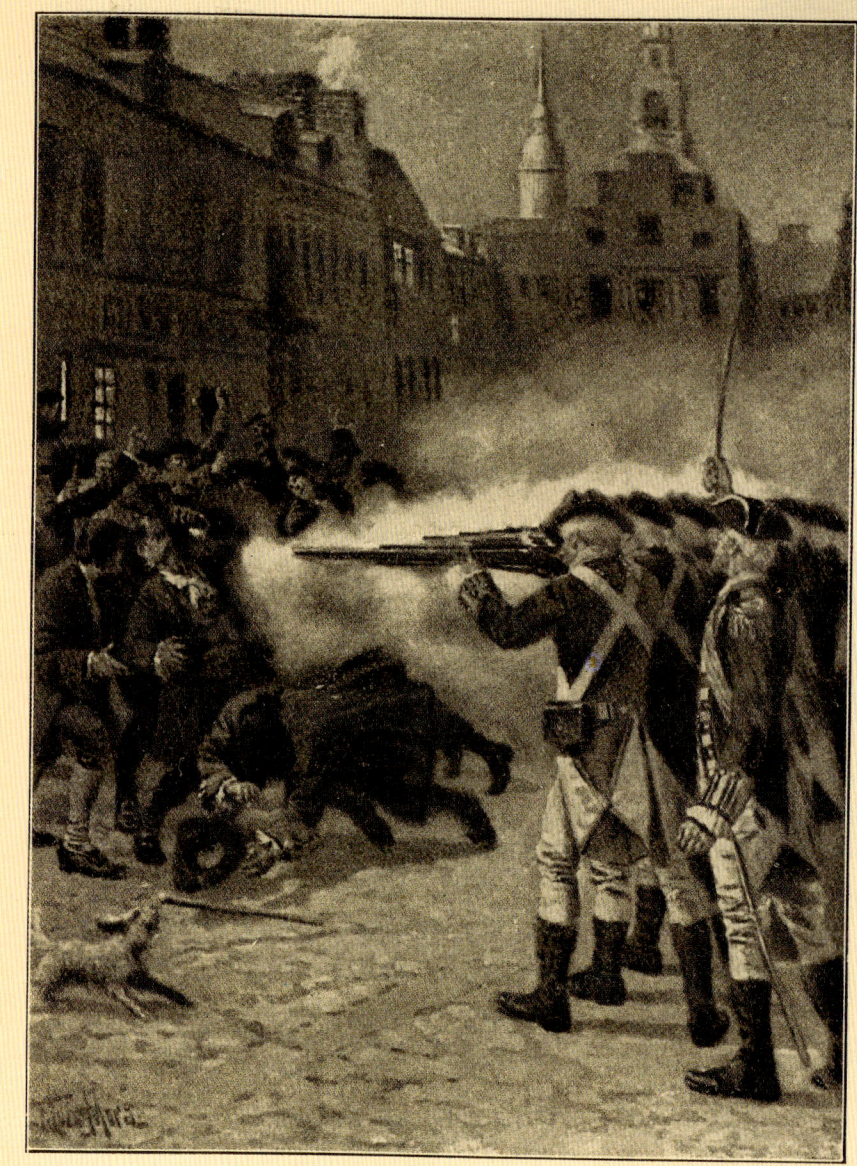

THE BOSTON MASSACRE

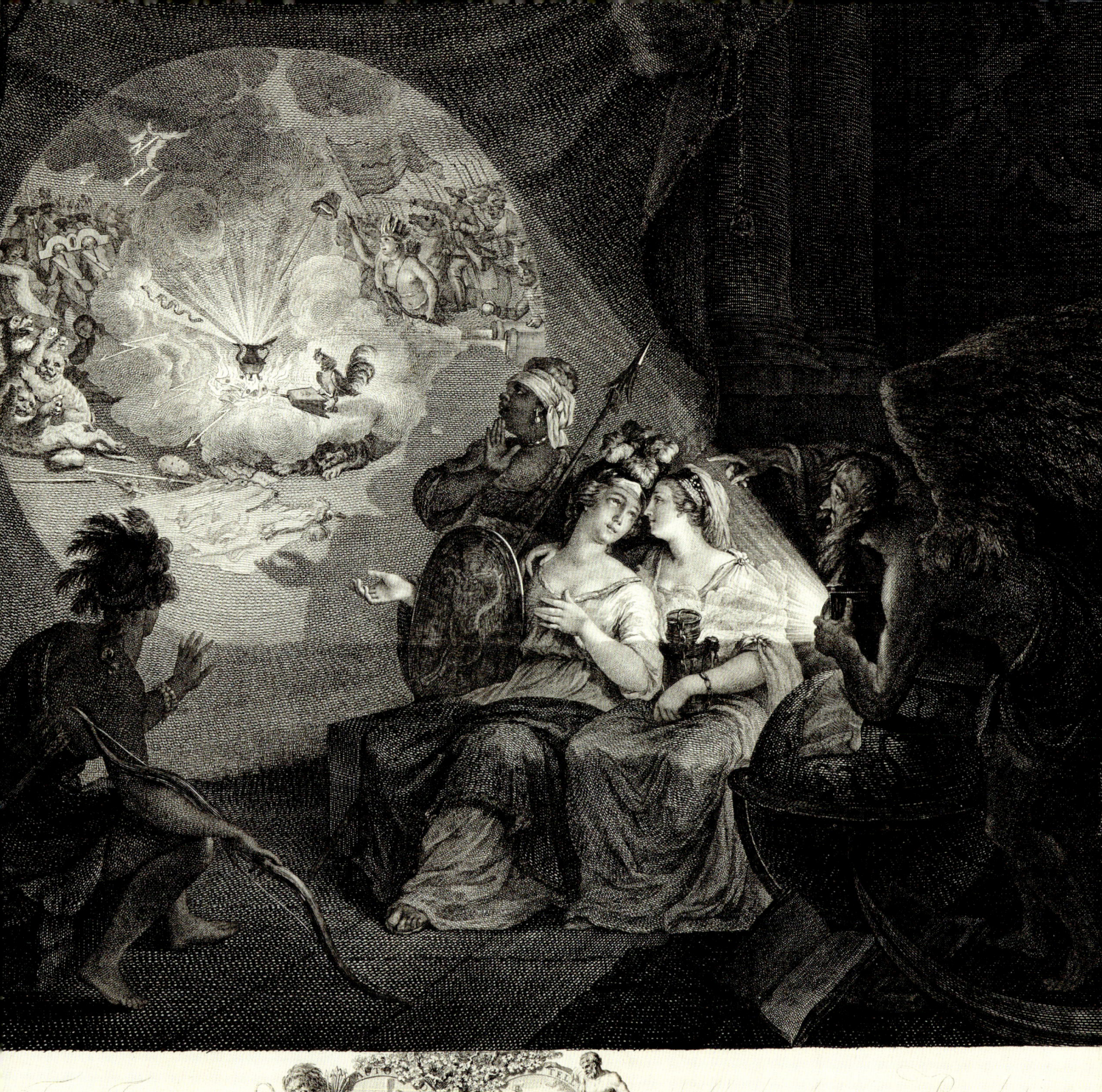

THE TEA-TAX TEMPEST, Carl Guttenberg. Engraving,
1778. GM 1576.203

In this engraving, Father Time depicts scenes from
the Boston Tea Party that took place on December 16,
1773. The four women in his audience represent the
continents of North America, Africa, Europe, and Asia.
America, dressed as a Native American, sits separately
from her sister continents and watches herself guide the
forces that are chasing the fleeing British army of yoked
soldiers and lion cubs.

A Message to the Governor from the Assembly.

May it please your Honor,

When we considered your Message of the 29th of January, recommending the Support of a Garison at Fort Pitt, founded on Apprehensions, in the Back Inhabitants, of Danger from the Indians, at a Time when we imagined the Treaties of Friendship were perfectly observed between his Majesty and them, we thought it our Duty to enquire into the Reason and Grounds, if any, for those Apprehensions. We were therefore induced to apply to Government for Information whether there appeared a Disposition in the Natives to violate those Treaties, and from your last Message we cannot find that there is the least Cause for such a Suspicion, otherwise we have no Doubt you would, on our Request, have communicated it. From whence we are led to conclude that the Uneasiness of the Back Settlers is without Foundation, and by no Means a sufficient Reason for a Measure, which we fear may be productive of the very Mischiefs it may be intended to avert.

We well know, that from the first Settlement of the Province down to the late French and Indian War, the most perfect good Understanding and Friendship were preserved between this Government and those People by a Conduct uniformly just and kind towards them; that since the late Indian War, the like happy Effects have been produced by the like Policy, and that, on the Contrary, the maintaining of Garisons in or near

their

He had underestimated colonial will, however. Tension mounted between the redcoats and civilians in the occupied city and on March 5, 1770, erupted in a cobbled square into the Boston Massacre when a group of soldiers fired into an angry and armed mob. Five colonists were killed, and although the force had been provoked, colonists spun it as further evidence of British severity. Some in Great Britain even began questioning the legitimacy of royal actions and began to voice support for the colonial cause. The Townshend Act was repealed and all but a tea tax abandoned, but the colonists' protest continued and culminated in 1773 with the Boston Tea Party. Parliament responded by passing the Coercive Acts, known in America as the Intolerable Acts. Intended to punish Massachusetts, it forbade ships from loading and unloading in Boston Harbor, protected royal officials by allowing cases brought against them to be moved to England, and granted the crown authority to appoint most government officials. In a final move, it also passed the Quartering Act that stipulated British troops could be quartered anywhere, including private homes. Hope of reconciliation dwindled as populations on both sides of the Atlantic became increasingly polarized.

Although early frustrations had been isolated to individual colonies, a collective sense of being wronged began to develop, and in 1774 colonial leaders convened at the First Continental Congress in Philadelphia to discuss potential courses of action. Most in attendance still favored compromise and negotiation

FACING AND ABOVE: LETTER FROM JOSEPH GALLOWAY TO THE GOVERNOR OF PENNSYLVANIA, FEBRUARY 19, 1773. GM 4026.4534

In this letter, Galloway rejected the idea of building a garrison at Fort Pitt to ease the minds of back inhabitants. The treaties with local tribes were good, he argued, and constructing a fort "might be productive of the very Mischiefs it may be intended to avert."

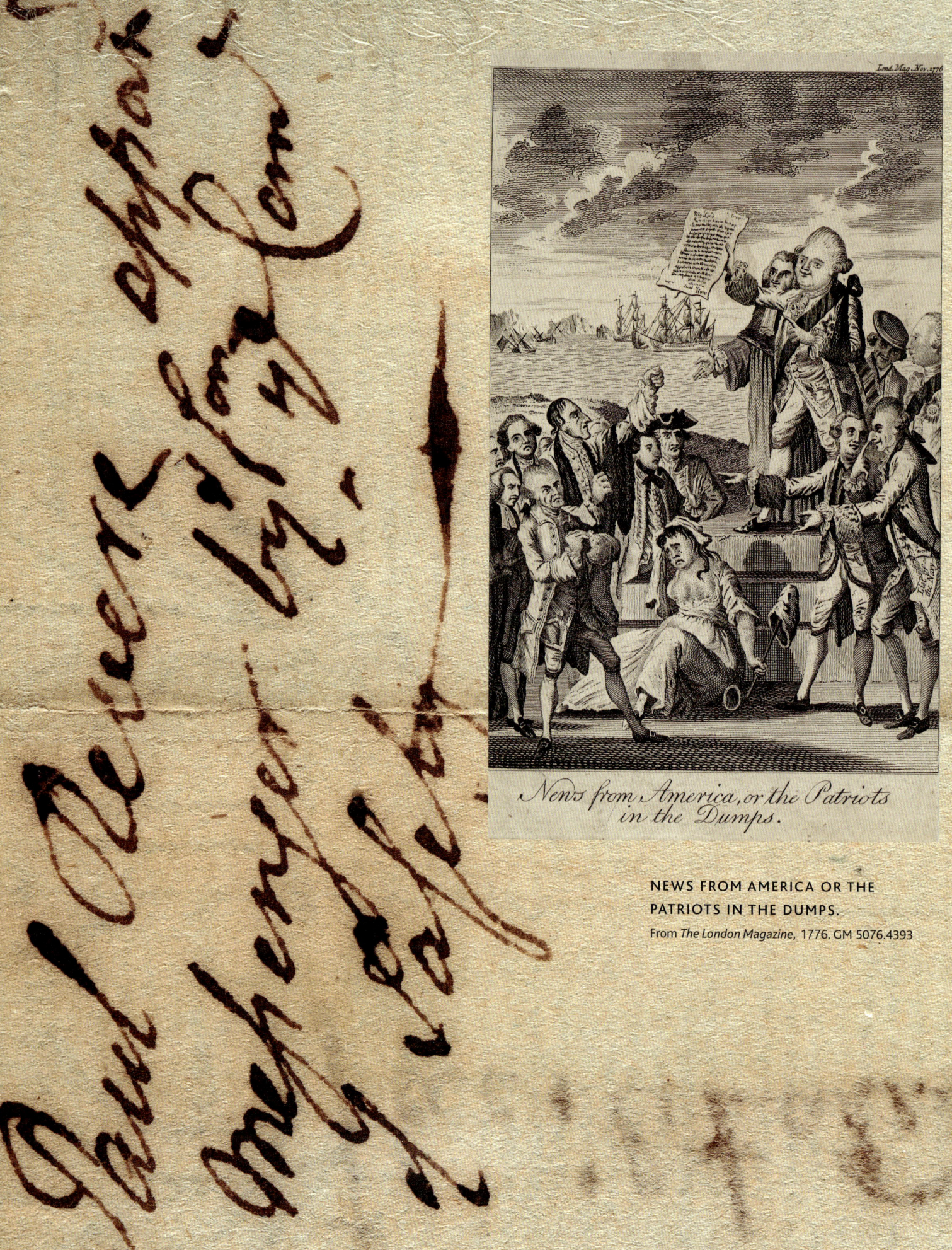

News from America, or the Patriots in the Dumps.

NEWS FROM AMERICA OR THE
PATRIOTS IN THE DUMPS.
From *The London Magazine*, 1776. GM 5076.4393

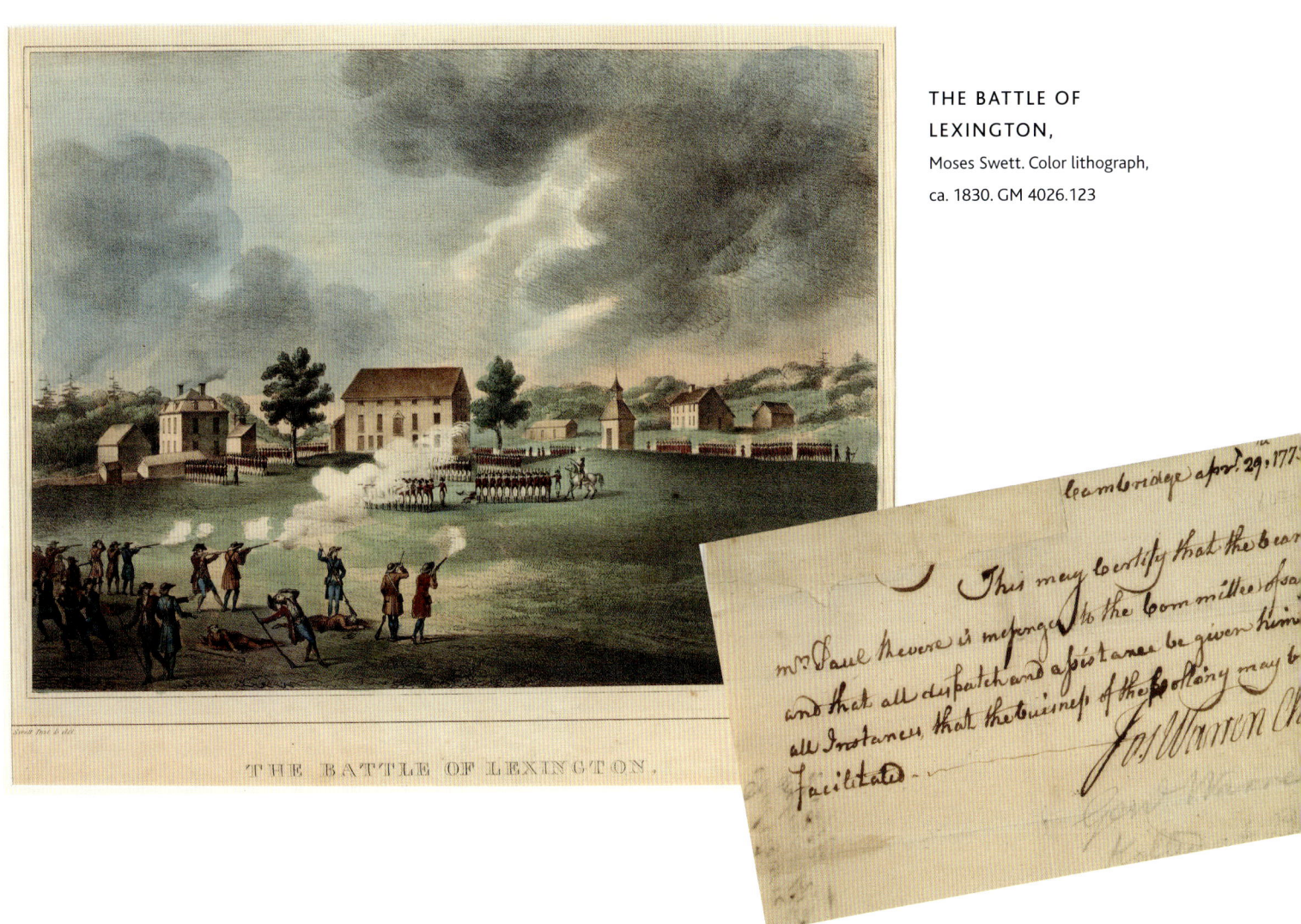

THE BATTLE OF LEXINGTON.

with the crown, placing their faith in reason and logic. They agreed, however, to collectively disobey the taxes. Massachusetts, the epicenter of resistance, even formed a Committee of Safety charged with alerting local militias of any British approach. Special militias prepared to respond instantly were fittingly named minutemen. On April 19, 1775, they were called to service at Lexington and Concord to intercept British troops sent to destroy ammunition.[8] It was the first battle in a war that would last seven years. In a final attempt at reconciliation, the colonies offered the Olive Branch petition, asking the king to call off his military and negotiate. Instead, the king declared the colonies to be in open rebellion. Some in Britain warned of the possible consequences of militarily engaging the colonies, one even predicting "for on the fate of America depends the fate of Britain."[9] What had once been a civil war had become a revolution.[10]

This brief dispatch written by Joseph Warren (1741–1775) identifies Paul Revere (1734–1818) as an official messenger for the Massachusetts Committee of Safety. Written ten days after the battles at Lexington and Concord, the document authorizes Revere to perform "business for the colony." From April 21 through May 7, 1775 Revere journeyed throughout the region and some of these travels took him to areas where he was not well known and therefore needed identification. Warren had been involved in the struggle against Britain since the passing of the Townshend Acts in 1767 and had published several articles under pseudonyms. After Lexington and Concord, he abandoned his comfortable career as a physician in service to the Revolution. He was killed two months later at the Battle of Bunker Hill.

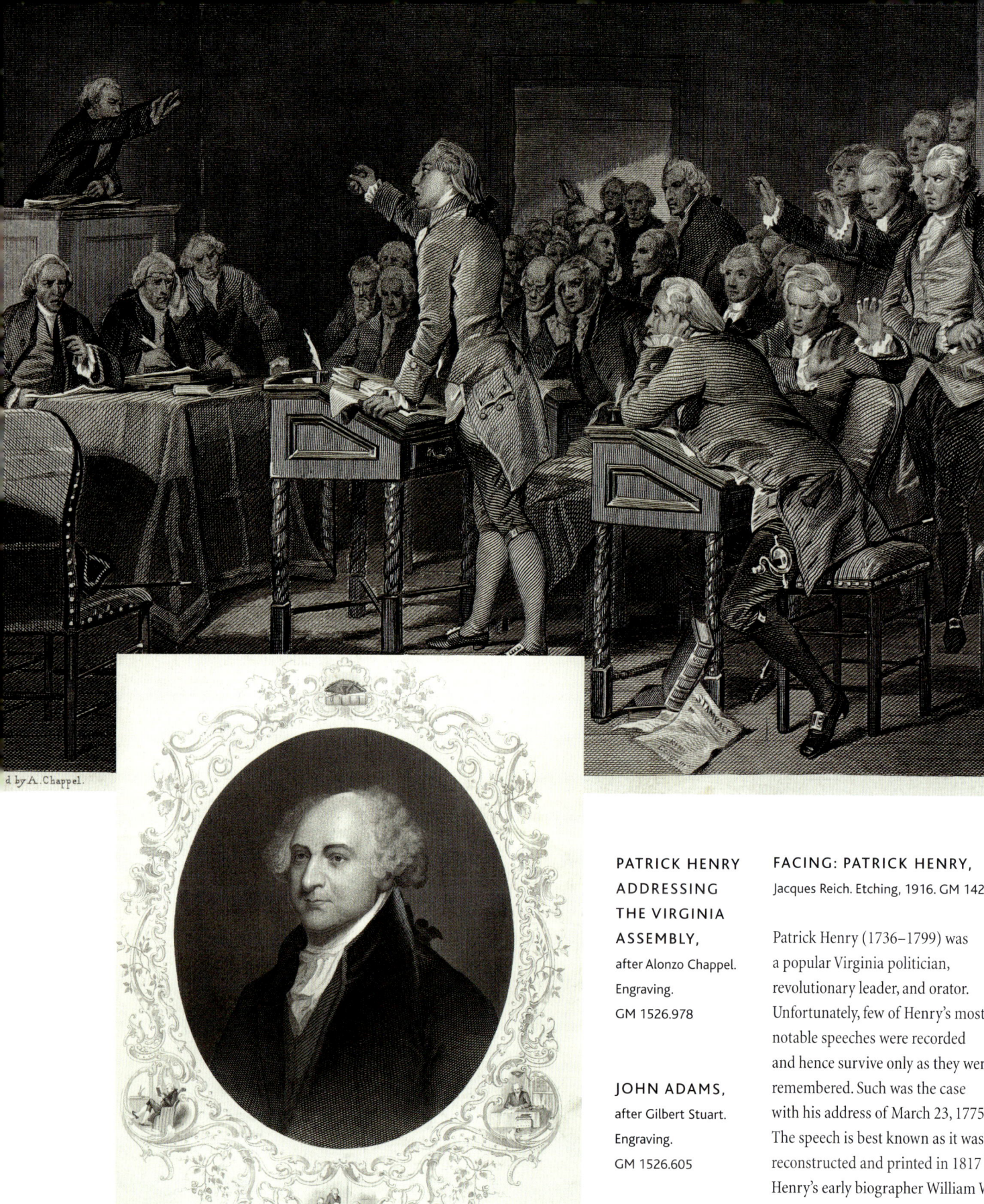

d by A. Chappel.

Engraved by H.B.I

John Adams

PATRICK HENRY
ADDRESSING
THE VIRGINIA
ASSEMBLY,
after Alonzo Chappel.
Engraving.
GM 1526.978

JOHN ADAMS,
after Gilbert Stuart.
Engraving.
GM 1526.605

FACING: PATRICK HENRY,
Jacques Reich. Etching, 1916. GM 1427.5

Patrick Henry (1736–1799) was
a popular Virginia politician,
revolutionary leader, and orator.
Unfortunately, few of Henry's most
notable speeches were recorded
and hence survive only as they were
remembered. Such was the case
with his address of March 23, 1775.
The speech is best known as it was
reconstructed and printed in 1817 by
Henry's early biographer William Wirt.

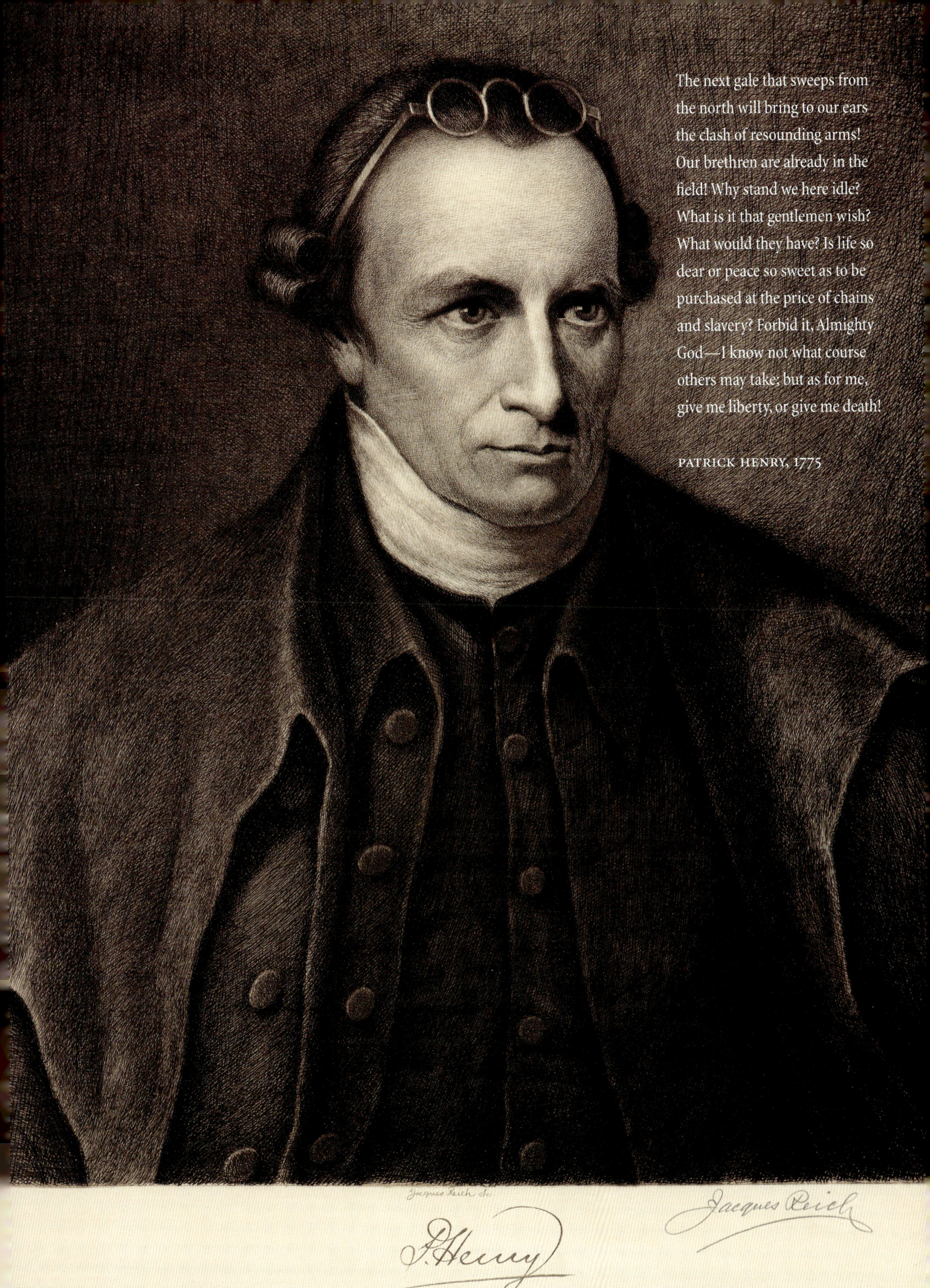

The next gale that sweeps from the north will bring to our ears the clash of resounding arms! Our brethren are already in the field! Why stand we here idle? What is it that gentlemen wish? What would they have? Is life so dear or peace so sweet as to be purchased at the price of chains and slavery? Forbid it, Almighty God—I know not what course others may take; but as for me, give me liberty, or give me death!

PATRICK HENRY, 1775

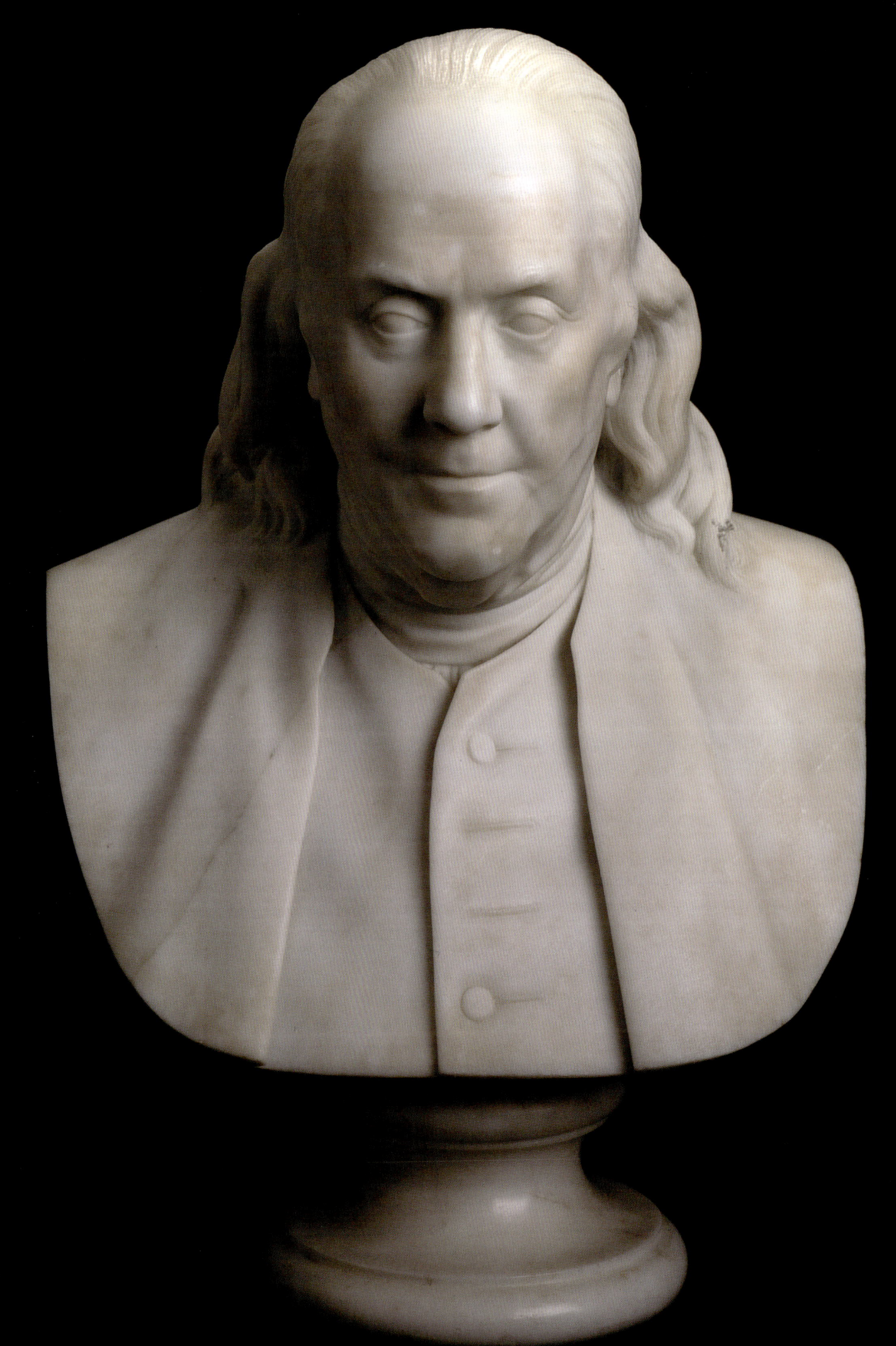

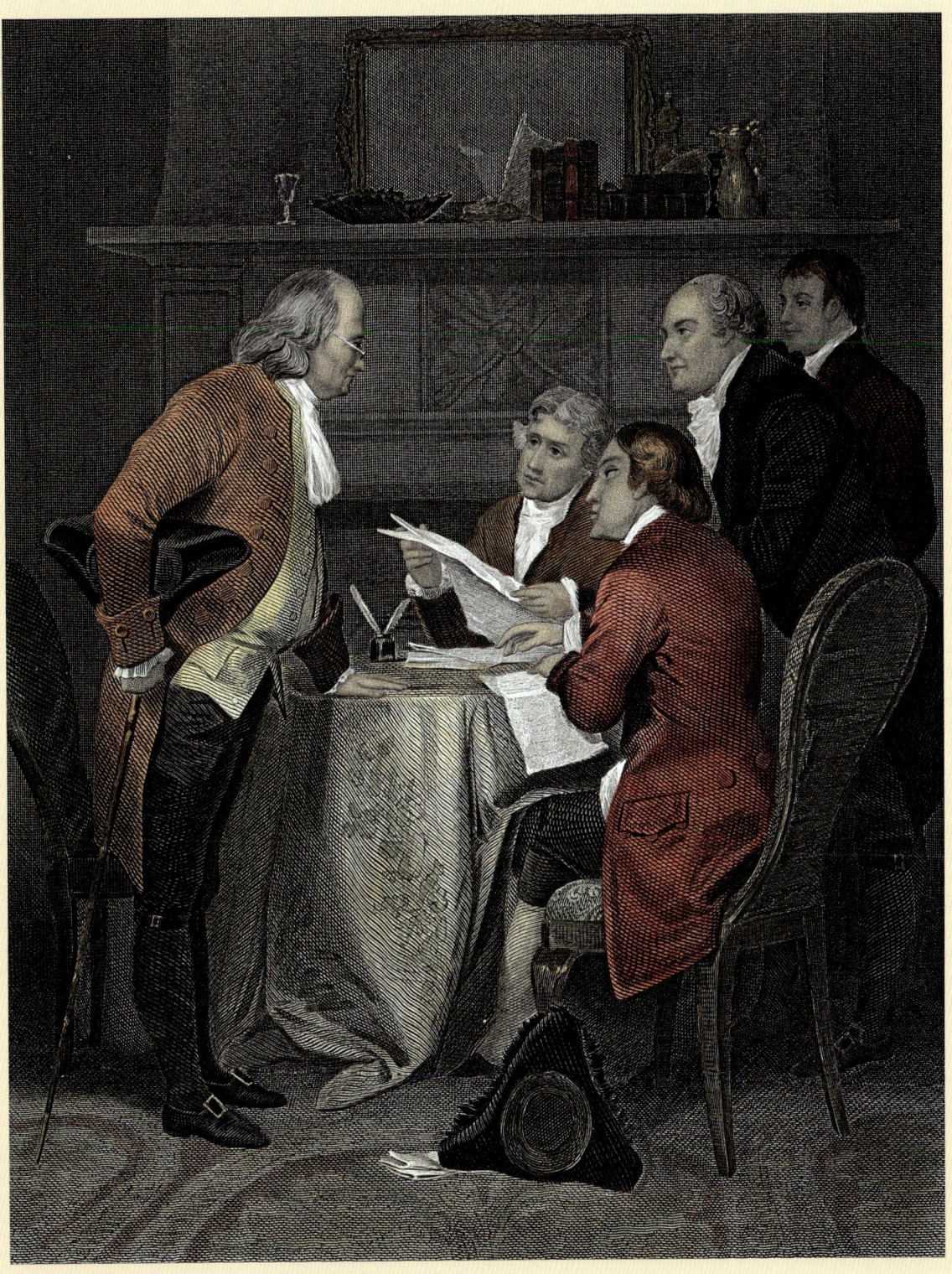

THE DECLARATION COMMITTEE. Engraving. GM 15.1129

Thomas Jefferson, John Adams, Benjamin Franklin, Robert Livingston, and Roger Sherman
were appointed to the Declaration Committee in June of 1776 at the Second Continental Congress.

BENJAMIN FRANKLIN, Hiram Powers. Marble. GM 0926.6

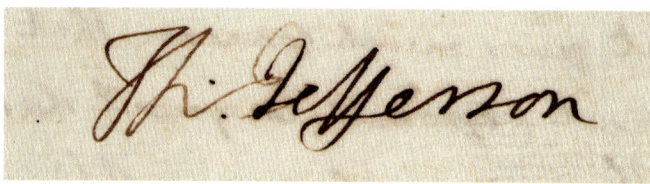

THOMAS JEFFERSON, James Earle Fraser. Bronze. GM 0817.168

Thomas Jefferson (1743–1826), the third president of the United States, was a statesman, diplomat, author, scientist, and architect. Following the adoption of his most famous writing, the Declaration of Independence, Jefferson left the Continental Congress and returned to activities in the government of Virginia.

In 1784, Jefferson was appointed to assist Benjamin Franklin and John Adams in Europe during treaty negotiations. The following year he succeeded Franklin as minister to France. He proved a diligent and skillful diplomat, remaining among the French until 1789. Upon his return, Jefferson became the first secretary of state under the Constitution. Supported by the Republicans for president in 1796, but running second (by only three electoral votes) to Federalist John Adams, he became vice-president. In 1800 Jefferson was elected to the presidency and was the first to be inaugurated in Washington. Despite excessive condemnation in Federalist newspapers, Jefferson won an easy reelection to a second term. The most notable achievement of his presidency was the purchase of the Louisiana Territory in 1803.

By the summer of 1776, the American Revolution was in its infancy, gaining momentum as opposition to the crown increasingly replaced the loyalty once pledged to it. King George III had abandoned attempts to quiet the minds of his subjects in America and had turned instead to an oppressive militant policy. Although unthinkable less than a decade before, many colonists began to embrace independence from Great Britain, and at the Pennsylvania State Hall the historic decision fell to the Second Continental Congress—among its members John Adams, Benjamin Franklin, Patrick Henry, and a young Virginian, Thomas Jefferson. At only thirty-three, he was the youngest Virginia delegate at the Congress but already possessed of a reputation for quick-mindedness and an able pen. Like many educated men of his age, he was heavily influenced by the Scottish Enlightenment and the belief in reason and logic and above all, the ability of men to effect change. Guided by this belief and under appointment of the Congress, he drafted a formal document severing all ties with Great Britain. In moving language, Jefferson set forth an idea—that all men were created equal. It was an inescapable contradiction—a country combating tyranny while practicing the worst tyranny possible in slavery. A country that committed atrocities against Native Americans in the name of progress.

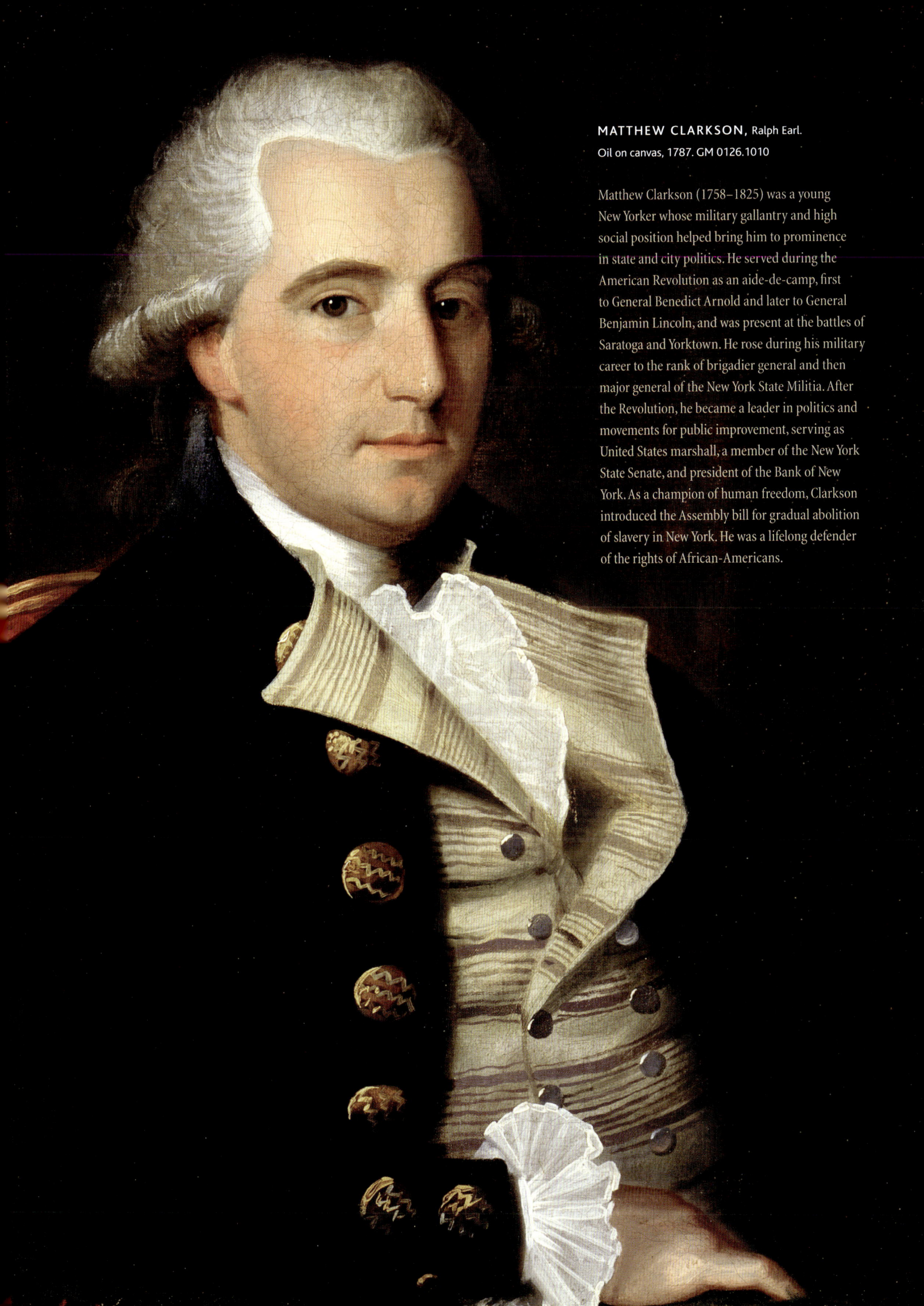

MATTHEW CLARKSON, Ralph Earl.
Oil on canvas, 1787. GM 0126.1010

Matthew Clarkson (1758–1825) was a young
New Yorker whose military gallantry and high
social position helped bring him to prominence
in state and city politics. He served during the
American Revolution as an aide-de-camp, first
to General Benedict Arnold and later to General
Benjamin Lincoln, and was present at the battles of
Saratoga and Yorktown. He rose during his military
career to the rank of brigadier general and then
major general of the New York State Militia. After
the Revolution, he became a leader in politics and
movements for public improvement, serving as
United States marshall, a member of the New York
State Senate, and president of the Bank of New
York. As a champion of human freedom, Clarkson
introduced the Assembly bill for gradual abolition
of slavery in New York. He was a lifelong defender
of the rights of African-Americans.

Dear Fleming   Philadelphia July 1. 1776.

yours of 22d. June came to hand this morning and gratified me much as this with your former contains interesting intelligence.

Our affairs in Canada go still retrograde, but I hope they are now nearly at their worst. the fatal sources of these misfortunes have been want of hard money with which to procure provisions, the ravages of the small pox with which one half of our army is still down, and an unlucky choice of some officers. by our last letters, Genl. Sullivan was retired as far as Isle au noix with his dispirited army and Burgoyne pursuing him with one of double or treble his numbers. it gives much concern that he had determined to make a stand there as it exposes to great danger of losing him & his army; & it was the universal sense of his officers that he ought to retire. Genl. Schuyler has sent him positive orders to retire to Crown point but whether they will reach him time enough to withdraw him from danger is questionable. here it seems to be the opinion of all the General officers that an effectual stand may be made & the enemy not only prevented access into New york, but by preserving a superiority on the lakes we may renew our attacks on them to advantage as soon as our army is recovered from the small pox & recruited. but recruits, tho' long ordered, are very difficult to be procured on account of that dreadful disorder.

The Conspiracy at New York is not yet thoroughly developed, nor has any thing transpired, the whole being kept secret till the whole is got through. one fact is known of necessity, that one of the General's lifeguard being thoroughly convicted was to be shot last Saturday. General Howe with some ships (we know not how many) is arrived at the Hook, & as is said, has landed some horse on the Jersey shore. the famous major Rogers is in custody on violent suspicion of being concerned in the conspiracy.

I am glad to hear of the Highlanders carried into Virginia. it does not appear certainly how many of these people we have but I imagine at least six or eight hundred. great efforts should be made to keep up the spirits of the people the succeeding three months: which in the universal opinion will be the only ones in which our trial can be severe.

account of the late nomination of delegates. I have no other state of it but the number of votes for each person. the omission of Harrison & Braxton & my being next to the lag give me some alarm. it is a painful situation to be 300. miles from one's country, & thereby open to secret assassination without a possibility of self-defence. I am willing to hope nothing of this kind has been done in my case, & yet I cannot be easy. if any doubt has arisen as to me, my country will have my political creed in the form of a 'Declaration &c.' which I was lately directed to draw. this will give decisive proof that my own sentiment concurred with the vote they instructed us to give. had the post been to go a day later we might have been at liberty to communicate this whole matter.

July. 2. I have kept open my letter till this morning but nothing more new. Adieu.

Th. Jefferson

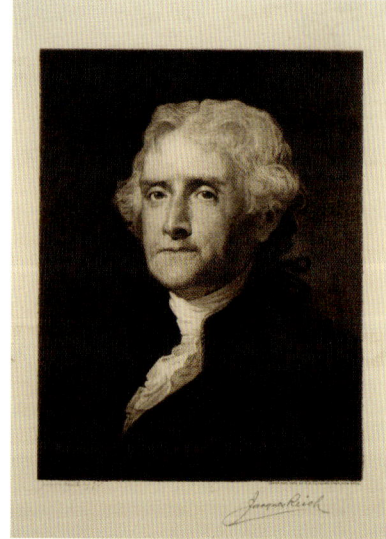

THOMAS JEFFERSON, Jacques Reich. Engraving. GM 1527.128

LETTER FROM THOMAS JEFFERSON TO WILLIAM FLEMING, JULY 1-2, 1776. GM 3826.71

Two days before the Continental Congress adopted the Declaration of Independence, Thomas Jefferson wrote his old college friend, William Fleming. The two had begun a lifelong friendship as students at the College of William and Mary. In July 1776, Fleming was in Williamsburg, Virginia, and Jefferson was drafting the Declaration of Independence in Philadelphia. Jefferson paused in his work to write Fleming. His letter expressed concern over a recent election in which he received barely enough votes for reappointment to the Virginia delegation. Worried that his constituents questioned his commitment to the cause, he told Fleming that his countrymen would soon see his resolve in a "Declaration etc." he was drafting.

Jefferson was known internationally as a scholar and patron of learning. Some twenty years after his drafting of the Declaration of Independence, in 1797, he was elected president of the American Philosophical Society, a position he retained until 1815. Throughout this later period of his life, he labored for the advancement and dissemination of knowledge, pioneering numerous branches of science, notably paleontology, ethnology, geography, and botany. Jefferson's twin wishes were to be remembered as the author of the Declaration of Independence and the father of the University of Virginia.

A country that left no place for women except the home. Still, it was an idea to aspire to, and the Declaration set forth the reason for independence in language so clear and true that anyone could see its validity.[11] After several drafts and revisions, Congress adopted the Declaration of Independence on July 4, 1776.

For the majority of colonists, the Declaration put into words a sentiment that had been growing for some time. "The Revolution was effected before the war commenced," John Adams later noted. It "was in the minds and hearts of the people; a change in their religious sentiments, of their duties and obligations. . . .This radical change in the principles, opinions, sentiments, and affections of the people was the real American Revolution."[12] As the Declaration was read in public squares and from pulpits across the colonies, the response was visceral and sometimes violent. Statues of King George were pulled down and royal arms defaced,[13] as people shouted "God save the Free Independent

BELOW LEFT: THOMAS PAINE, W. Sharp. Mezzotint, 1793. GM 1576.199

Thomas Paine (1737–1809) arrived in the American colonies from Britain in 1774, and played an active role in the political affairs of the United States and France. Known for his writings, his works included *Common Sense* (published in January 1776) and a series of patriotic tracts entitled *The Crisis* (published from 1776 through 1783). *Common Sense* addressed a wide audience with simple language and metaphors derived from the Bible. Paine argued that the entire American conflict was the fault of the "royal brute" King George III, and that the very idea of monarchy was contrary to good government. In *The Crisis,* Payne argued for complete independence. Following the revolution, he held several positions in both state and federal government. He returned to Europe in 1787 and later, as a naturalized French citizen, was chosen as a member of the National Convention. In 1802, he traveled again to America and remained in New York for his final years.

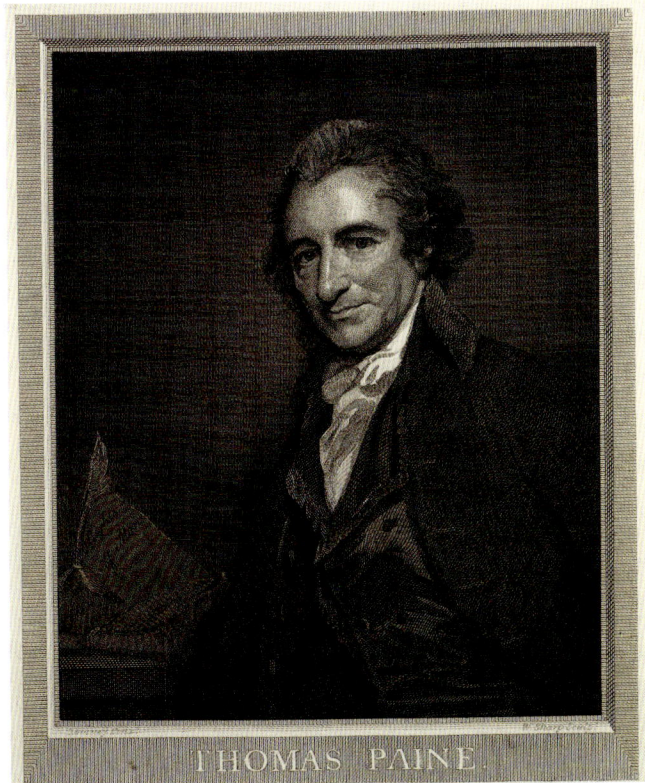

RIGHT: NATHAN HALE, Frederick W. MacMonnies. Bronze, 1890. GM 0826.2

From *Freeman's Journal,* September 26, 1776—"Inhuman barbarity! One Hale in New York, on suspicion of being a spy was taken up & dragged without ceremony to the execution post, and hung up—" Forty-three years later, the *Genius of Liberty* would report that Hale's final statement was his regret that he had "but one life to lose for his country."

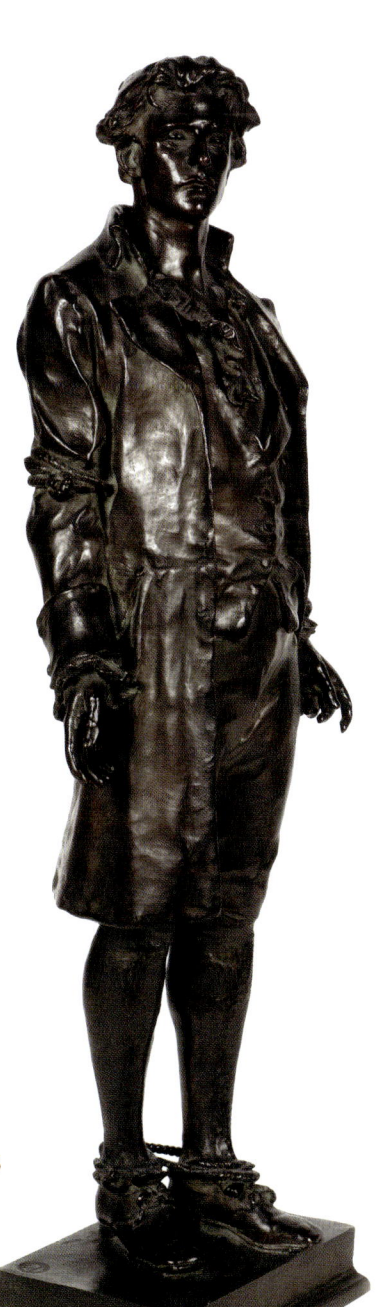

The American History Collection at Gilcrease Museum 65

In Congress July 4, 1776

A Declaration By the Representatives of the
United States of America In General Congress
assembled.

When In the course of human Events, it becomes necessa
-ry for one People to dissolve the political bands which
have connected them with an another, and to assume a-
-mong the Powers of the Earth, the seperate and equal Station
to which the Laws of Nature & Natures God entitle them
A decent respect to the Opinions of Mankind requires that
they should declare the causes which impel them to the

Separation.

We hold these truths to be self evident, that all men are
created equal, that they are endow'd by their Creator
with certain unalienable rights, that among these are
Life, Liberty & a pursuit of happiness — That to secure
these rights Government are instituted among Men, deri-
-ving their just powers from the consent of the Governed,
that whenever any form of Government becomes destruc-
-tive of these Ends, it is the right of the People to alter
or to abolish it, and to institute new Government, lay-
-ing its foundation on such principles and organizing
its powers in such form, as to them shall seem most
likely to effect their safety & happiness, Prudence, indeed

States of America.[14] These were uncertain times that famously tried men's souls,[15] but the colonists were not without support. The British Parliament was an unlikely source for such support, but it did contain members, such as Isaac Barré, who publicly argued the American cause and predicted that the colonists would not be intimidated or strong-armed. Their greatest support, however, came from the solace they found in the familiar figure appointed to lead the Continental Army nearly twenty years to the day after his defeat as a British soldier—George Washington.

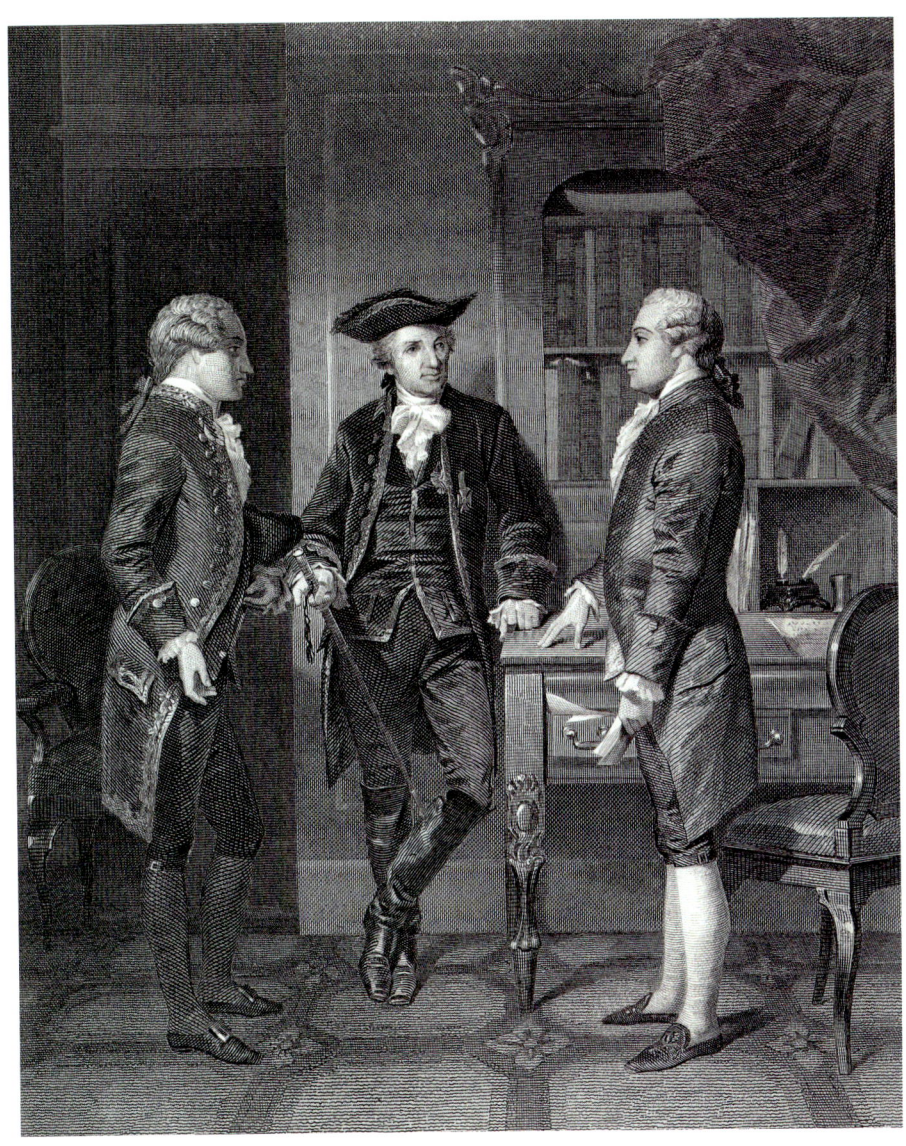

FACING: CERTIFIED COPY OF THE DECLARATION OF INDEPENDENCE, ATTESTED AND SIGNED BY SILAS DEANE AND BENJAMIN FRANKLIN, 1777. GM 4026.901

In June of 1776, Richard Henry Lee of Virginia presented a resolution that called for American independence. John Adams, Benjamin Franklin, Thomas Jefferson, Robert Livingston, and Roger Sherman were appointed to draft a declaration of reasons for the impending separation. Only thirty-three years old, Jefferson was not a highly visible member of Congress, though known for his "masterly pen." He prepared the draft and submitted it to the committee for consideration. Adams and Franklin suggested minor changes, and some further alterations were made after it was presented to the Congress on June 28. The final words were still largely those of Jefferson.

On July 2, Lee's resolution was passed and two days later the delegates to the Second Continental Congress formally adopted the Declaration. At its passage it was signed only by John Hancock, the presiding officer of the Congress. Later the Declaration of Independence was read aloud in the city of Philadelphia at what came to be known as Independence Square. Printed copies were made, sent to legislatures and published throughout the colonies. The other members of the Congress did not sign the Declaration until August 2, when a copy engrossed on parchment was witnessed with the delegates' names.

BARON DE KALB INTRODUCING LAFAYETTE TO SILAS DEANE, after Alonzo Chappel. GM 15.1130

Born in Bavaria, Johann de Kalb rose above his humble origins and earned the title of Baron through his military service to the French crown. In 1777 he and Lafayette arrived in the colonies and joined the Continental ranks.

Articles of Confederation and perpetual
Union between the States of.

New-Hampshire,	The counties of New-Castle
Massachusetts Bay,	Kent and Sussex on Delaware,
Rhode-Island,	Maryland
Connecticut,	Virginia
New-York,	North Carolina
New-Jersey	South Carolina
Pennsylvania	and Georgia.

Art. 1. The name of this Confederacy shall be
"The united States of America".

Art. 2. The said States hereby severally enter into a
firm league of Friendship with each other, for their
common defense, the security of their Liberties and
their mutual and general welfare, binding themselves
to assist each other against all force offered to or attacks
made upon them or any of them, on account of
Religion, Sovereignty, Trade, or any other pretence
whatever.

Art. 3. Each State reserves to itself the sole and
exclusive regulation and government of its internal
police in all matters that shall not interfere with
the Articles of this Confederation.

Art. 4. No State without the consent of the United
States in Congress assembled, shall send any Embassy
to, or receive any Embassy from, or enter into any
conference

them considered, and if approved by them,
they are advised to authorise their Delegates to
ratify the same in the Assembly of the United
States, which being done, the Articles of this
Confederation shall inviolably be observed by
every State, and the Union is to be perpetual:
Nor shall any alteration at any time hereafter
be made in these Articles or any of them,
unless such Alteration be agreed to in an
Assembly of the United States, and be afterwards
confirmed by the Legislatures of every State.

A True Copy of the Original Articles

Test

B Franklin

Silas Deane

ARTICLES OF CONFEDERATION, 1777. GM 4026.899

In 1776, a committee led by John Dickinson of Delaware was charged with designing a form of shared government between the colonies. The Dickinson draft was presented to Congress on July 12. It took nearly two years for the final form of the document, called The Articles of Confederation, to be accepted, and another three years for all thirteen states to ratify it. As approved by the Continental Congress, signed by Silas Deane and Benjamin Franklin, and sent to Frederick the Great of Prussia, this document represented the first effort at building a national government. In many ways it functioned as a treaty between small nations rather than as a structure for true national government. Each state, regardless of population or geographic area, had one vote in Congress. Congress could declare war and peace, send and receive ambassadors, enter into treaties, regulate Indian affairs, coin money, and establish a post office. It could not, however, levy taxes or regulate commerce. There was no federal executive and no national court system, and the states retained any power not expressly delegated within the Articles. With a national government hampered by such restrictions, a convention was held in 1787 to revise the Articles. They would eventually be replaced by the Constitution two years later.

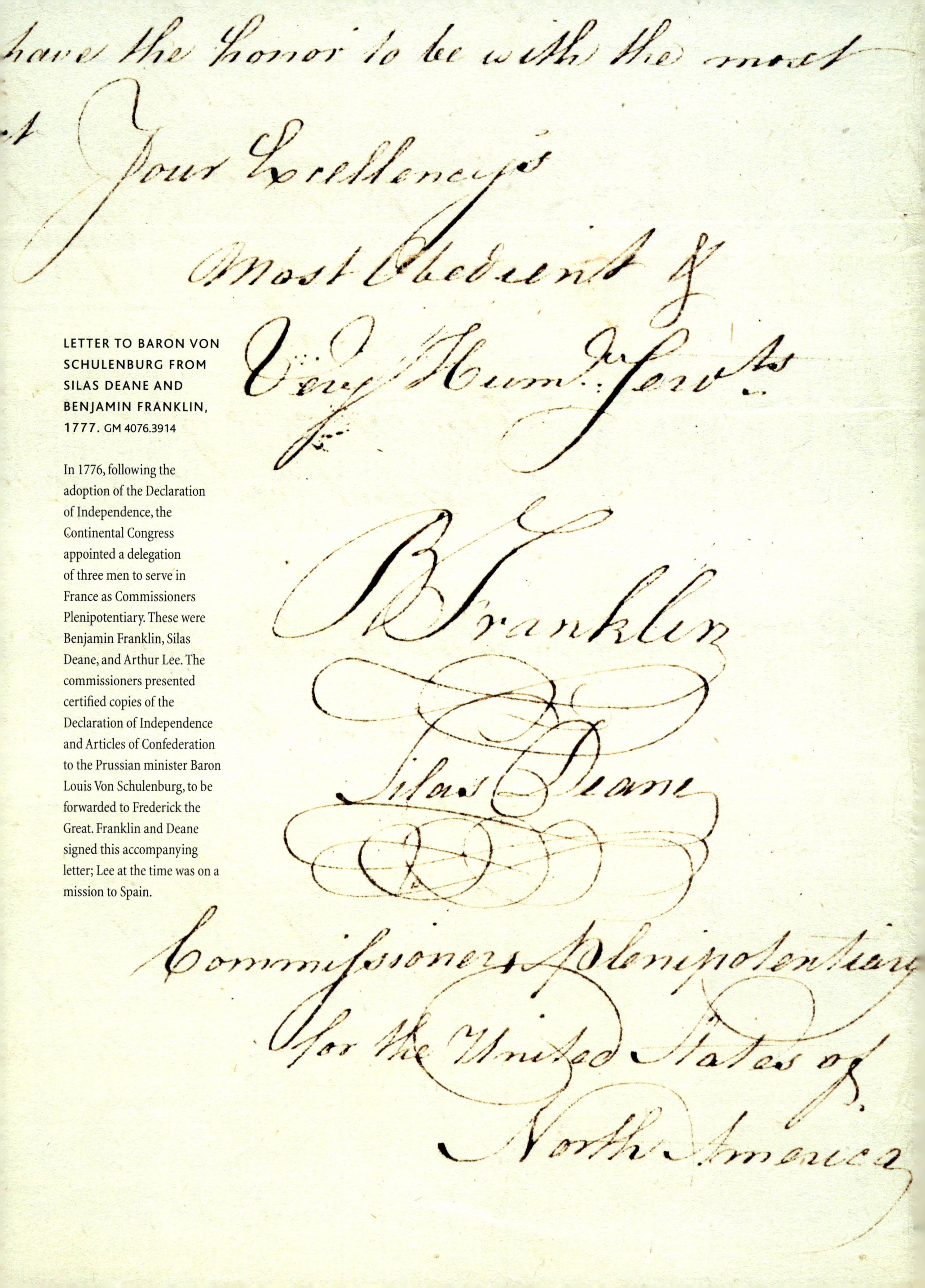

have the honor to be with the most

Your Excellency's

Most Obedient &

Very Hum: Serv.ts

B Franklin

Silas Deane

Commissioners Plenipotentiary

for the United States of

North America

LETTER TO BARON VON SCHULENBURG FROM SILAS DEANE AND BENJAMIN FRANKLIN, 1777. GM 4076.3914

In 1776, following the adoption of the Declaration of Independence, the Continental Congress appointed a delegation of three men to serve in France as Commissioners Plenipotentiary. These were Benjamin Franklin, Silas Deane, and Arthur Lee. The commissioners presented certified copies of the Declaration of Independence and Articles of Confederation to the Prussian minister Baron Louis Von Schulenburg, to be forwarded to Frederick the Great. Franklin and Deane signed this accompanying letter; Lee at the time was on a mission to Spain.

For the next six years, Washington led the troops in the "common cause of America,"[16] fighting in the fields and on the shores of the struggling new nation. It was a difficult and uncertain task marked by early losses, but the Continentals persevered and scored victories at the battles of Trenton and Princeton. Supplies, however, became increasingly scarce over the following two years and by October of 1779, Washington's army was in poor condition. Quartered at Morristown, New Jersey, for the winter, Washington now not only faced assaults from the British army, but also from his own. Mutinies would remain a threat for the remainder of the Revolution. Sacrifice was not made only by the soldiers, however, and from families sharing their grain to wives and mothers waiting for loved ones to return, all paid the price of war.[17] Year after year, battle after battle, the Continentals persevered with a singular determination to defeat Great Britain. Despite Britain's superior military, she could not defeat the determination and resolve of the American forces, and in 1781, the diversity of the young nation was visible as Native American, African American, and colonial soldiers watched General Cornwallis surrender his sword at Yorktown, effectively bringing the war to an end. The transition of a rebellion into a revolution was complete.[18] As an added insult, American victory was due in no small part to an alliance it formed in 1778 with Britain's historic enemy—France.[19] Although the Treaty of Paris formally recognized the independence and creation of the United States of America, the country remained united in name only—states maintained their individual identities as an unlikely experiment in self-government began, guided by the Articles of Confederation. Even at this early point, many worried over the strength of the new country. "The cords of union," one newspaper reported, were "but a rope of sand."[20] Many thought the new government would quickly revert to a monarchy with Washington as king, but he quickly quelled those anxieties when he resigned his commission and returned to his home at Mount Vernon.

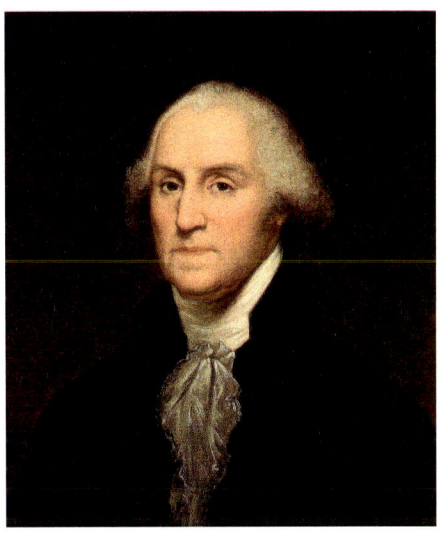

GEORGE WASHINGTON, Rembrandt Peale. Oil on canvas, 1795. GM 0126.1005

George Washington sat for Charles Willson Peale and his son Rembrandt Peale in 1795. Rembrandt described the sitting: "The hour he appointed was 7 o'clock in the morning, I was up before daylight, putting everything in the best condition for the sitting with which I was to be honored, but could scarcely mix my colors, and was conscious that my anxiety would overpower me and that I should fail in my purpose unless my father would agree to take a canvas alongside me and thus give me an assurance that the sittings would not be unprofitable, by affording the double chance for a likeness. This had the effect to calm my nerves, and I enjoyed the rare advantage of studying the desired countenance whilst in familiar conversation with my father."

Later in life, Rembrandt Peale decided that his artistic aim was to "multiply the countenance of Washington," and so he painted several copies from his earlier work, including this rendering from the Gilcrease collection.

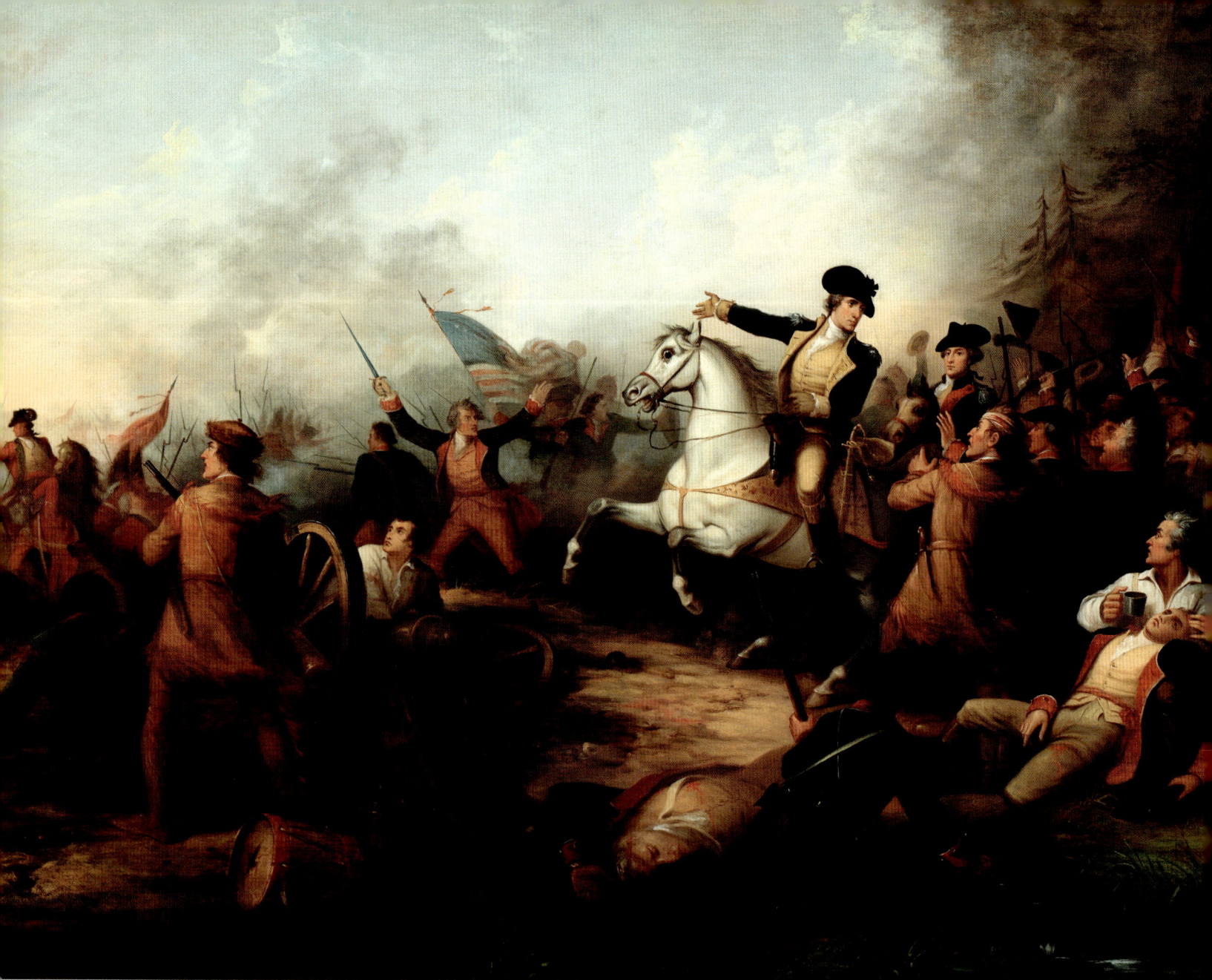

WASHINGTON AT THE BATTLE OF PRINCETON, JANUARY 3, 1777, William T. Ranney. Oil on canvas. GM 0126.2108

The Revolution moved into New Jersey during the final days of 1776. In a campaign that lasted three weeks, Americans earned victories at the battles of Trenton and Princeton, demonstrating George Washington's military acumen and the fortitude of some 5,000 American troops.

The fighting outside Princeton almost became a rout, however, following the death of American General Hugh Mercer. Washington personally rallied his men and forced the British to retreat into the town of Princeton, and on January 3 the British regiments were defeated. Following this successful campaign, Washington and his army took up winter quarters at Morristown in northern New Jersey.

PORTRAIT OF GEORGE WASHINGTON, Charles Willson Peale. Oil on canvas, ca. 1795. GM 0126.1013

George Washington (1732–1799) was the first president of the United States and commander of the Continental Army during the American Revolution, but began his career of public service twenty years earlier as a member of the Virginia House of Burgesses, justice of Fairfax County, delegate to the First and Second Continental Congresses, and president of the Constitutional Convention.

Charles Willson Peale is known as the principal painter of Washington. Between 1772 and 1795, he painted Washington seven times from life, and eventually he produced sixty portraits of the man. Peale was well known to colonial leaders. He was active in the American Revolution as a commissioned captain and involved in the Battles of Trenton and Princeton. He served on several military and civil committees and in 1779 was elected one of Philadelphia's representatives to the General Assembly of Pennsylvania. John Adams wrote: "Peale is from Maryland, a tender, soft, affectionate creature. He is ingenious. He has vanity, loves finery, wears a sword, gold lace, speaks French, is capable of friendship, and strong family attachments and natural affections." By contrast, Peale described himself as "a thin, spare, pale-faced man."

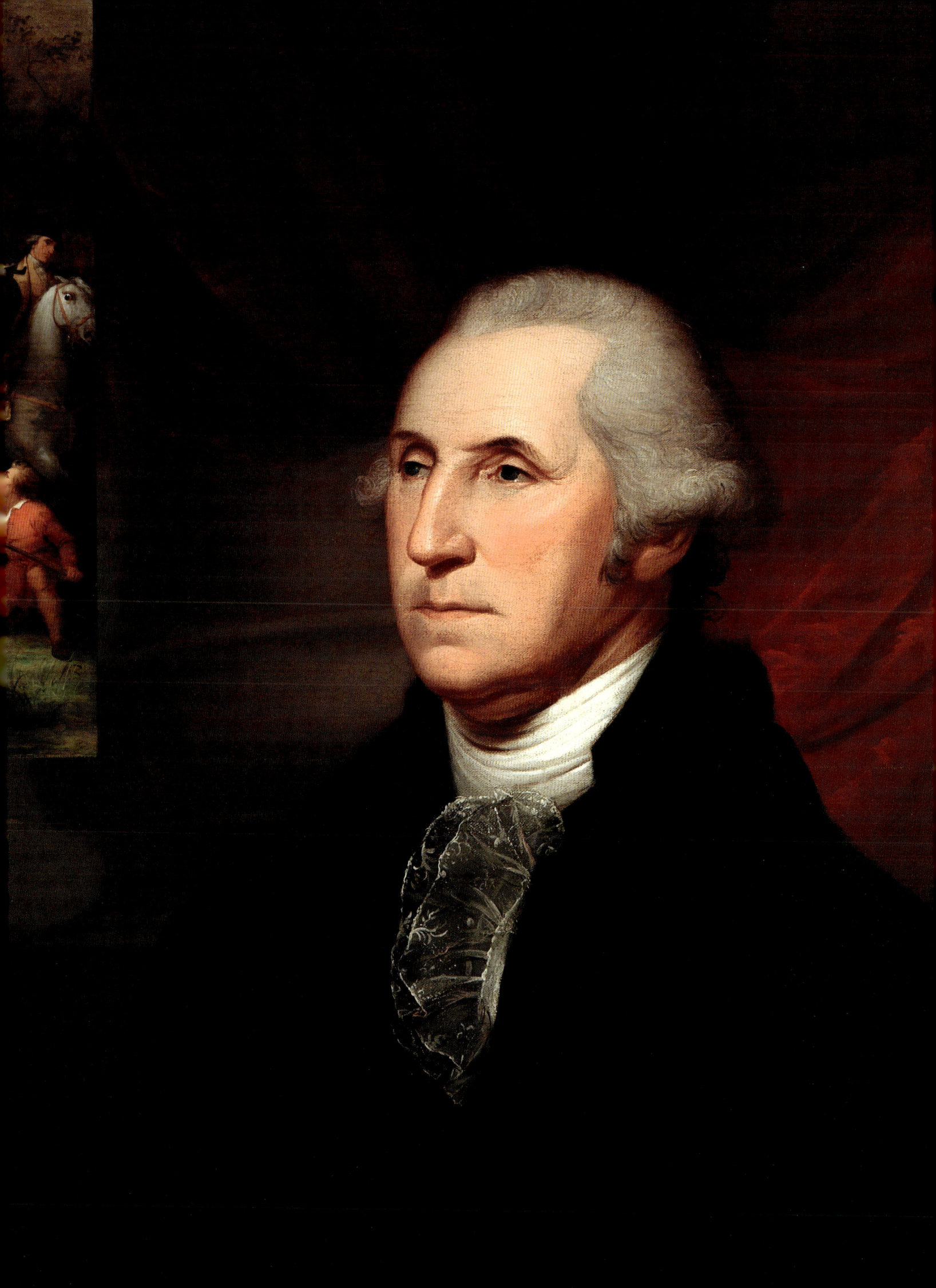

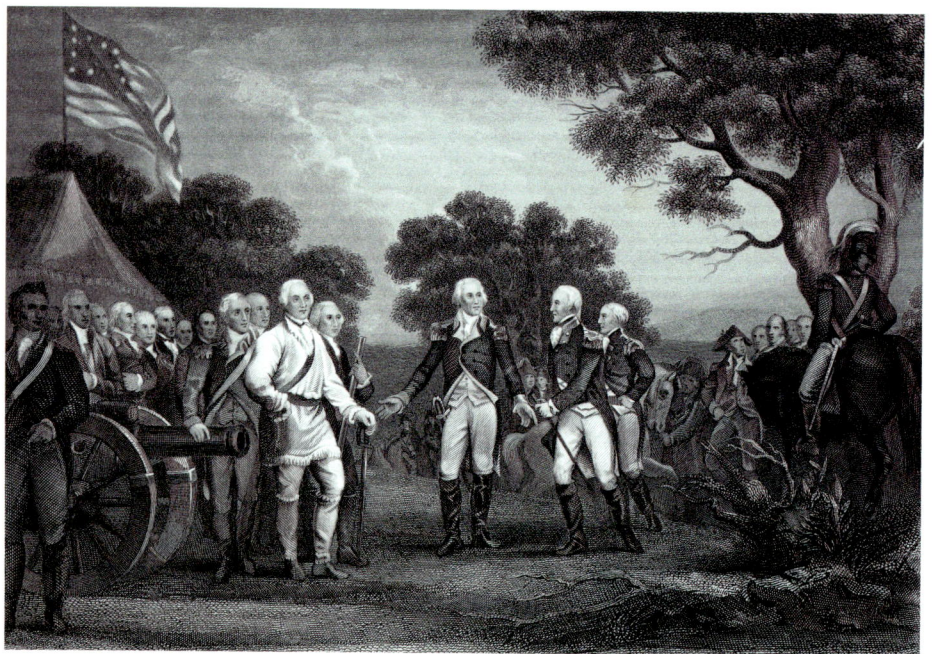

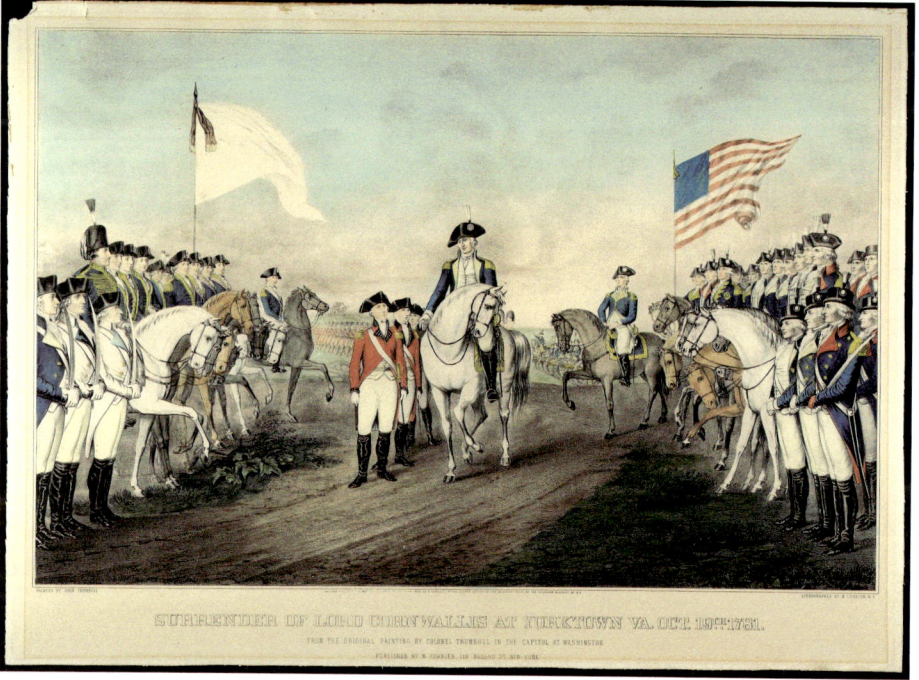

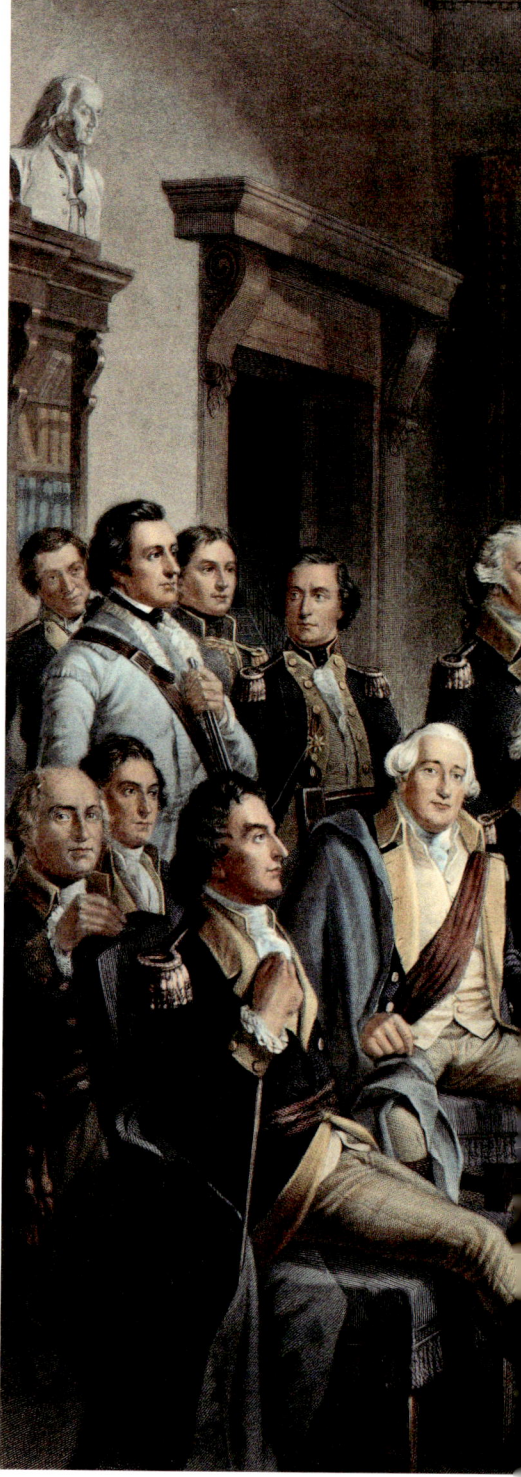

After the Battle of Yorktown, Cornwallis was forced to surrender to the American
and French forces. He did not, however, personally relinquish his sword, but
instead sent his second in command, Brigadier Charles O'Hara, who initially tried
to surrender the sword to General Rochambeau, the leader of the French forces.
Rochambeau, however, reminded O'Hara that it was to Washington he should
surrender the sword.

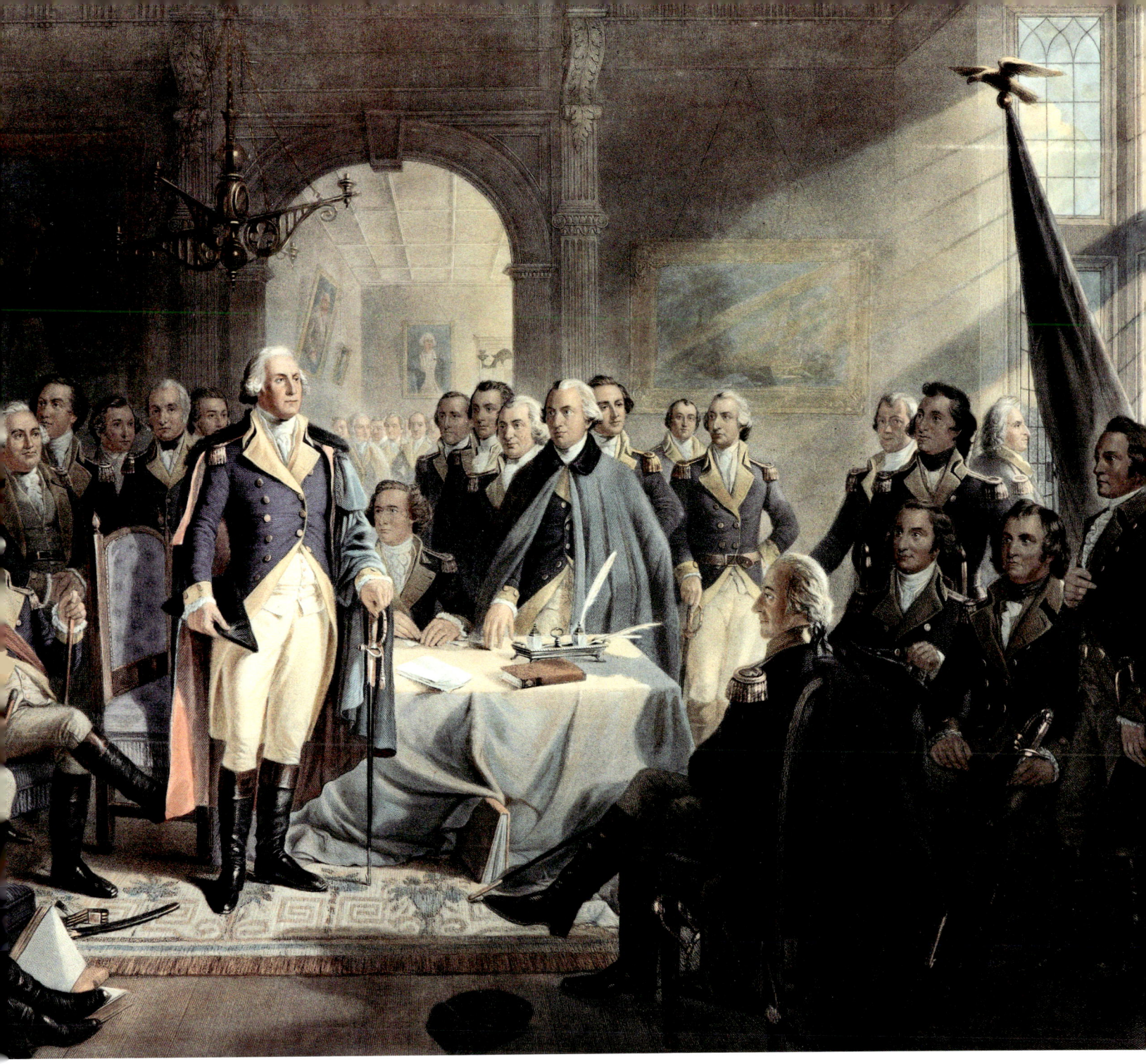

WASHINGTON AND HIS GENERALS, James Troyle. Color engraving, 1856. GM 1526.116

The British surrender at Yorktown in October 1781 did not end the war. British forces still occupied parts of Georgia, South Carolina, and New York. However, in Britain support for the war was disintegrating, and by April 1782 informal peace talks were initiated. The Peace of Paris was finally signed in September 1783. Only after British troops departed in November 1783, could General Washington leave his position. On Thursday, December 4, he said farewell to his officers in the Long Room of Fraunces Tavern in New York City. According to a contemporary newspaper account the group was comprised of a few generals, some lower officers, and other acquaintances. Washington raised a glass, saying, "With a heart full of love and gratitude I now take leave of you, and most devoutly wish your latter days may be as prosperous and happy as your former ones have been glorious and honorable." He then drank a toast to those present and asked that each take leave and shake his hand. Afterwards, Washington and his officers walked to the Hudson River, where a barge waited. As church bells rang and onlookers crowded streets and windows, Washington boarded the boat in silence, took off his hat and waved farewell.

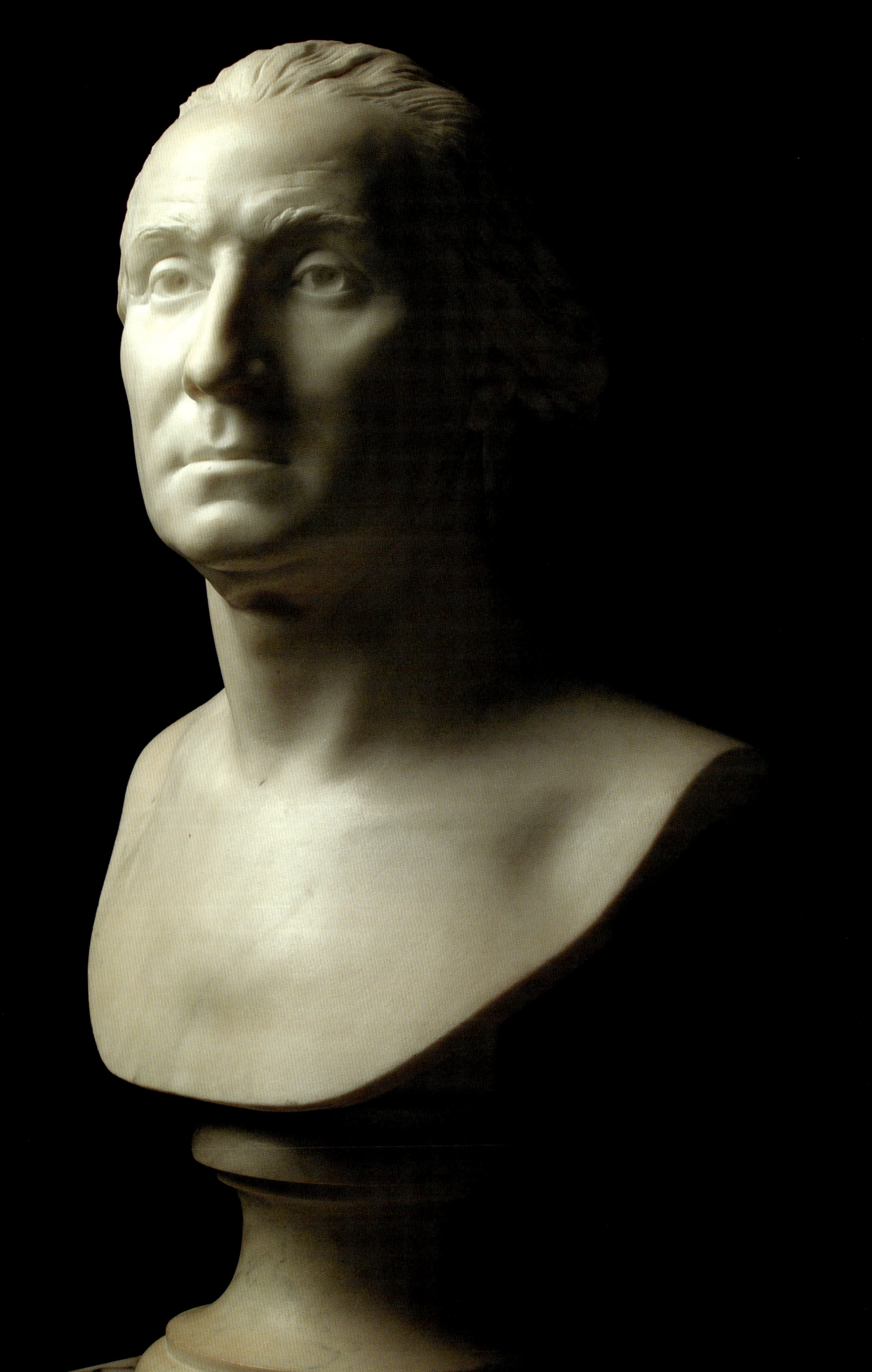

Over the next six years, the country struggled to define itself and its government. The United States did not have an ancient, collective past to build upon like most countries—no inherited identity founded on centuries of shared history. They had only the present and in the absence of cultural memory turned instead to American symbols. The flag, the seal of the United States, the bald eagle, and even George Washington were among the most prominent.[21] So too was the number thirteen, now intrinsically linked to the struggle of the thirteen colonies for independence. From the number of toasts given at celebrations to fireworks to cannon fire, thirteen was seen as anything but unlucky, and on no day was this more apparent than the Fourth of July,[22] the anniversary of American independence celebrated by citizens every year.

As Americans struggled with the nuances and intricacies of new citizenship in their daily lives, state governments tried to navigate the challenges and surprises of self-government. The inefficiencies of the current system quickly surfaced, and it became clear a more centralized government was necessary. In May of 1787 politicians once again gathered in Philadelphia, this time to "revise the federal system of Government" during the Constitutional Convention. Washington, after much persuasion, agreed to preside over the convention, but it was James Madison who largely directed the discussion and substance of the Constitution. After five months of deliberation, the document was adopted. The United States would be a republic, with three branches of government—the executive, legislative, and judicial. Incorporating a system of checks and balances, the Constitution insured no branch had disproportionate power. The most unprecedented aspect of the government, however, was the power it gave to its citizens. Americans, not divine right, would determine who led them as president, and the choice for the first president was unanimous.

As George Washington traveled to New York for his inauguration, the complexity of the new colonial identity was evident in displays that at times seemed more regal than republican, residuals perhaps of a monarchical past. Rose petals were thrown at his feet and people addressed him as "Your Excellency." Thousands crowded the streets, eager to catch a glimpse of the man already known as the father of the country.[23] The once defeated British soldier had become the first president of the United States, and the message to Europe was clear.

GEORGE WASHINGTON, Jean Antoine Houdon. Seravezza marble, 1788. GM 0976.4

At the close of the Revolutionary War, Virginia voted to erect a statue of Washington. Thomas Jefferson and Benjamin Franklin arranged for Jean Antoine Houdon, the most important sculptor of the period, to receive the commission. Houdon was so pleased that he voluntarily journeyed to Virginia to meet Washington instead of working from a painting. Franklin accompanied the French sculptor on his voyage from France to Washington's home, Mount Vernon, in the fall of 1785. Houdon made sketches and clay models from sittings and also took a life cast. He returned to France to complete the life-size, full figure marble, which he brought back in 1788. Because of Washington's almost universal popularity, Houdon carved many busts based on his original sittings.

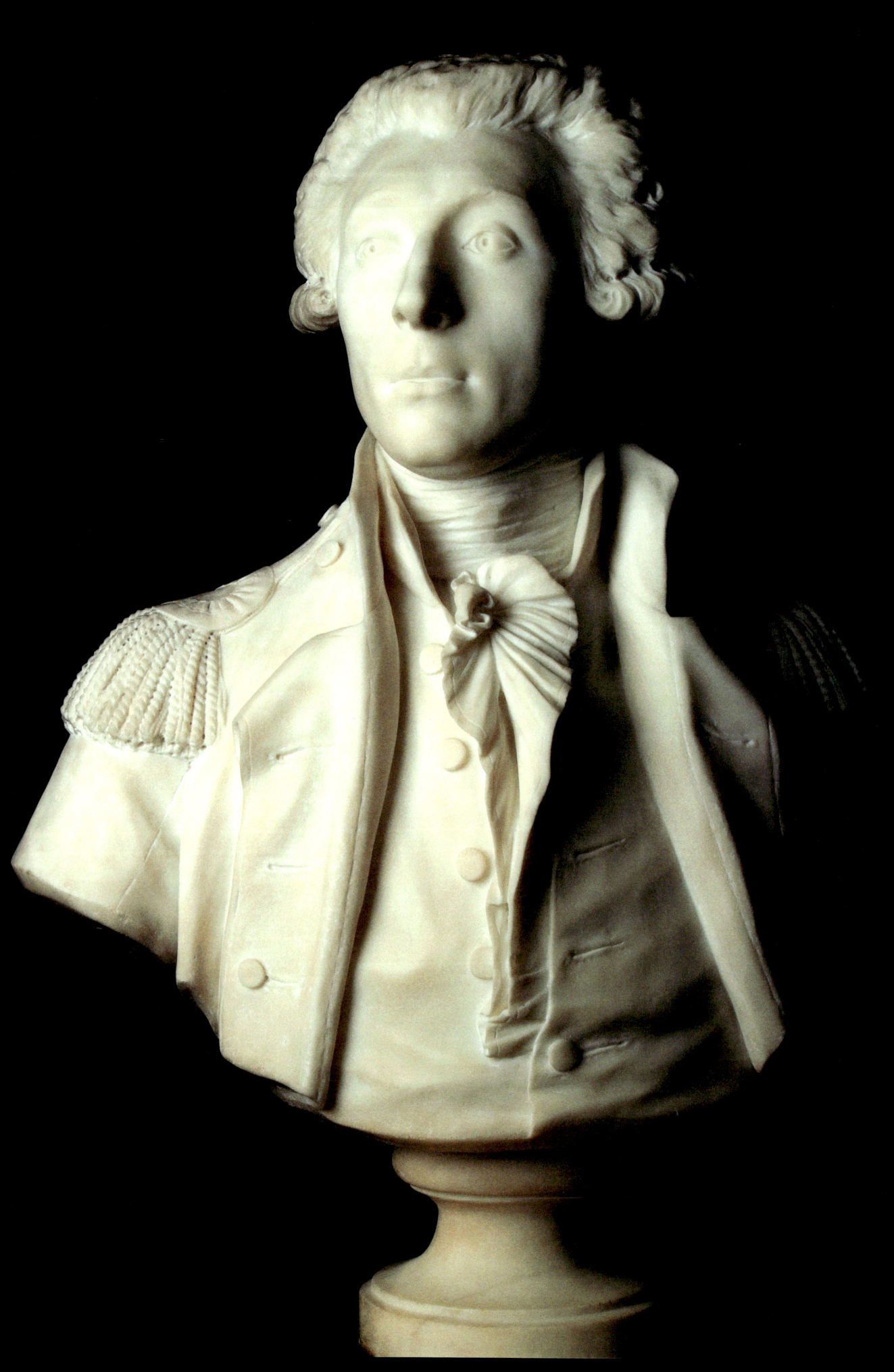

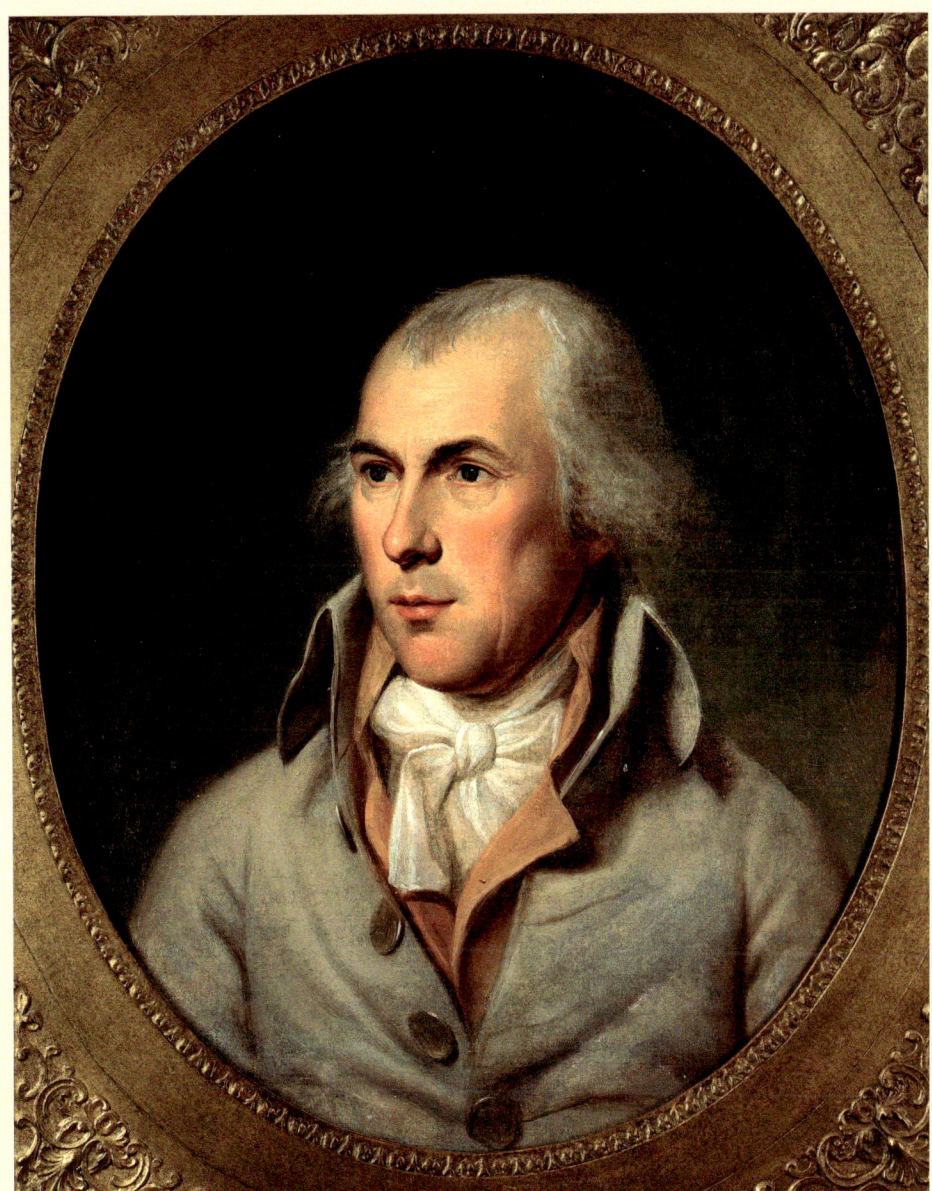

GENERAL LAFAYETTE,
Jean Antoine Houdon. Seravezza marble,
1789. GM 0976.3

Lord Maria Joseph Paul Yves Roch
Gilbert du Motier, Marquis de Lafayette
(1757–1834) was a wealthy idealist,
French aristocrat, and enthusiastic
supporter of liberty. In 1777, he arrived
in the American colonies aboard a ship
equipped at his own expense to offer his
service to the military effort. Congress
commissioned him a major general in
the Continental Army just before his
twentieth birthday, and Washington gave
him a small independent command
in 1777. He distinguished himself in
battle and is considered a hero of the
American Revolution. Lafayette's greatest
service, however, was political. In 1779
while on a mission home, he persuaded
King Louis XVI of France to send out an
expeditionary force to North America.
Under the command of Comte de
Rochambeau, the French troops helped
Washington win the decisive battle of
Yorktown.

This marble portrait of Lafayette in the
uniform of commander of the guard
is one of two busts of the hero by Jean
Antoine Houdon. This one, done for
Lafayette, remained in his family until
sold to Thomas Gilcrease. French art
historians consider it t to be one of
Houdon's best works.

JAMES MADISON, Charles Willson Peale.
Oil on canvas, 1792. GM 0126.1006

This portrait of James Madison (1751–1836) was painted fourteen
years before his election as the fourth president of the United States. It
commemorates his role as the "father of the Constitution." Madison's record
of public service was impressive. He was a member of the Continental
Congress, the Annapolis and Constitutional Conventions, and the U. S. House
of Representatives, and he served as secretary of state. A brilliant American
political thinker, he led the development of the first ten amendments to the
Constitution, known as the Bill of Rights.

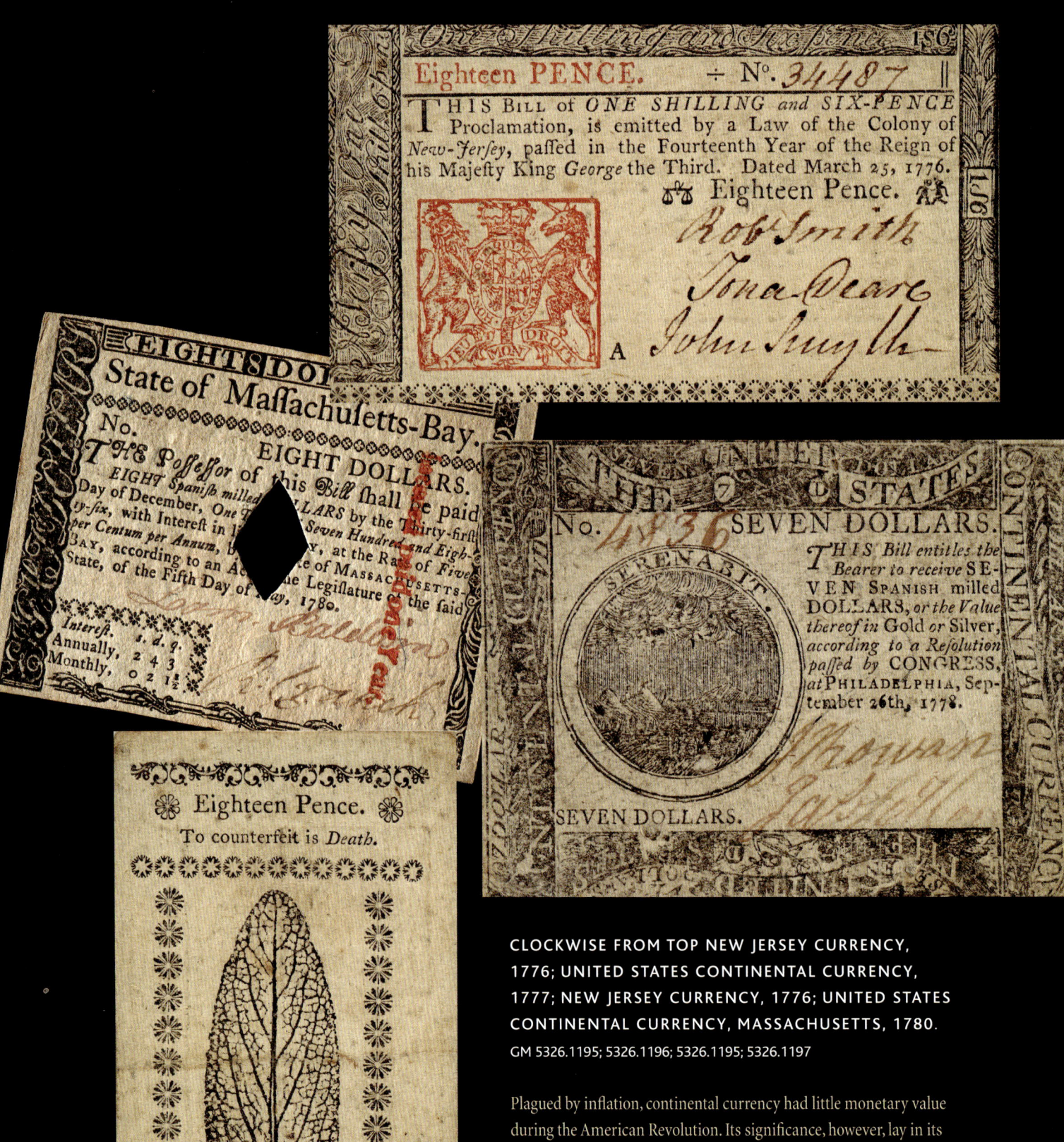

CLOCKWISE FROM TOP NEW JERSEY CURRENCY,
1776; UNITED STATES CONTINENTAL CURRENCY,
1777; NEW JERSEY CURRENCY, 1776; UNITED STATES
CONTINENTAL CURRENCY, MASSACHUSETTS, 1780.
GM 5326.1195; 5326.1196; 5326.1195; 5326.1197

Plagued by inflation, continental currency had little monetary value
during the American Revolution. Its significance, however, lay in its
role as colonial propaganda—as physical evidence that the United
States was no longer bound to Great Britain.

FACING: NATIONAL GAZETTE, P. Freneau.
Wednesday, April 17, 1793. GM 5026.4394

National Gazette.

By P. FRENEAU: Published WEDNESDAYS and SATURDAYS, at THREE DOLLARS per annum.

NUMB. 49 of VOL. II.] WEDNESDAY, April 17, 1793. [Total No. 153.]

Mr FRENEAU,

THE two enclosed pieces appeared in the Hartford American Mercury of April 1st. They seem to have been calculated more particularly for the meridian of Connecticut, but may also be very acceptable to a number of readers in "*the latitude of Philadelphia.*" A. B.

AS the origin of all power is in the people, a government recognizing that principle, and securing the rights of representation and election, is said to be a free government. The constitution of the United States, and of the individual States of America, fall within this description; for the people in whom the source of power resides, impart the first impulse and moving force to the political machine, by election—This right forms the basis of our freedom—it is the grand check to the encroachments of the magistrates, and that degree of influence which they might otherwise obtain over the subjects of their authority. The history of past ages, as well as the known principles of human nature, afford the fullest evidence of the tendency of all government toward absolute dominion—Therefore, in its constitution and formation, that it be ballanced, checked and secured, against this natural tendency as far as the case will admit, is not of itself enough; there is a duty continually to be performed by the people; they are to watch and employ the checks left in their hands. The continuation of their liberty does not so much depend upon the existence of the right of election, as upon a vigilant and careful exercise of it.—They are the proprietors of government, and the ruler, the person who is entrusted with the management of the estate. If the owners neglect their proprietary interest, the manager may easily run off with the profit, leaving them to share in nothing but the expence. A progression of small and imperceptible encroachments may in course of time grow into system and acquire the force of precedent. From the same cause, the sentiments, manners and habits of a country, may suffer a slow revolution, and elections retain nothing of their original, but the name.

These observations, though they contain no new or uncommon sentiments to recommend them, are, from the nature of the subject, worthy of some attention, and may lead us to reflect, that the liberty we enjoy is an inheritance we are bound to transmit to posterity unimpaired. If the use or abuse of the right of election is the medium through which it may be either preserved or lost, the conclusion is obvious, that an attentive exercise of this right is an indispensible duty incumbent on every Freeman. The chief magistrates in Connecticut are often elected by less than one twentieth part of the legal voters—But a small part of the Freemen assemble, and but a small portion of that part attend when the most important branch of the business is transacting—the *Tools* and *Connections* of those who seek for office are left to execute their designs unmolested. When such inattention prevails, it is neither strange or unaccountable, that men sometimes gain an election, and afterwards hold their place against the choice of a majority of the people.

It may be urged that the Freemen cannot have personal knowledge of every man held up to view, as meriting their suffrages throughout a whole State; and must either be guided by the opinion of others, or must many times neglect to act.

But if it be a business of such moment, every Elector ought to inform himself, and always to give his suffrage according to the best information he can obtain. Men who have gained important offices, whether deserving or undeserving, are, from their condition and situation, always able to secure to themselves friends.

The longer such office has been in the possession of one man, or one family, the more numerous will be his adherents ready to cover his faults, and exhibit only the fairest part of his character. Hence arises a question worthy the attention and examination of every Free Elector—Whether public discussion of the qualifications and merits of candidates for office, be not necessary for the formation of a right judgment on that subject—Men who occupy elevated stations in life, are surrounded with sycophants and flatterers, ready on every occasion to *pimp*, *cabal*, and *intrigue* for their patron. Nothing affords so great security against their designs as a free public discussion of every one, opens the sources of intelligence, and excites men to develope the truth. He who fears to be tried by this test, ought never to come forth as a candidate for office.

Another thing deserving of notice in the exercise of the right of election, is, that the highest offices be not continued too long in one *family* or *person*.

In Connecticut the compensations given for public services are in no cases so great as to produce a dangerous accumulation of wealth in the hands of those who receive them, but it is very obvious, that the long continuance of dignified and important offices in the same family, begets an influence more dangerous to a republican government than that which is derived from wealth. Aristocratic sentiments, and aristocratic manners are here generated, nursed and matured. A man born and educated with exalted ideas of his own greatness and that of his ancestors, will never consider his fellow-men as his equals, or as partaking of the same rights—Invest him with the powers of magistracy, and all subordinate offices of trust and emolument, within his reach, will be seized upon for his own family and connections, to the exclusion of those who are much better qualified. By such means he will form an atmosphere of influence tending directly to sap the foundation of free government. The first article of the creed of a republican, is that all men are equal, and are distinguished only by their ability and their merit.

But when power has been suffered to flow in the same channel until it has produced to itself a bulwark against the hands who gave it, these principles are reversed—"It then becomes the Electors to be sensible of their just rights, in order, that by understanding in the first place what as men they owe to themselves, they may in the second make their rulers know, and if necessary feel, what they, as servants of the people, owe to them."

ALGERNON SIDNEY.

In a preceding paper I suggested a few thoughts on the importance of elections, and the dangerous consequence of negligence in the elective body; in pursuing the subject we shall naturally notice the operation, influence, and effect of parties.

IT will be found in all free governments, where full liberty of thought & action is allowed, that the public sentiment will be divided on many questions respecting the principles of the government, the administration, or some other circumstance connected with the general police, from whence parties are produced. At the commencement of the late war, *some persons* of *haughty* and *imperious minds* became leaders in the revolution, not from an attachment to republican principles, but from a regard to the honors expected to be shared under the new government.

From this source originated two parties in Connecticut, the one contending for the good of the whole, proceeded on democratic ground, and endeavoured by their practice to verify their professions in the cause of liberty—the other seemed to aim at the good of *the few*, and the aggrandizement of particular families, clamoured for more *energy* and a *higher tone* to the administration, inveighed against the imbecility, timidity, and dependance of the magistrates, and ridiculed every republican argument opposed to their system. The cabals and intrigues of this party in course of time, increased its strength by advancing its principal leader to a higher and more influential station.

Though this was not the act of the Freemen at large, but the result of skilful management in the Legislature, yet it was considered by the successful partizans as a subject of triumph, and from this time their attempts to influence succeeding elections, became more direct, open and notorious. The *ribaldry* of Billingsgate was let loose upon their opponents from a *mercenary groupe* of *grubstreet scriblers*, through the medium of a *prostituted press*.

Low ridicule, with them was forcible argument, and the application of unmeaning nicknames, such as *Bubo*, *Weglog*, *Wronghead*, *Wimble*, and *Copper*, conclusive evidence. In short, men of the most established reputation for integrity and worth, who appeared on the other side of the question, were traduced, vilified, and scurrilously abused; and if I may use the language … *shuffle* and *cut the pack* until *all the honors* should be dealt into their own hands. No serious answer could very well be given to a piece of vulgar ridicule, especially if it had no other foundation than the place of one's residence, or the corpulent, or slender proportions of his body: hence some men of too weak nerves to bear the force of such weapons, retreated from the conflict and left the game to terminate as chance should direct. To recount the worthy characters, which have been displaced from important offices, and sacrificed to the designs of this party, would exceed the limits I have assigned; they are well known, and fresh in the minds of many of the good people of this state.

It is remarkable that through the whole period of time in which these divisions have existed in the state, and the great struggles that have been made to increase the weight in the *Aristocratic Scale*, there has scarce any thing appeared on that side, addressed to the understanding and good sense of the people. The dependance seems to have been upon the *wit*, rather than the *logic* of their writers. Neither the *Patient*, the *Client*, nor even the solemn *service of the Altar*, could detain these witty scriblers from the more important business of their party.

I have taken but a summary review of the parties in this State; whoever gives the subject a more careful examination, and enters more minutely into the history of it, will agree in the position endeavored to be supported by these papers, that the whole *fabric of our liberty*, depends on *vigilance and attention in the exercise of the rights of election*. Unless the Freemen look for themselves, they are liable to imposition from all quarters. The extensive circulation of Newspapers through this State, might afford a competent share of information respecting the affairs of the public to every individual. Whatever appears in the style of candid discussion, and is addressed to the understanding of the people, ought to receive their attention, but if *Irony*, *Satire*, and *Ridicule*, are adopted as the guide of their judgment, they are certain to err.

At the last annual election, a sentiment prevailed in all parts of the State, that it was best to make a change in the office of Lieut. Governor. Judge Ellsworth was generally thought of, as a suitable character for that place. But what was the opposition? Not that Mr. Ellsworth was less capable of presiding in the Court of Errors, than the gentleman then in office—Not that his abilities were inferior to the other in any point of view—Not that his integrity was doubted—Not that he did not merit and possess the highest confidence of the people. No arguments or objections of this kind were ever suggested, but the public papers teemed with the same kind of ridicule which has ever been the chief instrument of the party in opposition. The Freemen were to be laughed out of their opinions, and eighteen hundred and ninety-four independant Electors who honored him with their suffrages, would be nothing less than a *Faction*, in a state of *actual rebellion* against the *reigning powers*. Why? Because they judged it conducive to the public interest to break up the hereditary descent of an overgrown family, and introduce a man more *universally esteemed*, into the line of succession. Have the people of Connecticut no power to change their rulers? Have they no discretion to determine on whom the honors of government ought to be conferred? Are they placed under the *conservation* of a *junto* of *blackguard scriblers*? Or are they at liberty to examine, judge, and act for themselves? If the latter be the case, let not the arts of the *intriguing partizan*, or the mean ridicule of the *mercenary Wit*, divert them from the great objects of their duty; let them enquire with diligence, decide with deliberation, and act with firmness—let them guard their rights with care and defend them with spirit.

ALGERNON SIDNEY.

Mr. PAINE'S REASONS FOR PRESERVING THE LIFE OF LOUIS CAPET—AS DELIVERED TO THE NATIONAL CONVENTION.

CITIZEN PRESIDENT,

MY hatred and abhorrence of monarchy are sufficiently known; they originate in principles of reason and conviction, nor, except with life, can they ever be extirpated; but my compassion for the unfortunate, whether friend or enemy, is equally …

I voted that Louis should be tried, because it was necessary to afford proofs to the world of the perfidy, corruption and abomination of the monarchical system. The infinity of evidence that has been produced, exposes them in the most glaring and hideous colours. Thence it results, that monarchy, whatever form it may assume, arbitrary or otherwise, becomes necessarily a centre, round which are united every species of corruption, and that the *kingly trade* is no less destructive of all morality in the human breast, than the trade of an executioner is destructive of its sensibility.

I remember, during my residence in another country, that I was exceedingly struck with a sentence of M. Autheine, at the Jacobins, which corresponds exactly with my own idea, "Make me a king to-day," said he, "and I shall be a robber to-morrow."

Nevertheless, I am inclined to believe, that if Louis Capet had been born in an obscure condition, had he lived within the circle of an amiable and respectable neighbourhood, at liberty to practise the duties of domestic life, had he been thus situated, I cannot believe that he would have shewn himself destitute of social virtues: we are in a moment of fermentation like this, naturally little indulgent to his vices, or rather to those of monarchical governments, we regard them with additional horror and indignation; not that they are more heinous than those of his predecessors, but because our eyes are now open and the veil of delusion at length withdrawn, yet the lamentable, degraded state to which he is actually reduced, is surely far less imputable to him, than to the constituent assembly, which, of its own authority, without consent or advice of the people, restored him to the throne.

I was in Paris at the time of the flight or abdication of Louis XVI. and when he was taken and brought back. The proposal of restoring to him the supreme power struck me with amazement; and although at that time, I was not a French citizen, yet as a citizen of the world, I employed all the efforts that depended on me to prevent it.

A small society, composed only of five persons two of whom are now members of the convention, took, at that time, the name of the Republican Club, (Societe Republicaine). This society opposed the restoration of Louis, not so much on account of his own personal offences, as in order to overthrow the monarchy, and to erect on its ruins the Republican System, and an equal Representation.

With this design I traced out in the English language certain propositions, which were translated, with some trifling alterations, and signed by Achilles Duchatlet, actually lieutenant-general in the army of the French Republic, and at that time one of the five members which composed our little party; the law requiring the signature of a citizen at the bottom of each printed paper.

The paper was indignantly torn by Malouet and brought forth in this very room as an article of accusation against the person who had signed it, the author and their adherents; but such is the revolution of events, that this paper is now revived, and brought forth for a very opposite purpose; —To remind the nation of the error of that unfortunate day, that fatal error of having not then banished Louis XVIth. from its bosom, & to plead this day in favour of his exile, preferably to his death.

The paper in question was conceived in the following terms:

"*Brethren and Fellow Citizens,*

The serene tranquility, the mutual confidence which prevailed amongst us, during the time of the late king's escape, the indifference with which we beheld him return, are unequivocal proofs that the absence of a king is more desirable than his presence, and that he is not only a political superfluity, but a grievous burthen pressing hard on the whole nation.

Let us not be imposed on by sophisms; All that concerns this man, is reduced to four points.

He has abdicated the throne in having fled from his post. Abdication and desertion are not characterized by the length of absence; but by the single act of flight. In the present instance, the act is every thing, and the time nothing.

The nation can never give back its confidence to a man who, false to his trust, perjured to his oath, conspires a clandestine …

The president of the United States was similar to a king, but inherently better. He was one of the people, chosen by the people. Sensitive to the new precedent of breaking precedent, Washington weighed each decision, careful to promote respect and reverence for the new office. He surrounded himself with men pivotal to the Revolution. John Adams served as his vice president, John Jay as secretary of state, and Alexander Hamilton as secretary of treasury. Thomas Jefferson would replace Jay roughly one year later. Washington realized that by virtue of being first, every action he took or did not take, would shape or at the least influence future presidents and protocol. "We are a young nation," he once wrote, "and have a character to establish."[24] It paralleled the difficulties in forging a new nation. There was no manual, no instruction. There were only men and their decisions, and Washington was forced to make a significant one in 1793.

As his presidency progressed, the country had experienced significant turmoil concerning the role and reach of the government. Burdened with debt from the Revolution and eager to raise funds, Congress had imposed a tax on all distilled spirits. Americans had predictably protested, citing the same arguments they had used against the Stamp and Townshend Acts. The resultant Whiskey Rebellion grew particularly heated and violent in the western states. Washington knew a failure to quell it would undermine the power of his presidency. If he succeeded, he would restore stability. He called nearly 13,000 militia to western Pennsylvania, where they put down the rebellion with little force. While the Whiskey Rebellion had demonstrated conflict between civilians and government, there was also conflict, however, rising within the government.

During the Revolution, colonial leaders had been united in the common cause of independence. But now that the war was over, factions had quickly formed over beliefs on the structure and role of the federal government. Federalists like John Adams and Alexander Hamilton believed in a strong, central government not dissimilar from a monarchy, governing a society and economy built on industrialization. Republicans like Thomas Jefferson and James Madison, however, believed in a smaller central government and the power of state governments, arguing for agrarian-based socioeconomics. Men who had sat shoulder to shoulder in Independence Hall now found themselves on opposing sides, and it was a division that eventually threatened the survival of the Union.

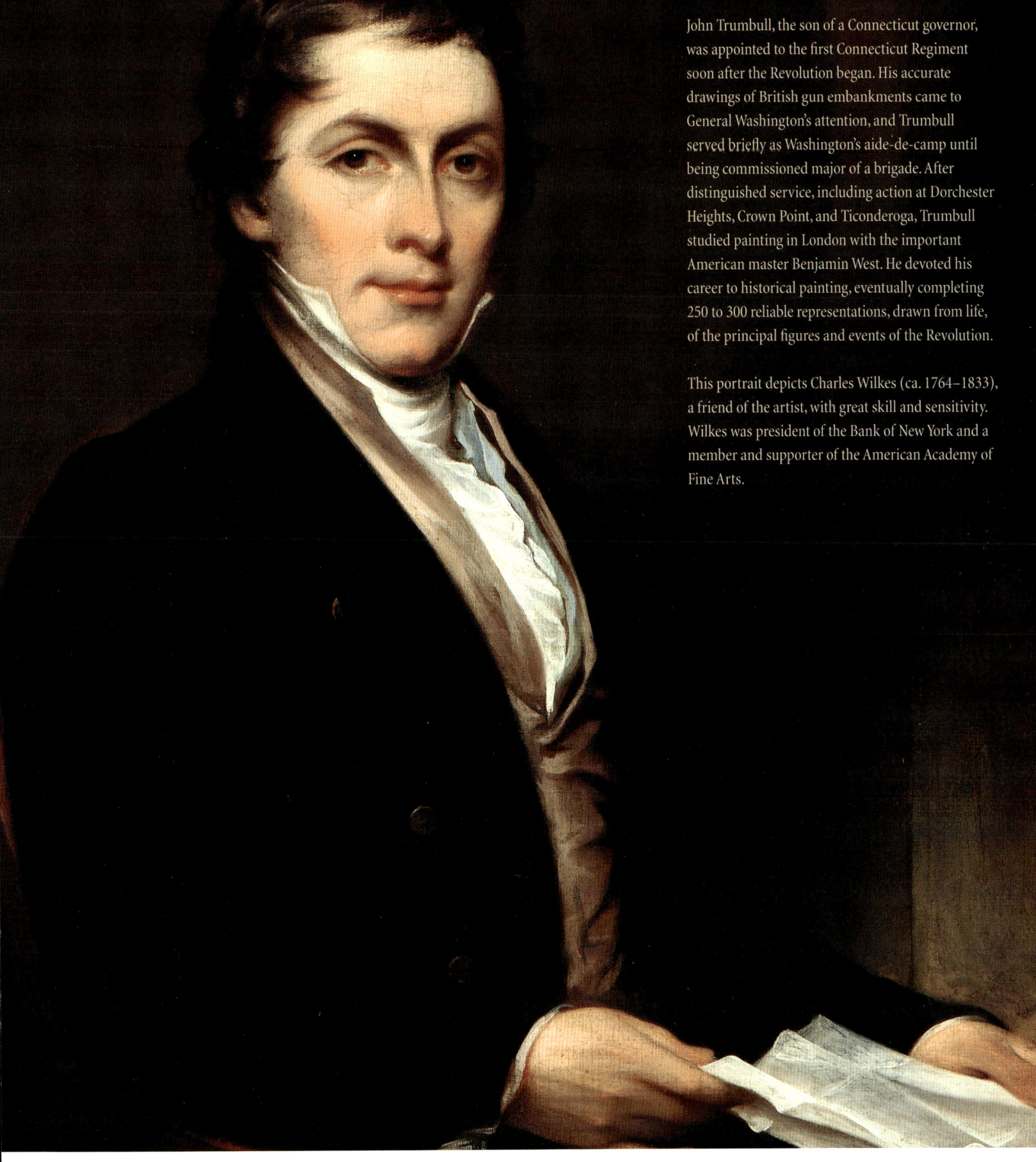

John Trumbull, the son of a Connecticut governor, was appointed to the first Connecticut Regiment soon after the Revolution began. His accurate drawings of British gun embankments came to General Washington's attention, and Trumbull served briefly as Washington's aide-de-camp until being commissioned major of a brigade. After distinguished service, including action at Dorchester Heights, Crown Point, and Ticonderoga, Trumbull studied painting in London with the important American master Benjamin West. He devoted his career to historical painting, eventually completing 250 to 300 reliable representations, drawn from life, of the principal figures and events of the Revolution.

This portrait depicts Charles Wilkes (ca. 1764–1833), a friend of the artist, with great skill and sensitivity. Wilkes was president of the Bank of New York and a member and supporter of the American Academy of Fine Arts.

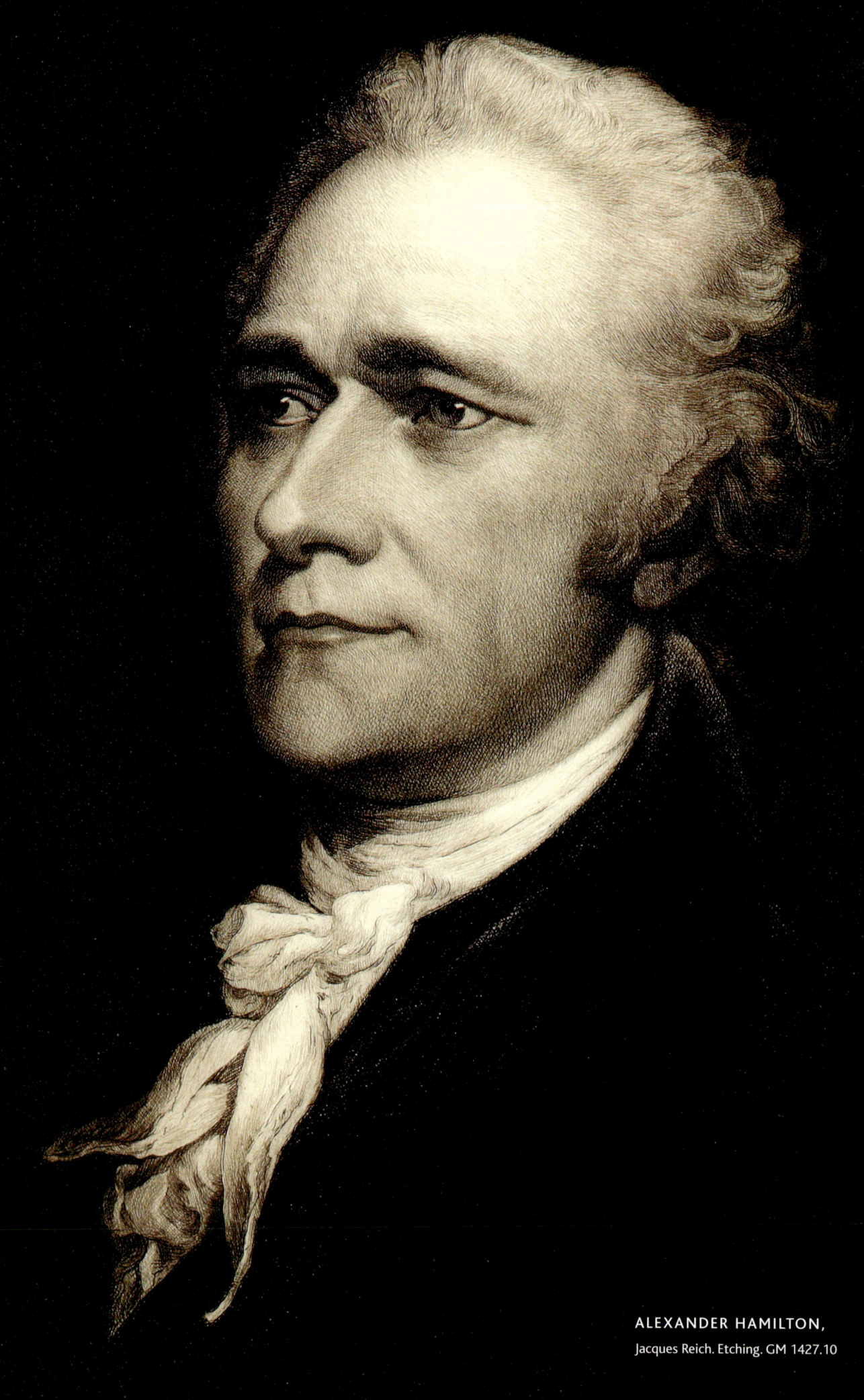

ALEXANDER HAMILTON,

Jacques Reich. Etching. GM 1427.10

In December 1799, however, the parties briefly set aside this debate when George Washington died at the age of sixty-seven, only two years after the end of his second term as president. The country grieved as though it had lost a parent, eulogizing and mythologizing the man who had been a constant in American political and popular culture. In many ways, his life had paralleled that of the young nation. Born as a British citizen and colonist, he had fought as a British soldier during the French and Indian War only to lead American forces against the empire twenty years later, and ultimately govern the new nation as its first president.

It had not been an easy transition or one that happened quickly. From ambiguity over identity to the French and Indian War, from the Revolution to its aftermath, it was an era characterized by conflict and resolution. Unlike the image of a young and united set of states often conjured, the reality was starkly different. Social factionalism, not cohesion, was the norm, as different groups with different goals and motivations vied against one another. It was a pattern that re-emerged after the Revolution as the difficult work of constructing a nation began; but this diversity was not a new element in the American society. It had always been present, and the political leaders cemented the country's pluralistic heritage in the nation's official motto: *E Pluribus Unum*—out of many, one.

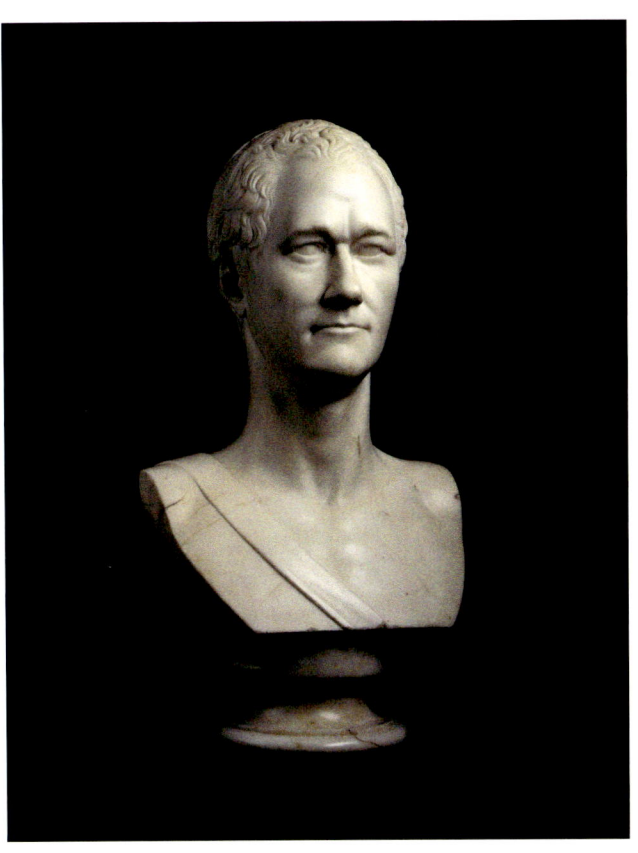

ALEXANDER HAMILTON, Giuseppe Ceracchi. Marble. GM 0976.5

Alexander Hamilton (1757–1804) arrived in the American colonies from the West Indies in 1773. During the Revolutionary War, he distinguished himself on a number of military missions. At the Battle of Princeton (January 3, 1777) his artillery company's action forced the British troops barricaded in Nassau Hall to surrender. At the Battle of Monmouth (June 28, 1778) he rallied fleeing American troops. During the siege at Yorktown (September to October 1781), he was conducted a brilliant attack on one of the two principal British fortifications. He also became a personal friend of the Marquis de Lafayette. Hamilton was a believer in the necessity of a strong central government, and his essays in *The Federalist Papers* supported the ratification of the Constitution. He was a friend and close advisor of President Washington, some of whose decisions and speeches reflect Hamilton's views.

Hamilton was the first secretary of the treasury. He instituted judicious fiscal policies and established the credit of the new nation at home and abroad. He also recommended the institution of various excise taxes and import duties, which became law although contested by Jefferson and Madison. Overall, Hamilton's fiscal system worked to strengthen the central government, develop resources of the nation, stimulate capitalistic enterprises and trade, and balance industry and agriculture. Reflecting the connection drawn between the American and the Roman republics, Ceracchi portrayed Hamilton here as a Roman senator dressed in a toga.

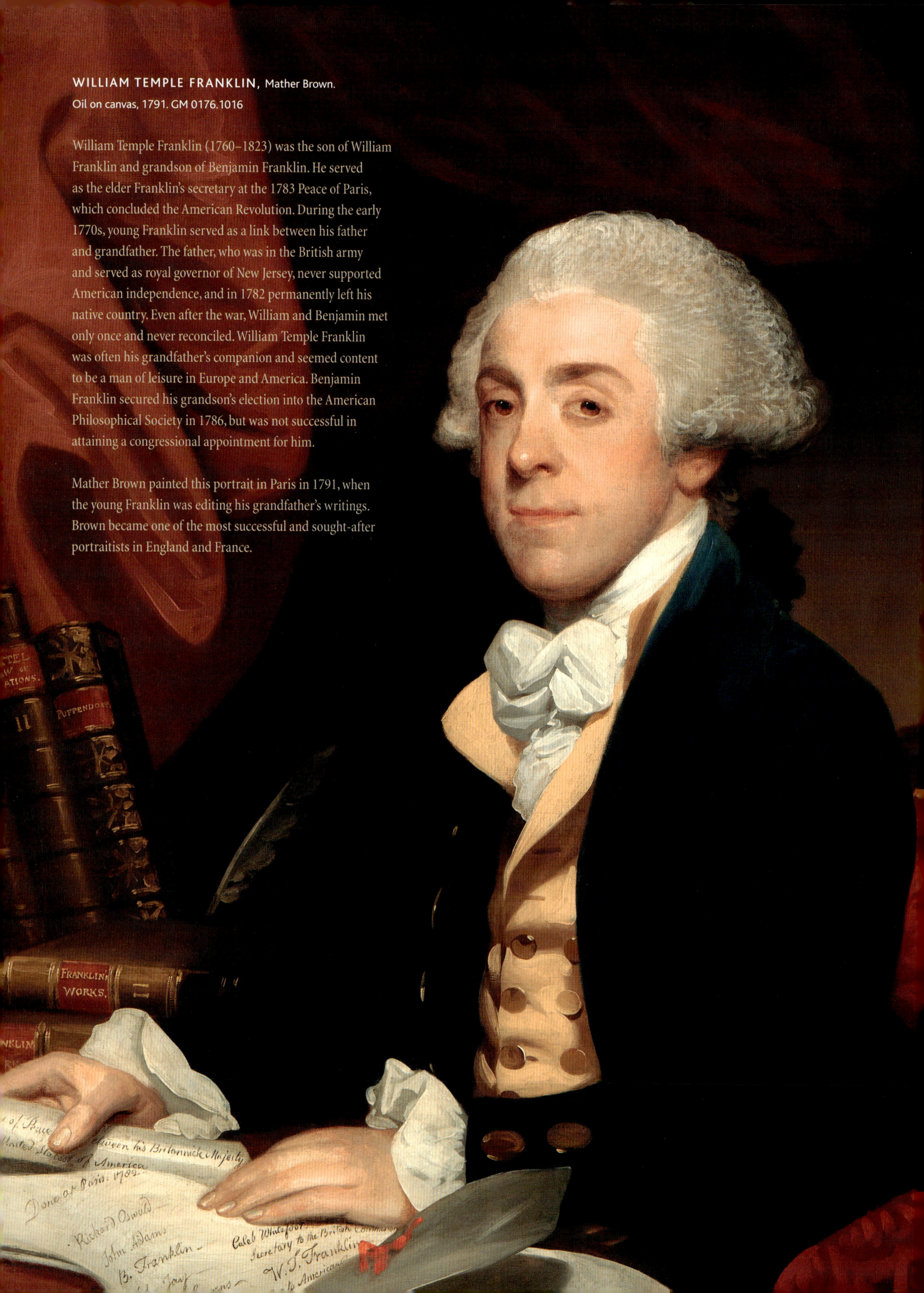

WILLIAM TEMPLE FRANKLIN, Mather Brown.
Oil on canvas, 1791. GM 0176.1016

William Temple Franklin (1760–1823) was the son of William Franklin and grandson of Benjamin Franklin. He served as the elder Franklin's secretary at the 1783 Peace of Paris, which concluded the American Revolution. During the early 1770s, young Franklin served as a link between his father and grandfather. The father, who was in the British army and served as royal governor of New Jersey, never supported American independence, and in 1782 permanently left his native country. Even after the war, William and Benjamin met only once and never reconciled. William Temple Franklin was often his grandfather's companion and seemed content to be a man of leisure in Europe and America. Benjamin Franklin secured his grandson's election into the American Philosophical Society in 1786, but was not successful in attaining a congressional appointment for him.

Mather Brown painted this portrait in Paris in 1791, when the young Franklin was editing his grandfather's writings. Brown became one of the most successful and sought-after portraitists in England and France.

In less than 200 years, a disparate group of colonies had improbably become a country. It was a time of remarkable expansion as settlers pushed into the frontier, populations diversified, political parties emerged, and as the turn of the century approached, Americans turned inexorably from the East towards the West.

NOTES

1. "Kingdoms, Countries, and Places Subject to, or claimed by, his Brittanic Majesty, and Elector of Hanover," *Boston Gazette*, February 12, 1754, issue 59, p. 2.

2. "Philadelphia, February 5," *Pennsylvania Gazette*, February 5, 1754, issue 1311, p. 2. Article begins, "Mr. Washington, the Ambassador sent to the Indian Country, is return'd."

3. Jack Rakove, *Revolutionaries: A New History of the Invention of America* (Boston: Houghton-Mifflin, 2010), p. 12.

4. "The Terms of Capitulation granted by Monsieur de Villier, Captain and Commander of the Infantry of his most Christian Majesty, to those English troops actually in Fort-Necessity, which is built on the Land of the King's Dominions," *Boston Evening-Post*, July 29, 1754, issue 987, p. 2.

5. Gordon Wood, *Revolutionary Characters: What Made the Founders Different* (New York: Penguin Books, 2007), p. 21. In 1763, Lord Halifax stated that while Americans were subjects of the crown, they were ultimately foreigners.

6. "A Declaration by the Representatives of the United Colonies of North-America," *Pennsylvania Evening Post*, July 11, 1775, volume I, issue 73, p. 291. A document sent to Parliament listing the grievances.

7. "London, January 24," *Newport Mercury*, April 17, 1775, issue 867, p. 1. In a speech made by the Earl of Chatham arguing for the removal of British troops from Boston, he stated, "Had the early situation of the people been attended to, my Lords, it would not have come to this; but the infant complaints of Boston were literally treated like the capricious squalls of a child."

8. "Norwich, April 20," *Norwich Packet*, April 20, 1775, issue 81, p. 3. Addressed to *all the Friends of American Liberty*, the article reports the battle at Lexington between a British brigade and a colonial militia.

9. "London, January 21," *Providence Gazette*, April 15, 1775, volume XII, issue 589, p. 4.

10. "Salem, April 25," *Essex Gazette*, April 18, 1775, volume VII, issue 352, p. 3. Article reports the colonies are "involved in all the Horrors of a civil War."

11. Thomas Jefferson to Henry Lee, May 8, 1825.

12. John Adams to H. Niles, February 13, 1818.

13. "Philadelphia, July 8," *New York Gazette*, July 15, 1776, issue 1292, p. 1. "Suneday, in the evening, the statue of King George the Third, on horseback, in the Bowling Green, was taken down, broken to pieces, and its honour leveled with the dust."

14. "New York, August 19," *New York Gazette*, August 19, 1776, issue 1292, p. 2. Article describing the reaction to a public reading of the Declaration at Ticonderoga: "Now we are a People! We have a Name among the States of this World."

15. "The American Crisis," *Pennsylvania Packet*, December 27, 1776, volume VI, issue 268, p. 1. The opening line of Thomas Paine's series called "The American Crisis."

16. "To his Excellency," *Massachusetts Spy*, July 12, 1775, volume V, issue 229, p. 1.

17. "By His Excellency," *Pennsylvania Packet*, December 31, 1777, p. 1. Request by General Washington for nearby colonists to share their grain with troops at Valley Forge.

18. "London, February 9," *Essex Gazette*, March 28, 1775, issue 349, p. 2. In an address to King George III, the Lord-Mayor proclaimed that "a successful resistance is a Revolution, not a Rebellion." He went on to say the Americans "will sooner declare themselves independent, and risk every consequence of such a contest, than submit to the yoke which Administration is preparing for them."

19. Thomas Fleming, *The Perils of Peace: America's Struggle for Survival after Yorktown* (New York: Smithsonian Books, 2008), p. 4.

20. *Salem Gazette*, May 29, 1783, volume II, issue 85, p. 1.

21. "New York, July 8," *Independent Journal,* July 8, 1786, issue 272, p. 2. The article presents a description of a theater in New York decorated for the Fourth of July, complete with the name of Washington inscribed alongside the eagle.

22. "Savannah, Georgia," *South Carolina Weekly Gazette*, July 17, 1784, volume II, issue 96, p. 2.

23. "Trenton, April 21, 1789," *New York Packet*, May 1, 1789, issue 902, p. 2. The article describes Washington's arrival and march through Trenton, New Jersey, on his way to his inauguration.

24. Wood, *Revolutionary Characters: What Made the Founders Different*, p. 57. Wood examines the personalities and proclivities of the leading figures of the American Revolution.

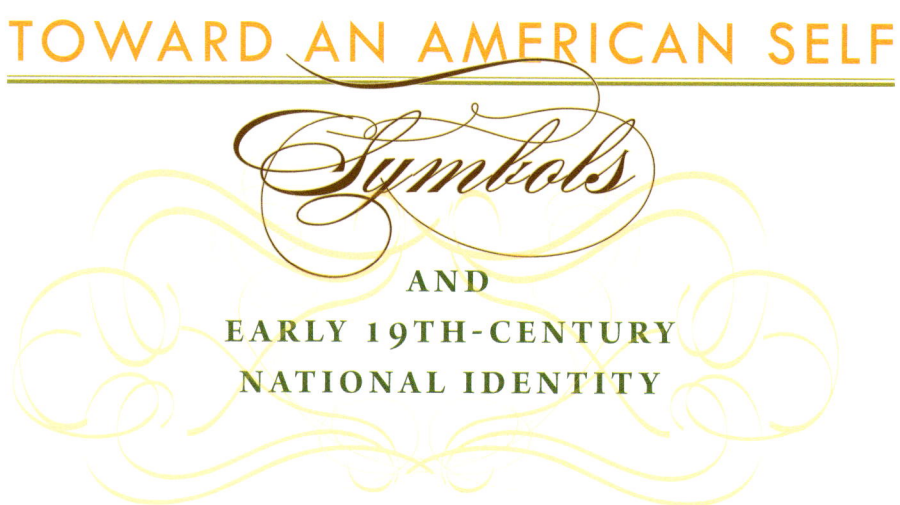

TOWARD AN AMERICAN SELF

Symbols

AND
EARLY 19TH-CENTURY
NATIONAL IDENTITY

RANDY RAMER

History can be seen as the interpretation of cultural symbols across time, of the recollection and assessment of social meanings attributed to people, places, actions and other things of the past. These meanings are symbols—cultural artifacts that reveal both profound and nuanced insights into the lives of individuals long removed from contemporary understanding.

Symbols are social constructions. They convey information that relays or enhances collective thoughts, values and emotions. Symbols can be material, tangible things. They can be naturally occurring phenomena, such as Grand Canyon, or human-made, such as the carved faces on Mount Rushmore (literally outsized American heroes). Actions and events can be symbolic, even those that exist only in the shared imagination. Symbols can also be living things, including people. The bald eagle, Marilyn Monroe, and Daniel Boone all symbolize particular qualities for most Americans. Cultural symbols emerge from the collective imagination. They are derived from both reality and fantasy to convey ideals that support and shape common understandings. Across time and space, such symbols promote social cohesion and provide a framework for the exposition of group values. Cultural symbols speak in a language without words. They reveal the thoughts, emotions and dreams of a people—the fundamental desires, notions, and feelings that strike chords of understanding within the social group. They "represent the thinking and feeling which correspond to the limits of man's knowledge" about the world and a given society's place within it.[1]

The United States of the early 1800s was a nation in search of itself. Its social history can be read in the symbols it invented to communicate with itself about its identity and its role in a complex world. Symbols from the period reinforced an expanding popular mythology as a broader American ethos emerged and regional identities linked primarily to statehood gradually gave way to a larger view of the American cultural Self. As populations and national territory continued to increase, new ideas regarding the nation's future and its perceived potential led to the development of more unifying nationalistic sentiments. These ideas, embodied in symbols, forged a uniquely American character that has shaped the nation and influenced much of the larger world. It remains potent after some two centuries.

BEAVER HAT AND DETAIL OF ITS MANUFACTURER'S TRADEMARK.
Beaver fur, felt, leather, late 19th century. GM 85.99

Throughout western Europe and in the fledgling United States, a man's beaver-fur hat was a significant sartorial symbol that denoted the wearer's power and status. The production of hats using beaver pelts spurred the fur trade of the early 1800s.

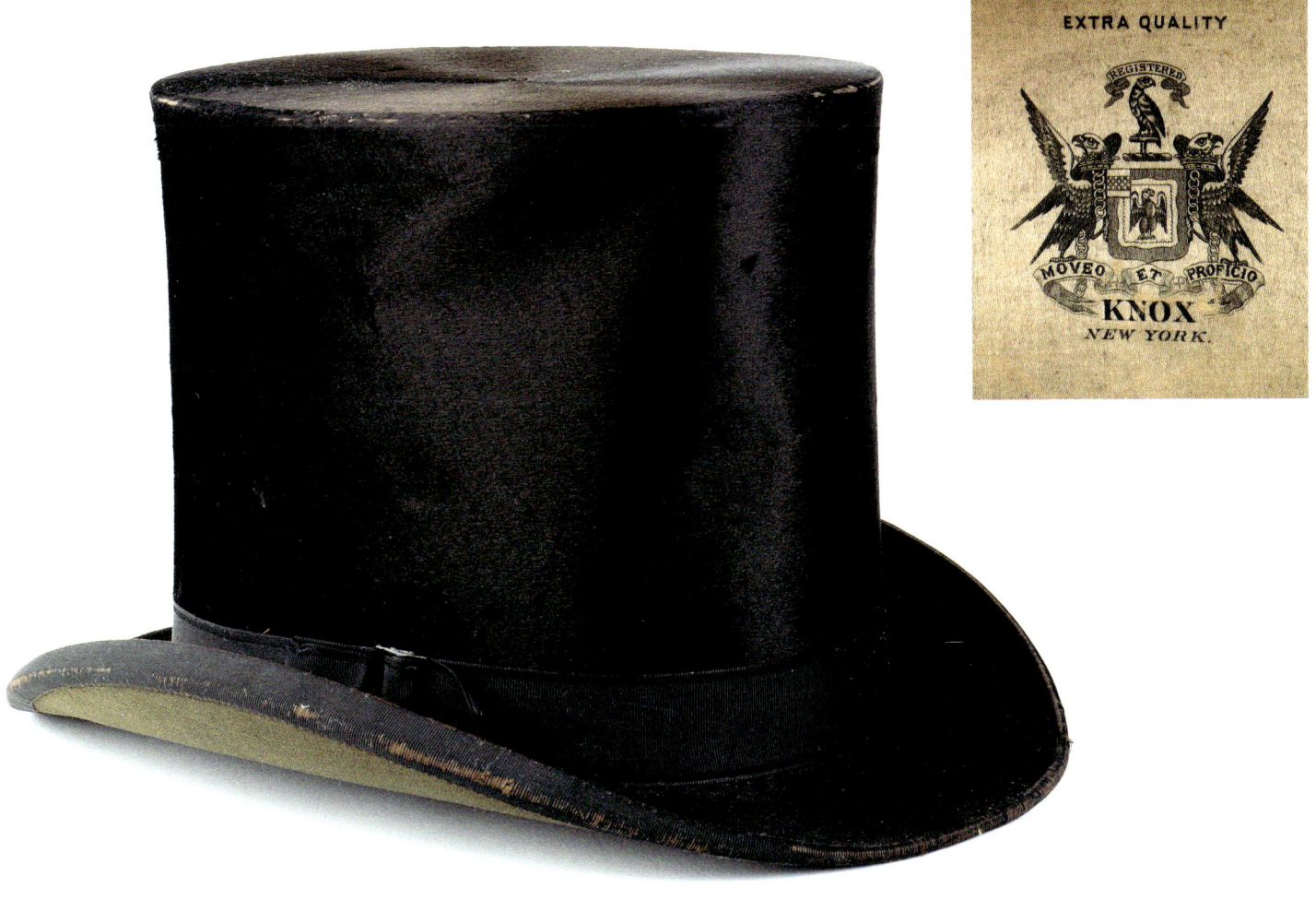

CALLING CARDS OF EMPIRE

In the early morning hours of July 27, 1806, in a campsite along the Two Medicine River in present day Montana, Meriwether Lewis woke from a sound sleep to the shouts and commotion of violent conflict. He and three fellow travelers from Thomas Jefferson's intrepid Corps of Discovery found themselves engaged in a fight with a small band of Piegan Blackfeet they had encountered the previous afternoon. The Indians were attempting to steal the sleeping explorers' guns but the plan erupted into a skirmish as the Americans unexpectedly roused. As the Piegans attempted to flee with the guns, one of the explorers gave chase and killed a would-be thief with a knife to the chest. As the Americans secured their weapons, Lewis cautioned his men against further bloodshed. The deadly encounter continued to escalate, however, as the Piegans now eyed the expedition's horses. Lewis gave the order to shoot any horse thieves as he and the others ran quickly to ensure the safety of their mounts. In his journal Lewis wrote:

CAPTAIN LEWIS SHOOTING AN INDIAN, unknown artist. Etching, 1810. Library of Congress LC-USZ62-19231

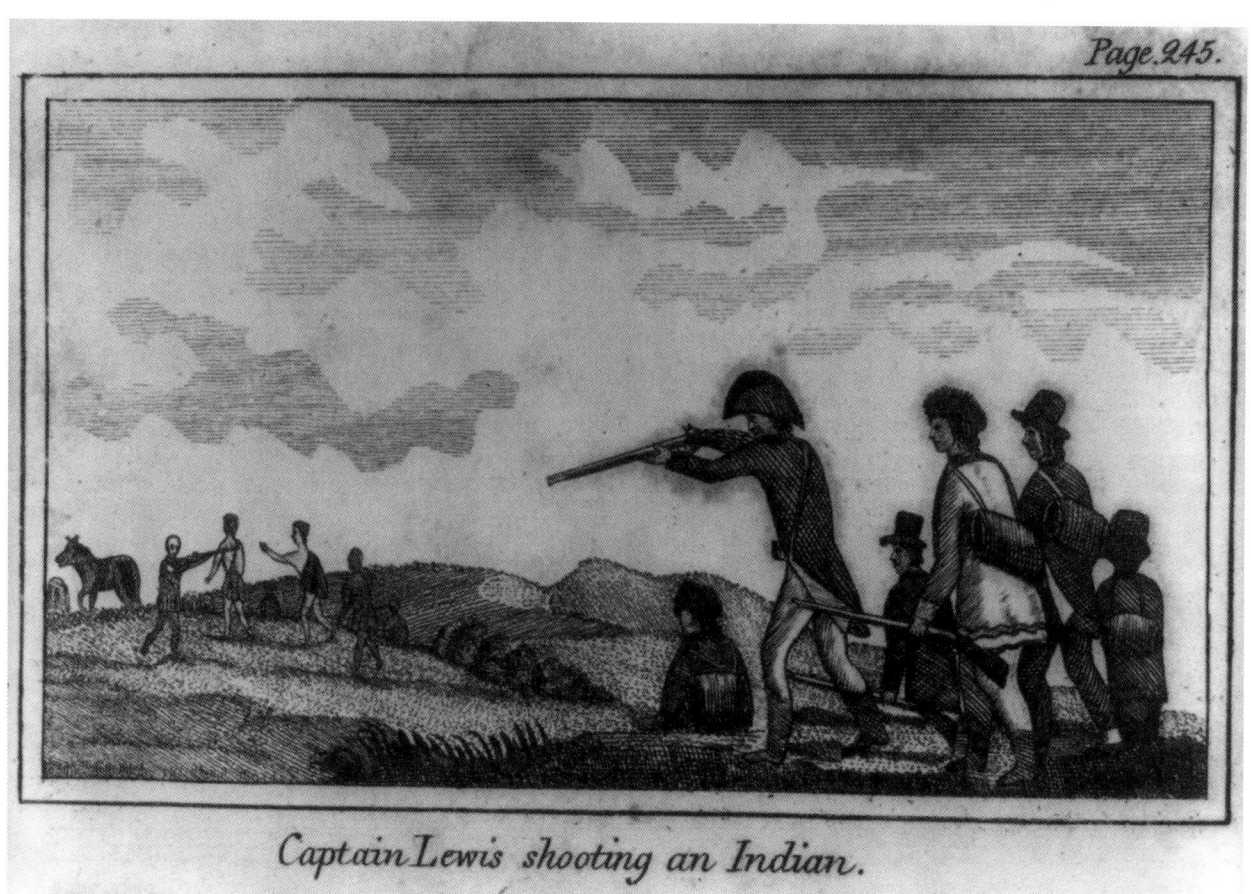

Captain Lewis shooting an Indian.

"…being nearly out of breath I could pursue no further, I called to them as I had done several times before that I would shoot them if they did not give me my horse and raised my gun, one of them jumped behind a rock and spoke to the other who turned around and stoped at the distance of 30 steps from me and I shot him through the belly…"[2]

During a journey that ultimately lasted some three years and covered more than 3,500 miles of unfamiliar territory, the killing of the two Piegans along the Two Medicine River was remarkably the only taking of human life in the elusive pursuit of a Northwest Passage. The previous afternoon, Lewis had given gifts to three of the Piegans. These included a handkerchief, a flag, and—significantly—an American peace medal. After the deadly altercation, the explorer and his companions surveyed the bodies, then gathered the Indians' weapons and burned them. Historian James P. Ronda refers to Lewis's final act in the aftermath of the Two Medicine fight as a "moment of Imperial bravado." The explorer "took the sacred amulets from the dead men's shields and then hung a peace medal around the neck of one Indian so that 'they might be informed who we were.' A peace medal had become the calling card of empire."[3]

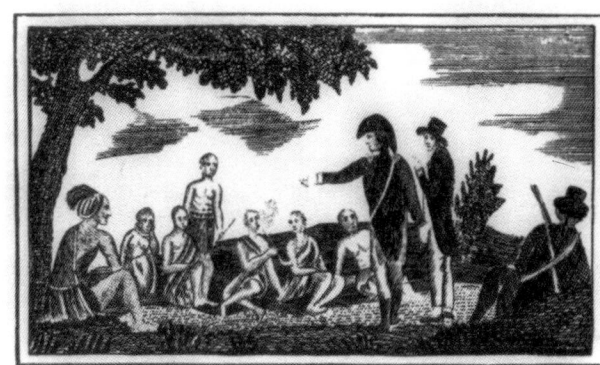

Captains Lewis & Clark holding a Council with the Indians Page 17

CAPTAIN LEWIS AND CLARK HOLDING A COUNCIL WITH THE INDIANS. Etching, 1810.
Library of Congress
LC-USZ62-17372

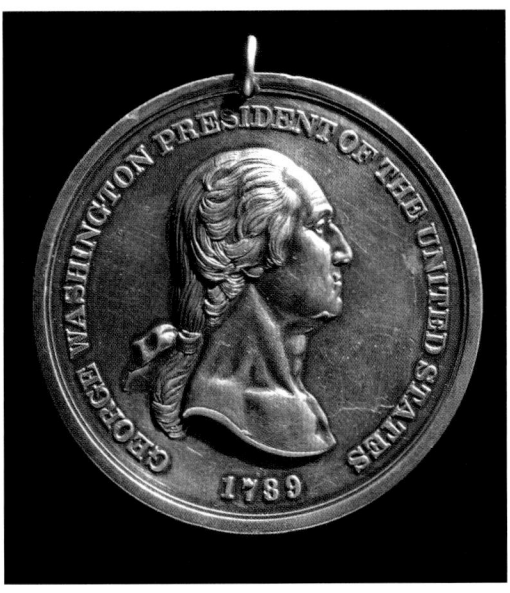
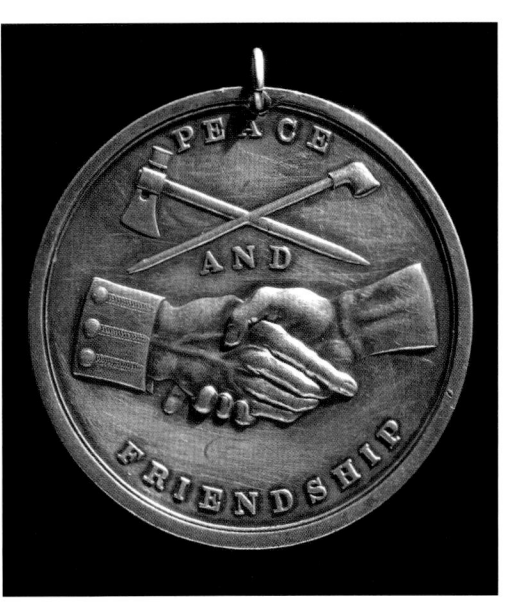

WASHINGTON PEACE MEDAL.
Silver, 1789. GM 6527.18

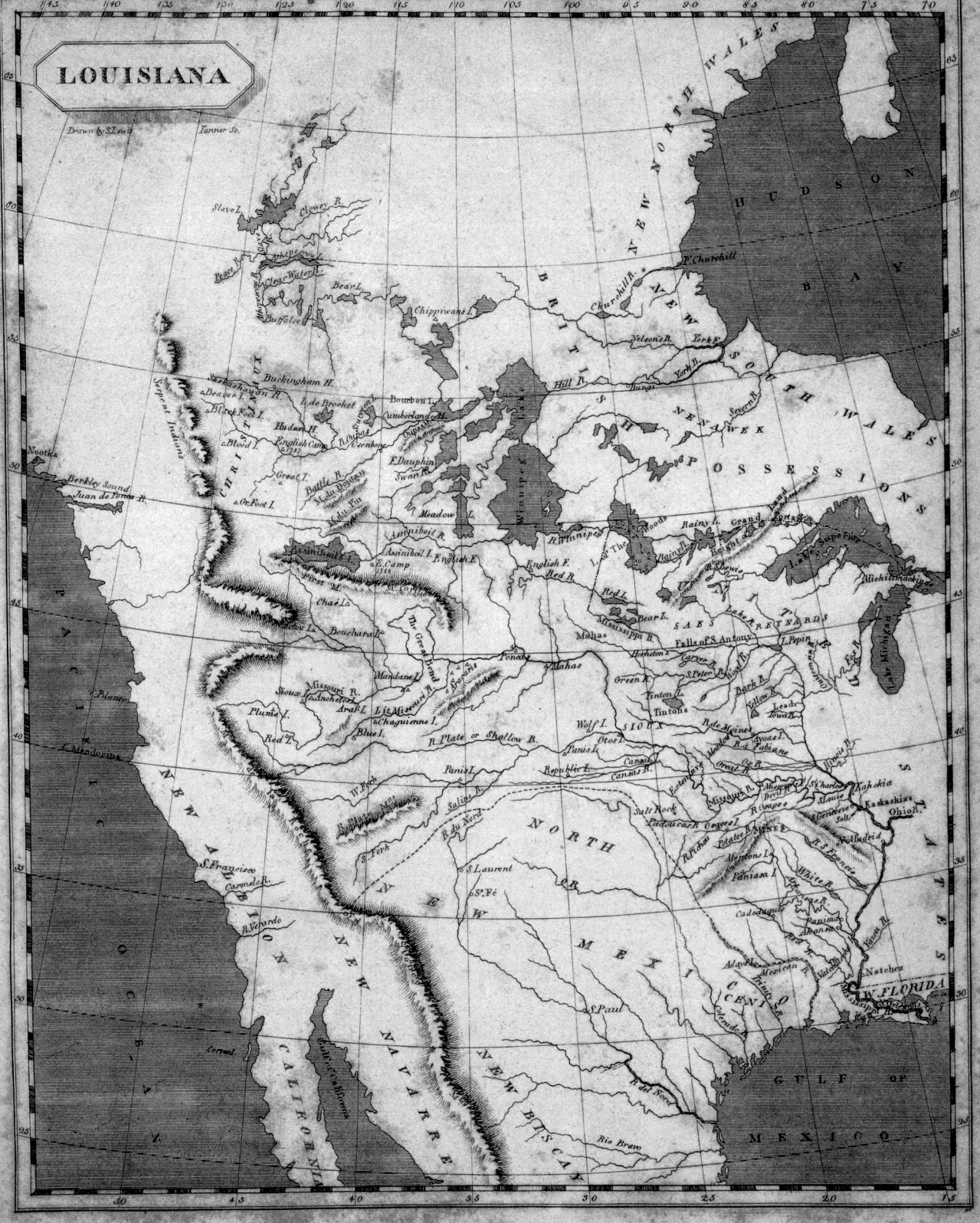

LOUISIANA

Drawn by S. Lewis.   Turner Sc.

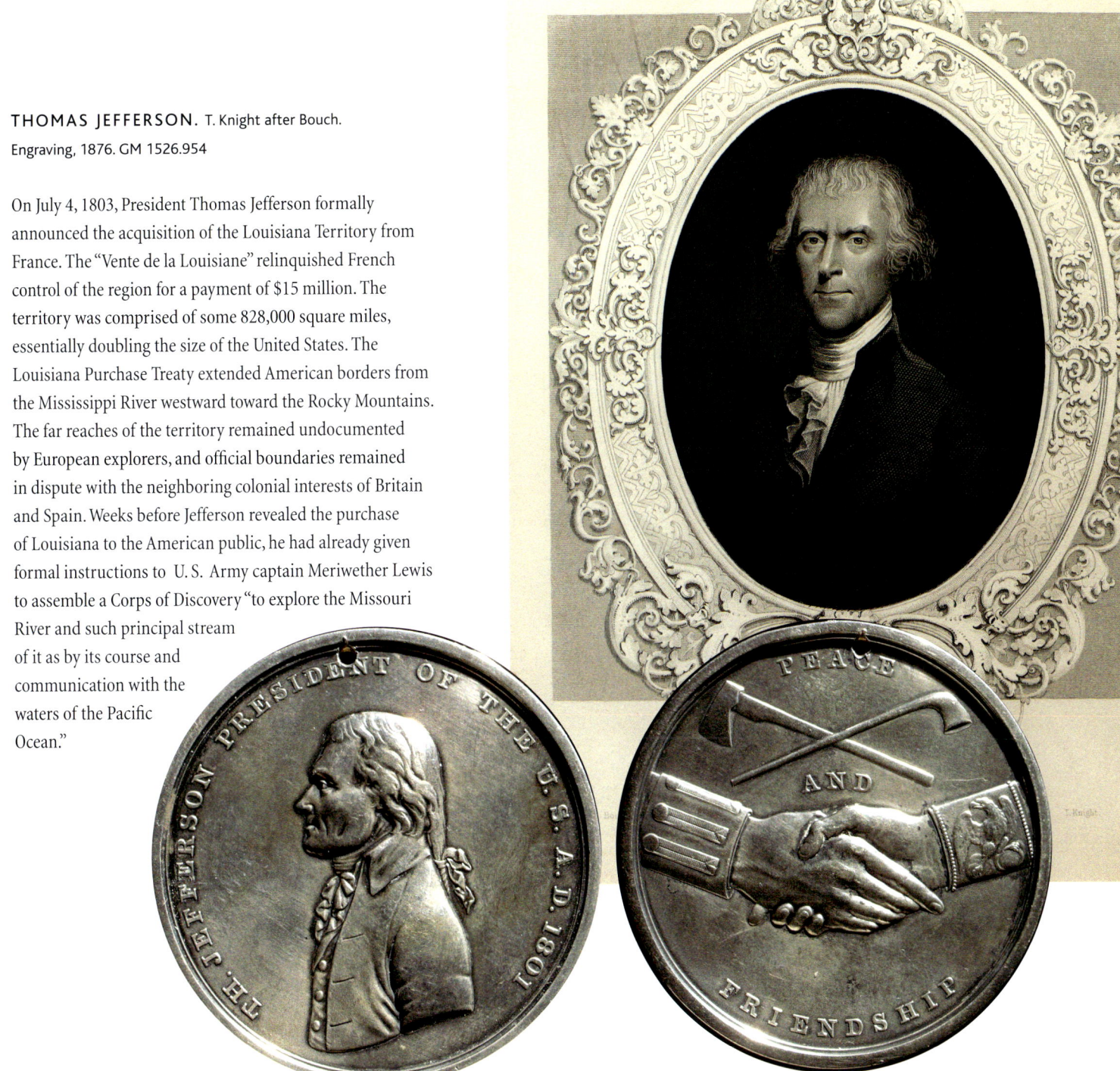

THOMAS JEFFERSON. T. Knight after Bouch.
Engraving, 1876. GM 1526.954

On July 4, 1803, President Thomas Jefferson formally announced the acquisition of the Louisiana Territory from France. The "Vente de la Louisiane" relinquished French control of the region for a payment of $15 million. The territory was comprised of some 828,000 square miles, essentially doubling the size of the United States. The Louisiana Purchase Treaty extended American borders from the Mississippi River westward toward the Rocky Mountains. The far reaches of the territory remained undocumented by European explorers, and official boundaries remained in dispute with the neighboring colonial interests of Britain and Spain. Weeks before Jefferson revealed the purchase of Louisiana to the American public, he had already given formal instructions to U. S. Army captain Meriwether Lewis to assemble a Corps of Discovery "to explore the Missouri River and such principal stream of it as by its course and communication with the waters of the Pacific Ocean."

FACING: MAP OF LOUISIANA IN 1894. Henry S. Tanner.
Published by John Conrad & Co. GM 3926.257

The efforts of Lewis and Clark and the Corps of Discovery were fundamental to the nation's expanding knowledge of the continent. The expedition allowed for a better understanding of just how large the newly acquired territory actually was and what the Louisiana Purchase could ultimately portend for future generations. Information regarding plants, animals, locations of Native settlements, and accurate maps of waterways and mountain ranges effectively changed how the nation saw itself. This knowledge also soon urged a reevaluation of the commercial potential of the region. In the years following the 1806 conclusion of the expedition, business interests in the new territory dramatically increased as fur trading companies extended their domains throughout the Northwest. The population of the United States continued to expand as well, nearly doubling in the U. S. census reports between the years 1790 and 1810 with some 7.2 million individuals recorded—including almost 1.2 million slaves.

JEFFERSON PEACE MEDAL.
Silver, 1801. GM 6516.17

Peace medals were seen by many Native Americans as possessing "bad medicine" and were often given away by the original recipients to tribal enemies "in hope the ill-luck would be conveyed to them." (Alexander Henry)

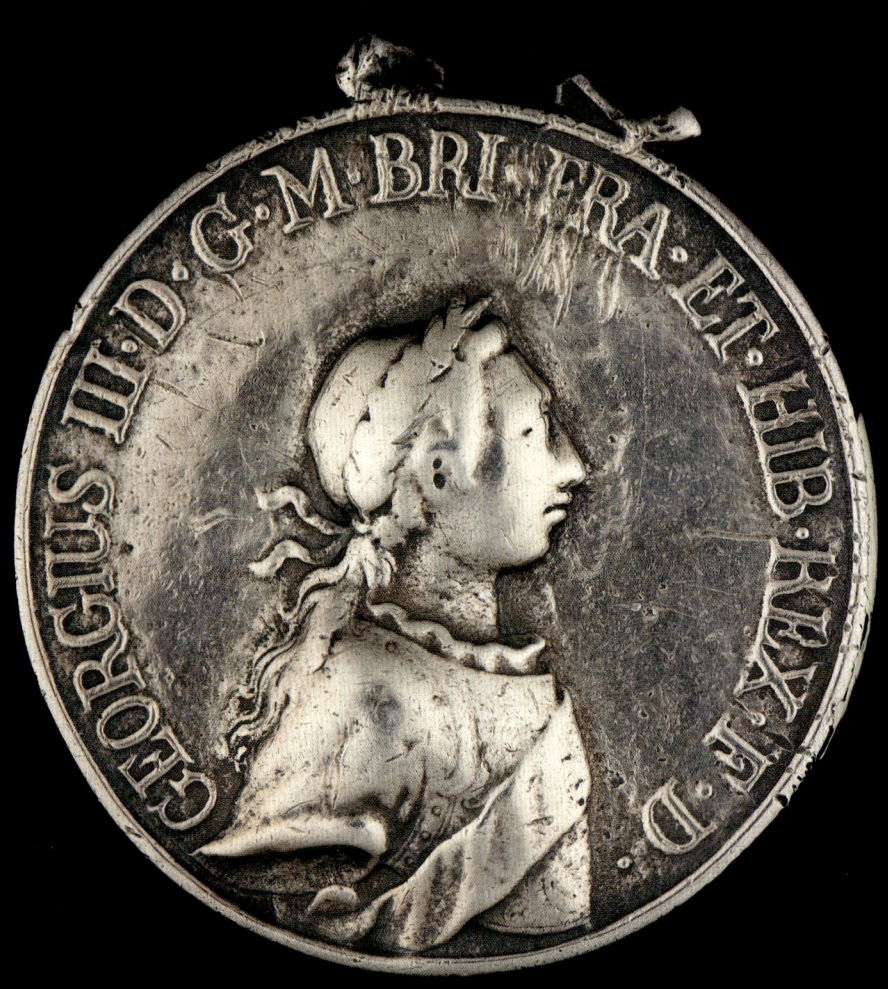

GEORGE III PEACE
MEDAL. Silver, 1764.
GM 65.57

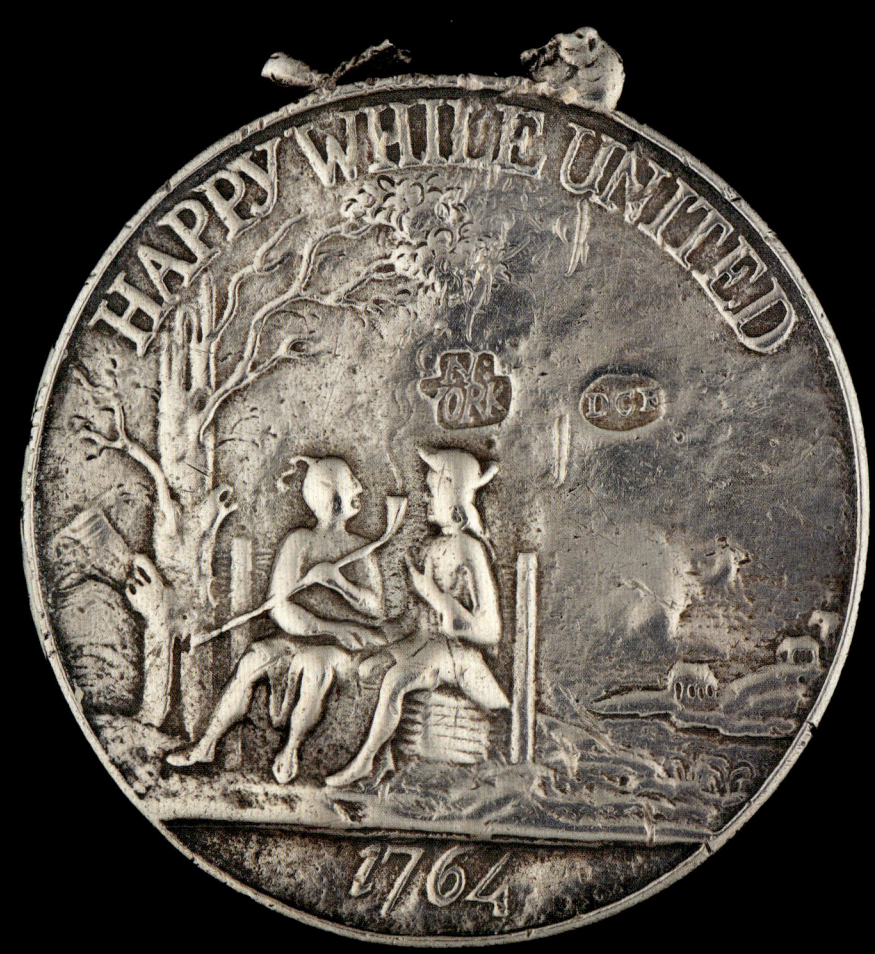

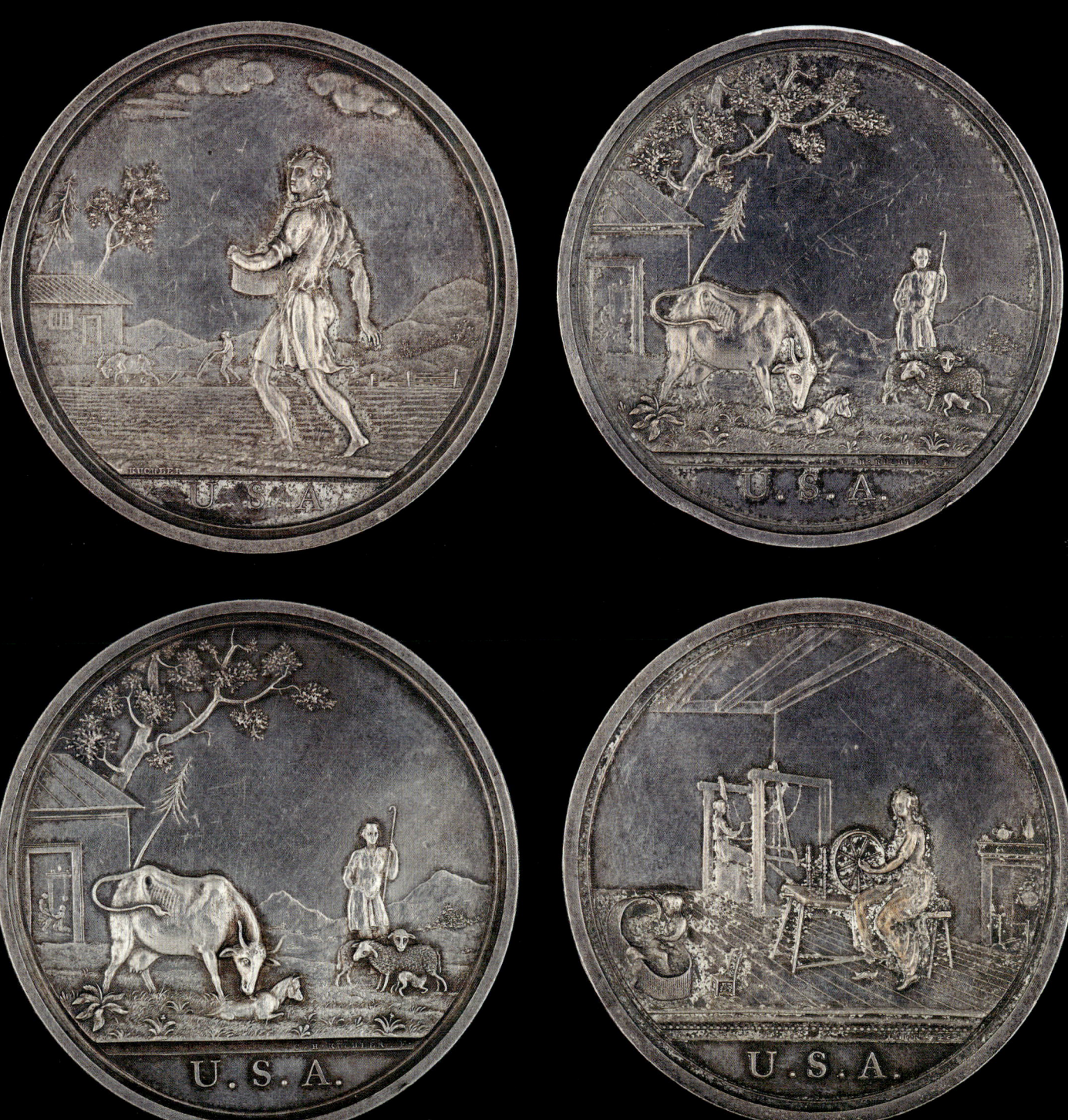

WASHINGTON SEASON MEDALS. Silver, 1796.
GM 60.155, 60.156, 65.14, 65.43

Washington "season" medals were designed by artist
John Trumbull (American, 1756–1843).

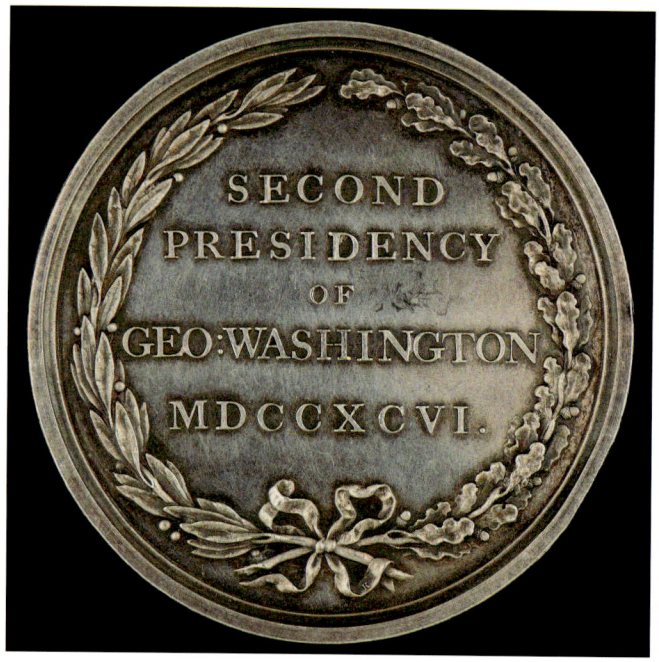

WASHINGTON
SEASON MEDAL.
Silver, 1796. GM 65.43b

TOMAHAWK PIPE.
Wood, German silver,
steel, early 19th century.
GM 8436.1102

Tomahawk pipes were
popular trade items.
Typically manufactured
in Europe, they became
important symbols in
the display of status and
authority within a given
tribe.

TOMAHAWK PIPE.
Wood, metal, 19th century.
GM 8436.1100

Produced ostensibly as gifts between representatives of the United States government and prominent Native American leaders, peace medals were indeed employed as emblems of American imperial desires. They were unique political symbols, given less as tokens of peace and friendship than as a tangible evidence of American influence over a region and its people. While the Native American recipients of medals largely viewed them as "signs of respect from one equal to another," their acceptance was viewed quite differently by the United States government. According to Ronda, peace medals were often accepted by Native Americans as part of "a ritual symbolizing a balanced relationship, a moment of mutual regard. But the medals and the act of giving them and receiving them signified something else for the American explorers and the president who sent them. Medals represented sovereignty and national power. Once a chief or headman accepted one, that act was interpreted as acknowledging the sovereign authority of the United States."[4]

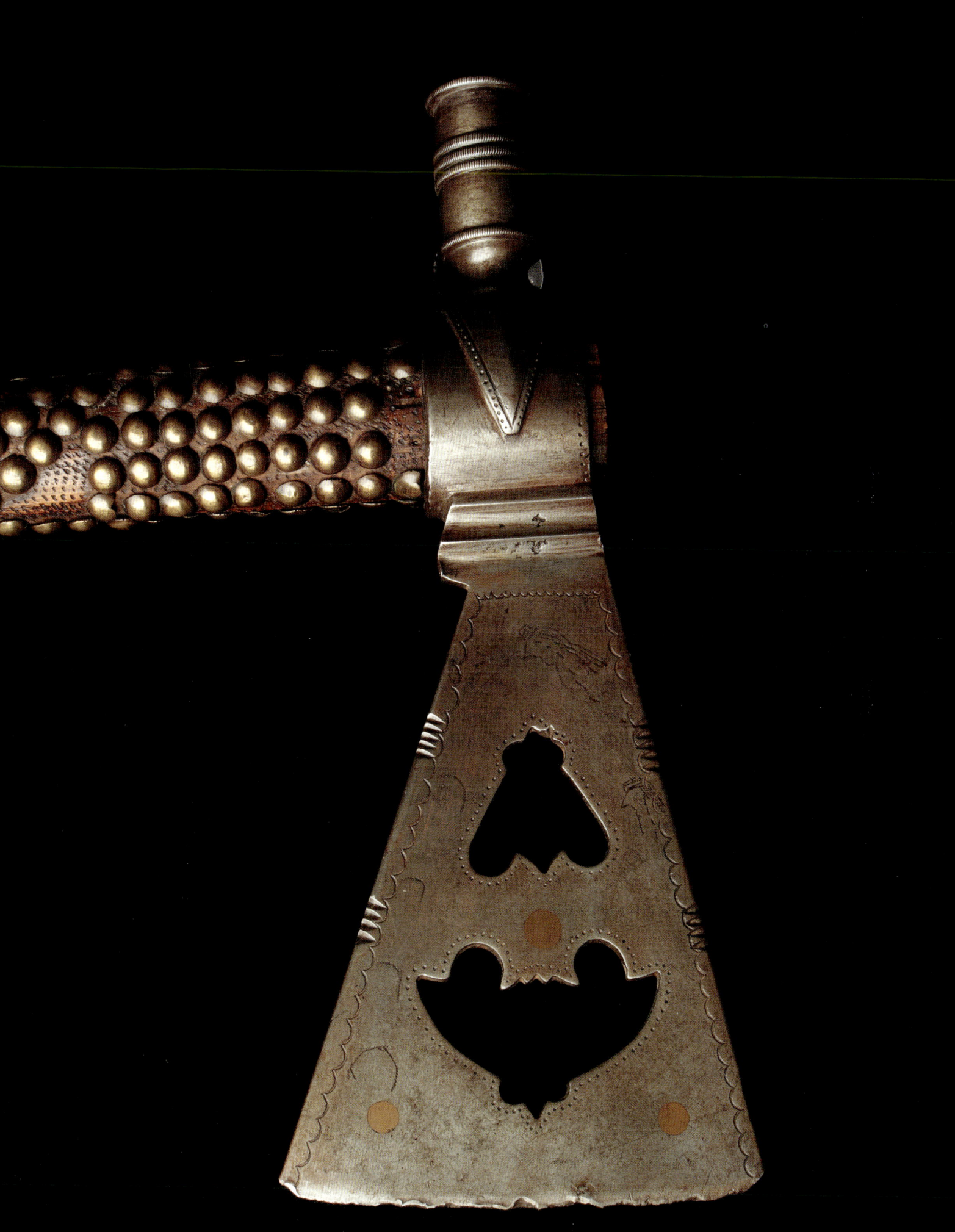

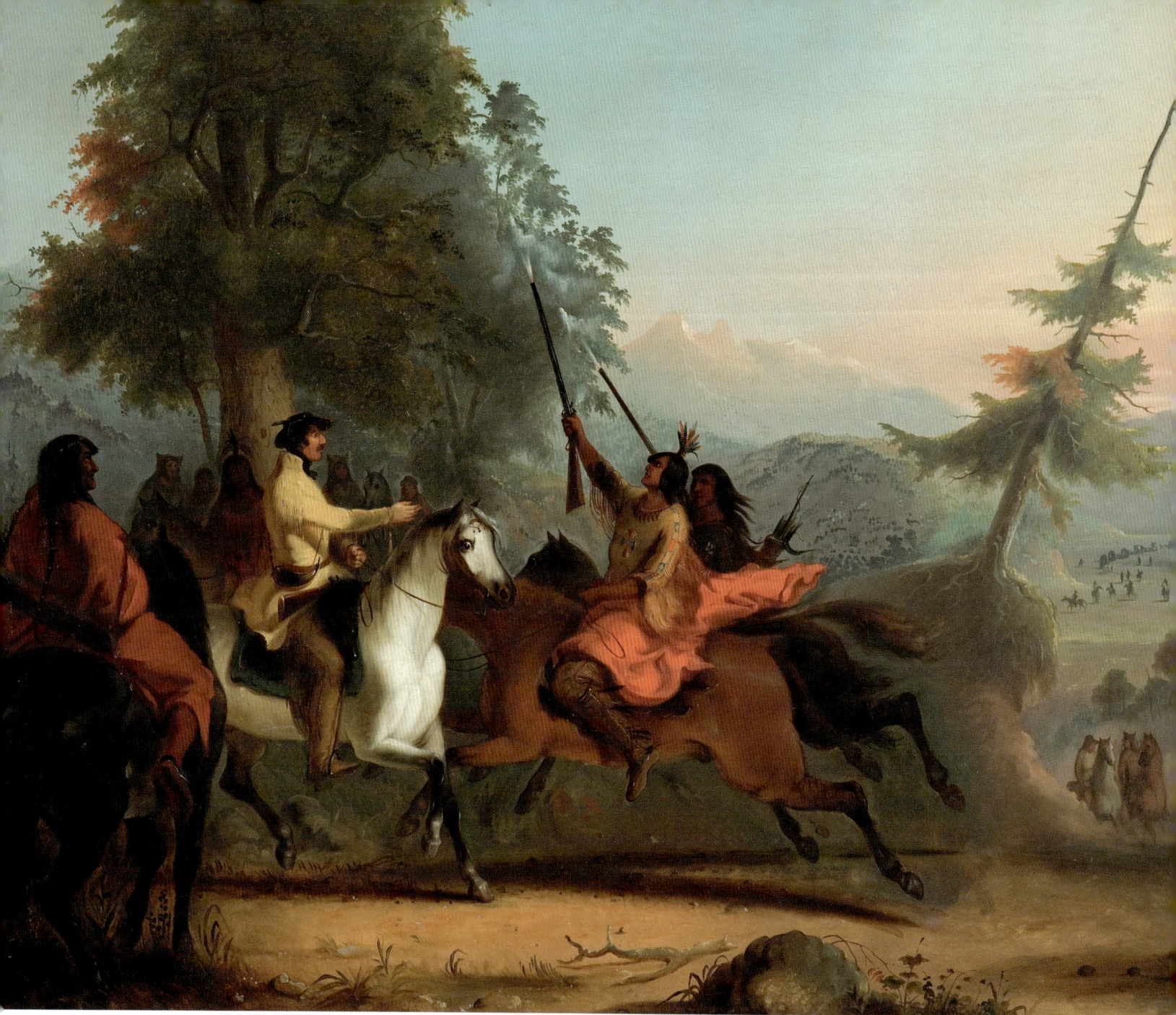

SIR WILLIAM DRUMMOND
STEWART MEETING INDIAN CHIEF,
Alfred Jacob Miller. Oil on canvas, ca. 1840s.
GM 0126.738

FACING, LEFT: RENT-CHA-WAS-ME, MAK-HOS-KAH'S WIFE,
Charles Bird King. Oil on canvas, 1825. GM 0126.1202

FACING: RIGHT: MAK-WE-HAH-MAK, GOWAY CHIEF (GREAT WALKER),
Charles Bird King. Oil on wood,1825. GM 0126.1194

All of Charles Bird King's Indian portraits were destined for the Indian Gallery, a collection of Indian memorabilia and portraits. The idea came about in part due to John C. Calhoun, who in 1821 first summoned tribal chiefs to Washington. He agreed with Thomas L. McKenney, chief of the Bureau of Indian Affairs, who had a plan for a gallery of Indian likenesses. King, who had painted Calhoun in 1818, was recommended for the government commissions. King worked for McKenney for twenty years, painting 143 Indian portraits for the War Department, as well as replicas for presentation to the sitters.

TRADE BEAD NECKLACE. Wood, bone, metal, shell, glass beads, ca. 1830. GM 8436.166

This necklace employs glass beads manufactured around the world, with examples from Venice, Bohemia, and China, amid beads of Native American manufacture. The necklace also includes a rare Phoenix button made for the military uniforms of King Henri Christophe of Haiti. The necklace demonstrates scope of global trade in the early 19th century.

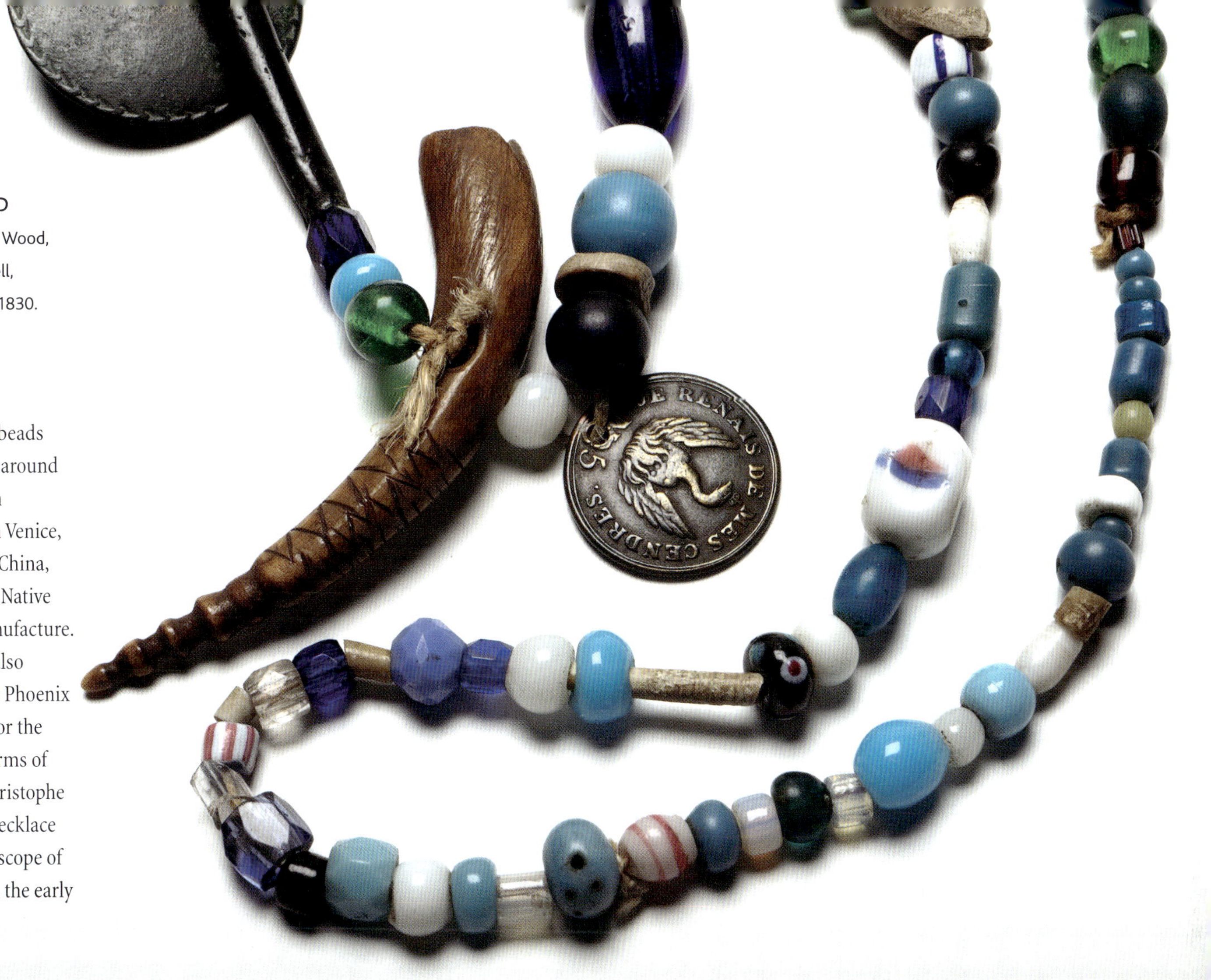

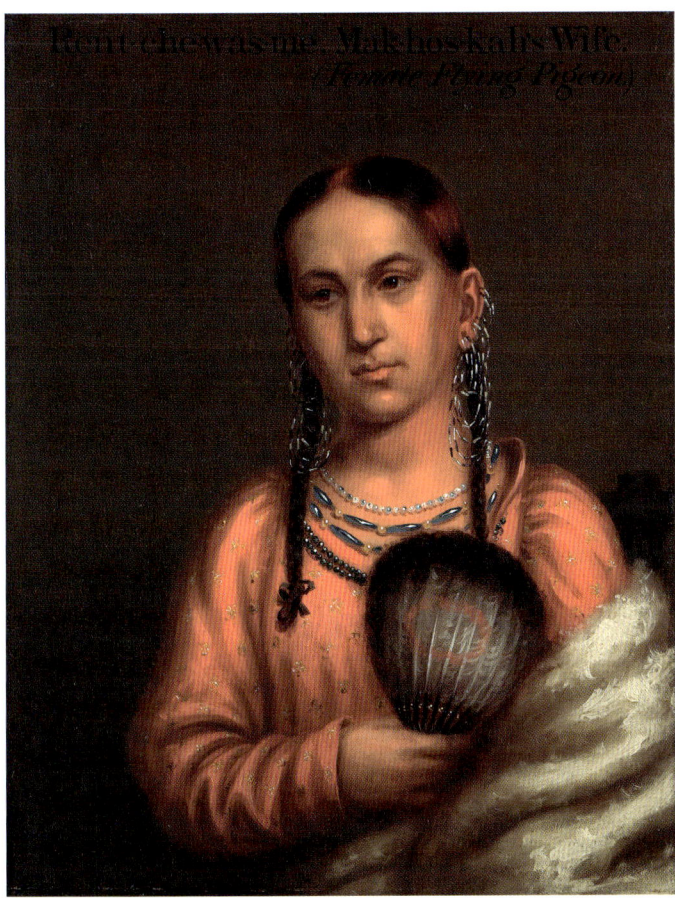

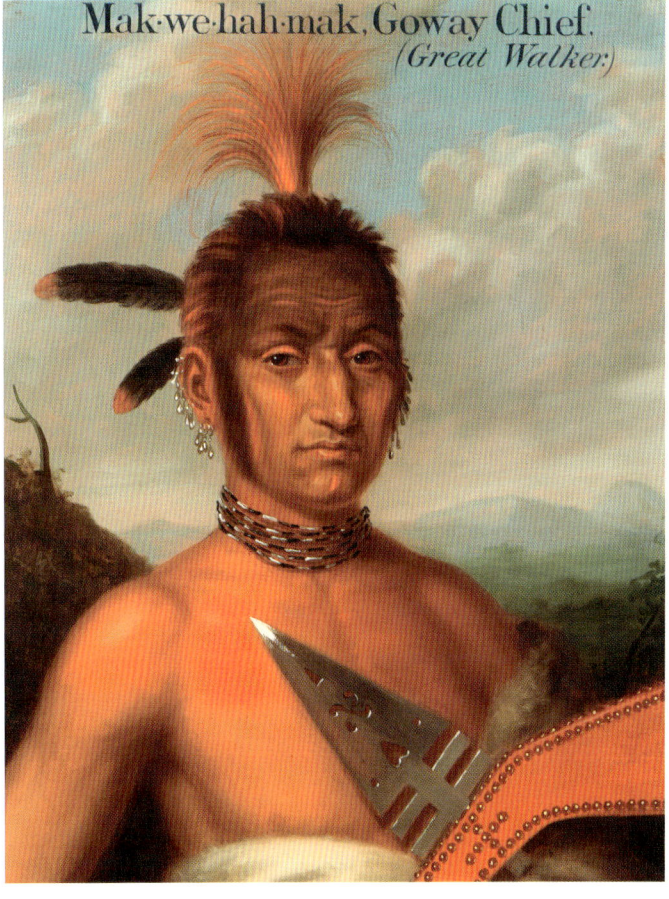

Mak·we·hah·mak, Goway Chief. (Great Walker.)

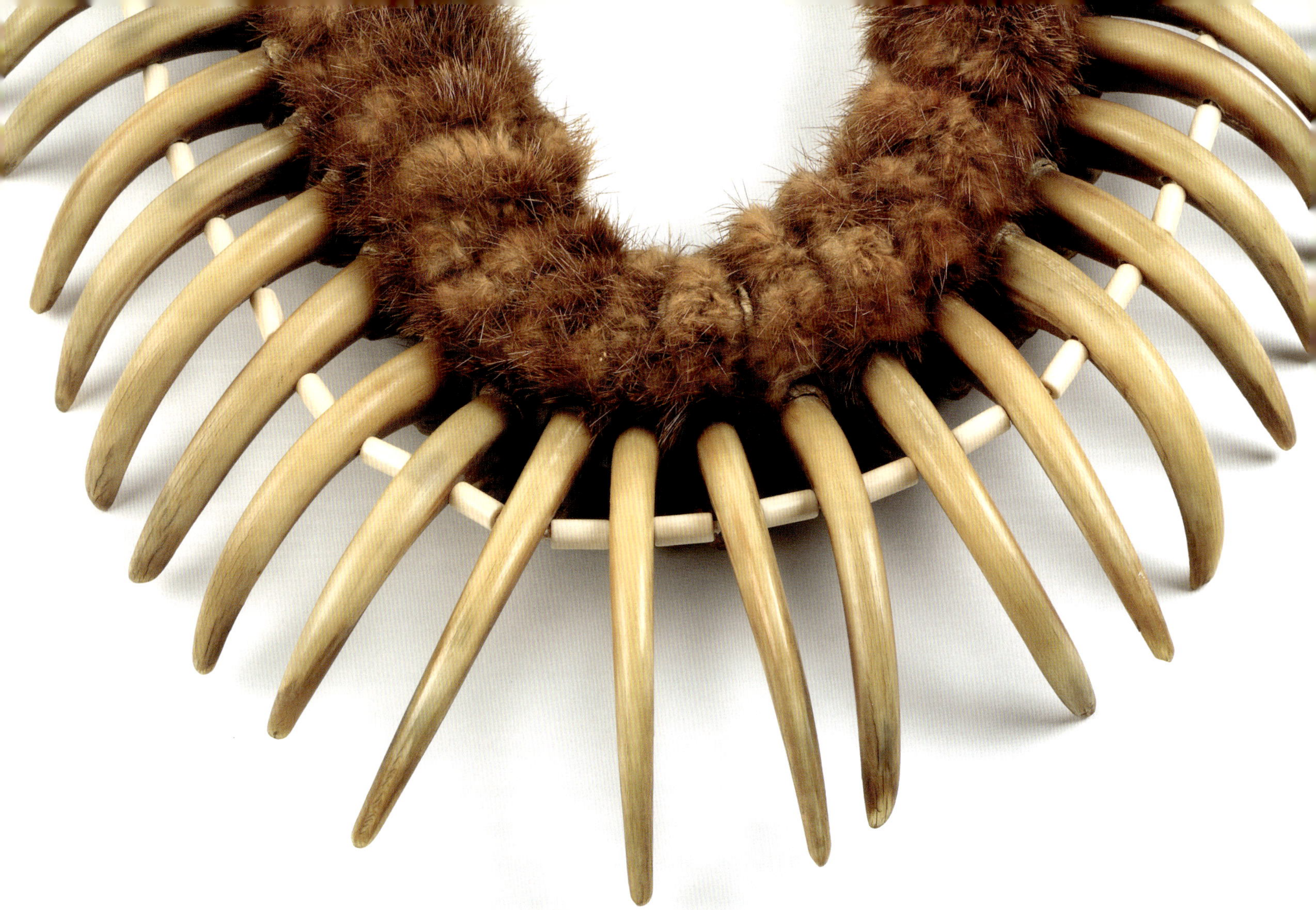

BEAR CLAW NECKLACE. Bear claws, otter fur, bone, glass beads, leather, early 19th century. GM 84.2159

Bear claw and otter fur necklaces were often worn by tribal leaders as symbols of stature and prominence.

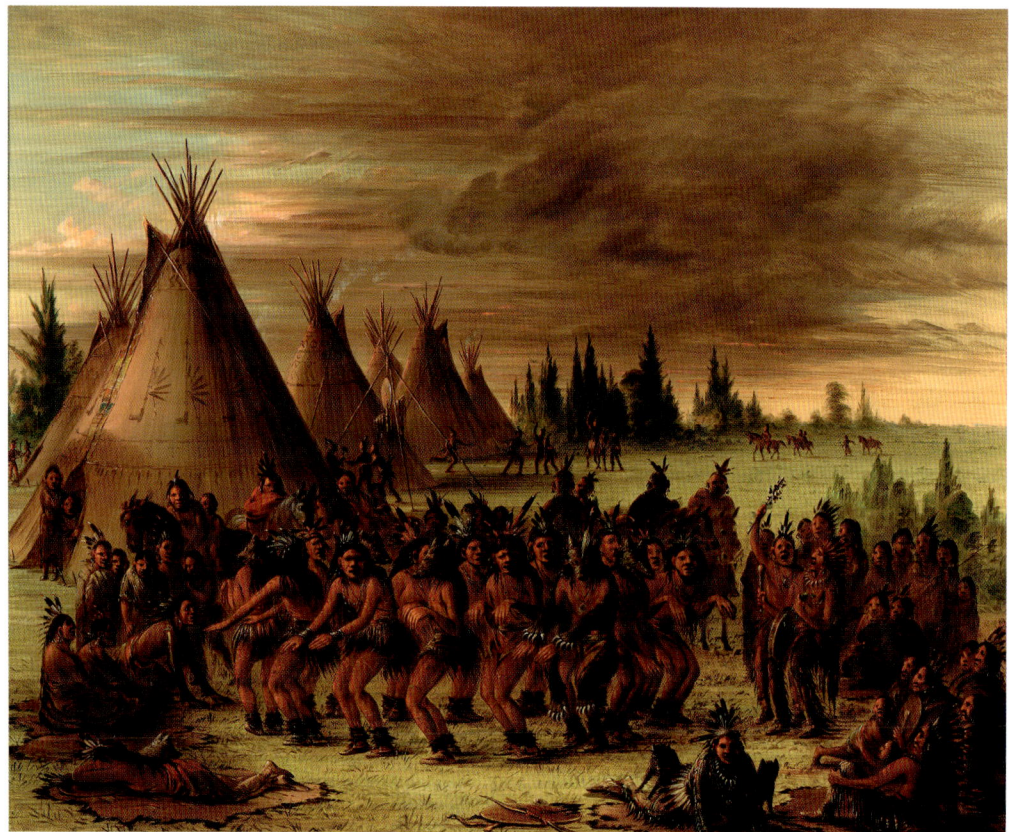

BEAR DANCE, George Catlin. Oil on canvas, 1847. GM 0126.2171

Mak-hos-kah, chief
(White Cloud.)

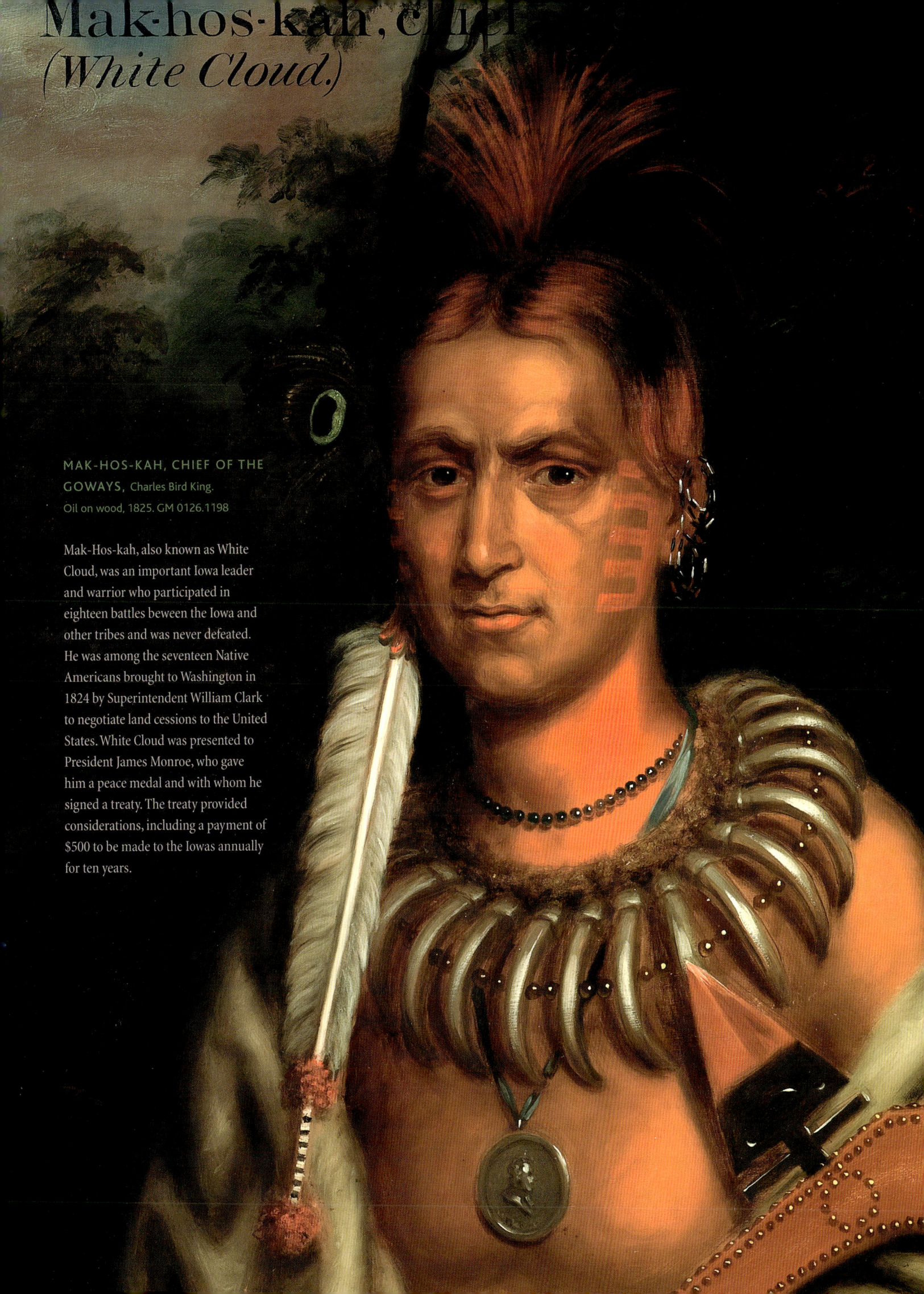

MAK-HOS-KAH, CHIEF OF THE GOWAYS, Charles Bird King.
Oil on wood, 1825. GM 0126.1198

Mak-Hos-kah, also known as White Cloud, was an important Iowa leader and warrior who participated in eighteen battles beween the Iowa and other tribes and was never defeated. He was among the seventeen Native Americans brought to Washington in 1824 by Superintendent William Clark to negotiate land cessions to the United States. White Cloud was presented to President James Monroe, who gave him a peace medal and with whom he signed a treaty. The treaty provided considerations, including a payment of $500 to be made to the Iowas annually for ten years.

By the time of Thomas Jefferson's election in 1800, peace medals had been used by European colonial powers in North America for generations. When the United States emerged in the late 18th century, it continued the traditional practice of manufacturing peace medals for ritual distribution among foreign groups. Peace medals were designed and used as fundamental symbols of national vitality and interest—notably those interests that expanded and enriched the economic and political horizons of a given power. For the fledgling American republic, peace medals can be seen as emblems of the intent to assert influence against the going concerns and interests of rival powers, particularly those of Great Britain in the thriving fur trade. As the United States' ability to compete continued to expand in the early nineteeth century, the production and use of peace medals continued to increase as well. Medals invoked the authority of the federal government and demonstrated to European imperial powers an American willingness to vie for the ongoing economic and political relationships with Native peoples. They signified an American presence with which the Europeans would ultimately have to contend.

MILITIA HELMET PLATE. Brass, 1812. GM 63.691

The peace medal is unique among artifacts of early 19th-century American material culture. Its symbolic attributes remind us of the diverse meanings of things across time and space. The individual human interactions associated with the giving and receiving of peace medals demonstrate their power to convey ideas and attitudes without words. The medals represented not only the intents and aspirations of their makers but also the thoughts and fears of those who received them. Ultimately, peace medals symbolize the larger policies and power of the United States—not only the broader expansionist desires of the Republic but also the expanding American hegemony over Native peoples in the competitive acquisition of new territory. They represent an era of interaction between cultural Others and the legacy of empire and conquest that continues to remain deeply woven into the fabric of American life.

In June 1812, the twelfth United States Congress received a confidential message from President James Madison "on the subject of our affairs with Great Britain." The message contained an account of grievances against America's imperial ancestor. It was an indictment of "the conduct of her Government" regarding "a series of acts, hostile to the United States as an independent and neutral nation." Madison's formal remonstration covered an expansive narrative of complaints, largely concerning disagreements over trade, British impressment of sailors serving in America's merchant fleet, and the incitement of Indian insurrection.[5] In only a matter of weeks, Congress voted for a formal declaration of war, the first in the history of the nation. The conflict that followed—which came to be known as the War of 1812—lasted some three years, cost combatants on each side thousands of lives, expended millions in terms of both dollars and pounds, and exposed the insecurities and hubris of two peoples still caught up in a contest of governmental will largely unsettled since the end of the American Revolution.

The War of 1812 began after years of political and economic discord between the United States and Great Britain. The tensions were ignited in June 1807 by the attack on the U.S.S. *Chesapeake* by the H.M.S. *Leopard* in the course of its mission to discover deserters from the Royal Navy. To supply troops for its war with Napoleon's France, the Royal Navy had for years engaged in the impressment of sailors for service to the crown. Thousands of British sailors had become

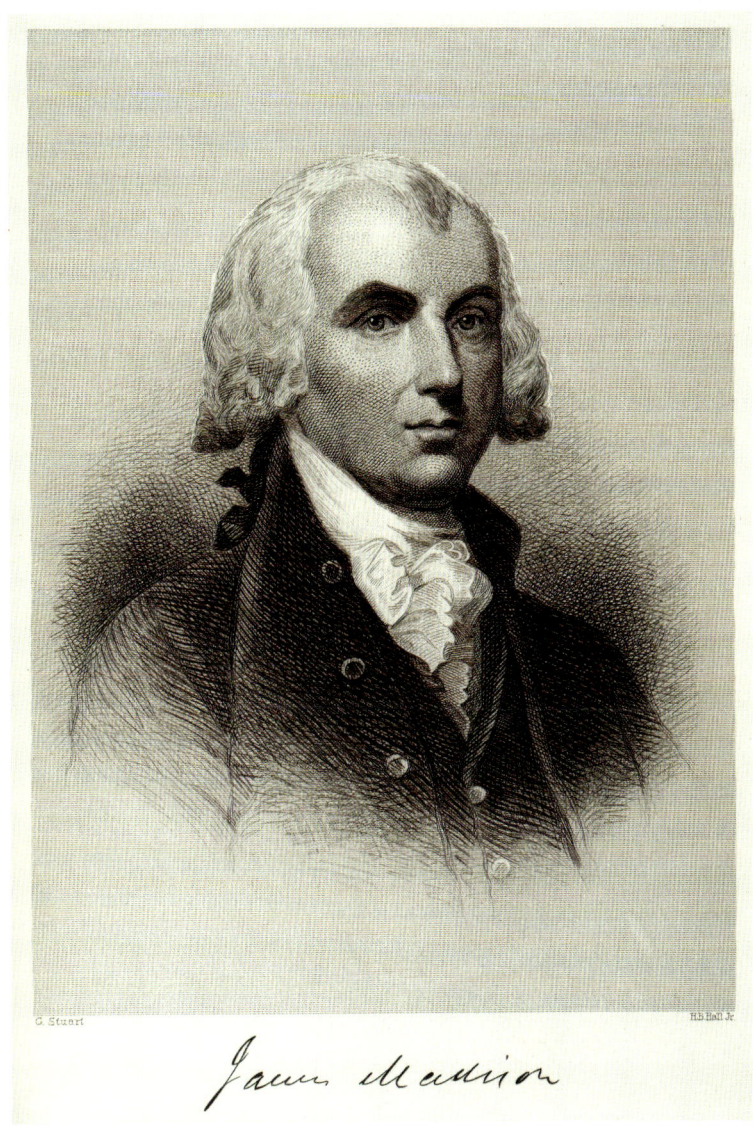

C. Stuart   H.B. Hall Jr.

James Madison

JAMES MADISON.
James Grant Wilson after Gilbert Stuart, from *The Presidents of the United States* (D. Appleton & Co.). Engraving, 1898. GM 2316.329

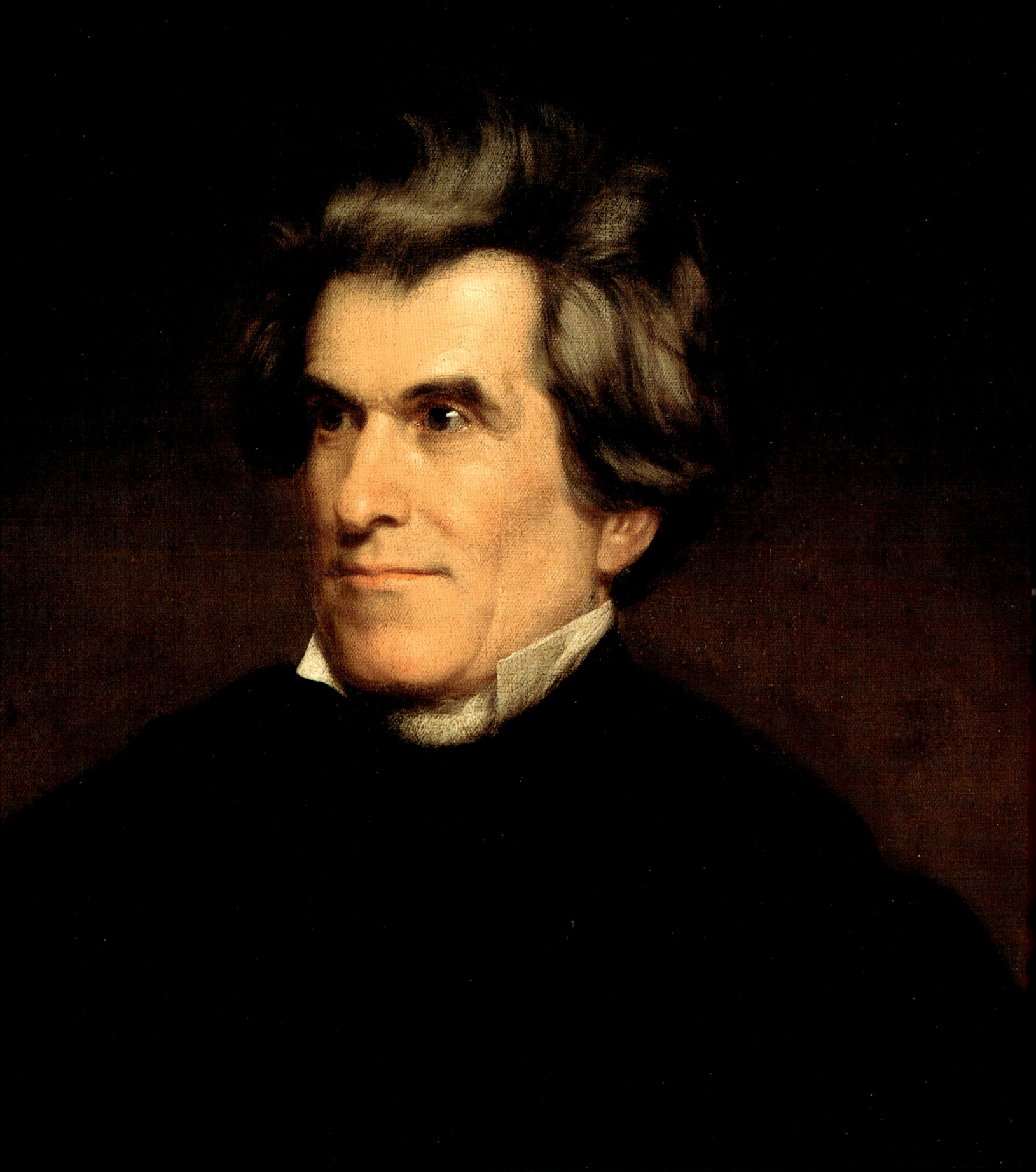

JOHN C. CALHOUN,
James Bogle. Oil on canvas,
1847. GM 0126.1014

naturalized American citizens—
some perhaps in an attempt to avoid
wartime service—yet Britain did
not recognize the right to renounce
British citizenship and viewed these
sailors as subject to English maritime
law. The attack on the *Chesapeake*
in American waters just off the
Virginia coast immediately incited
American anger. The "*Chesapeake-
Leopard* Affair" roused nationalist
sentiments. President Jefferson wrote
of the nation's collective outrage,
"Never since the Battle of Lexington
have I seen this country in such a
state of exasperation as at present
and even that did not produce such
unanimity."[6] In retaliation and in an
effort to protect American economic
interests, Jefferson successfully urged
the passing of the Embargo Act of
1807 which restricted all trade with
foreign powers.

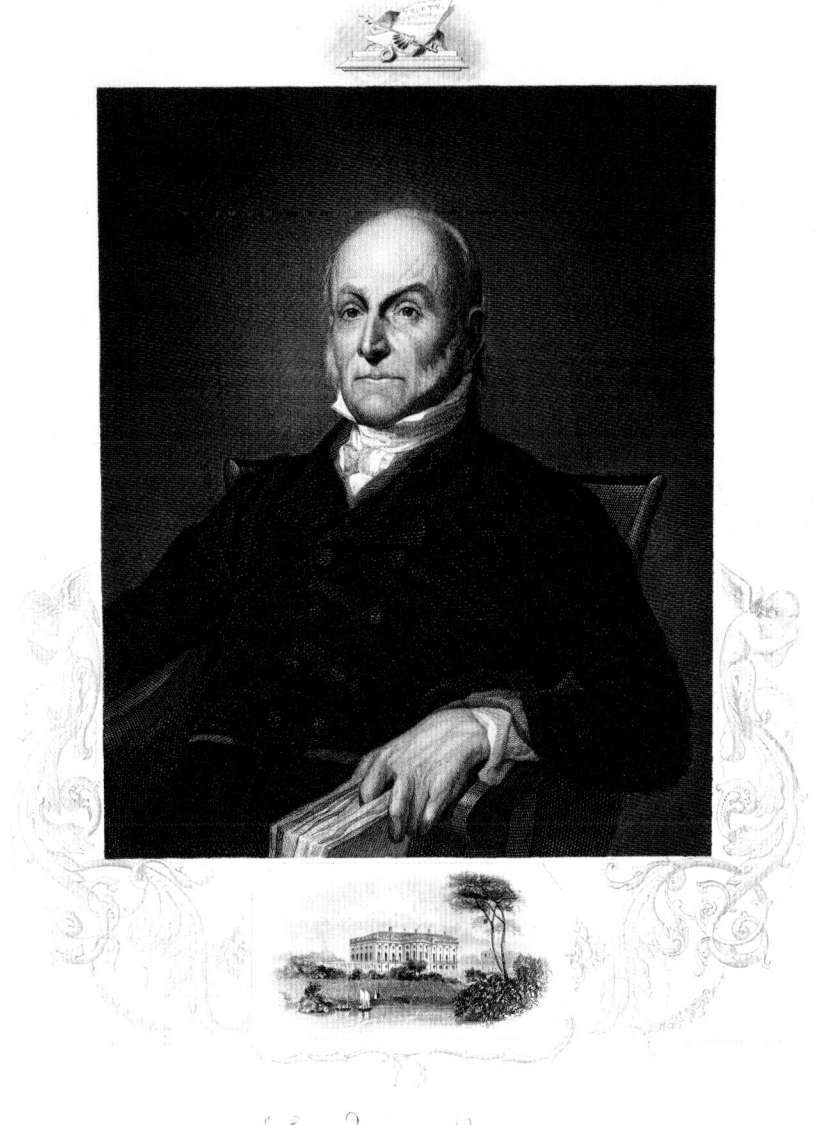

JOHN QUINCY
ADAMS, R. E. Babson and
J. Andrews after George Peter
Alexander Healy. Engraving,
ca. 1858. GM 15.1132

   Over the next few years, the
tenuous relationship between the United States and Great Britain continued to
deteriorate. As the impressment of sailors escalated with England's growing need
for manpower in the war with France, American frustrations continued to build
as well. In the Northwest, the increasingly organized Native resistance to American
expansionism caused both alarm and suspicion regarding Great Britain's support
of wholesale insurrection. In the fall of 1811, the debate over war with Great Britain
became heated in the U. S. Congress as the so-called "war hawks" Henry Clay,
John C. Calhoun, and others urged the nation toward all-out military conflict. For
some, the prospect of war coincided with growing expansionist desires. Historian
Carl Benn describes this mix of motives:

As relations degenerated towards war from 1807 to 1812, many Americans argued that the United States ought to seize the British provinces that lay to the north of the republic in order to get even with Britain, to realize America's destiny, or even to profit personally through territorial expansion. Others, such as President James Madison, desired conquest because these colonies were emerging as a competitor to the United States in the export of North American products. Annexation would benefit U. S. expansion elsewhere too: in the west against the aboriginal tribes, who would be deprived of help from British officials and Canadian fur traders; and in the south, where filibusters and expansionists hoped that the subjugation of Canada would help them in realizing their goal of taking the Floridas from Britain's new European ally, Spain.[7]

Even Thomas Jefferson's eye glanced to Britain's northern provinces in the early months of the war. In a letter to William Duane in August 1812, the former president alluded to the sense of ease that many Americans had with regard to the potential conquest. "The acquisition of Canada this year, as far as the neighborhood of Quebec, will be a mere matter of marching, and will give us the experience for the attack on Halifax, the next and final expulsion of England from the American continent."[8] Jefferson's comments reflected a growing national impulse toward the ultimate domination of North America.

EAGLE POMMEL SWORD. Steel, bone, 1812.
GM 84.3402a

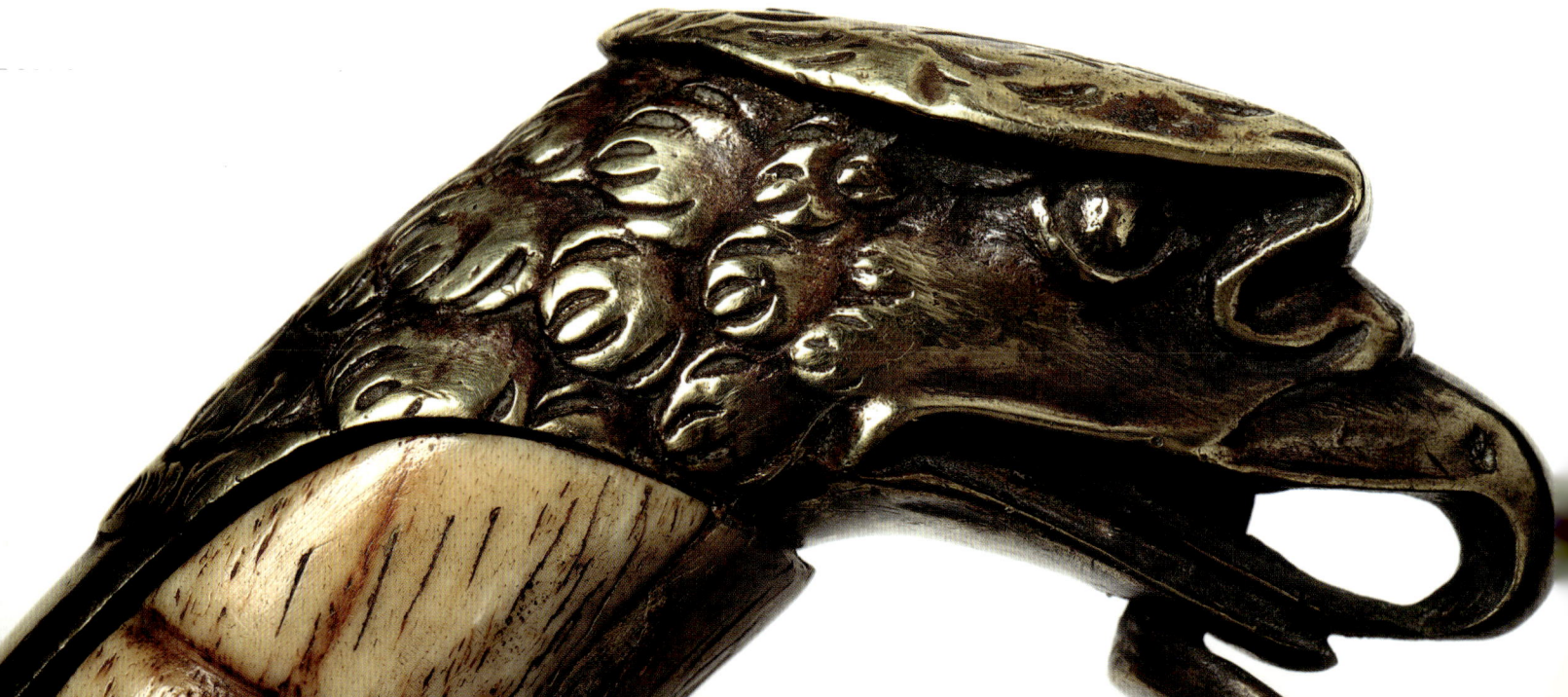

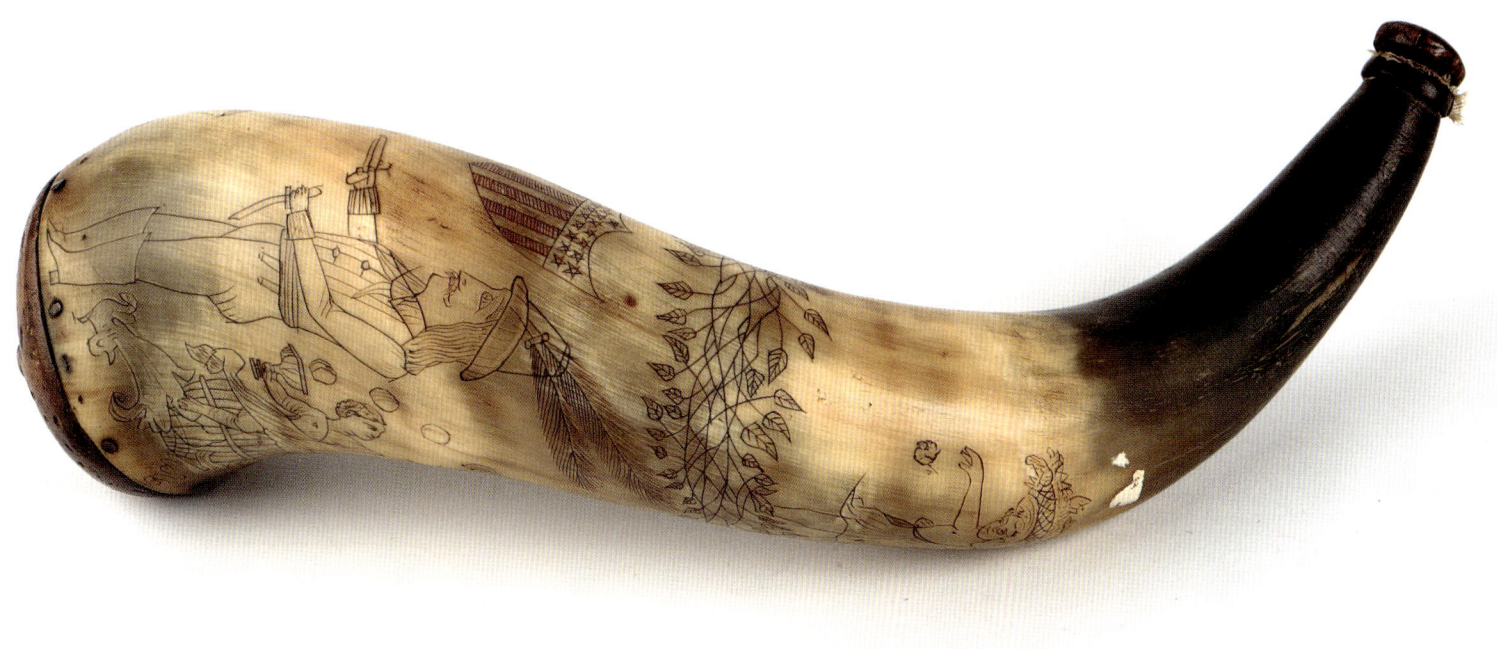

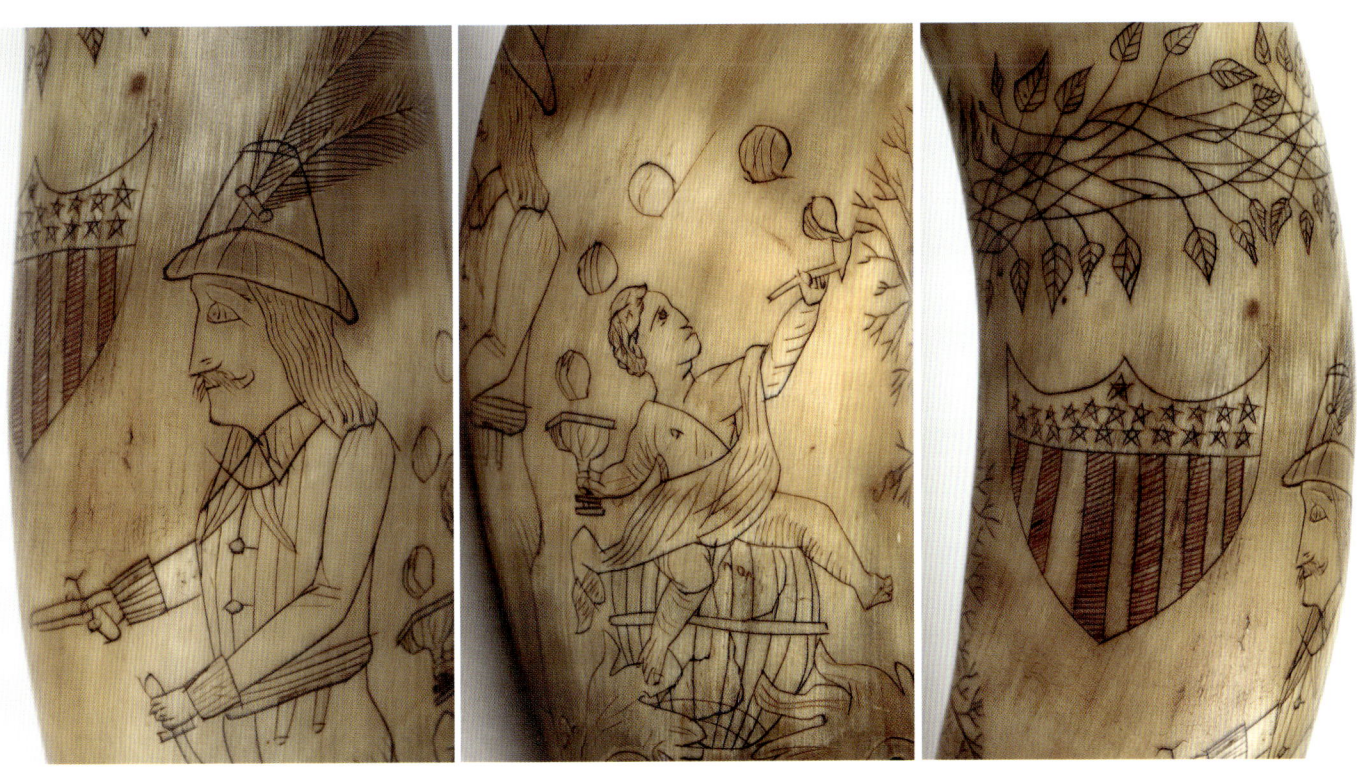

INCISED POWDER HORN. Horn, metal, wood, 19th century. GM 8436.1215

The War of 1812 emerged from a set of ideas—not only about American rights and economic interests but about the concept of American nationhood itself. It can be seen as an assertion of growing national pride. Both governments claimed aggrieved status, yet neither fully comprehended the full political, social, and economic ramifications of their contentions. On both sides, the conflict roused nationalist passions that encouraged aggressive and retaliatory actions in response to perceived affronts to a given collective prestige.

For America, the war emerged out of the looming insecurities of a young nation still attempting to find its way in a world it saw as comprised of equals. For Great Britain, the conflict involved giving a long due comeuppance to its former colonies whose complaints were seen as a petty distraction in England's ongoing and more legitimate war with France.

The years leading up to America's second war with Great Britain were characterized by an expansion of ambition and self-assurance by the leaders of the United States government. Since the time of Jefferson, a new American Self was emerging. It was a Self that had been propelled with the promise of a new century and the fantasies of unsettled territories with the acquisition of new lands.

The years between the purchase of the Louisiana Territory and the outbreak and aftermath of the War of 1812 reveal a nation enlarging not only its sovereign borders but ultimately its sense of cultural identity—its collective psychological place in an increasingly complex and changing world. As historian Robert Kagan asserts:

America in the first quarter of the 19th century was expansive not only in a territorial sense. As national confidence grew with the acquisition of more land and more security, Americans took an increasingly expansive view of their role in the world, beyond territorial boundaries. Oddly enough, it was the nearly futile War of 1812 that boosted American confidence and brought to the fore qualities in the American character that had been submerged during the trying decades of the 1780s and 90s. If the acquisition of Louisiana and the ratification of the Transcontinental Treaty determined the physical contours of the American continental empire for the remainder of the century, the War of 1812 both revealed and significantly shaped the character of the nation that was to inhabit it.[9]

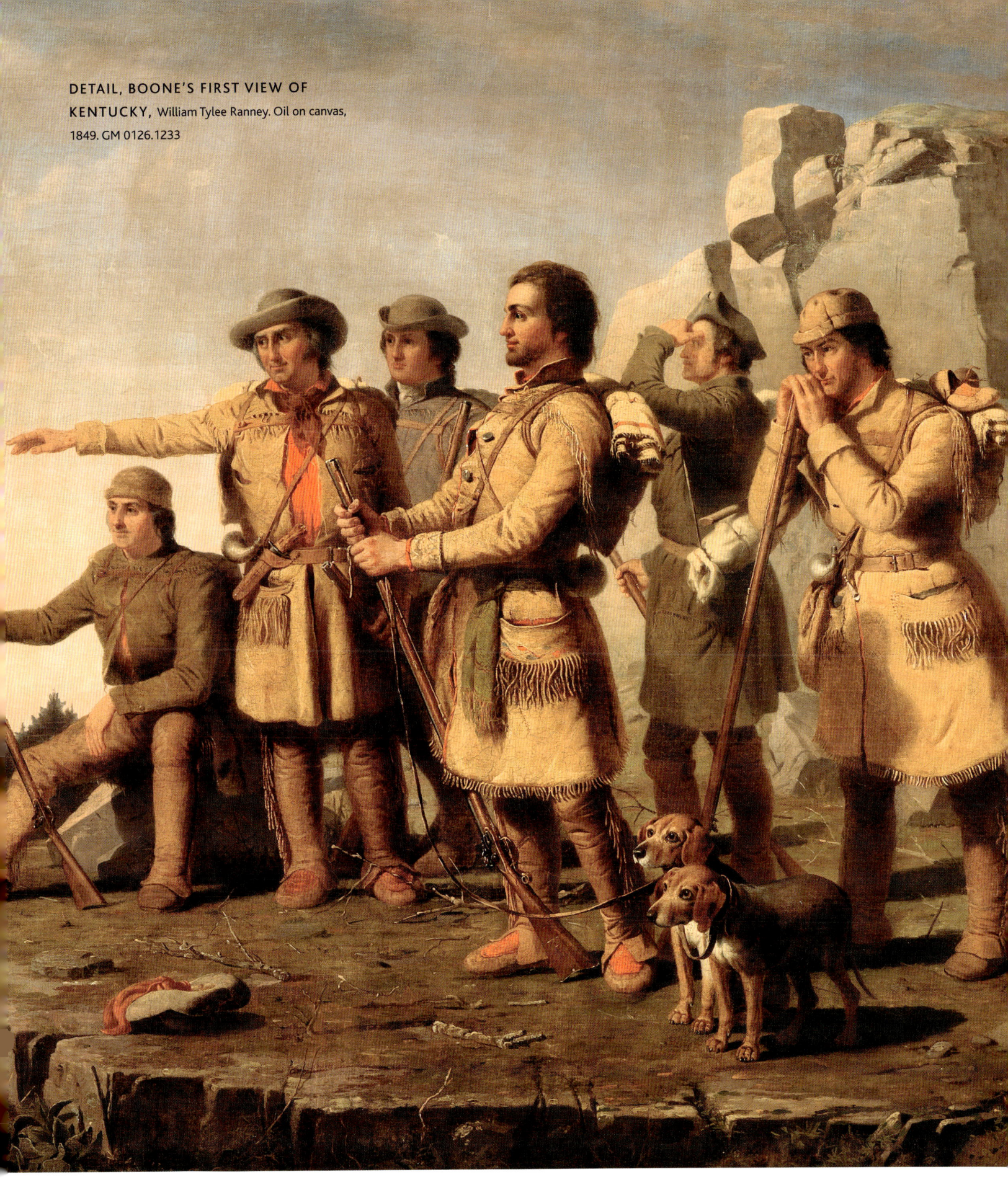

DETAIL, BOONE'S FIRST VIEW OF
KENTUCKY, William Tylee Ranney. Oil on canvas,
1849. GM 0126.1233

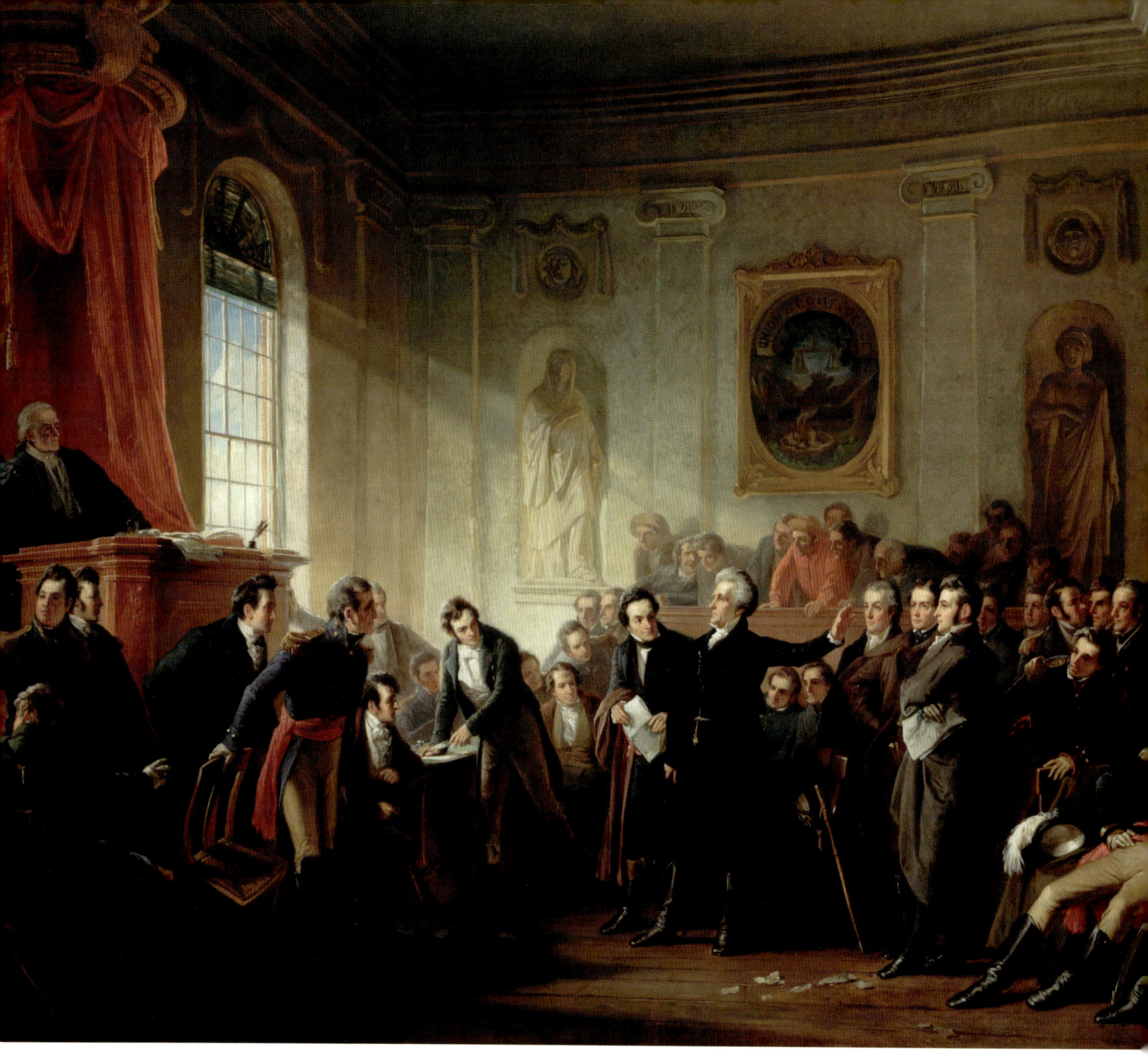

The American character that emerged during the War of 1812 was shaped by an intense patriotism in which regional identities were overshadowed by nationalistic fervor. With the British defeat of Napoleon's forces in 1814, however, American nationalist sentiments took on an added sense of dread. Victory over France now allowed Great Britain to devote more effort and resources to the war in North America—a change in circumstance for which the United States was both politically and militarily unprepared. The British invasion of America in the summer of 1814 set into motion a series of events that ultimately changed the course of the history of the continent. The occupation of Washington, D.C., by

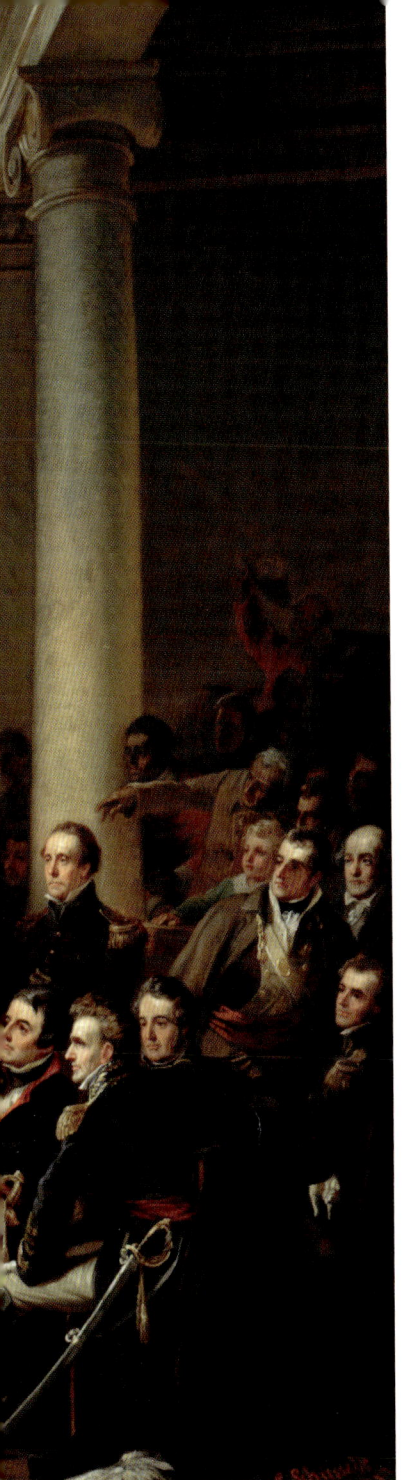

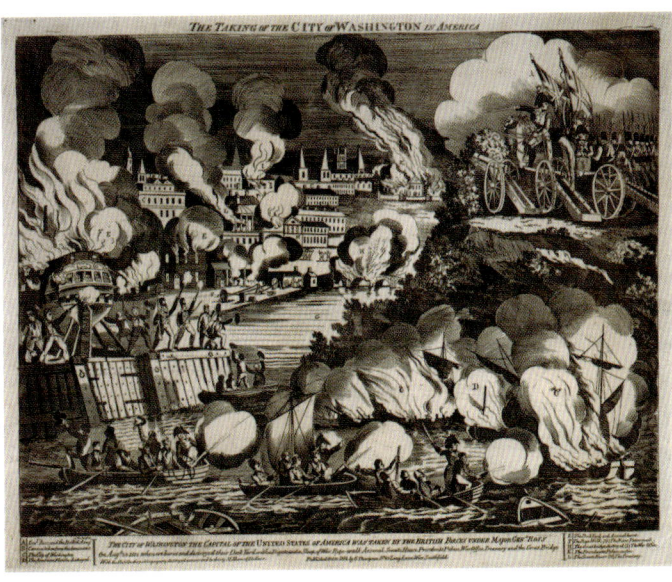

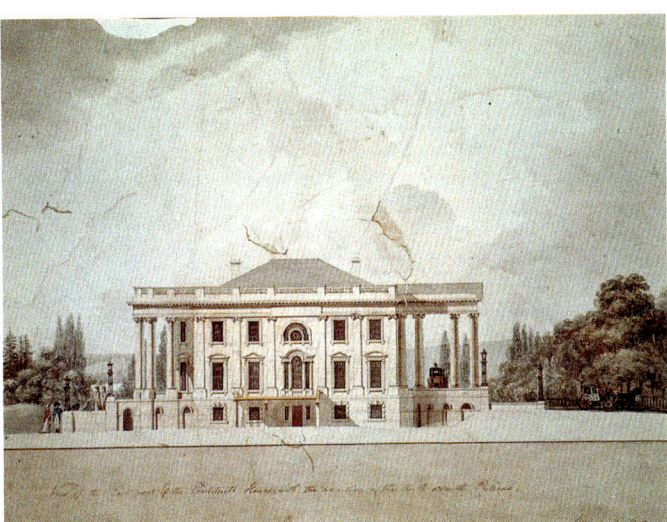

FACING: ANDREW JACKSON BEFORE JUDGE HALL, NEW ORLEANS, Christian Schussele. Oil on canvas, 1859. GM 0126.2023

Preparing for the defense of New Orleans in what proved to be the final campaign of the War of 1812, General Andrew Jackson imposed martial law throughout the city. This state of crisis continued from December 1814 through the defeat of the British on January 8, 1815, and continued until the official announcement of the end of the war reached Jackson in late February.

Earlier in February, as news of the peace filtered into New Orleans, a letter critical of Jackson's policy was published in the *New Orleans Courier.* Jackson immediately arrested the letter's author, state legislator Louis Louaillers. When Judge Dominick Hall granted Louaillers a *writ of habeas corpus,* General Jackson also arrested the federal judge. Hall was released but ordered to leave New Orleans. When martial law was rescinded, Judge Hall summoned Jackson before his court to prove why he should not be held in contempt. Jackson was found guilty, but Hall announced that in view of Jackson's service to the nation a fine of $1,000 would be suspended. General Jackson rejected the suspension and immediately paid the fine.

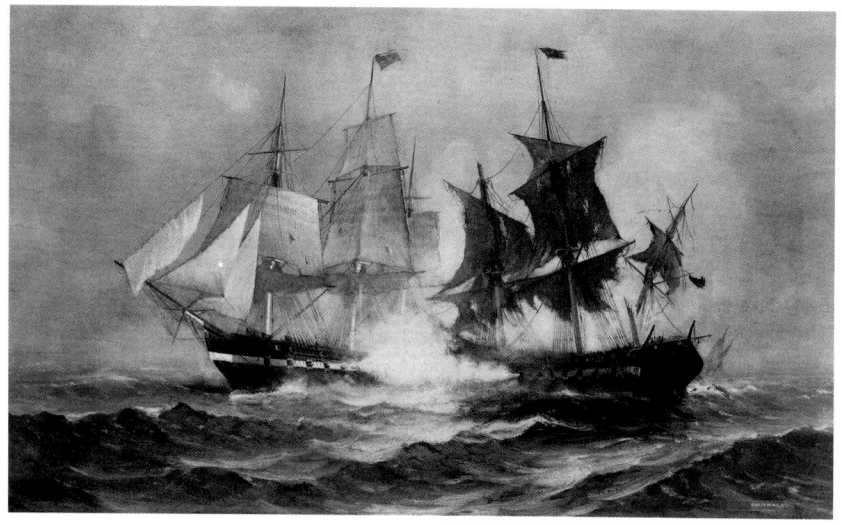

British forces and the destruction of key government buildings that followed —including the burning of the president's mansion—were intended to diminish public morale for the "greater political effect likely to result."[10] As one British officer noted, it would "lessen the dignity and pomp of a misjudged and impolitic people."[11] The destruction of the capital, however, ultimately did more to establish the righteousness of the American cause in the minds of the people. Even President Madison expressed moral outrage over the "barbarous policy" of British forces that "has not even spared those monuments of the arts and models of taste with which our country had enriched and embellished its infant metropolis."[12] It mattered little to the nation that American forces had similarly sacked British houses of government during the invasion of Canada in the early years of the war. The American identity that was emerging assumed a position of innocence and virtue regardless of the facts on the ground. By the war's end, the nation saw only what it wanted to see. As Carl Benn relates:

> Most Americans seemed to forget why their country had gone to war, the failure of their soldiers, sailors, and diplomats to achieve their objectives, and instead embraced the memories of successes at Plattsburgh, Baltimore, and especially New Orleans to bolster an interpretation of the peace that affirmed the independence and dignity of their country, going so far as to proclaim that they had won a 'second war of independence...As time passed, the legends of American victory grew. The famous Democratic-Republican party newspaper *Niles Register,* on 14 September 1816, crowed: '...we did virtually dictate the treaty of Ghent to the British,' ignoring completely that it had been a scramble just to get the status quo of 1812, let alone achieve any war aims, while vague affirmations that Britain had come out of the war with a new-found respect for the United States helped to solidify such views. This attitude has remained dominant in the American public consciousness.[13]

The War of 1812 can be seen as the symbolic enactment of the American Self. The American character that emerged was a response to collective uncertainty about the nation's place in the world. The markers of that character are revealed in the attitudes that started the war and those that influenced and oversaw its implementation. The symbolic aspects of the emerging American identity

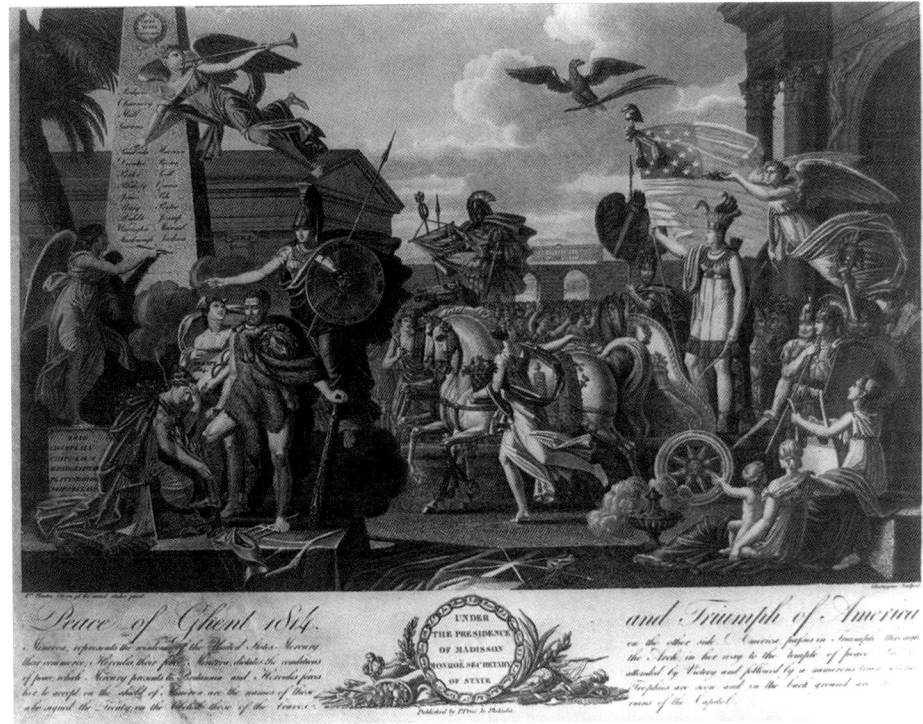

are revealed in the nation's overwhelming focus on the war's successes and in its nearly complete disregard for the lessons that could have been learned from its failures. Across time, the manner in which Americans have remembered the War of 1812 demonstrates its power as a symbolic moment in the collective mind. The popular accounts of heroism, sacrifice, and defiance in the face of peril all reinforce the ongoing notions of national strength and virtue but continue to ignore the insecurities and weaknesses that have existed at the very foundations of the republic. Leland Dewitt Baldwin's observations from over a half century ago remain profound:

> The generation of the War of 1812 saw the emergence of the American character in the form it was to bear for a century, with only minor changes. We usually have been materialistic, vaguely idealistic, rashly optimistic, emotional, sentimental, and easily diverted from the pursuit of difficult objectives – in other words, immature. These characteristics in an older nation would rightly be called psychopathic; of course nations, no more than individuals, exhibit all the characteristics of immaturity. In this immaturity lies the explanation for many of the vagaries which have marked our social, economic, and political policies as a people.[14]

ATROCIOUS SAINTS

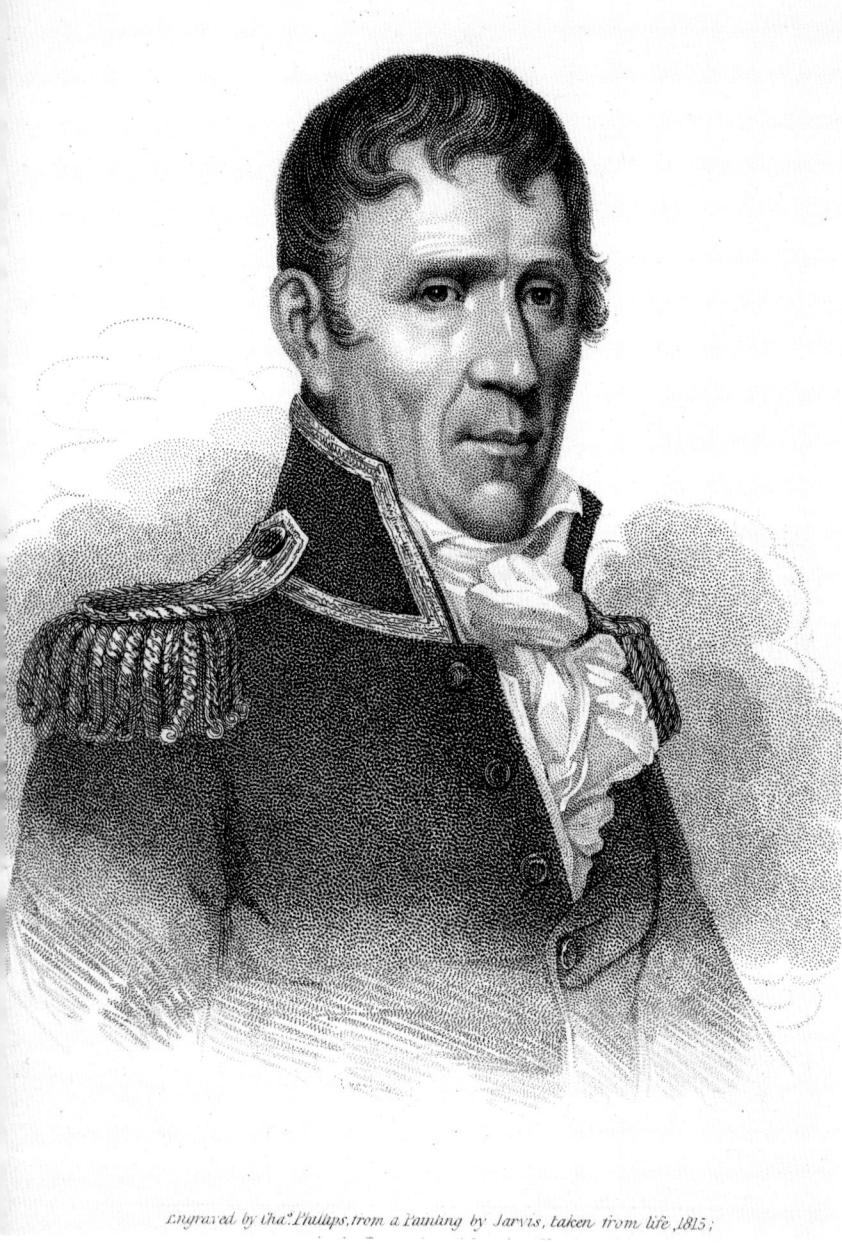

Engraved by Thos Phillips, from a Painting by Jarvis, taken from life, 1815;

ANDREW JACKSON,
after J.W. Jarvis. Engraving.
GM 15.1133

The victory at New Orleans did not affect the terms of peace with Britain, as the Treaty of Ghent was signed before the fighting occurred. The Battle of New Orleans did establish Andrew Jackson as the major hero of the War of 1812 and a national figure.

In 1860, biographer James Parton published one of his most noted works, a three-volume study titled *Life of Andrew Jackson*. Among the most prolific biographers of his time, Parton anguished over the complexities involved in his attempt to assess the life and career of the nation's seventh president. After months of poring over a "unique, bewildering collection" of books, newspaper articles and the like, Parton found himself increasingly perplexed about what had been written on the general, perhaps the most controversial, celebrated, and reviled political leader in American history. To Parton, Jackson was an enigma. It had been only a handful of years since the president's death in 1845, yet the details of Jackson's life were seemingly comprised of one profound contradiction pitted against another. The biographer expressed his deep frustration in the preface to his work:

> If any one, at the end of a year even, had asked what I had yet discovered respecting General Jackson, I might have answered thus: 'Andrew Jackson, I am given to understand, was a patriot and a traitor. He was one of the greatest of generals, and wholly ignorant of the art of war. A writer brilliant, elegant, eloquent, and without being able to compose a correct sentence, or spell words of four syllables. The first of statesmen, he never devised, he never framed a measure. He was the most candid of men, and was capable of the profoundest dissimulation. A most law-defying, law-obeying citizen. A stickler for discipline, he never hesitated to disobey his superior. A democratic aristocrat. An urbane savage. An atrocious saint.'[15]

Parton's assessment reflected the conflicting views of Jackson by his contemporaries and the press throughout a military and political career that had spanned nearly half a century. "So difficult it is to attain information respecting a man whom two-thirds of his fellow citizens deified, and the other third vilified," Parton wrote. The biographer clearly understood that Jackson had become far more than the sum of his life's efforts. Beyond his status as soldier or statesman, Jackson had become a national symbol—a primary lightning rod of early 19th-century American political, economic, and social life. He had become the physical embodiment of contradictions existing deep in the collective character of the nation. In Jackson, the people saw what they wanted to see, a reflection of their own attitudes and perspectives, shaped by their own ambitions and desires.

As a symbol, Jackson had emerged in a number of incarnations well before his election to the presidency in 1828. The widely-proclaimed "hero of New Orleans" had long been a figure on the American stage. With his victory over British forces at the closing days of the War of 1812, Jackson became an immediate folk sensation—an emblem of national stamina—representing the character and strength of the American Self against a European Other. Against a backdrop of foreign invasion and the national humiliation endured with the invasion of British forces on American soil, Jackson emerged a national celebrity in a culture that had known very few. Jackson's later military exploits in the First Seminole War and his conquest of Spanish Florida helped to solidify his status as a national icon. The general's broad popularity among the people encouraged his candidacy for the U. S. presidency in the election of 1824. While Jackson led his opponents, John Quincy Adams, William H. Crawford, and Henry Clay, he failed to win a majority of the vote. The election was then decided in the House of Representatives, where Jackson was defeated by Adams who had drawn support from Henry Clay. Adams then appointed Clay secretary of state, outraging Jackson supporters who saw the arrangement as a "corrupt bargain." Ironically, Jackson's loss only encouraged his popularity among the masses. He became a symbol of public indignation against the corruption of economic and political elites.

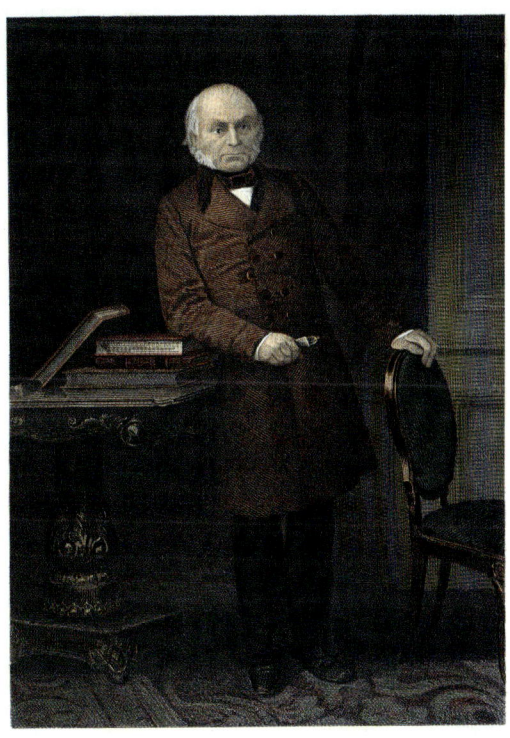

J. Q. Adams

JOHN QUINCY
ADAMS, Johnson, Fry, &
Co. after Alonzo Chappel.
Engraving, 1861.
GM 15.1132

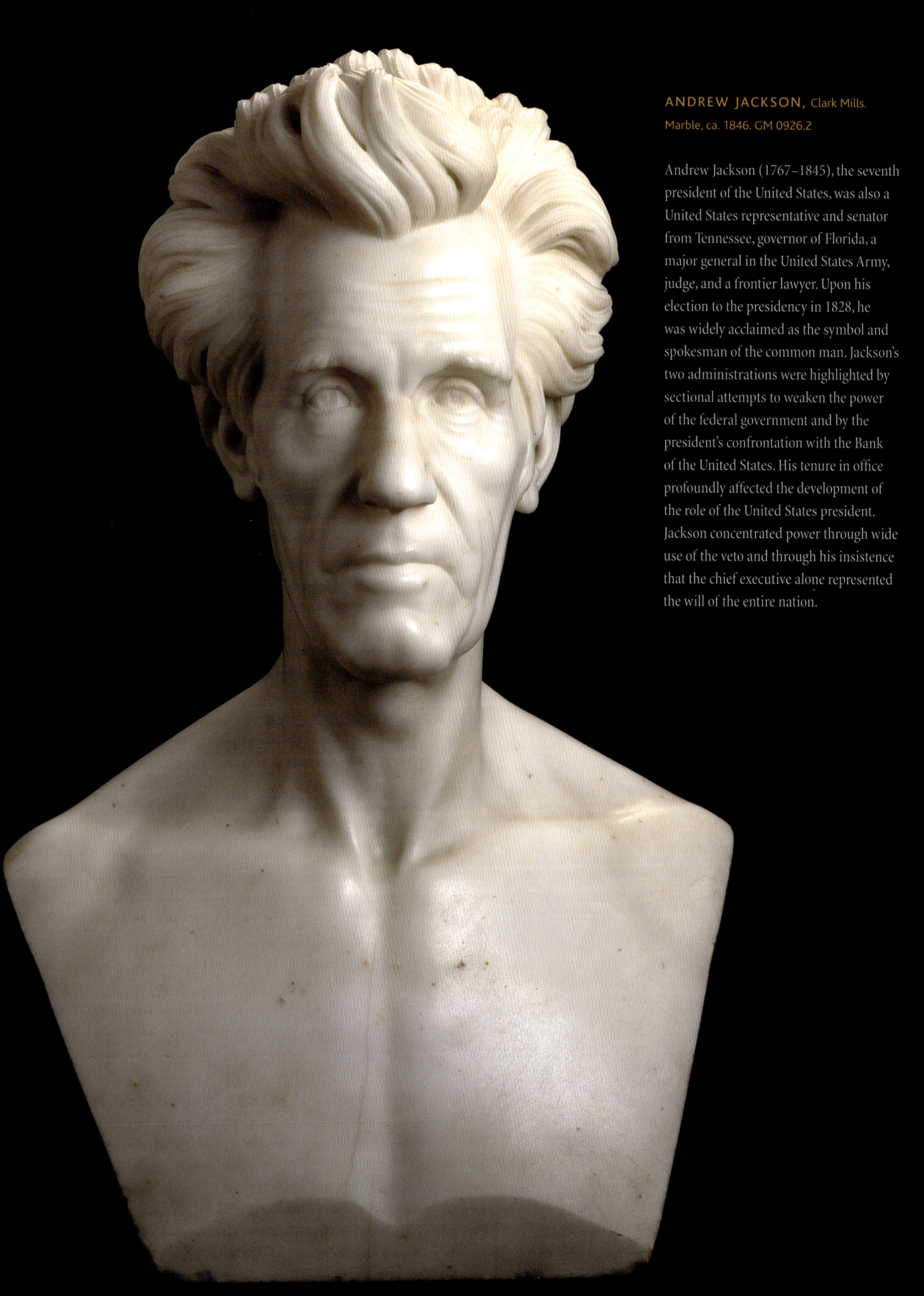

ANDREW JACKSON, Clark Mills.
Marble, ca. 1846. GM 0926.2

Andrew Jackson (1767–1845), the seventh president of the United States, was also a United States representative and senator from Tennessee, governor of Florida, a major general in the United States Army, judge, and a frontier lawyer. Upon his election to the presidency in 1828, he was widely acclaimed as the symbol and spokesman of the common man. Jackson's two administrations were highlighted by sectional attempts to weaken the power of the federal government and by the president's confrontation with the Bank of the United States. His tenure in office profoundly affected the development of the role of the United States president. Jackson concentrated power through wide use of the veto and through his insistence that the chief executive alone represented the will of the entire nation.

This growing distrust helped to propel Jackson to the White House in the election of 1828. Combined with the self-perpetuating mythology regarding the general's early life and military exploits was now the belief that the new president embodied the bootstrap values of common citizens—he became the first popularly elected president in the history of the republic. The 1828 election ushered in a new era in American social and political life. The expanding mythology that continued to surround Jackson served the interests of the new administration, yet the profound divisions within American culture remained. As a soldier and newly-elected president, Andrew Jackson had inherited the mantle of George Washington in the popular mind. Still, many were not as enthusiastic. "Some Americans thought of the president-elect as a second Father of His Country. Others wanted him dead."[16]

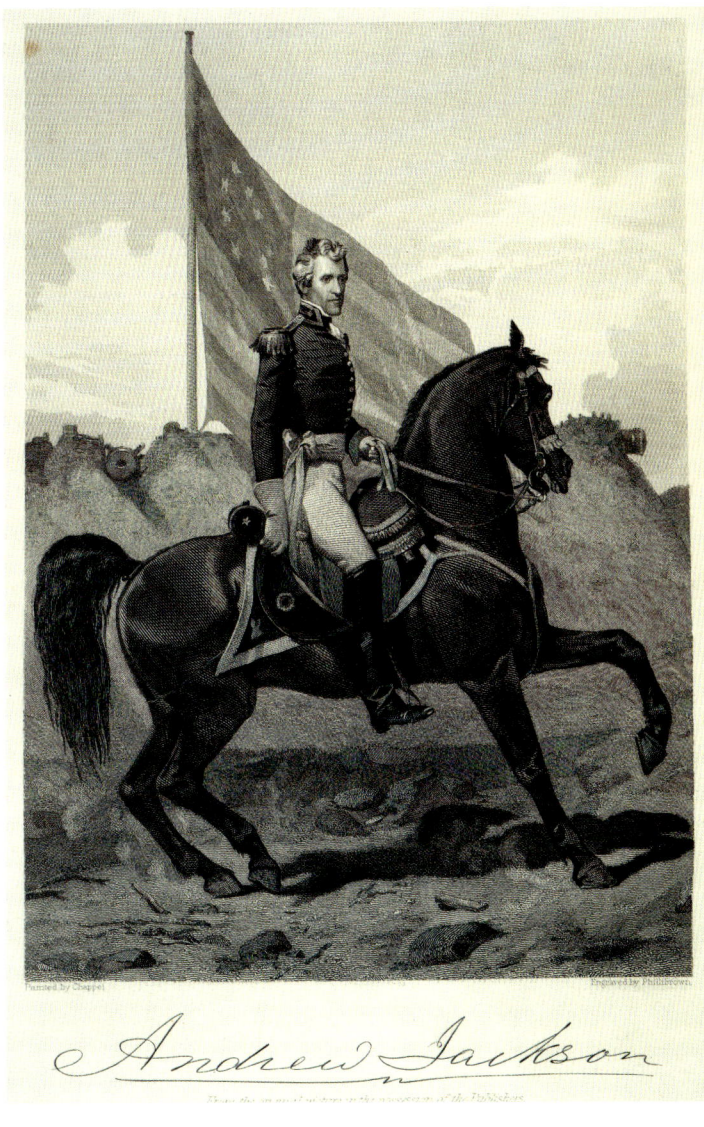

ANDREW JACKSON, Johnson, Fry and Co., after Alonzo Chappel. Engraving, 1858. GM 15.1134

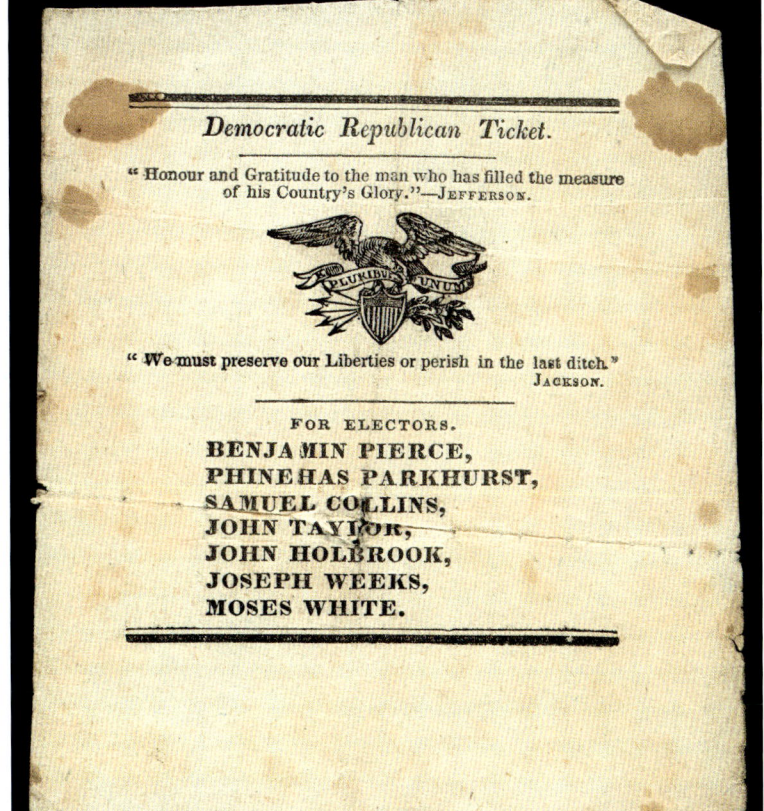

DEMOCRATIC REPUBLICAN TICKET, 1832. GM 5326.1198

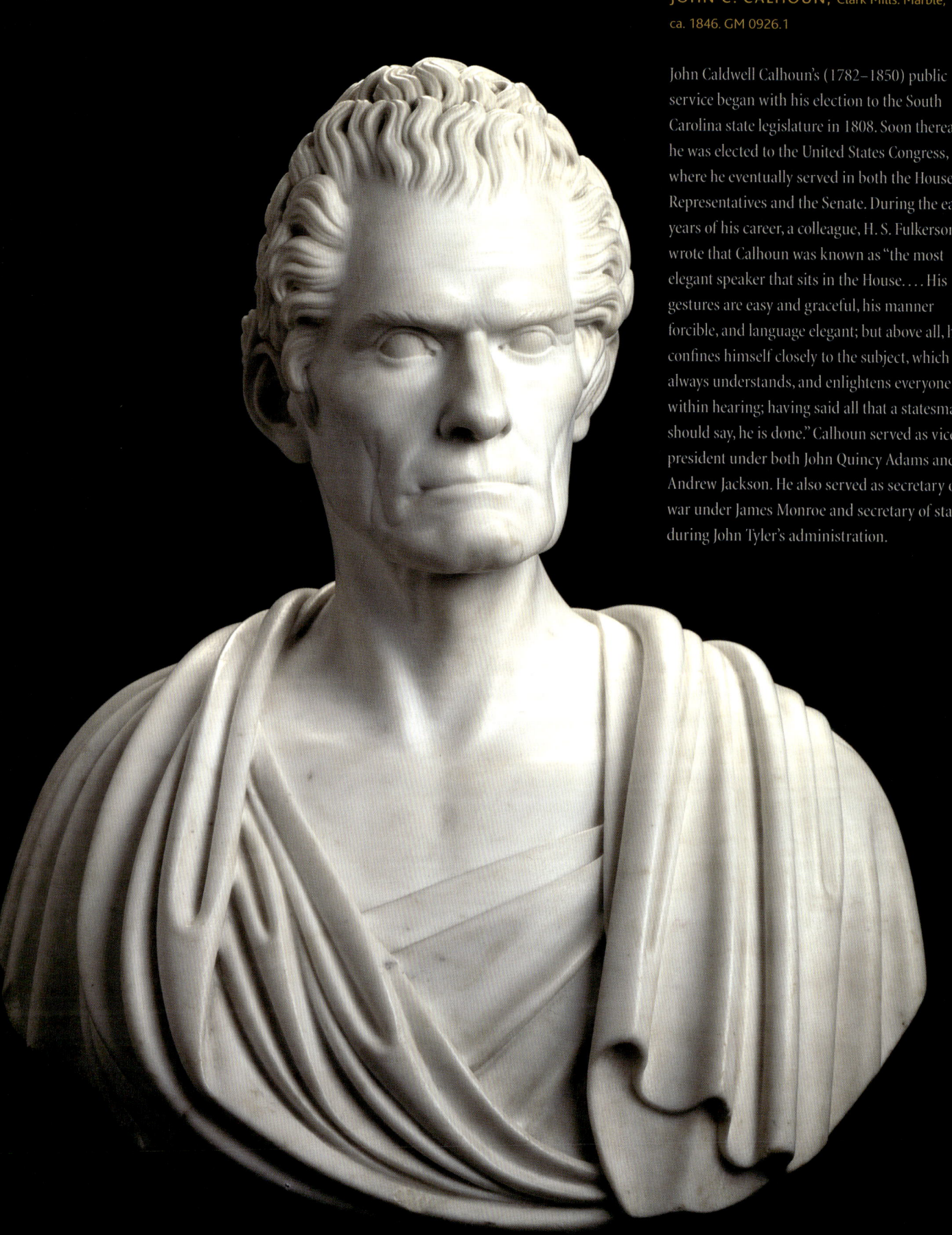

JOHN C. CALHOUN, Clark Mills. Marble, ca. 1846. GM 0926.1

John Caldwell Calhoun's (1782–1850) public service began with his election to the South Carolina state legislature in 1808. Soon thereafter he was elected to the United States Congress, where he eventually served in both the House of Representatives and the Senate. During the early years of his career, a colleague, H. S. Fulkerson, wrote that Calhoun was known as "the most elegant speaker that sits in the House.... His gestures are easy and graceful, his manner forcible, and language elegant; but above all, he confines himself closely to the subject, which he always understands, and enlightens everyone within hearing; having said all that a statesman should say, he is done." Calhoun served as vice president under both John Quincy Adams and Andrew Jackson. He also served as secretary of war under James Monroe and secretary of state during John Tyler's administration.

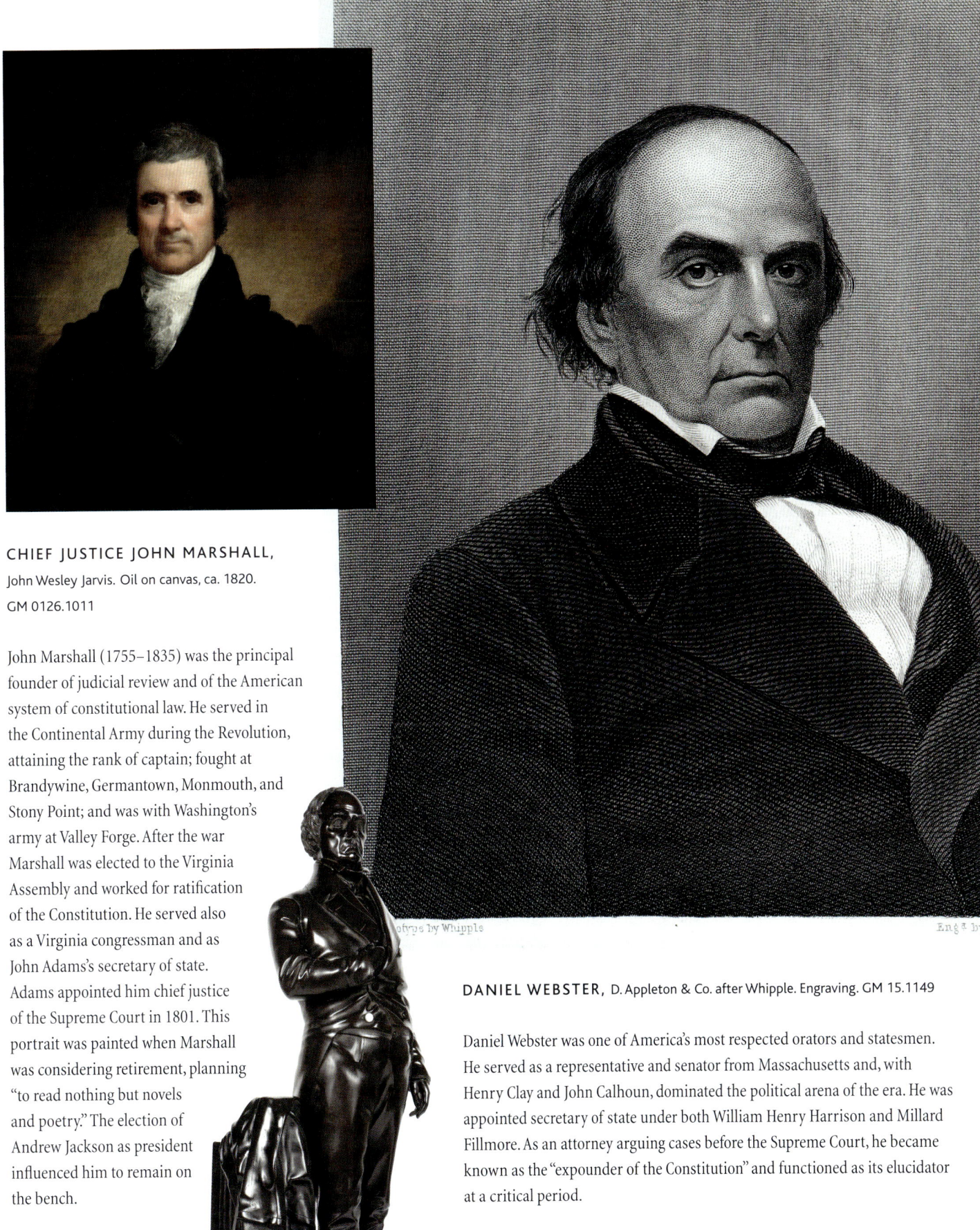

CHIEF JUSTICE JOHN MARSHALL,
John Wesley Jarvis. Oil on canvas, ca. 1820.
GM 0126.1011

John Marshall (1755–1835) was the principal
founder of judicial review and of the American
system of constitutional law. He served in
the Continental Army during the Revolution,
attaining the rank of captain; fought at
Brandywine, Germantown, Monmouth, and
Stony Point; and was with Washington's
army at Valley Forge. After the war
Marshall was elected to the Virginia
Assembly and worked for ratification
of the Constitution. He served also
as a Virginia congressman and as
John Adams's secretary of state.
Adams appointed him chief justice
of the Supreme Court in 1801. This
portrait was painted when Marshall
was considering retirement, planning
"to read nothing but novels
and poetry." The election of
Andrew Jackson as president
influenced him to remain on
the bench.

DANIEL WEBSTER, D. Appleton & Co. after Whipple. Engraving. GM 15.1149

Daniel Webster was one of America's most respected orators and statesmen.
He served as a representative and senator from Massachusetts and, with
Henry Clay and John Calhoun, dominated the political arena of the era. He was
appointed secretary of state under both William Henry Harrison and Millard
Fillmore. As an attorney arguing cases before the Supreme Court, he became
known as the "expounder of the Constitution" and functioned as its elucidator
at a critical period.

DANIEL WEBSTER, Thomas Ball. Bronze, 1858. GM 0826.93

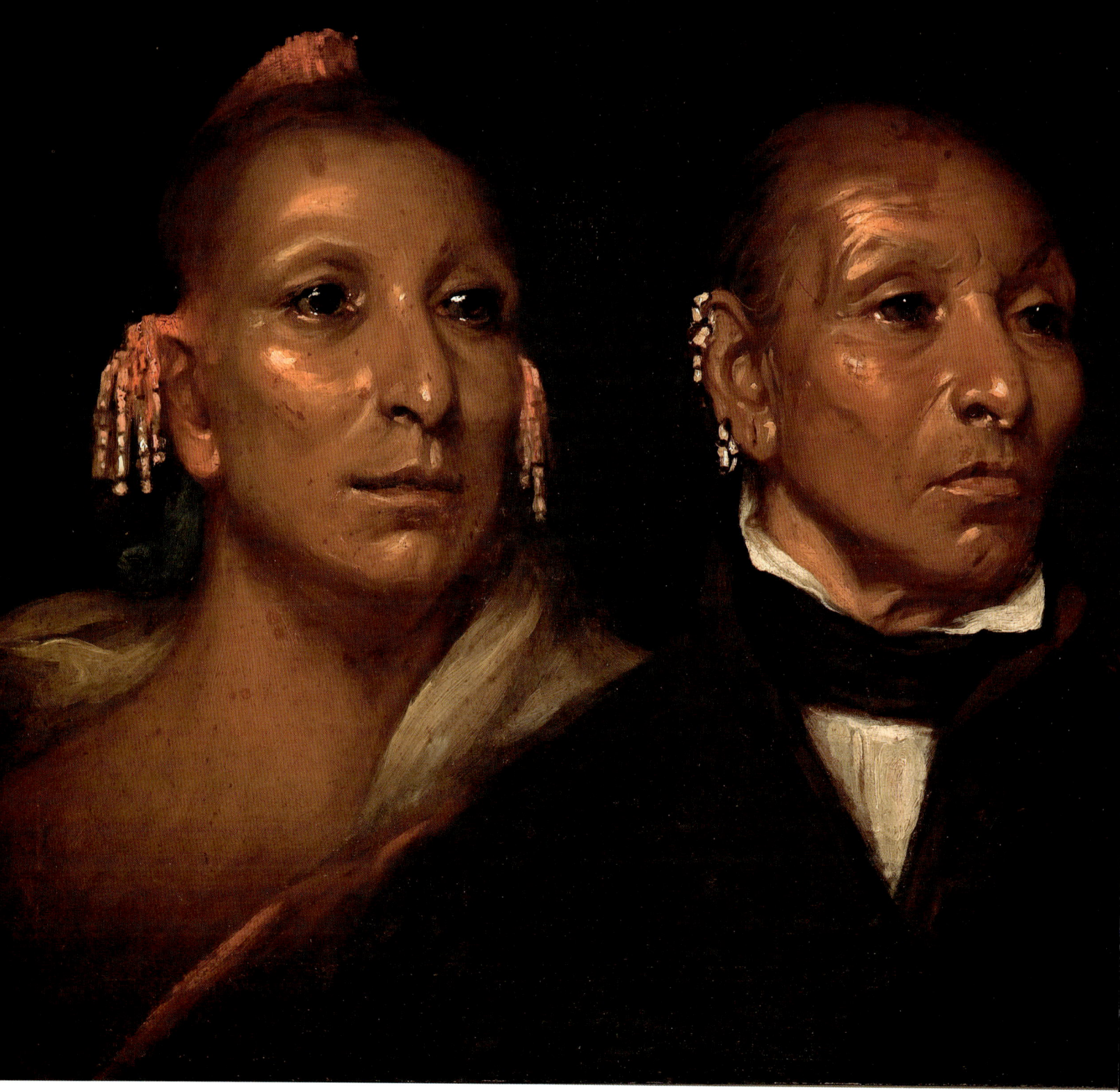

BLACK HAWK AND HIS SON, WHIRLING THUNDER, John Wesley Jarvis.
Oil on canvas, 1833. GM 0126.1007

Sauk leader Black Hawk's defeat in the Black Hawk War of 1832 ended Sauk and Fox claims
to lands east of the Mississippi River. Governmental policies regarding the removal of Native
people from their traditional homelands can be seen as a symbolic enactment of the larger
national will. American notions of racial superiority became a powerful rationalization for
the pursuit of expansionist desires.

PIPE BOWL—TREATY OF DANCING RABBIT CREEK (CHOCTAW). Stone, 1832. GM 61.1739

The Treaty of Dancing Rabbit Creek, the first treaty signed under the Indian Removal Act, gave nearly 11 million acres of Choctaw land in what is now Mississippi to the United States government in exchange for 15 million acres of land in Indian Territory. On September 15, 1830, more than 6,000 members of the Choctaw tribe gathered at Dancing Rabbit Creek to meet with government officials and discuss terms that would eventually open Choctaw-held lands to white settlement. Thomas Gilcrease acquired this stone pipe from a descendant of Greenwood LeFlore, one of the Choctaw signers of the treaty. The pipe is characteristic of those dating to the Mississippian Period, which ended prior to contact with Europeans.

Throughout the 1830s, the United States expanded the lands within its direct control. A growing population as well as broadening economic and political interests urged the acquisition of new territories—particularly those traditionally held by Native Americans. The election of Andrew Jackson to the presidency in 1828 accelerated a process that would ultimately lead to the cession of Native lands to the United States, and passage of the Indian Removal Act of 1830 set into motion the eventual government confiscation of Native American homelands east of the Mississippi. Indian removal was completed both by treaty and through military coercion. In the largest forced displacement, often referred to as the "Trail of Tears," thousands of Native people died from cold, starvation, and disease while on the march to lands set aside by the federal government as "Indian Territory" in present-day Oklahoma.

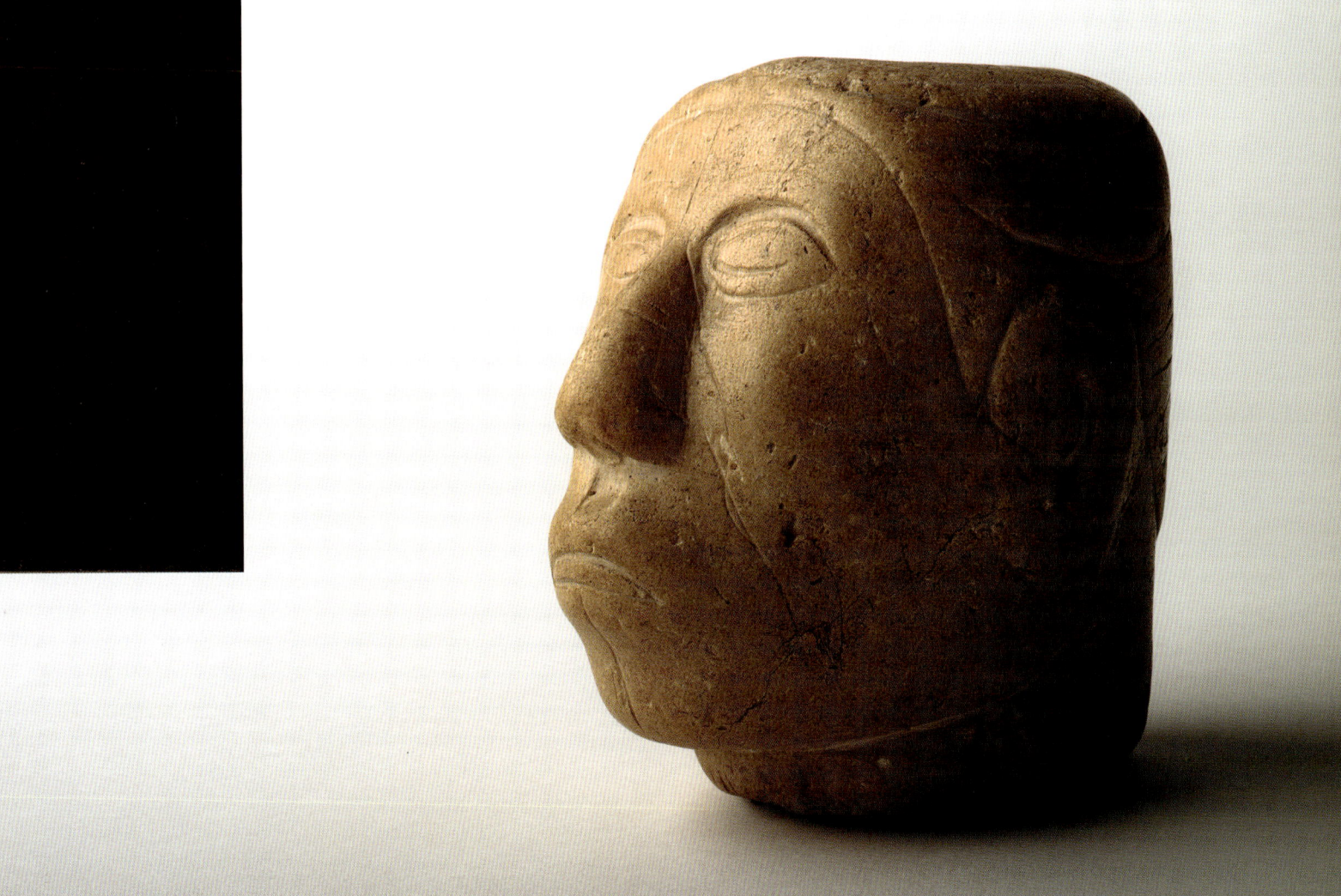

JOHN W. QUINNEY, Charles Bird King.
Oil on wood, 1842. GM 0126.1200

A member of the Stockbridge band of
Mahicans and based in New York, John W.
Quinney led a delegation to Wisconsin in
an effort to purchase lands and relocate
his tribe. While many members made the
move, others did not. When tribal members
arrived at their new home near the Fox
River, they found the Menominee Tribe
had already sold the land to the United
States government. Quinney traveled to
Washington, D.C., in an effort to regain
the lands. Over the course of twenty years,
the Stockbridge tribe and the federal
government signed numerous treaties in
an effort to secure their lands, Quinney
representing his tribe in the discussions. By
1852, with no resolution in sight, Quinney,
by then in his fifties, petitioned to the
government to grant him the deed to his
personal land, giving up his tribal rights
and becoming a citizen of the United States.
George Catlin described Quinney as "a
civilized Indian, well educated—speaking
good English. He is a Baptist missionary
preacher, and a very plausible and eloquent
speaker." In a speech to Congress in 1852,
Quinney referred to himself simply as "a
true Native American."

Muster Roll of Capt. John Benge's Detachment of Emigrating Cherokees —

Sally	"	"	"	"	1	2	"	"	3	3	"	"	3	2
Geo C Lowry	1	1	1	4	1	1	"	"	2	6	"	2	2	8	2
Witch & Wife	1	1	"	2	1	1	"	"	2	4	"	"	4	"
Geo Baldridge	"	"	"	1	1	"	3	1	"	4	5	"	3	3	8	1
James Orr	3	2	"	"	5	2	1	"	"	3	8	"	1	1	9	4
Edward Lea	1	3	1	"	5	1	1	"	"	2	7	"	"	"	7	4
Rising Fawn & Widow	"	"	"	2	1	"	"	"	3	3	"	"	3	3
Moses Lea	"	3	"	3	1	1	"	"	2	5	"	"	5	2
Jefe Lea	"	1	"	1	1	1	"	"	2	3	"	"	3	2
Speaker	3	"	2	2	7	"	"	"	"	7	"	"	7	"
Dick Astring	"	1	"	4	5	"	"	"	5	"	"	5	"
Young Dick	1	2	1	"	4	"	"	"	4	"	"	4	"
E Guater	2	3	2	3	10	"	"	"	10	12	20	32	42	"
Geo Gunter	1	4	1	3	9	"	"	"	9	6	16	22	31	"
Martin Benge	2	2	"	"	4	2	1	"	3	7	"	2	2	9	3
Robt Benge	1	3	1	"	5	1	1	"	2	7	"	"	7	1
Wm Alexander	2	"	"	"	2	1	2	"	3	5	"	"	5	1
Jack Miller	"	1	"	1	2	1	2	"	3	5	"	"	5	5
H Langley	3	2	"	1	6	2	2	"	1	5	11	"	"	11	1
Jas Smith	1	"	"	1	1	1	"	1	2	"	"	2	6
Johnson Smith	1	"	"	1	1	1	"	3	4	"	4	4	8	8
Peter Will	1	1	1	"	3	1	1	"	2	5	"	"	5	4
Young Beaver	4	"	1	"	5	1	3	"	"	4	9	"	"	9	5
Young Chicken	"	"	"	"	1	1	"	"	2	2	"	"	2	"
Chariey	1	2	1	"	4	2	"	"	2	6	"	"	6	"
Corn Tassle	3	1	"	"	4	3	4	"	"	7	11	"	"	11	"
Rising Fawn	2	2	1	1	6	3	2	"	"	5	11	"	"	11	"
Frau McLemore	"	1	"	"	1	1	7	"	"	8	9	"	"	9	5
Turtin Head	1	1	1	"	3	2	2	"	"	4	7	"	"	7	1

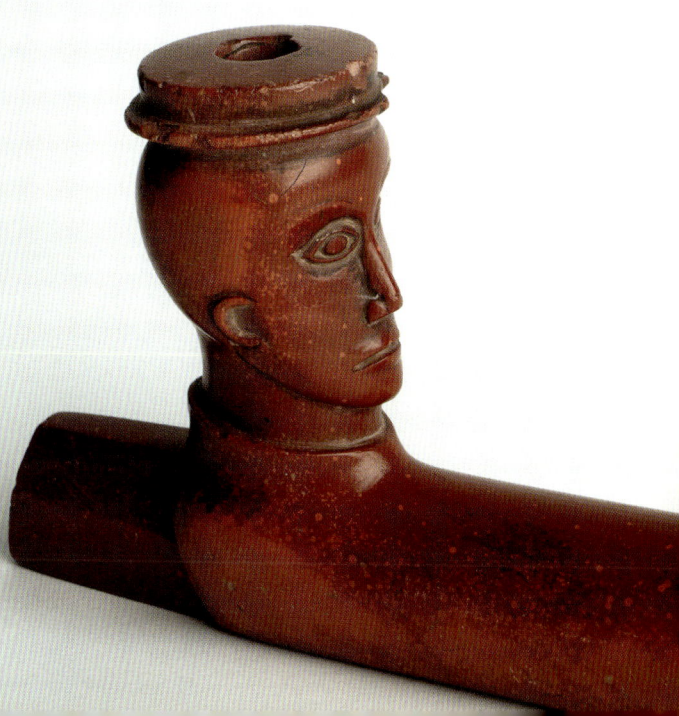

The contradictions described in James Parton's biography of Jackson reflect the deep social, economic, and political divisions among the American people during the general's ascendency and role on the national stage. Jackson's was a life marked by continual conflict, both on the battlefield and in the political arena. Perhaps his greatest conflict, however, lay in the public imagination as "historical actuality imposed little restriction on the creation of the symbolic role the people demanded Andrew Jackson to play."[17] This role was scripted simultaneously by partisan factions on both sides of the Jackson fence. The contradictions exposed during Jackson's presidency belong not so much to the nation's chief executive as to the nation at large. Jackson's ascent to and tenure in the White House revealed and exacerbated a fundamental rift in public thought regarding the status and future of the republic. It revealed profound differences not only in the approach to solving problems but in defining the nature of the problems themselves.

"The symbolic Andrew Jackson is the creation of his time," wrote historian John William Ward in his 1962 study *Andrew Jackson: Symbol for an Age*. "Through the age's leading figure were projected the age's leading ideas. Of Andrew Jackson, the people made a mirror for themselves…the symbol was not the creation of Andrew Jackson… the symbol was a creation of the times. To describe the early 19th century as the age of Jackson misstates the matter. The age was not his. He was the age's."

Andrew Jackson is often regarded as the first modern president, largely because of his dramatic expansion of executive powers, which continue to be exercised by presidents nearly two centuries later. In this way, Jackson's influence continues to reverberate. But in less direct ways, the contradictory turbulence of his persona is also a perennial presence—in the heated political exchanges that erupt in the houses of Congress, in the popular media, and in the arena of public life, in an ever-continuing discourse that seems so often at war with itself.

As historians continue to struggle with the enigma of Jackson's greatness, tempered by his great flaws, we perhaps must also continue to struggle with the greatness, flaws, and contradictions that remain firmly embedded within the character of the national Self.

SYMBOLIZING IDENTITY

People see through the filter of their own circumstances and experiences—including their personal insecurities, ambitions, and desires. Shared rituals, iconic personalities, and meaningful material objects—symbols—distill broad social and political meanings and give individuals an important tool for communicating with each other. The American use of symbols is not unique in the long trajectory of human social life. Yet the varied ways in which Americans have used symbolic communication remain distinct. In the early years of the republic, Americans interpreted the world around them with the aim of promoting their own interests, primarily expansionist desires. These willful ambitions pitted the early 19th-century American Self against a host of foreign Others. The national identity emerged against the array of definitions Americans gave to those Others who stood in the way of American ideals and ambitions. Through the complex language of symbols, the United States conveyed that sense of identity—to the larger world, but even more importantly, to the American people themselves.

NOTES

1. W. Lloyd Warren, *The Living and the Dead: A Study of the Symbolic Life of Americans* (New Haven: Yale University Press, 1959), 524.

2. Journals of Lewis and Clark

3. James P. Ronda, *Finding the West: Explorations with Lewis and Clark.* Albuquerque: University of New Mexico Press, 2001.

4. James P. Ronda, *Jefferson's West: A Journey with Lewis and Clark* (Charlottesville, Virginia: Thomas Jefferson Foundation, 2000).

5. *The Debates and Proceedings in the Congress of the United States. 17th Congress, 1st Session.* ed. Washington: Gales and Seaton, 1855.

6. Thomas Jefferson and Paul Leicester Ford, *The Writings of Thomas Jefferson: 1807-1815* (New York: G.P. Putnam's Sons, 1898).

7. Carl Benn, *The War of 1812* (New York: Routledge, 2003).

8. Thomas Jefferson and Paul Leicester Ford, *The Writings of Thomas Jefferson*, p. 365.

9. Robert Kagan, *Dangerous Nation: America in the World, 1600-1898* (London: Atlantic, 2006).

10. Roger Morriss, *Cockburn and the British Navy in Transition: Admiral Sir George Cockburn, 1772–1853* (Columbia: University of South Carolina Press, 1997).

11. Jon Latimer, *1812: War with America* (Cambridge: Belknap Press of Harvard University Press, 2007).

12. Annals of Congress, Senate, 13th Congress, 3rd Session.

13. Carl Benn, *The War of 1812.*

14. Leland Dewitt Baldwin, *The Meaning of America: Essays toward an Understanding of the American Spirit* (Pittsburgh: University of Pittsburgh Press, 1955).

15. James Parton, *Life of Andrew Jackson: In Three Volumes.* Vol.1 (New York: Mason Brothers, 1860).

16. Jon Meacham, *American Lion: Andrew Jackson in the White House* (New York: Random House, 2008).

17. John William Ward, *Andrew Jackson, Symbol of an Age* (New York: Oxford University Press, 1962).

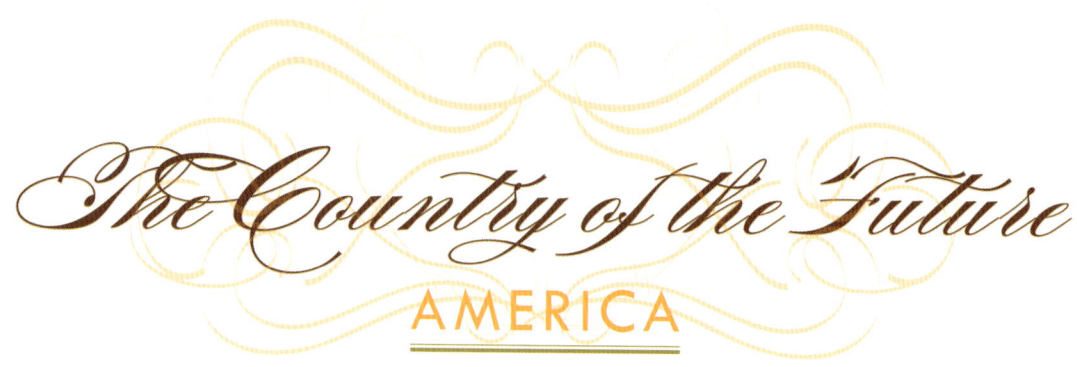

The Country of the Future

AMERICA

IN THE MID-19TH CENTURY

AMANDA LETT

O n a warm summer day in August 1845, Frederick Douglass, an escaped slave turned lecturer, stepped aboard the ship *Cambria*, in the company of James Buffum, an American abolitionist, and the Hutchinson Family Quartet of Singers, all bound for a lecture tour of Great Britain in support of Douglass's recently published *Narrative of the Life of Frederick Douglass*.[1] Before Douglass even embarked, he encountered the ingrained prejudice prevalent throughout the country—originally booked in a stateroom, he was forced to take a room in steerage because of his skin color. As word of his presence on the ship grew, fanned in part by the Hutchinson family who passed out copies of Douglass's *Narrative*, many of the abolitionists aboard pressured the man to give a lecture during the two-week journey.[2] Douglass expressed reservations, due in no small part to the pro-slavery faction on the ship who had not been quiet in venting its hostile displeasure at the celebrity in their midst. Despite the threat of being thrown overboard, Douglass agreed to speak, at the captain's pleasure.[3] The captain, a reformed slaveholder, agreed. However, as the crowd gathered for the afternoon lecture, hecklers attacking Douglass at every turn prevented him from speaking. In an attempt to keep the peace, the Hutchinson family sang hymns and Buffum

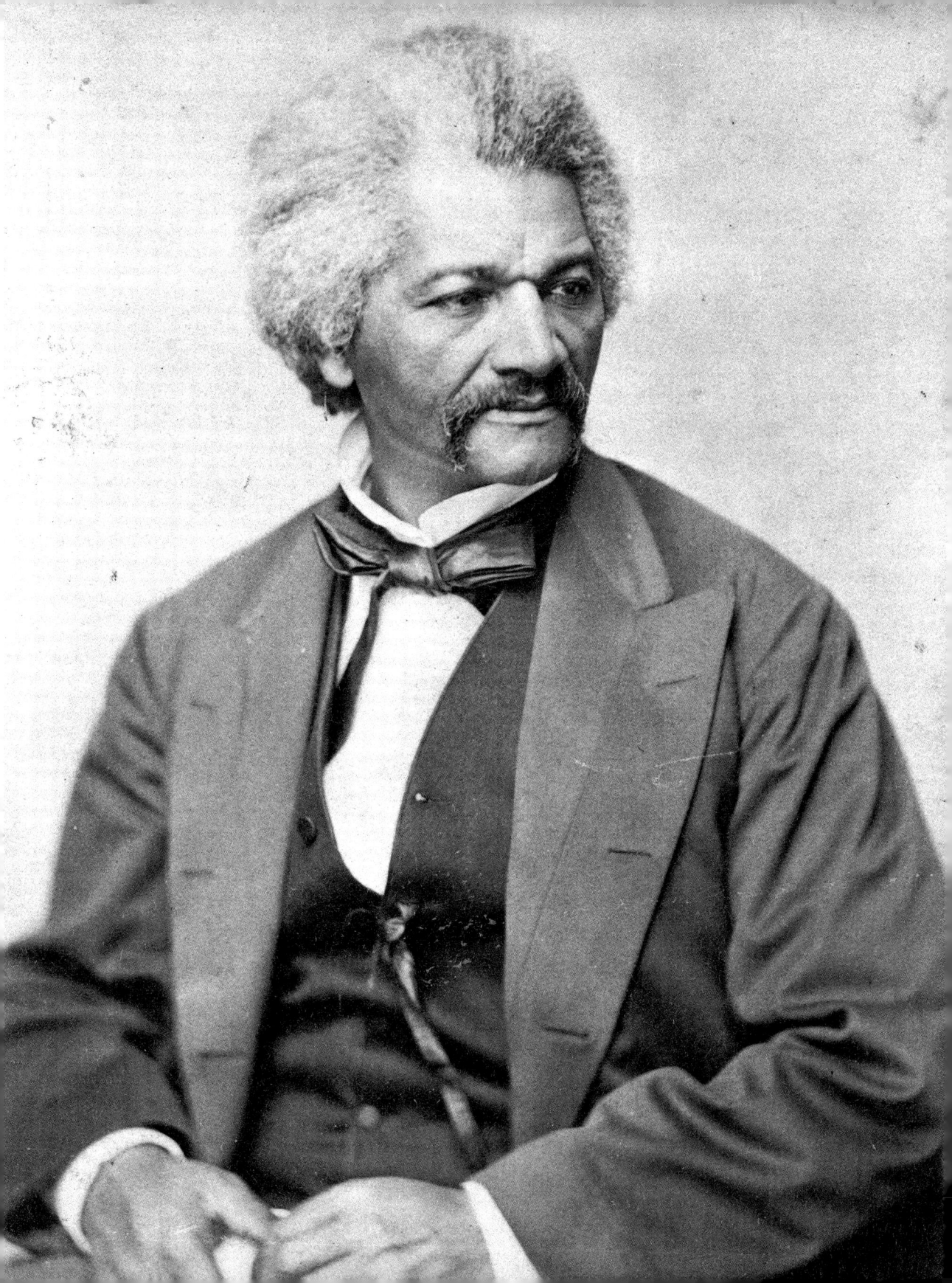

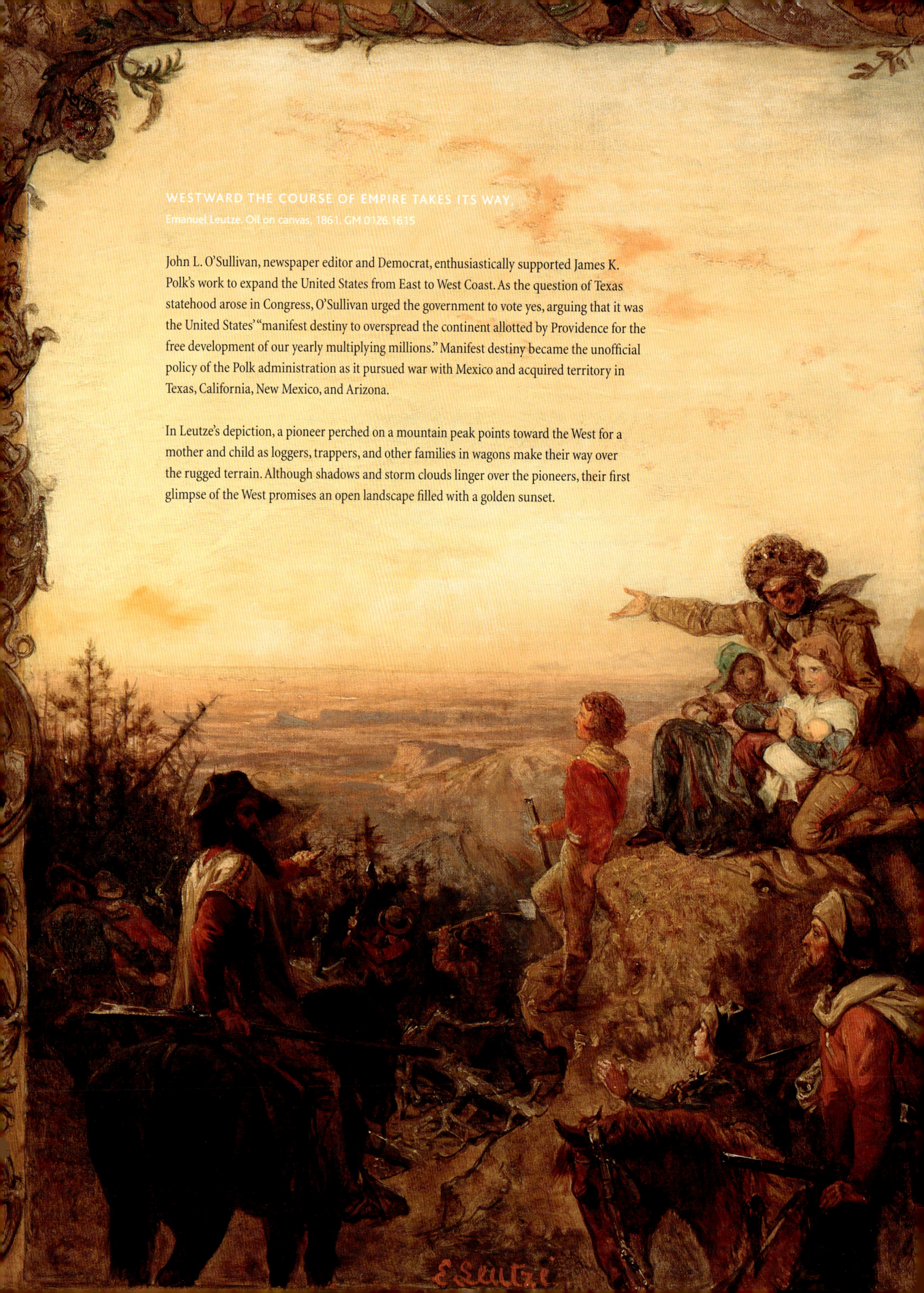

John L. O'Sullivan, newspaper editor and Democrat, enthusiastically supported James K.
Polk's work to expand the United States from East to West Coast. As the question of Texas
statehood arose in Congress, O'Sullivan urged the government to vote yes, arguing that it was
the United States' "manifest destiny to overspread the continent allotted by Providence for the
free development of our yearly multiplying millions." Manifest destiny became the unofficial
policy of the Polk administration as it pursued war with Mexico and acquired territory in
Texas, California, New Mexico, and Arizona.

In Leutze's depiction, a pioneer perched on a mountain peak points toward the West for a
mother and child as loggers, trappers, and other families in wagons make their way over
the rugged terrain. Although shadows and storm clouds linger over the pioneers, their first
glimpse of the West promises an open landscape filled with a golden sunset.

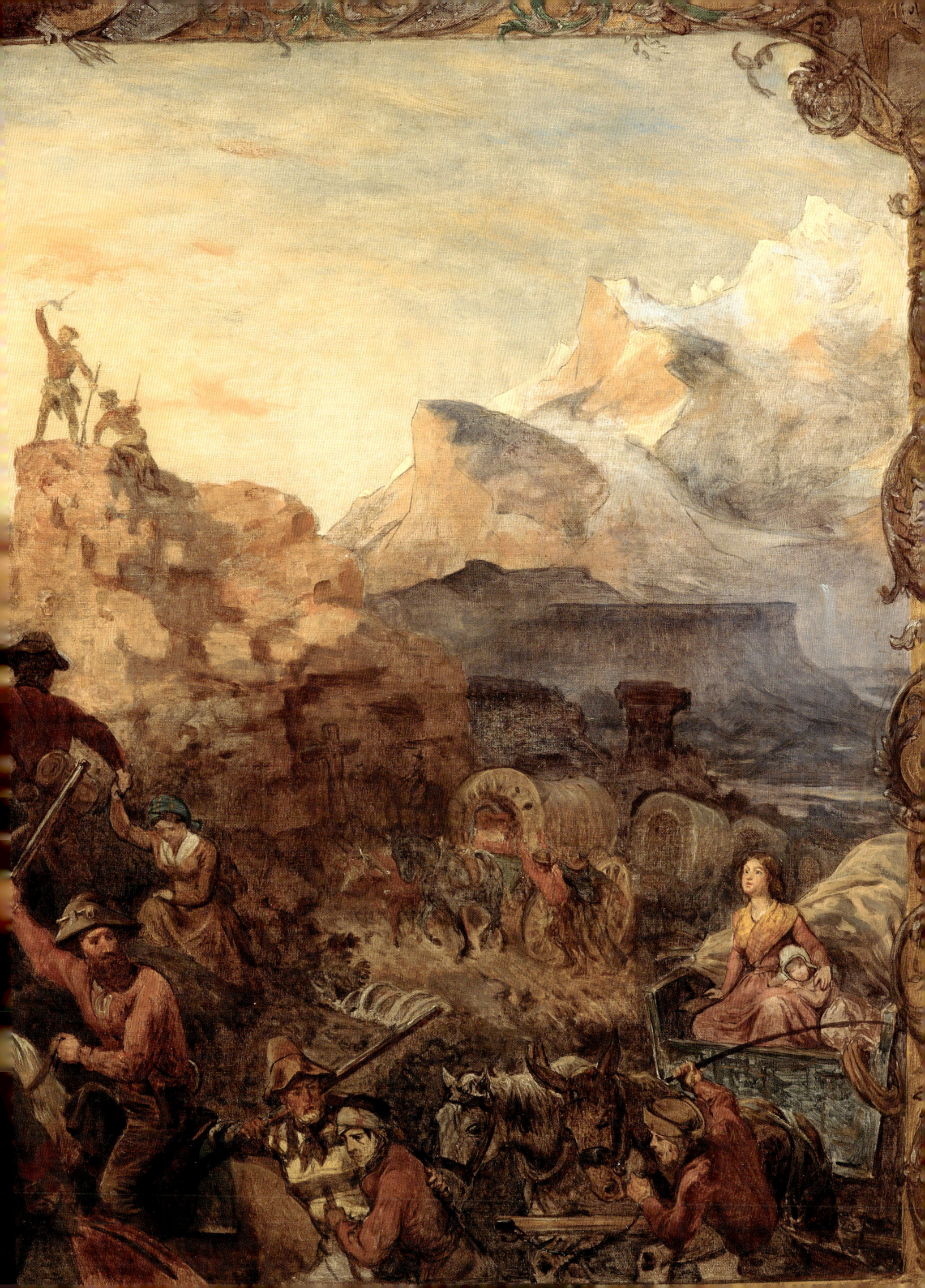

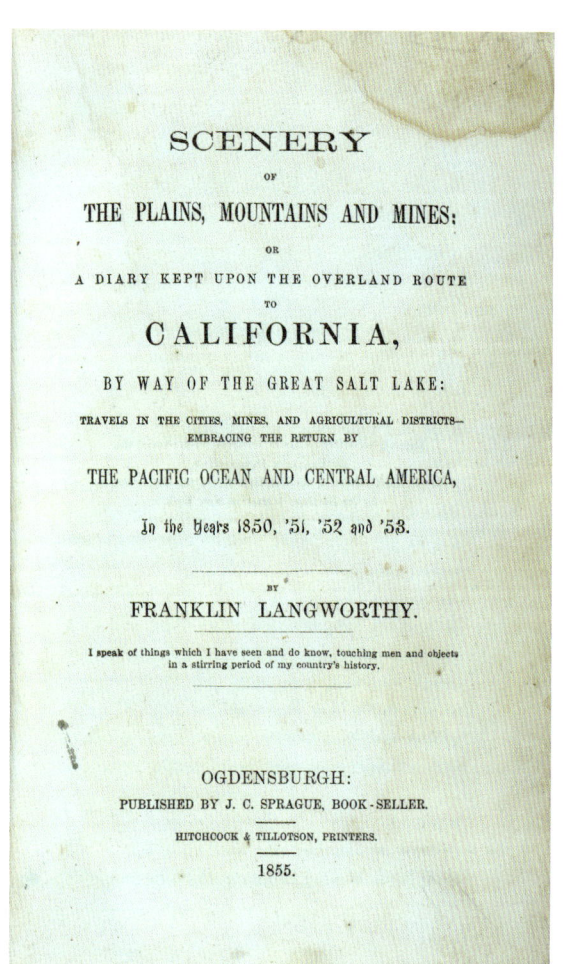

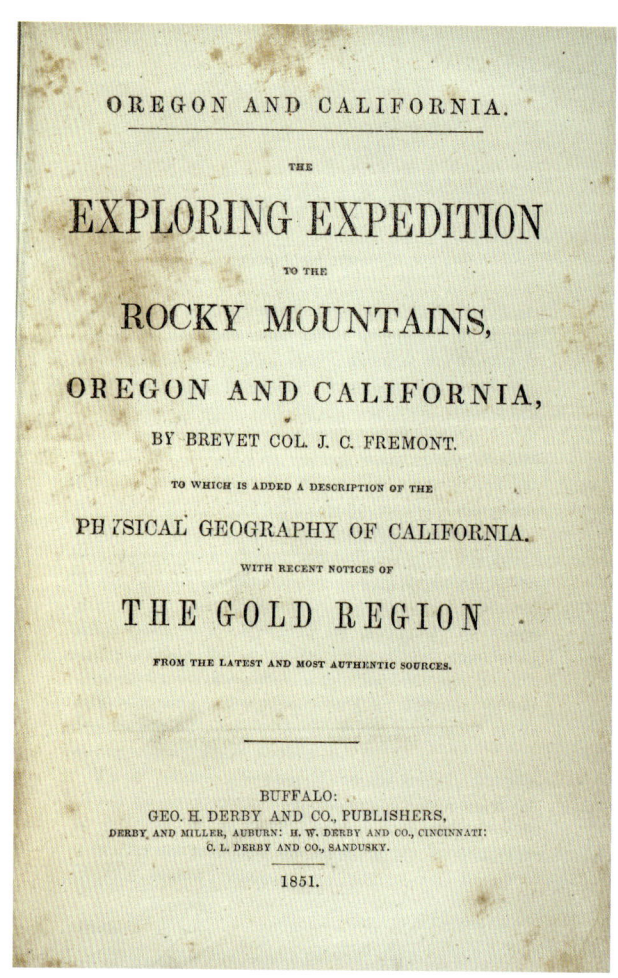

OREGON AND CALIFORNIA,
John Charles Fremont. 1851. GM 2124.77

The acquisition of territory in the Pacific Northwest was a major plank in the Democratic platform of 1844. Shouting the slogan "Fifty-four Forty or Fight!" agitators pressed the United States government to pursue land up to the latitude of the northern boundary with Russia. In quiet negotiations with the British, who claimed that region for themselves, President Polk came to an agreement that established the country's northern boundary at the upper edge of present day Washington State. California, acquired through war with Mexico, completed Polk's march to the Pacific. The new territories generated interest back home and books like Fremont's *Oregon and California* described the new territories to eager readers in the East.

tried to appeal to common decency.[4] In the end, though, only threat of the brig convinced the pro-slavery mob to leave. Douglass finished his lecture to a smaller, yet enthusiastic, crowd. It was an auspicious start to what would be a wildly successful tour, one that secured his freedom in the United States. After Douglass finished his speaking tour of Great Britain, he remarked, "I go back to the United States not as I landed here—I came a slave; I go back a free man; I came here a thing, I go back as a human being."[5] Douglass spoke to an England that had abolished its slave trade nearly forty years earlier. The economic crises that were predicted regarding Britain's trade with her colonies did not come to pass, and the formerly enslaved people who were now British subjects certainly proved to be just as loyal as her other subjects.[6] But in the United States, these arguments were more nuanced. In areas where the economy was more industrialized, the abolition movement seemed to flourish, yet a good portion of the nation, more agriculturally based, depended on slavery as the backbone of its economy. Both sides of the argument were represented on the *Cambria*.

In the two decades leading to the Civil War, the westward momentum of the United States sparked confrontations with other countries in both the Pacific Northwest and in the Southwest. Manifest Destiny—the 19th-century belief that the United States was destined to spread from ocean to ocean—was no longer a philosophical concept but an active pursuit. Innovations in communication and transportation, including the telegraph and the railroad, meant that Americans knew what was happening in the world faster than ever and had the freedom to move around the country in a new way. At the same time, everyday people concerned themselves with another, social frontier. Movements intended to better mankind—and indeed, the nation—sprang up in parlors, churches, and lecture halls across the country, using advancements in communication to spread their messages. While these groups enriched many lives and inspired thousands to agitate for women's rights, abolition, and temperance, they also further divided the nation ideologically. The political landscape, already contentious, also divided the United States as Whigs and Democrats moved further from each other, sharing less common ground. As the country added territory and expanded its reach, the visions for two very different countries with competing goals emerged. While views differed, what underlay them was the same—an optimistic belief that ordinary citizens could shape the nation and its future. Despite raucous political times, the new social goals of Americans would change the way we thought of ourselves not only in the 1840s, but well into the 20th century and beyond.

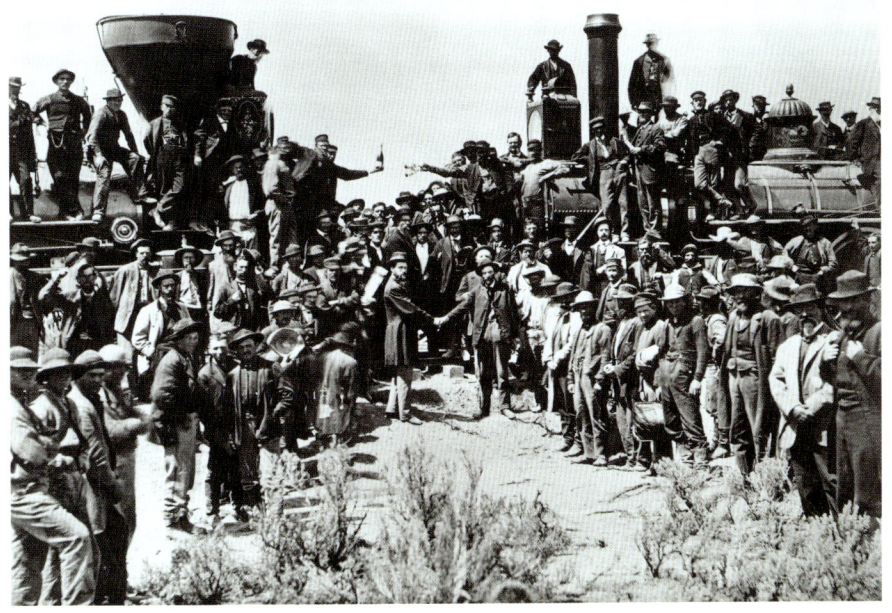

EAST AND WEST SHAKE HANDS.
Photograph. GM 4316.3314

The transcontinental railroad was built by two separate companies: The Union Pacific Railroad and the Central Pacific Railroad. At the height of construction nearly 10,000 ex-soldiers, ex-convicts, and Irish immigrants worked alongside an equal number of draft animals laying track for the railroads for the Union Pacific Railroad. The Central Pacific employed 12,000 Chinese laborers, which constituted 90 percent of its workforce. The Transcontinental Railroad was completed in 1869, just six years after it had begun. Workers met at Promontory Summit, Utah, on May 10 to officially drive in the last stake.

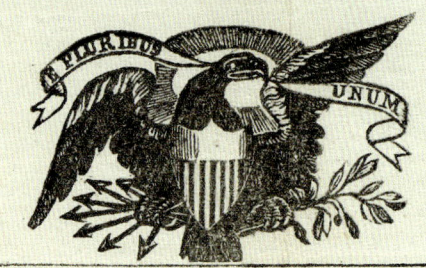

By the President of the United States of America.

A PROCLAMATION.

Whereas the Congress of the United States, by virtue of the constitutional authority vested in them, have declared by their act, bearing date this day, that, "by the act of the republic of Mexico, a state of war exists between that government and the United States:"

Now, therefore, I, JAMES K. POLK, President of the United States of America, do hereby proclaim the same to all whom it may concern; and I do specially enjoin on all persons holding offices, civil or military, under the authority of the United States, that they be vigilant and zealous in discharging the duties respectively incident thereto : and I do moreover exhort all the good people of the United States, as they love their country, as they feel the wrongs which have forced on them the last resort of injured nations, and as they consult the best means, under the blessing of Divine Providence, of abridging its calamities, that they exert themselves in preserving order, in promoting concord, in maintaining the authority and the efficacy of the laws, and in supporting and invigorating all the measures which may be adopted by the constituted authorities for obtaining a speedy, a just, and an honorable peace.

In testimony whereof, I have hereunto set my hand, and caused the seal of the United States to be affixed to [L. S.] these presents. Done at the city of Washington the thirteenth day of May, one thousand eight hundred and forty-six, and of the independence of the United States the seventieth.

JAMES K. POLK.

By the President :
JAMES BUCHANAN,
Secretary of State.

PROCLAMATION DECLARING A STATE OF WAR BETWEEN THE UNITED STATES AND MEXICO, MAY 10, 1846. GM 3526.257

When the United States annexed Texas in 1845, the boundary between the new territory and Mexico was the Nueces River. Many Texans argued that the boundary should be the Rio Grande River, allowing Texans to expand their farmlands and encourage settlement. The flame was fanned by the newspapers of the day that described the full annexation of Texas as a part of the United States' "manifest destiny" to, in their opinion, turn unused land into productive farms and cities. On April 24, 1846, an American unit performing reconnaissance work in the Mexican territory along the Rio Grande River was surrounded by Mexican forces. The Mexican army allowed one soldier to leave in order to inform General Zachary Taylor of the news. General Taylor reported to Washington that "Hostilities may now be considered as commenced." This minor skirmish signaled the beginning of the Mexican-American War.

JAMES K. POLK, Johnson Fry & Co. Engraving, 1862. GM 1526.951

Democrat James K. Polk, a protégé of Andrew Jackson, believed the future of America lay westward. Polk promised in his 1844 inaugural address to pursue territory in the Pacific Northwest and in Texas, and he largely accomplished his political goals in his one term as president, expanding the nation from the Atlantic to the Pacific. A controversial figure, Polk frequently clashed with Whig members of Congress who accused him of fighting an unfounded war against Mexico and of expanding his powers beyond their scope. In return, Polk was suspicious of the political leanings of his generals, especially Winfield Scott and Zachary Taylor, the heroes of the Mexican War, and actively campaigned against them.

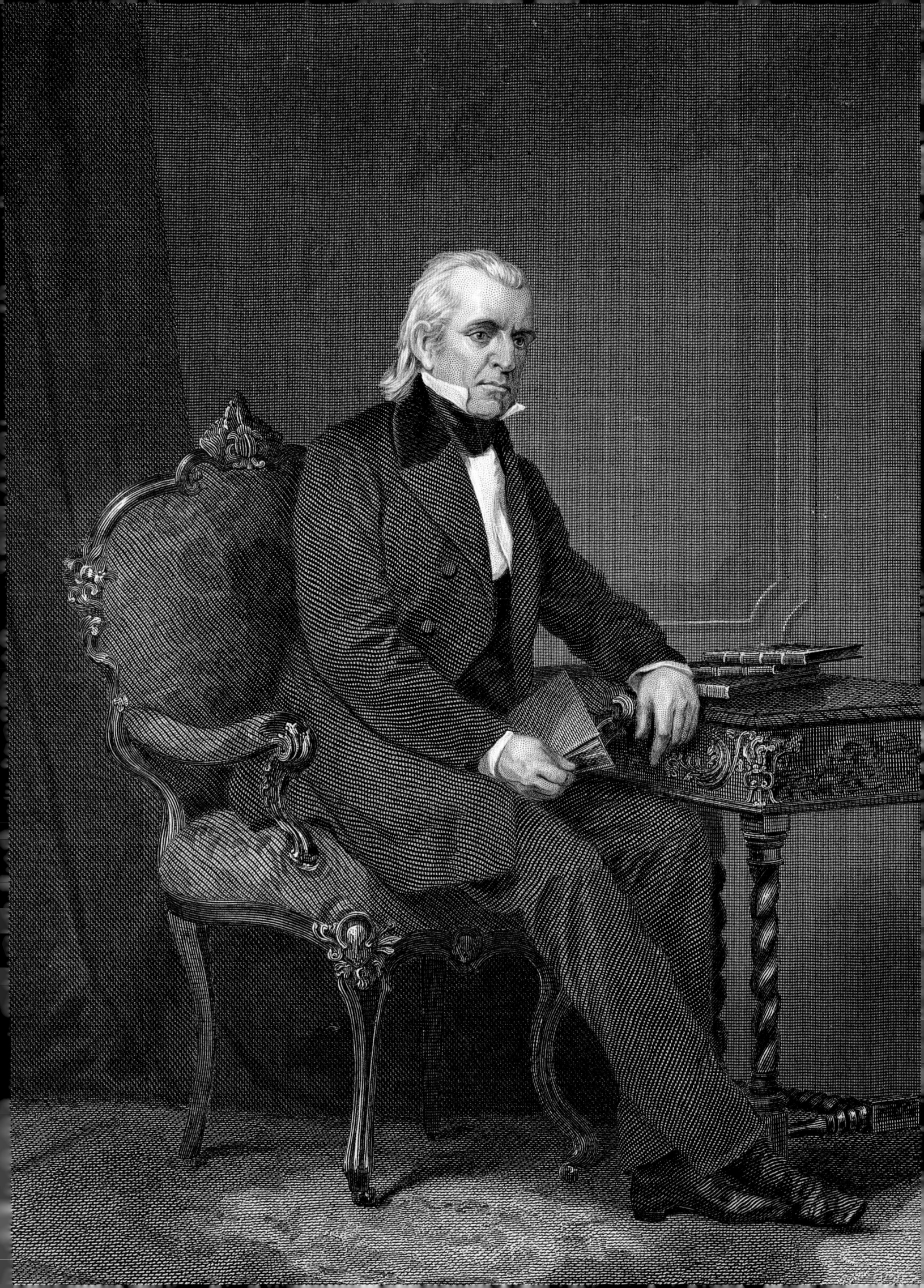

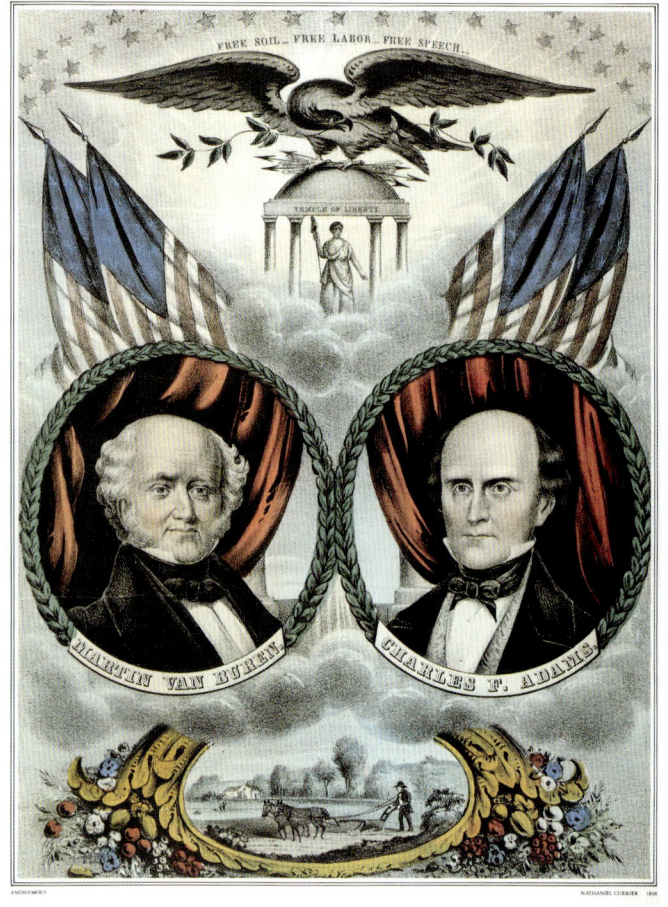

At the heart of the division in American life was politics. Whigs, led by Henry Clay, and Democrats, led by John C. Calhoun, squabbled over issues like the national bank, national planning, expansionism, and slavery. In effect, these differences of opinion masked a deeper, fundamental issue that would eventually divide them and the country—a differing view of the world. Democrats, while not opposing opportunities for economic growth that were favorable to farmers, were still very much tied to the idea of an agriculturally based America, rooted in the values of Thomas Jefferson and the founding fathers.[7] Democrats felt that America's strength lay in its agricultural roots, especially as new lands were acquired. Whigs, on the other hand, felt that the future lay in diversifying the economy. This included agriculture, but also industry and new technologies. They felt they had a

GRAND DEMOCRATIC FREE SOIL BANNER,
Nathaniel Currier. Lithograph, 1848. GM 16.967

moral obligation to better the nation through education, economic development, and social reform.[8] As historian Daniel Howe notes, the "extension of the nation's boundaries appealed to them little unless it promised economic development."[9]

These tensions were brought to the fore under the James K. Polk administration. President Polk's handling of the Oregon Territory question, as well as the pursuit of the Mexican War, divided many in both parties. A protégé of Andrew Jackson, Polk was elected in 1844 and made it clear that he would work for claims in both Oregon and Texas, arguing "wherever Americans choose to settle, the federal government should extend its protection over them."[10] Supporting him were land speculators, farmers looking for better lands, industrialists interested in economic expansion, those who feared Catholic encroachment into the United States, and many who wanted to expand slavery's reach.[11] While the settlement with Britain, not without its own controversy, ended peacefully and resulted in a gain of both present day Oregon and Washington states, a more bellicose approach was applied to Mexico. On May 10, 1846, after an initial skirmish begun by American troops—

yet blamed on the Mexican army—war was declared. A few days later, General Zachary Taylor and his men, with their superior firepower, crossed the Rio Grande River into Mexican territory and subdued the city of Matamoros.[12] The United States' skill with advanced weaponry and tactics resulted in victories at places like Palo Alto, the previously impenetrable Gulf fortress at Vera Cruz, and Buena Vista, site of the largest battle of the war.[13] With leaders like General Taylor and General Winfield Scott, and talented lieutenants like James Longstreet and Ulysses S. Grant, the Americans were able to defeat a much larger army, although at great expense, both in terms of money and blood, over the course of the two-year war.[14] The war sparked dissent, even among officers. The key generals, Taylor and Scott, were Whigs, opposed to Polk's party, and were viewed with suspicion by the Democratic president, who feared the conflict would create heroic soldiers turned Whig politicians. Ethan Hitchcock, a lieutenant colonel, wrote in his diary, "We have not one particle of right to be here. It looks as if the government sent a small force on purpose to bring on a war, so as to have a pretext for taking California and as much of this country as it chooses."[15] This dissent, however, did not keep American forces from pursuing the war.

On February 2, 1848, Nicholas Trist, under orders from Polk, worked with the Mexican government to secure a peace treaty acceptable to both Mexico and the United States. The terms were harsh. Mexico, in return for an end to hostilities and the sum of $15 million dollars, ceded California, New Mexico, and all of Texas north of the Rio Grande.[16] Trist hoped the treaty would mollify Democrats in Congress and be "as little exacting as possible from Mexico," due to his feelings on "the iniquity of the war."[17] Although publically displeased with the treaty, Polk submitted it to Congress, and it was ratified in March of 1848. Whigs bitterly

SERVICE REVOLVER.
Metal, wood, ca. 1850s.
GM 61.63

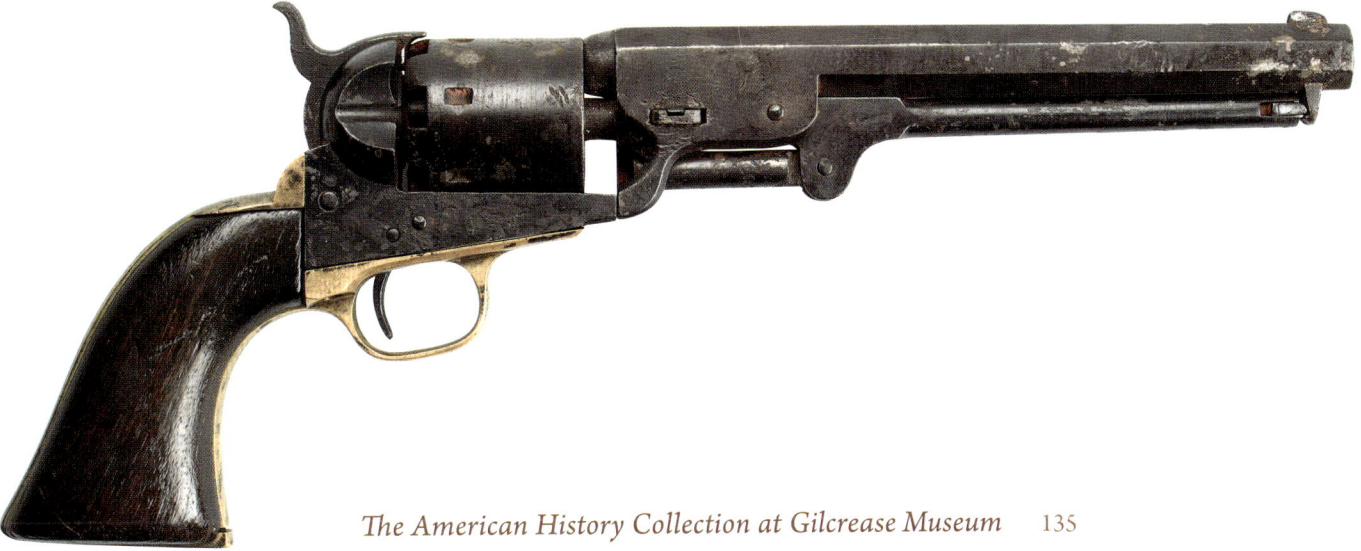

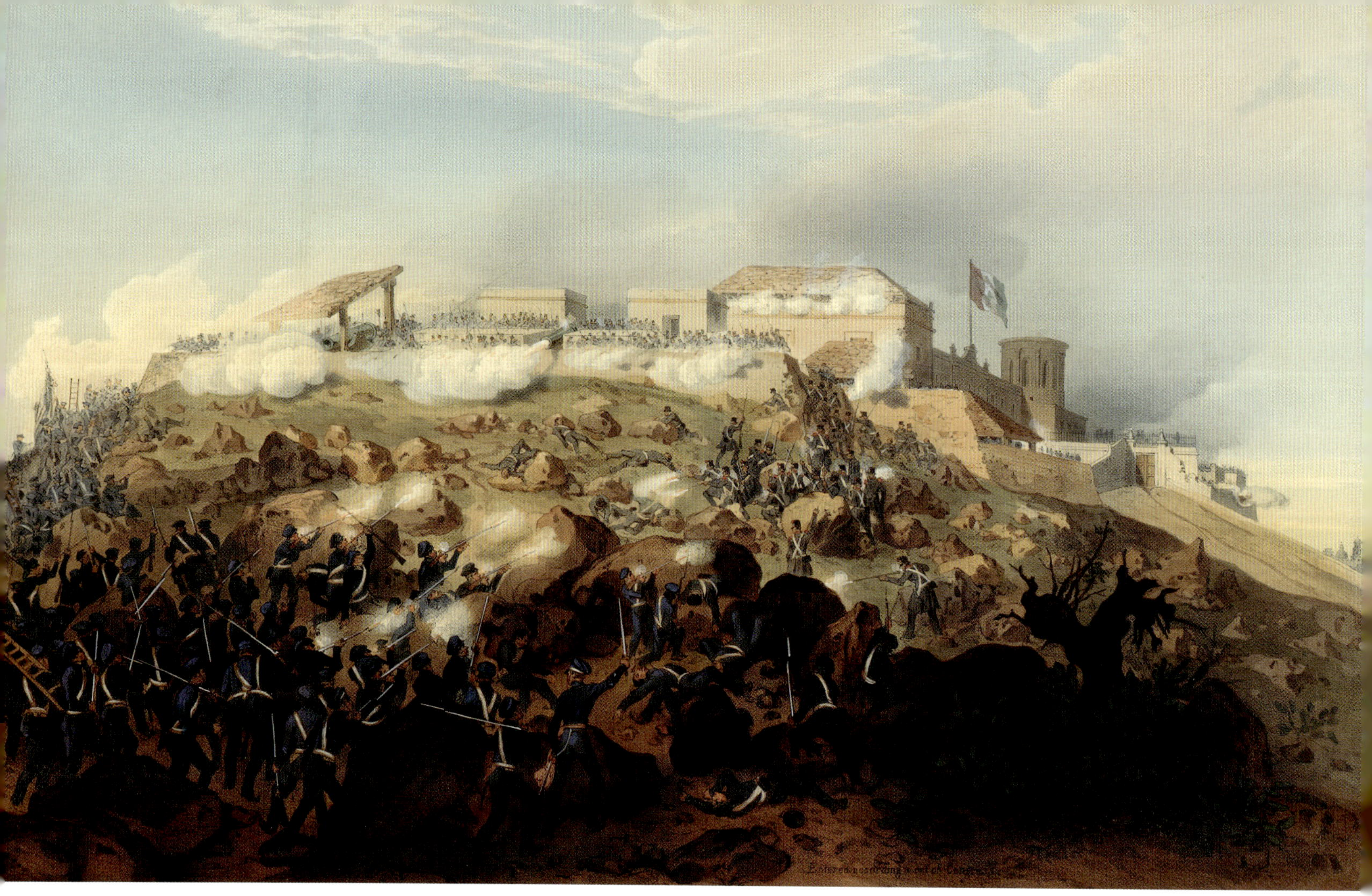

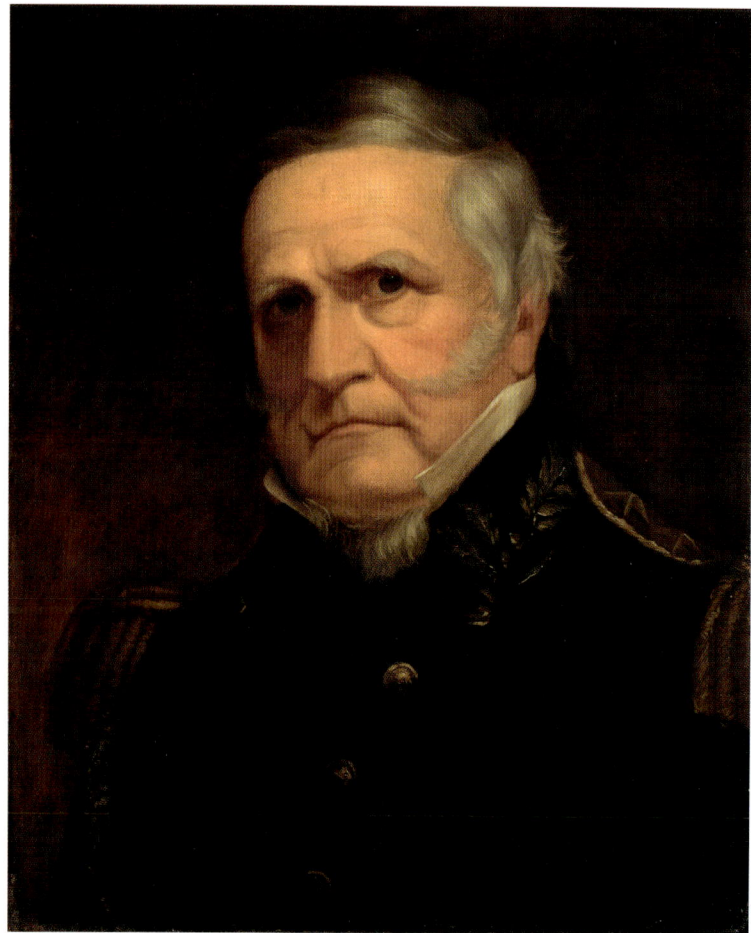

BOMBARDMENT AT VERA CRUZ.
From *The War Between the United States and Mexico Illustrated*, by Carl Nebel, 1851. GM 2526.3008a

PORTRAIT OF GENERAL WINFIELD SCOTT,
unknown artist. Oil on canvas. GM 01.1540

Winfield Scott, known as "Old Fuss n' Feathers" to his men, served as general in three American wars—the War of 1812, the Mexican War, and the Civil War. Politically a Whig, Scott earned the trust of his men through his tactical expertise and judgement in the heat of battle. Scott also earned high praise from his peers. The Duke of Wellington, the British hero of the Napoleonic Wars, declared Scott "the greatest living soldier." As commander of the largest amphibious assault the United States would undertake until D-Day, Scott led his men in taking the Mexican fortress city of Vera Cruz, previously thought impenetrable. They then marched onward to Mexico City. Although he was a Virginian, Scott felt his loyalty lay with the federal government and so served on the Union side.

opposed the war and cited its dubious start, the loss of life, and the possibility that the slave trade could expand into new territories as reasons to end the war and take no territory from the Mexican government. Polk persevered, stating that while the new territory "remained of little value" to the Mexicans, "as part of our Union they will be productive of vast benefits to the United States."[18] Despite Polk's victory, the legacy of the Mexican-American War for the United States was its impact on the growth of slavery. Would these new territories accept slavery, or would they ban it? Americans became increasingly divided over that sentiment throughout the 1850s.

VIEW IN THE RUINS OF THE ALAMO.

From *Historical Collections of the Great West,* by Henry Howe, 1851. GM 2526.1548

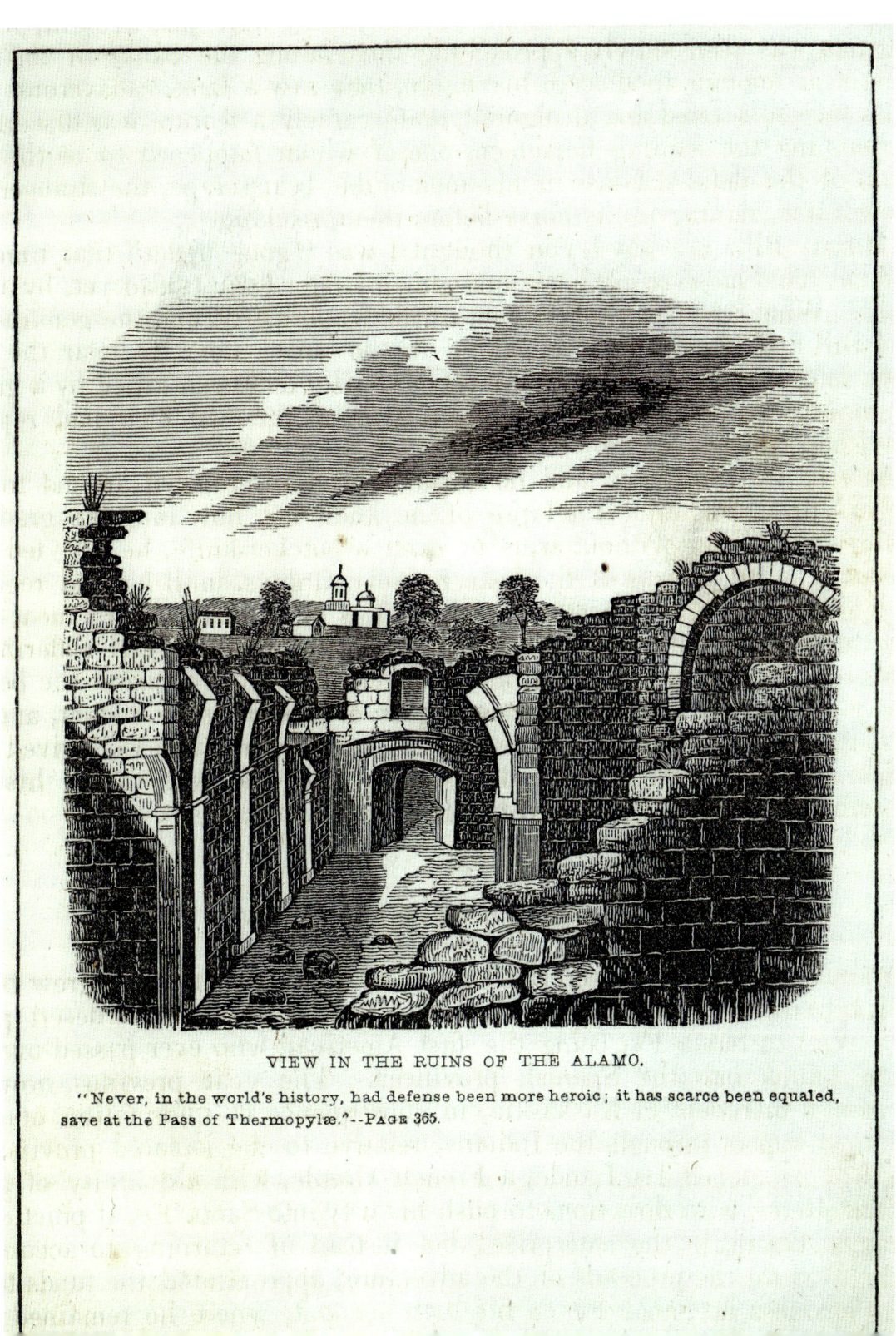

VIEW IN THE RUINS OF THE ALAMO.

"Never, in the world's history, had defense been more heroic; it has scarce been equaled, save at the Pass of Thermopylæ."--PAGE 365.

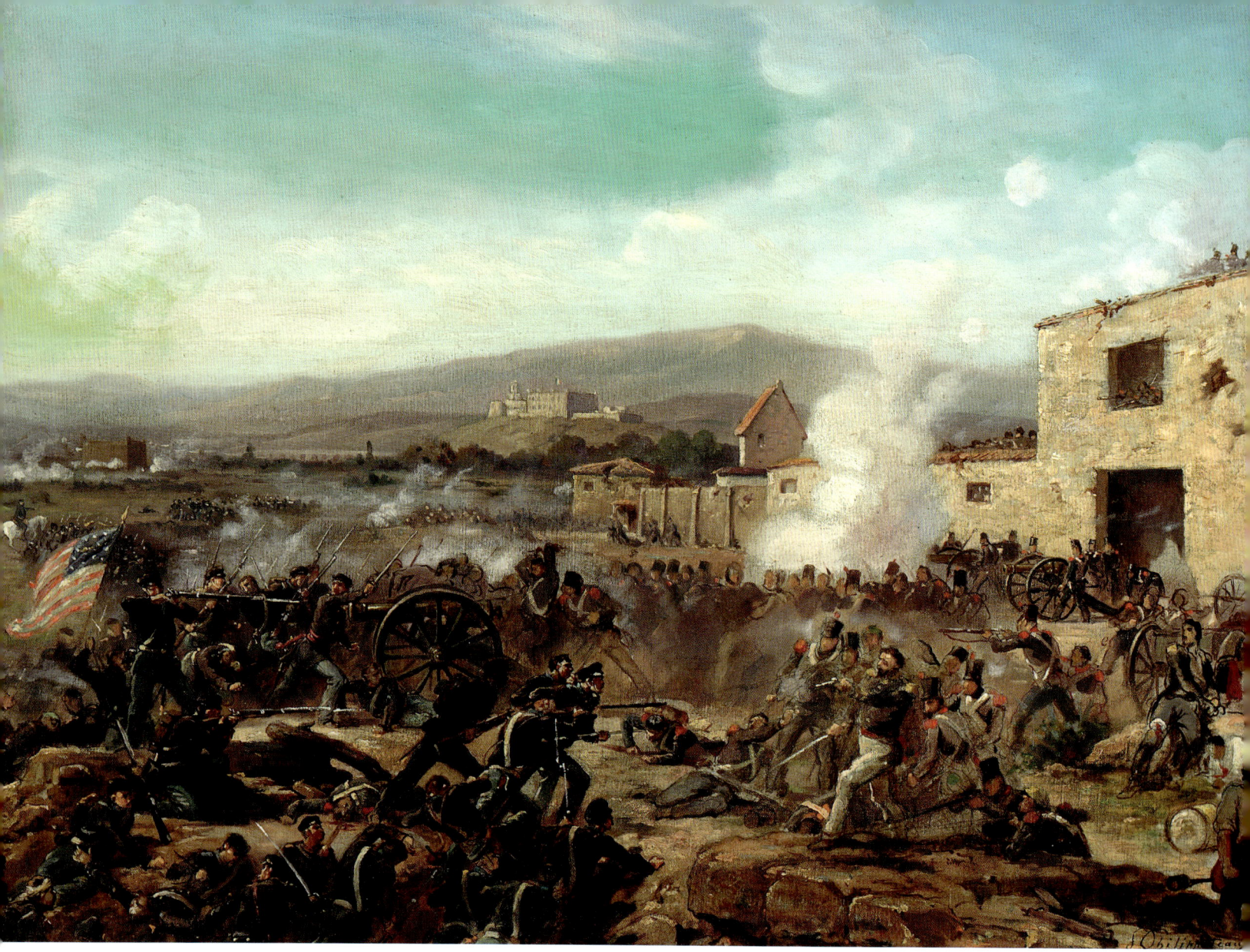

THE BATTLE OF BUENA VISTA,
James Walker. Oil on canvas. GM 0126.1633

Over the course of the three-day battle later called the Battle of Buena Vista, General Zachary Taylor and his men—including a battalion lead by Jefferson Davis—faced a much larger Mexican army lead by General Santa Anna. While the American forces had a technological advantage over their Mexican counterparts, superior numbers on the Mexican side meant that fighting was intense and casualties high. At one point, Taylor left the battle to check on troops at another position. When he was informed upon his return that the battle was lost, Taylor replied, "That is for me to determine." In the end, exhaustion, hunger, and a lack of supplies led the Mexican troops to retreat, handing victory to the Americans.

GENERAL D. ANTONIO LOPEZ DE SANTA ANNA,
Alfred Hoffy. Color lithograph, 1847. GM 1526.83

Elected president of Mexico in 1833 and serving numerous non-consecutive terms, General D. Antonio Lopez de Santa Anna influenced Mexican politics for much of the 19th century, coming into conflict as often with his American neighbors to the north as he did his own countrymen. Infamous in the United States for his attack on the Alamo mission during the Texas Revolution, Santa Anna would once again face American forces during the U. S.-Mexican War. Despite promises that he would work to end the war and sell all disputed territory to the United States, Santa Anna marched on Mexico City and declared himself president, immediately launching new offenses against the American army. After the defeat at Mexico City and the loss of large amounts of territory to the U. S., the self-styled "Napoleon of the West" went into exile, reappearing sporadically on the political scene with little success until his death in 1876.

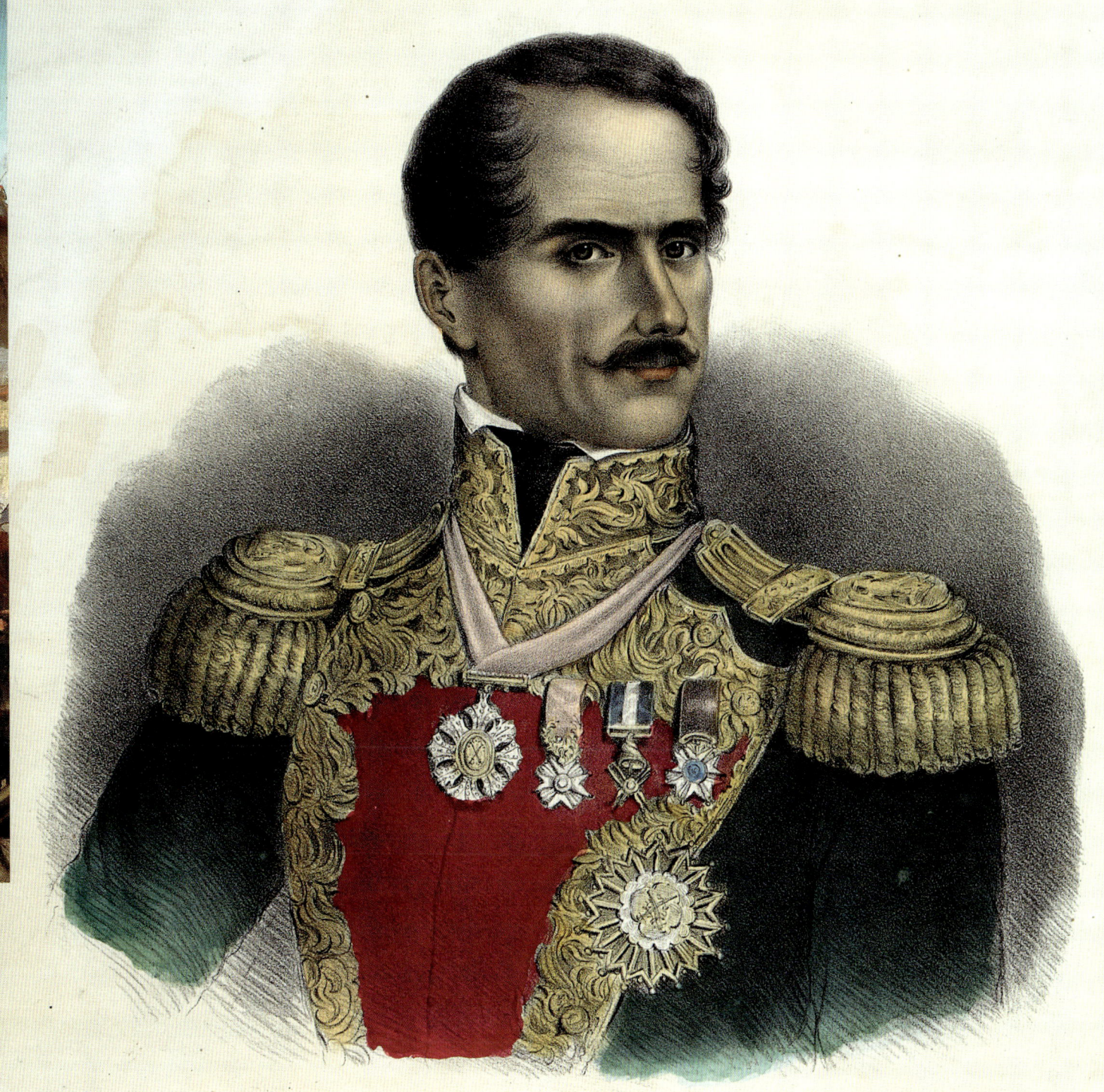

GENERAL D. ANTONIO LOPEZ DE SANTA-ANNA,

PRESIDENT OF THE REPUBLIC OF MEXICO.

By **A. Hoffy**, from an original likeness taken from life at **Vera-Cruz.**

The above is a correct likeness from our personal observation

E. W. Moore
Com'late Texas Navy.

Alex. C Blount.

Published July 1847, by **A. HOFFY**, N°. 20, South, Third S.t near Chesnut, Philad.ª

& by **JOHNSON & BROCKETT**, N°. 28, South Seventh S.t bet. Chesnut & Walnut.

Entered according to act of Congress in the year 1847, by A. Hoffy, & Johnson & Brockett, in the Clerks office of the district Court of the Eastern district of Pennsyl.ª

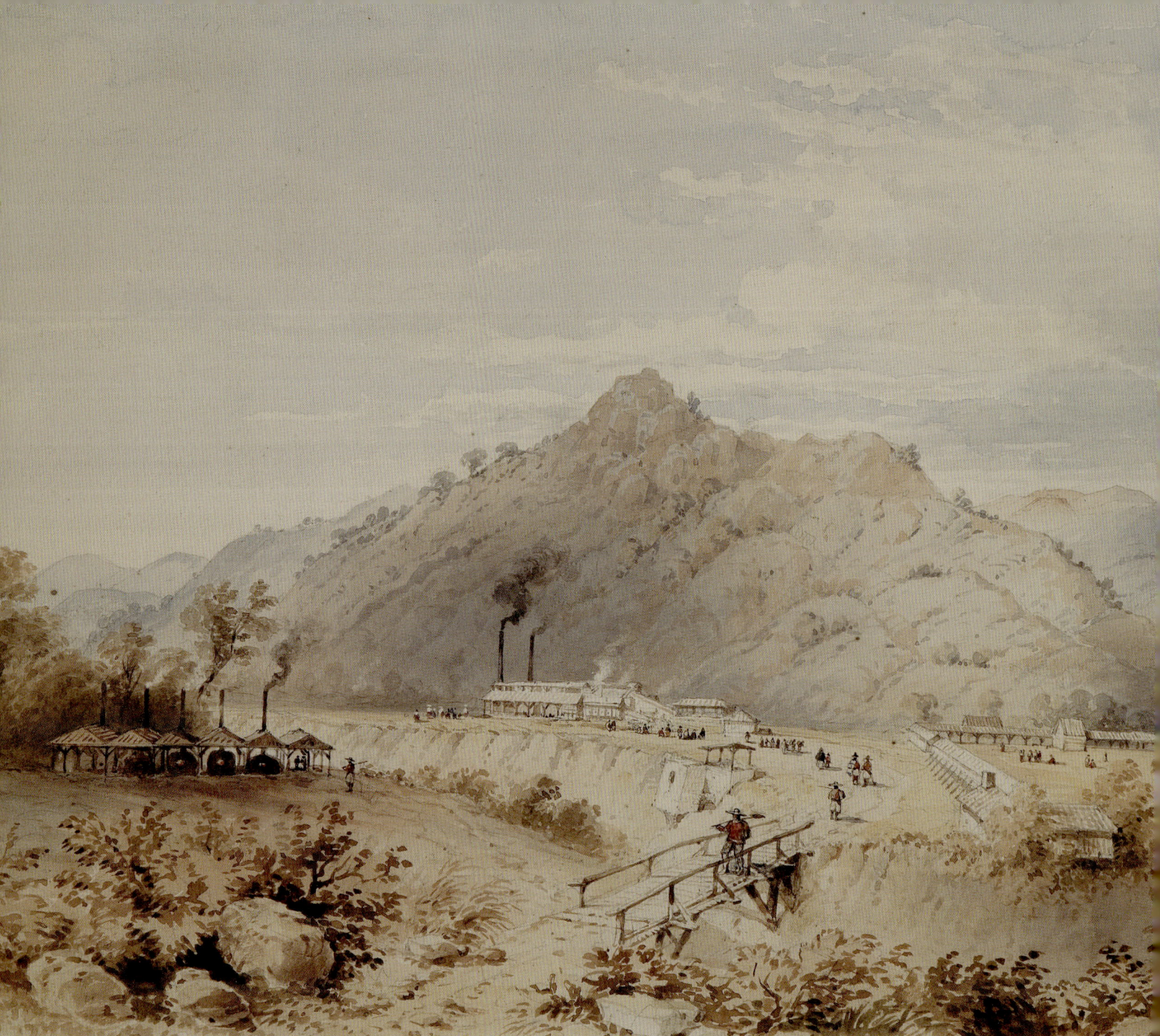

GOLD MINING IN CALIFORNIA,
Frederick Edwin Church. Watercolor.
GM 0236.1438

FACING: CRESCENT SILVER
COMPANY STOCK CERTIFICATE.
GM 5316.1199

FACING: SUTTER'S MILL. From *Historical Collections of the Great West,*
by Henry Howe, 1851. GM 2526.1548

On January 4, 1848, gold was discovered at Johann Sutter's mill outside of present-day
Coloma, California. By the end of the year, with victory over Mexico secured, President
James K. Polk proudly announced in his annual message that "The accounts of the
abundance of gold in that territory are of such an extraordinary character as would
scarcely command belief." Within a year miners had extracted over $10 million worth
of gold, increasing the value of U. S. currency. By 1851, that amount would grow to over
$200 million. Settlers began pouring into California territory, lured by the promise of
quick riches. Boom towns sprang up rapidly, many exemplifying the worst excesses of
life in the West. Encroachment on Native American lands, violence, and lawlessness
helped to foster the myth of the "Wild West" far beyond the reaches of "civilized" life.

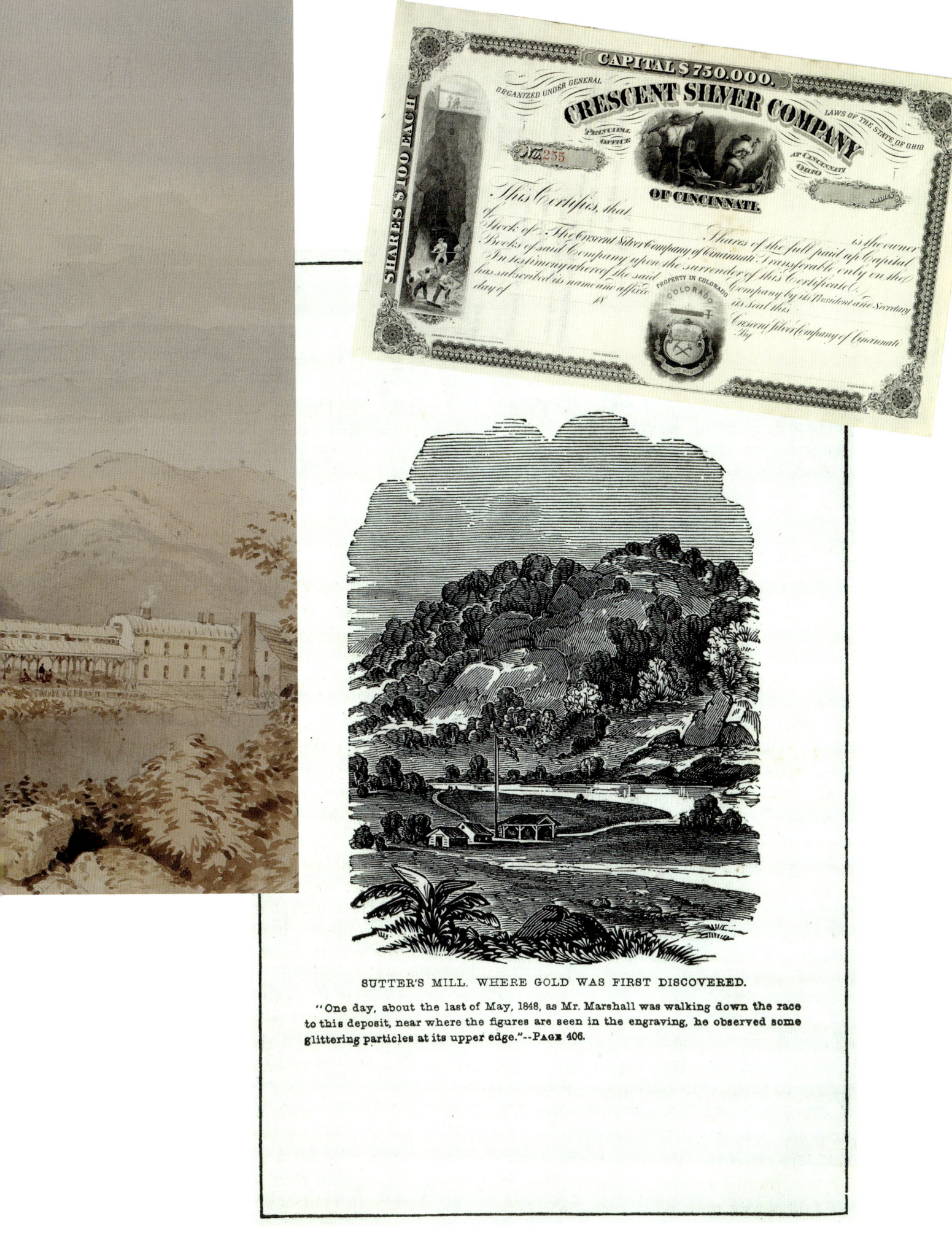

SUTTER'S MILL, WHERE GOLD WAS FIRST DISCOVERED.

"One day, about the last of May, 1848, as Mr. Marshall was walking down the race to this deposit, near where the figures are seen in the engraving, he observed some glittering particles at its upper edge."--PAGE 406.

JENNY LIND.
Johnson, Fry & Co.
Engraving. GM 1526.989

When Jenny Lind, "The
Swedish Nightingale,"
toured the United States in
the 1850s, she was one of
the most famous singers
of her day. She came to
America in response to
a lucrative offer from
P. T. Barnum, and the
entertainment maestro
mounted such a massive
publicity campaign prior
to her ninety-three–venue
tour that Lind became
a household name. The
singer won over American
audiences with her talent
and her commitment to
charity—much of her
proceeds went to various
churches in the cities in
which she performed.
She proved so popular,
in fact, that so-called
"Lindomania" broke
out, and manufacturers
attached her name to
hundreds of products in
their advertising, hoping to
cash in on her notoriety.

Despite the war and increasingly partisan politics, immediate social concerns engaged the average American. Itinerant lecturers expounded on every possible point of view, capturing the imaginations of many.[19] Indeed, fads for every sort of movement, from temperance to hypnotism, gripped the nation. Many of these movements had a fundamentally religious base, rooted in the deep confidence in divine Providence nearly universal at this time. The belief that Americans were a "chosen people," able to witness Providence manifest itself, spurred citizens to act according to their faith.[20] Evangelicals, for example, believed that because they had been saved, they, in turn, were called to save the world by changing society.[21] Faith influenced everything from revival movements to the Transcendentalists, but also informed the temperance, women's, and abolitionist movements. Ralph Waldo Emerson, in his first book of essays, wrote,

"O my brothers, God exists. There is a soul at the centre of nature, and over the will of every man, so that none of us can wrong the universe. It has so infused its strong enchantment into nature, that we prosper when we accept its advice, and when we struggle to wound its creatures, our hands are glued to our sides, or they beat our own breasts. The whole course of things goes to teach us faith. We need only to obey."[22]

Emerson and his fellow Transcendentalists, although outside mainstream belief, still felt the pull of Providence, allowing that those who followed God's will prospered spiritually, while those who did not struggled against themselves. John O'Sullivan, editor of the *United States Magazine and Democratic Review*, described America's westward expansion as "our manifest destiny to overspread the continent allotted by Providence for the free development of our yearly multiplying millions."[23] Even in the face of everyday tragedy, average Americans obeyed "the will of divine Providence." Thomas Hayter, a young man living in Oregon Territory, sent word home to his sister that their father and another brother had passed away. In his letter, he resigned himself to these losses and reminded his sister, "it has pleased the good Lord to Remove them and I Can but Submit and say His Will Be Done."[24] Considerations of faith informed early 19th-century American life from governmental policy to expressions of personal grief and higher philosophical thought. These expressions of faith would find an outlet in other, unexpected sources.

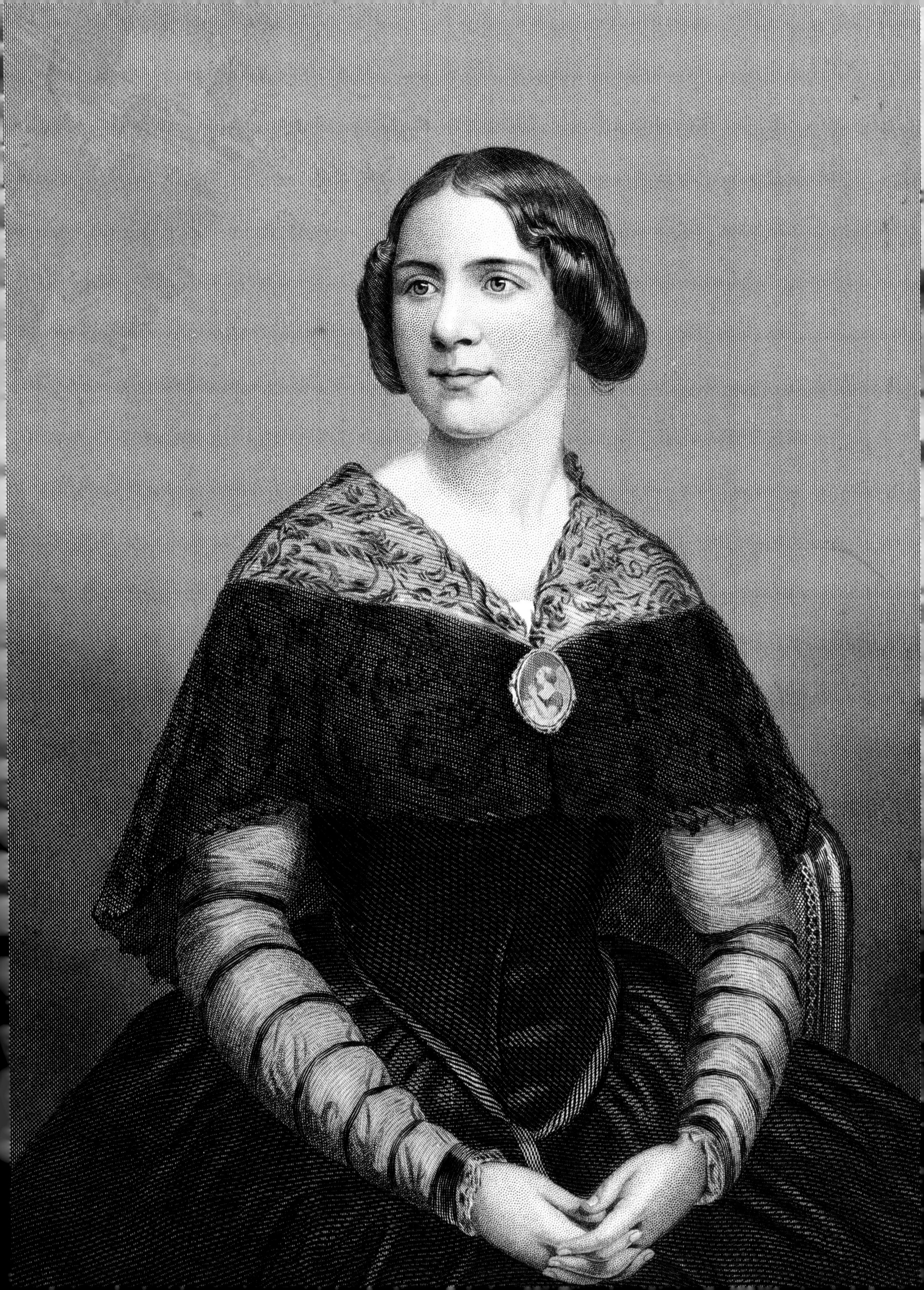

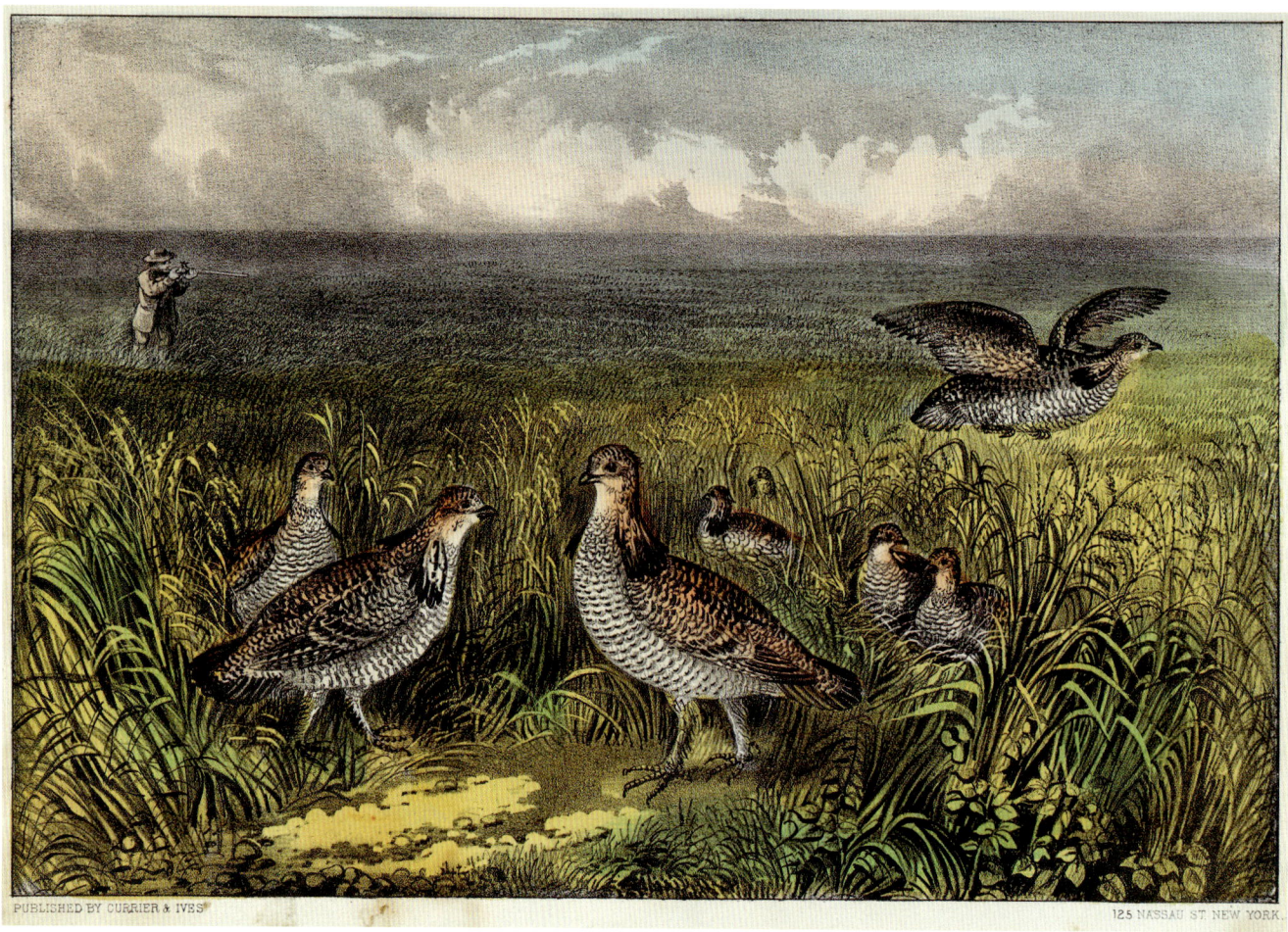

PUBLISHED BY CURRIER & IVES®   125 NASSAU ST NEW YORK.

SHOOTING ON THE PRAIRIE, Nathaniel Currier
after Arthur Fitzwilliam Tait. Lithograph. GM 1526.35.

Retailing at twenty cents per print, Currier and Ives
lithographs became a decorative staple of American
homes. Nathaniel Currier and James Merritt Ives
partnered in 1857 to sell affordable prints to a mass
market, employing factory women to hand color each
lithograph and sending out an army of salesmen to sell
their prints door to door. In business for seventy-two
years, the firm published nearly 7,500 images and worked
with several important artists, including George Inness,
Eastman Johnson, Thomas Nast, and Arthur Fitzwilliam
Tait. The latter's sporting scenes became some of the
most popular prints Currier and Ives produced. *American
Woman's Home,* a homemaking manual written by
Catharine Beecher and Harriet Beecher Stowe in 1869,
prescribed proper art for the home that could "express the
sincere ideas and tastes of the household." For the general
public, Currier and Ives prints represented their culture,
values, and ideals. In 1907, with the growing popularity
of photography, the company closed its doors.

THE COUNTY ELECTION, George Caleb Bingham.
Engraving, ca. 1852. GM 1526.569

The American Art-Union was founded in New York City in 1841 to educate
the public about art and inspire a national aesthetic. For five dollars a year,
subscribers received a few prints of Art-Union pieces each year and were entered
into a drawing for an oil painting annually. Artists submitted their works to the
Art-Union committee, which judged each piece on artistic and nationalistic merit.
Pieces determined to capture the American spirit or impart American values were
purchased and displayed in the Art-Union Gallery in New York. In the end, rivals
caused the demise of the Art-Union, forcing it to close their doors after the state of
New York determined it was operating an illegal lottery.

Bingham, a frequent Art-Union contributor, demonstrates his grasp on American
culture with this scene of an election. Depicting a cross-section of American
types, the artist gently satirizes all walks of life and all political persuasions.
Bingham's scene features men interested in the election, those more interested
in the crowd, and those who are simply there to gamble and drink. This piece,
created in the Art-Union's last days, was not shown at its gallery in New York.
Instead, Bingham took the painting with him on a tour of western cities, bringing
the genre the Art-Union popularized to a new audience.

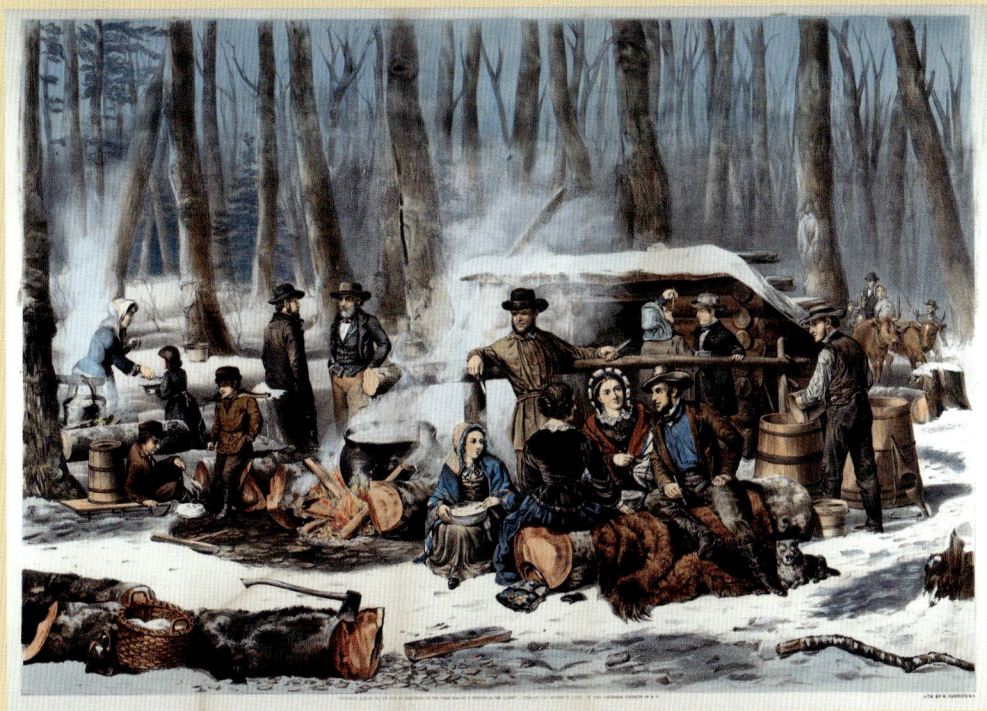

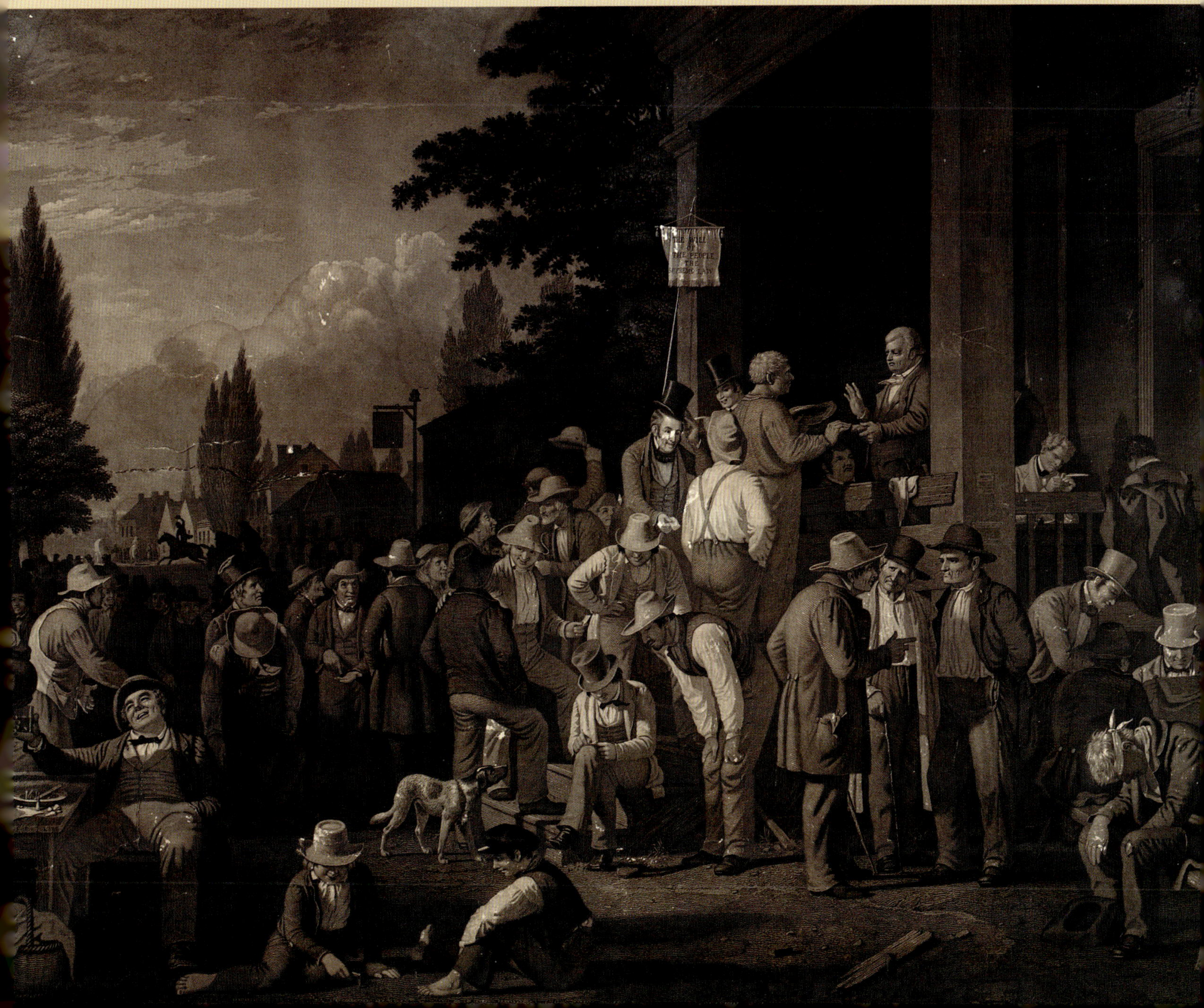

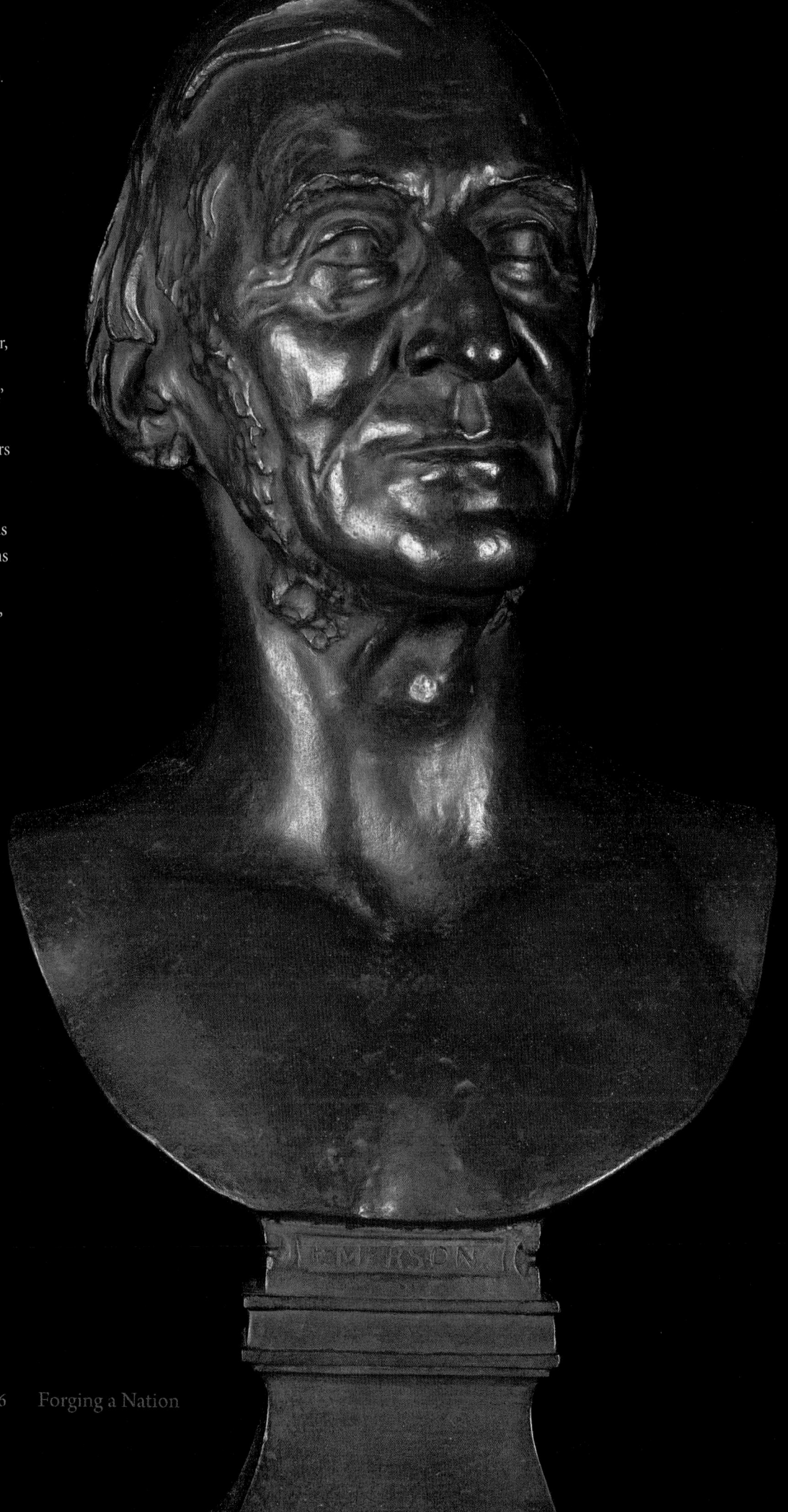

RALPH WALDO EMERSON,
Daniel Chester French. Bronze, 1879.
GM 0826.58

A leader of the Transcendentalist
movement in the United States,
Ralph Waldo Emerson became
one of America's most influential
thinkers. The Transcendentalists
believed that a new order, one
based on reason and democracy,
was at hand. Trained as a minister,
Emerson achieved fame through
his essays, such as "Self-Reliance,"
and books, including *Nature,* and
embarked on popular lecture tours
throughout the country.

Advocating the ideas that God was
present in nature and that humans
had a divine purpose, Emerson
and his fellow Transcendentalists,
including Henry David Thoreau,
questioned traditional theology
and were denounced by more
mainstream religious leaders.

Many of the social movements of the 19th century were rooted in Protestant morality. Groups advocating for temperance believed that the tenets of Christianity were not only for the benefit of the individual but for the whole society, and they likened indulgence in alcohol to the sin of gluttony. The elimination of alcohol, they urged, would remove a host of abuses, namely violence and other illegal behavior, from the American character.[25] Sermons and lectures stressed the ills caused by liquor and the need for total abstinence from intoxicating drinks. Temperance supporters who signed pledges stating that they would refrain from all alcohol marked their names with a "T" beside them, giving birth to the word, "teetotaler."[26]

Temperance was also embraced in the factories, where workers were encouraged to stay sober during working hours by both factory owners and by Working Men's groups, who believed it improved their quality of life in the cities.[27] Smaller women's organizations worked to ban "the ring leader of all the vices…this earth-blighting and soul-destroying demon."[28]

Although gains in sobriety were made, the complete abolition of alcohol remained an impossible goal. These temperance movements, however, had a much larger role to play in American society. Growing from a small collection of individuals, religiously based temperance groups like the American Temperance Society, founded in 1826, spread and changed shape depending upon community needs. In New York City, for example, temperance advocates organized relief efforts for the deserving poor, especially aiding women whose husbands had left or died, leaving them with children and few ways to support themselves.[29] By taking up various causes, these crusaders for moral improvement crossed regional and denominational lines, and attracted like-minded citizens throughout the nation, spurring action for women's rights and the abolition of the slavery.

The temperance movement acted as a model for other groups who followed in its wake. For women, philanthropic and religious organizations provided a new, public role—one previously dominated by men. One summer day in Seneca Falls, New York, a group of women, including Elizabeth Cady Stanton, met for what they called a "Women's Rights Convention."

Trust thyself: every heart vibrates to that iron string. Accept the place the divine providence has found for you, the society of your contemporaries, the connection of events. Great men have always done so, and confided themselves childlike to the genius of their age, betraying their perception that the absolutely trustworthy was seated at their heart, working through their hands, predominating in all their being. And we are now men, and must accept in the highest mind the same transcendent destiny; and not minors and invalids in a protected corner, not cowards fleeing before a revolution, but guides, redeemers, and benefactors, obeying the Almighty effort, and advancing on Chaos and the Dark.

—Ralph Waldo Emerson, from "Self-reliance"

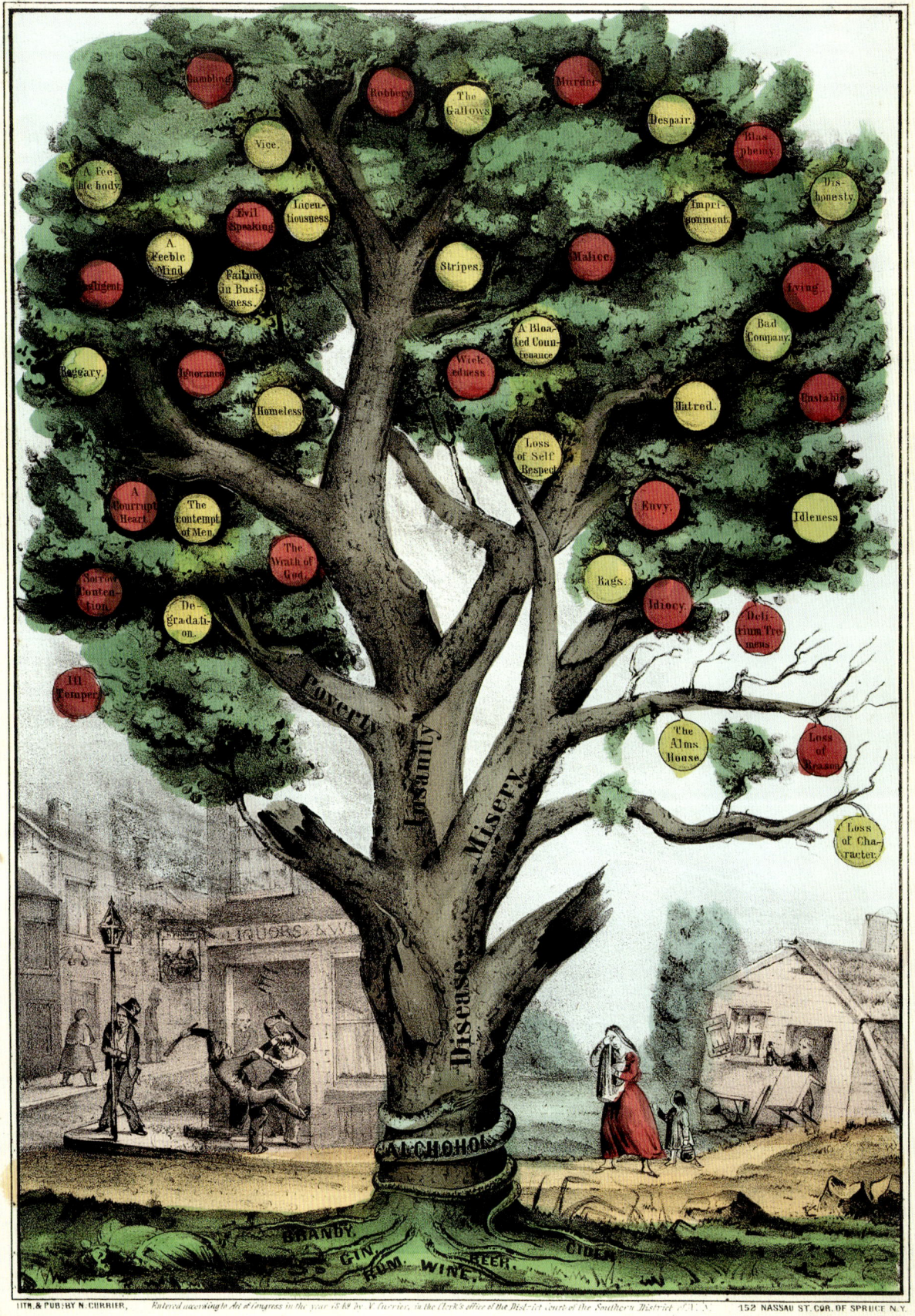

LITH. & PUB. BY N. CURRIER, Entered according to Act of Congress in the year 1849 by N. Currier, in the Clerk's office of the District Court of the Southern District of N.Y. 152 NASSAU ST. COR. OF SPRUCE N.Y.

THE TREE OF INTEMPERANCE.

Wine is a mocker, Strong drink is raging, and whosoever is deceived thereby is not wise. Proverbs XX. *At the last it biteth like a Serpent, and stingeth like an Adder;* Prov. XXIII 3° *For the Glutton and the Drunkard shall come to Poverty and drowsiness shall clothe a man with rags.* Proverbs XXIII. 2

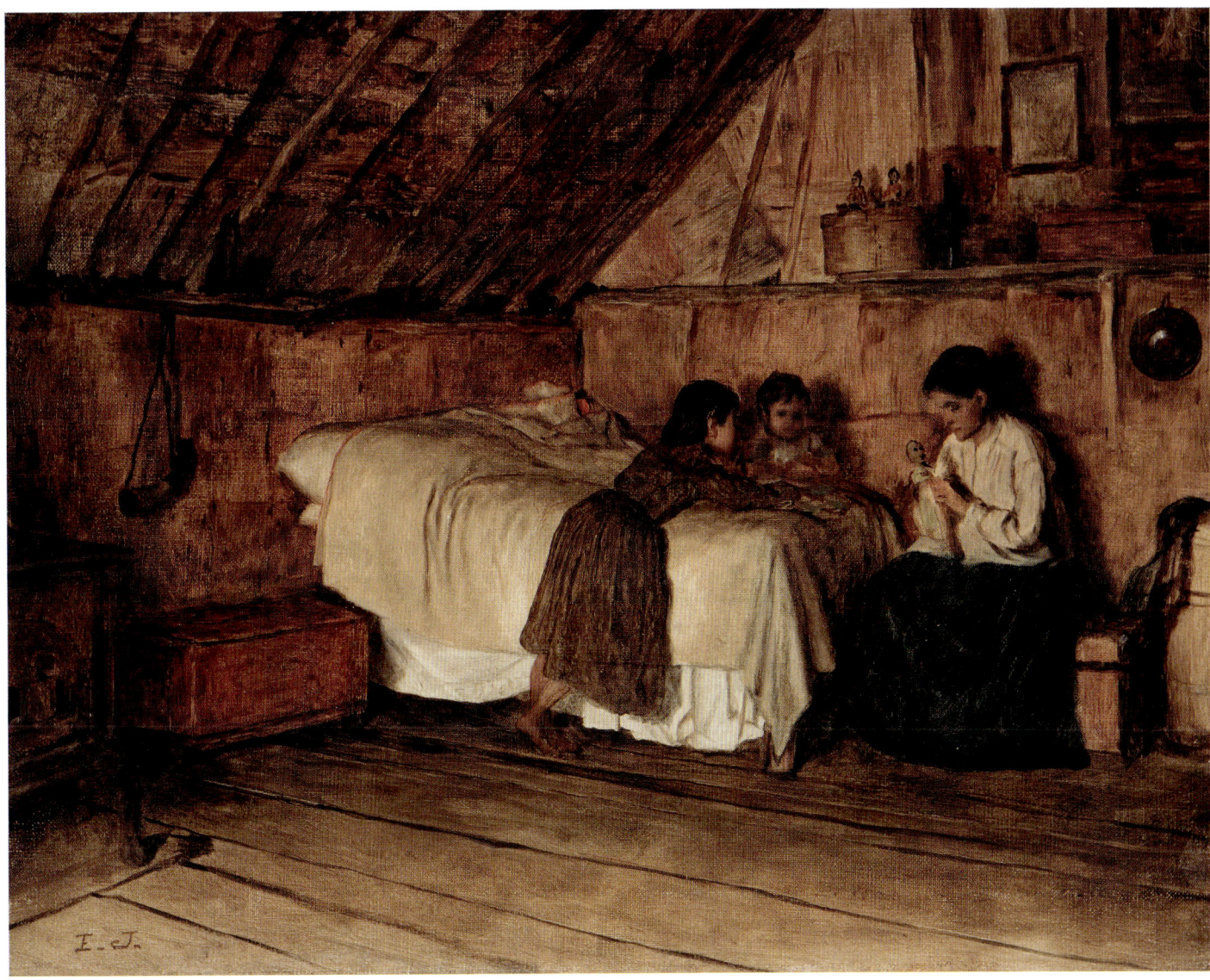

The small group adopted a "Declaration of Sentiments" urging the government to give them full rights under the law, including the right to own property, access to education, job opportunities, and the right to vote. "We insist," they wrote, "that [women] have immediate admission to all the rights and privileges which belong to them as citizens of the United States."[30] Newspaper accounts of the movement, although disparaging, encouraged others to form similar groups across the country. Inspired by the new movement, women entered the workforce in increasing numbers. One such employee, fifteen-year-old Mary Paul, described her desire to work at the Lowell mills in a letter to her father. "I could earn much more to begin with than I can anywhere about here," she wrote. "I think that the factory is the best place for me and if any girl wants employment I advise her to come to Lowell."[31]

THE DOLL,
Eastman Johnson. Oil on canvas. GM 0126.1508

FACING: THE TREE OF TEMPERANCE,
Nathaniel Currier. Engraving, 1849. GM 1526.30

ST. PAUL'S, BROADWAY,
NEW YORK, Alexander Davis.
Engraving, 1840. GM 1526.1094

In the first half of the 19th century, New York City grew from a city of about 200,000 to one of about 800,000. By 1850, well over 60 percent of those living in the city were foreign-born. As the merchant capital of the United States, New York attracted immigrants, especially those from Ireland fleeing the potato famine, with a promise of opportunities. Many, however, found instead inadequate housing, poor temporary jobs, and disease. Women could find work as domestic laborers, factory workers, or through other, illegitimate venues. Many men had harder times finding stable work and took advantage of opportunities in the western territories to make their fortune. By the middle of the 19th century, New York and other major cities had developed a reputation for crime, poverty, and disease, mainly due to the overcrowded and unsanitary living conditions in poor immigrant neighborhoods.

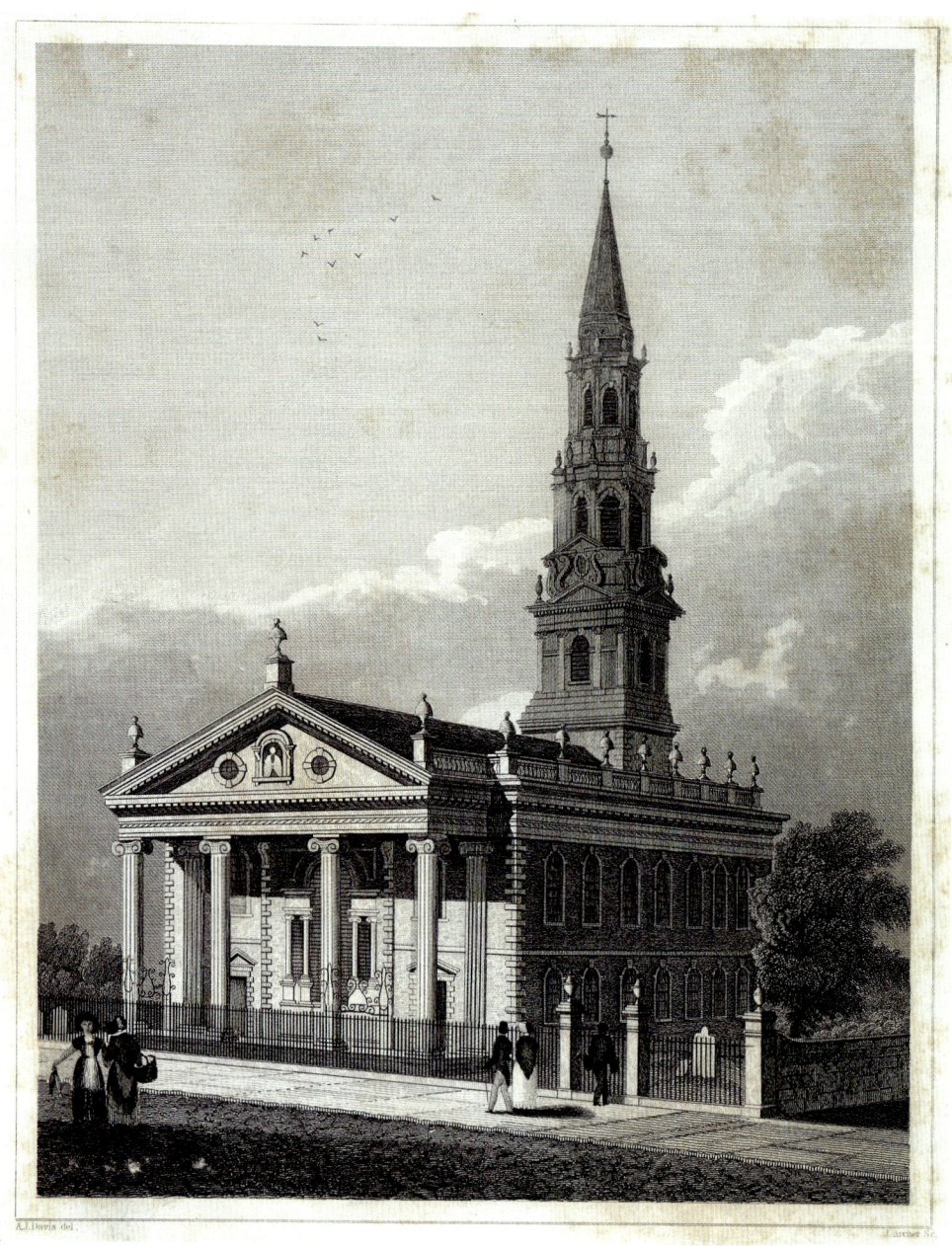

FACING: TITLE FOR A QUARTER SECTION OF LAND TO CIN-CON-TUM-BE, UNITED STATES GOVERNMENT, 1846. GM 5126.509

Although Polk focused mainly on foreign affairs during his tenure as president, he continued to implement the Native American policies put forth by his predecessors. In this document, Cin-con-tum-be, a young Choctaw boy, was granted a quarter section of land, approximately 160 acres, by the United States government as stipulated in the Treaty of Dancing Rabbit Creek of 1830. Cin-con-tum-be and his family were among the 5,000 to 6,000 Choctaw members who chose to remain in Mississippi rather than make the uncertain journey to Indian Territory. The Treaty of Dancing Rabbit Creek stated that any Choctaws who remained in Mississippi became United States citizens and would submit to the laws of both the State of Mississippi and the United States and relinquish their rights as members of the Choctaw Nation.

THE UNITED STATES OF AMERICA,

To all to whom these Presents shall come, Greeting:

WHEREAS, under the *fourteenth Article of* the Treaty, concluded at Dancing Rabbit Creek, on the twenty-seventh day of September, in the year of our Lord one thousand eight hundred and thirty, by the Commissioners on the part of the United States, and the Chiefs, Captains, and Head Men of the Choctaw Nation, on the part of said Nation, *Cun-oon-tam-be* became entitled, out of the lands ceded to the United States by the said Treaty, to *a quarter Section* of land; And whereas, *it appears from a return reported November 22d 1845 by the Commissioner of Indian affairs to the General Land Office that the Commissioners under the Act of Congress approved 23d August 1842, entitled "An Act to provide for the satisfaction of claims arising under the fourteenth and nineteenth Articles of the treaty of Dancing Rabbit Creek concluded in September one thousand eight hundred and thirty" have made an award which was approved on the 23d July 1845 by the Secretary of War in favor of the said Cun-oon-tam-be as a child under ten years of age at date of treaty of the following described tract, viz: the North East quarter of Section twenty one containing One hundred and sixty acres, and fourteen hundredths of an acre in township eight (North) of Range Nine East (of the Choctaw Meridian) in the District of Lands subject to sale at Columbus, Mississippi*_____;

NOW KNOW YE, That the UNITED STATES OF AMERICA, in consideration of the premises, and in conformity with the provisions of the said Treaty, HAVE GIVEN AND GRANTED, and by these presents DO GIVE AND GRANT, unto the said *Cun-oon-tam-be, and to the heirs of the same* ~~and to heirs,~~ the said tract of land above described: TO HAVE AND TO HOLD the same, together with all the rights, privileges, immunities, and appurtenances of whatsoever nature thereunto belonging, unto the said *Cun-oon-tam-be* and to ~~the~~ heirs and assigns for ever, *of the said Cun-oon-tam-be*_____.

IN TESTIMONY WHEREOF, I, *James K. Polk* PRESIDENT OF THE UNITED STATES OF AMERICA, have caused these Letters to be made PATENT, and the SEAL of the GENERAL LAND OFFICE to be hereunto affixed.

GIVEN under my hand, at the CITY OF WASHINGTON, the *second* day of *September* in the year of our Lord one thousand eight hundred and *forty six* and of the INDEPENDENCE OF THE UNITED STATES the ~~sixty~~ *seventy first.*

BY THE PRESIDENT: *James K. Polk*

Recorded Vol. *2* Page ____

Ex d.

S.H. Laughlin, Recorder of the General Land Office.

When the Civil War began in 1861, nearly 4 million men, women, and children were slaves, considered property to be bought or sold at their owner's discretion. As the country expanded, the issue of slavery in new territories divided the nation politically and created a bitter rivalry between northern industrialists who opposed the trade and southern plantation owners who depended upon it. Men and women like Frederick Douglass and Sojourner Truth wrote elegant accounts of the horrors of life as a slave and spoke to enthusiastic groups hoping to abolish the grim trade. Congress passed a measure that it hoped would stave off conflict, the Compromise of 1850. The Compromise banned slavery in California, but left other territories the right to determine the slavery question for themselves. The measure did little, however, to appease either party.

Complete Listing of 42 Slaves of the Robert M. Compton estate with Ages and approximate Value. MADISON County, TENN 1848.

SAL, OLD WOMAN ABOUT 90 No Value

OLD TAB MAN ABOUT 70 No Value

Name	Value	Name	Value
VENUS AGE 38 Value	$400.00	SARAH, AGE 4 YEARS	200.00
CHARLES AGE 34 Value	600.00	ESSY AGE 25 Value	450.00
JENN AGE 17 Value	600.00	NOLLY AGE 28 & Child	
MINDER AGE 15 Value	550.00	AMANDA 3 YEARS	550.00
BURWELL AGE 30 Value	400.00	MARTHA AGE 12 YEARS	550.00
NERO AGE 9 Value	425.00	EMANUAL AGE 15 Value	625.00
JULIA AGE 8 Value	350.00	SILAS AGE 39 Value	575.00
CLEO AGE 6 Value	275.00	MANISH AGE 30 & Child	
SILAS AGE 2 Value	200.00	HARRILT 5 months	550.00
OLD BEN AGE 65 No Value	— 6 —	LUCY, AGE 17 YEARS	600.00
JACK AGE 39 Value	550.00	ANDREW AGE 12 Value	525.00
SYLVIA AGE 37 Value	250.00	JERRY AGE 9 Value	475.00
MARY AGE 18 & Child		MAHALA AGE 6 Value	300.00
AGE 2 Value	725.00	STEPHEN AGE 4 Value	300.00
AMER AGE 14 Value	550.00	MARY ANN AGE 2 Value	260.00
KANE AGE 12 Value	500.00	DAVID AGE 60 Value	175.00
JOHN AGE 9 Value	475.00	SOPHIA AGE 18 Value	425.00
LIZA AGE 5 Value	275.00		
STEPHEN AGE 25 Value	650.00		
LEZA AGE 3 Value	200.00		
LITTLE BEN AGE 30 Value	650.00		
BINER AGE 28 & Child			
WINNEY 15 months	500.00		
ROSE AGE 8 Value	325.00		
VIOLA AGE 6 Value	250.00		

Total Value of 42 Slaves $16,200.00

Respectfully submitted

Charles Templeton
Administrator of the Robert M. Compton estate.

* Madison County Court Copy

Despite the drudgery and danger of most factory work, the women who worked in Lowell and other places stood as an emblem for the rights lobbied for by the Seneca Falls conventioneers.[32] As women stepped into their new role as advocates not only for their own causes, but also for those concerning Indian Removal policies, treatment of criminals and the mentally ill, and the war with Mexico, they found themselves aligned with a cultural shift in the United States that would draw the fiercest debate, the abolition movement.

The abolition movement in America traced its roots back to England and men like Thomas Clarkson and Granville Sharp, who had worked through the British legal system to oppose and abolish the slave trade. Many of those reformers traveled to the United States to encourage fledging American movements to agitate for abolition. By the 1840s, many of those who worked stridently for abolition were women. Frederick Douglass declared, "When the true history of the antislavery cause shall be written, women will occupy a large space in its pages, for the cause of the slave has been peculiarly woman's cause."[33] The fear of the extension of slavery was on the minds of many reformers, men and women, especially in the wake of the Mexican-American War. With the United States gaining vast amounts of territory, the slavery question became a hotly contentious one. Texas, which had fought for most of its territory in the 1830s, was a slaveholding state. Proposals that suggested slavery should not be extended to new territories were voted down, and the Compromise of 1850, though enacted in the hopes of staving off a war, did little to quiet fears on both sides of the slavery debate.[34]

REWARD FOR RUNAWAY SLAVE. From the *National Intelligencer,* March 19, 1845, Washington, D.C. GM 5326.1201

METAL BELT BUCKLE. GM 69.224

ONE HUNDRED DOLLARS REWARD.--Ran away from the subscriber on Monday, the 24th instant, my boy PATRICK, without the least provocation. He is about 18 years old, 5 feet 5 or 6 inches high, of a light copper color, with very large cheek bones for a negro ; and is so fond of talking that he will continue to declare his innocence, if accused, though ordered to keep silence. I purchased him of the estate of the late Thos. Magruder, near Good Luck, in this county, with whose widow his mother now resides. He is also in the habit of visiting frequently Mr. Frederick Skinner's, near Centreville, where it is believed he last was seen.

To have him apprehended I will give $25 if taken in Prince George's county or the District of Columbia, $50 if taken in any other slave State, and the above reward if taken in a free State ; in either case he must be delivered to me or secured in a public jail, so that I get him again. Any information may be directed to me near Upper Marlborough, Prince George's county, Maryland.

mar 28—tf   THO. W. CLAGETT.

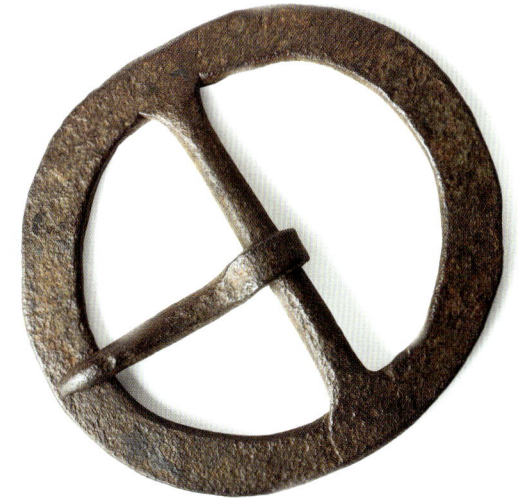

LIFE AT THE SOUTH:

OR

"UNCLE TOM'S CABIN" AS IT IS.

BEING

NARRATIVES, SCENES, AND INCIDENTS

IN THE

REAL "LIFE OF THE LOWLY."

By W. L. G. SMITH.

BUFFALO:
GEO. H. DERBY AND CO.
CLEVELAND: TOOKER AND GATCHEL.
SANDUSKY: C. L. DERBY AND CO.
CHICAGO: D. B. COOKE AND CO.
1852.

UNCLE TOM'S CABIN;

OR,

LIFE AMONG THE LOWLY.

BY

HARRIET BEECHER STOWE.

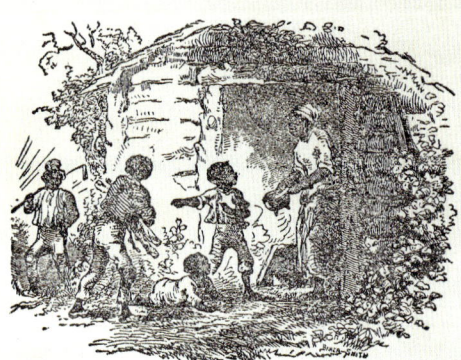

VOL. I.

BOSTON:
JOHN P. JEWETT & COMPANY.
CLEVELAND, OHIO:
JEWETT, PROCTOR & WORTHINGTON.
1852.

LIFE AT THE SOUTH OR UNCLE TOM'S CABIN AS IT IS, 1862, by W. L. G. Smith. GM 3426.4069

Books such as *Life at the South* were written to correct the "distortions and falsehoods" in the account of slavery contained in Harriet Beecher Stowe's *Uncle Tom's Cabin*. These books took the plot of Stowe's novel— a slave forced to leave his family by his owner—and inverted it to demonstrate that the slaves were happy with their lives on the plantations. These novels often painted abolitionists as the villains, luring innocent slaves away from the protection of their owners to live lives of misery and hardship in the industrial cities of the north. Although numerous "anti-*Uncle Tom*" books were published, they could not compete with the overwhelming popularity of *Uncle Tom's Cabin,* and were largely forgotten after the Civil War.

UNCLE TOM'S CABIN, VOL. 1, 1852,
by Harriet Beecher Stowe. GM 2426.378

Harriet Beecher Stowe's 1852 *Uncle Tom's Cabin* became an international bestseller, selling 300,000 copies in its first year. Detailing the fate of slaves separated from their families through sale, it brought the horrors of slavery into the homes of thousands of readers. Many cities in the South tried to ban the novel for its depiction of southern plantation owners, yet the book was so popular that stores could not keep it in stock. Queen Victoria was said to have wept while reading it, and Abraham Lincoln, when he met Stowe in 1862, reportedly said, "So you're the little woman who wrote the book that made this great war."

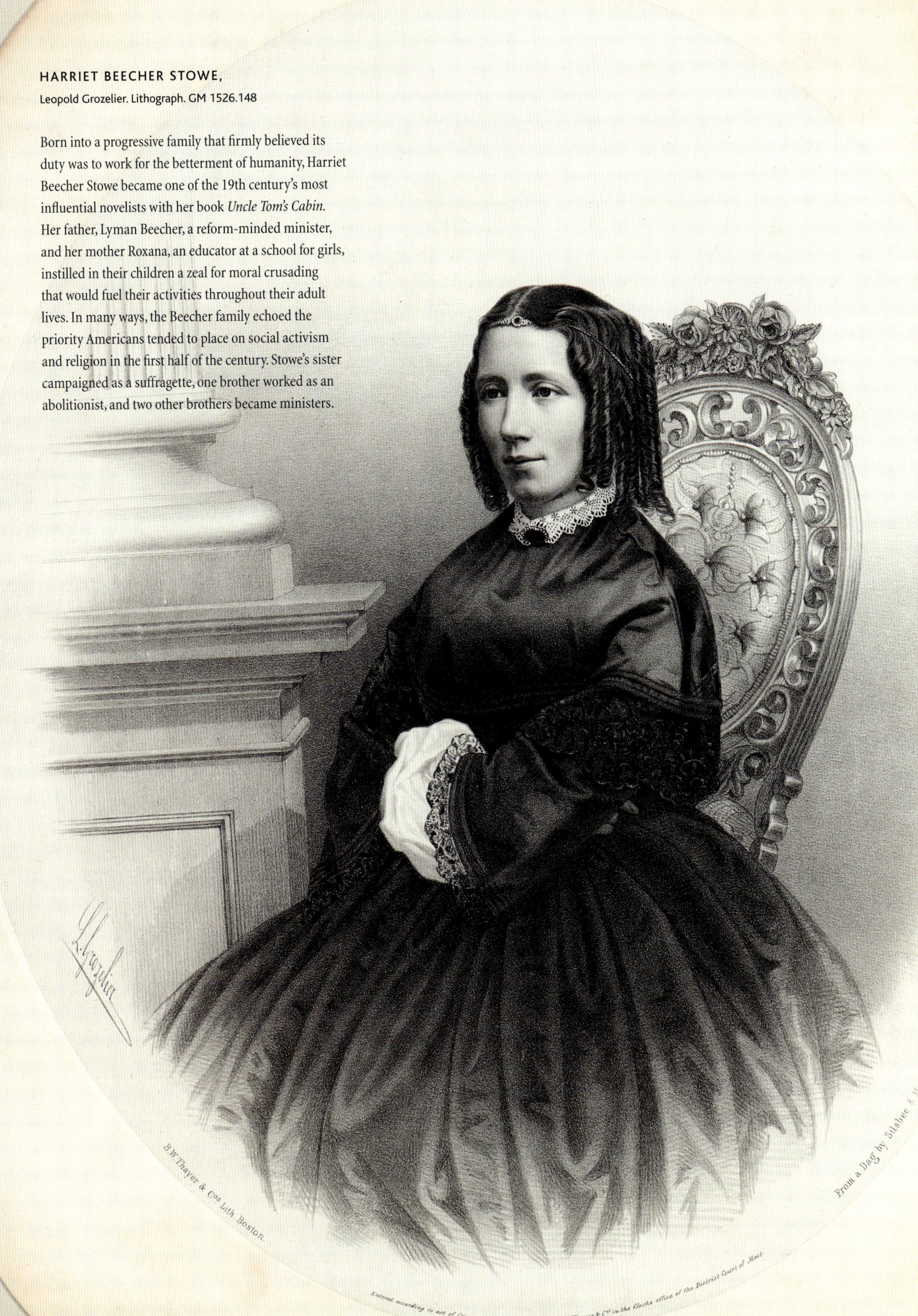

HARRIET BEECHER STOWE,

Leopold Grozelier. Lithograph. GM 1526.148

Born into a progressive family that firmly believed its
duty was to work for the betterment of humanity, Harriet
Beecher Stowe became one of the 19th century's most
influential novelists with her book *Uncle Tom's Cabin.*
Her father, Lyman Beecher, a reform-minded minister,
and her mother Roxana, an educator at a school for girls,
instilled in their children a zeal for moral crusading
that would fuel their activities throughout their adult
lives. In many ways, the Beecher family echoed the
priority Americans tended to place on social activism
and religion in the first half of the century. Stowe's sister
campaigned as a suffragette, one brother worked as an
abolitionist, and two other brothers became ministers.

B.W. Thayer & Co's Lith Boston.

From a Dag by Silsbee & Mowry.

Entered according to act of Congress in the year 1853, by B.W. Thayer & Co. in the Clerks office of the District Court of Mass.

The core issues underlying the support of abolition were both practical and moral. Some supporters focused primarily on economic forces. While many feared that freed African-Americans from the South would compete for factory jobs in the North, abolitionists believed that slave labor harmed white workers as well. They argued that slave labor devalued the work done by free men and equated manual labor with servitude, driving wages down for all. This aspect of abolition appealed to politicians in the bourgeoning Free Soil and Republican parties.[35] Those who focused on the moral implications of slavery found a leader in Joseph Priestley, an English minister and scientist who left Britain for America in 1794. A vocal supporter of the antislavery movement in England and the United States, Priestley insisted there were "common rights of humanity" and that all men "were equally men and therefore equally entitled to all the natural and just rights of man."[36] Building upon those themes, newspaper editor William Lloyd Garrison developed a "Declaration of Sentiments" for the American Anti-Slavery Society. In it, he declared that the treatment of enslaved people in the United States was

> "an audacious usurpation of the Divine prerogative, a daring infringement on the law of nature, a base overthrow of the very foundation of the social compact, a complete extinction of all the relations, endearments and obligations of mankind, and a presumptuous transgression of all the holy commandments."[37]

The most strident abolitionists needed no convincing that God was on their side. Abolition as a moral issue did not allow for differing viewpoints, and these arguments ignited violent skirmishes. An already passionate debate gained momentum due to innovations in communication. "Thanks to steam navigation and electric wires," Frederick Douglass wrote, "a revolution now cannot be confined to the place or the people where it may commence, but flashes with lightning speed from heart to heart, from land to land, until it has traversed the globe."[38] At the end of the 1850s, John Brown and his men would invoke God's will to rationalize their futile plot at Harper's Ferry.

Despite the fury and passion the anti-slavery cause aroused in its followers and detractors, its hope, as with most social movements of the 1840s and 1850s, was to build the better America promised by the Declaration of Indpendence. The fervor for this ideal America would ultimately pull the nation apart.

NOTES

1. Simon Schama, *Rough Crossings: Britain, the Slaves, and the American Revolution* (New York: Harper Collins, 2006), p. 415-416. See Schama for a fascinating look at the early roots of the abolition cause in both England and the United States. For a fine account of Douglass's exploits in England, see pages 415-422.

2. Ibid., p. 416.

3. Ibid., p. 417.

4. Schama, *Rough Crossings*, p. 417. Douglass described the scene, stating that the hymns "which like the angels of old, closed the lions' mouths so that for a time, silence prevailed."

5. Ibid., p. 421. One of Douglass's admirers in England paid for his manumission papers.

6. Thomas Clarkson, *History of the Rise, Progress, and Accomplishment of the Abolition of the African Slave Trade by the British Parliament: A New Edition with Prefatory Remarks on the Subsequent Abolition of Slavery* (West Strand, London: John W. Parker, 1839), pp. 44-45.

7. Howe, *What Hath God Wrought*, p. 582.

8. Howe, *What Hath God Wrought*, p. 686.

9. Ibid., p. 583.

10. Ibid., p. 702. Polk also stated that he felt the United States' "title to Oregon is clear and unquestionable." This led him in to direct conflict with Great Britain, who also had claim to the Oregon Territory.

11. Ibid., p. 705.

12. Ibid., p. 745.

13. Howe, *What Hath God Wrought*, pp. 746-747.

14. Ibid., p. 752.

15. Ethan Hitchcock, "Diary Entry," in Howe, *What Hath God Wrought*, p. 739. Hitchcock's sentiments were echoed by politician Henry Clay and Lt. Ulysses S. Grant.

16. Howe, *What Hath God Wrought*, p. 803.

17. Nicholas Trist, "Letter to his Wife," Howe, *What Hath God Wrought*, p. 805. Trist's decision to submit the treaty came at great personal sacrifice. Polk disapproved of the terms, and had Trist arrested and brought back to the United States. His political life was ruined. Trist went unpaid for his work until 1871.

18. Howe, *What Hath God Wrought*, p. 809.

19 Lewis O. Saum, *The Popular Mood of Pre–Civil War America* (Westport, Connecticut: Greenwood Press, 1980), p. 159.

20. Ibid., p. 5.

21. Daniel Walker Howe, *Making the American Self: Jonathan Edwards to Abraham Lincoln* (Oxford, England: Oxford University Press, 1997), p.117.

22. Ralph Waldo Emerson, "Spiritual Laws," in Irwin Edman, ed., *Emerson's Essays* (New York: Harper Colophon, 1951), p. 99.

23. John L. O'Sullivan, "Annexation," *United States Magazine and Democratic Review*, 17 July, 1845, in Sarah Burns and John Davis, *American Art to 1900: A Documentary History* (University of California Press, 2009), p. 427.

24. Saum, *The Popular Mood of Pre–Civil War America*, p. 22.

25. Howe, *What Hath God Wrought*, pp. 166-167. Lyman Beecher put this theory forth in the 1830s.

26. Ibid., p. 167.

27. Ibid., p. 543.

28. Saum, *The Popular Mood of Pre-Civil War America*, p. 163. This quote comes from an address by Hannah Coffin and Adaline Wright to the Economy Union of the Daughters of Temperance in 1853.

29. Christine Stansell, *City of Women: Sex and Class in New York, 1789–1860,* (Urbana: University of Illinois Press, 1987), p. 69. Stansell provides a wonderful insight into the lives of working-class and poor women living in New York before the Civil War.

30. Howe, *What Hath God Wrought*, pp. 838-839.

31. Saum, *The Popular Mood of Pre–Civil War America*, pp. 161-162.

32. Stansell, *City of Women*, p. 125

33. Howe, *What Hath God Wrought*, p. 653.

34. Stanley Harrold, ed., *The Civil War and Reconstruction: A Documentary Reader,* (Malden, Massachusetts: Blackwell Publishing, 2008), p. 34. The Compromise of 1850 banned slavery in California, allowed settlers in New Mexico and Utah to vote on slavery themselves, and strengthened the fugitive slave act.

35. Howe, *What Hath God Wrought*, pp. 545-546.

36. Isaac Kramnick, "18th-Century Science and Radical Social Theory: The Case of Joseph Priestley's Scientific Liberalism," *The Journal of British Studies*, Vol. 25, No. 1, Jan. 1986, p. 18.

37. William Lloyd Garrison, "Declaration of Sentiments of the American Anti-Slavery Society," December 5, 1833 in Harrold, *The Civil War and Reconstruction:*

38. Howe, *What Hath God Wrought*, p. 848.

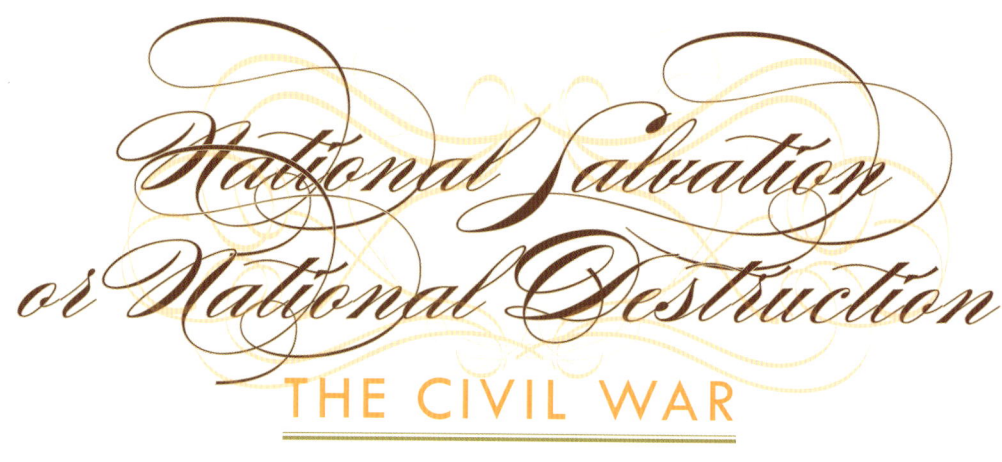

National Salvation or National Destruction

THE CIVIL WAR

AND ITS AFTERMATH

AMANDA LETT

By November 9, 1860, most of the nation had heard the news. The Republican nominee, Abraham Lincoln, a man who was not even on the ballot in ten states, had been elected president. Newspapers from New York to San Francisco discussed the result and possible reactions from the southern states. As the breathless wire reports came in at *The New York Times,* the consensus was that dark days lay ahead. News from Georgia and South Carolina revealed that they were forming conventions to discuss their next steps in a threatened secession. In San Francisco, the editors clung to the belief that moderation by President Lincoln would put the vexing questions of state's rights and slavery back in the realm of Congress, where southern politicians could nurse their political wounds and might still have some effect.[2] Virginia newspapers proclaimed that the nation was "on the brink of a revolution" and ended their dispatch with a cautious "Let us hope for the best."[3] Throughout the nation, the election of Abraham Lincoln was greeted with a strange mixture of uncertainty, fear, and jubilation. The anti-slavery faction excitedly declared that, indeed, a revolution had come and that "the country has once and for all thrown off the domination of the Slaveholders."[4] The southern faction felt the election of a Republican president was calamitous. "Will you be slaves or will you

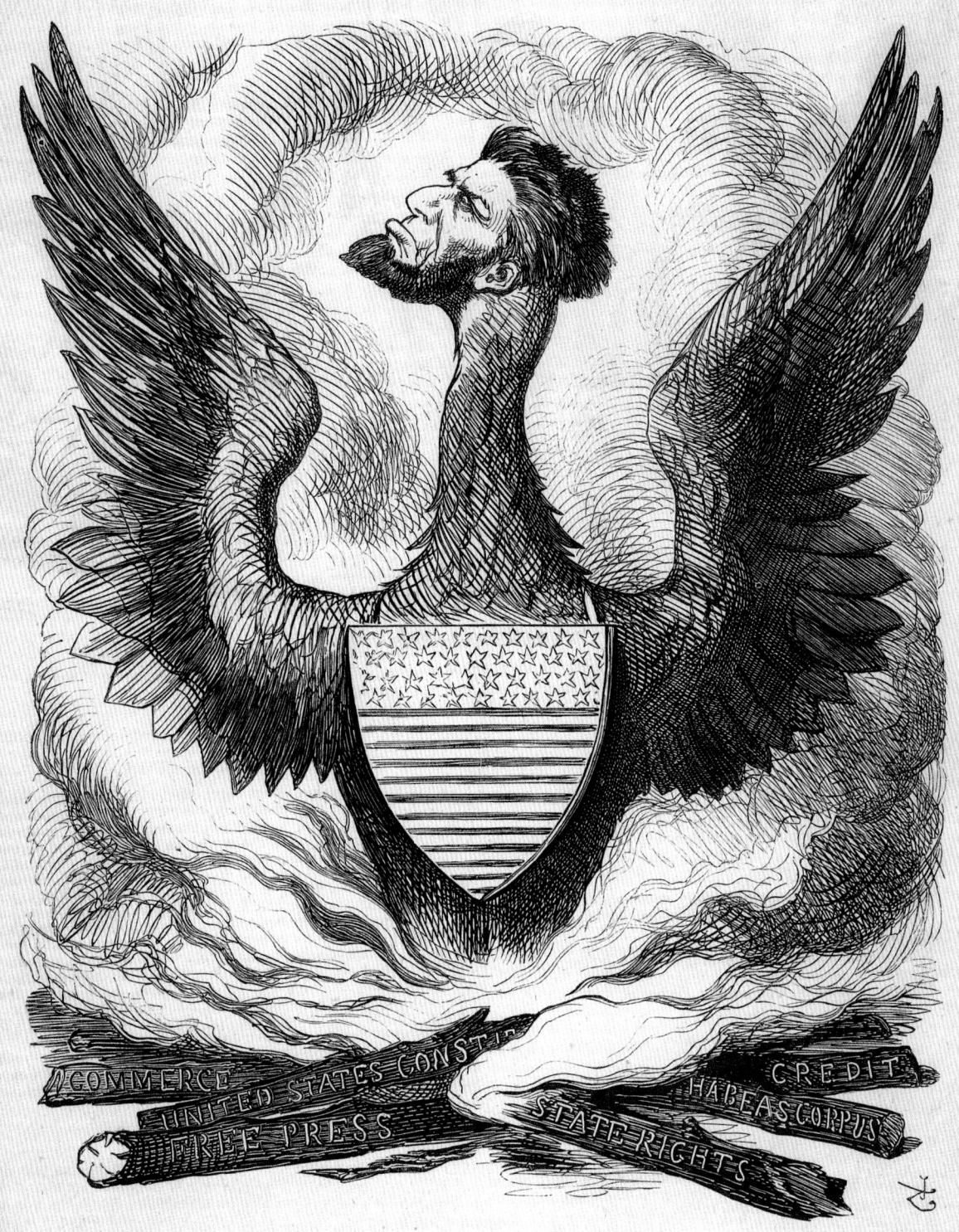

THE FEDERAL PHŒNIX.

STEPHEN DOUGLAS, George Peter Alexander Healy.
Oil on canvas, 1857. GM 0126.1112

A career politician, Stephen Douglas served the state of
Illinois throughout the turbulent years leading up to the
Civil War. Known to many as "Little Giant" for his short
stature but forceful nature, Douglas was the chief architect
of the Compromise of 1850 and supported President
James K. Polk's decision to go to war with Mexico. When
Douglas sought reelection to his Senate seat in 1858 he
faced a younger opponent named Abraham Lincoln.
Douglas won the election, but electoral debates between
the two contenders catapulted Lincoln into the national
spotlight. Douglas once again faced Lincoln as the
Northern Democratic candidate for president in 1860, but
factiousness brewing between Northern and Southern
Democrats ensured the party a loss. A supporter of the
Union until he died in 1861, Douglas worked to find a
compromise to threatened secession, and, when that failed,
worked with President Lincoln to secure the border states
for the North.

be independent?" Jefferson Davis asked. "Will you consent to be robbed of your property, or will you strike bravely for liberty, property, honor, and life?"[5] The next four and a half years would change the country in ways unfathomable in the fall of 1860. The United States would be stretched almost to a breaking point, as family and friends were pitted against each other at a terrible cost. The war marked the transition from an America in her infancy to a more mature, united country, and spurred the inventiveness and industry that accompanied the country through the last half of the 19th century.

The seeds of the Civil War were planted long before the cannons fired at Fort Sumter. Division, whether through political affiliation, economic situation, or due to strong regional ties, marked the decades before the war. The country's ever-changing boundary magnified these internal rifts. As each new territory was claimed and each new state added, the opportunity for political parties to expand their sphere of influence produced vicious exchanges—exchanges eagerly reproduced in the newspapers of the day. Lincoln himself admitted as much when he was nominated to the Illinois state senate in 1857. "I believe this government cannot endure," Lincoln stated, "permanently half slave and half free."[6] As the country had grown up, the two halves, North and South, had grown apart. In the northern states, industry had become the engine of the economy, putting men—and for the first time, women—to work in numbers unimaginable in previous decades. Northern cities grew exponentially during the decades leading up to the Civil War, bolstered by immigrants, but also by native-born Americans looking for more opportunities than rural life could afford.[7] Northern industries produced the vast majority of both raw materials and finished goods—such as guns, shoes, and cloth—needed to outfit an army, and had double the amount of railroad lines for transportation of both goods and people.[8] Although the North had embraced new technologies and the ideas of competitive, free-labor capitalism, the South remained tied to the older, Jeffersonian notions of America.

DRESS. Cotton, mid-19th century. GM 94.89

LEVEE AT NEW ORLEANS, William Aiken Walker.

Oil on Canvas. GM 0126.1208

Born in Charleston, South Carolina, in 1838, William Aiken Walker
often painted scenes of the South, such as plantations, cotton fields, and
shipping docks. Although the artist was primarily self-taught, his work
gained attention from the noted publisher Currier & Ives, who published
some of his lithographs, including *Levee at New Orleans*.

The first American steamboats embarked in 1811 from Philadelphia to
New Orleans. The new vessels powered by both steam and traditional
paddle wheels allowed riverboat captains to more easily navigate inland
rivers and increased the scope of trade.

W.A.Walker. 1883.

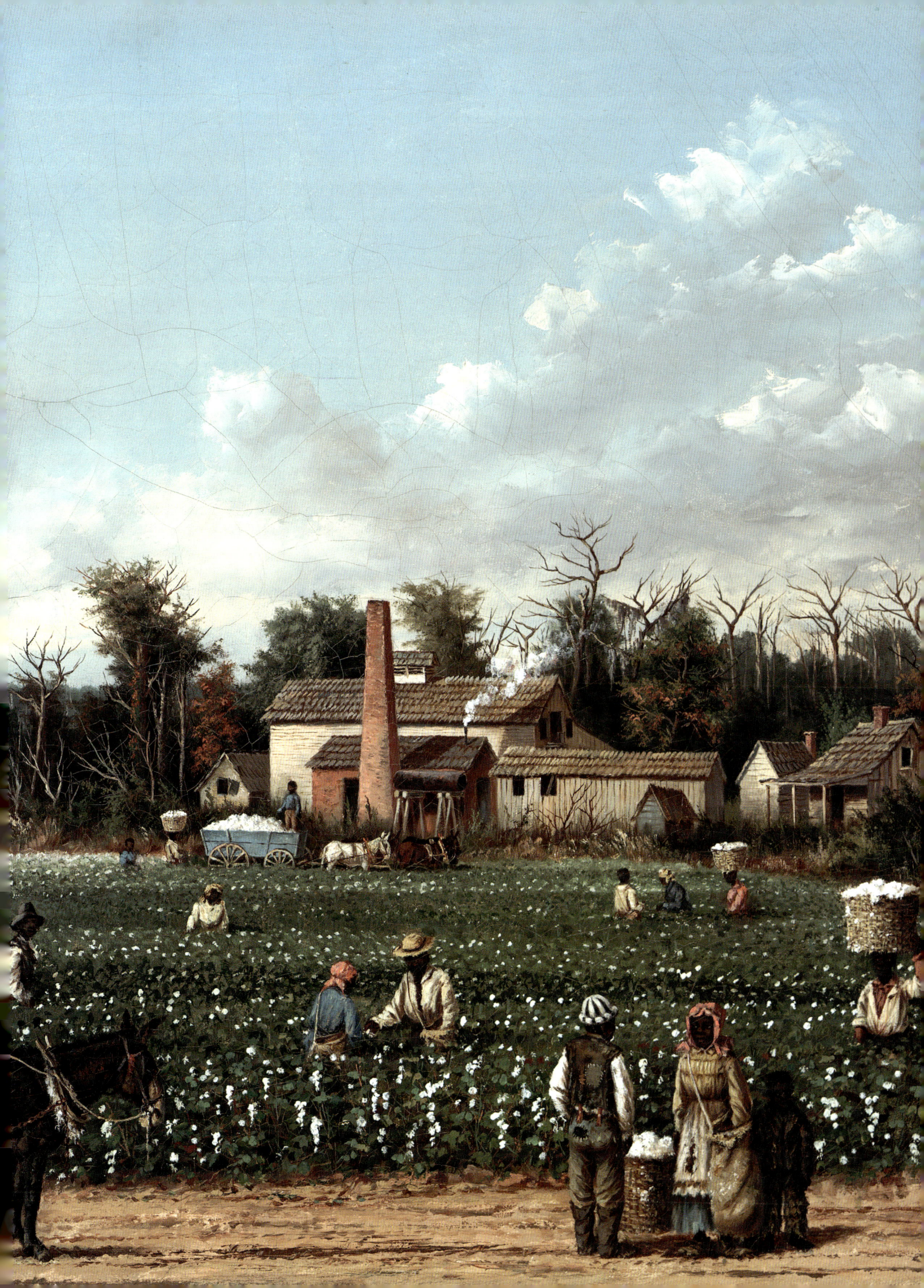

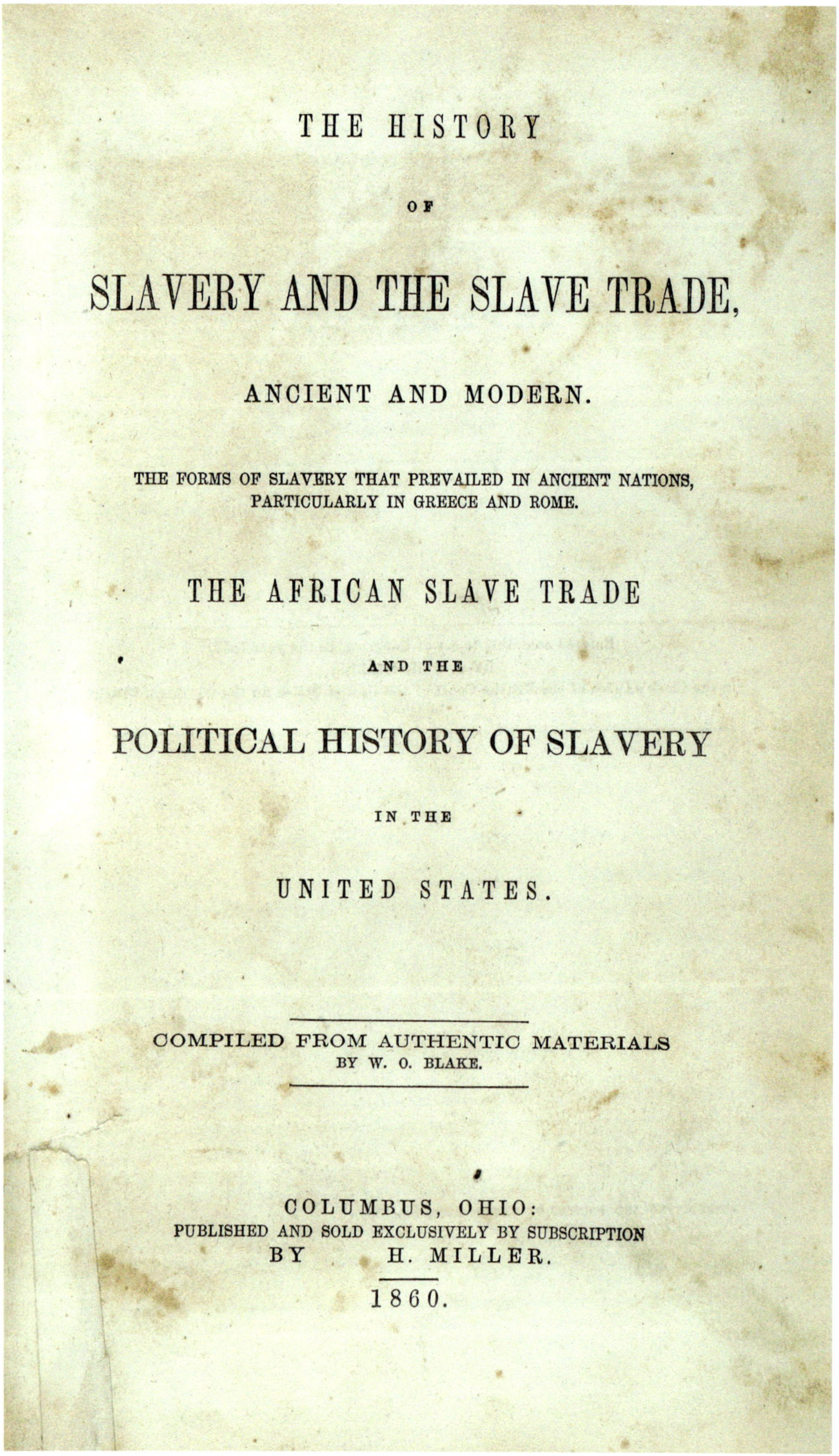

THE HISTORY

OF

SLAVERY AND THE SLAVE TRADE,

ANCIENT AND MODERN.

THE FORMS OF SLAVERY THAT PREVAILED IN ANCIENT NATIONS,
PARTICULARLY IN GREECE AND ROME.

THE AFRICAN SLAVE TRADE

AND THE

POLITICAL HISTORY OF SLAVERY

IN THE

UNITED STATES.

COMPILED FROM AUTHENTIC MATERIALS
BY W. O. BLAKE.

COLUMBUS, OHIO:
PUBLISHED AND SOLD EXCLUSIVELY BY SUBSCRIPTION
BY H. MILLER.
1860.

NATIONAL ANTI-SLAVERY STANDARD, 1861. GM 5326.1202

By the end of the Civil War, the abolitionists had succeeded in their primary goal—the United States government had made slavery illegal in the South with the Emancipation Proclamation, and throughout the rest of the Union with the thirteenth amendment. With passage of the fourteenth and fifteenth amendments, the government further secured rights for African-Americans, guaranteeing men the right to vote and both sexes all other rights and privileges as citizens of the United States. At the beginning of the hostilities, however, many abolitionists felt that President Lincoln's pursuit of the war purely to preserve the Union did not go far enough. Men like newspaper editor Horace Greeley wrote impassioned pleas to the president encouraging him to free the slaves. By 1862, Lincoln privately agreed with the abolitionists in the North and began constructing his proclamation. Although former slaves were free, abolitionists continued to work on their behalf, building schools and churches, working as educators, and traveling to southern states to ensure African-Americans were allowed to exercise their hard-won rights.

BILL OF SALE FOR 16 SLAVES, 1857. GM 5326.1203

SHACKLES. Iron, 19th century. GM 66.228

National Anti-Slavery Standard.

Rev F Frottingham

VOL. XXI. NO. 48.

NEW YORK, SATURDAY, APRIL 13, 1861.

WHOLE NO. 1,088.

THE CHURCH ANTI-SLAVERY SOCIETY.

National Anti-Slavery Standard.

PUBLISHED WEEKLY, ON SATURDAY,
AT TWO DOLLARS PER ANNUM,
BY THE
AMERICAN ANTI-SLAVERY SOCIETY,
At its Office, No. 5 Beekman Street, New York,
AND AT THE OFFICE OF THE
PENNSYLVANIA ANTI-SLAVERY SOCIETY,
107 N. Fifth St., above Arch, Philadelphia.

Selections.

Life in the Land of Chivalry.

From The Cincinnati Gazette, March 29.

THREE MONTHS IN PRISON FOR HAVING YOUR OWN OPINION.

Mr. Arthur Robinson, a young man about twenty-eight years of age, who was expelled from New Orleans for entertaining views not favorable to slavery...

INHUMAN TREATMENT OF A BLACK MAN.

From The Newbern (N. C.) Press.

HANGING A MICHIGAN MAN.

WHIPPING A WOMAN TO DEATH.

Received Columbia January 1st 1857 of Andrew Wallace ten thousand four hundred dollars in full for the purchase of the following negroes, to wit, Randolph, Dinah, Louisa, Clara, Julia, Lisbon, Sophy, Nelly, Sam, Rogers, William, Keziah, Mosy, Solomon, Absalom, Sylvia and I hereby bind myself my executors, administrators and assigns to warrant and forever defend the said Slaves unto the said Andrew Wallace his heirs executors and administrators against myself and against all other persons whomsoever lawfully claiming or to claim the same or any part thereof. Witness my hand & seal this 1st day of January 1857. Signed. Sealed and delivered in the presence of

Wm Wallace

Sam. W. Evans (L S)

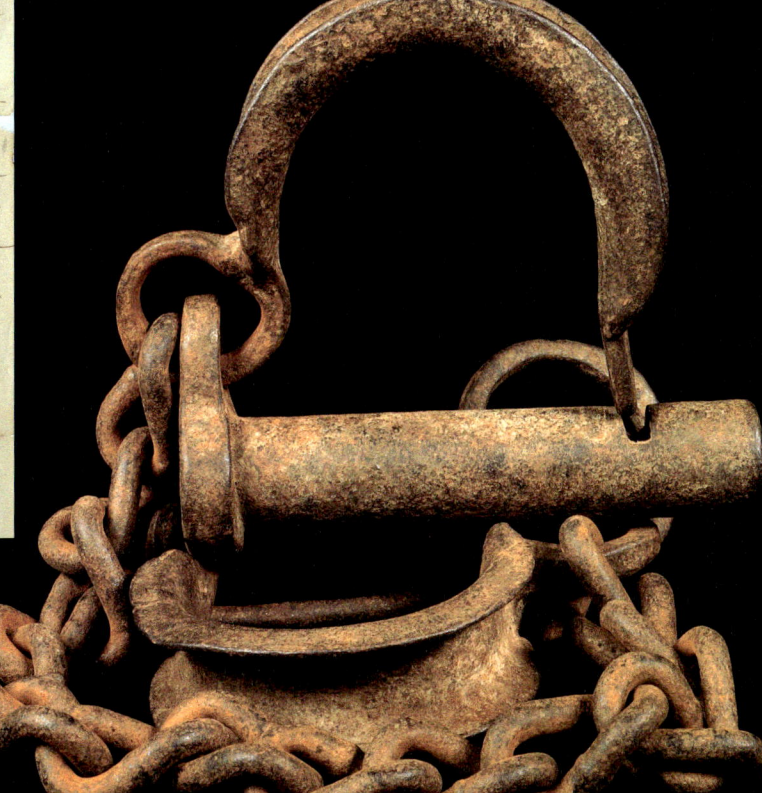

HARPER'S WEEKLY.
A JOURNAL OF CIVILIZATION.

Vol. IX.—No. 448.]   NEW YORK, SATURDAY, JULY 29, 1865.   [SINGLE COPIES TEN CENTS.
[$4.00 PER YEAR IN ADVANCE.

Entered according to Act of Congress, in the Year 1865, by Harper & Brothers, in the Clerk's Office of the District Court for the Southern District of New York.

FOURTH OF JULY AT ALBANY AND SARATOGA.

THE fact that General GRANT was to be present at Albany on the Fourth rendered that place a great centre of attraction during that day.

The ceremonies of the day took place on the Washington Parade-Ground. Besides the Lieutenant-General, several other distinguished military men were present, among whom were Generals SCHOFIELD, HUNTER, KAUTZ, KILPATRICK, and SICKLES. Having arrived on the Parade-Ground, after the prayer and the reading of the Declaration General BUTTERFIELD presented to the Government

and people of New York two hundred battle-flags, accompanying the presentation with an eloquent speech. Governor FENTON was too weak to deliver the responsive address, which was read by his private secretary. The oration of the day was pronounced by Dr. E. H. CHAPIN. After the oration, which was one of CHAPIN's finest efforts, there was the usual rush after General GRANT, who with difficulty fought his way to his carriage. We give an illustration of the presentation of the flags on page 468.

Independence Day was celebrated at Saratoga also under brilliant auspices, being made the occasion for a grand reunion of the Army of Tennessee.

The most noticeable characteristic of the celebration here was the absence of noise, the city government, frightened by the late fires, having forbidden the ignition of gunpowder in any shape during the day. The reunion of the army took place at LELAND's Union Hotel. Most of the officers who had been at Albany were present at the grand dinner which the LELANDS gave to the army. WILLIAM ROSS WALLACE recited a poem on the occasion. We give an illustration of the dinner on page 468. We publish also on page 469 three other illustrations—one of the ball which took place in the evening in the new Opera House just completed by the Messrs. LELANDS, another of the drive to Saratoga

Lake, and the third gives a fine view of the Lake itself. Saratoga Lake is three and one half miles from the town, and has on its borders several hotels. Pickerel, perch, and other fish abound in the Lake, and the disciples of WALTON can here indulge to their heart's content in their favorite amusement. This Lake is the favorite resort of the visitors at the Springs, and is the terminus of the best drives about the town. On the Fourth these drives were frequented by a large number of fashionable turn-outs. It would not tend to diminish the pleasures of Independence Day if it were always and every where celebrated with the quietness which characterized the celebration this year at Saratoga.

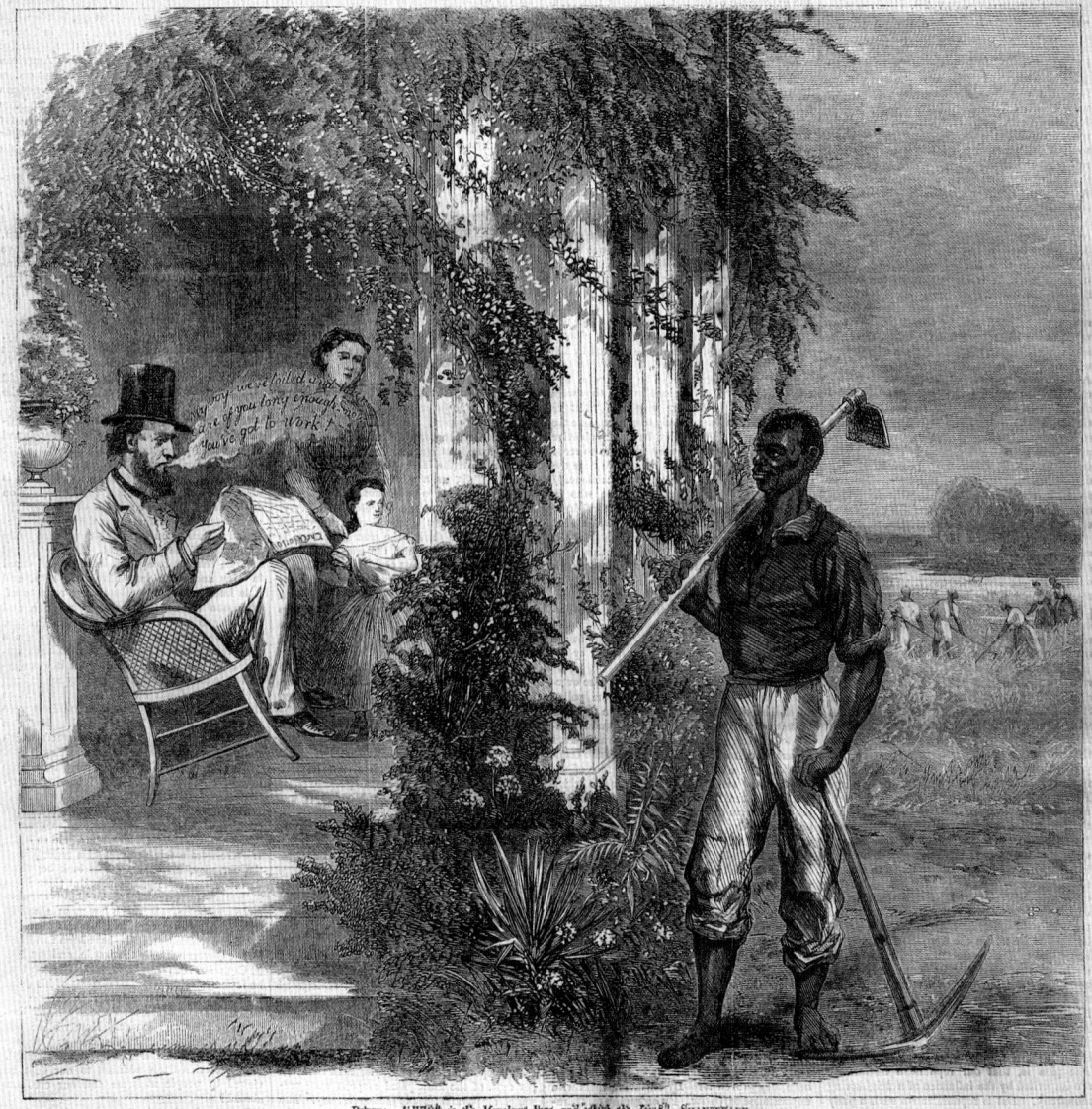

PORTIA.—"Which is the Merchant here, and which the Jew?"—SHAKSPEARE.

THE GREAT LABOR QUESTION FROM A SOUTHERN POINT OF VIEW.—[BY JOHN.]

The South's agriculturally based economy, in many ways unchanged since the turn of the 19th century, remained vested in the celebration of the gentleman farmer, the rights of property, and limited government.[9] While the southern states could grow enough food to feed its army and had a cash crop—cotton, potentially worth millions—its lack of infrastructure crippled supply lines and potential trade routes.[10]

Moral and political beliefs also marked the vast difference between North and South. Many of the most influential writers and speakers in the North, including philosopher Ralph Waldo Emerson, newspaper editor Horace Greeley, and author Harriet Beecher Stowe, advocated for abolition. As the debate over the slaveholding rights of new territories escalated, the factions supporting both abolition and slavery became more aggressive, to the point of violence. The 1850s came to a bloody close in Kansas, where agitators from the North and South sponsored settlers in the hope that they could sway the wording of the state constitution to either include or exclude slavery.[11] For some abolitionists, the slavery question was tied not only to beliefs, but to economics. Historian James McPherson argues that "Yankees [felt] slavery degraded labor, inhibited economic development, discouraged education, and engendered a domineering master class determined to rule the country in the interests of its backward institutions."[12] Many southerners felt that by isolating slavery to just their states, they would become marginalized from the rest

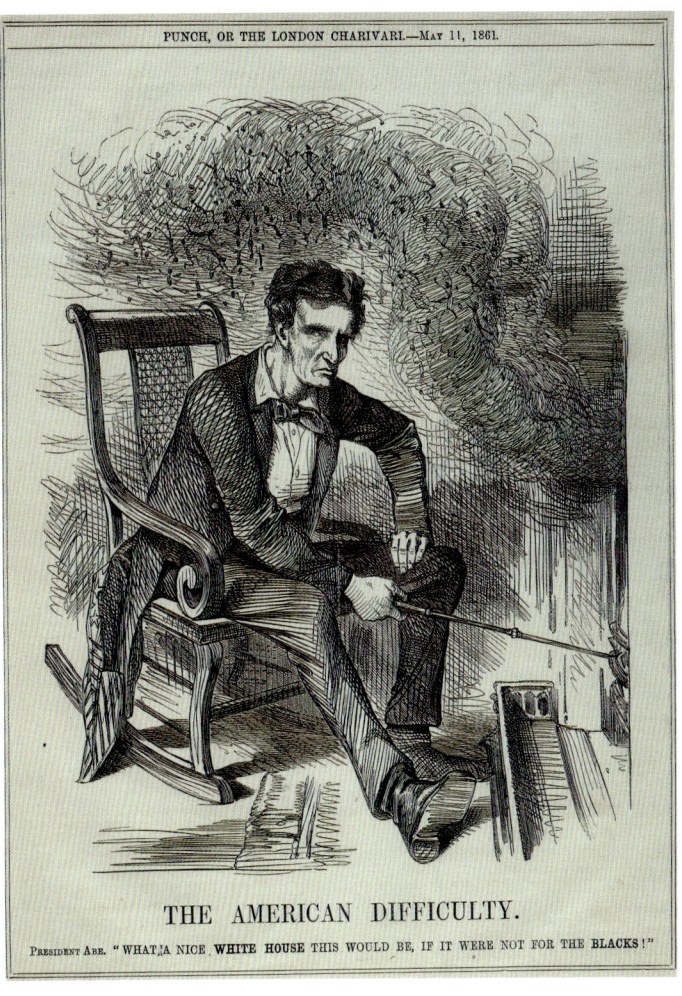

THE AMERICAN DIFFICULTY. *Punch, or the London Charivari,* May 11, 1861. GM 5076.4398

President Abraham Lincoln won only 40 percent of the popular vote, yet captured sufficient electoral vote-rich states to win the election. The outcome was met with trepidation in the South, where some counties had not even had him on their ballots. Almost immediately some southerners began to speak of secession. In Lincoln's first inaugural address, he called for calm, assuring the nation that he had no intention of altering the laws regarding slavery in the United States. He closed his speech with these words: "We are not enemies, but friends. We must not be enemies. Though passion may have strained, it must not break our bonds of affection. The mystic chords of memory, stretching from every battle-field and patriot grave to every living heart and hearthstone all over this broad land, will yet swell the chorus of the Union when again touched, as surely they will be, by the better angels of our nature."

FACING: THE GREAT LABOR QUESTION FROM A SOUTHERN POINT OF VIEW. *Harper's Weekly,* July 29, 1865. GM 5026.4397b

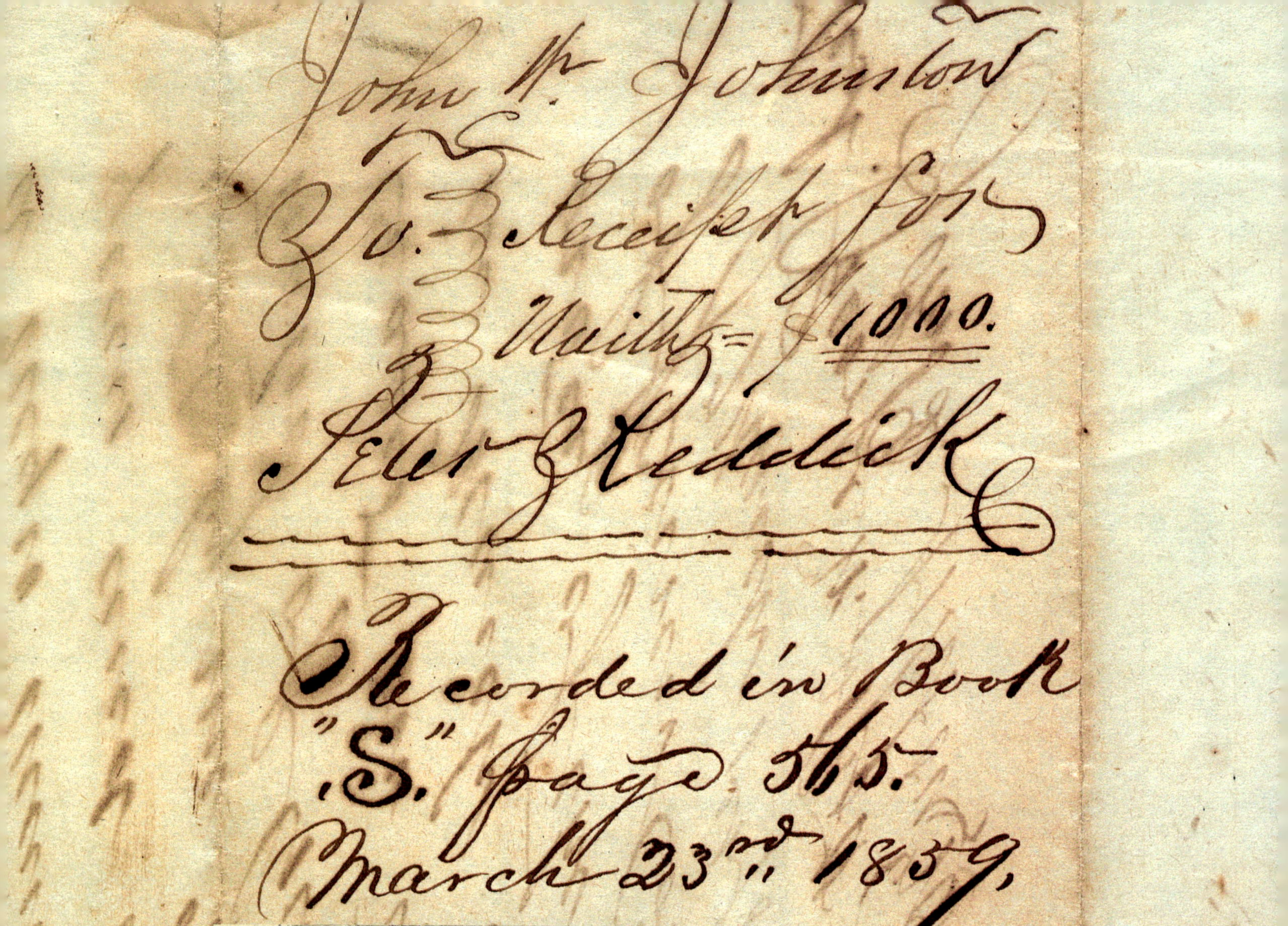

John W. Johnston

To Receipt for

Naith = $1000.

Peter Reddick

Recorded in Book
"S." page 565.
March 23rd 1859.

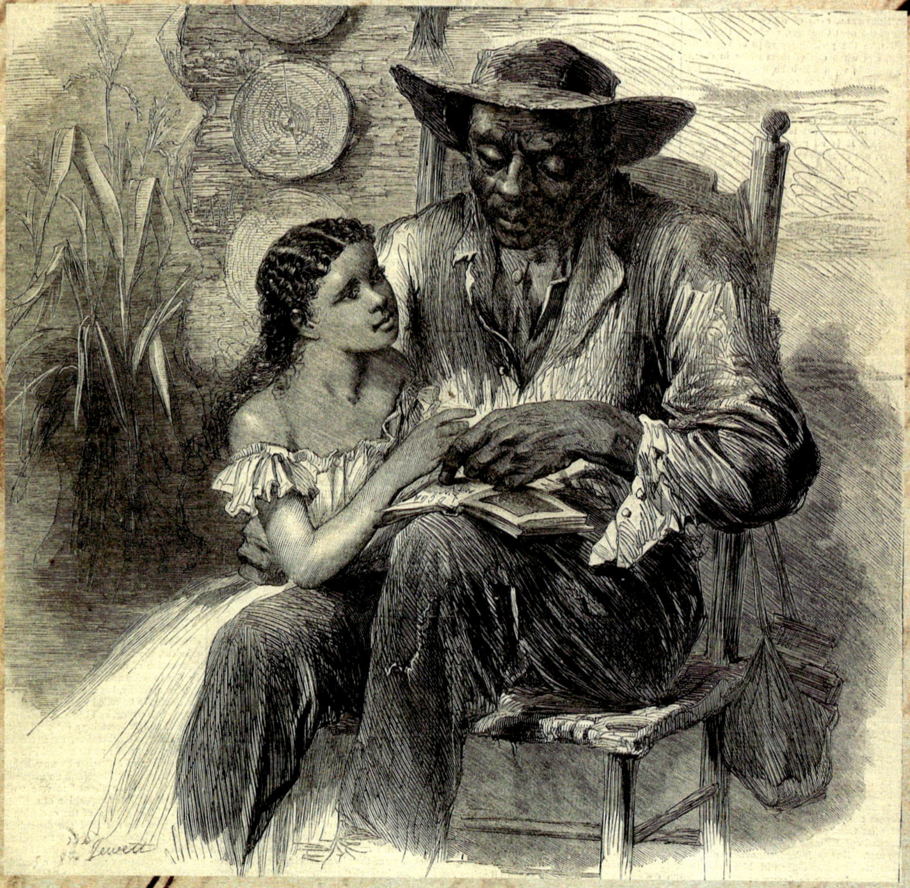

UNCLE TOM AND HIS
GRANDCHILD. *Harper's Weekly.*
November 3, 1866. GM 5026.4399

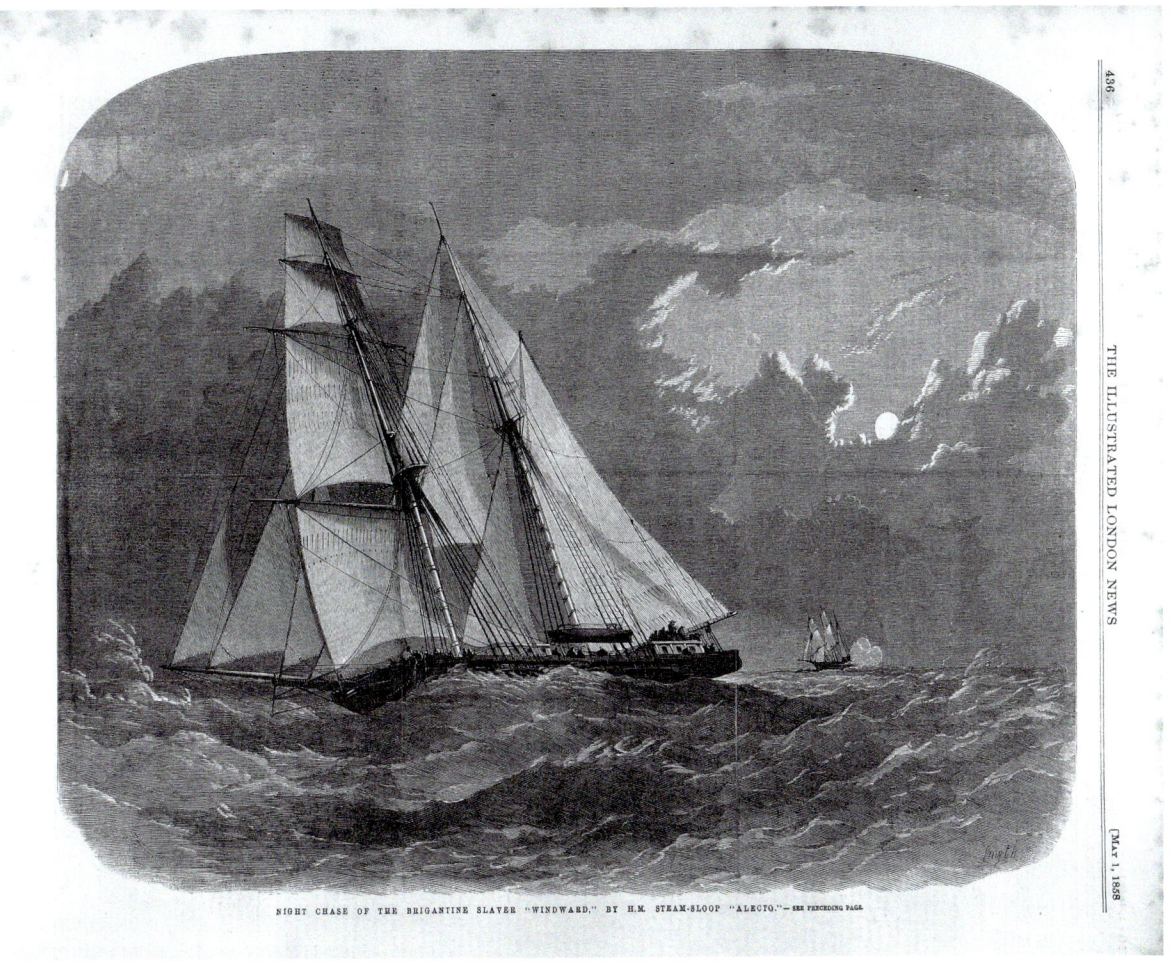

NIGHT CHASE OF THE BRIGANTINE SLAVER "WINDWARD," BY H.M. STEAM-SLOOP "ALECTO."— SEE PRECEDING PAGE.

of the country, despite the fact that their dependence on agriculture supported and enlarged the slave population in the United States.[13] This idea of being passed over as the rest of the country changed direction seems to have caused the most fear in many southerners and led them to believe that if the choice was to remain in the Union or preserve their way of life, they would rather fight for their lives.

If the skirmishes of "Bleeding Kansas" were the opening salvo in a larger war, then John Brown's raid on Harper's Ferry in Virginia on October 16, 1859, proved that the war had moved much closer to home for most Americans. Believing that slavery must be abolished at any cost, Brown was an active fighter for a free-state Kansas. He went so far as to participate in raids on pro-slavery homes, liberating slaves where he found them, and arousing the ire of the government in Missouri, as well as the pro-slavery adherents in the Kansas territory.[14] Believing he could start a slave revolt by seizing a government armory, Brown and twenty-two of his followers tried to forcibly take control of the armory at Harper's Ferry, fully expecting that once the building was in their hands, others would rally to the

NIGHT CHASE OF THE BRIGANTINE SLAVER "WINDWARD," BY H. M. STEAMSHIP "ALECTO." *The Illustrated London News,* May 1, 1858. TL2009.35.64m

JOHN BROWN, Currier and Ives. Lithograph. GM 16.968

John Brown's raid on the Harpers Ferry armory in 1859 was the opening salvo in what would become the Civil War. A survivor of "Bleeding Kansas"—the fight over slavery in Kansas Territory—Brown became a fervent supporter of the abolitionist cause. Believing that violence was the only way to free slaves, Brown and a small group of supporters planned to raid the national armory in Harpers Ferry, Virginia (now West Virginia), and instigate a riot among the local slaves. Brown and his men were quickly arrested, tried, and convicted for treason.

By the day of Brown's execution, many in the North began to see him as a martyr to the cause of abolitionism. Henry Wadsworth Longfellow and William Cullen Bryant both saw him as a hero. Said Bryant, "History, forgetting the errors of the nobleness of his aims will record his name among those of its martyrs and heros."

This copy of a Currier and Ives lithograph depicts Brown comforting those for whom he fought while stoically facing death.

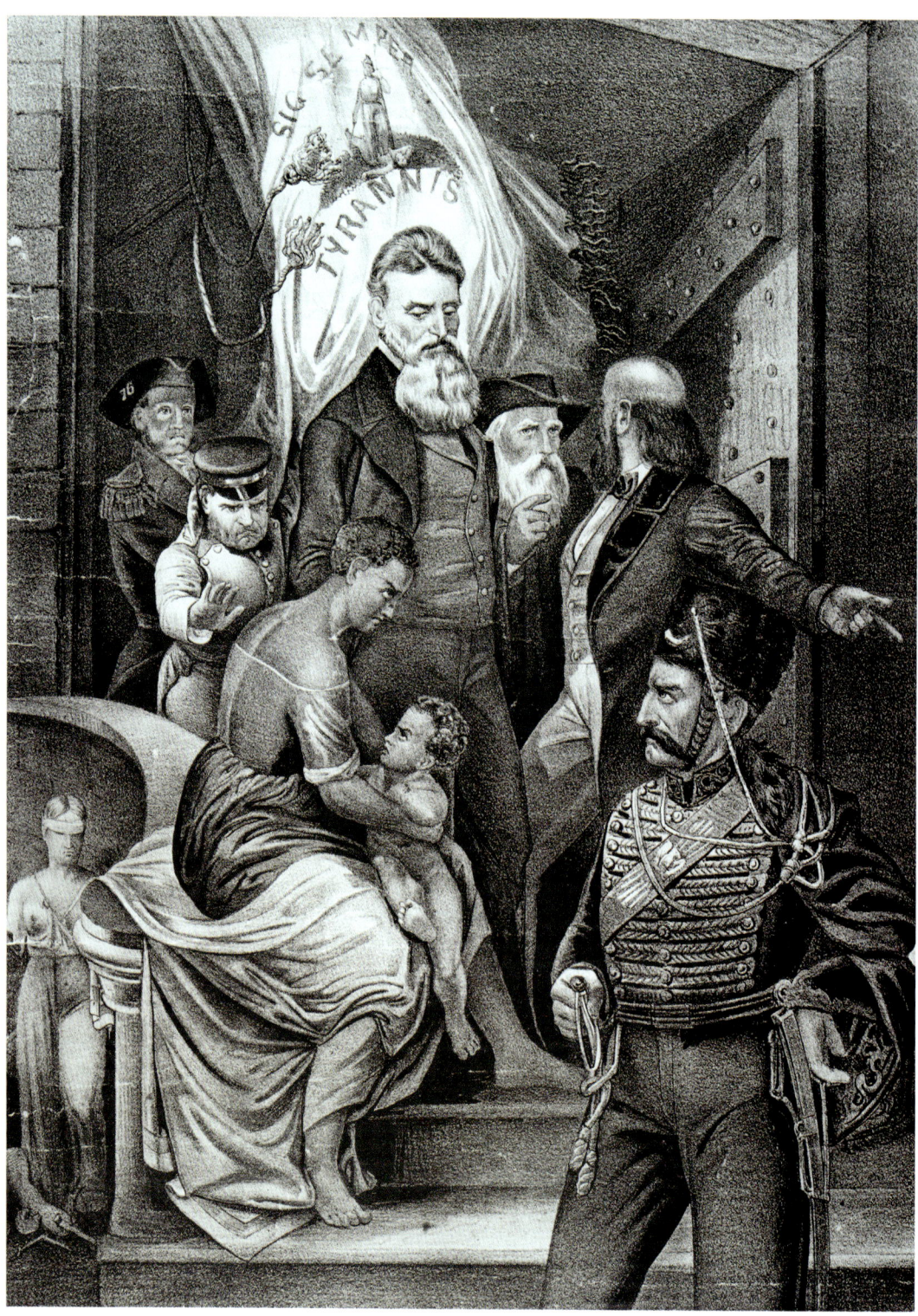

"Now, if it is deemed necessary that I should forfeit my life for the furtherance for the ends of justice, and mingle my blood further with the blood of my children and with the blood of millions in this slave country whose rights are disregarded by wicked, cruel, and unjust enactments—I submit; so let it be done!"

—John Brown, in his last speech before the court, prior to his execution, December 2, 1859

cause.[15] Despite confirming the worst fears about abolitionists in the South, and despite the fact that Brown was captured and executed, he became a folk hero of sorts in the North. "This will be a great day in our history," Henry Wadsworth Longfellow noted in his diary the day of Brown's execution, "the date of a new Revolution—quite as much needed as the old one."[16] William Cullen Bryant stated, "History, forgetting the errors of the nobleness of his aims, will record his name among those of martyrs and heroes."[17] In 1861, one Massachusetts regiment would adopt the song "John Brown's Body" as its anthem, proving that for many in the Union, as one observer wrote, "Brown has become an idea, a thousand times purer and better and loftier than the Republican idea."[18] With each side so opposed to the other and no compromise appealing to either, the country was on the precipice of a devastating war.

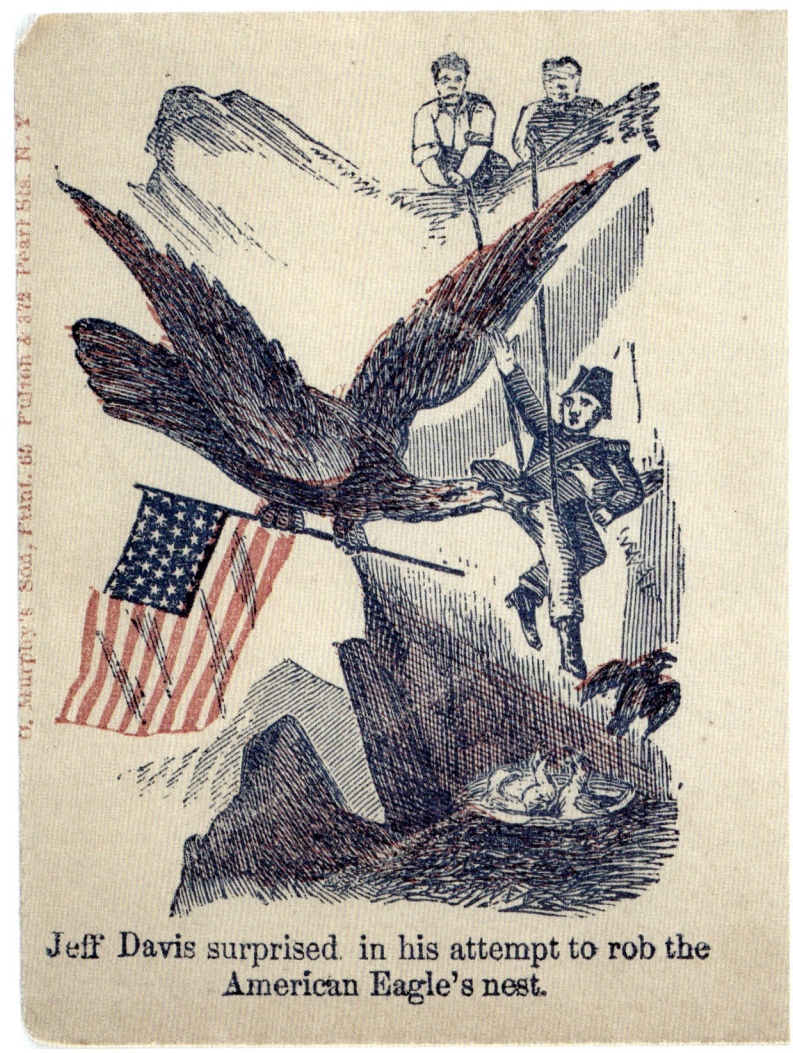

Jeff Davis surprised in his attempt to rob the American Eagle's nest.

ENVELOPE. Engraving, ca. 1862. GM 5326.1204

The reaction to the election of 1860 was fairly swift. Starting with South Carolina, states began seceding in December, one month after Lincoln's election. On January 21, 1861, Jefferson Davis withdrew himself from his Senate seat, citing his allegiance to his state, Mississippi, and his belief that the federal government had violated the sovereignty of the southern states.[19] The belief that a government out of southern hands would be a hostile government towards the southern states encouraged those remaining, including Mississippi, Florida, Alabama, Georgia, Texas, and Louisiana to leave the Union before Lincoln's inauguration.[20] Virginia, Arkansas, Tennessee, and North Carolina left soon after. Forming their own government, the Confederate States of America elected Jefferson Davis president and Alexander Stephens vice president. A little

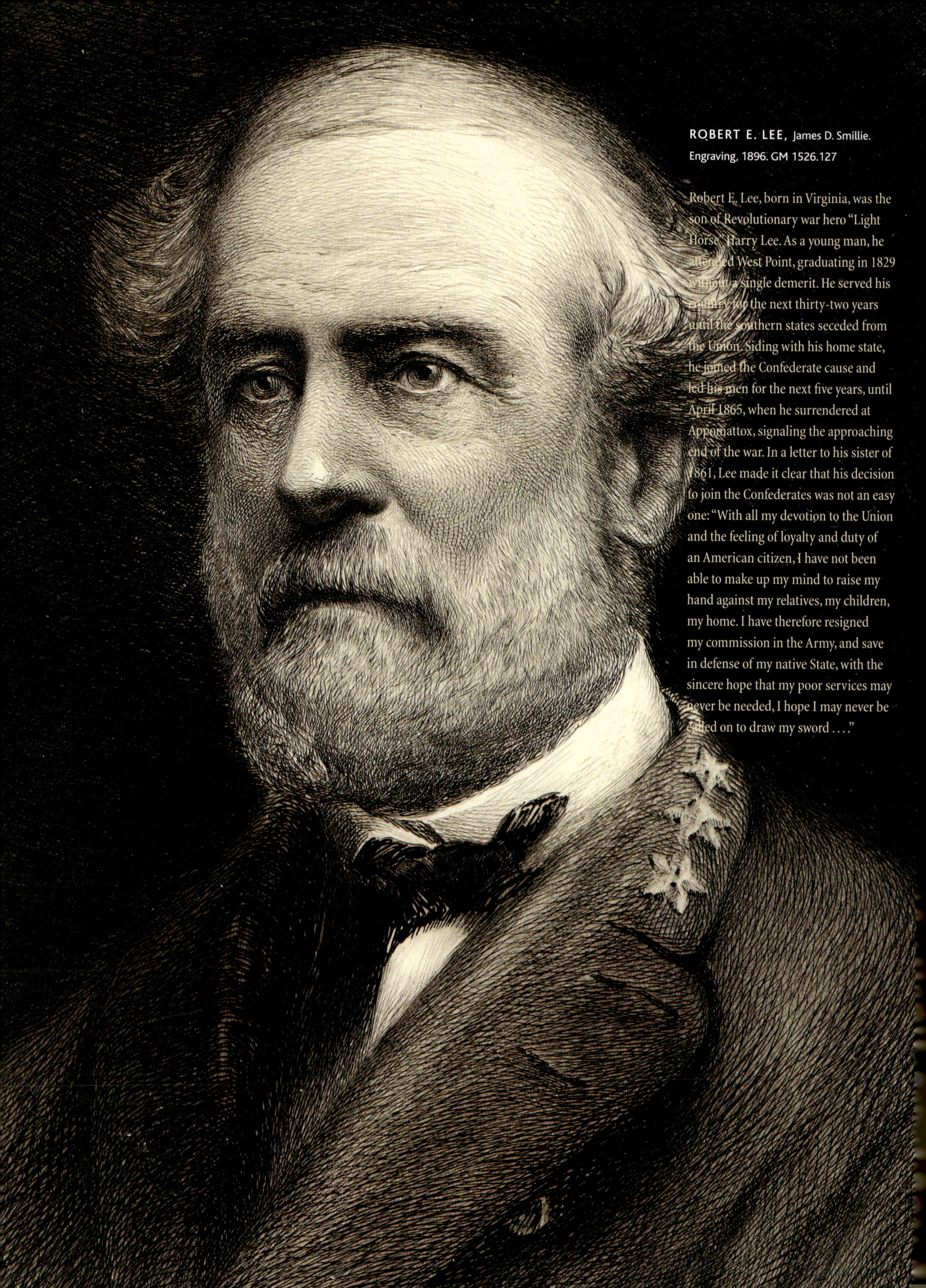

ROBERT E. LEE, James D. Smillie.
Engraving, 1896. GM 1526.127

Robert E. Lee, born in Virginia, was the son of Revolutionary war hero "Light Horse" Harry Lee. As a young man, he attended West Point, graduating in 1829 without a single demerit. He served his country for the next thirty-two years until the southern states seceded from the Union. Siding with his home state, he joined the Confederate cause and led his men for the next five years, until April 1865, when he surrendered at Appomattox, signaling the approaching end of the war. In a letter to his sister of 1861, Lee made it clear that his decision to join the Confederates was not an easy one: "With all my devotion to the Union and the feeling of loyalty and duty of an American citizen, I have not been able to make up my mind to raise my hand against my relatives, my children, my home. I have therefore resigned my commission in the Army, and save in defense of my native State, with the sincere hope that my poor services may never be needed, I hope I may never be called on to draw my sword . . . ."

over a month after Lincoln's inauguration in March of 1861, Davis and his new cabinet decided to strike Fort Sumter, a federal garrison in South Carolina. As a federal outpost located in a breakaway state, Fort Sumter held great symbolic meaning, even as the Union struggled to find a way to get supplies and support to it. On April 12, 1861, confederate troops, led by General Pierre Gustave Toutant Beauregard, opened fire on the fort. The battle, which lasted a day and half, resulted in surrender, and on April 14, "the American flag came down and the Confederate stars and bars rose over Sumter."[21]

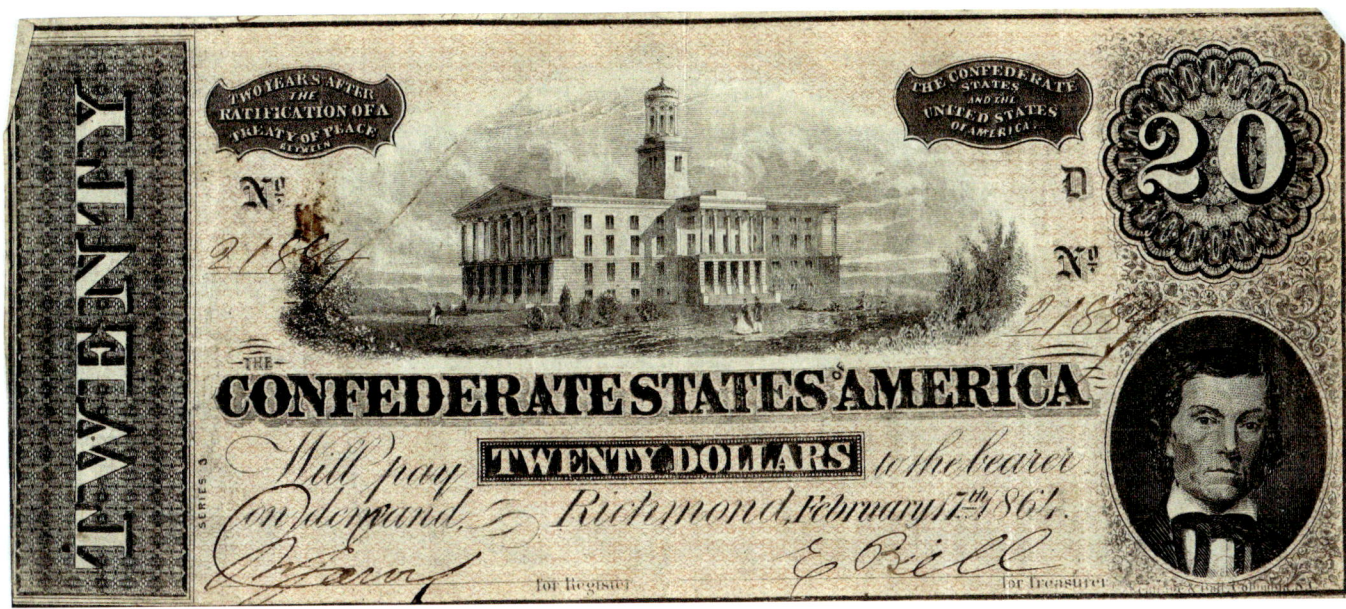

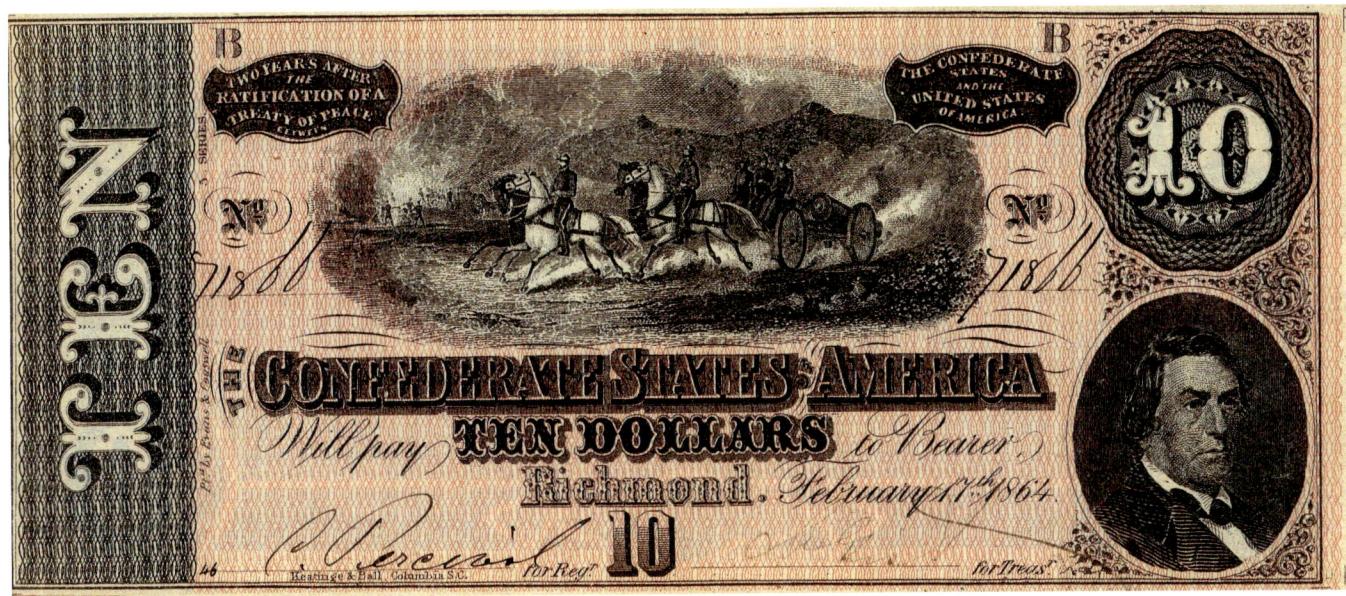

HARPER'S WEEKLY
A
JOURNAL OF CIVILIZATION.

VOL. VI.—No. 271.]   NEW YORK, SATURDAY, MARCH 8, 1862.   [SINGLE COPIES SIX CENTS.
$2 50 PER YEAR IN ADVANCE.

Entered according to Act of Congress, in the Year 1862, by Harper & Brothers, in the Clerk's Office of the District Court for the Southern District of New York.

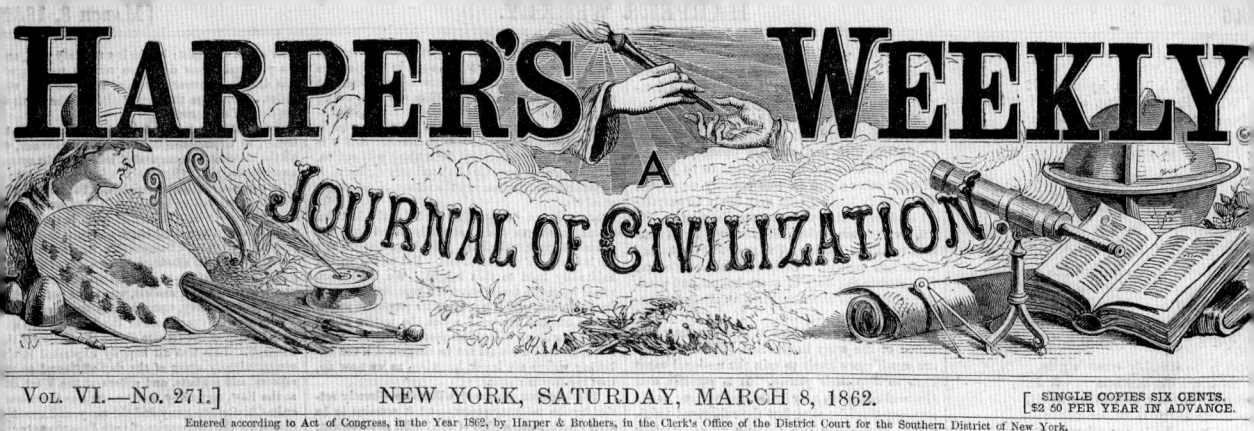

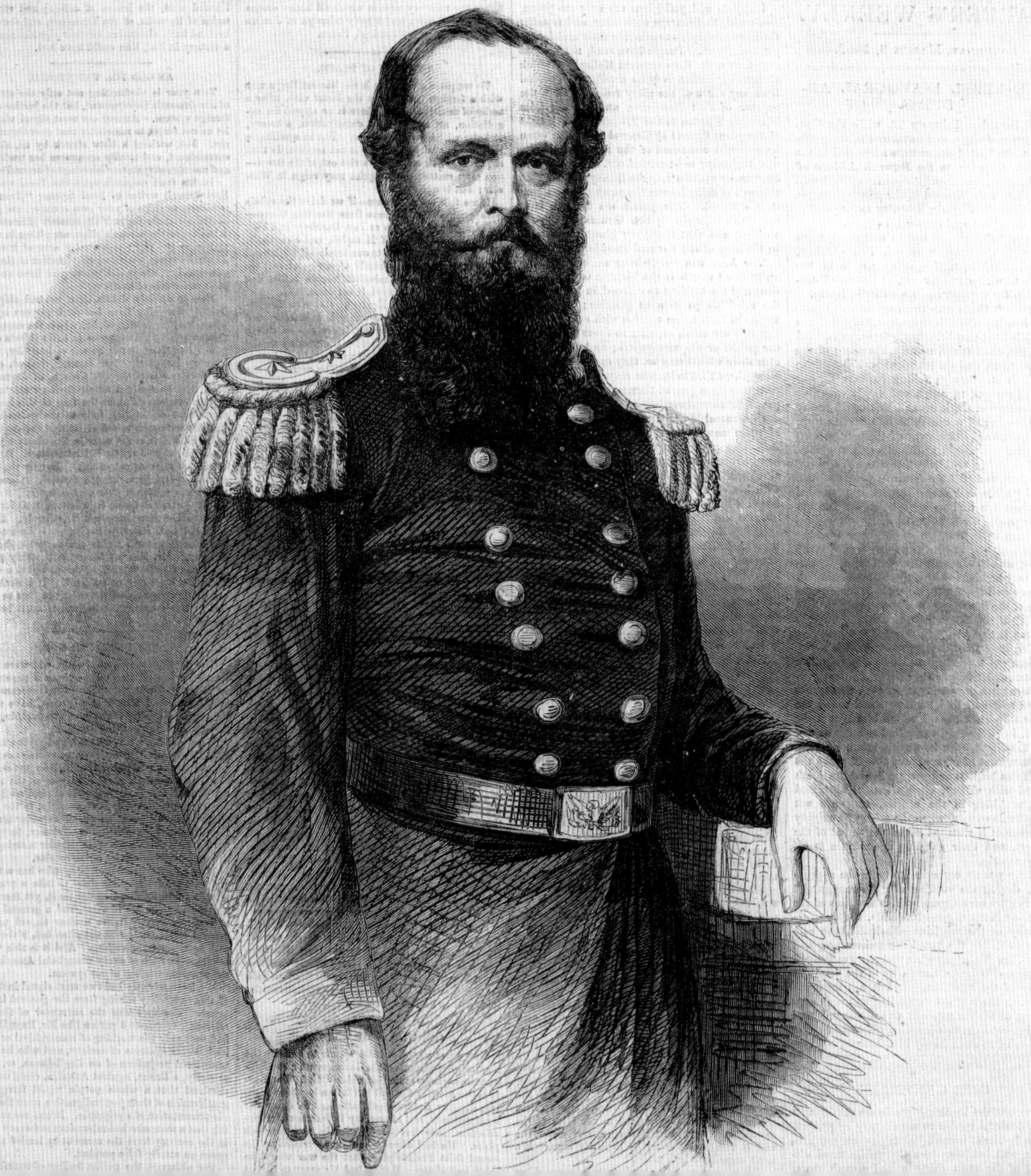

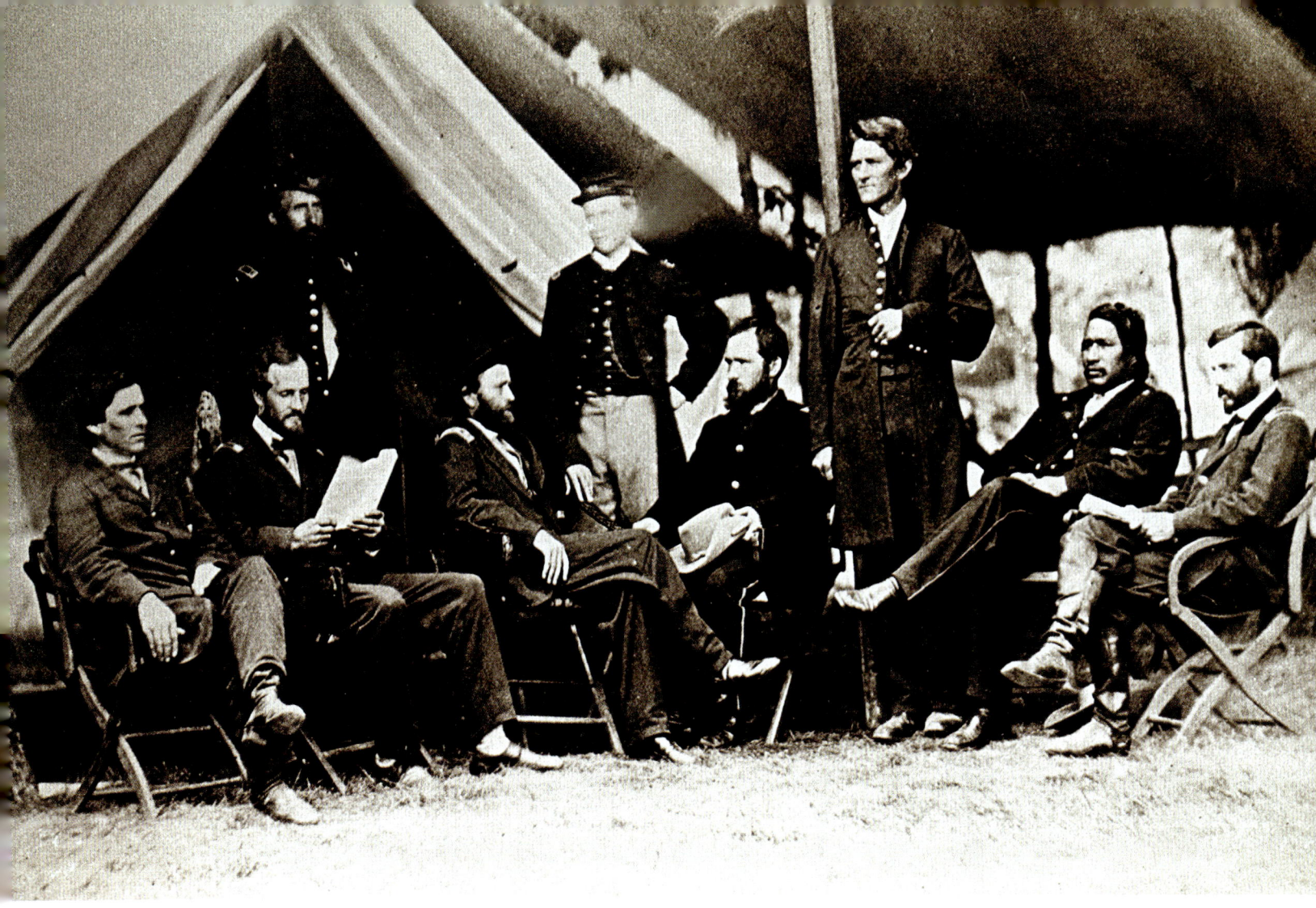

FACING: MAJOR ULYSSES
S. GRANT. *Harper's Weekly,*
March 8, 1862. GM 5026.4397jj

GENERAL ULYSSES S. GRANT AND HIS MEN,
unknown photographer. Photograph, ca. 1864. GM 4326.9072

Ulysses S. Grant, born in Ohio in 1822, rose through the army ranks to become
general in chief of the Army of the Potomac, and the man responsible for
determining the military strategy that ultimately won the Union the war. Grant
served under Zachary Taylor during the war with Mexico alongside Robert E.
Lee. Afterwards he tried his hand at farming and at running a business but found
little success with either. In the Civil War Grant once again found success as a
military leader, training Illinois volunteer corps. His victories on the battlefield
brought him to the attention of President Lincoln, who was in desperate need of
leaders. Grant was not always successful in battle (his detractors on both sides
depicted him as a drunk) but Lincoln supported his leadership, saying that "I
can't spare the man. He fights." As the war drew to a close, Grant coordinated
all of the major campaigns with Generals Sherman, Sheridan, and Thomas
and negotiated a peace with Robert E. Lee's Army of Virginia that allowed the
South to reenter the Union without war trials. After the war, Grant's popularity
soared, and in 1868 he was elected president. Although Grant worked to ensure
African-American participation in government and sought to reverse the policy
regarding Native American tribes, his terms in office were marred by corruption
scandals within his cabinet and an unstable economy. He died in 1885, still
struggling to achieve success in civilian life.

The war began ominously for the Union. Over its course, hopes of victory would be raised and dashed repeatedly. With its first major loss at the Battle of Bull Run in 1861 and a series of frustrating false starts by General George McClellan and his Army of the Potomac, hopes that the war would end quickly faded. The grimness of a nation at war became reality. Many battles had up to 30 percent casualties, and in the Battle of Shiloh, the first major Union victory, 20,000 soldiers either died or were injured.[22] High casualties and missed opportunities would be the hallmarks of the war. The Battle of Antietam in September of 1862 pitted McClellan's forces against General Robert E. Lee and the Army of Northern Virginia. Despite McClellan's superior numbers and the discovery of Lee's battle plan, the Union general drew down and allowed the Confederate troops to retreat.[23] Battles like Fredericksburg in 1863 saw over 15,000 killed, while other battles, like Vicksburg in Mississippi, turned into a protracted siege for General Ulysses S. Grant. Gettysburg was a turning point. Over the first few days of July 1863, the Union armies successfully defended, and then defeated, the Confederate army, ending with Major General George Pickett's disastrous charge against General George Meade's men. The Confederate army was decimated, and General Lee's army would never get so far into Union territory again.[24] For the first time since 1860, the Union had a reason to celebrate the Fourth of July. The celebration was tempered, however, by the staggering loss of life. Of the 140,000 who fought at Gettysburg, there were over 50,000 casualties, with some companies losing every single one of their men.[25] It is little wonder then, that when Lincoln arrived to dedicate the field at Gettysburg as a national cemetery on November 19, 1863, he stated "that from these honored dead we take increased devotion to that cause for which they gave the last full measure of devotion; that we here highly resolve that these dead shall not have died in vain."[26] Lincoln's statement renewed the nation's resolve to see the war through to the end.

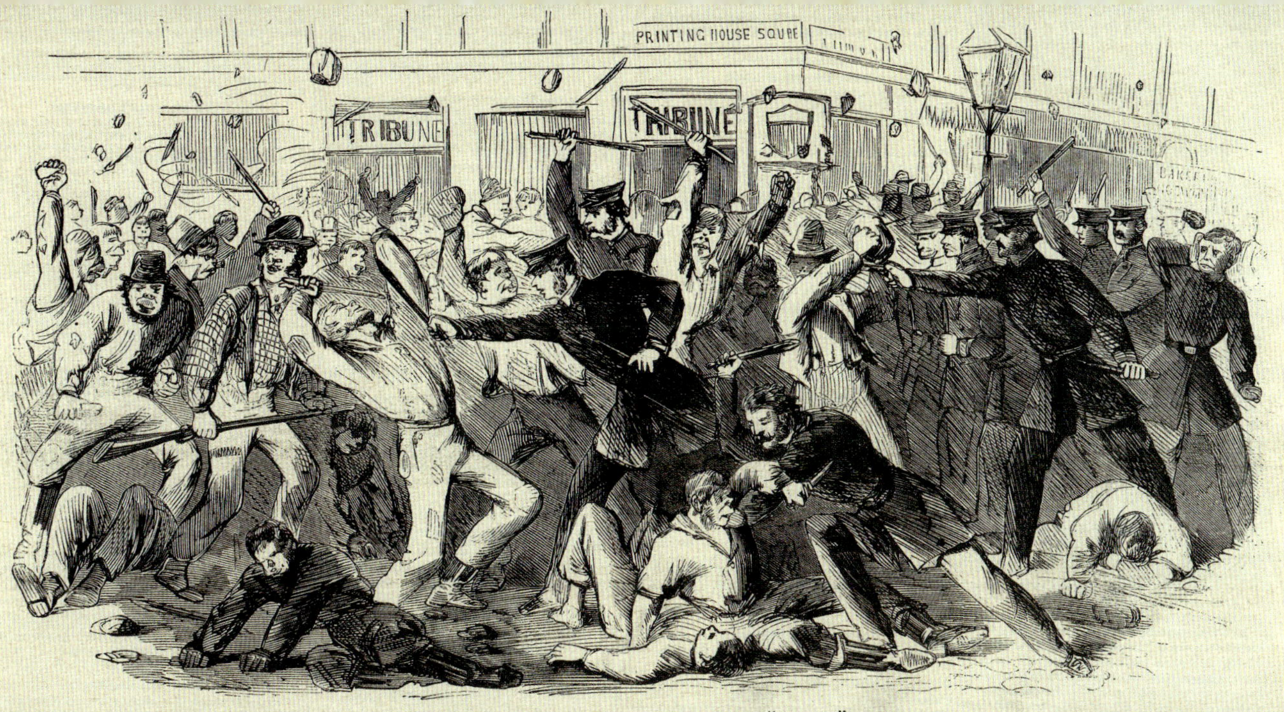

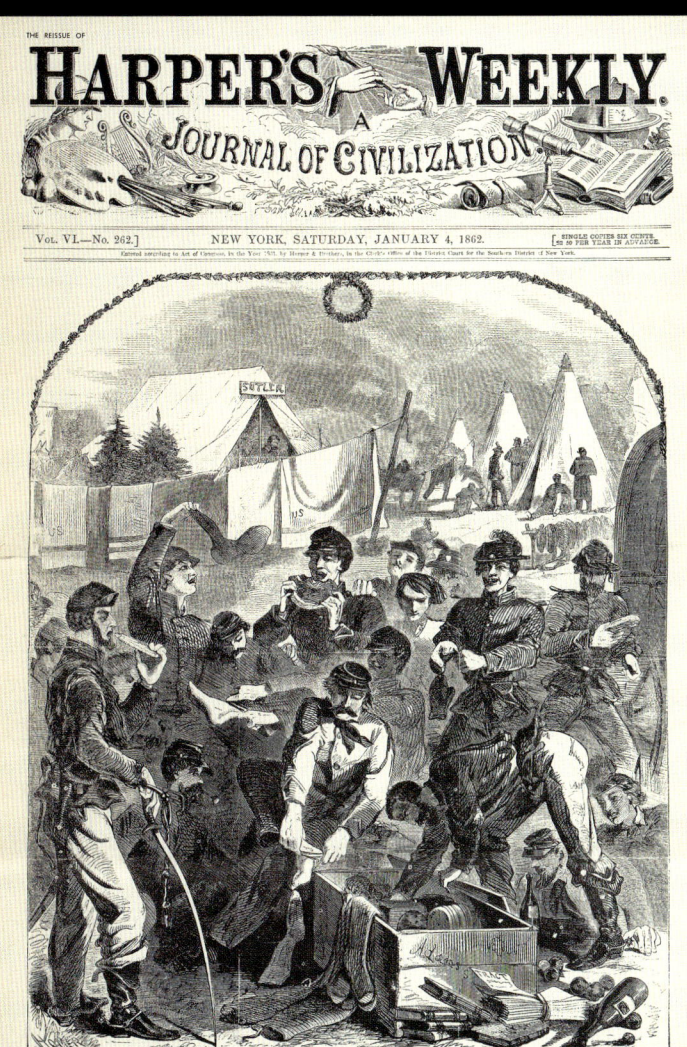

CHARGE OF THE POLICE ON THE RIOTERS AT THE "TRIBUNE" OFFICE.

As the war dragged on, both sides found it difficult to encourage new recruits. In 1862, the Confederacy began drafting men to fight, and in 1863 the Union followed suit. Although any man of age could be drafted, wealthier men could pay $300 or provide a man to take their place, causing many to remark that this was "a rich man's war, but a poor man's fight." This idea took root in many among the Irish-American community in New York City, where men were conscripted right off the boat. With the date for the draft looming, the city plunged into anarchy. Targeting their anger at the government and at African-Americans, who were seen as competition for work, rioters rampaged through the city for five days in July 1863. By the time Union troops moved in to quell the mob, over 100 people had been killed. Churches, prosperous homes, the draft office, and the *New York Tribune* building were burned or destroyed.

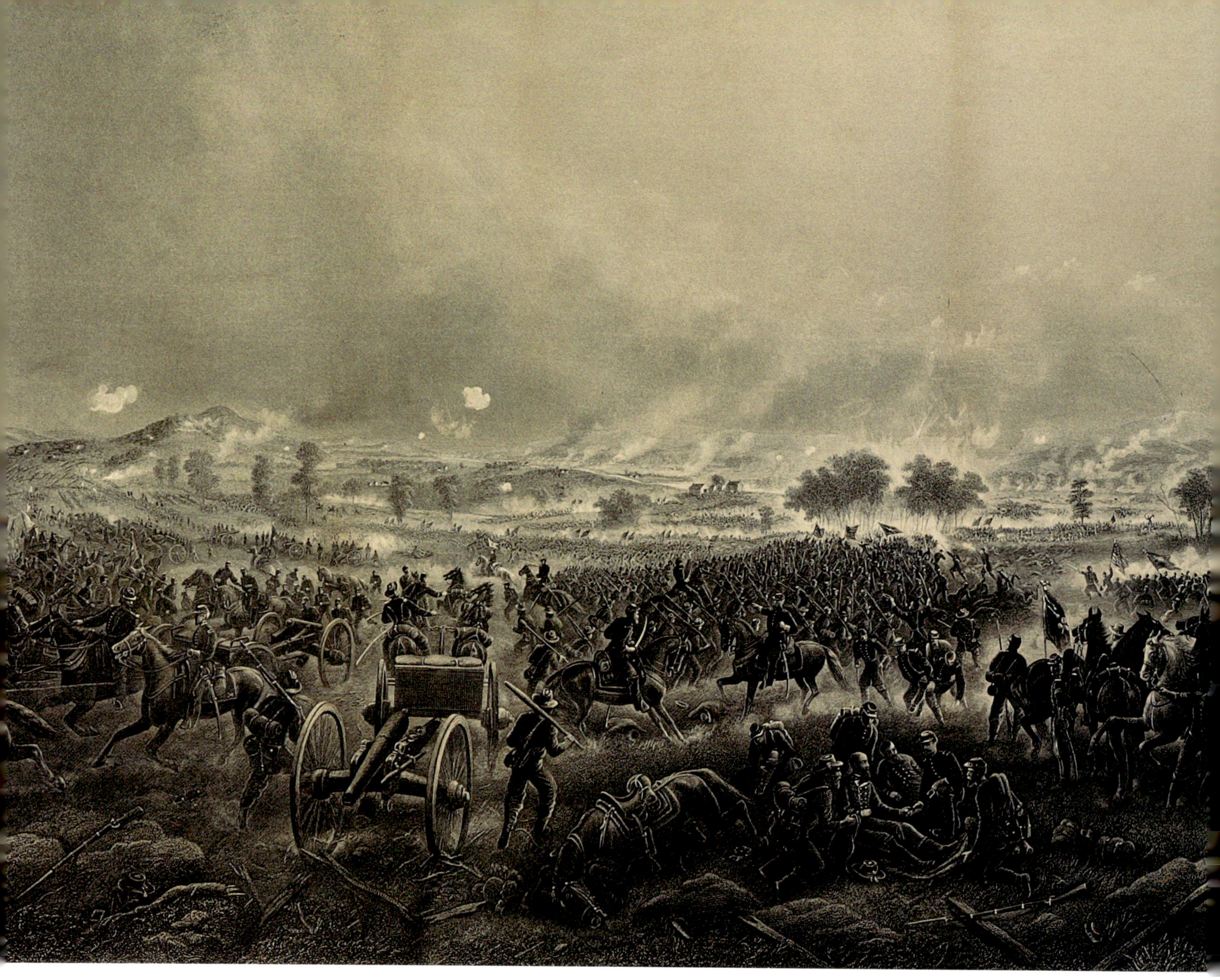

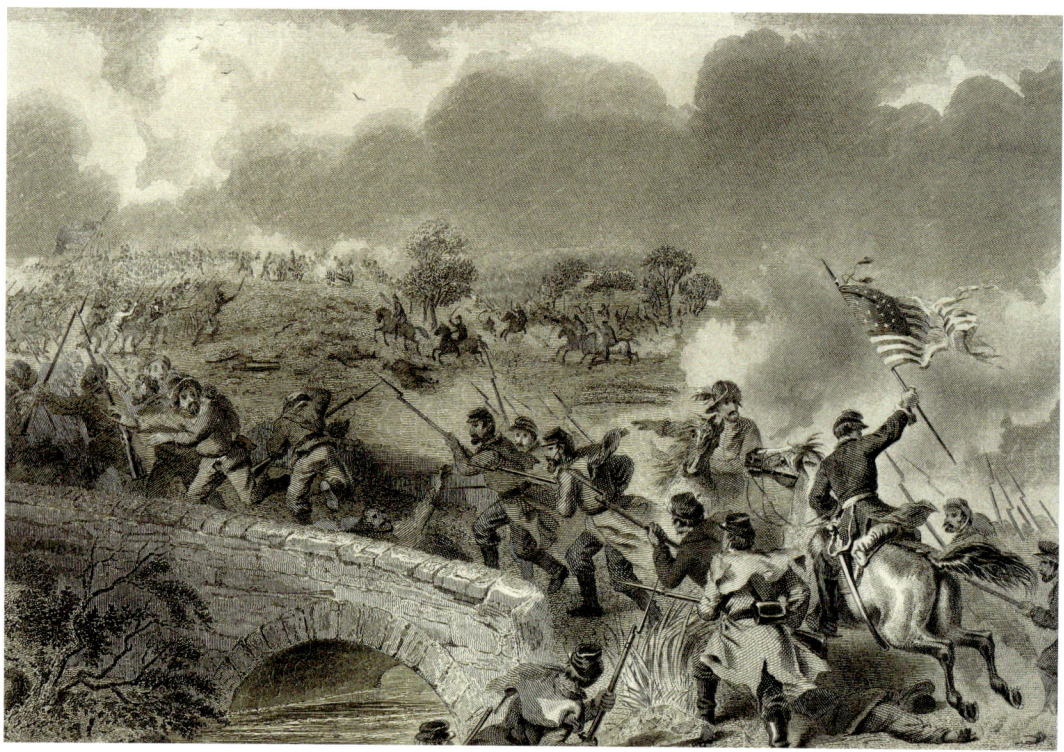

BATTLE OF ANTIETAM.

From *The Great Rebellion: A History of the Civil War in the United States* by J. T. Headley. American Publishing Company, 1866. GM 2726.134

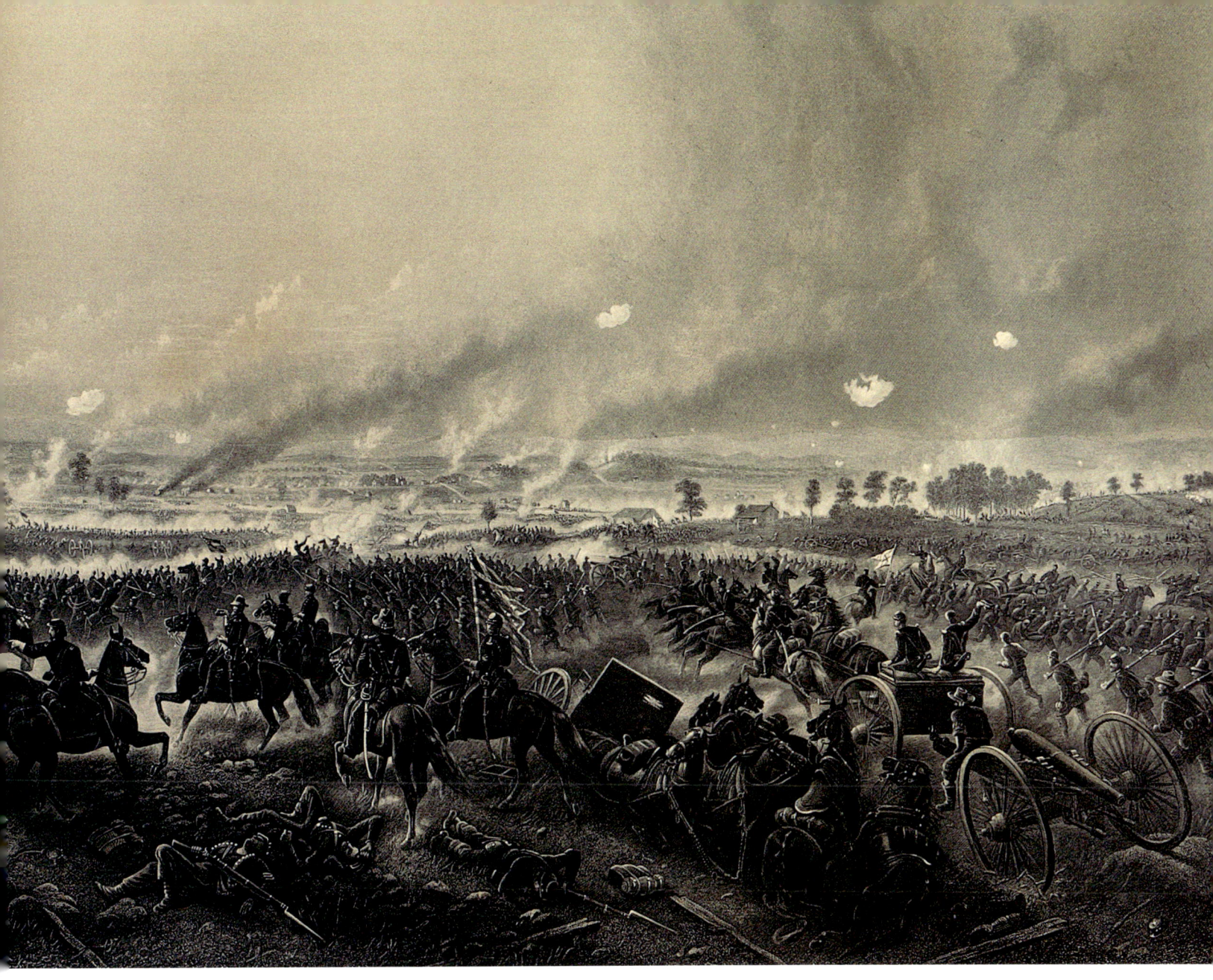

GETTYSBURG—REPULSE OF LONGSTREET'S ASSAULT, James Walker. Engraving. GM 1526.118a

The Battle of Gettysburg, fought during the first three days of July 1863, proved to be a turning point for the Union army. Northern troops led by General George Meade arrived in the town of Gettysburg, Pennsylvania, before the Confederates and were able to occupy the high ground. Confederate soldiers led by General Robert E. Lee arrived a day later and attacked, eventually pushing the Union army back from its position. As troops regrouped the next day, fighting began at the Peach Orchard, Little Round Top, and the Wheatfield. Despite heavy losses, the Union maintained its line. The battle reached its apex on July 3 at Cemetery Ridge. There, Major General George Pickett, under the command of Confederate Lt. General James Longstreet, launched an assault on the Union forces holding the line. Pickett planned to attack after Confederate shelling had disabled the North's cannons. Although a Confederate success initially seemed possible, the Union artillery revived, proving it had not been destroyed after all. Pickett lost two-thirds of his men, and although the battle was not yet over, Gettysburg was lost. Longstreet later recalled that he had disagreed with Lee's order to attack, stating, "I could see the desperate and hopeless nature of the charge and the hopeless slaughter it would cause. That day at Gettysburg was one of the saddest of my life."

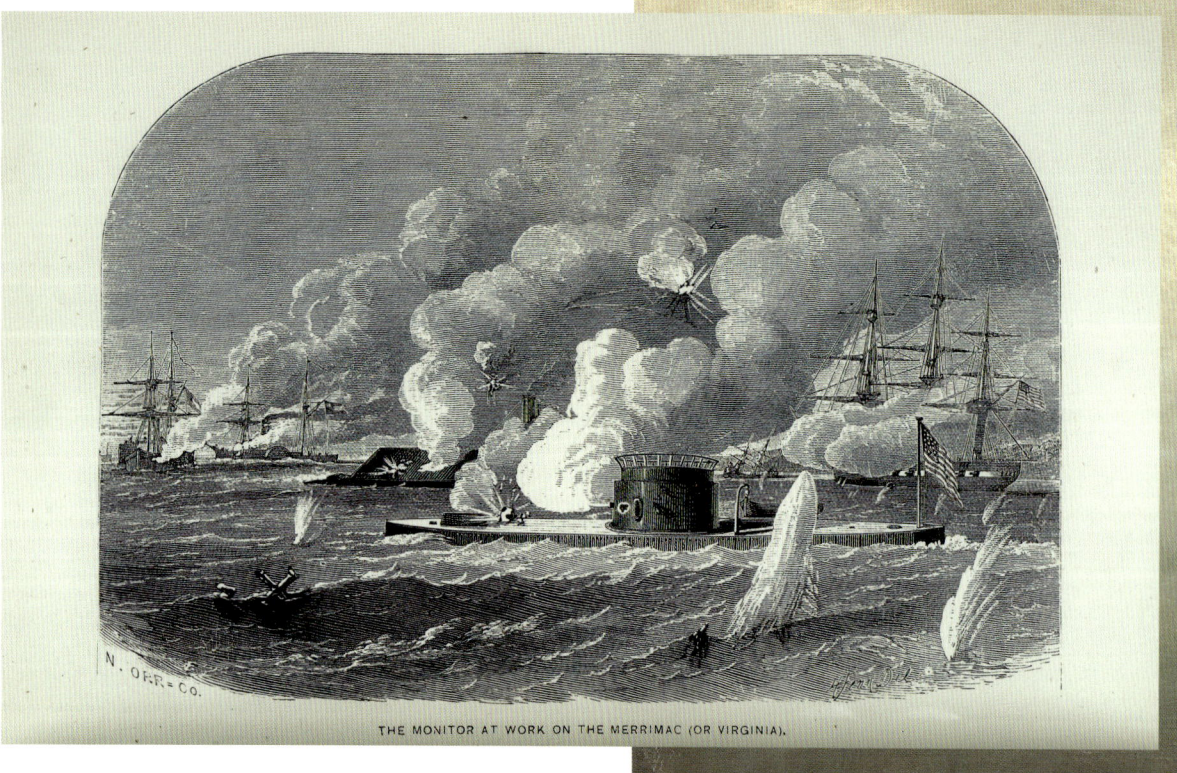

THE MONITOR AT WORK ON THE MERRIMAC (OR VIRGINIA).

THE MONITOR AT WORK ON THE MERRIMAC
(OR VIRGINIA). From *The American Conflict*, by Horace Greeley, 1867. GM 2726.131.112

THE ENGAGEMENT BETWEEN THE MONITOR AND THE MERRIMAC, John Stuart. Oil on canvas. GM 0116.1558

On March 9, 1862, the *U.S.S. Monitor* and the *C.S.S. Virginia* (as the *U.S.S. Merrimac* was rechristened) made history when they clashed on the waters off Hampton Roads. The *C.S.S. Virginia* was the scuttled *U.S.S. Merrimac*, rebuilt and refitted as an ironclad. In two days time, it had already sunk the Union's *Cumberland* and *Congress*. The *U.S.S. Monitor*, however, was a more difficult opponent. Launched in January of 1862, it was somewhat smaller than the *Virginia*, but had a state-of-the-art armored turret. Roughly twenty feet in diameter, the turret rotated by steam power, allowing for all-around fire. One crewman described the shock as the two vessels "eyed" each other. "You can see surprise in a ship just as you can see it in a man, and there was surprise all over the *Merrimac*." After their first skirmish, the two ships never engaged the other again; both were destroyed by the end of 1862. The *C.S.S. Virginia* was sunk by her men rather than be captured by the Union. The *Monitor* sank in a storm off Cape Hatteras as it was being towed for a new assignment.

CIVIL WAR MILITARY DRUM. Animal hide and wood, ca. 1861. GM 84.3404

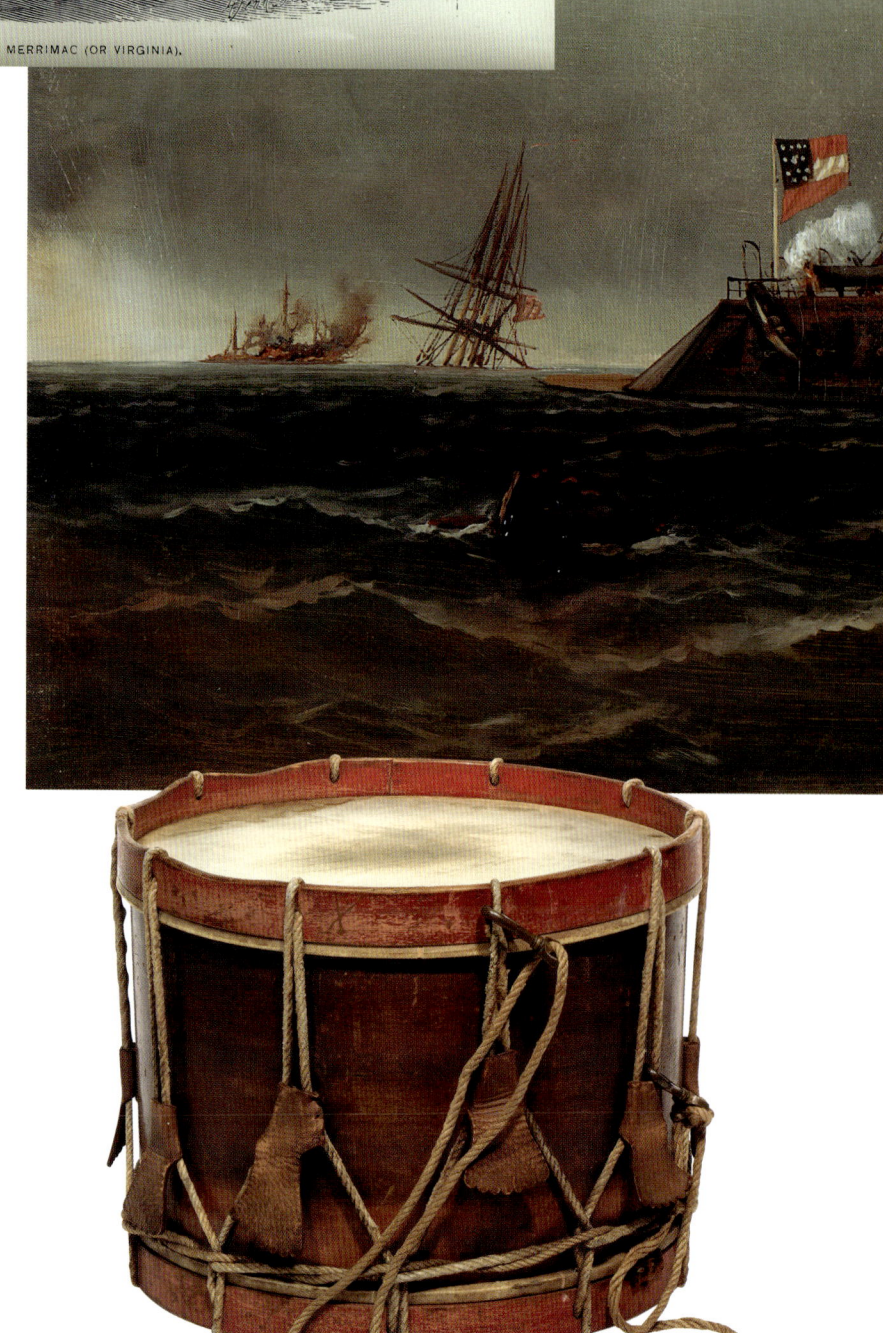

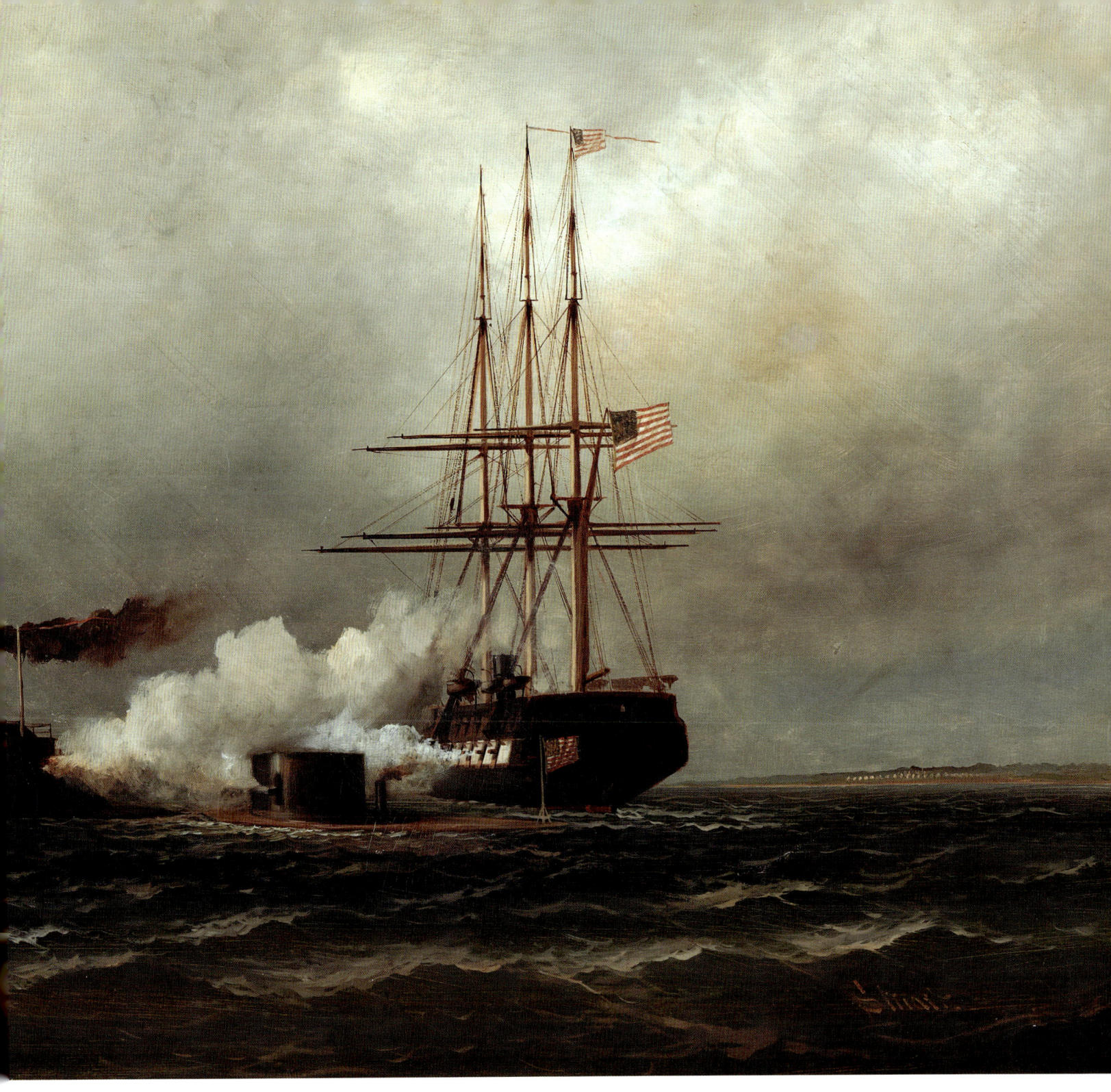

Throughout the war, the nation's resolve rested on the fighting men. After each battle, the letters home from the soldiers on both sides gave their loved ones a glimpse into their lives, the fear, the hope, and even the boredom that accompanied their day-to-day routines. For many on the front lines, the little things kept them going. One soldier wrote, "I was much disappointed to hear that you was not agoing to send me that box. Don't be afraid to send it for it would kill nobody if I shouldn't get it."[27]

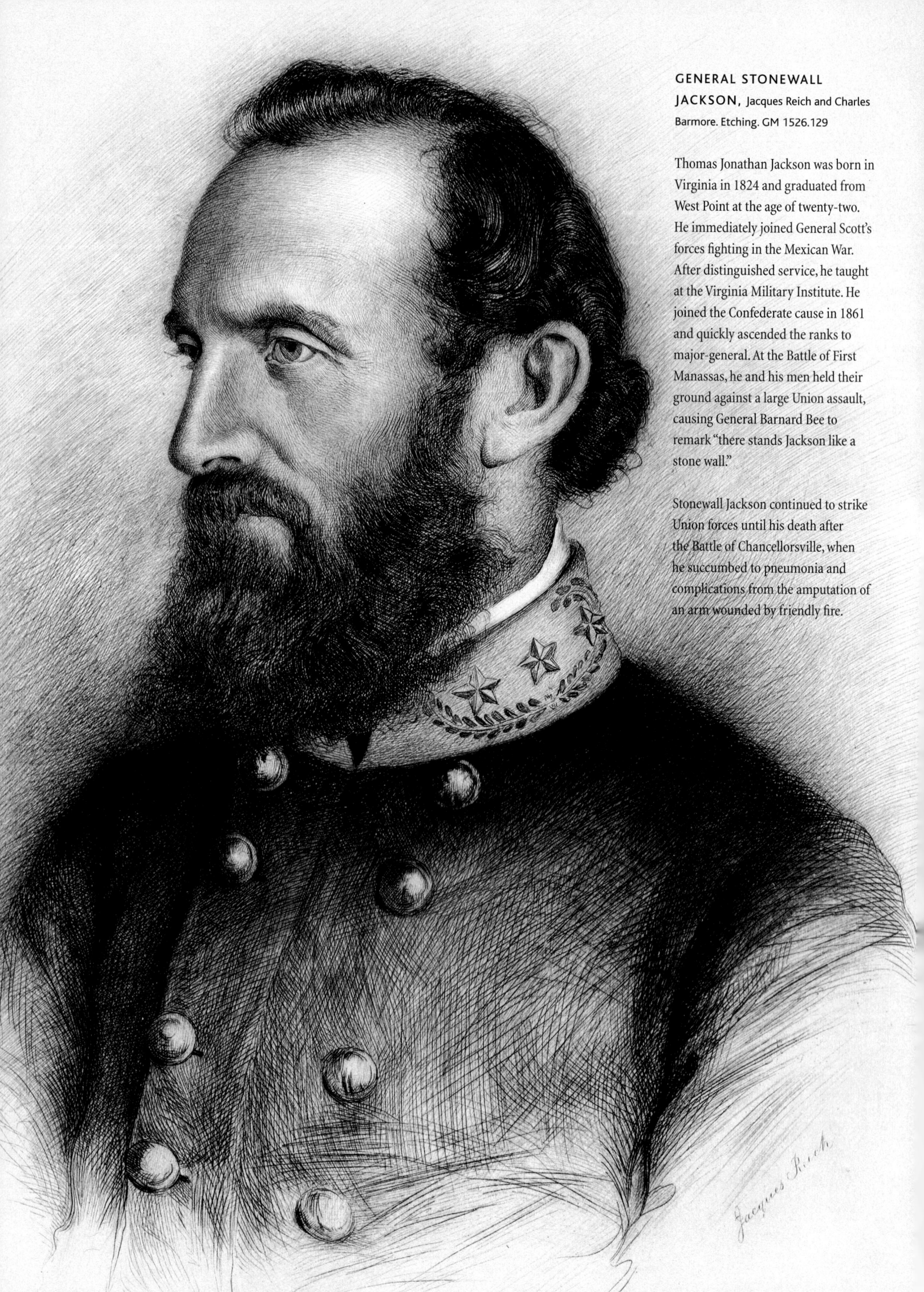

GENERAL STONEWALL JACKSON, Jacques Reich and Charles Barmore. Etching. GM 1526.129

Thomas Jonathan Jackson was born in Virginia in 1824 and graduated from West Point at the age of twenty-two. He immediately joined General Scott's forces fighting in the Mexican War. After distinguished service, he taught at the Virginia Military Institute. He joined the Confederate cause in 1861 and quickly ascended the ranks to major-general. At the Battle of First Manassas, he and his men held their ground against a large Union assault, causing General Barnard Bee to remark "there stands Jackson like a stone wall."

Stonewall Jackson continued to strike Union forces until his death after the Battle of Chancellorsville, when he succumbed to pneumonia and complications from the amputation of an arm wounded by friendly fire.

Another complained, "I have taken cold and have a headache and a fever. I believe the terrible dust has much to do with it and the hard fare. I can get little or nothing to eat, the best is blue-looking beef and the terrible bread cooked in camp. We have no coffee, tea or sugar."[28] Some sent more hopeful words home, relying on their faith in the purpose of the war. "I am willing—perfectly willing—to lay down all my joys in this life, to help maintain this government," wrote one soldier, while another felt enlisting was "a duty I owe to my country and to my children to do what I can to preserve this government."[29] More often than not, though, letters home detailed the battles and their aftermath. After the battle of Shiloh, one soldier wrote, "I never realized the 'pomp and circumstance' of the thing called glorious war until I saw this. Men lying in every conceivable position; the dead with their eyes wide open, the wounded begging piteously for help. I seemed in a sort of daze."[30] General William T. Sherman would go on to state that the sight of mangled bodies on a battlefield "would cure anybody of war."[31] For those who fought on both sides, General Sherman's statement summed up their feelings as they returned to their lives.

Not all those who remained at home needed letters to explain the horrors of battle. The new medium of photography, led by Matthew Brady and Timothy O'Sullivan, brought images of war to newspapers and to Main Street galleries. In a review of an 1862 showing of Brady's

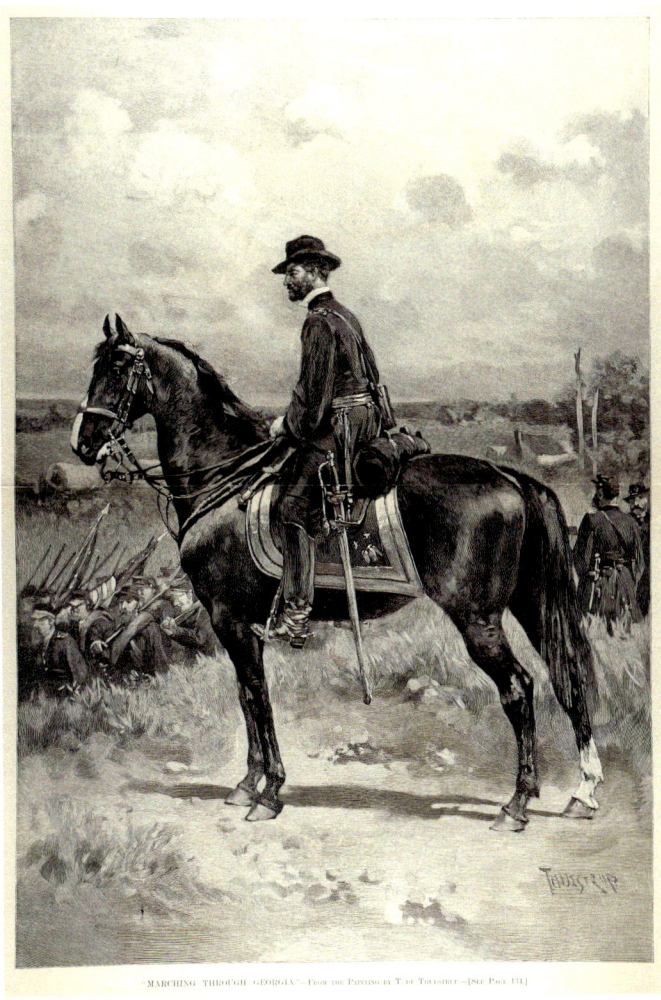

MARCHING THROUGH GEORGIA, Thure de Thulstrup. *Harper's Weekly,* February 21, 1891. T. F. Healy Collection, Gilcrease Museum Archive

William Tecumseh Sherman earned fame on the battlefield by enacting the concept of "total war" to bring an end to Confederate hostilities. While Sherman's strategy left an uncompromising legacy, he personally disliked battle, stating that the sight of its bloodshed "would cure anyone of war." After laying siege to Atlanta, Sherman and his men began their "March to the Sea." Turning towards Savannah and then north to the Carolinas, they destroyed crops and railroad tracks in an effort to illustrate the futility of continued warfare against the Union army. When the city government of Atlanta asked Sherman to call off a forced evacuation of the city due to the hardship it would cause civilians, he responded that "You cannot qualify war in harsher terms than I will. War is cruelty, and you cannot refine it; and those who brought war into our country deserve all the curses and maledictions a people can pour out. I know I had no hand in making this war, and I know I will make more sacrifices today than any of you to secure peace. But you cannot have peace and a division of our country." After the Civil War, Sherman commanded the U. S. Army under President Grant, orchestrating military policy during the Plains Indian Wars. Asked to run for president several times, Sherman famously said, "I will not run if nominated and I will not serve if elected."

photographs of battle scenes, the reviewer for the *New York Times* grappled with the tragedies depicted in the photos, but also with the public's fascination with them. The author writes that

> Mr. Brady has done something to bring home to us the terrible reality and earnestness of war. If he has not brought bodies and laid them in our dooryards and along the streets, he has done something very like it. Crowds of people are constantly going up the stairs; follow them, and you find them bending over photographic views of that fearful battle-field, taken immediately after the action. Of all objects of horror one would think the battle-field should stand preeminent, that it should bear away the palm of repulsiveness. But, on the contrary, there is a terrible fascination about it that draws one near these pictures, and makes him loathe to leave them. These pictures have a terrible distinctness.[32]

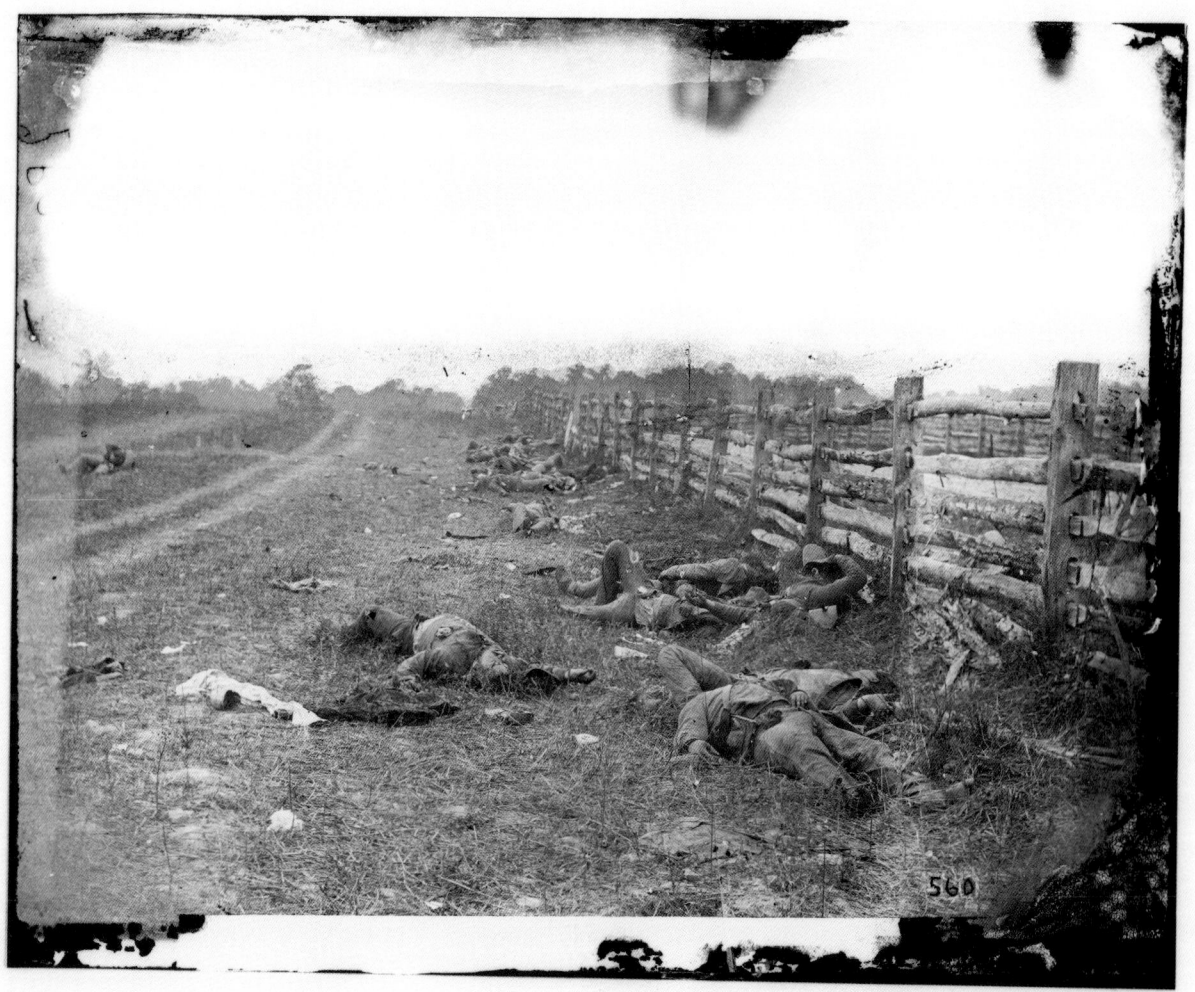

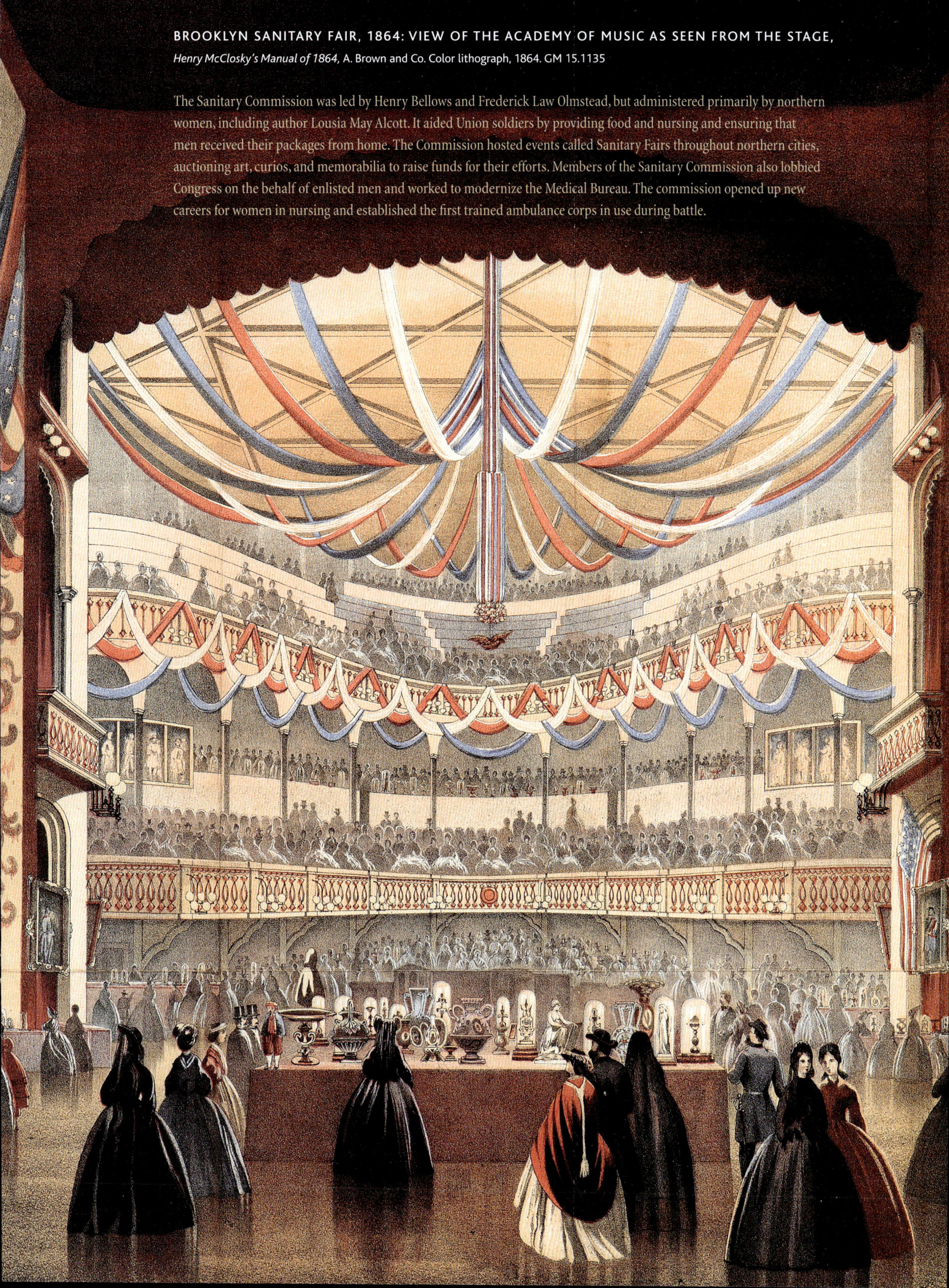

BROOKLYN SANITARY FAIR, 1864: VIEW OF THE ACADEMY OF MUSIC AS SEEN FROM THE STAGE,

Henry McClosky's Manual of 1864, A. Brown and Co. Color lithograph, 1864. GM 15.1135

The Sanitary Commission was led by Henry Bellows and Frederick Law Olmstead, but administered primarily by northern women, including author Lousia May Alcott. It aided Union soldiers by providing food and nursing and ensuring that men received their packages from home. The Commission hosted events called Sanitary Fairs throughout northern cities, auctioning art, curios, and memorabilia to raise funds for their efforts. Members of the Sanitary Commission also lobbied Congress on the behalf of enlisted men and worked to modernize the Medical Bureau. The commission opened up new careers for women in nursing and established the first trained ambulance corps in use during battle.

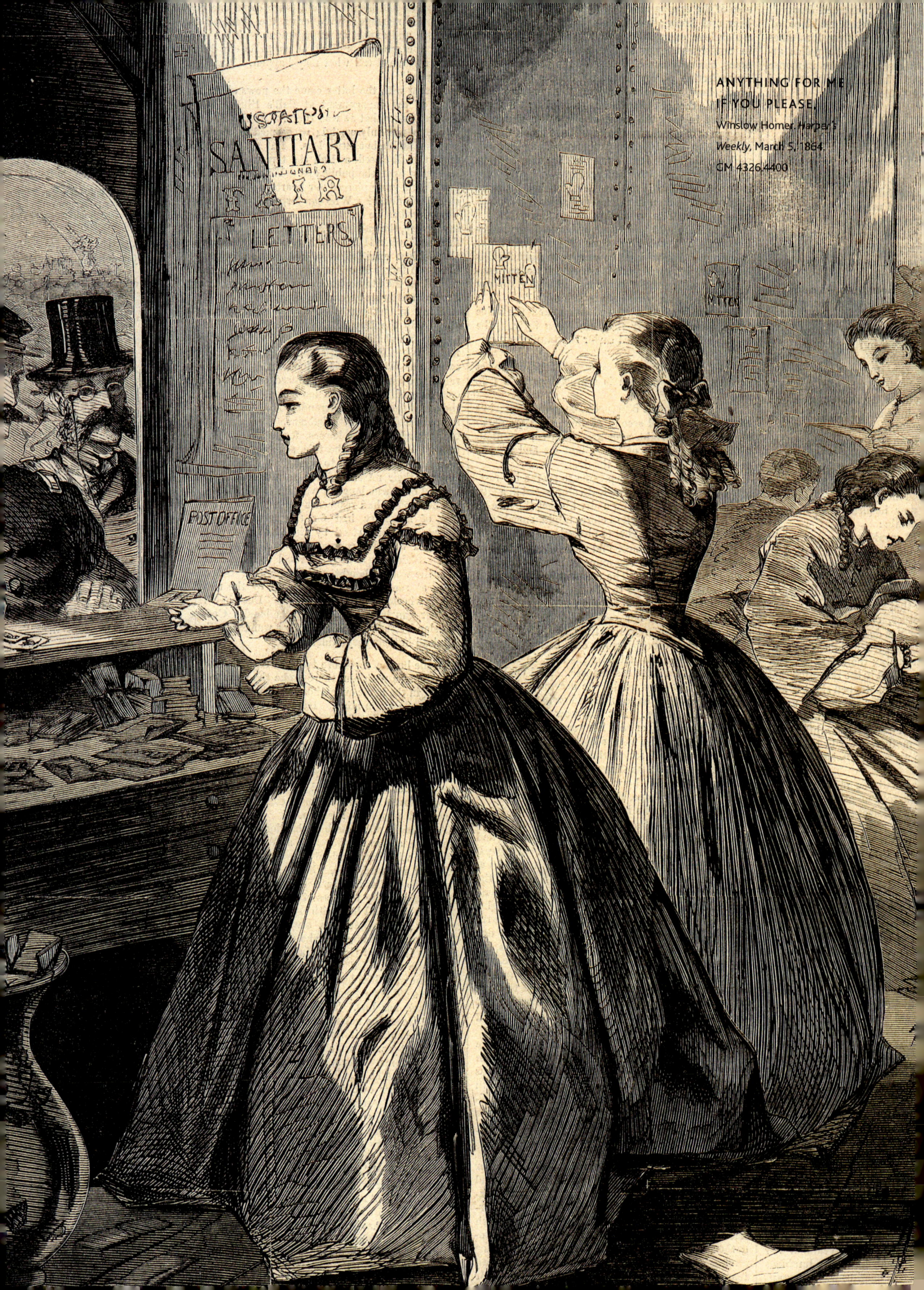

ANYTHING FOR ME
IF YOU PLEASE.
Winslow Homer, *Harper's*
Weekly, March 5, 1864
CM 4326.4400

Others experienced the horrors of war firsthand, especially in the Confederate states. In Richmond, one woman wrote, "We lived in one immense hospital and breathed the vapors of the charnel house."[33] Another woman, Dora Miller, kept a diary about her life during the siege of Vicksburg. "The slow shelling of Vicksburg goes on all the time, and we have grown indifferent," she wrote, three months into the siege. "It does not at present interrupt or interfere with daily avocations, but I suspect they are only getting the range of different points; and when they have them all complete, showers of shot will rain on us all at once."[34] Author Louisa May Alcott served as a nurse at a Union hospital outside of Washington, D. C., and turned her experiences into a story collection entitled *Hospital Sketches*. She described her duties as "washing faces, serving rations, giving medicine, and sitting in a very hard chair, with pneumonia on one side, diptheria on the other, five typhoids on the opposite, and a dozen dilapidated patriots, hopping, lying, and lounging about."[35]

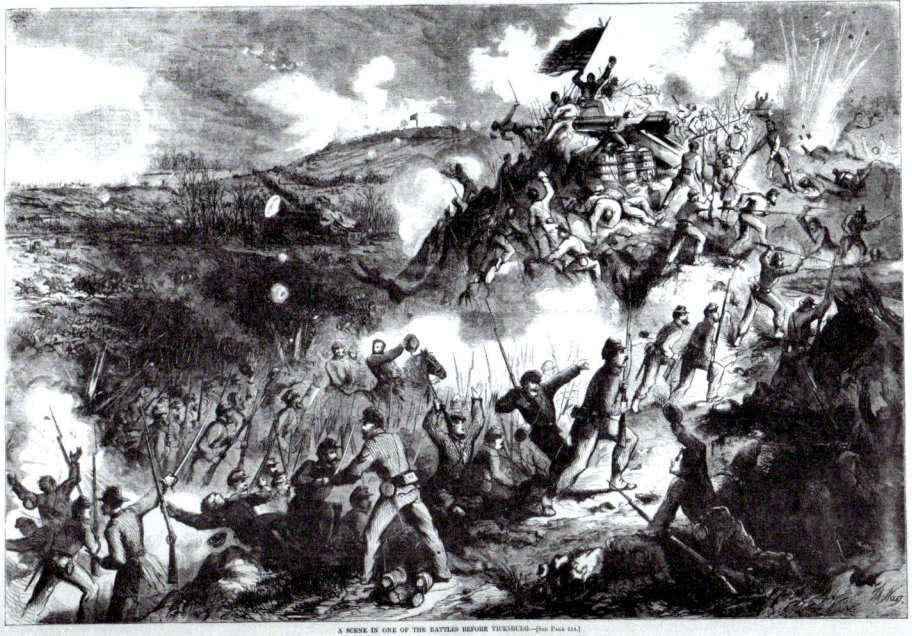

A SCENE IN ONE OF THE BATTLES BEFORE VICKSBURG.—[See Page 154.]

A horrible day. The most horrible yet to me, because I've lost my nerve. We were all in the cellar, when a shell came tearing through the roof, burst up-stairs, tore up that room, and the pieces coming through both floors down into the cellar, one of them tore open the leg of H's pantaloons. This was the tangible proof the cellar was no place of protection from them. On the heels of this came Mr. J. to tell us that young Mrs. P. had had her thigh-bone crushed. When Martha went for the milk, she came back horror-stricken to tell us the black girl there had her arm taken off by a shell. For the first time, I quailed. — Dora Miller, citizen of Vicksburg, June 25, 1863

THE BATTLE OF VICKSBURG,
Thomas Nast. *Harper's Weekly,* March 7, 1863. GM 5027.1729

With a spring offensive in April 1863, Major General Ulysses S. Grant and his army faced Lt. General John C. Pemberton's Army of Mississippi in the long siege of Vicksburg, Mississippi. The city was important strategically to both the Union and Confederate armies, since its occupation meant control of vital supplies and communications that flowed along the Mississippi River. As the population of Vicksburg literally dug in—building caves to avoid the constant barrage of shells from the Union army—supplies ran short, and the threat of death was ever present.

On July 4, 1863, a mere day after the Union victory at Gettysburg, heavy casualties, lack of supplies, and no reinforcements led Pemberton to surrender. Union control cut the Confederacy in two, dividing Confederate troops in the West with the government in the East. The Confederate defeat at Vicksburg loomed large in the city's memory. Legend states that the city of Vicksburg would not celebrate Independence Day until World War II.

For some, the sights and sounds of the battlefield were far removed from their daily lives; for others, the war came home in a tangible way. Those who volunteered, those who had the misfortune to live next to a battlefield, and those who bought tickets to see Matthew Brady's photographs—all witnessed the horrors of war, and all hoped that the war would end quickly.

In 1864, Lincoln faced reelection. A series of losses and draws throughout much of the spring and summer made the odds of a second term seem bleak at best.[36] The Emancipation Proclamation, declaring that all slaves residing in states in rebellion from the Union were free, issued after the Northern victory at Antietam, and enacted on January 1, proved to be unpopular among some of the troops and many of the voters in the Union. Others, however, rallied to the new focus in the war. One Indiana colonel noted that although there were few abolitionists in his unit, his men still wanted "to destroy everything that in aught gives the rebels strength," and that "this army will sustain the emancipation proclamation and enforce it with the bayonet."[37] In addition to a national draft, the Union army began to accept African-American soldiers, many of whom were freed slaves, and in the summer of 1864, paid the men the same wages as their white counterparts.[38] In the South, meanwhile, the successes of the war proved small comfort to the loss of life and poor supplies. Any attempt by the Confederate government to mobilize states to help the central government fight the war was met with suspicion and a lack of compliance. Wealthy men, able to hire others to fight for them, led to some derisively calling it "a rich man's war, but a poor man's fight."[39]

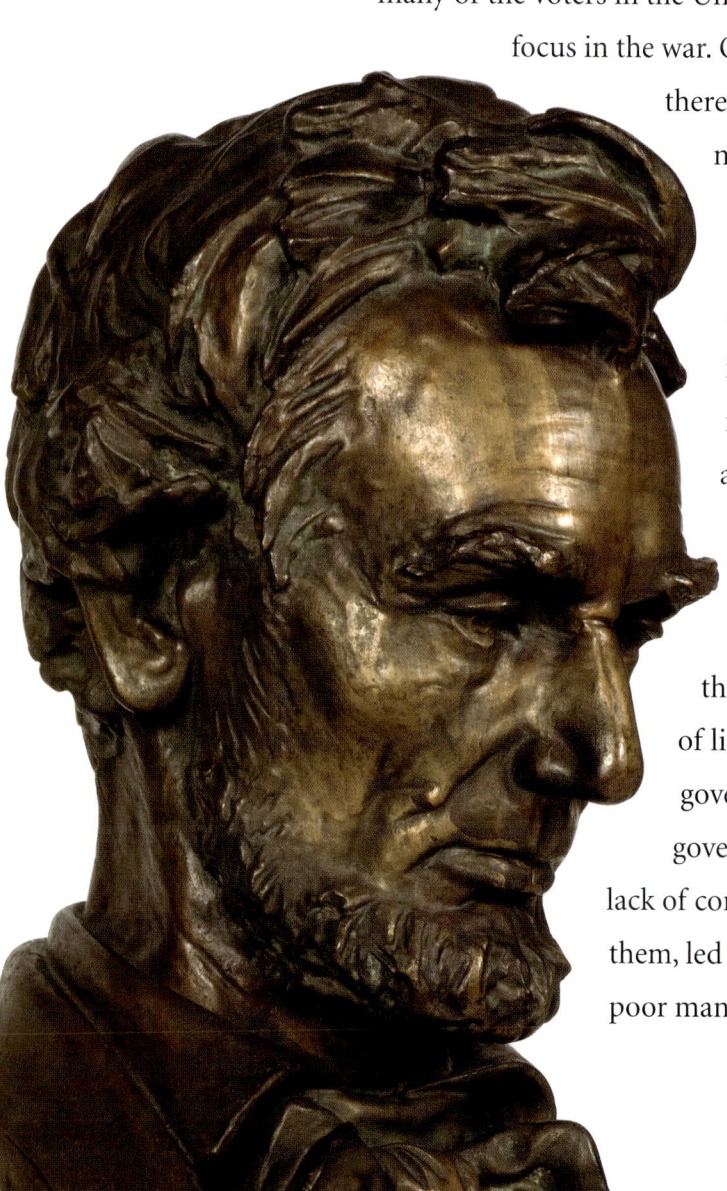

ABRAHAM LINCOLN,
Augustus Saint-Gaudens.
Bronze. GM 0826.113

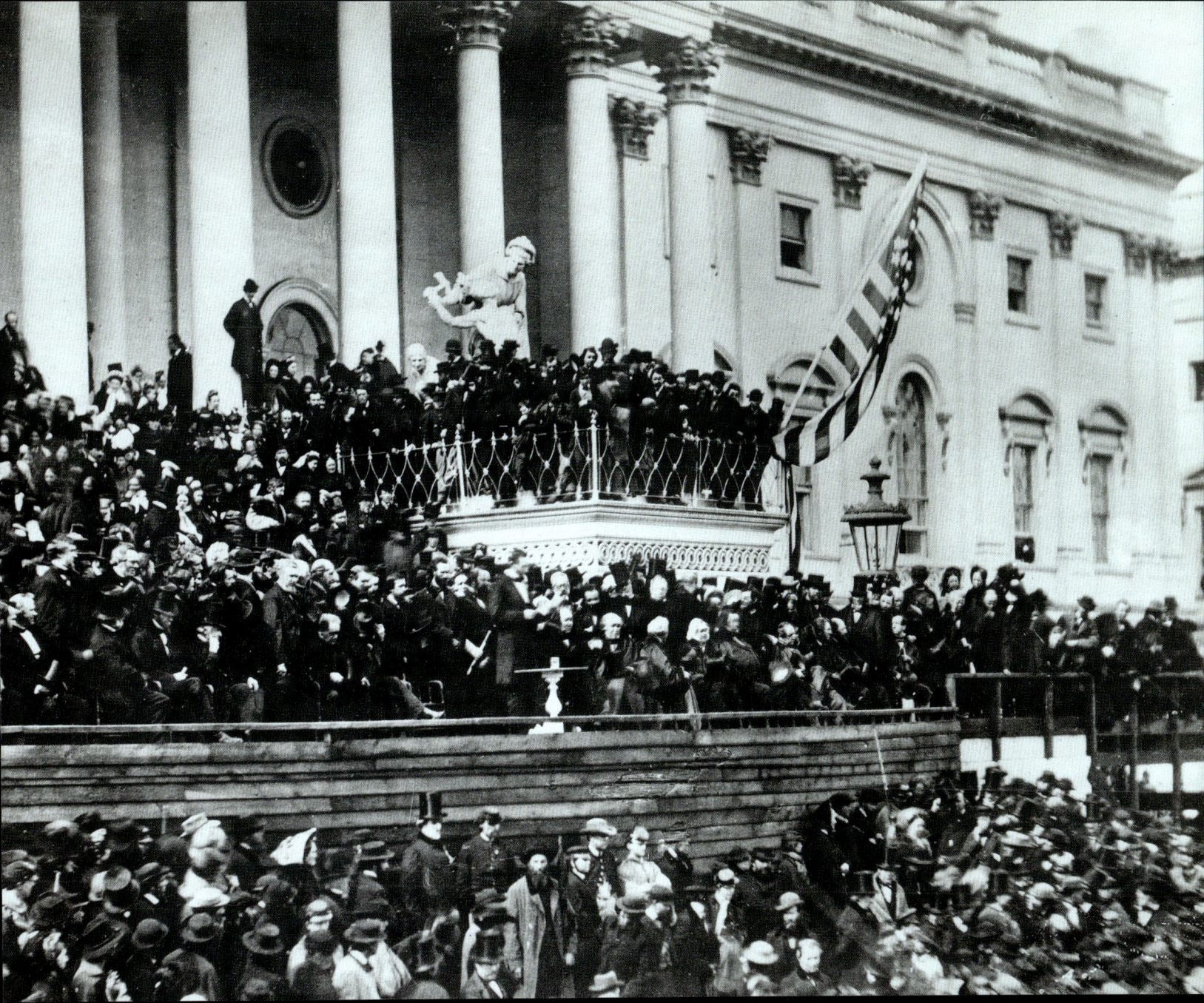

With malice toward none; with charity for all; with firmness in the right, as God gives us to see the right, let us strive on to finish the work we are in; to bind up the nation's wounds; to care for him who shall have borne the battle, and for his widow, and his orphan—to do all which may achieve and cherish a just and lasting peace among ourselves, and with all nations.

— Abraham Lincoln, March 4, 1865

ABRAHAM LINCOLN'S SECOND INAUGURATION, 1865. Photograph. GM 4326.3156

In 1864, Lincoln faced reelection. A series of losses and draws throughout much of the spring and summer made the odds of a second term seem bleak at best. The Emancipation Proclamation, declaring that all slaves residing in states in rebellion from the Union were free, issued after the northern victory at Antietam and enacted on January 1, proved unpopular among some of the troops and many of the voters in the Union. But in the fall of 1864, a series of last-minute successes by the North, including General Sherman's movement into Atlanta and General Grant's victory at Vicksburg, handed Lincoln the election.

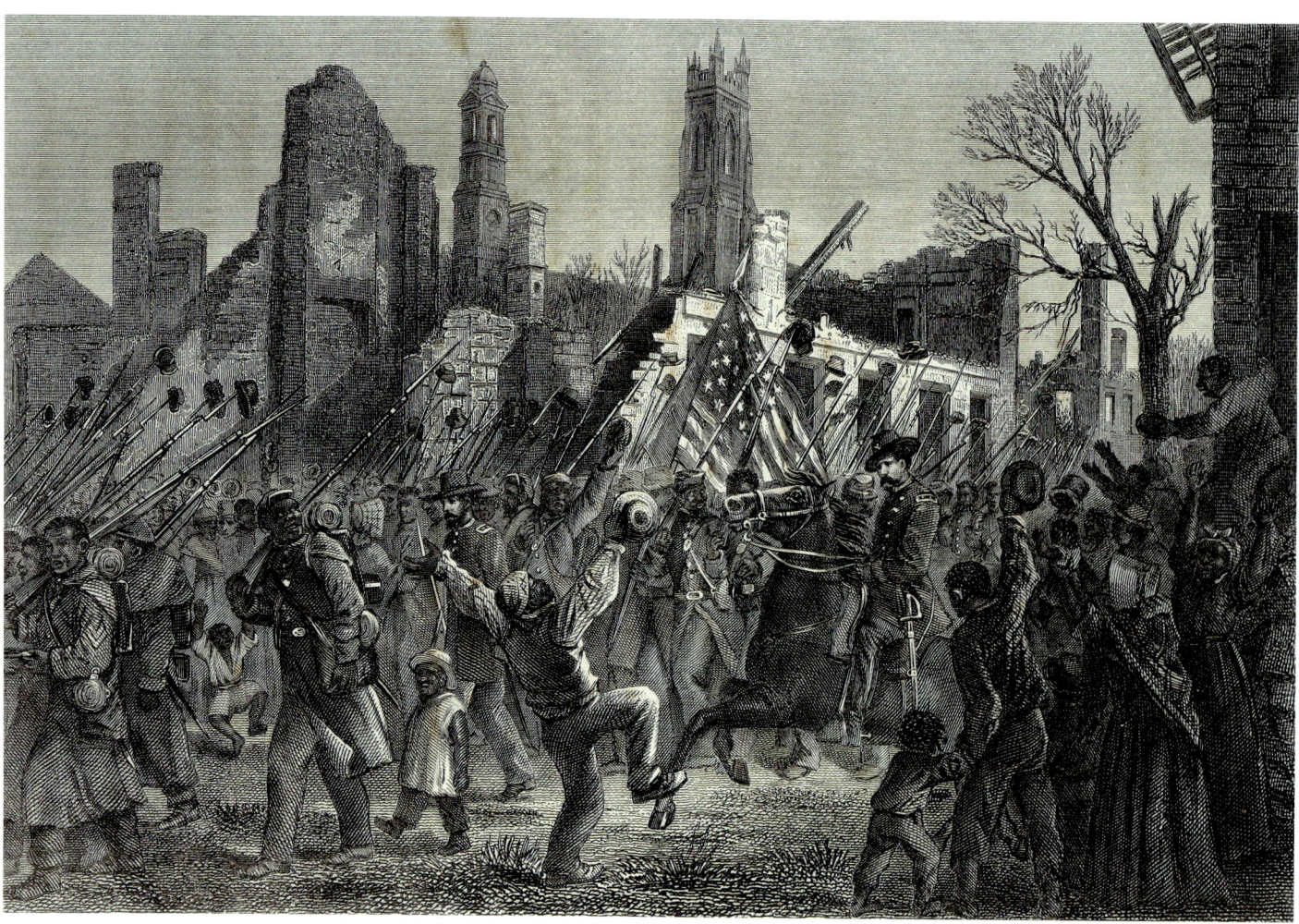

BLACK TROOPS. From *The Great Rebellion: A History of the Civil War in the United States,* by J. T. Headley, 1866. GM 2726.134

African-American troops were an important part of the Union's strategy during the war. Early on, abolitionists argued that black men should be allowed to fight for Union and their freedom. Slaves who surrendered to or were captured by the northern army were known as "contrabands" and were employed to do various work around the army camps. Many provided vital assistance to Union generals by working as guides and spies, offering crucial insider information. In July 1862, Congress passed an act allowing black soldiers to enlist in the military, and in August the first all-African American regiment, the First South Carolina Volunteers, reported for duty. With the issue of the Emancipation Proclamation, enrollment by blacks in the Union army continued to grow, encouraged by leaders like Frederick Douglass. Although they were only paid ten dollars a month while their white counterparts were paid thirteen, black recruits rapidly formed new regiments that faced fierce battles, proving their mettle time and again. By the end of the war, twenty-three black soldiers had been awarded medals of honor, and black soldiers made up nearly a tenth of the Union's fighting force.

EMANCIPATION PROCLAMATION, 1864.
GM 5326.801

This document, one of only forty-eight printed copies of President Lincoln's Emancipation Proclamation, is known as the Leland-Boker Edition. Each was signed by President Lincoln and Secretary Seward. During the Civil War, epidemics of measles, dysentery, typhoid, and malaria swept through army ranks, killing two soldiers for every one killed in battle. To raise money for the sick and wounded, and to improve conditions in military camps, the Sanitary Commission began holding fairs. The printed facsimiles of the proclamation were sold at the 1864 Philadelphia Sanitary Fair, one of the most successful such events and the only one attended by President Lincoln. While there he gave an emotional speech: "War at its best, is terrible, and this war of ours, in its magnitude and in its duration is one of the most terrible…it has carried mourning to almost every home, until it can almost be said that the 'heavens are hung in black.' Yet the war continues…"

BY THE PRESIDENT OF THE UNITED STATES OF AMERICA,

A Proclamation.

·····

Whereas, on the twenty-second day of September, in the year of our Lord one thousand eight hundred and sixty-two, a proclamation was issued by the President of the United States, containing, among other things, the following, to wit:

"That on the first day of January, in the year of our Lord one thousand eight hundred and sixty-three, all persons held as slaves within any State or designated part of a State, the people whereof shall then be in rebellion against the United States, shall be then, thenceforward, and forever, free; and the Executive government of the United States, including the military and naval authority thereof, will recognize and maintain the freedom of such persons, and will do no act or acts to repress such persons, or any of them, in any efforts they may make for their actual freedom.

"That the Executive will, on the first day of January aforesaid, by proclamation, designate the States and parts of States, if any, in which the people thereof, respectively, shall then be in rebellion against the United States; and the fact that any State, or the people thereof, shall on that day be in good faith represented in the Congress of the United States, by members chosen thereto at elections wherein a majority of the qualified voters of such State shall have participated, shall, in the absence of strong countervailing testimony, be deemed conclusive evidence that such State, and the people thereof, are not then in rebellion against the United States."

Now, therefore, I, ABRAHAM LINCOLN, PRESIDENT OF THE UNITED STATES, by virtue of the power in me vested as commander-in-chief of the army and navy of the United States, in time of actual armed rebellion against the authority and government of the United States, and as a fit and necessary war measure for suppressing said rebellion, do, on this first day of January, in the year of our Lord one thousand eight hundred and sixty-three, and in accordance with my purpose so to do, publicly proclaimed for the full period of one hundred days from the day first above mentioned, order and designate as the States and parts of States wherein the people thereof, respectively, are this day in rebellion against the United States, the following, to wit: ARKANSAS, TEXAS, LOUISIANA, (except the Parishes of St. Bernard, Plaquemines, Jefferson, St. John, St. Charles, St. James, Ascension, Assumption, Terre Bonne, Lafourche, St. Mary, St. Martin, and Orleans, including the City of New Orleans,) MISSISSIPPI, ALABAMA, FLORIDA, GEORGIA, SOUTH CAROLINA, NORTH CAROLINA, AND VIRGINIA, (except the forty-eight counties designated as West Virginia, and also the counties of Berkeley, Accomac, Northampton, Elizabeth City, York, Princess Ann, and Norfolk, including the cities of Norfolk and Portsmouth,) and which excepted parts are for the present left precisely as if this proclamation were not issued.

And by virtue of the power and for the purpose aforesaid, I do order and declare that all persons held as slaves within said designated States and parts of States are and henceforward shall be free; and that the Executive government of the United States, including the military and naval authorities thereof, will recognize and maintain the freedom of said persons.

And I hereby enjoin upon the people so declared to be free to abstain from all violence, unless in necessary self-defence; and I recommend to them that, in all cases when allowed, they labor faithfully for reasonable wages.

And I further declare and make known that such persons, of suitable condition, will be received into the armed service of the United States, to garrison forts, positions, stations, and other places, and to man vessels of all sorts in said service.

And upon this act, sincerely believed to be an act of justice warranted by the Constitution upon military necessity, I invoke the considerate judgment of mankind and the gracious favor of Almighty God.

In witness whereof I have hereunto set my hand and caused the seal of the United States to be affixed.

Done at the CITY OF WASHINGTON this first day of January, in the year of our
[L. S.]   Lord one thousand eight hundred and sixty-three, and of the Independence of the United States of America the eighty-seventh.

By the President:

Abraham Lincoln

Will. H. Seward, Secretary of State.

A true copy, with the autograph signatures of the President and the Secretary of State.

Jno. G. Nicolay,
Priv. Sec. to the President.

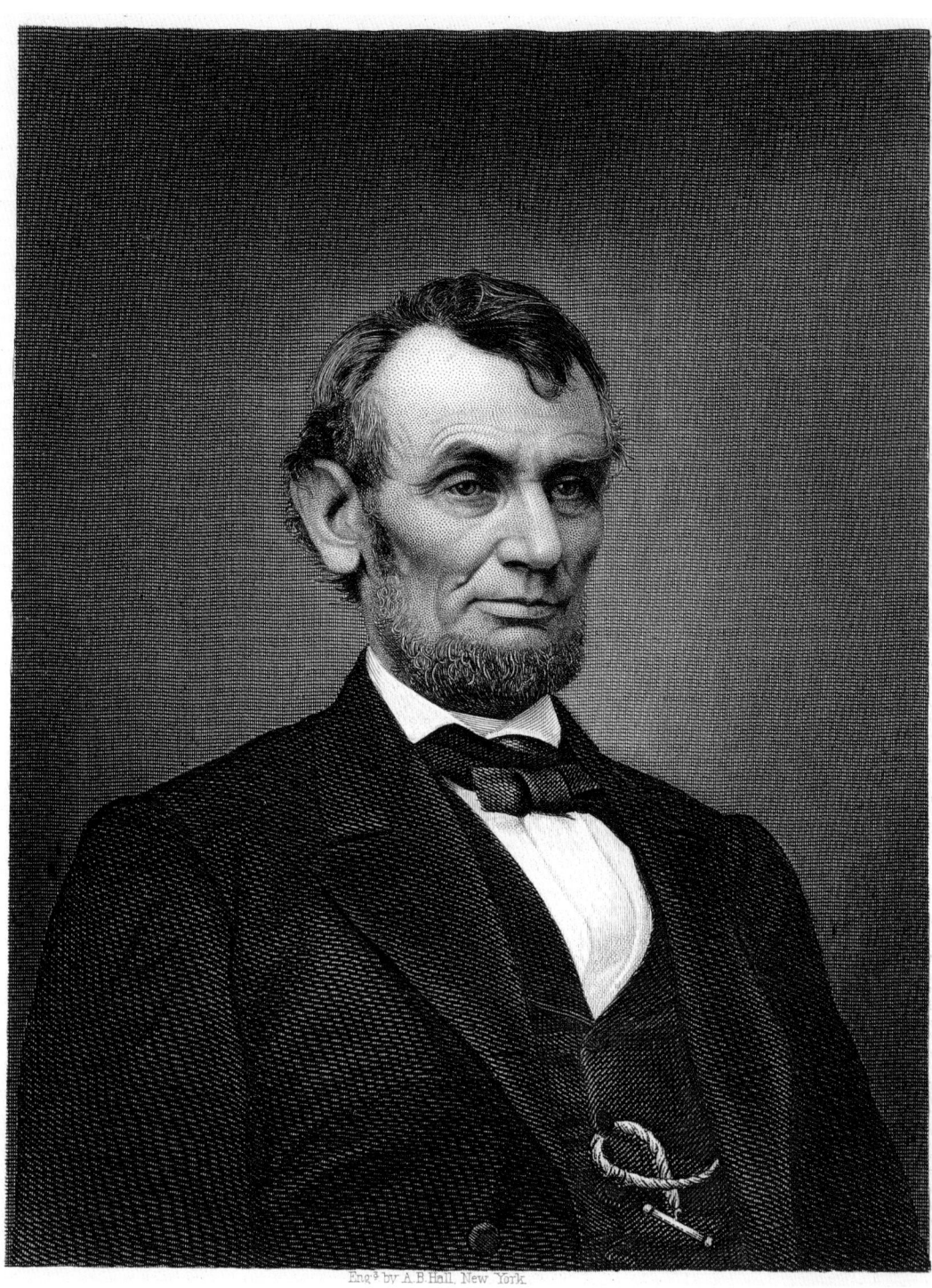

Eng.ᵈ by A.B Hall. New York.

A lack of organizations like the Sanitary Commission, which provided food, established hospital conditions, and general comfort to the Union soldiers, meant that average homes were turned into hospitals, bringing the horrors of war into the parlors of the South.[40] By the fall of 1864, a series of last minute victories by the North, including General Sherman's movement into Atlanta and General Grant's victory at Vicksburg, handed Lincoln the election. The tide of the war had turned.

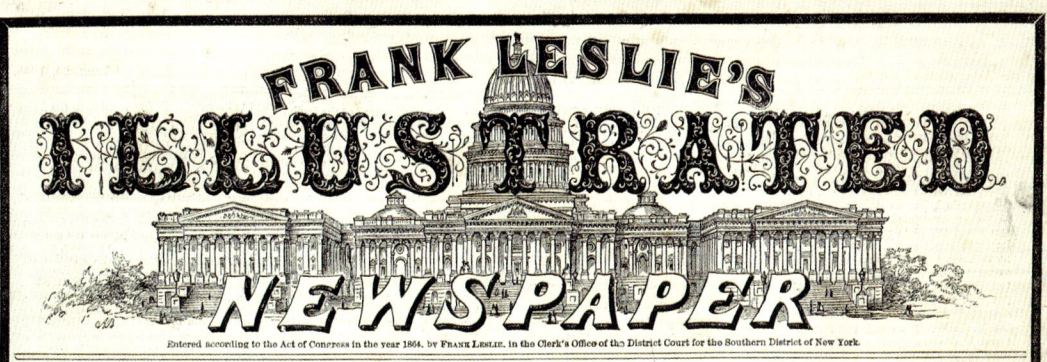

Entered according to the Act of Congress in the year 1864, by FRANK LESLIE, in the Clerk's Office of the District Court for the Southern District of New York.

No. 500—VOL. XX.]   NEW YORK, APRIL 29, 1865.   [PRICE 10 CENTS. $4 00 YEARLY. 13 WEEKS $1 00.

ABRAHAM LINCOLN.
Assassinated Good Friday, 1865.
BY EDMUND C. STEDMAN.

"Forgive them, for they know not what they do!"
He said, and so went shriven to his fate—
Unknowing went, that generous heart and true.
Even while he spoke the slayer lay in wait,
And when the morning opened Heaven's gate
There passed the whitest soul a nation knew.
Henceforth all thoughts of pardon are too late;
They, in whose cause that arm its weapon drew,
Have murdered MERCY. Now alone shall stand
Blind JUSTICE, with the sword unsheathed she wore.
Hark, from the eastern to the western strand,
The swelling thunder of the people's roar:
What words they murmur—FETTER NOT HER HAND!
So LET IT SMITE, SUCH DEEDS SHALL BE NO MORE!
N. Y. Tribune.

The Martyr President.

ON the 14th of April, 1861, the flag of the United States went down on the beleaguered walls of Fort Sumter. Its little garrison of seventy men succumbed to the thousands of traitors who had been permitted to pile up, unmolested, battery on battery around it, and the treason nursed so long in South Carolina had there its first triumph. The rebellion, then commenced in cowardice, ended on the fourth anniversary of that eventful day in assassination. Every step in its progress had been marked by some crime more heinous than the last. Persecution and murder of men and women for their adhesion to the flag of their fathers; Fort Pillow massacres; systematic starvation of Union prisoners; plots to burn crowded cities, and to dash railway trains down precipices, to say nothing of wholesale incendiarism on the high seas, have been among the common incidents of the war on the part of the South, and have passed into history as the characteristics of the rebellion. But one thing was necessary to complete the deep damnation of the monster treason of the 19th century. That hideous culmination was achieved on the night of April 14th, 1865, when ABRAHAM LINCOLN, the loved and honored head of the nation, was slain by a rebel assassin! Slain while unarmed and unsuspicious, slain from behind, with every incident that could lend a darker hue to the atrocity of the act. Almost at the same moment, a maimed and wasted statesman, helpless on a couch of suffering in a dimly-lighted sick chamber, was assaulted and stabbed by another foul emissary of the monster crime! Nor was there a single accessory of cowardice and brutality wanting here. Nothing indeed was wanting in the design, scope and execution of both acts, to invest them with a character more horrid and repulsive than attaches to any similar events in the wide annals of murder! The commencement, the progress, and the close of the rebellion—treason, wanton barbarity, assassination! Unrelieved by a single trait, lightened up by no single act of generosity, it stands in history one black, hideous blotch on civilization and mankind! Posterity will regard it, even through the haze of time, with a shudder, and parallels for its atrocities will only be found in the records of the darker days of the French Revolution, or in the bloody traditions of Dahomey! Abraham Lincoln has joined the noble army of Freedom's Martyrs. "Christ died to make men holy; he died to make men free!" When that great, kind, expansive heart ceased to beat, humanity lost not alone its first representative man, but mankind lost its truest and best friend. Even the red-handed, dismayed and skulking traitors of the South found room in his broad sympathies, and a mercy there which perhaps encroached on God's first attribute of justice. Passing strange that the two men highest in position in the nation, and most disposed to leniency and forgiveness, were these that this hell-born treason selected for its last and most distinguished victims! Did Heaven order that its ultimate act should be to shut fast and bar for ever the half-opened door of national sympathy? Did Providence frown on the possible weakness that would condone treason and betray the cause for which five hundred thousand of our brothers have died and still fester in uncoffined graves!

Far be it from us to attempt lightly to interpret the inscrutable ways of the Almighty, but

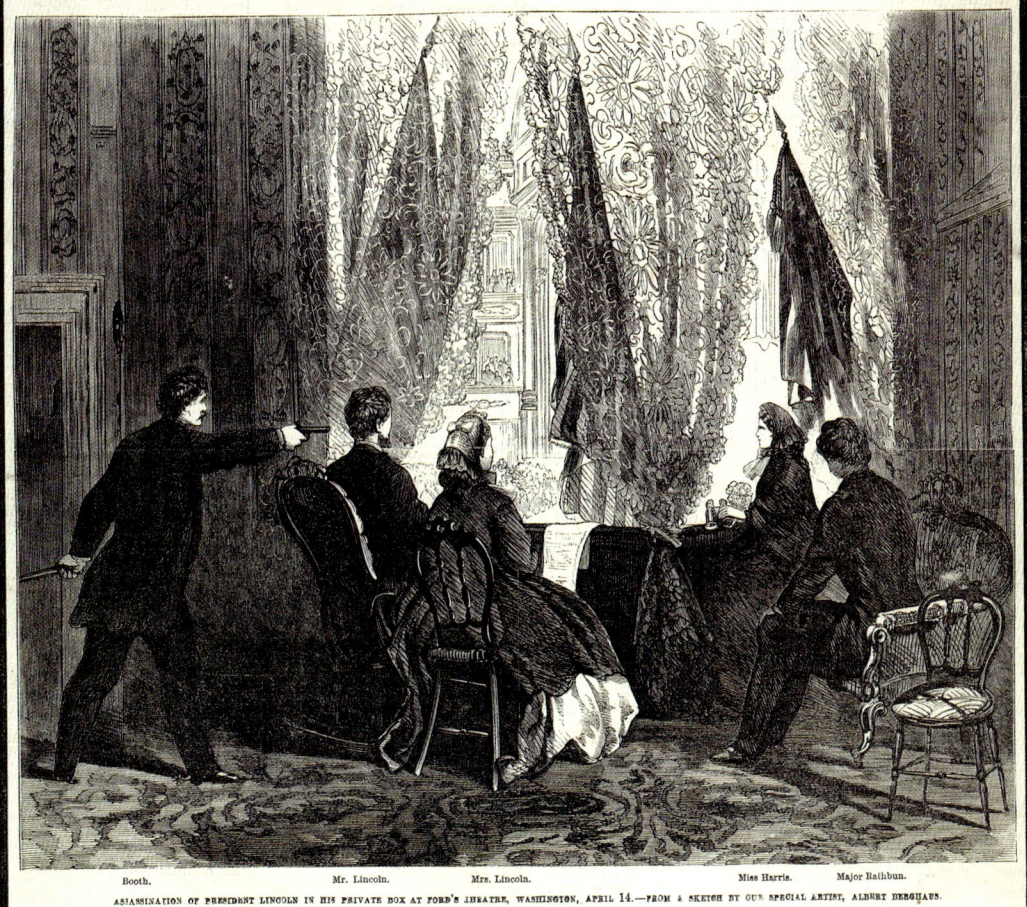

Booth.   Mr. Lincoln.   Mrs. Lincoln.   Miss Harris.   Major Rathbun.

ASSASSINATION OF PRESIDENT LINCOLN IN HIS PRIVATE BOX AT FORD'S THEATRE, WASHINGTON, APRIL 14.—FROM A SKETCH BY OUR SPECIAL ARTIST, ALBERT BERGHAUS.

ASSASSINATION OF PRESIDENT LINCOLN,

Frank Leslie's Illustrated Newspaper, April 29, 1865.
GM 4126.774

One week after General Robert E. Lee surrendered the Army of Virginia to General Ulysses S. Grant, President Lincoln began the transition from a wartime president to a peacetime leader. On April 14, he took a well-deserved evening off to attend the play *Our American Cousin* at Ford's Theater in the company of his wife Mary, Major Henry Rathbone, and Clara Harris, Rathbone's fiancée. John Wilkes Booth, an actor turned southern sympathizer, used his fame to get into the theater. Booth crept into the president's box and shot him. Although Rathbone attempted to seize the assailant, Booth leapt out of the box and onto the stage, breaking his leg. He then fled into the night and eluded capture for twelve days before being shot in a barn in Virginia, where he had hidden. Booth was part of a larger plot to kill the leading statesmen in the government—Vice President Andrew Johnson and Secretary of State William Seward were also attacked, but survived. President Lincoln, however, died on April 15 of the wound he sustained at the theater.

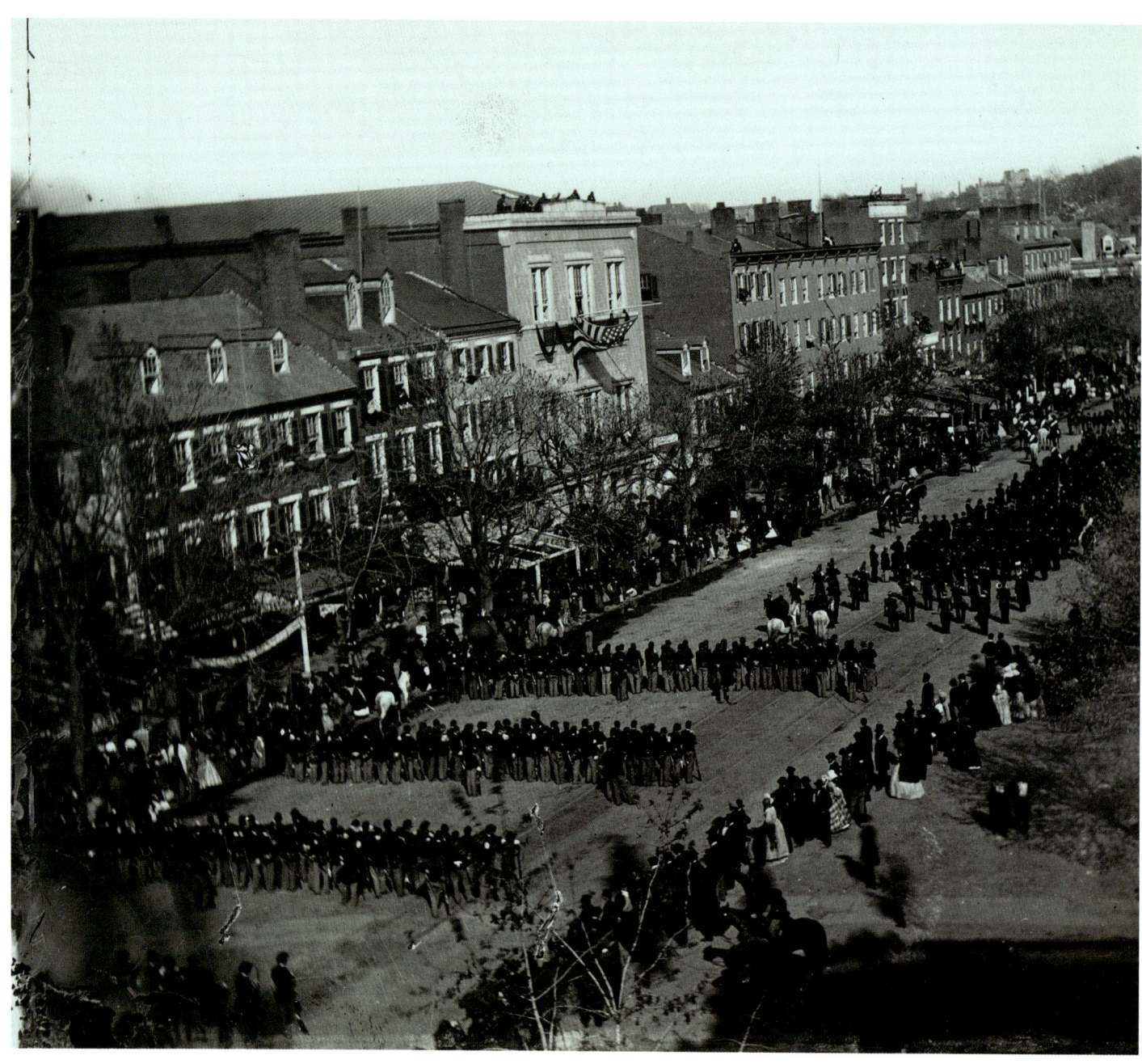

FUNERAL PROCESSION OF ABRAHAM LINCOLN, 1865.
Photograph. GM 4326.3153a

Lincoln's assassination shook the country. The shooting left Americans—both in the North and the South—doubly saddened in the brutal aftermath of war. Lincoln became a martyr for the nation, uniting the country in a way that would have been unimaginable when General Lee surrendered on April 9, 1865. Lincoln lay in state at the Capitol Building for several days before his body began the 1,700 mile trek from Washington, D.C., to Illinois, covering the same route President-elect Lincoln had taken on his journey to Washington in 1861. Stops included Philadelphia, New York City, Cleveland, and Chicago. On May 4, 1865, Lincoln was laid to rest in Springfield, Illinois. This photo, from a negative by Matthew Brady, captures just some of the thousands who paid their final respects on Pennsylvania Avenue.

At the end of Lincoln's second inaugural address on March 4, 1865, he implored the nation to rise to an elevated and compassionate effort and "With malice toward none; with charity for all . . . to bind up the nation's wounds; to care for him who shall have borne the battle, and for his widow, and his orphan—to do all which may achieve and cherish a just and lasting peace among ourselves, and with all nations."[41]

Although the fighting continued, the war seemed to be in hand. A little over a month later, on April 7, General Grant would confront General Lee's army for what would be the last time near Appomattox Court House. After a brutal defeat, Lee accepted Grant's terms of surrender. Grant allowed the Confederate soldiers to keep their horses and mules and allowed the officers to keep their sidearms, provided that they go back home and fire them in war no more.[42] The major fighting of the war was over. Grant recalled that after the surrender was official, soldiers of both armies "came in great numbers, and seemed to enjoy the meeting as much as though they had been friends separated for a long time while fighting battles under the same flag."[43] Three and a half million men went to war and 620,000 of those would never return home.[44] The rest tried their best to pick up their lives and move forward. This was harder for many in the South. A farmer from Louisiana noted in his journal that "Society has been completely changed by the war. The [French] Revolution of '89 did not produce a greater change in the 'Ancien Régime' than this has in our social life."[45] For Lincoln, any return to normalcy was short lived. On April 15, barely a week after fighting ceased and on Good Friday, John Wilkes Booth assassinated Lincoln while he was attending a play at Ford's Theater.

Thoroughly believing that he was acting heroically and bitterly disappointed when he realized that popular opinion did not

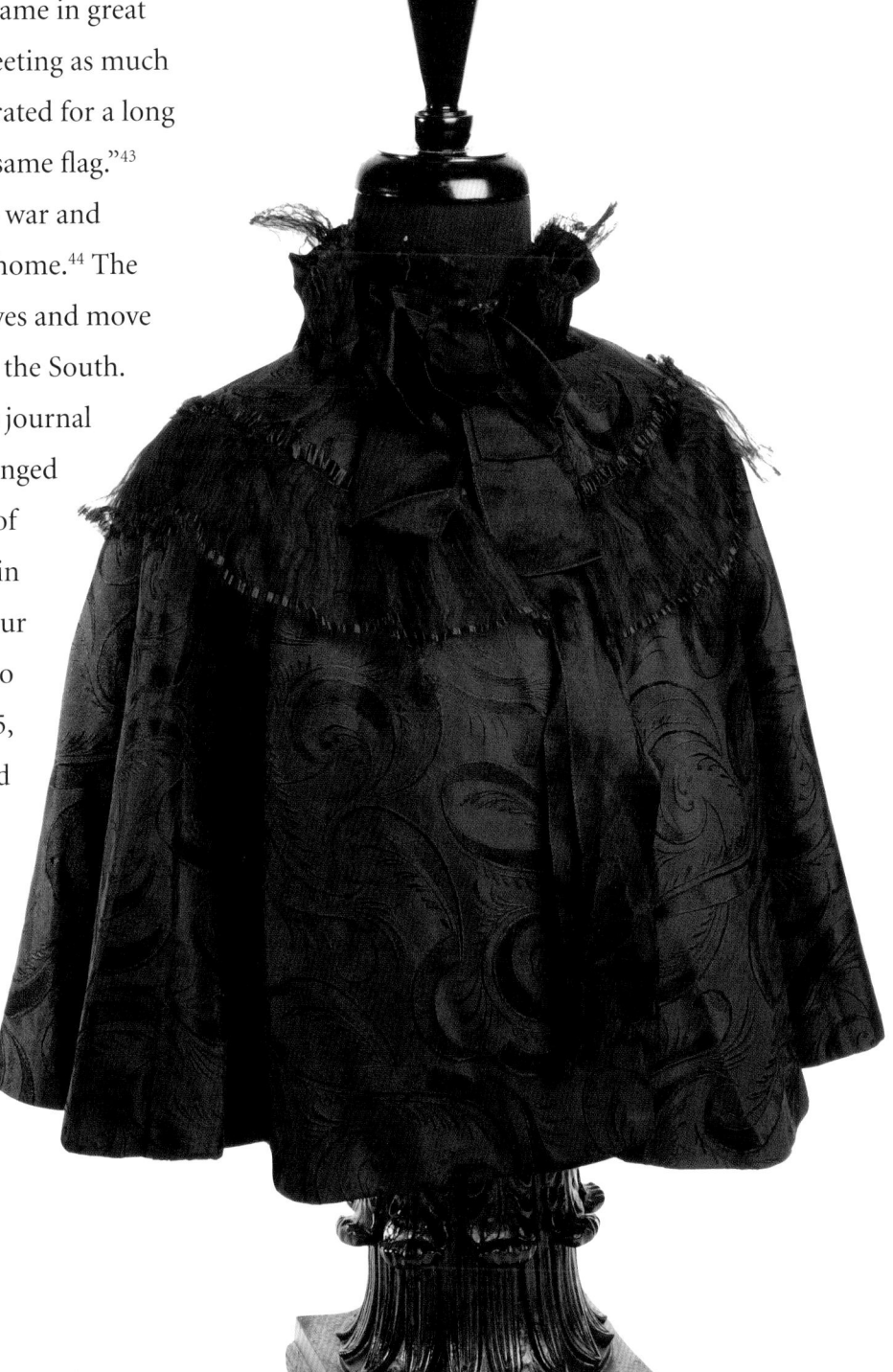

Casualties were high throughout the Civil War. Of soldiers wounded, nearly 15 percent died from their injuries due to insufficient medical care. The number killed in battle was unlike anything seen before. In the Battle of the Seven Days, fought in Virginia in 1862, nearly 30,000 men from both sides were killed. At Gettysburg, approximately 50,000 died. By war's end in 1865, the human cost of four years of fighting amounted to 620,000 lives lost. The sheer number of injuries and deaths meant that many families experienced the loss of husbands, brothers, and sons; many of those fortunate enough to come home suffered life-changing injuries.

agree with him, Booth was the subject of a massive manhunt. He died at the hands of federal agents.[46] As the nation, especially the northern states, mourned its president, citizens returned to their homes and businesses.

As the war ended and the business of the nation resumed, many of the men who had made their mark in the war turned to public life and the tasks of rebuilding and reunifying the country. Lincoln had laid out preliminary plans for southern reconciliation, but it would fall to his successor, Andrew Johnson, to initiate them. The thirteenth, fourteenth, and fifteenth amendments to the Constitution were passed in 1865, enforcing the Emancipation Proclamation and guaranteeing African-Americans the right to vote. The initial phase of the Civil Rights movement was over, although it would take 100 years and a new movement to secure those rights. Gradually, and not without argument, the Confederate states were reintegrated into the Union. In the end, despite the loss of life, a new, united nation was born from the ashes of the war. Historian Shelby Foote noted the change in the way Americans perceived themselves after the war. "Before the war," Foote notes, "people would say 'the United States are.' After the war, people began to say, 'the United States is.' That's the change."[47] America changed from an association of states into one united country. With these divisions in the past, Americans looked ahead to a limitless future. That future lay in the West.

NOTES

1. Frederick Douglass, "The Mission of the War," in Ian Frederick Finseth, *The American Civil War: An Anthology of Essential Writings* (New York: Routledge, 2006), p. 264. The phrase occurs in a speech Mr. Douglass gave in Philadelphia in 1863, while the outcome of the war was still undecided.

2. "What Effect Will Lincoln's Election Have on the Union," *Daily Evening Bulletin*, San Francisco, California, November 8, 1860.

3. "How the Result is Received," *New York Times*, November 9, 1860, p. 1.

4. James M. McPherson, *Battle Cry of Freedom: The Civil War Era* (Oxford, England: Oxford University Press, 1988), p. 233. McPherson's book is a thorough overview of the American Civil War,

discussing not only battles and tactics, but also covering the political and social concerns surrounding the war.

5. McPherson, *Battle Cry of Freedom*, p. 241.

6. Ibid., p. 179. This followed his more famous phrase that "a house divided against itself cannot stand."

7. Elizabeth Johns, *American Genre Painting: The Politics of Everyday Life* (New Haven: Yale University Press, 1991), p. 176. Johns notes that in New York, for example, the population increased from 200,000 in 1830 to 800,000 in 1860. Coastal cities were not the only ones to experience such growth. Inland cities, such as Cincinnati, St. Louis, and Memphis, also saw rapid growth during this time.

8. McPherson, *Battle Cry of Freedom*, p. 318.

9. Ibid., pp. 860-861.

10. Ibid., p. 318. McPherson notes that the real problem lay in the fact that once the railroads were damaged, the Southern states had no way to make the material with which to replace them.

11. *The Civil War*, directed by Ken Burns, American Documentaries, Inc, Hollywood, California, 1990, episode 1. This nine-part series provides an excellent overview of the Civil War, using contemporary photographs and relying on diaries, letters, and newspapers to explain the impact of the war on those who fought in it and how it still shapes our country today.

12. McPherson, *Battle Cry of Freedom*, p. 39.

13. Ira Berlin, *Generations of Captivity: A History of African-American Slaves*, (Boston: Harvard University Press, 2003), p. 9.

14. "The Kansas War," *The New York Times*, January 28, 1859, p. 2. In retaliation, Brown's home had been burned and one of his sons killed by pro-slavery men.

15. "The Harper's Ferry Rebellion," *New York Times*, October 20, 1859, p. 1.

16. McPherson, *Battle Cry of Freedom*, p. 210.

17. Ibid., p. 210.

18. Finseth, *The American Civil War*, p. 375 and McPherson, *Battle Cry of Freedom*, p. 210. The quote is from William Dean Howells.

19. Jefferson Davis, "Farewell Address, January 21, 1862," quoted in Finseth, *The American Civil War*, pp. 35-36.

20. McPherson, *Battle Cry of Freedom*, p. 241. One Georgia secessionist stated, "On the 4th of March, 1861 [the date of Lincoln's inauguration], we are either slaves in the Union or freemen out of it."

21. Ibid,. p. 274.

22. Ibid., p. 413. McPherson states that this total "was nearly double the 12,000 killed at Manassas (Bull Run), Wilson's creek, Fort Donelson, and Pea Ridge combined."

23. Burns, *The Civil War*, episode 3.

24. Ibid., episode 5.

25. Ibid., episode 5.

26. Abraham Lincoln, "Address at the Dedication of the Gettysburg National Cemetery," in Finseth, *The American Civil War*, p. 113.

27. Sarah Rosetta Wakeman (aka Edwin), "Letter dated January 15, 1863," in Stanley Harrold, ed, *The Civil War and Reconstruction: A Documentary Reader* (Malden, Massasschusetts: Blackwell Publishing, 2008), p. 109. Ms. Wakeman was one of approximately 400 women who disguised themselves as men and fought in the Civil War. She served from 1862 until her death from disease in New Orleans in 1864.

28. Charles Minor Blackford, "Letter, July 17th 1864," in Harrold, *The Civil War and Reconstruction*, p. 121. Captain Blackford was a Confederate judge advocate at Petersburg when he sent this letter home.

29. McPherson, *Battle Cry of Freedom*, p. 309.

30. McPherson, *Battle Cry of Freedom*, p. 413.

31. Ibid., p. 413.

32. "Brady's Photographs," *The New York Times*, October 20. 1862 in Sarah Burns and John Davis, *American Art to 1900: A Documentary History* (Berkeley: University of California Press, 2009), p. 520.

33. McPherson, *Battle Cry of Freedom*, p. 477. This woman was writing during the fighting between May and June of 1862.

34. Dora Miller, "Diary Entry, March 20, 1863," in Harrold, *The Civil War and Reconstruction*, p. 137.

35. Louisa May Alcott, "Chapter III: A Day," *Hospital Sketches*, in Finesth, *The American Civil War*, p. 106. Alcott goes on to describe some of the men's deaths, as well as her participation in an amputation.

36. Burns, *The Civil War*, episode 6. There were several small skirmishes the Union encountered as they moved to Richmond that resulted in high casualties. General William T. Sherman's forces were stalled near Atlanta, and General Grant was still locked in a stalemate in Vicksburg.

37. McPherson, *Battle Cry of Freedom*, p. 588.

38. Burns, *The Civil War*, episode 7.

39. Ibid., episode 2.

40. Ibid., episode 5.

41. Abraham Lincoln, "Second Inaugural Address," March 4, 1865, in Finseth, *The American Civil War*, p. 488.

42. Ulysses S. Grant, *Personal Memoirs of U. S. Grant*, "Chapter 67: Negotiations at Appomattox," in Finseth, *The American Civil War*, pp. 162-163.

43. Ibid., p. 165.

44. Burns, *The Civil War*, episode 9.

45. McPherson, *Battle Cry of Freedom*, p. 861.

46. John Wilkes Booth, "Diary Entries, April 17, 1865 and April 22, 1865," in Finseth, *The American Civil War*, pp. 494-495.

47. Shelby Foote, quoted in Burns, *The Civil War*, episode 9.

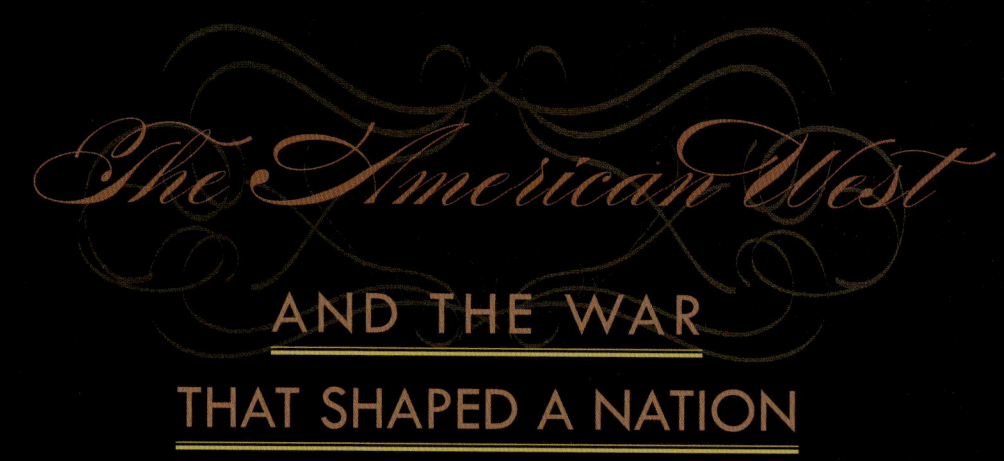

The American West

AND THE WAR

THAT SHAPED A NATION

ERIC SINGLETON

The morning of December 29, 1890, was cold on the flats of the Pine Ridge Reservation where a band of Lakota men, women, and children were encamped. On the previous day they had been following their leader Big Foot toward the south when they were intercepted by a detachment of the U. S. Seventh Cavalry Regiment and herded toward Wounded Knee Creek. There they had spent the night, surrounded by soldiers. ❖ Things had been bad a long time for the Lakota. They had signed away more and more land in exchange for peace, protection, and provisions. But whites encroached on their lands, U. S. agents cut their rations, and their traditonal source of life, the bison, had become nearly extinct. Some had danced the Ghost Dance to renew the earth and restore traditional ways. But the Ghost Dance had caught the attention of a fearful white population. Now the Army had orders to confiscate all weapons from the Lakota—including Big Foot's group. ❖ In the Lakota camp, troops began stripping blankets from the backs of people, in search of guns. A commotion ensued. Shots rang out, and the ground once covered in a mantle of white began to show stains of red. In the bloody chaos that followed, hundreds of Lakota women, men, and children were shot down—many in the back as they ran for their lives. The event would be known as the Massacre of Wounded Knee, and it would signal the end of the Plains Indian Wars.

SCENE OF THE
WOUNDED KNEE
MASSACRE.
Photograph. GM 4326.4985

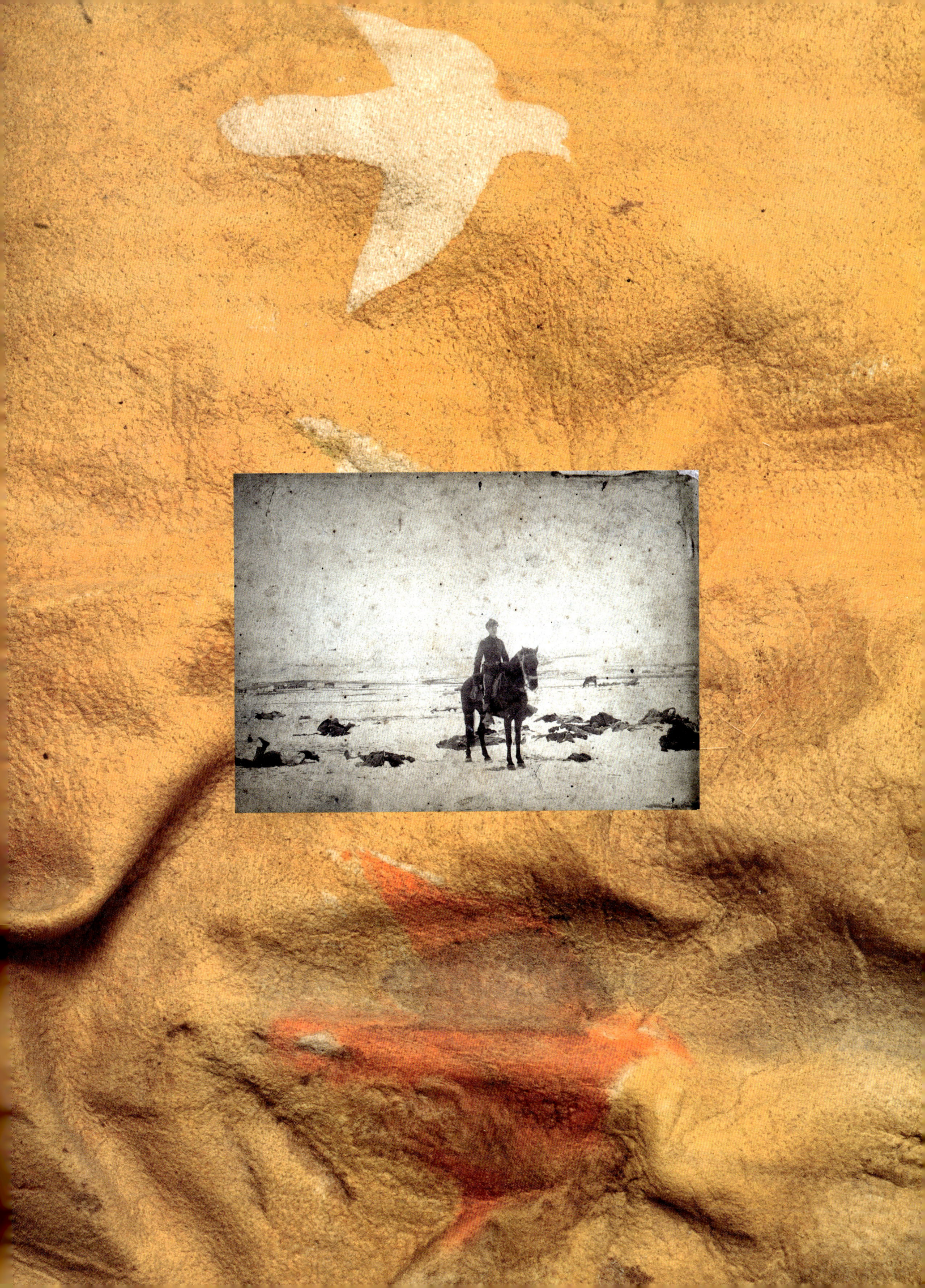

Native Americans resisted U. S. settlement in the West throughout the 19th century, with the struggle playing out in more than a thousand separate battles and altercations. As railroads and the Homestead Act brought wave upon wave of settlers, the wildlands shrank, and hunting grounds, once so plentiful, diminished.[2] The United States had battled Native people for control of land and resources since the nation's inception, but after the Civil War, America had transformed as a nation. While previously the United States had seen itself as a country that spanned North and South, it now also saw itself in terms of East and West, and as the nation looked west at the potential wealth the land offered, only the indigenous people stood in its way. The cost of white expansion to Native people would be the loss of everything they had known. Relegated to reservations and stripped of their land, they battled the military and settlers in an effort to preserve their way of life. For the United States, interactions with Native Americans became willful displays of force, demonstrating that the nation was prepared to do whatever it took to control land occupied by the tribes.

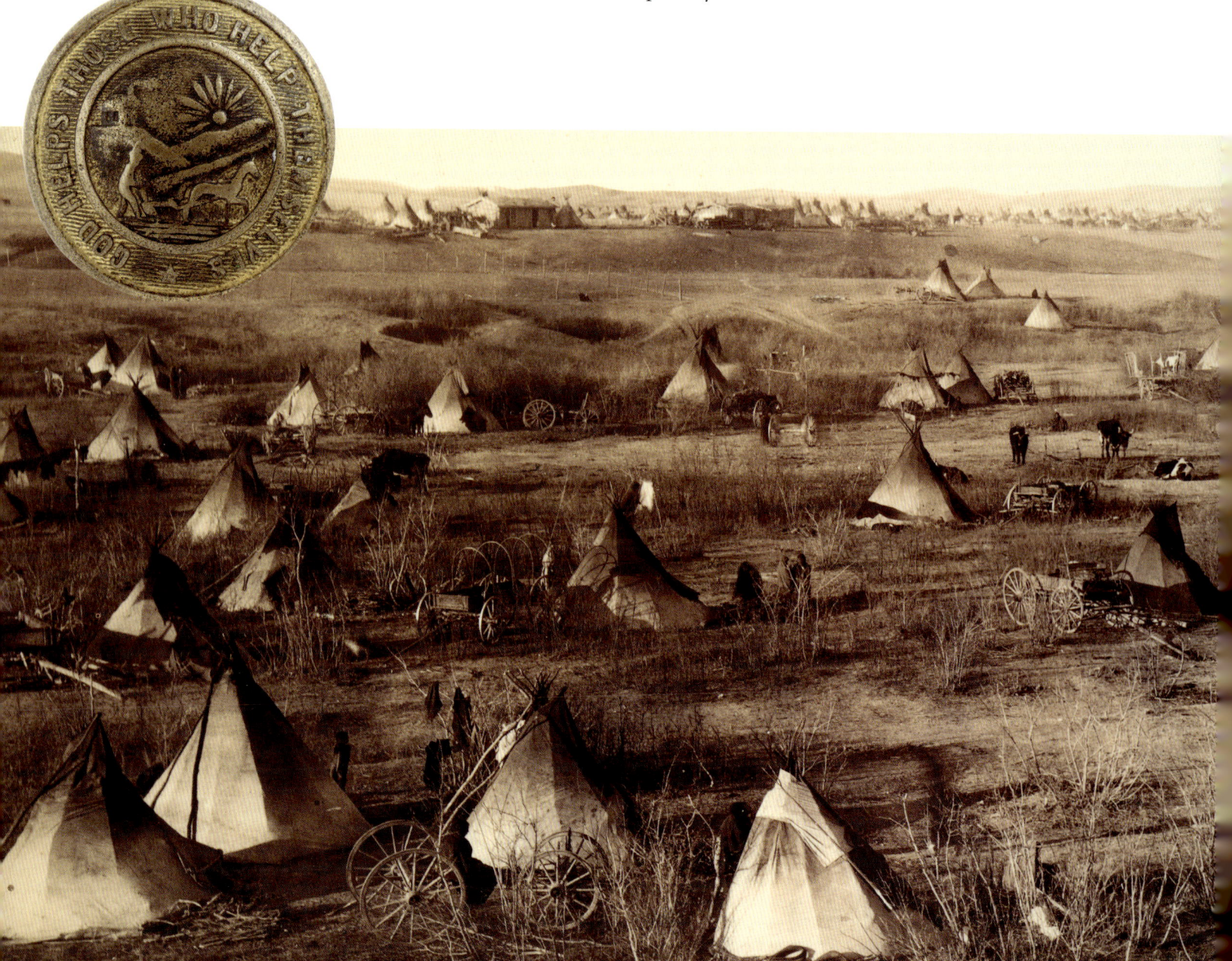

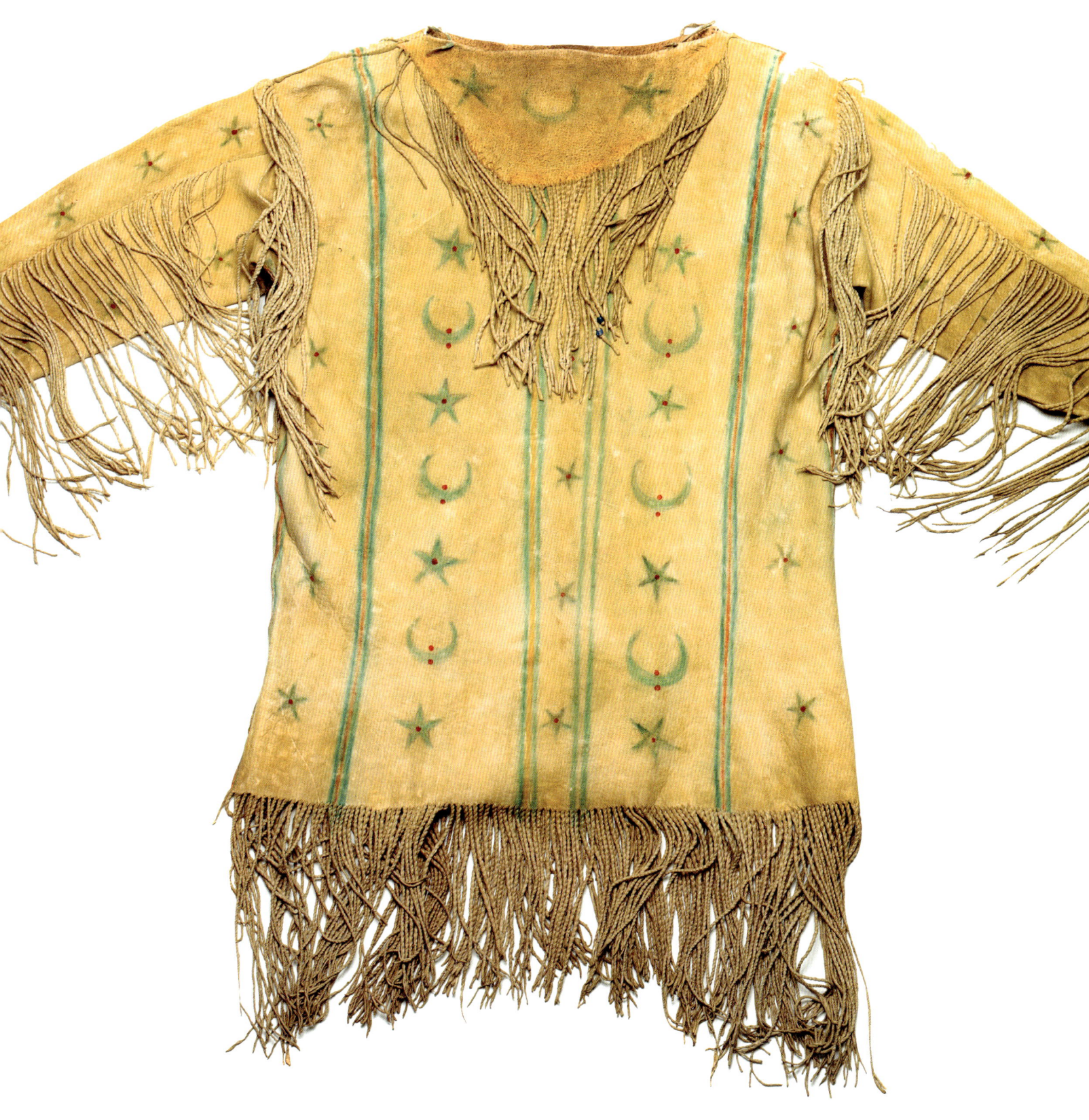

KIOWA GHOST DANCE SHIRT. Buckskin, late 19th century. GM 8427.1824

The Ghost Dance began in the visions of a Paiute by the name of Wovoka. In his native tongue, his name means "Cutter," but whites in Nevada also knew him as Jack Wilson. Wovoka, who lived in the solitary landscapes of Nevada all his life, was born to a father described as a "dreamer" with supernatural powers. Wovoka's message about the new religion began with his ascension to heaven. He related that while out cutting wood one day he heard a noise. As he moved towards the noise he fell down dead. God then took him to heaven and described the upcoming apocalypse that would sweep across the world, bringing life and hope back to the Native peoples. The dance, which is the focus of the religion, lasted for five days and was to be performed every six weeks until the coming of the apocalypse. These conditions, however, changed for every American Indian tribe depending on their own religious beliefs and needs at the time.

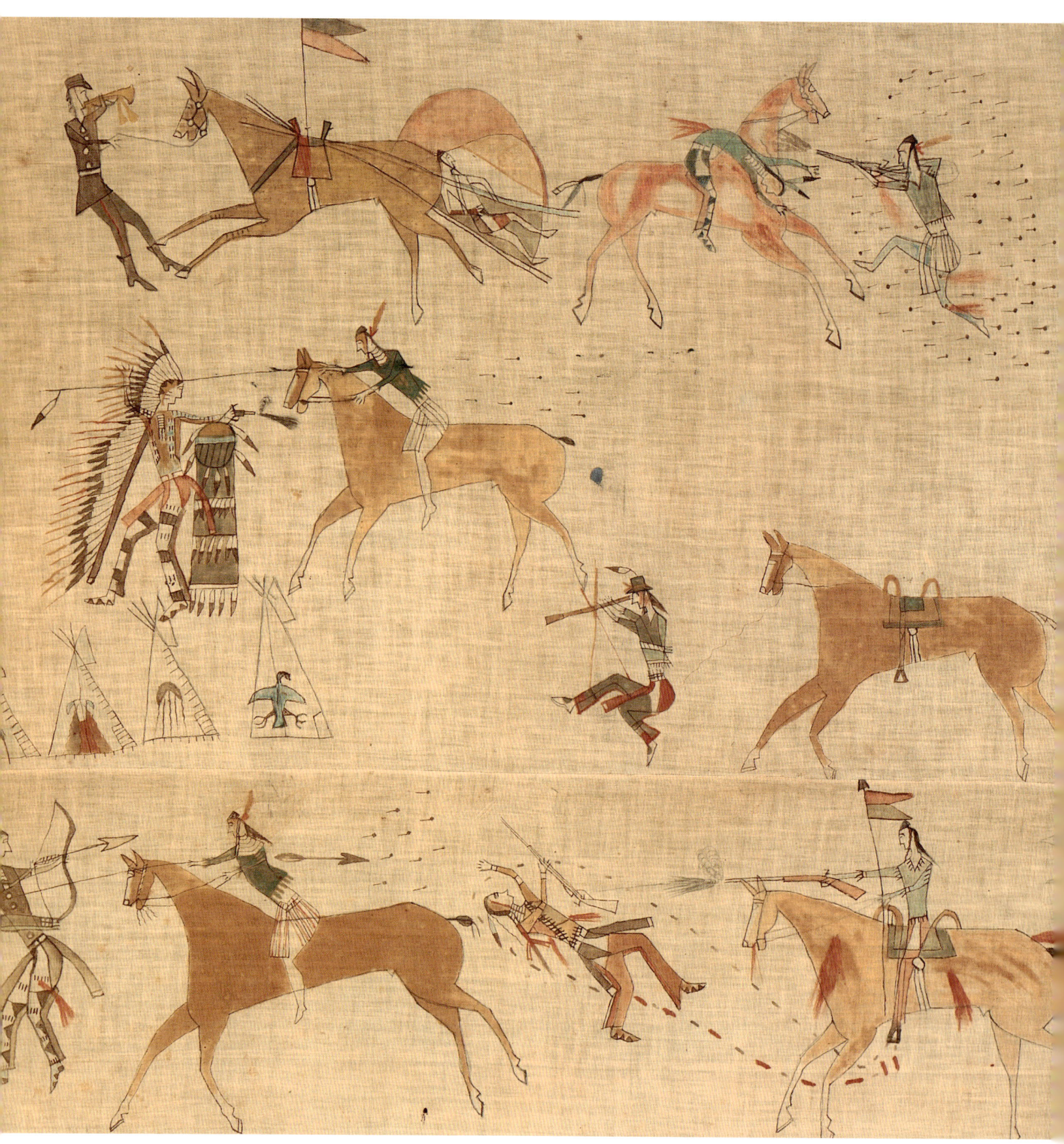

WAR RECORD. White Swan, Crow. Watercolor, ink, and pencil on muslin, late 19th century. GM 0226.589

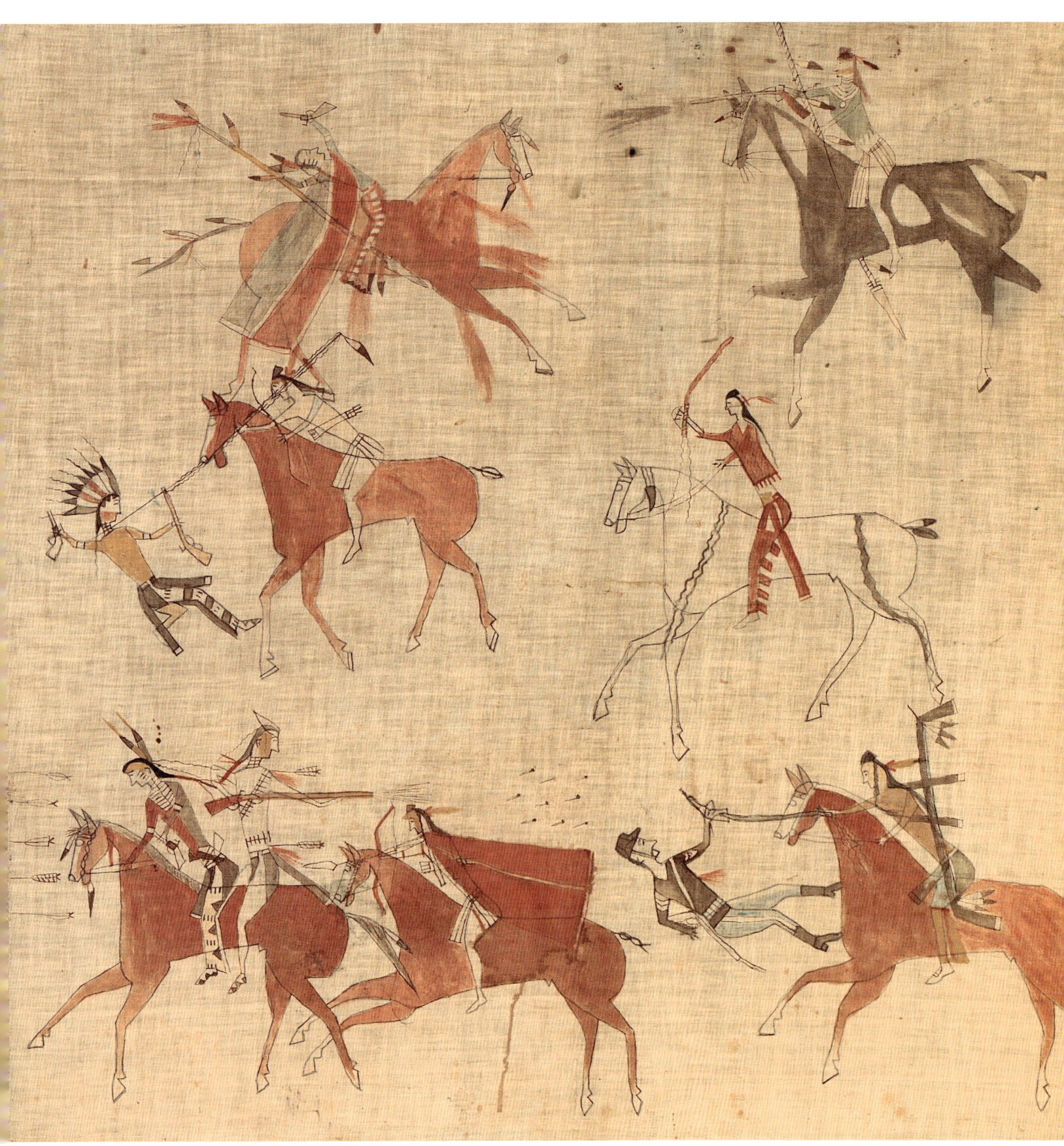

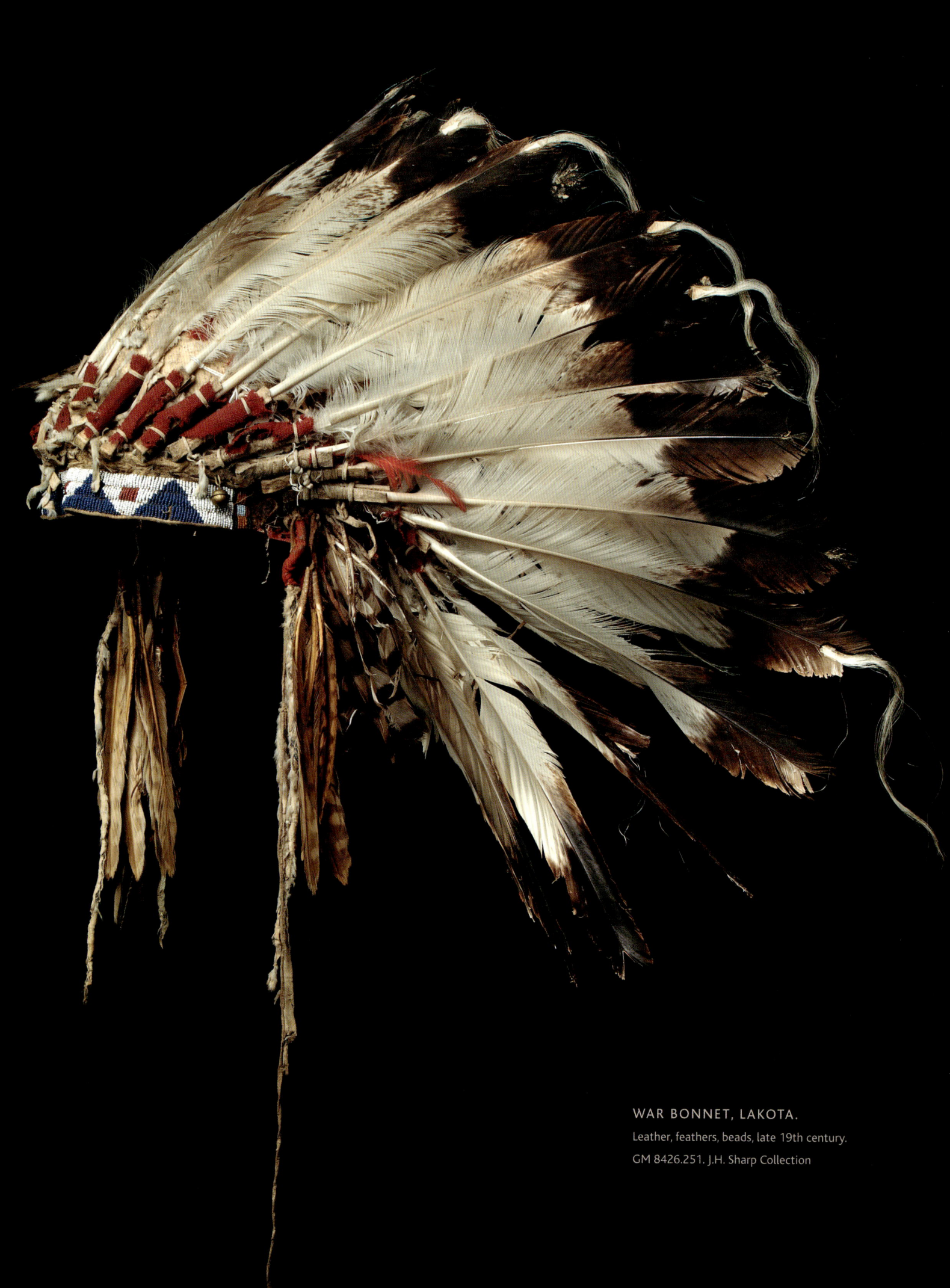

WAR BONNET, LAKOTA.
Leather, feathers, beads, late 19th century.
GM 8426.251. J.H. Sharp Collection

When Europeans first migrated into North America, the Lakota lived in the timberlands of Wisconsin and Minnesota and were a much different people than the Lakota of Wounded Knee. The early Lakota lived on a lake, farmed, hunted, and resided primarily in semi-permanent abodes constructed of deerskin.[3] As the Lakota moved onto the Plains, life changed for them. Before the introduction of the horse, these people traversed the vast, semi-arid plains on foot and in canoes, endowing mountains and lakes with sacred attributes and creating communities that venerated the environment that gave them their livelihood.[4] However, life for the Lakota was about to change.

Dispatched by President Thomas Jefferson to find a land route to the Pacific, Meriwether Lewis and William Clark and members of their expedition embarked on a nearly two-year journey across the North American continent, exploring lands Americans hoped soon to possess. During the initial stages of the expedition, in September 1804, they encountered the Lakota.

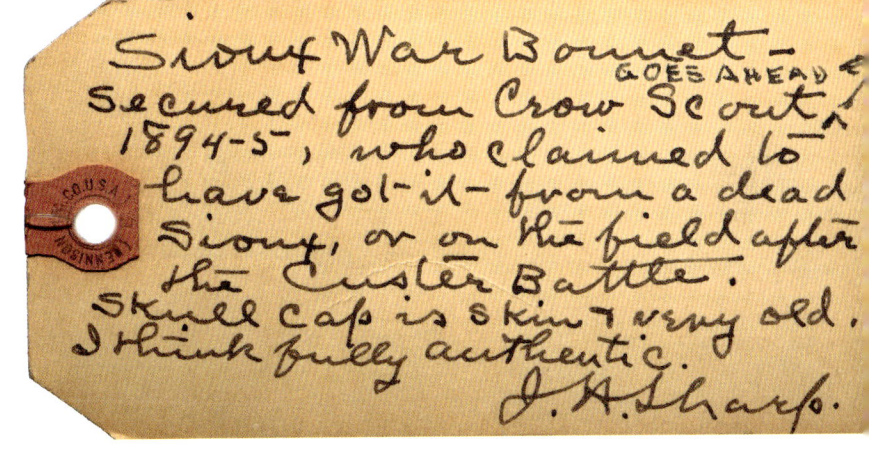

TAG ACCOMPANYING LAKOTA WAR BONNET

This tag accompanied the bonnet shown on the facing page, purportedly procured from a Crow scout, Goes Ahead, in 1894-1895. He claimed he obtained it from a Lakota killed in battle.

It would become the first of many tense altercations between the Lakota and the United States. Fearing these new explorers would endanger their trade relationships with other nations, the Lakota halted the explorers' progress, demanding payment from the travelers in exchange for allowing their passage over the land and rivers occupied by the tribe.[5] Although the parties managed to avoid bloodshed, neither could avoid trying to impress upon the other that they were the dominant culture. The explorers' attitude toward the Lakota was reflected in journals kept during the expedition: "the Sioux [are] the vilest miscreants of the savage race, and must ever remain the pirates of the Missouri".[6] Other explorers who encountered the tribe recorded different observations, reporting that the Lakota "treated them kindly" and that the Lakota practice was "never [to] attack until attacked… and [to] keep their word strictly."[7] Nevertheless, the exchange between the tribe and the Lewis and Clark expedition was a harbinger of how the two peoples' relationship would play out.

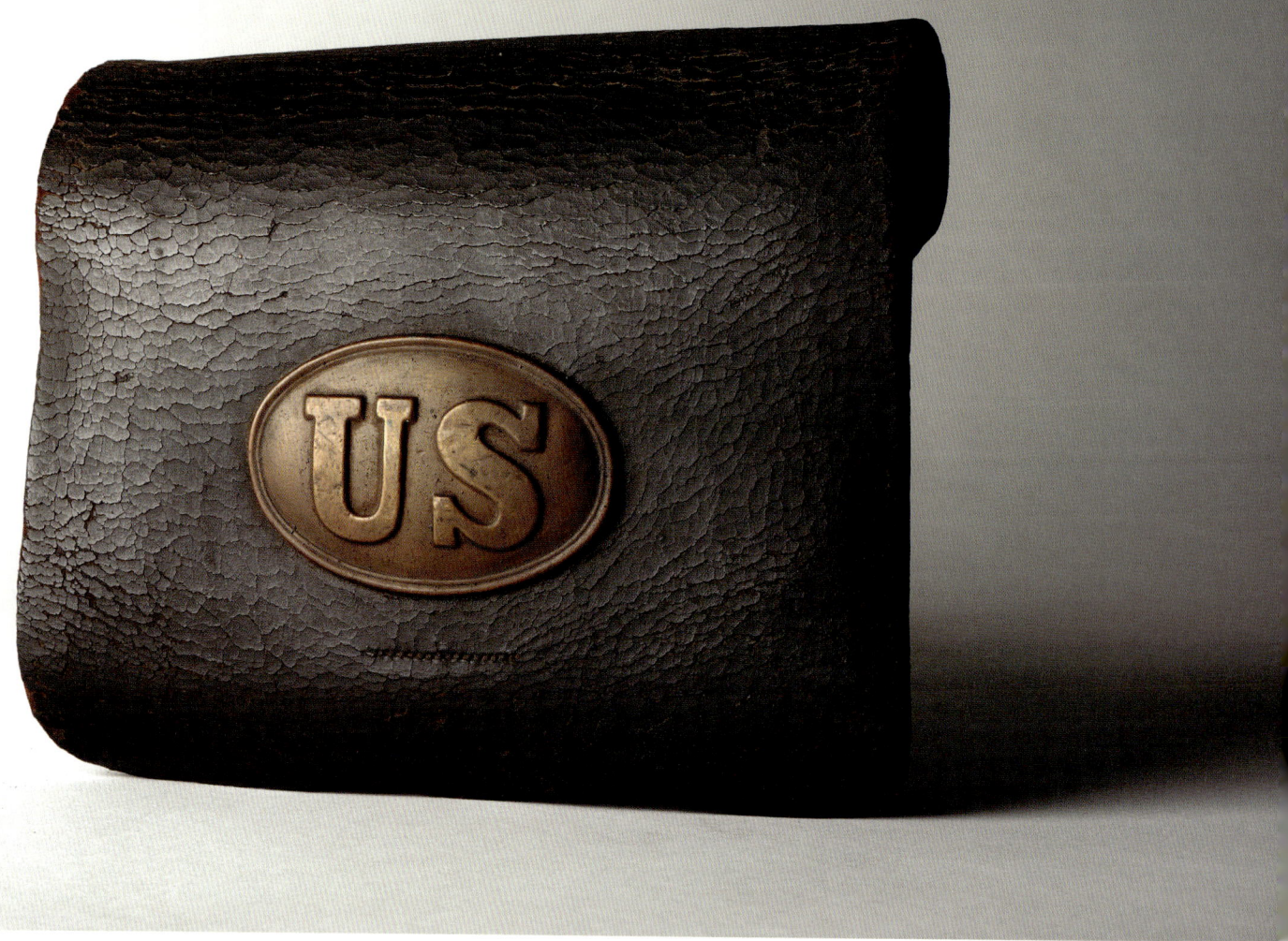

AMMUNITION POUCH. Leather and brass, mid-19th century. GM 8716.42

BLACK HILLS PROCLAMATION, APRIL 6, 1872. Broadside. GM 3526.59

This proclamation informed Americans that the Black Hills were off limits to settlement and mining. However, by 1876 the government had disavowed the 1868 Treaty of Fort Laramie, which this proclamation protected, and opened the region to American citizens.

Over the next few decades, Lakota encounters with western settlers and traders increased. At first, most of these meetings were confined primarily to exchanges between the Natives and fur traders. However, as the United States expanded, and the county's desire for more resources grew, settlers and profiteers moved into land held by the tribe. According to historian Francis Parkman, Jr., who visited the Lakota in the early 1840s,

> When the emigrants began to pass through their territory on the way to Oregon, they [the Lakota] had seen no whites except the handful employed about the Fur Company's posts. They esteemed them a wise people, inferior only to themselves, living in leather lodges, like their own, and subsisting on buffalo. But when the swarm of Meneaska [whites], with their oxen and wagons, began to invade them, their astonishment was unbounded. They could scarcely believe that the earth contained such a multitude of white men. Their wonder is now giving way to indignation; and the result, unless vigilantly guarded against, may be lamentable in the extreme.[8]

BY THE GOVERNOR OF DAKOTA TERRITORY.

A PROCLAMATION.

Information having reached the office of the Executive of said Territory, through various sources, to the effect that combinations of men have been and are now being made with a view to entering and occupying the region of country known as the "Black Hills" of Dakota, which is within the Reservation belonging to the Sioux Indians, under the plea that the said Black Hills country has valuable mineral deposits, as well as quantities of timber fit for lumber. Now, therefore,

I, EDWIN S. McCOOK,

Secretary and Acting Governor of the Territory of Dakota, by the direction of the President of the United States, through the Hon. COLUMBUS DELANO, Secretary of the Interior, do hereby warn all such unlawful combinations of men, of whatever locality, or under whatever plea or excuse operating, that any such attempt to violate our Treaty stipulations with these Indians, or disturb the peace of the said Territory, by an effort to invade, occupy or settle upon said Reservation, will not only be illegal, and likely to disturb the peace between the United States and said Indians, but will be disapproved by the Government. And if such efforts are persisted in, the Government will use so much of its civil and military as may be necessary to remove from this Indian Territory all persons who go there in violation of law.

In Testimony Whereof, I have hereunto set my hand, and affixed the Seal of the said Territory.

GIVEN at my office, in the City of Yankton, this 6th day of April, A. D. 1872.

EDWIN S. McCOOK,

Secretary and Acting Governor of Dakota Territory.

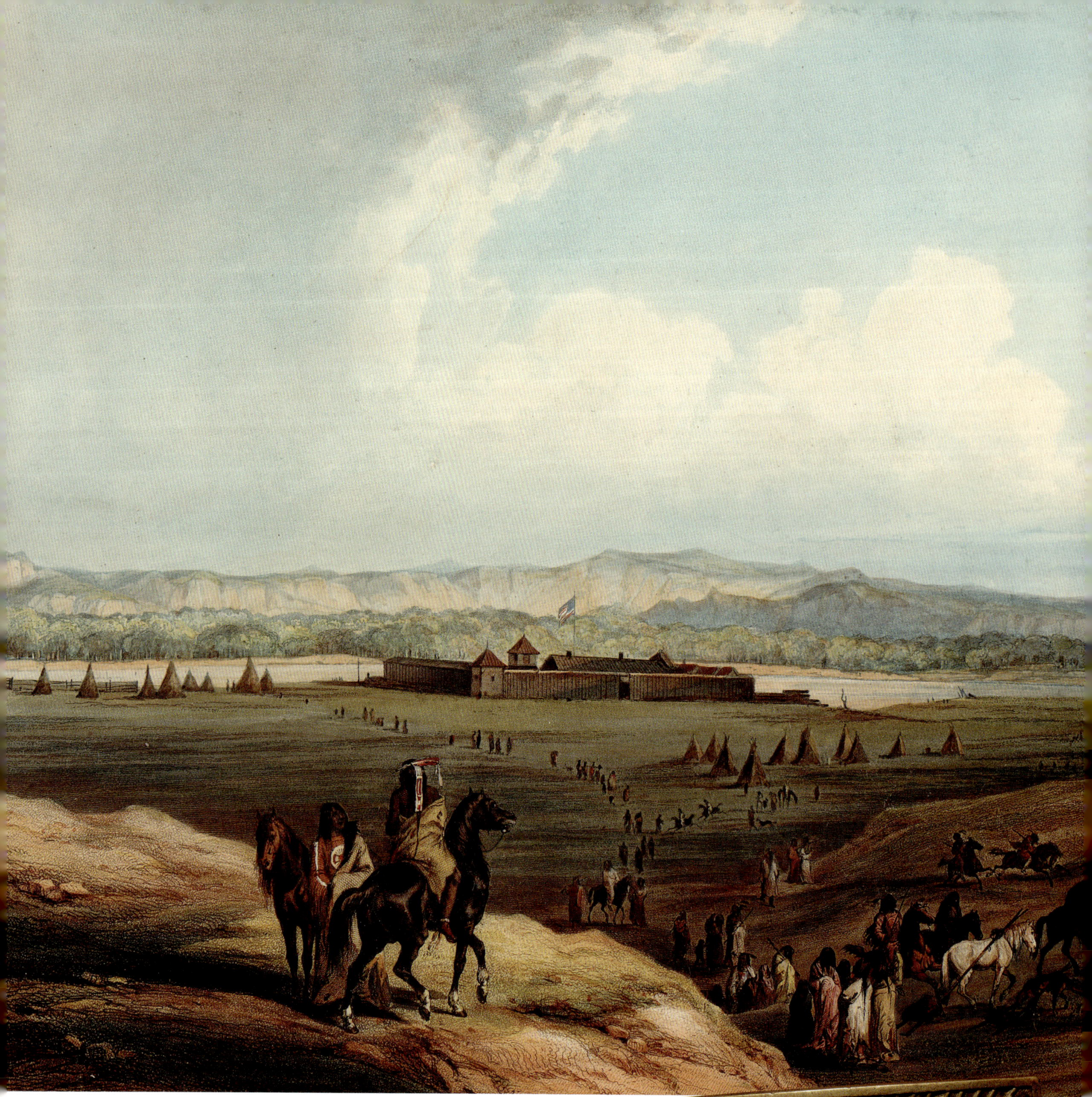

FORT UNION, Karl Bodmer, ca. 1845.
Engraving of a watercolor. GM 4576.91.62b

MILITARY BELT BUCKLE. Brass.
GM 69.125

The American Trading Company established the Fort Union
Trading Post in 1828. It remained active until 1867, when
the United States Army purchased it for building supplies to
construct Fort Buford. Located on the upper Missouri River,
Fort Union was an active trade center that purchased buffalo and
other animal hides from various Native American tribes.

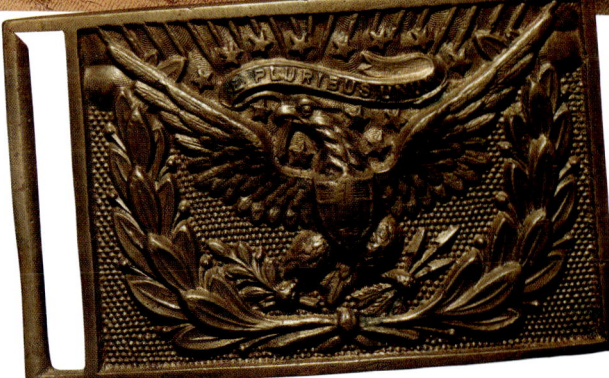

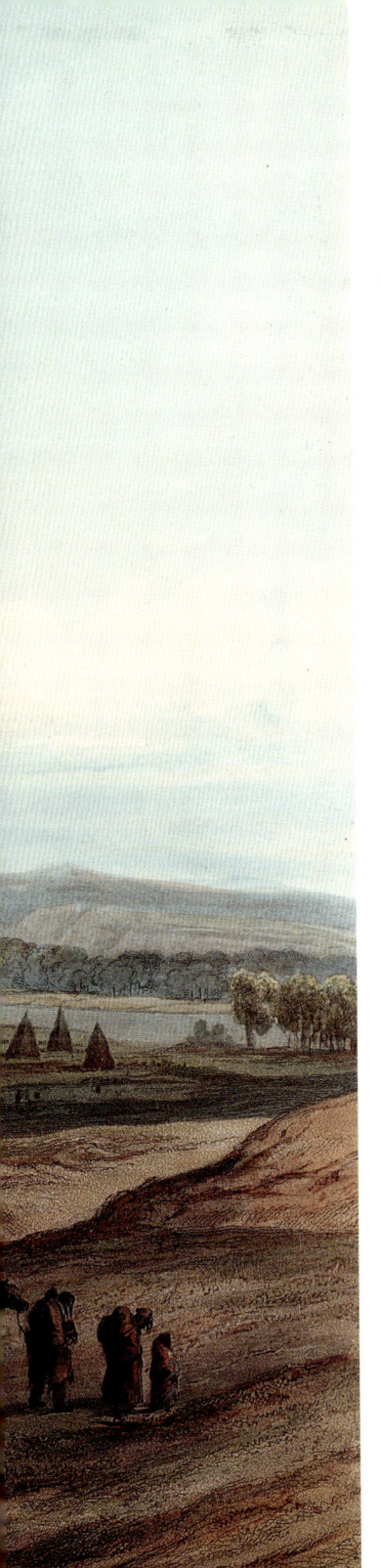

This influx would have dire consequences for the Lakota. The increased movement of whites upon their territorial land drove game from the territory and began diminishing the bison herds that once had been so vast. By 1845, the Platte Valley had seen such a dramatic decrease in the bison population that it forced the Lakota to hunt in the lands of their enemies, the Utes and Shoshones, west of the Laramie Mountains.[9] The destruction of the bison herds would have an even greater effect later as the government used their destruction to further disenfranchise the people of the Plains.

In 1863, thousands of miners and profiteers encroached onto Lakota land.[10] Gold had been discovered in Montana Territory and those anxious to exploit it began moving along the Bozeman Trail in order to gain access to the area. The region became a battleground. Led by Red Cloud, a Lakota chief and future statesmen, the Lakota fought the intrusion, attacking miners and the United States Army throughout their territory. Red Cloud's war, as it became known, inflicted heavy casualties on the Army and on American civilians, and soon became one of the only wars that American Indians ever won against the United States.[11]

In 1868, the U. S. government signed the Treaty of Fort Laramie in response to the war. This treaty established the Black Hills, land sacred to the Lakota, as well as lands in Montana territory, as a reservation belonging to the Lakota and stated that "no white person or persons shall be permitted to settle upon or occupy any portion of the [reservation]."[12] Treaties such as this were easy for the government to uphold as long as it was believed that the land was worthless.

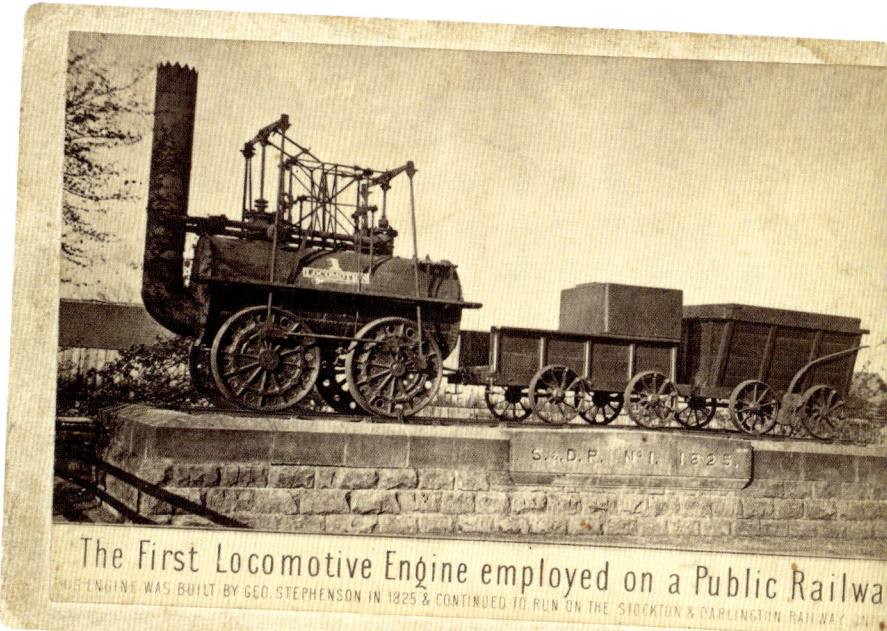

FIRST LOCOMOTIVE ENGINE EMPLOYED ON A PUBLIC RAILWAY. GM 4326.1988

Railroads had a dramatic impact on western development, making travel quicker, safer, and more economically friendly. For the cattle industry, railroads meant that cattle could be moved east, which would open up more markets and increase the price of beef. For immigrants it meant jobs, and for the government it meant the introduction of more states. Between the years 1836 and 1864 the United States had only 400 miles of railroads operating in twelve states. By the second half of the 18th century, that number had increased to approximately 90,000 miles. (John F. Stover, *American Railroads*.)

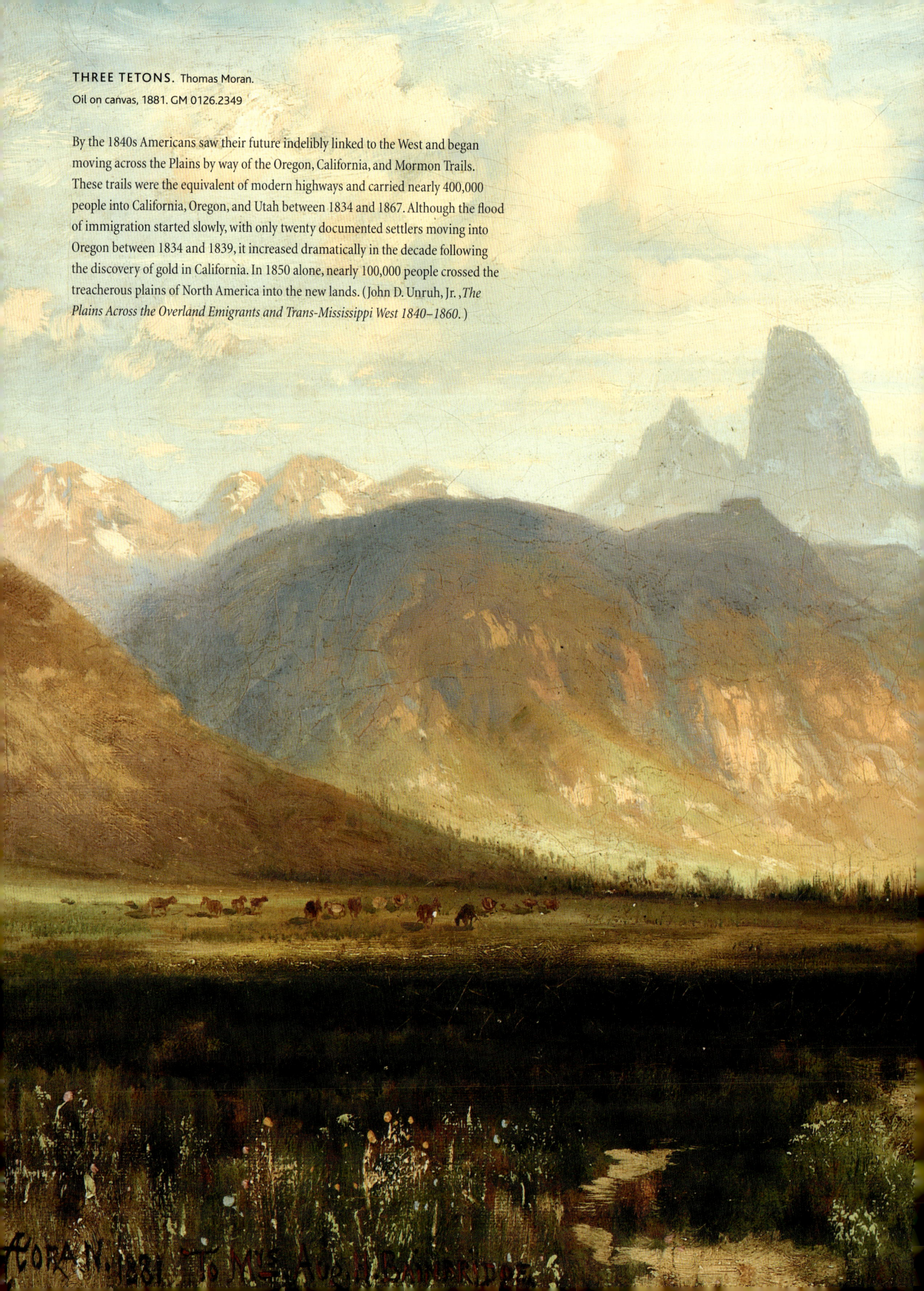

THREE TETONS. Thomas Moran.

Oil on canvas, 1881. GM 0126.2349

By the 1840s Americans saw their future indelibly linked to the West and began moving across the Plains by way of the Oregon, California, and Mormon Trails. These trails were the equivalent of modern highways and carried nearly 400,000 people into California, Oregon, and Utah between 1834 and 1867. Although the flood of immigration started slowly, with only twenty documented settlers moving into Oregon between 1834 and 1839, it increased dramatically in the decade following the discovery of gold in California. In 1850 alone, nearly 100,000 people crossed the treacherous plains of North America into the new lands. (John D. Unruh, Jr., *The Plains Across the Overland Emigrants and Trans-Mississippi West 1840–1860.*)

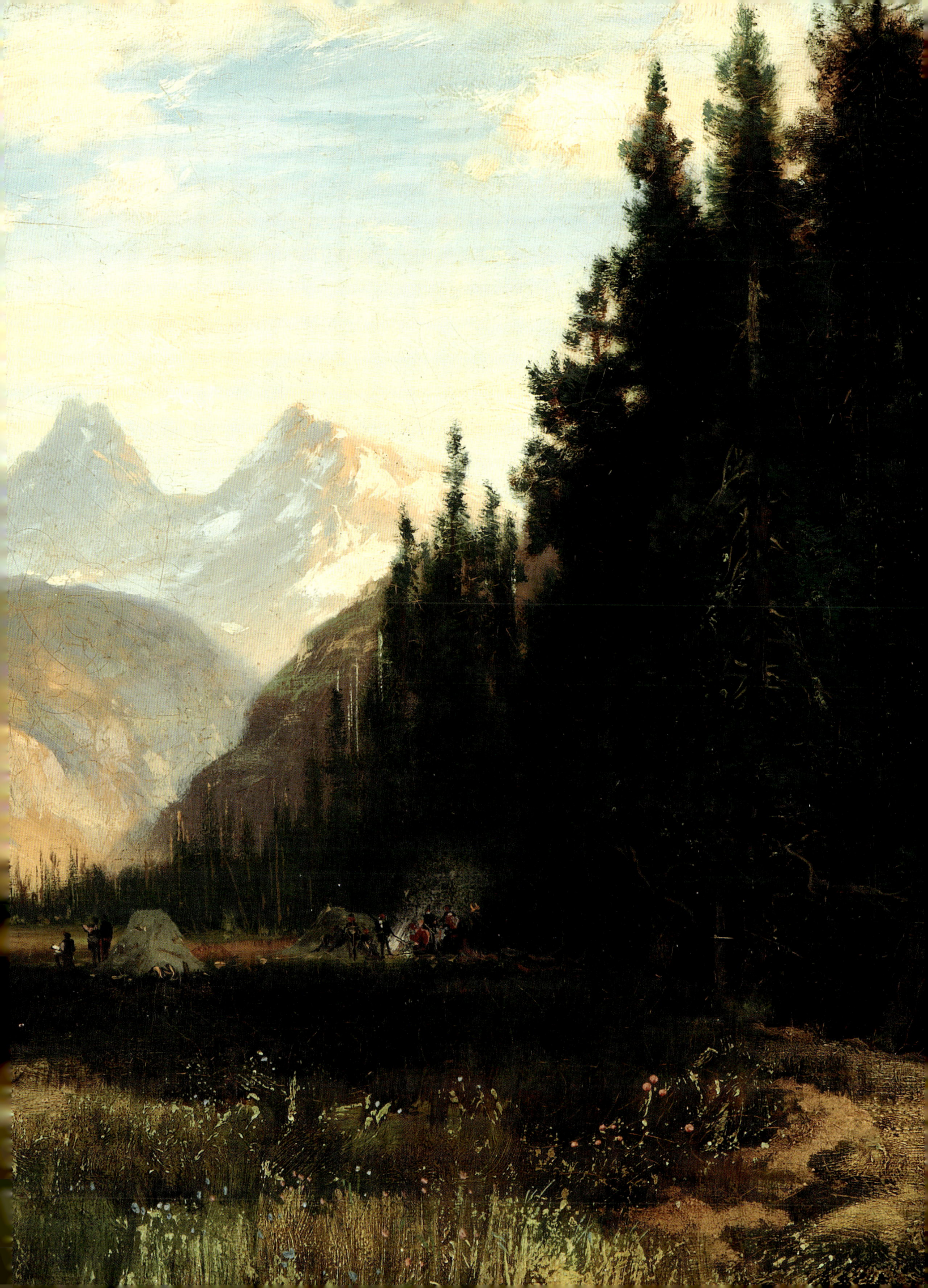

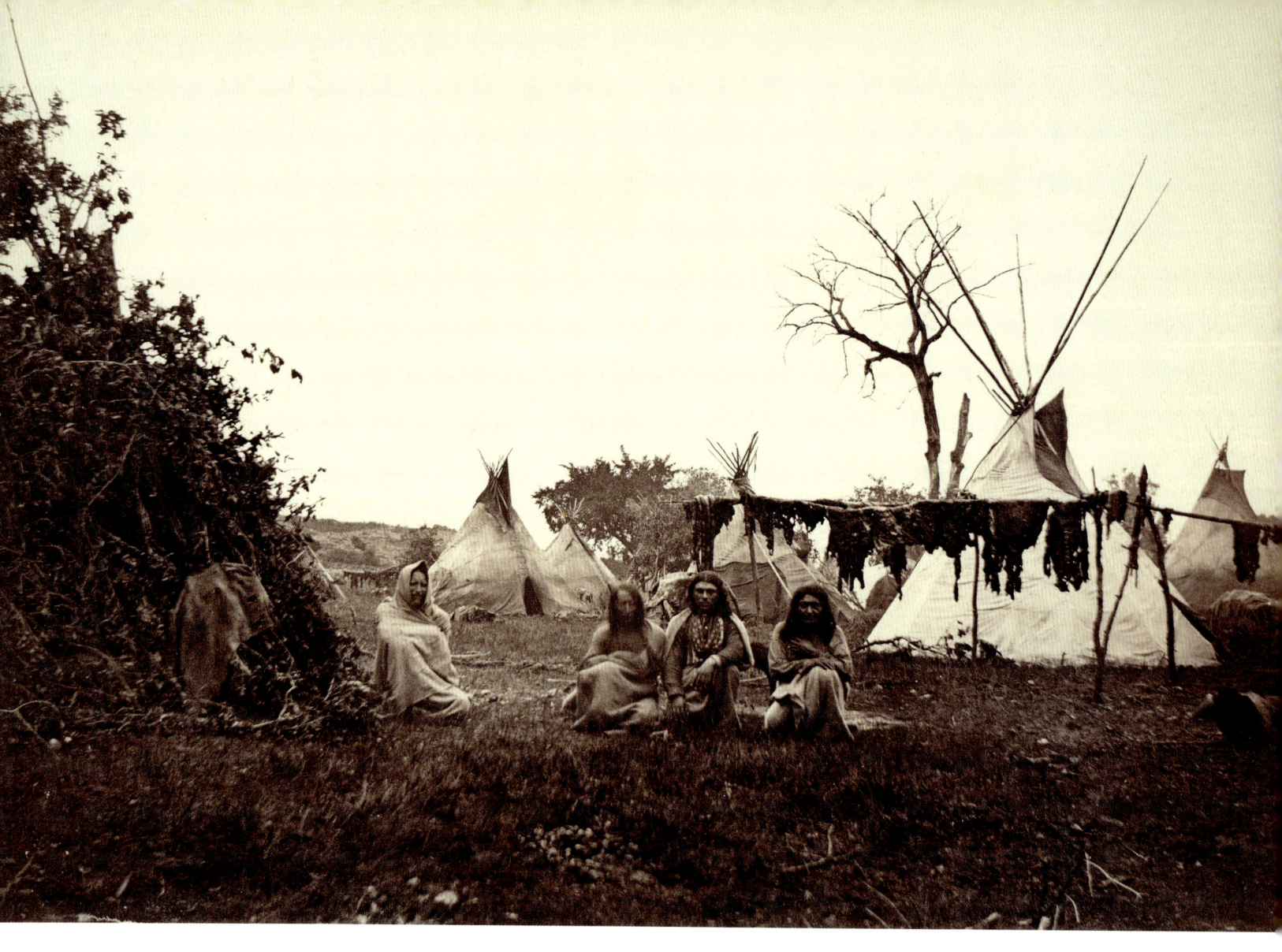

With the discovery of gold in the Black Hills in 1875, the United States government began exploring ways to disavow the Fort Laramie Treaty. Any encroachment by Americans into the region was illegal, yet Americans quickly moved into the Black Hills by the thousands, and the government did very little to stop the onslaught.[13] As described in the *Milwaukee Daily Sentinel* in March 1875, "there are plenty of people who can be relied on to prove that the treaty securing the Sioux to the reservation in which the Black Hills are situated is null and void."[14] The Indians, it concluded, should acknowledge that if they could not understand how important the Black Hills were to Americans, it was their own fault, not the white man's, that they suffered.[15] To enforce the government's claim on the Black Hills, the United States Army moved into Lakota territory. Because the Army could not directly attack the Lakota who continued to stay on the established reservation, a military expedition was designed by the U. S. government to attack those Lakota and their allies who had become embittered towards reservation life

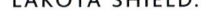

LAKOTA SHIELD.

Feathers, buffalo hide, buckskin, cloth, late 19th/early 20th century. GM 8427.2170

Shields made from horse or bison hide were the only defensive apparatus available to American Indians on the Plains. Before use in battle, shields were blessed by a religious leader. They were handled with great care due to their religious significance.

FACING: CHEYENNE DRYING MEAT.

Photograph. GM 4526.128.22

The Cheyenne were allies of the Lakota in many battles against the United States. In November 1864, Colonel John M. Chivington led one of the most horrific massacres in U.S. history against the Cheyenne at Sand Creek. Chivington's troops engaged an unprepared and virtually defenseless Cheyenne camp. During the attack many Indians began waving white flags hoping to prevent the deaths of their loved ones, but to no avail. The Cheyenne were slaughtered, and the troopers scalped and mutilated every Indian body left at the scene. General Nelson A. Miles would later declare the massacre the "foulest and most unjustifiable crime in the annals of America." (Robert M. Utley, *The Story of the West: A History of the American West and its People.*)

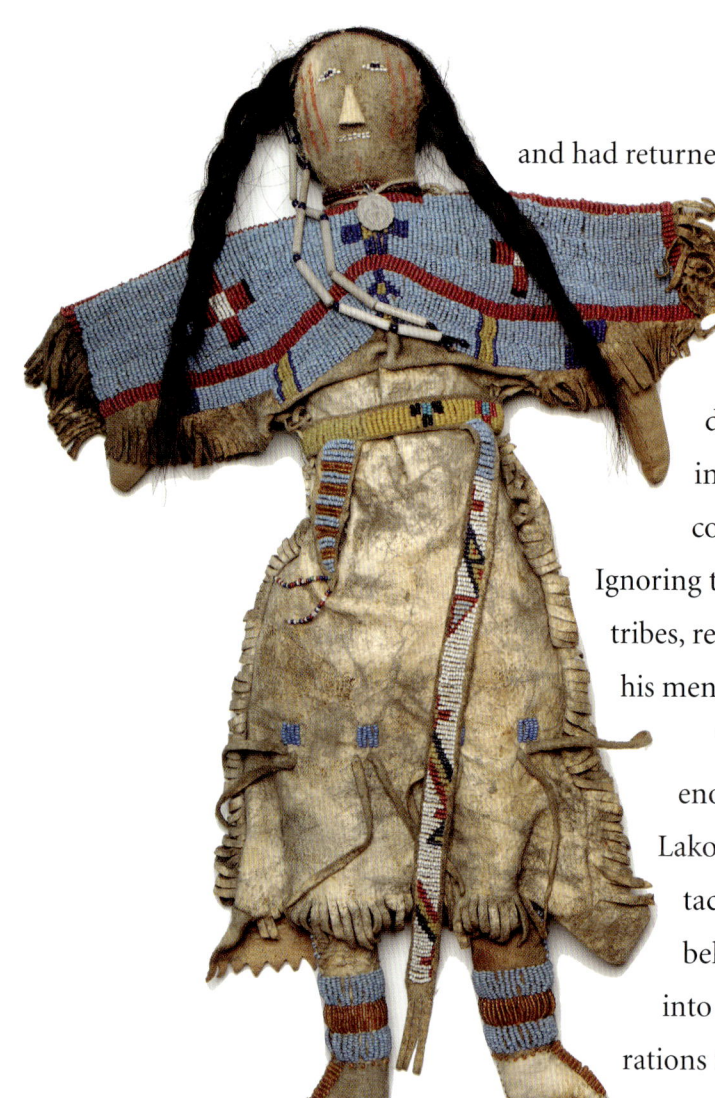

LAKOTA DOLL.
Buckskin, feathers, beads,
hair, late 19th century.
GM 84.901, Walker
Collection

The doll has beaded
facial features with a
raised leather nose, and
human hair.

and had returned to hunting in Wyoming and Montana. On June 26, 1876 Lt. Colonel George Armstrong Custer, under the command of General Alfred Terry, located the Lakota and their allies at Little Big Horn in Montana territory. Under orders to simply discover the Native American position, Custer was to immediately report back, so that a consolidated force could be used to engage the Lakota and their allies. Ignoring the commands of his superiors, Custer engaged the tribes, resulting in the complete annihilation of himself and his men.

The public outcry surrounding this disaster was enormous and brought swift retribution upon the Lakota by the United States government. A change in tactics was quickly implemented. The government believed it could weaken the Lakota by moving deeper into their territory, creating new forts, and withholding rations from the agencies assigned to provide food to American Indians living on reservations. Since 1876 was America's centennial, the government also used the battle as a propaganda tool to drum up public support against the Lakota and their allies. The public was more than happy to believe the illusion created by the government, which glorified Custer as an American hero. To Custer's defeat "the public reaction was instantaneous, universal, and instinctive. The Indians had launched a bloody war. They were massacring the army. The honor and security of the nation were in jeopardy. Exterminate the red devils!"[16] However, not every American agreed with this public condemnation of the Lakota. The Omaha *Daily Herald* of July 13, 1876, declared that

The next settlement of the Sioux should be made final by their removal from a country in which they will never be allowed to live in peace. We are confessedly a nation of mercenaries and land thieves, and have been since the nation was born. The African is the only being of an inferior race whose rights a majority of the people of this country ever felt bound to respect, all because he had no land to steal.[17]

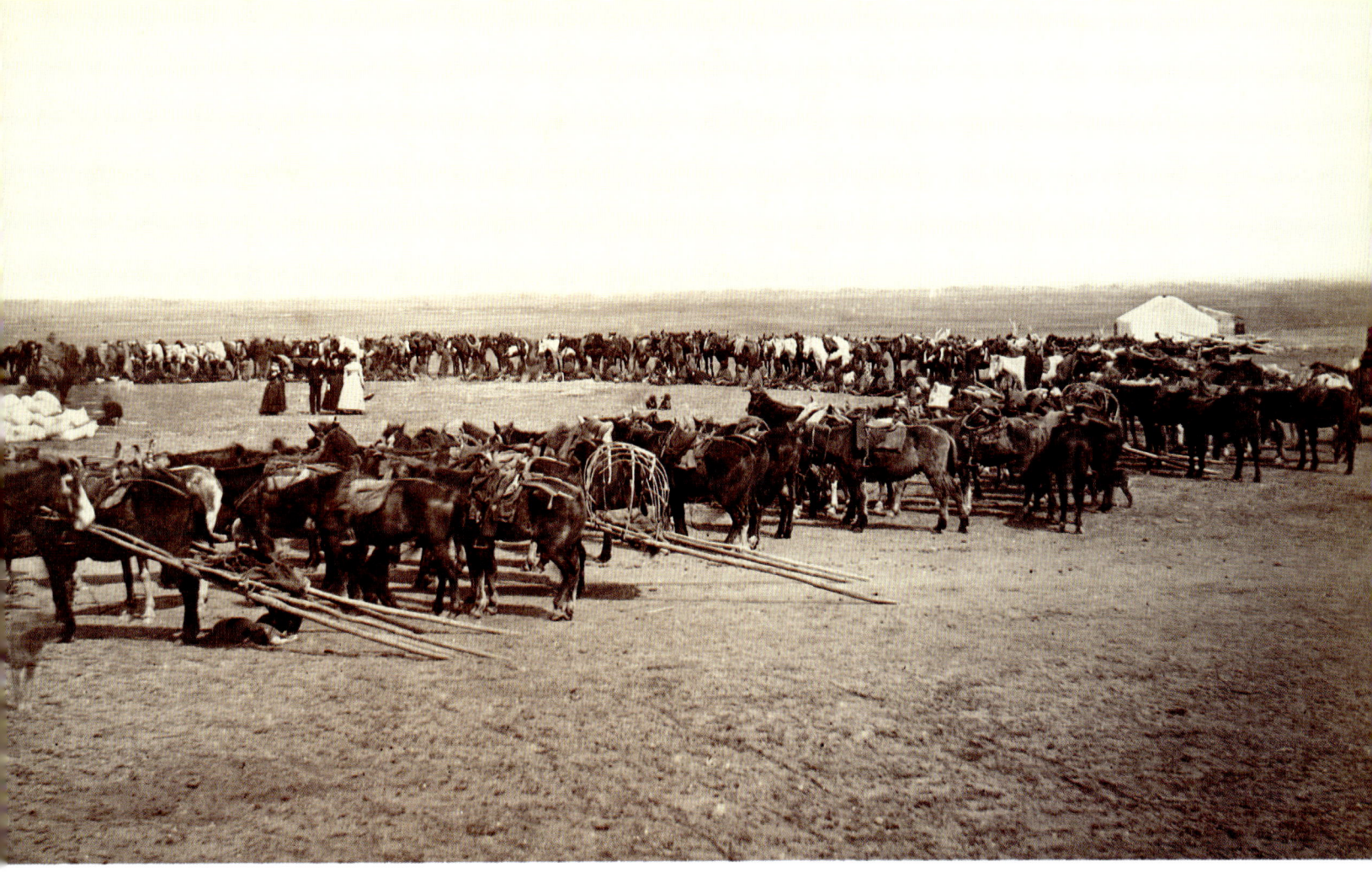

INDIANS RECEIVING
RATIONS, LATE 19TH
CENTURY. Photograph.
GM 4526.128.8

Ironically, just as the United States ended the Civil War—a war fought in part to liberate a subjugated people—it began ever more aggressively to withdraw those same liberties from another people—Native Americans.

Following the War of 1876-1877, the Lakota were forced into the reservation system. Government agents, knowing that the Lakota and their allies could do little to stop the incursion onto their lands, coerced Indian nations into parting with additional tracts and further reduced their rations. This created hunger, starvation, and disease.[18] Several years later, in 1889, the United States government would create the Pine Ridge Reservation and several others. These reservations would be the new home of the Lakota, forever depriving them of the Black Hills.

Now with access to Lakota territory, settlers, sportsmen, and entrepreneurs began a fatal second assault—hunting the bison to near extinction. Bison were central to Lakota religious beliefs and their main source of food. Without them, the Lakota had little chance of fighting back against the United States. As far as the government was concerned, the slaughter of bison helped ranchers, provided commercial opportunities, and coaxed Native Americans onto reservations—their choice being either to enter the reservation or to starve. As General Philip Sheridan

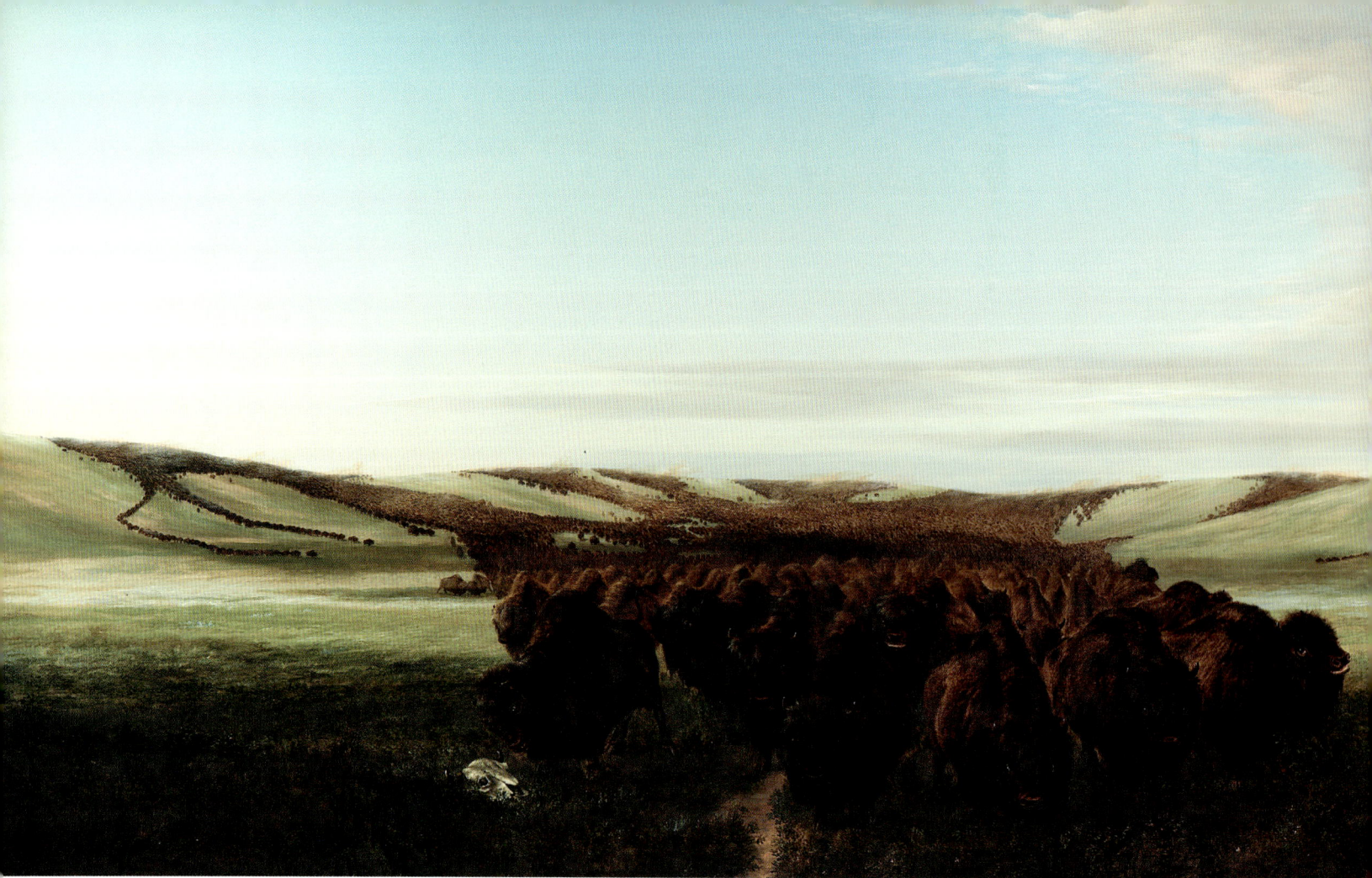

noted in the 1870s, "These men [bison hunters] have done more in last two years…
to settle the vexed Indian question than the entire regular army has done in the
last thirty years." In 1874, Columbus Delano, secretary of the interior, further
noted, "the buffalo are disappearing rapidly, but not faster than I desire. I regard
the destruction of such game… as facilitating the policy of the government…
destroying [Indian] hunting habits, [and] coercing them on reservations."[19]

By the late 1880s, the Lakota were completely dependent on the United States
for survival. Their way of life was shattered. In their despair, many turned to the
Ghost Dance. This new religion preached that "a time will come when the whole
Indian race, living and dead, will be reunited upon a regenerated earth, to live a
life of aboriginal happiness, forever free from death, disease, and misery."[20] Started
in the late 1880s by Wovoka, a Paiute Indian, the Ghost Dance was meant to bring
back the world its followers once had known. As word of the new messiah spread,
a hope for renewal began to form in the minds of Native Americans. This ideal
appealed to many communities. However, for many Americans it was one more
excuse to reduce Native American resistance through the reservation system and
acculturation. Western settlers' mischaracterizations of the Ghost Dance swept

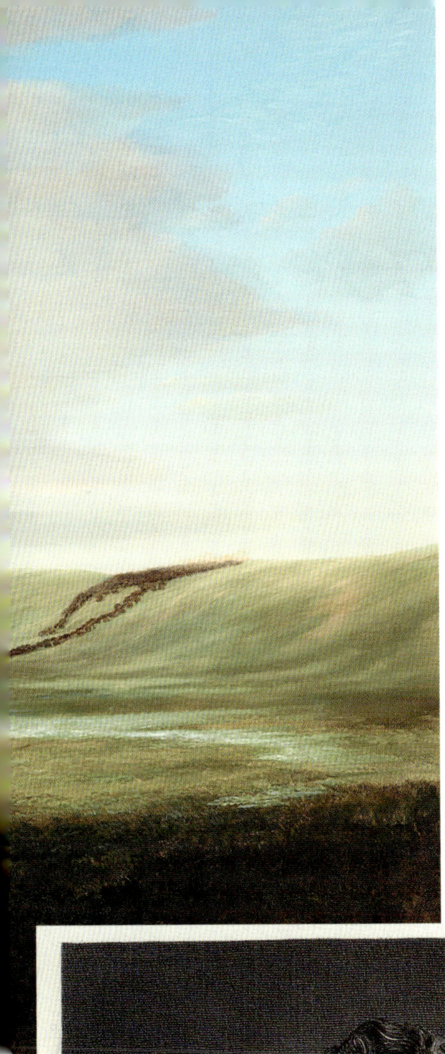

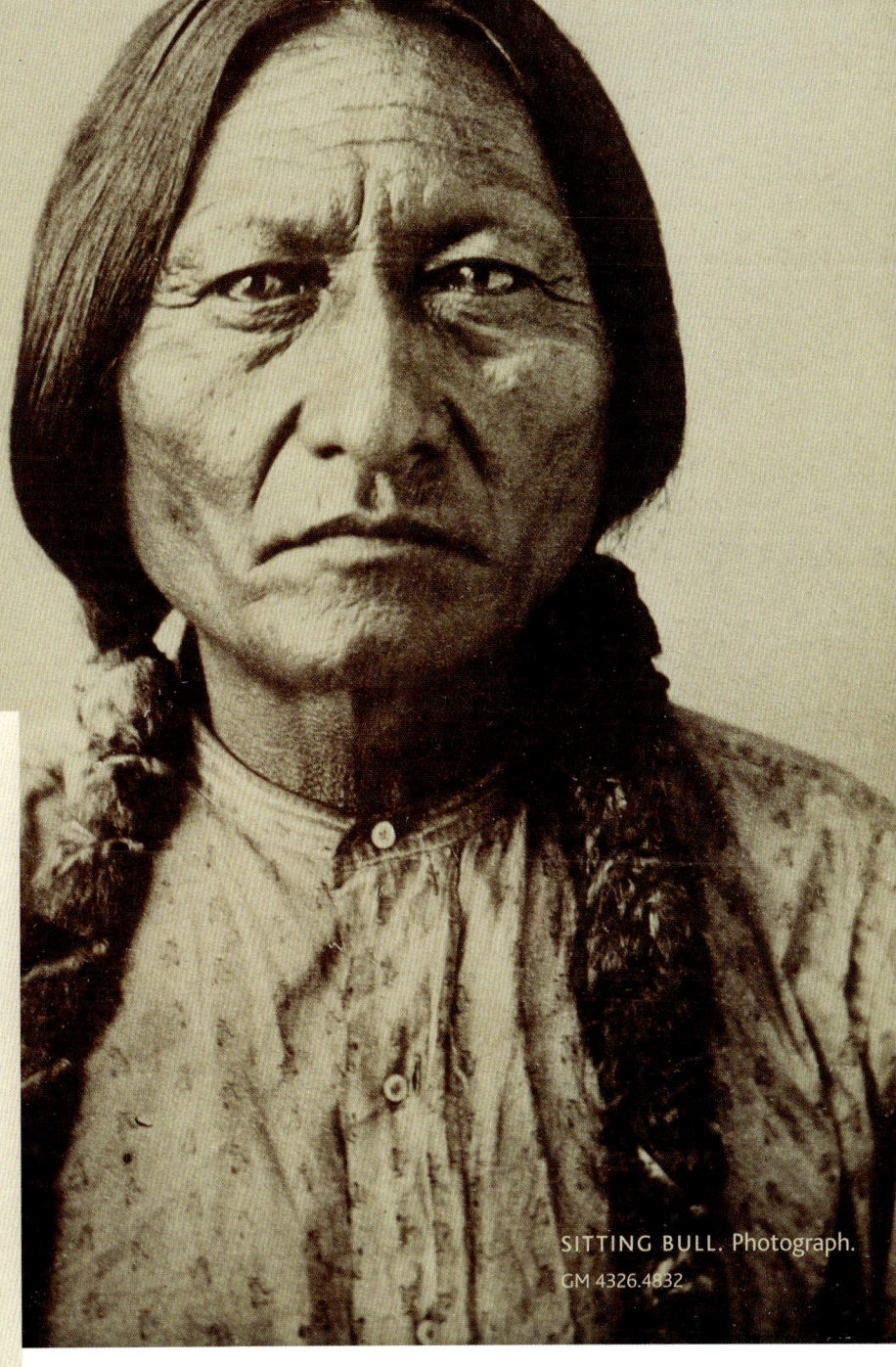

SITTING BULL. Photograph.
GM 4326.4832

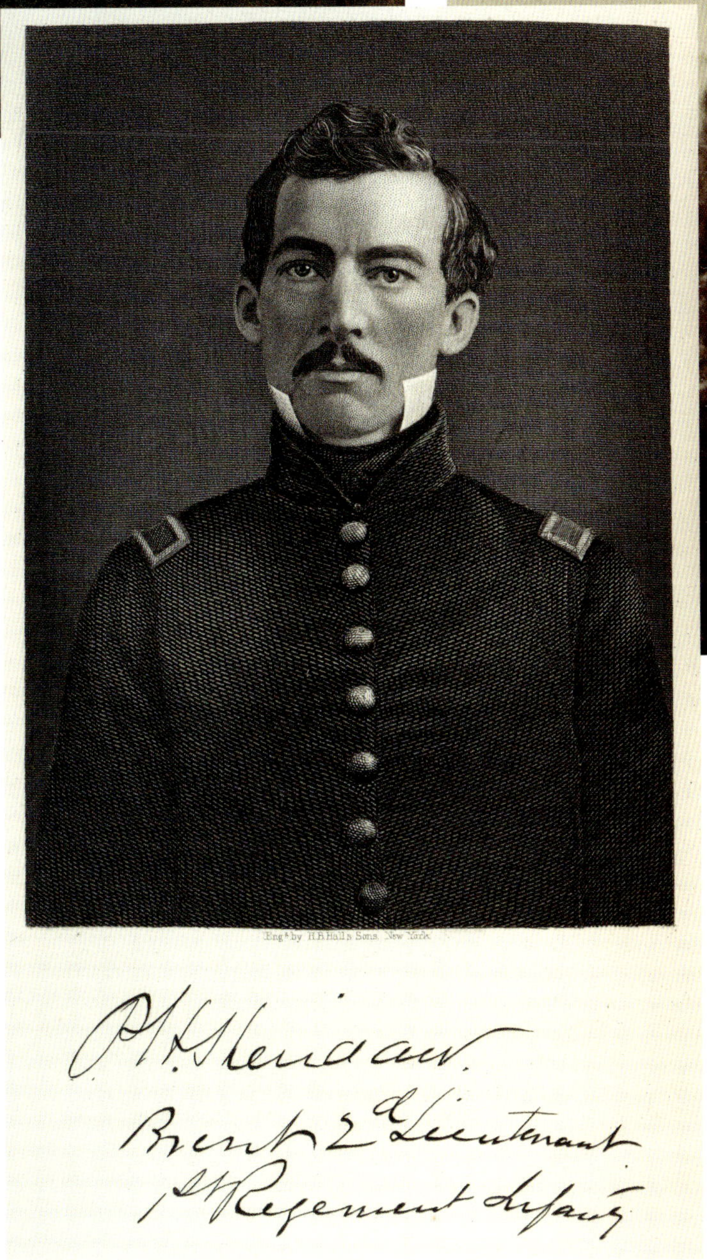

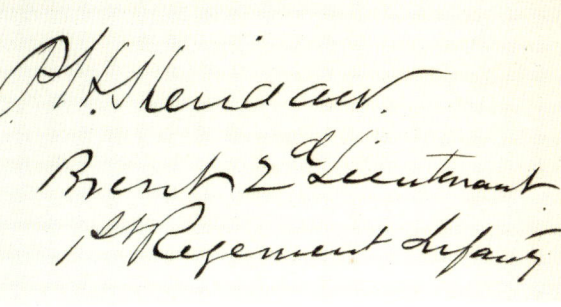

GENERAL P. H. SHERIDAN. From *Philip H. Sheridan, Personal Memoirs of P. H. Sheridan*, Vol. I (New York: Charles L. Webster and Company, 1888), p. 345. GM 2317.1268

General Philip Sheridan's military career began in 1848 when he received an appointment to the United States Military Academy. Quickly rising in rank, Sheridan acquired a well deserved reputation for being one of the North's most daring generals during the Civil War. After the war he was appointed head of the Department of the Missouri, which put him in command of the U. S. Army's campaigns against Native Americans in the West. He is famously purported to have said, "the only good Indian I ever met was dead." Troops under Sheridan's command fought 619 engagements, sustaining 565 deaths and 691 injuries. (Paul Andrew Hutton, *Phil Sheridan and His Army*.)

through the United States. Newspapers around the country wrote headlines such as "Fear Indian Uprising"[21] and "Horrible Antics of the Indians at Pine Ridge Growing out of Religious Fanaticism."[22]

The Lakota therefore, turned to leaders within their tribe who preached that an apocalypse could be brought forth through the immediate destruction of the white population. Following one of their more militant leaders, Sitting Bull, and wearing "ghost shirts"—shirts that were supposed to deflect bullets from the white man's guns—the Lakota embraced a version of the dance that was radically different from the original. Fearing that the Lakota could be mounting a new resistance, the government sent forty-three Indian police officers to arrest Sitting Bull at the Standing Rock reservation. Instead, they murdered him. After his death on December 15, 1890, L. Frank Baum, future author of the *Wizard of Oz*, wrote in the *The Aberdeen Saturday Pioneer*

With [Sitting Bull's] fall the nobility of the Redskin is extinguished, and what few are left are a pack of whining curs who lick the hand that smites them. The Whites, by law of conquest, by justice of civilization, are masters of the American continent, and the best safety of the frontier settlements will be secured by the total annihilation of the few remaining Indians. Why not annihilation? Their glory has fled, their spirit broken, their manhood effaced; better that they die than live the miserable wretches that they are.[23]

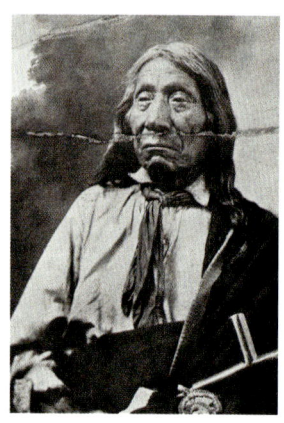

RED CLOUD. From *Chief Flying Hawk's Tales* by Major Israel McCreight (New York: Alliance Press, 1936), p. 10. GM 2927.66a

Born in 1821 in western Nebraska, Red Cloud led the Lakota to victory over the U. S. Army in 1868 and thereafter assumed the role of statesman on behalf of his nation. He traveled twice to Washington, D. C., in 1870 and 1875, hoping to gain a compromise that would allow the Lakota and the United States to live in peace.

WAR CLUB "SKULL CRACKER." Stone, wood, feathers, cotton, silk, leather, 19th century. GM 8426.1065

FACING: LAKOTA SHIRT. Buckskin, feathers, beads, late 19th century. GM 84.1822

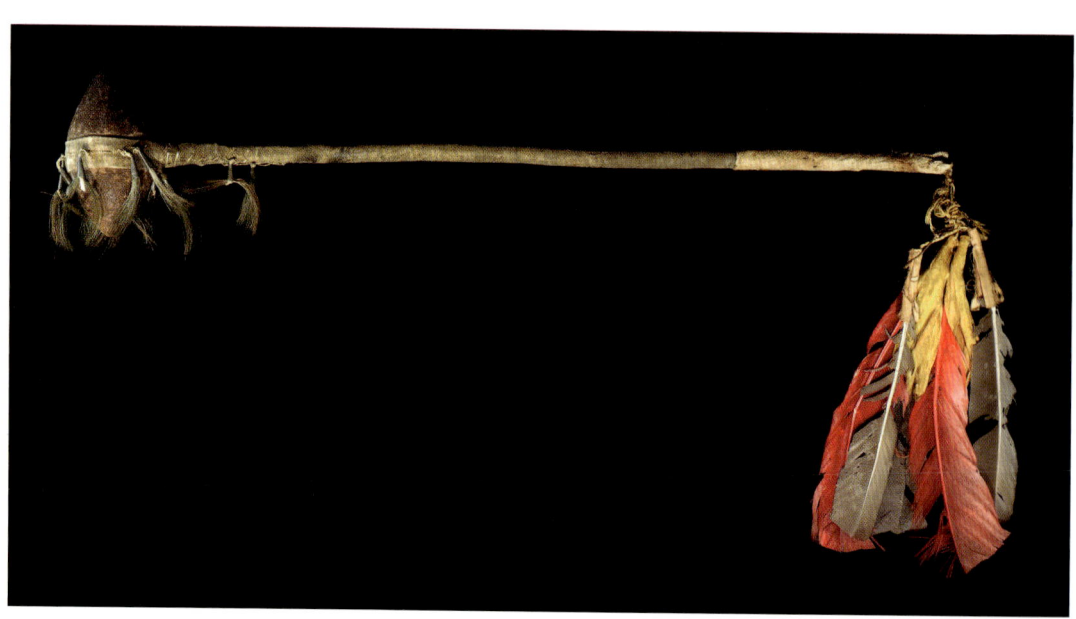

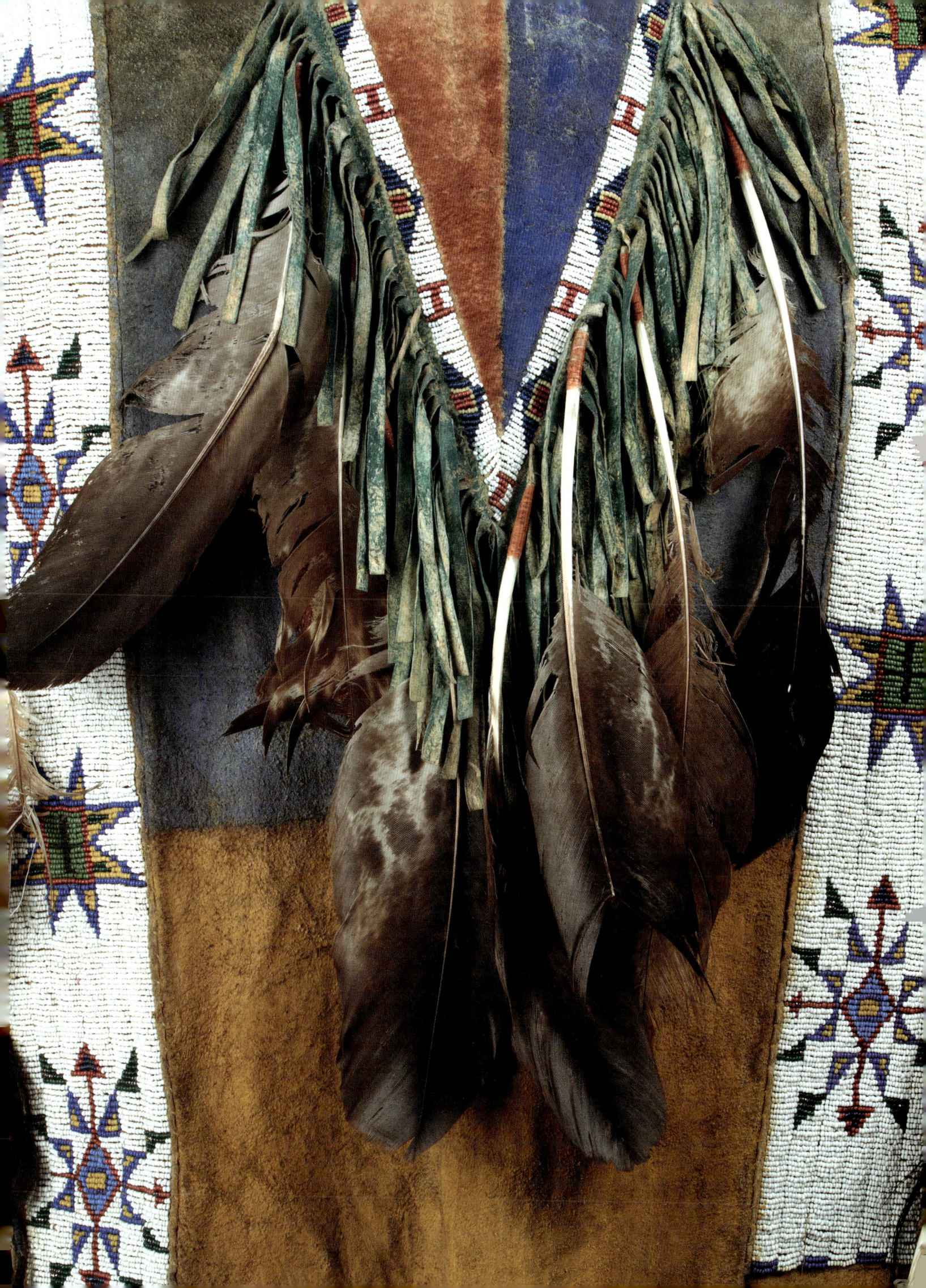

To the Senate and House of Representatives

IN CONGRESS ASSEMBLED.

Your Memorialists, on behalf of the General Committee of the United States Indian Commission, beg leave to call the attention of your Honorable bodies to the condition and treatment of our Indian tribes.

We are the more encouraged to make this appeal, by the humane spirit which has been so distinctly manifested in your recent legislation. The appointment amid the excitement of impending hostilities, of the Peace Commission, and the gratifying results of that Commission in averting an apparently inevitable and general Indian war, one year since, afford assurance of a deep desire to do justice, and a willingness to make sacrifices for that end, which it gives us the most sincere pleasure to acknowledge.

It has long been the conviction of the humane amongst us, that our Aboriginal inhabitants have been the victims of great wrongs, cruelties and outrage; but it is only recently that the particular nature, the atrocious character, and the frightful results of these crimes have been brought distinctly before us. The recent reports of the Indian Peace Commissioners, and of the Joint Special Committee of the two Houses of Congress, have in some degree disclosed the nature and sources of them; and the disclosure is at once so painful and humiliating, as to call for the most prompt and vigorous measures of redress and remedy, for the reason that it concerns alike the honor and the interests of the nation.

We stand charged before the civilized world, by the testimony of our own witnesses, with having been "uniformly unjust to the Indians;" and it is stated by Gen. SHERMAN and his associate commissioners, that this injustice has been the cause of all the wars which they have waged against us.

Among the chief causes of these wars which have entailed the loss of many lives, and been the pretext upon which the people of the United States have been robbed of millions of hard earned treasure, we enumerate the following:

I.—The dissatisfaction of the Indians in consequence of having sometimes been betrayed into the cession of their lands by pretended treaties.

II.—The constant failure of the Government to fulfil in good faith its treaty obligations with the tribes.

III.—The frequent and unprovoked outrages and murders of Indians by soldiers and white citizens.

IV.—The impossibility of obtaining justice in local courts, or of punishing white criminals, for the reason that the testimony of Indians is not allowed in those courts.

V.—The unlawful occupation, by the whites, of lands not ceded nor treated for.

VI.—The shameful fact, that of all the appropriations made by Congress for their benefit, but a small part ever reaches them.

It is also affirmed, by the same authorities, that the Indian race is becoming not only morally degraded, but also physically undermined, by the most loathsome disease which infests our civilization; that one of the finest physical types of man has already become seriously enfeebled; and that tribes, originally comparatively pure, are fast sinking into a grossness of vice which threatens their utter extinction.

This latter evil, in all its destructive extent, seems to be an inevitable attendant of the presence of our troops in the Indian country. All these, and

The government, however, was not finished with the Lakota. Soon, at the behest of reservation officials, it would undertake its final act in the country's war with the tribe.

On December 29, 1890, American troops under the command of Colonel James W. Forsyth moved into territory belonging to the Lakota. As they advanced, they spotted a group of Lakota on their way to the Standing Rock reservation to join Red Cloud, the Lakota chief who had been an activist for peace since the Fort Laramie Treaty. The soldiers, believing that the Lakota were armed, encircled the group on that cold day in late December. Forsyth's orders were simply to disarm them, but something much more terrible transpired. Accounts vary about the exact sequence of events, but within a matter of hours the United States Army had chased down and murdered the retreating Lakota. Sources cite varying death tolls, but according to the Office of Indian Affairs, 469 men, women, and children were killed, wounded, or captured.[24] Bodies were scattered across a broad distance and soon covered with snow. Few Lakota, if any, escaped, according to General Nelson A. Miles.[25] With Wounded Knee, the country's defeat of Native Americans was complete. It was the final act in a bloody drama that had lasted nearly a century.

When Horace Greeley, editor of the *New York Tribune,* joined his contemporaries in hailing western lands as the source of fortune and prosperity in 1838, he was espousing a basic ideal of American life—individual opportunity. "If any young man is about to commence into the world, we say to him, publicly and privately, Go to the West; there your capacities are sure to be appreciated."[26] But a United States that showed so little regard for the unique lives and cultures it displaced as it spread west betrayed an equally basic founding ideal—that all are created equal, with equal rights to life, liberty, and the pursuit of happiness. "Many, if not most, of our Indian wars have had their origin in broken promises and acts of injustice upon our part," remarked President Rutherford B. Hayes in December 1877.[27] America had "won the West" at a very high cost.

FACING: CONGRESSIONAL DOCUMENT, JULY 14, 1868. GM 5127.508

This document describes the unjust treatment of Native Americans by the U. S. government. It acknowledges, "We stand charged before the civilized world, by testimony of our own witness, with having been 'uniformly unjust to the Indians,' [and]… that this injustice has been the cause of all the wars which they [American Indians] have waged against us."

FACING: DETAIL, GHOST DANCE SHIRT, KIOWA. Leather, late 19th century. GM 8427.1824

U. S. INDIAN POLICE BADGE. Metal, late 19th century. GM 69.159

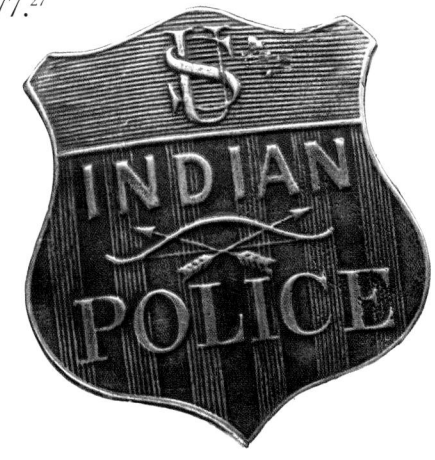

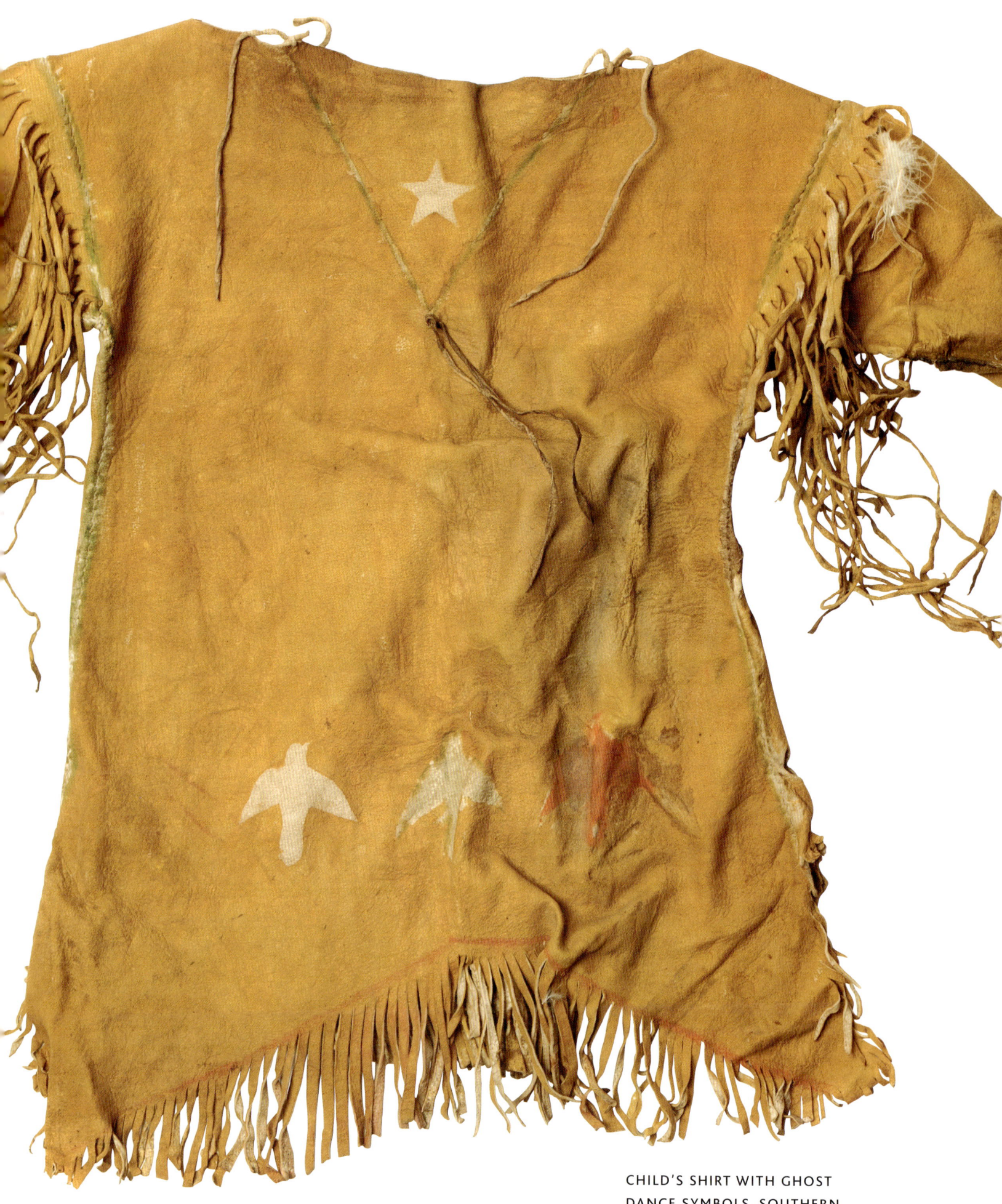

CHILD'S SHIRT WITH GHOST
DANCE SYMBOLS. SOUTHERN
PLAINS/ARAPAHO. Leather, feathers,
late 19th century. GM 8926.142

NOTES

1. For an account of the occurrences at Wounded Knee, see James Mooney, *The Ghost Dance Religion and Wounded Knee* [Fourteenth Annual Report of the Bureau of Ethnology to the Secretary of the Smithsonian Institution 1892–1893 part 2] (New York: Dover Publications, 1973).

2. The Homestead Act, signed into law in 1862, divided large tracts of land into 160-acre allotments for redistribution. Approximately 1.6 million homesteads were granted under the act and 270,000,000 federal acres privatized between 1862 and 1934, a total of 10 percent of all land in the United States.

3. Doane Robinson, *A History of the Dakota or Sioux Indians* (Aberdeen, South Dakota: News Printing Co, 1904), p. 33.

4. Robert Lowie, *Indians of the Plains* (Lincoln: University of Nebraska Press, 1954), p. 19.

5. Elin Woodger and Brandon Toropov, *Encyclopedia of the Lewis and Clark Expedition* (New York: Checkmark Books, 2004), p. 53.

6. Reuben Gold Thwaites, ed. *Original Journals of the Lewis and Clark Expedition, Volume 6* (Digital Scanning, Inc., 2001, originally published 1904), p. 98.

7. Robinson, *A History of the Dakota or Sioux Indians*, p. 31.

8. Francis Parkman, *The Oregon Trail: Sketches of Prairie and Rocky Mountain Life* (New York: Charles Scribner's Sons, 1915), p. 135.

9. Charles M. Robinson III, *The Plains Wars: 1757–1900* (Long Island, New York: Osprey Publishing, 2003), p. 18.

10. Grace Raymond Hebard and Earl Alonzo Brininstool, *The Bozeman Trail: Historical Accounts of the Blazing of the Overland Routes into the Northwest, and the Fights with Red Cloud's Warriors* (Cleveland, Arthur H. Clark Company, 1922) p. 205.

11. Viegas, *The Fort Laramie Treaty, 1968: A Primary Source Examination of the Treaty That Established a Sioux Reservation in the Black Hills of Dakota*, p. 44.

12. Fort Laramie Treaty, 1868 http://avalon.law.yale.edu/19th_century/nt001.asp

13. Thomas D. Griffith and Dustin D. Floyd, *Insiders' Guide to South Dakota's Black Hills and Badlands* (Kearney, Nebraska: Morris Book Publishing LLC, 2007), p. 27.

14. *Milwaukee Daily Sentinel*, March 19, 1875.

15. Ibid.

16. John Stephens Gray. *Centennial Campaign: The Sioux War of 1876* (Norman: University of Oklahoma Press, 1988), p. 256.

17. Continued quote: "We must accept the facts of the situation. The brave men of a dying race who guide in its council must be made to see that this conflict is hopeless as the results are inevitable for them. This done, the best welfare of the red man will be gained, the future civilization of the continent ensured and the Indian, hunted down no longer by the merciless spirit of the superior race, will be allowed the poor privilege of perishing in peace." Hugh J. Reilly, *The Frontier Newspapers and the Coverage of the Plains Indian Wars* (Santa Barbara, California: Greenwood Publishing Group, 2010), p. 57.

18. Robert M. Utley, *Frontier Regulars: The United States Army and the Indian, 1866–1891* (Lincoln: University of Nebraska Press, 1973), p. 402.

19. House Reports, 43rd Cong., 1st sess., No. 384, pg 99, quoted in Robert Wooster, *The Military and United States Indian policy 1865–1903* (Lincoln: University of Nebraska Press, 1995), p. 171.

20. James Mooney, *The Ghost Dance Religion and Wounded Knee* [Fourteenth Annual Report of the Bureau of Ethnology to the Secretary of the Smithsonian Institution 1892–1893 part 2] (New York: Dover Publications, 1973), p. 777.

21. *The Milwaukee Journal*, April 18, 1889.

22. *The Daily Inter Ocean* (Chicago), November 21, 1890.

23. Robert Venables. *Looking Back at Wounded Knee 1890*, in *Northeast Indian Quarterly* (Spring 1990). http://www/dickshovel.com/TwistedFootnote.html

24. Indian Rights Association Papers. *Letter from the Office of Indian Affairs Feb. 7, 1891* [Oklahoma State University Library]. Microfilm.

25. Mooney, *The Ghost Dance Religion and Wounded Knee*, p. 871.

26. Robert C. Williams, *Horace Greeley: Champion of American Freedom* (New York: New York University Press, 2006) p. 43.

27. James D. Richard, *A Compilation of the Messages and Papers of the Presidents 1789–1889*. vol. 7. (Washington: Government Printing Office, 1898), p. 475.

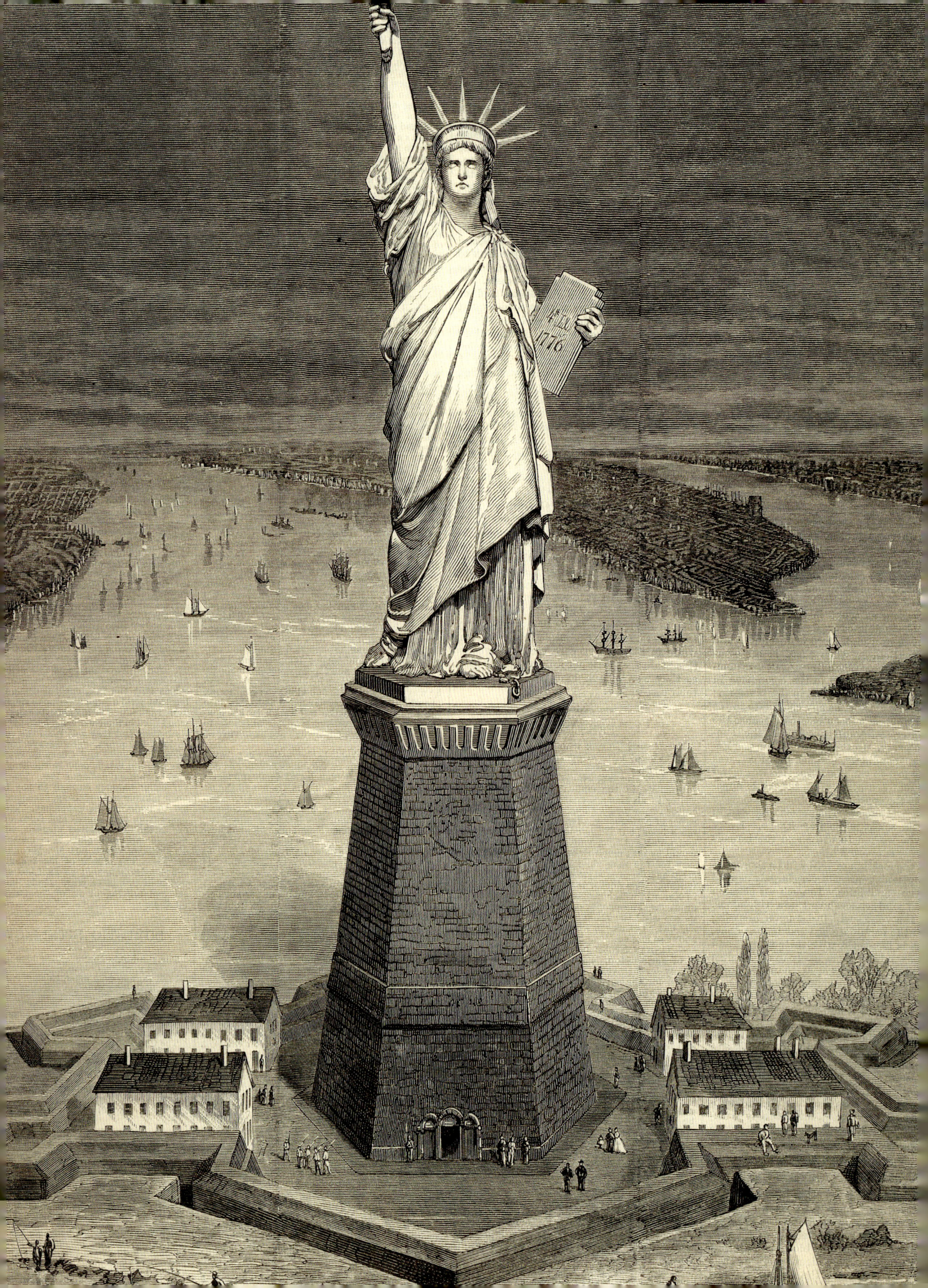

EPILOGUE: THE ETERNAL FRONTIER

The president's assassination in 1901 . . . offered a somber reminder of the precariousness of human events and how the hopes and dreams of the future can shift in an instant. Yet, the collective will of the people endured. Vast new frontiers remained to be imagined across a landscape of ever-expanding American ambition, desire, and search for meaning. The American character that had been shaped over time and through experience stood poised to reveal itself to the larger world.

I n 1893, historian Frederick Jackson Turner presented a lecture to the American Historical Association at the World's Columbian Exposition in Chicago. His paper, entitled "The Significance of the Frontier in American History," argued that westward expansion had been a fundamental process in determining the nature of the American character. Turner's thesis linked American identity and cultural uniqueness to the frontier—in his view, the social, economic, and geological space that existed between "savagery and civilization." Turner's presentation and its more widely received publication caused concern among many Americans, for he also noted the findings of the 1890 census which declared that the area of the American frontier had closed and no longer had a "place in the census reports."

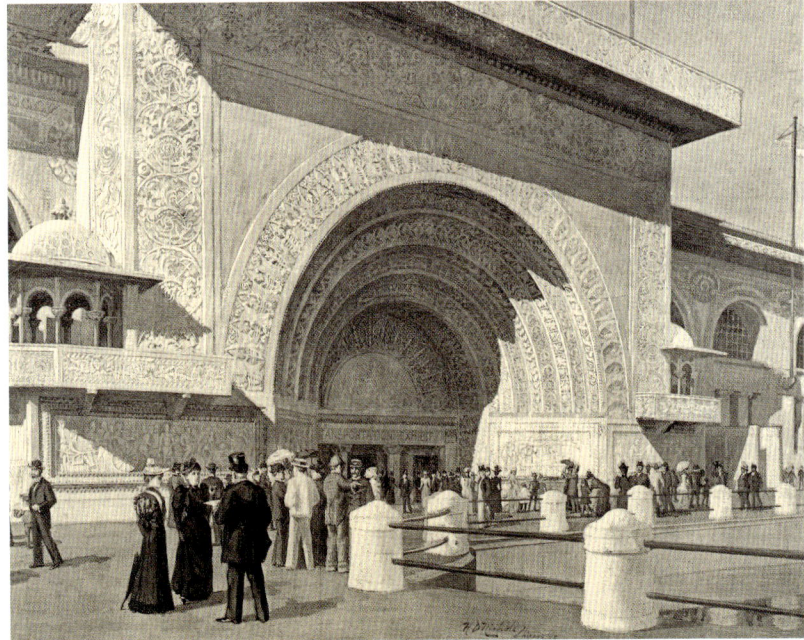

COLUMBIAN EXPOSITION – GOLDEN DOORWAY TO THE TRANSPORTATION BUILDING, *Harper's Weekly,* May 13, 1893. GM 3426.8532

PROJECTED STATUE OF LIBERTY FOR NY HARBOR, *Harper's Weekly,* November 27, 1875. GM 3426.3347

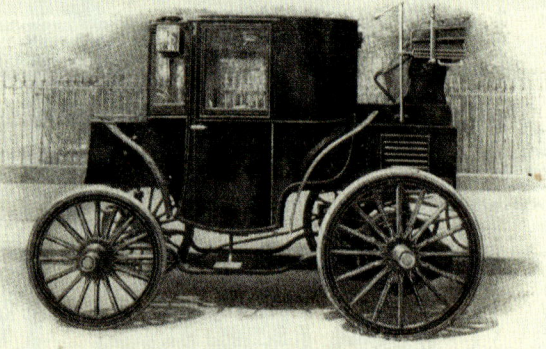

Riker Electric Vehicles

Represent the last step in the perfection of Automobiles. Vibration has been completely overcome; absolute control of speed and direction has been secured. The minimum cost of operation and the highest degree of durability has been attained. Every requirement of pleasure or business, every demand for beauty and service is fully supplied by a Riker Electric Vehicle—

RIKER ELECTRIC DEMI COACH.

The Perfect Automobile.

...ll tell us whether you want a carriage for pleasure or a wagon for business we will mail ...gue accurately describing them in pictures and words.

THE RIKER ELECTRIC VEHICLE CO., Elizabethport, N. J.

ADVERTISEMENT FOR RIKER ELECTRIC VEHICLES, 1900. GM 5327.1207

EDISON PHONOGRAPH AND CYLINDER, Wood, metal, wax, paper, ca. 1901. GM 84.3506

FACING: APPLICATIONS OF PROFESSOR BELL'S NEW TELEPHONE. *Scientific American,* Vol. XXXVII, No. 14, October 6, 1877. GM 5026.4401

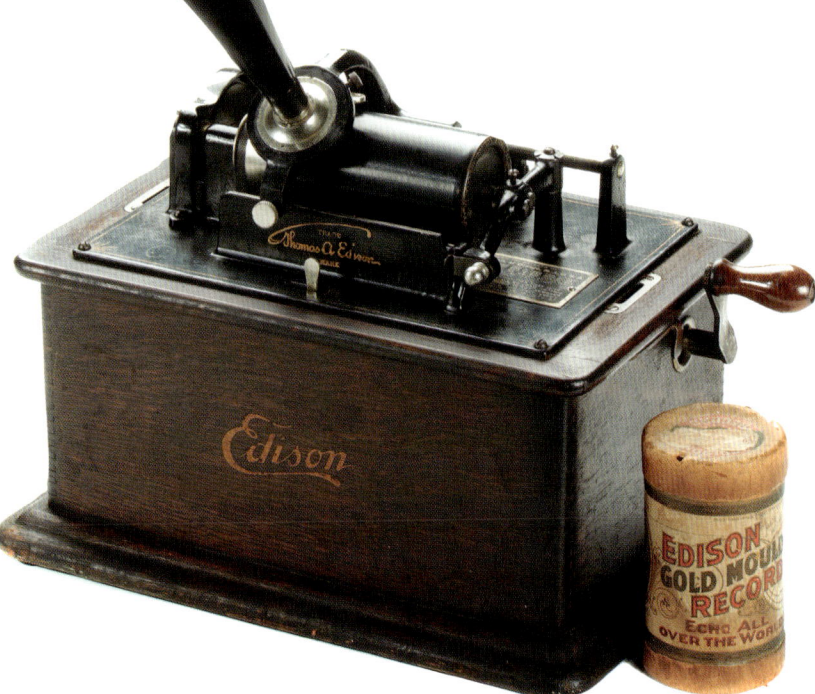

SCIENTIFIC AMERICAN

A WEEKLY JOURNAL OF PRACTICAL INFORMATION, ART, SCIENCE, MECHANICS, CHEMISTRY, AND MANUFACTURES.

Vol. XXXVII.—No. 14.
[NEW SERIES.]

NEW YORK, OCTOBER 6, 1877.

$3.20 per Annum.
[POSTAGE PREPAID.]

THE NEW BELL TELEPHONE.

Professor Graham Bell's telephone has of late been somewhat simplified in construction and also arranged in more compact portable form. It consists now of but three metal portions and is contained in a casing of wood or light hard rubber, but five and five eighths inches in length and two and seven eighths inches in diameter at the enlarged end. It will be remembered that this telephone differs from all others in that it involves the use of no battery nor of any extraneous source of electricity whatever. The only current employed is that generated by the voice of the speaker himself.

The simplicity of the construction is clearly shown in Fig. 1 of our engravings, in which both sectional and exterior views of the device are given. Referring to the sectional view, A is a permanent magnet, held by the screw shown in the rear. Around one end of this magnet is wound a coil, B, of fine insulated copper wire (silk covered), the ends of which are attached to the larger wires, C, which extend to the rear and terminate in the binding screws, D. In front of the pole and

coil, B, is a soft iron disk, E. Finally the whole is inclosed in a wooden casing having an aperture in front of the disk, and which, besides serving to protect the magnet, etc., acts somewhat as a resonator.

The principle of the apparatus we have already explained in some detail, but it may be summarized here as follows: The influence of the magnet induces all around it a magnetic field, and the iron diaphragm, E, is attracted towards the pole. Any alteration in the normal condition of the diaphragm, produces an alteration in the magnetic field, by strengthening or weakening it, and any such alteration of the magnetic field causes the induction of, a current of electricity in the coil, B. The strength of this induced current is dependent upon the amplitude and rate of vibration of the disk, and these depend in turn upon the air disturbance made by the voice in speaking, or in any other similar source. Therefore, first, a wave of air throws the diaphragm into vibration; second, each movement produces a change in the magnetic field; and third, an induced

[Continued on page 212.]

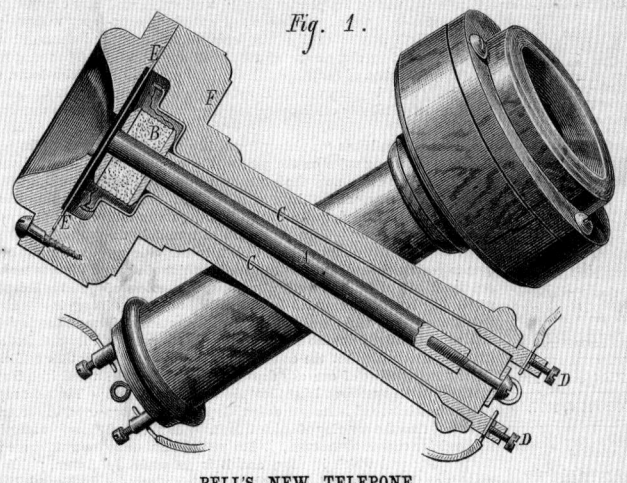

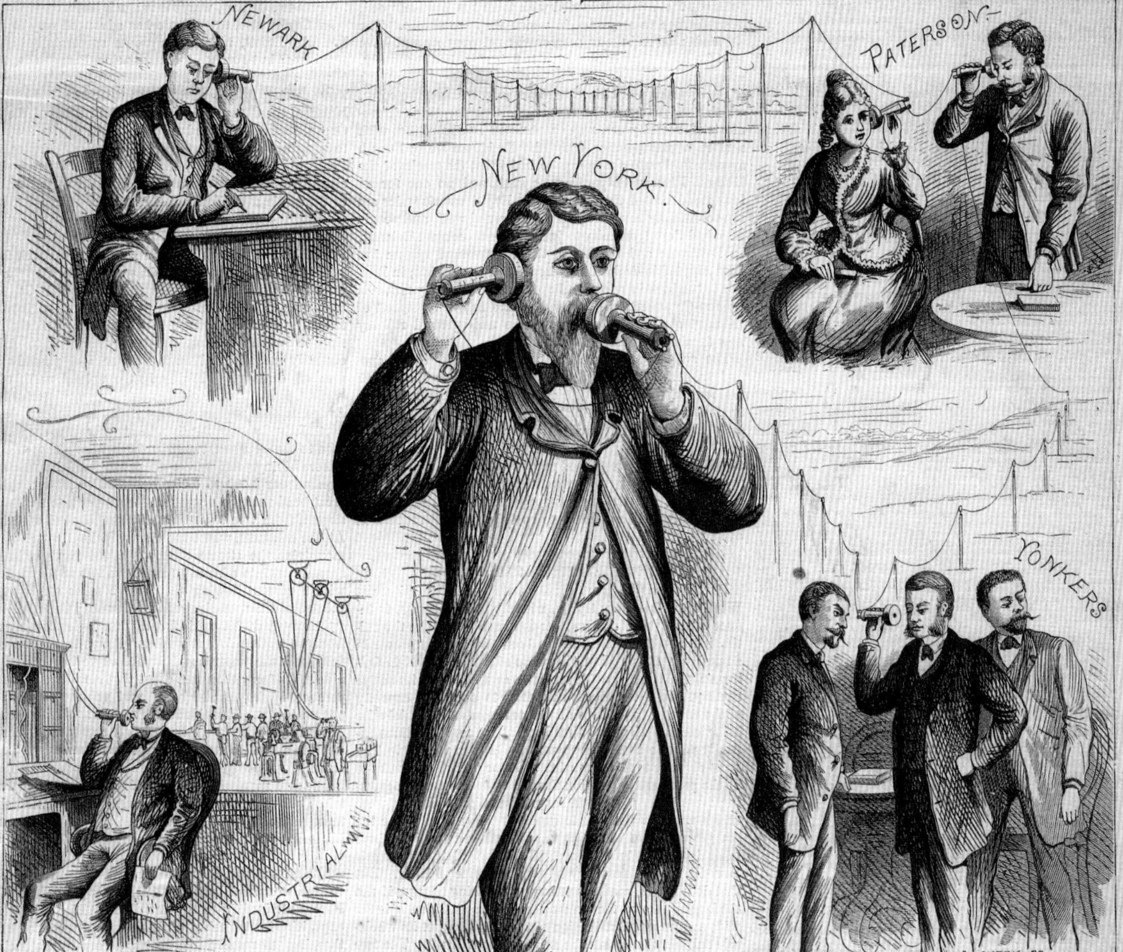

Fig. 1.

BELL'S NEW TELEPONE.

APPLICATIONS OF PROFESSOR BELL'S NEW TELEPHONE.

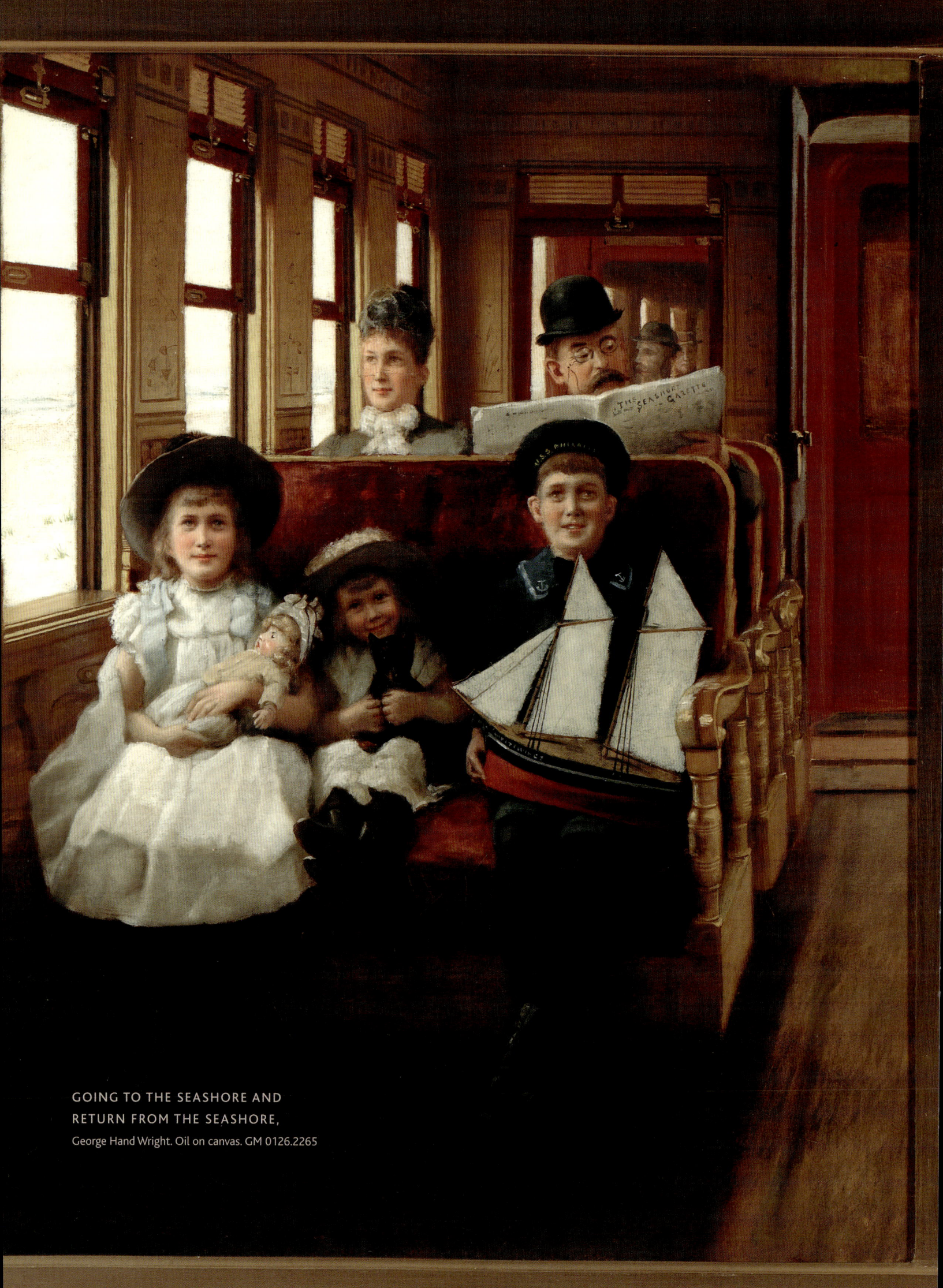

GOING TO THE SEASHORE AND
RETURN FROM THE SEASHORE,
George Hand Wright. Oil on canvas. GM 0126.2265

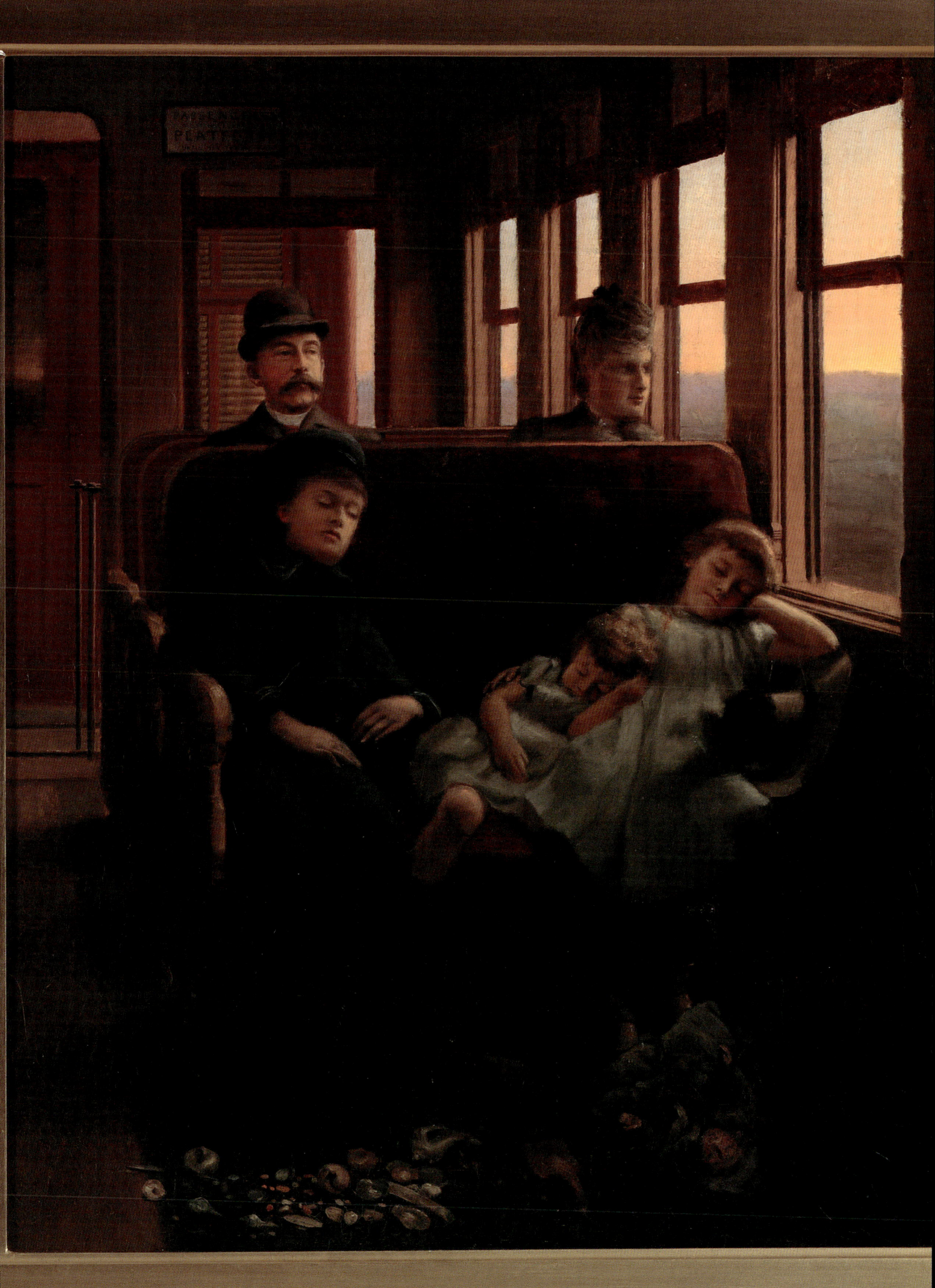

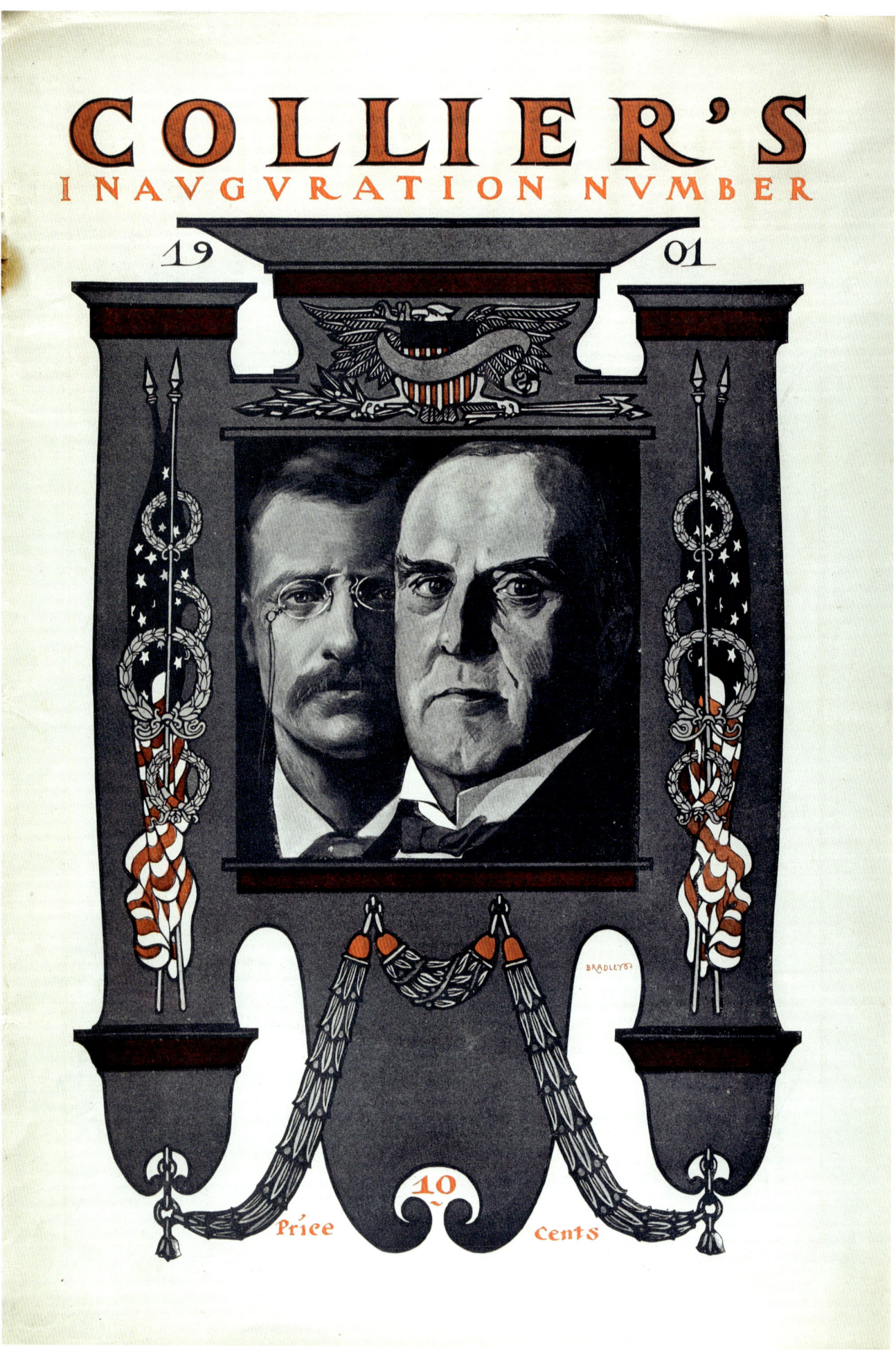

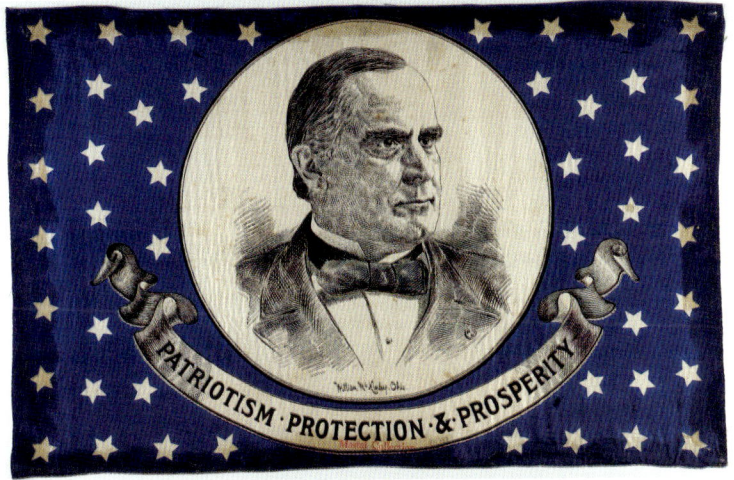

Between the end of the Civil War and the "closing of the frontier," the United States continued to become increasingly complex. Economic downturns and upturns cycled amid socio-political turmoil and change. European and Asian immigration surged while the push for expanding American territorial boundaries also found increasing public favor. The pre–Civil War technologies of railroad transportation and telegraphy were extended across the continent. The exploitation of natural resources—mineral deposits, timber, and open-range grasslands—encouraged economic growth and immigration. As the population of the United States increased, so too did the nation's sense of itself and its place in the world.

The onset of the Plains Indian Wars of the late 19th century marked the beginning of an end to military hostilities between the United States government and Native Americans. The July 4, 1876 centennial celebration was dramatically interrupted by news of the late June defeat of George A. Custer and the United States Army by Lakota and Northern Cheyenne forces along Greasy Grass Creek, also known as the Little Big Horn River, in Montana Territory. Custer's death was an international story, made famous not just by the press but also by the dramatization of the "Last Stand" in Buffalo Bill's Wild West Shows of the early 1880s. The defeat became an essential moment in the national story, its impact remaining vivid well into the 1900s with the increasing popularity of motion pictures and the eventual large-scale development of American cinema.

For the United States, the last decade of the 19th century marked the end of many eras, but also the beginning of numerous others. As technological advances continued to expand, so too did American notions of what was possible in the world. With new ways to communicate, either immediately by telephone or by the seemingly timeless phonographic recording, the potential for the application

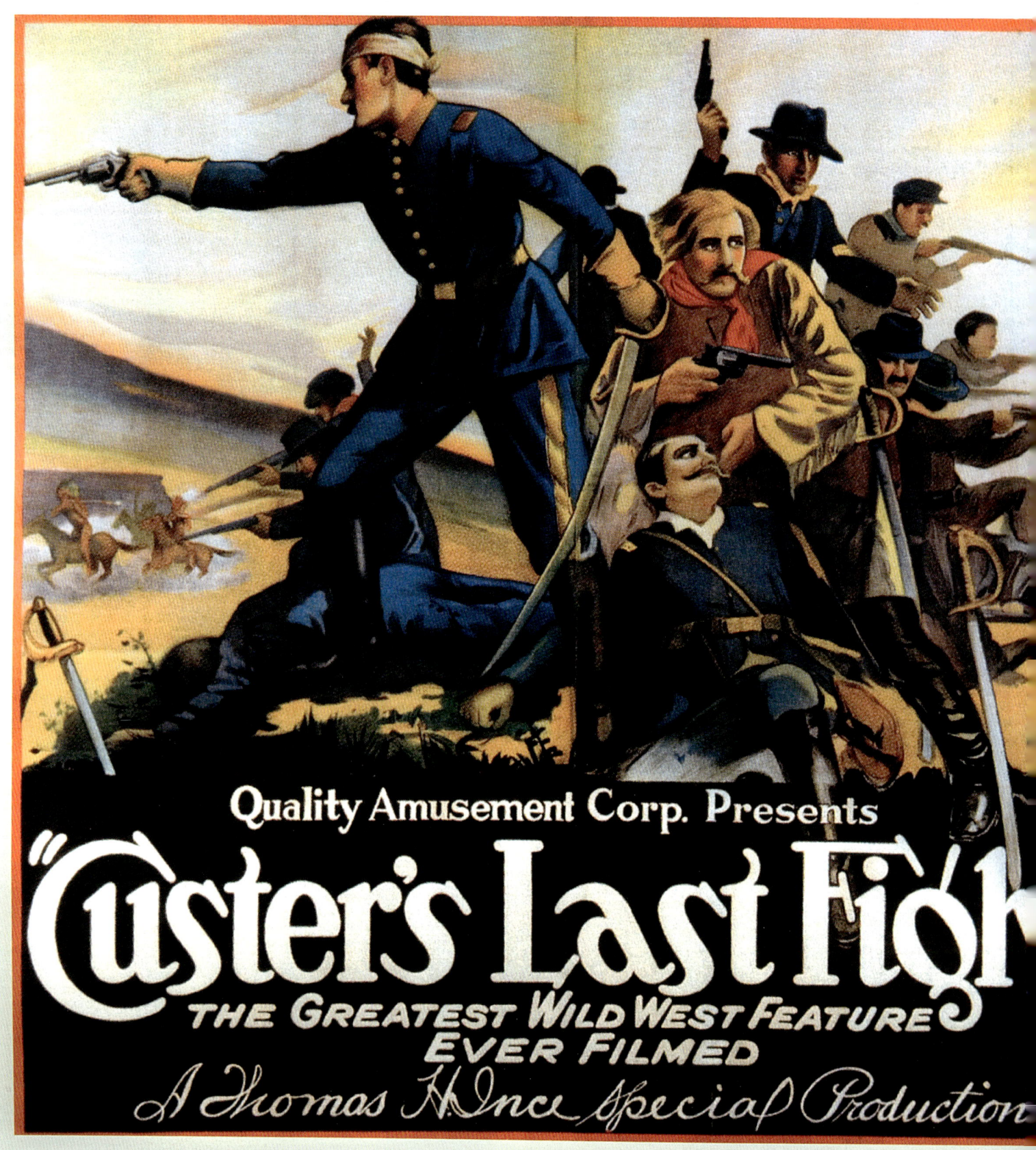

Quality Amusement Corp. Presents

"Custer's Last Figh

THE GREATEST WILD WEST FEATURE
EVER FILMED

A Thomas H. Ince Special Production

CUSTER'S LAST FIGHT
MOVIE POSTER. Quality
Amusement Corp., 1912. GM 16.961

of technology to day-to-day life seemed increasingly endless. The growing availability of artificial light produced by electric light bulbs allowed work and educational, civic, and recreational pursuits to carry on into the night. Advances in medicine spelled new promise for the future. While much of the nation lived in poverty—or without the essential rights of citizens—American identity still hinged on the ideas of the few. Advancing technology became a marker of the age as the restrictions of the past gave way to a new manner of being.

The American sense of the national character was dramatically changed with the defeat of Spain in the Spanish-American War in 1898. The defeat of the Spanish Empire in both the Caribbean and the Pacific fostered a new sense of American prowess—against the escalating colonial efforts of European powers. While the war ushered in a new level of patriotism among the American people, it also set the stage for decades of both ineffectual and autocratic regional governance, an ongoing disregard for human rights, and the over-arching pursuit of economic opportunity throughout the western hemisphere. The U. S. attempt at colonialism expanded not only national interests but also made clear the expanding range of American ideals to other nations around the globe.

The early months of the 20th century were marked by both portent and prodigy. In January of 1901, the American periodical *Collier's Weekly* published an issue covering the upcoming inauguration of William McKinley. President McKinley's re-election in the fall of 1900 set the stage for events that ultimately shaped the national character in ways that had up to that time been unforeseen. For the American people, the future appeared certain. The nation stood on the edge of a new century, waiting for the inevitable to unfold. McKinley's return to the White House was largely expected, with his new vice president, Theodore Roosevelt, the recent hero in the war against Spain, waiting dutifully in the wings. As the concerns of the new century awaited their attention, the triumphs of the past soon gave way to the unpredictable tragedies of the present.

In September 1901, President McKinley delivered a speech at the Pan-American Exposition in Buffalo, New York. The Exposition ceremoniously marked the turn of the new century and heralded the promises of the future. The following afternoon, at an open gathering near the Exposition's Temple of Music, the president greeted an overwhelmingly enthusiastic public. The event was seemingly innocuous, arranged largely for political purposes, yet just after four o'clock in the afternoon, William McKinley, Jr. was shot by a political anarchist. The president died eight days later of complications from his wounds. As the American people expressed disbelief, the workings of governmental office continued the unemotional transition of public office as Theodore Roosevelt was immediately sworn in as the 26th president of the United States.

For the American people of the year 1900, the 20th century loomed large. The coming decades would witness unforeseeable calamity—global warfare, famine, disease, and natural disaster. The new century would also bring about dramatic social and economic change that included the development of new technologies, advancements in medicine, and the expanding awareness of the unalienable rights held by all citizens. The Americans of 1900 moved toward the uncertainties of the future with characteristic fervor. The president's assassination in 1901, however, offered a somber reminder of the precariousness of human events and how the hopes and dreams of the future can shift in an instant. Yet, the collective will of the people endured. Vast new frontiers remained to be imagined across a landscape of ever-expanding American ambition, desire, and search for meaning. The American character that had been shaped over time and through experience stood poised to reveal itself to the larger world.

WATCHING THE BREAKERS, Winslow Homer. Oil on canvas, 1891. GM 0126.2664

At the close of the 19th century, Americans stood on the shores of a new world, the future

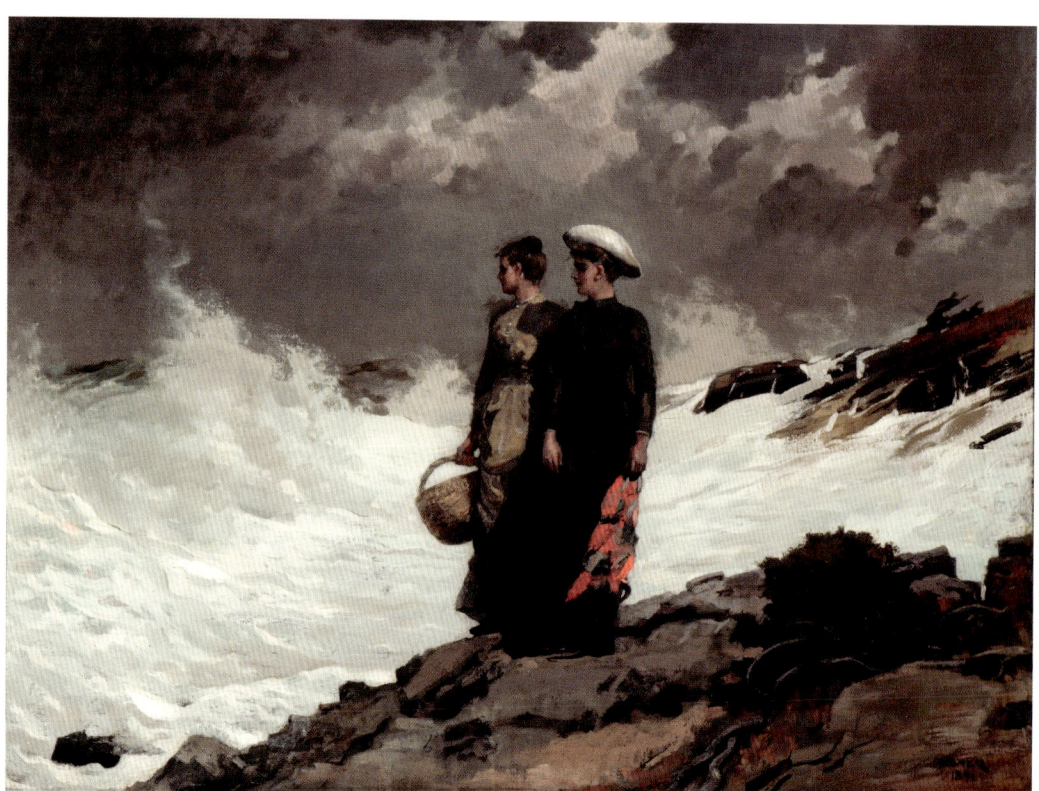

INDEX

ILLUSTRATIONS

Abraham Lincoln 188

Abraham Lincoln's Second
    Inauguration 189

A Complete Listing of 42 Slaves 152

John Adams 58

Advertisement for Riker Electric
    Vehicles 226

*A Herd of Buffaloes on the Bed of the
    River Missouri* 216

Alexander Hamilton 84

Alexander Hamilton 85

A Map of the Country of the Five
    Nations 41

America (1659 map) 27

American Forest Scene–Maple Sugaring
    145

ammunition pouch 206

Andrew Jackson 114

*Andrew Jackson before Judge Hall, New
    Orleans* 110-111

A New and Accurate Map of North
    America 46

Anglorumin Virginiam Aduentus 29

Antietam, MD, Confederate Dead by
    a Fence on the Hagerstown Road
    184

Applications of Professor Bell's New
    Telephone 227

Anything For Me, If You Please 186

Articles of Confederation 68-69

Assassination of President Lincoln 193

*Baron de Kalb Introducing Lafayette to
    Silas Deane* 67

bear claw necklace 100

Bear Dance 100

beaver hat 89

Benjamin Franklin 16

Benjamin Franklin (Hiram Powers) 60

Bill of Sale for 16 Slaves 164

*Black Hawk and His Son, Whirling
    Thunder* 120

Black Hills Proclamation, April 6, 1872
    207

black mourning cape 195

Black Troops 190

Bombardment at Vera Cruz 136

Boone's First View of Kentucky 109

Brooklyn Sanitary Fair, 1864 185

button from an Indian School
    Uniform, Crow, Montana Agency
    200

campaign banner for William
    McKinley 231

candle mold 33

*Captain John Smith and Party Landing
    at Jamestown May 14, 1607* 25

*Captain Lewis and Clark Holding a
    Council with the Indians* 91

Captain Lewis Shooting an Indian 90

Certification written by Joseph Warren
    for Paul Revere, April 29, 1775 57

Certified Copy of the Declaration of
    Independence 66

*Charge of the Police on the Rioters at the
    'Tribune' Office* 177

Charles Wilkes 83

Cherokee muster roll 123

Cheyenne drying meat 212

Chief Justice John Marshall 119

child's shirt with Ghost Dance symbols
    222

Christmas Boxes in Camp 177

Civil War artillery shell jacket 176

Civil War military drum 180

Codex Canadiensis 40

Columbian Exposition – Golden
    Doorway to the Transportation
    Building 225

Columbus Approaching San Salvadore
    23

Confederate ten-dollar bill 173

Confederate twenty-dollar bill 173

*Constitution and Guerriere, August 19,
    1812* 112

Crescent Silver Company stock
    certificate 141

Custer's Last Fight movie poster 232

Daniel Webster 119

Daniel Webster (Thomas Ball) 119

Declaration of Independence 10

Democratic Republican ticket, 1832
    117

Document of Indenture of Jonathan
    Chin to William Wanton, 1715 44

Document outlining the sale of
    Newisock, an Indian slave 43

eagle pommel sword 106

East and West Shake Hands 131

Edison phonograph and cylinder 226

Electric light bulb, ca. 1890 6

Emancipation Proclamation 191

*Equestrian Statue of Andrew Jackson,
    at Washington, Cast From British
    Cannon Captured by Jackson* 117

*First Locomotive Engine Employed on a
    Public Railway* 209

Fort Union Trading Post 208

Frederick Douglass 127

Funeral Procession of Abraham
    Lincoln 194

*General D. Antonio Lopez de Santa
    Anna* 139

General Lafayette 78

General P. H. Sheridan 217

General Stonewall Jackson 182

General Ulysses S. Grant and his Men
    175

George III peace medal 94

George Washington (Jean Antoine
    Houdon) 77

George Washington (Rembrandt Peale)
    71

*George Washington's Treaty with the
    Delaware* 13

Ghost Dance shirt (detail) 221

*Gettysburg—Repulse of Longsteet's
    Assault* 178-179

*Going to the Seashore and Return from
    the Seashore* 228-229

Gold Mining in California 140

Grand Democratic Free Soil banner
    134

Harriet Beecher Stowe 155

Hudson, Henry 18

incised powder horn 107

Indians receiving rations 215

James Madison (Charles Willson Peale
    painting) 79

James Madison (James Grant Wilson
    after Gilbert Stuart) 103

Jefferson peace medal 93

Jenny Lind 143

John C. Calhoun (Clark Mills) 118

John C. Calhoun (James Bogle) 104

John Quincy Adams 115

John Quincy Adams (Babson and
    Andrews after George Peter
    Alexander Healy) 105

John W. Quinney 122

Kiowa Ghost Dance shirt 201

King James II 14

Lakota doll 214

Lakota shield 213

Lakota shirt 218

Lakota war bonnet 204

lantern 34

Letter from Governor William Burnet
    to the Board of Trade, December
    4, 1726 39

Letter from Joseph Galloway to
    the Governor of Pennsylvania,
    February 19, 1773 55

Letter from Thomas Jefferson to
    William Fleming, July 1-2, 1776
    64

Letter to Baron von Schulenburg
    from Silas Deane and Benjamin
    Franklin, 1777 70

Levee at New Orleans 162-163

Liberty 2

*Life at the South or Uncle Tom's Cabin
    as it Is* 154

Log of Luke Fox 22

Major Ulysses S. Grant 174

Mak-Hos-Kah, Chief of the Goways 101

*Mak-We-Hah-Mak, Goway Chief
    (Great Walker)* 99

man's waistcoat 51

Map of Louisiana in 1894 92

Marching through Georgia 183

Massacre of Wounded Knee 199

Matthew Clarkson 63

metal belt buckle 153

military belt buckle 208

militia helmet plate 102

Nathan Hale 65

National Anti-Slavery Standard 165

New General Map of America 8-9

*News from America or the Patriots in the
    Dumps* 56

Oregon and California 130

peace medals 93, 94, 95

*Peace of Ghent 1814 and triumph of
    America / Mme. Plantou, Citizen of
    the United States pinxit; Chataigner*
    113

Penn's Treaty with the Indians 37

pewter charger 42

Philip H. Sheridan 217
Pine Ridge Reservation 215
pipe bowl 123
pipe bowl—Treaty of Dancing Rabbit
　　Creek 121
Pocohantas 25
Portrait of General Winfield Scott 136
Portrait of George Washington 73
Portrait of John Cotton 32
*Portrait of Mrs. John Apthorp, née
　　Hannah Greenleaf* 50
President Elect William McKinley and
　　Vice President Elect Theodore
　　Roosevelt 230
Proclamation by King James I 35
Proclamation Declaring a State of War
　　Between the United States and
　　Mexico, May 10, 1846 132
*Projected Statue of Liberty for NY
　　Harbor* 224
Proposition Made to Indians, July 30,
　　1684 38
Ralph Waldo Emerson 146
Red Cloud 218
*Rent-Cha-Was-Me, Mak-Hos-Kah's
　　Wife* 99
Reward for Runaway Slave 153
season medals (peace medals) 95
service revolver 135
shackles 165
Shooting On the Prairie 144
*Sir William Drummond Stewart
　　Meeting Indian Chief* 98
Sitting Bull 217
St. Paul's, Broadway, New York 150
Surrender of Lord Cornwallis 74
Sutter's Mill 141
The American Difficulty 167
The Battle of Buena Vista 138
The Battle of Lexington 57
The Boston Massacre 52
The County Election 145
The Declaration Committee 61
The Doll 149
*The Engagement Between the Monitor
　　and the Merrimac* 180-181
*The Great Labor Question from a
　　Southern Point of View* 166
The Landing of Christopher Columbus
　　19
*The Landing of Roger Williams at Slate
　　Rock* 36
The Monitor at Work on the Merrimac
　　180
*The Pilgrims Meet with Massasoit and
　　the Algonquins on the Shores of
　　Massachusetts Bay, 1621* 31
The Puritan 30

*The South Part of New-England, as it is
　　Planted this yeare, 1634* 33
*The Surrender of Burgoyne's Army at
　　Saratoga, October 17, 1777* 74
*The Taking of the City of Washington in
　　America* 111
The Tea-Tax Tempest 53
The Tree of Temperance 148
Thomas Jefferson 93
Thomas Jefferson (Reich engraving) 64
Thomas Paine 65
Three Tetons 210-211
Title for a Quarter Section of Land to
　　Cin-con-tum-be 151
tomahawk pipe 96, 97
trade bead necklace 99
Transcontinental Railroad 131
Uncle Tom and his Grandchild 168
Uncle Tom's Cabin, Vol. 1, 1852 154
*U. S. Capitol after Burning by the
　　British* 111
U. S. Indian police badge 221
View in the Ruins of the Alamo 137
*Village, Historia Americae Sive Novi
　　Orbis, I* 28
war bonnet, Lakota 204
war club 218
War Record 202-203
Washington and His Generals 75
*Washington at the Battle of Princeton,
　　January 3, 1777* 72
*Washington in Conference with
　　Representatives of Six Nations* 49
Washington season medal 96
Washington season medals 95
Washington peace medal 91
Watching the Breakers 234
*Westward the Course of Empire Takes Its
　　Way* 128-129
William Penn 37
William Temple Franklin 86

GENERAL INDEX

A
abolition 63, 130, 131, 147, 153, 156,
　　157, 167
abolitionists 126, 154, 155, 156, 164,
　　167, 171, 188, 190
Adams, John 5, 17, 52, 58, 61, 62, 65,
　　67, 72, 82, 87, 105, 115, 118, 119
African-Americans 63, 156, 164, 175,
　　177, 188, 196
African-American troops 190
Africans 18, 36
A History of the American People 52
Alabama 171
Alamo 138

Alcott, Louisa May 187
*America: Life, Liberty and the Pursuit of
　　a Nation* 15
American Anti-Slavery Society 156
American character 89, 108, 110, 113,
　　147, 225
American history 15, 17, 48, 114
American identity 12, 27, 40, 41, 47,
　　112, 113, 225, 233
American Indians (see also Indians,
　　Native Americans) 12
American Philosophical Society 64, 86
American Revolution 40, 49, 62, 63,
　　65, 72, 79, 80, 86, 87, 103, 157
American Self 47, 108, 113, 115, 125,
　　157
American Temperance Society 147
American Trading Company 208
American Woman's Home 144
America Painted to the Life 27
Andrew Jackson (Clark Mills) 116
Andrew Jackson: Symbol for an Age 124
Andrews, J. 105
Andros, Edmund 39
Annapolis 79
Antietam 188
Appomattox 195
Arizona 128
Arkansas 171
Army of Northern Virginia 176
Army of the Potomac 176
Arnold, Benedict 63
Articles of Confederation 15, 69, 70, 71
Art-Union 144
Atlanta 183, 189, 192, 197
Austria 51

B
Babson, R.E. 105
Baldwin, Leland Dewitt 113
Ball, Thomas 119
Baltimore 112
Barmore, Charles 182
Barnum, P. T. 142
Barré, Isaac 67
Battle of Antietam (see also Antietam)
　　176, 178
Battle of Buena Vista 138
Battle of Bull Run 176
Battle of Bunker Hill 57
Battle of Chancellorsville 182
Battle of First Manassas 182
Battle of Fredericksburg 176
Battle of Gettysburg (see also
　　Gettysburg) 179
Battle of Lexington (see also
　　Lexington) 105
Battle of Monmouth 85

Battle of New Orleans 114
Battle of Princeton 72, 85
Battle of Shiloh 176
Battle of Vicksburg (see also
　　Vicksburg) 176, 187
Battle of Yorktown 74
Bavaria 67
beads 99
Beauregard, Pierre Gustave Toutant
　　173
Bee, Barnard 182
Beecher, Catharine 144
Beecher, Lyman 155
Beecher, Roxana 155
Bellows, Henry 185
Bell telephone 226
Benn, Carl 105, 112, 125
Big Foot 198
Bill of Rights 12, 79
Bingham, George Caleb 144
bison 198, 209, 213, 215, 216
Black Hawk 120
Black Hawk War of 1832 120
Black Hills 206, 209, 212, 215
Bodmer, Karl 208
Bogle, James 104
Booth, John Wilkes 193, 195
Boston 34, 36, 47, 50, 51, 52, 53, 55,
　　87, 197
Boston Massacre 52
Boston Tea Party 53
Bozeman Trail 209
Bradford, William 41
Brady, Matthew 183, 188, 194
Britain 24, 27, 41, 46, 48, 51, 52, 55, 57,
　　62, 65, 71, 75, 80, 93, 102, 103, 105,
　　106, 108, 110, 112, 114, 126, 130,
　　134, 156, 157
British 4, 12, 18, 24, 34, 41, 48, 49, 51,
　　52, 53, 55, 57, 67, 71, 72, 75, 77,
　　83, 85, 86, 87, 103, 105, 106, 110,
　　111, 112, 115, 117, 125, 130, 136,
　　153, 157
Brown Bess rifle 48
Brown, John 156, 169, 170, 171, 197
Brown, Mather 86
Bryant, William Cullen 170, 171
Buena Vista 135
Buffalo Bill's Wild West Shows 231
Buffalo, New York 234
Buffum, James 126
Bureau of Indian Affairs 98
Burnet, William 39

C
Calhoun, John C. 98, 105, 118, 119,
　　134
California 128, 130, 135, 140, 152, 157,
　　196, 197, 210, 223

California territory 140
Canada 106, 112
capitalism 161
Carolina 45
Catholic 45, 134
Catlin, George 100, 122
Cayuga 38, 49
census 93, 225
Central Pacific Railroad 131
Ceracchi, Giuseppe 85
Chappel, Alonzo 58, 67, 115
Charleston 162
Cherokee 123
Chesapeake 105
Chesapeake-Leopard Affair 105
Cheyenne 213
Chin, Jonathan 45
Chivington, John M. 213
Choctaw 121, 150
Church, Frederick Edwin 140
Cin-con-tum-be 150
citizenship 45, 77, 105
Civil Rights movement 196
Civil War 131, 136, 152, 154, 157, 160, 161, 164, 170, 175, 178, 183, 190, 195, 196, 197, 200, 215, 217, 231
Clarkson, Matthew 63
Clarkson, Thomas 153
Clark, William 101
class divisions 45
Clay, Henry 105, 115, 119, 134, 157
Coercive Acts 55
College of William and Mary 64
Collier's Weekly 231, 233
colonial identities 41
colonial life 34
colonies 17, 31, 33, 39, 40, 41, 42, 45, 46, 50, 51, 52, 55, 57, 65, 67, 69, 77, 79, 85, 87, 106, 108, 130
colonists 18, 33, 34, 36, 40, 41, 45, 46, 48, 51, 52, 55, 62, 65, 67, 87
colonization 18, 24
Columbus, Christopher 18
Committee of Safety 57
Common Sense 65
Compromise of 1850 152, 153, 160
Concord 57
Confederate army 176
Congress 12, 55, 61, 62, 64, 65, 67, 69, 70, 79, 82, 103, 105, 111, 112, 118, 122, 123, 124, 125, 128, 132, 135, 152, 158, 180, 185, 190
Connecticut 39
conquistadors 14
Constitution 11, 12, 62, 69, 77, 79, 85, 112, 119, 196
Constitutional Convention 72, 77
Continental Army 67, 72, 79, 119
Continental Congress 55, 61, 62, 64,

67, 69, 70, 72, 79
Copley, John Singleton 50
Cornwallis, General 71, 74
Corps of Discovery 90, 93
Cotton, John 33
Crow 200, 205
C.S.S. Virginia 180
currency 80
Currier, Nathaniel 74, 134, 144, 145, 149, 162, 170
Currier and Ives 144, 145, 170
Custer, George Armstrong 15, 214, 231, 232

D
Dare, Virginia 18
Davis, Alexander 150
Davis, Jefferson 161, 171, 173
Deane, Silas 11, 17, 67, 69, 70
Declaration Committee 61
Declaration of Independence 11, 12, 15, 17, 62, 64, 65, 67, 70, 156
Declaratory Act 51
Deganawida 49
de Jumonville, Joseph Coulon 49
de Kalb, Baron 67
Delano, Columbus 216
Delaware Nation 12
Delawares 37
democracy 12, 15, 146
Democrats 128, 131, 132, 134, 135, 160
de Rochambeau 79
Dickinson, John 69
Dominion of New England 39, 40
Douglass, Frederick 126, 130, 152, 153, 156, 190
Douglas, Stephen 160
draft 177
Duane, William 106
Duke of Wellington 136
Dunlap Broadside 17
Dutch East India Company 18

E
Earl, Ralph 63
East Jersey 39
economy 42, 45, 82, 130, 134, 161, 167, 175
Edwards, Jonathan 45
electric light bulb 233
Emancipation Proclamation 11, 15, 164, 188, 189, 190, 196
Emerson, Ralph Waldo 142, 146, 167
emigrants 42, 206
England 22, 24, 25, 31, 33, 34, 39, 40, 41, 42, 45, 47, 55, 86, 105, 106, 108, 130, 153, 156, 157, 196, 237, 239
Enlightenment 17, 62
Evangelicals 142

expansionism 105, 134
F
farmers 42, 45, 134, 226
Federalist 62, 82, 85, 238
fifteenth anendment 164, 196
Fillmore, Millard 119
First Continental Congress 55
First Seminole War 115
Fleming, William 64
Florida 106, 115, 116, 171
Foote, Shelby 196
Ford's Theater 193, 195
Forsyth, James W. 221
Fort Buford 208
Fort Laramie Treaty 212, 221
Fort Necessity 48, 49
Fort Niagara 39
Fort Pitt 55
Fort Sumter 161, 173
Fort Union 208
founding fathers 12
fourteenth amendment 164, 196
France 12, 17, 34, 41, 47, 48, 51, 62, 65, 70, 71, 77, 79, 86, 93, 103, 105, 108, 110
Frank Leslie's Illustrated Newspaper 193
Franklin, Benjamin 4, 11, 15, 17, 61, 62, 67, 69, 70, 77, 86
Franklin, William Temple 86
Fraser, James Earle 62
Frederick the Great of Prussia 17
freedom of religion 11
freedom of speech 11
Fremont, John Charles 130
French 37, 39, 41, 45, 48, 49, 51, 62, 65, 67, 72, 74, 77, 79, 85, 93, 195,
French and Indian War 48, 49, 51, 85
French, Daniel Webster 146
Freneau, P. 80
Fulkerson, H. S. 118
fur traders 106, 206

G
Galloway, Joseph 55
Garner, Alexander 184
Garrison, William Lloyd 156
Generall Historie of Virginia, New-England, and the Summer Isles 25
Georgia 45, 75, 87, 158, 171, 183, 197
Gettysburg 176, 187
Ghost Dance 198, 201, 216, 221, 223
Gilcrease, Thomas 15, 17, 79, 121
Gleason's Pictorial 117
Gorges, Ferdinando 27
Grant, Ulysses S. 135, 175, 176, 183, 187, 189, 192, 193, 195
Greasy Grass Creek 231
Great Britain 24, 51, 55, 62, 71, 80, 102, 103, 105, 108, 110, 126, 130, 157

Great Treaty with the Delawares, 1682 37
Greeley, Horace 164, 167, 169, 180, 221
Greenleaf, Hannah 50

H
Hale, Nathan 65
Hall, A. B. 192
Hall, Dominick 111
Hamilton, Alexander 82, 84, 85
Hancock, John 67
Harper's Ferry 156, 169, 197
Harpers Ferry armory 170
Harper's Weekly 167, 168, 175, 177, 183, 186, 187, 225
Harrison, William Henry 119
Harvard University 33, 47, 125, 197
Hayes, Rutherford B. 221
Hays, William jacob 216
Hayter, Thomas 142
Headley, J. T. 178, 190
Healy, George Peter Alexander 105, 160
Henry McClosky's Manual of 1864 185
Henry, Patrick 58, 59, 62
Hiawatha 49
Historia Americae Sive Novi Orbis, I, 1634 29
Historia Americae Sive Novi Orbis, II, 1634 29
Historia Americae Sive Novi Orbis, XII, 1634 27
Historical Collections of the Great West 137, 140
Hitchcock, Charles 36
Hitchcock, Ethan 135
H.M.S. Leopard 103
Hoffy, Alfred 138
Homer, Winslow 177, 186, 234
Houdon, Jean Antoine 77, 79
Howard, Frances 24
Howard, Thomas Viscount 24
Howe, Daniel 134
Howe, Henry 137, 140
Hudson Bay 22
Hudson River 18, 75
Hutchinson Family Quartet of Singers 126

I
idealism 11
Illinois 157, 160, 161, 175, 194
immigrants 27, 33, 45, 131, 150, 161, 209
impressment 103
indenture 31, 45
indentured servants 27, 31, 42
Independence Hall 82
Indiana 188

Indian camp 201
Indian Gallery 98
Indian Removal 14, 121, 123, 153
Indian Removal Act 121
Indians (see also Native Americans) 12, 14, 34, 37, 38, 42, 47, 90, 91, 209, 212, 213, 214, 215, 218, 221, 223
Indian School 200
Indian slave 42
Indian Territory 121, 123, 150
inflation 80
Inman, Henry 37
Inness, George 144
Intolerable Acts 55
Iowas 101
Irish-American 177
Ives, James Merritt 144

J
Jackson, Andrew 14, 15, 111, 114, 115, 116, 117, 118, 119, 121, 123, 124, 125, 132, 134
Jackson, Frederick 225
Jackson, General Stonewall 182
Jackson, Thomas Jonathan 182
James II 14, 40
Jamestown 15, 24, 25, 41
Jarvis, John Wesley 114, 119, 120
Jay, John 82
Jefferson Peace Medal 93
Jefferson, Thomas 5, 15, 17, 61, 62, 64, 67, 77, 82, 85, 87, 90, 93, 102, 105, 106, 108, 125, 134, 138, 197, 205
Jewish 45
Johnson, Andrew 193, 196
Johnson, Cornelius 24
Johnson, Eastman 144, 149

K
Kagan, Robert 108
Kansas 167, 169, 170, 197
King, Charles Bird 98, 101, 122
King George III 17, 52, 62, 65, 87
King Henri Christophe of Haiti 99
King James 39
King James I 34
Knox, Henry 14

L
Lafayette, Lord Maria Joseph Paul Yves Roch Gilbert du Motier, Marquis 15, 67, 79, 85
Lakota 198, 204, 205, 206, 209, 212, 213, 214, 215, 216, 218, 221, 231
Laramie Mountains 209
League of the Iroquois 49
Lee, "Light Horse" Harry 172
Lee, Richard Henry 67

Lee, Robert E. 172, 175, 176, 179, 193, 194, 195
LeFlore, Greenwood 121
letters 15, 47, 181, 183, 196
Leutze, Emanuel 128
Lewis and Clark expedition 205
Lewis, Meriwether 90, 93
Lexington 57
Life of Andrew Jackson 114
Lincoln, Abraham 11, 15, 154, 157, 158, 160, 161, 164, 167, 171, 173, 175, 176, 188, 189, 190, 192, 193, 194, 195, 196, 197, 223
Lind, Jenny 142
Little Big Horn 214
Little Big Horn River 231
Livingston, Robert 61, 67
London, England 24, 31, 47, 56, 83, 87, 125, 157, 167
Longfellow, Henry Wadsworth 170, 171
Louaillers, Louis 111
Louisiana 48, 62, 93, 108, 171, 195
Louisiana Territory 62, 93, 108

M
MacMonnies, Frederick W. 65
Madison, James 15, 77, 79, 82, 85, 103, 106, 112
Magna Carta, 39
Mahicans 122
Maine 39
Manifest Destiny 128, 131, 132, 142
maps 4, 41, 46, 93
marriage 50
Marshall, John 15, 63, 112, 119
Massachusetts 39, 40, 57, 119
Massachusetts Assembly 52
Massachusetts Bay 31
Massachusetts Committee of Safety 11, 15, 57
Matamoros 135
Mather, Cotton 33
Matoaka (Pocahontas) 25
Mayer, Godfrey 17
McClellan, General George 176
McCreight, Israel 218
McKenney, Thomas L. 98
McKinley, William 233, 234
McPherson, James 167
Meade, George 176, 179
Menominee Tribe 122
Mercer, Hugh 72
Mexican-American War (see also Mexican War) 132, 137, 153
Mexican government 135, 137
Mexican War 132, 134, 136, 138, 182
Mexico 125, 128, 130, 132, 135, 136, 138, 140, 153, 157, 160, 175, 235,
Middle Passage 36

Miles, Nelson A. 213
militia 40, 48, 57, 82, 87
Miller, Alfred Jacob 98
Miller, Dora 187
Mills, Clark 116, 118
minutemen 57
Mississippi 121, 150, 171, 176
Mississippi River 93, 120, 187
Missouri 93, 169, 205, 208, 216, 217,
Missouri River 93, 208
Mohawks 49
Monroe, James 101, 118
Montana 90, 200, 209, 214, 231
Moran, Thomas 22, 210
Mormon Trail 210
Morristown 71, 72
Mount Vernon 77
Munger, George 111

N
Napoleon 110
Napoleonic Wars 136
Narraganset 36, 39
Narrative of the Life of Frederick Douglass 126
Nast, Thomas 144
National Gazette 80
National Intelligencer 153
nationhood 108
Native American policies 150
Native Americans 14, 18, 33, 34, 36, 53, 62, 93, 96, 101, 121, 175, 200, 215, 216, 217, 221, 231
Native groups 49
Native people 102, 120, 121
Nebel, Carl 136
Netherlands 34, 39
New Englanders 34
New England's Prospect 33
New France 41
New Hampshire 39
New Jersey 39, 71, 72, 80, 86, 87
New Mexico 125, 128, 135, 157
New Orleans 111, 112, 114, 115, 162, 197
Newton, Massachusetts, 33
New World 18
New York 39, 49, 77, 144, 147
New York City 75, 144, 147, 150, 177, 194
New York Tribune 177
Nicolas, Louis 41
Nine Years War 41
North Carolina 49, 171
Northern Cheyenne 231
Northwest Passage 22, 91

O
Office of Indian Affairs 221
O'Hara, Charles 74

Ohio River 48
Oklahoma 15, 121, 223
Olive Branch petition 57
Olmstead, Frederick Law 185
Omaha 214
Oneidas 38, 49
Onondagas 38, 49
Oregon 130, 134, 135, 142, 157, 206, 210, 223
Oregon Territory 134, 142, 157
Ortelius, Abraham 22
O'Sullivan, John 128, 142, 157, 183

P
Pacific Northwest 130, 131, 132
Paine, Thomas 65
Paiute 201, 216
Pan-American Exposition in Buffalo, New York 234
Parkman, Francis 206
Parliament 51, 52, 55, 67, 87, 157
Parton, James 114, 115, 124, 125
peace medal 91, 94, 94, 95, 96, 101, 102
Peace of Paris 75, 86
Peale, Charles Willson 71, 72, 79
Peale, Rembrandt 71
Pemberton, John C. 187
Pennsylvania 45, 47, 48, 55, 62, 72, 82, 87, 179, 194
Penn, William 37
Philadelphia 37, 47, 55, 64, 67, 72, 77, 87, 162, 190, 194, 196
Pickett, George 176, 179
Piegan Blackfeet 90
Piegans 90, 91
Pilgrims 31
Plains Indian wars 198, 200, 231
Plantation Act 45
plantation owners 42, 152, 154
plantations 42, 45, 154, 162
Platte Valley 209
Plattsburgh 112
Plymouth 34, 36, 39, 47
Pocahontas 25
Polk, James 128, 130, 132, 134, 135, 137, 140, 150, 157, 160
portraiture 50
Powers, Hiram 61
Powhatan 25
presidency 62, 82, 115, 116, 121, 124
Price, P. 113
Priestley, Joseph 156
Princeton, Battle of 72
Promontory Summit, Utah 131
pro-slavery 126, 130, 169, 197
Providence 36, 87, 128, 142
Puritan 30, 31, 33

Q

Quaker 37
Quartering Act 55
Quinney, John W. 122
quit-rents 39

R

railroad 131, 161, 183, 209, 231
Ranney, William Tylee 72, 109
Rathbone, Henry 193
Red Cloud 209, 218
Reich, Jacques 58, 64, 84, 182
Republican 62, 82, 112, 117, 156, 158, 171
Revere, Paul 11, 15, 57
Revolutionary War 12, 77, 85, 172
Rhode Island 39
Rio Grande River 132, 135
Roanoke 18
Rochambeau, General 74
Rocky Mountains 93
Rolfe, John 25
Ronda, James P. 91, 96, 125
Roosevelt, Theodore 231, 233, 234
Royal Proclamation of 1763 12
Russia 130

S

Saint-Gaudens, Augustus 30, 188
Salem 36
Sand Creek 213
San Francisco 158, 196
Sanitary Commission 185, 190, 192
Sanitary Fairs 185
San Salvadore 22
Santa Anna, General D. Antonio Lopez de Santa Anna 138
Sauk and Fox 120
Savage, Edward 4, 18
Schulenburg, Baron von 70
Schussele, Christian 111
Scientific American 226
Scott, Winfield 132, 135, 136
Second Continental Congress 61, 62, 67
Seneca Falls, New York 147
Senecas 49
settlers 12, 34, 36, 40, 41, 45, 47, 48, 87, 157, 167, 200, 206, 210, 215, 216
Seven Years War 49
Seward, William 193
Shackamaxon 37
Sharp, Granville 153
Sharp, W. 65
Sheridan, Philip 175, 215, 217
Sherman, William Tecumseh 175, 183, 189, 192
Sherman, Roger 61, 67
Shoshones 209

Sitting Bull 15, 217, 218
Six Nations 49
slaveholder 12, 126
slave owners 36
slave rebellions 36
slavery 33, 42, 45, 47, 59, 62, 63, 126, 130, 134, 137, 147, 152, 153, 154, 156, 157, 158, 164, 167, 169, 170, 197
slaves 12, 18, 27, 31, 33, 34, 36, 42, 45, 47, 93, 152, 154, 158, 164, 169, 170, 188, 189, 191, 197
slave trade 130, 137, 153
Smibert, John 33
Smillie, James D. 172
Smith, John 4, 24, 25
Smith, W. L. G. 154
social movements 147, 156
Sons of Liberty, 52
South Carolina 75, 87, 118, 125, 158, 162, 171, 173, 190
Spain 70, 93, 106, 233
Spanish-American War 233
Stamp Act 51, 52, 82
Stanley, John Mix 25
Stanton, Elizabeth Cady 147
Stearn, Julius 49
Stephens, Alexander 171
Stockbridge band (Mahicans) 122
Stowe, Harriet Beecher 144, 154, 155, 167
Stuart, Gilbert 58, 103
Stuart, John 180
Stuart, Ludovic 24
Supreme Court 119
Sutter, Johann 140
symbols 4, 42, 77, 88, 89, 96, 100, 102, 125

T

Tait, Arthur Fitzwilliam 144
Tait, Fitzwilliam 145
Tanner, Henry S. 93
tax 39, 40, 51, 55, 57, 69, 82, 85
Taylor, Zachary 132, 135, 138, 175
Theatrum Orbis Terrarum 22
temperance movements 147
Tennessee 171
Terry, Alfred 214
Texas 128, 132, 134, 135, 138, 153, 171
The Generall Historie of Virginia, New England and the Summer Isles 25
The Federalist Papers 85
The Great Rebellion: A History of the Civil War in the United States 178, 190
The New York Times 158
The Present State of His Majesties Isles and Territories in America, 1687 14

The Present State of North America, 1755 46
The Presidents of the United States 103
The War Between the United States and Mexico Illustrated 136
thirteenth amendment 164, 196
Thomas, General 175
Thompson, G. 111
Thoreau, Henry David 146
Townshend Act 52, 55, 57, 82
trade 25, 41, 85, 96, 99, 102, 103, 105, 130, 137, 152, 153, 162, 167, 205, 208
Trail of Tears 121
trails 210
Transcendentalist 142, 146
transcontinental railroad 131
treaties 14
Treaty of Dancing Rabbit Creek 121, 150
Treaty of Fort Laramie 206, 209
Treaty of Ghent 112, 114
Treaty of Hubertusburg 51
Treaty of Paris 12, 51
Treaty of Utrecht 48
Trist, Nicholas 135
Troyle, James 75
Trumbull, John 74, 83, 95
Truth, Sojourner 152
Turner, Frederick Jackson 225
Tuscaroras 49
Two Medicine River 90, 91
Tyler, John 118
Typus Orbis Terrarum 22

U

Uncle Tom's Cabin 154, 155
Union army 179, 183, 187, 188, 190
Union Pacific Railroad 131
United States Magazine and Democratic Review 142
U. S. Constitution 12
U.S.S. Chesapeake 103
U.S.S. Merrimac 180
U.S.S. Monitor 180
Utes 209

V

Valley Forge 119
Vera Cruz 135, 136
Vicksburg 187, 192
Villiers, Captain Louis Coulon 49
Virginia 18, 24, 25, 27, 34, 38, 45, 48, 58, 62, 64, 67, 72, 77, 105, 119, 125, 158, 169, 170, 171, 172, 175, 176, 180, 182, 193, 195
Virginia Company 24, 25
Voltaire 37
Von Schulenburg, Baron 17

W

Walker, James 138, 179
Walker, William Aiken 162
Wanton, William 45
War Department, 98
Ward, John William 124
War of 1812 103, 108, 110, 111, 113, 114, 115, 125, 136
Warren, Joseph 57
Washington, George 12, 13, 14, 48, 49, 51, 62, 67, 71, 72, 74, 75, 77, 79, 82, 83, 85, 87, 91, 95, 96, 98, 101, 111, 117, 119, 122, 125, 126, 130, 132, 135, 153, 194, 223
Washington, D.C. 15, 110, 187, 194, 218
Washington's Address to the Delaware Nation, 1779 12
Watching the Breakers 234
Webster, Daniel 119
West, Benjamin 17, 37, 83
western frontier 15
West Jersey 39
West Point 172, 182
Whig 131, 132, 134, 135, 136
Whirling Thunder 120
Whiskey Rebellion 82
White Cloud 101
Whitefield, George 45
White House 117, 124, 125, 233
White Swan 202
Wilkes, Charles 83
William of Orange 39, 40
Williams, Roger 36
Wilson, Jack 201
Wilson, James Grant 103
Wirt, William 58
Wise, John 39
Wood, William 33
World's Columbian Exposition in Chicago 225
Wounded Knee 205, 221
Wounded Knee Creek 198
Wovoka 201, 216
Wright, George Hand 228

Y

Yorktown 71, 75

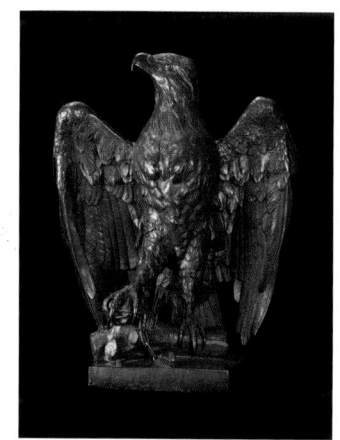